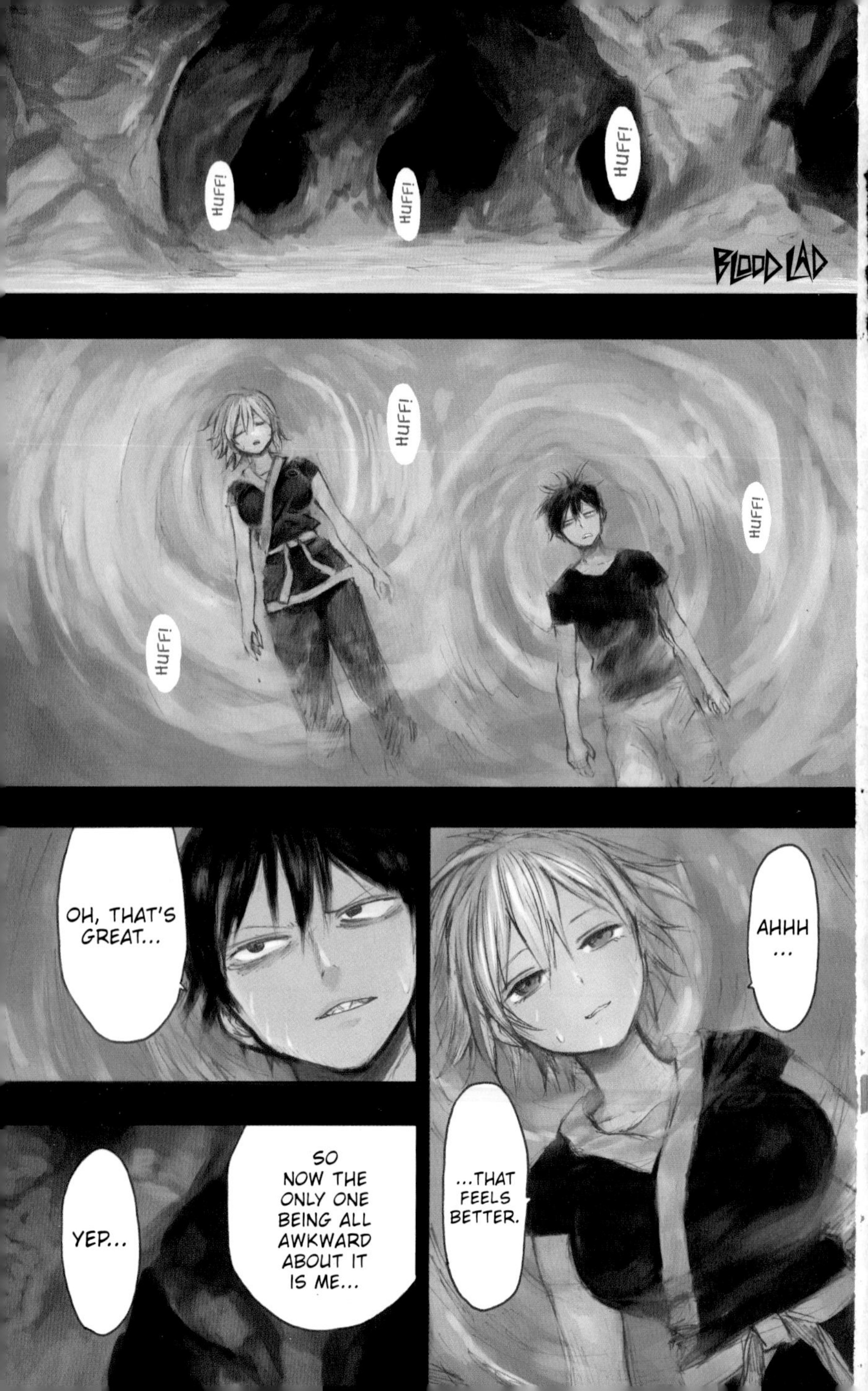
HUFF!
HUFF!
HUFF!
BLOOD LAD
HUFF!
HUFF!
HUFF!
AHHH ...
...THAT FEELS BETTER.
OH, THAT'S GREAT...
SO NOW THE ONLY ONE BEING ALL AWKWARD ABOUT IT IS ME...
YEP...

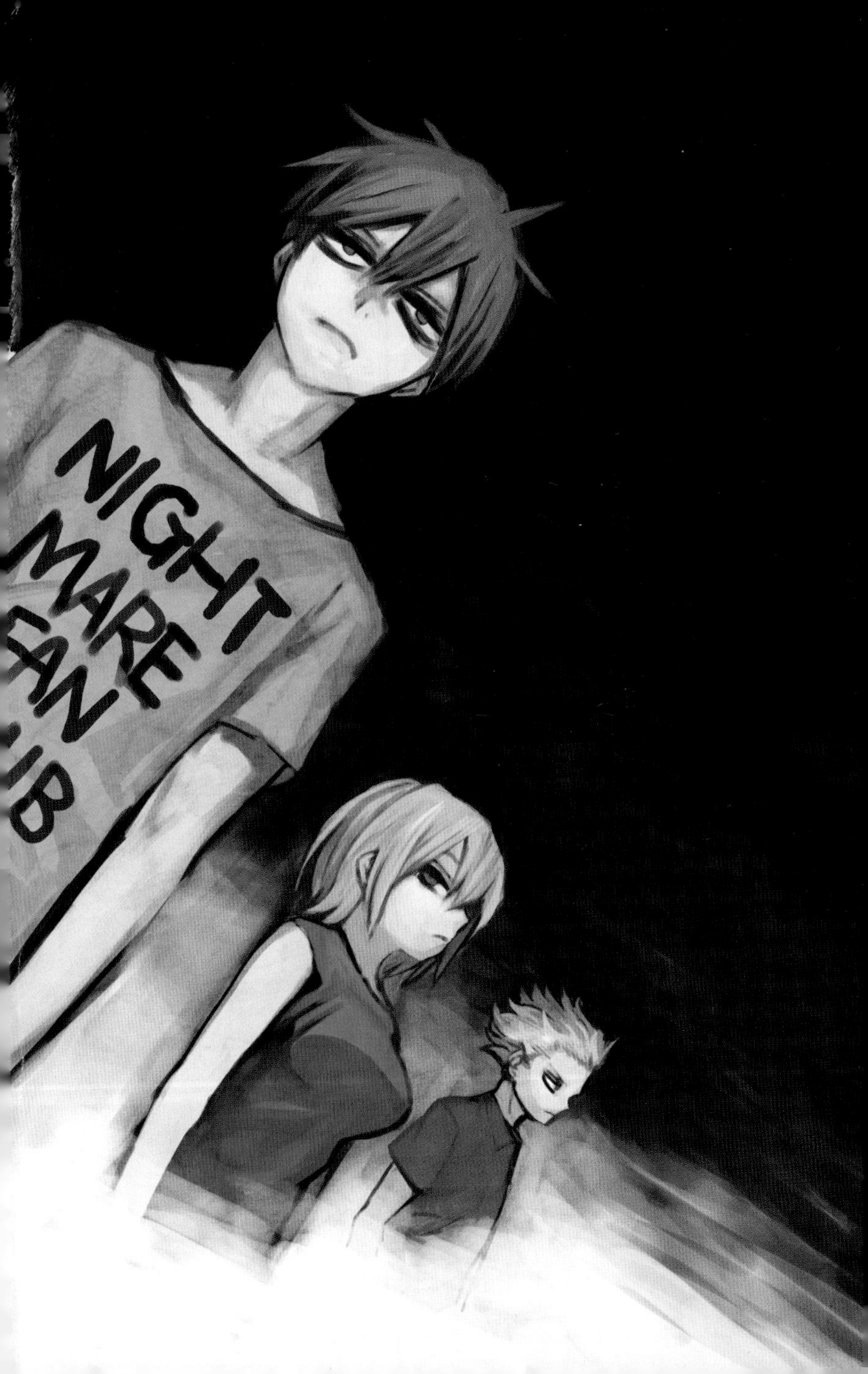
NIGHT
MARE
FAN

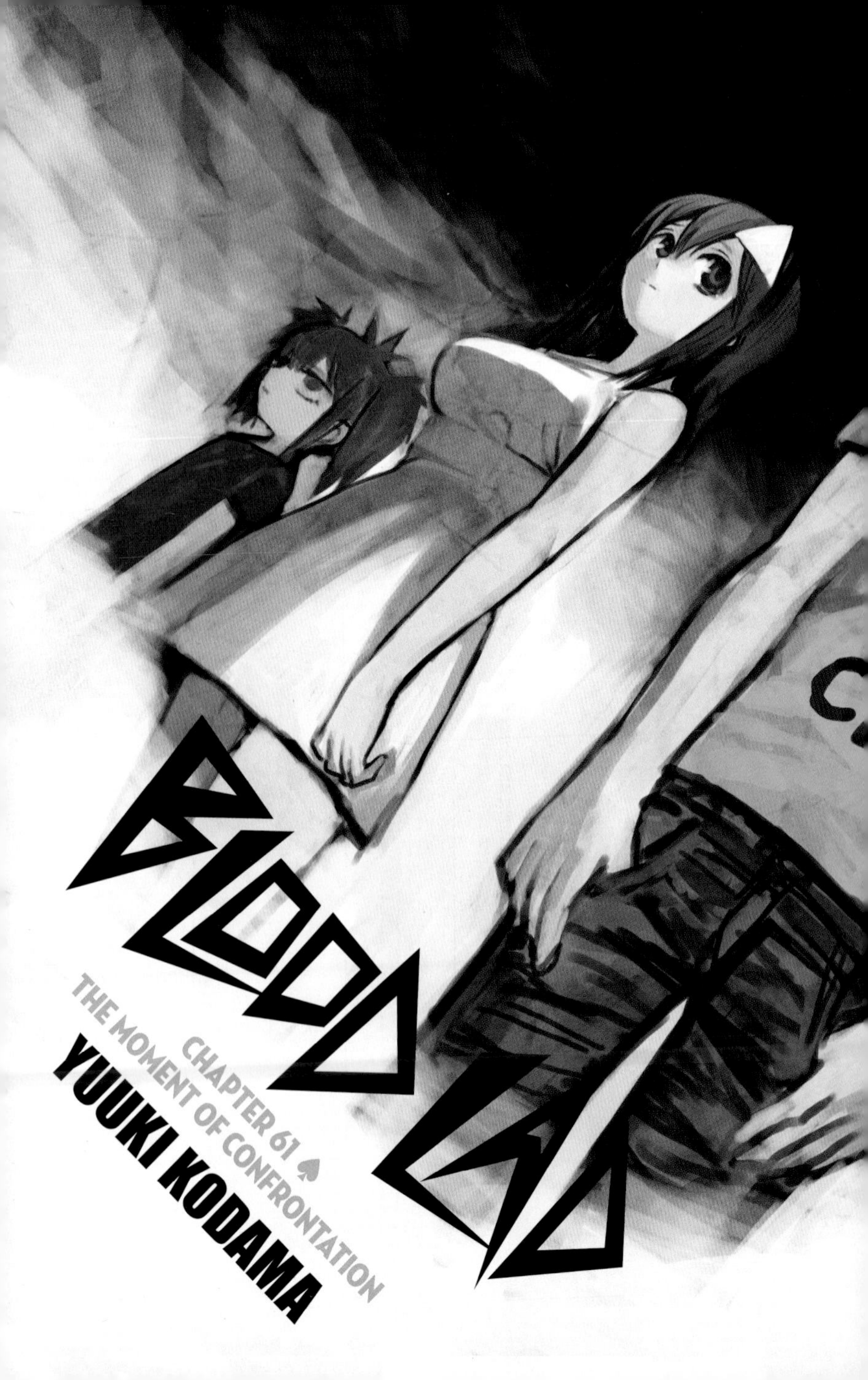
BLOOD LAD
CHAPTER 61 ♠
THE MOMENT OF CONFRONTATION
YUUKI KODAMA

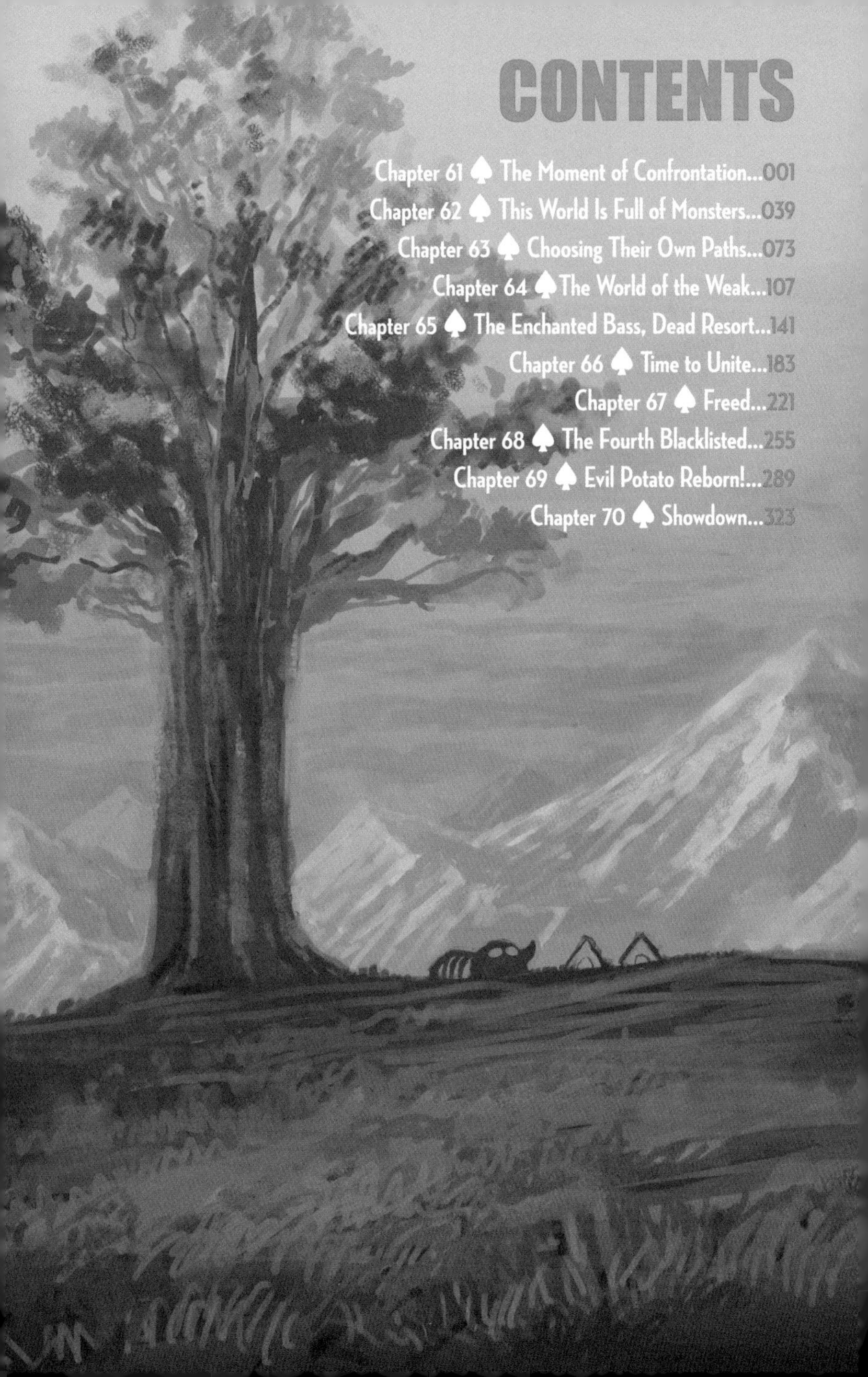

CONTENTS

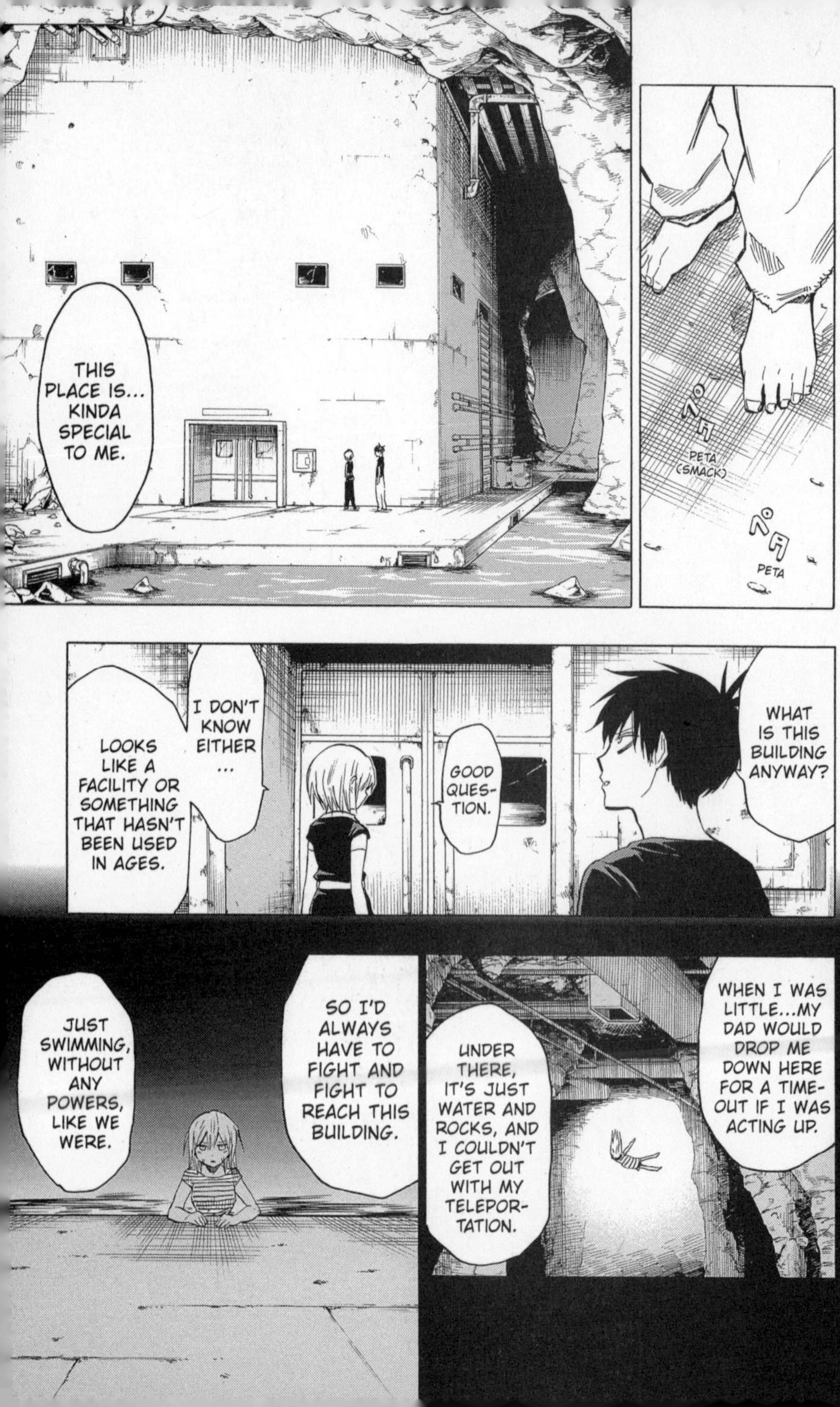
ペタ
PETA (SMACK)
ペタ
PETA
THIS PLACE IS... KINDA SPECIAL TO ME.
WHAT IS THIS BUILDING ANYWAY?
GOOD QUESTION.
I DON'T KNOW EITHER...
LOOKS LIKE A FACILITY OR SOMETHING THAT HASN'T BEEN USED IN AGES.
WHEN I WAS LITTLE...MY DAD WOULD DROP ME DOWN HERE FOR A TIME-OUT IF I WAS ACTING UP.
UNDER THERE, IT'S JUST WATER AND ROCKS, AND I COULDN'T GET OUT WITH MY TELEPORTATION.
SO I'D ALWAYS HAVE TO FIGHT AND FIGHT TO REACH THIS BUILDING.
JUST SWIMMING, WITHOUT ANY POWERS, LIKE WE WERE.

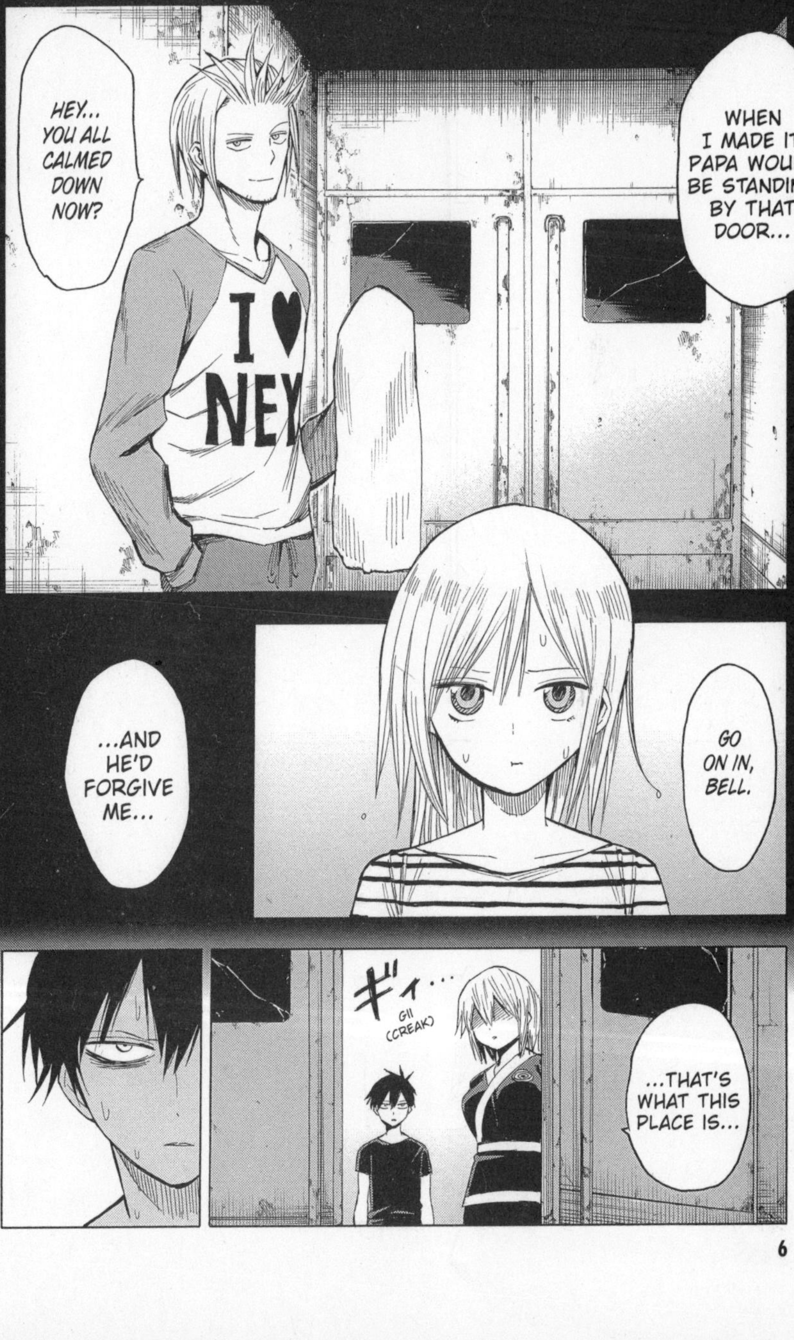
WHEN I MADE IT, PAPA WOULD BE STANDING BY THAT DOOR...
HEY... YOU ALL CALMED DOWN NOW?
GO ON IN, BELL.
...AND HE'D FORGIVE ME...
ギィ...
GII (CREAK)
...THAT'S WHAT THIS PLACE IS...

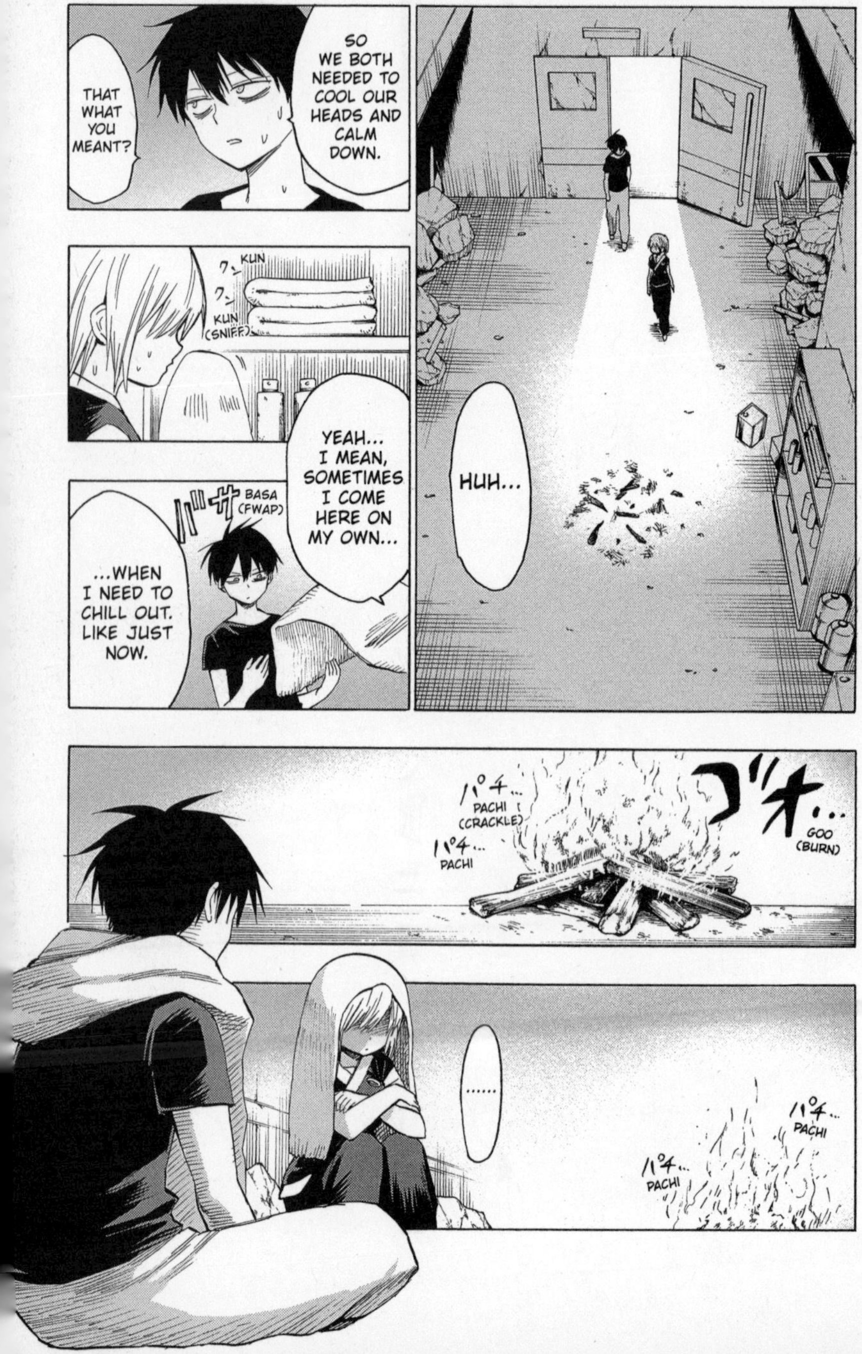
HUH...
SO WE BOTH NEEDED TO COOL OUR HEADS AND CALM DOWN.
THAT WHAT YOU MEANT?
クン KUN
クン KUN (SNIFF)
YEAH... I MEAN, SOMETIMES I COME HERE ON MY OWN...
バサ BASA (FWAP)
...WHEN I NEED TO CHILL OUT. LIKE JUST NOW.
ゴオ... GOO (BURN)
パチ... PACHI (CRACKLE)
パチ... PACHI
......
パチ... PACHI
パチ... PACHI

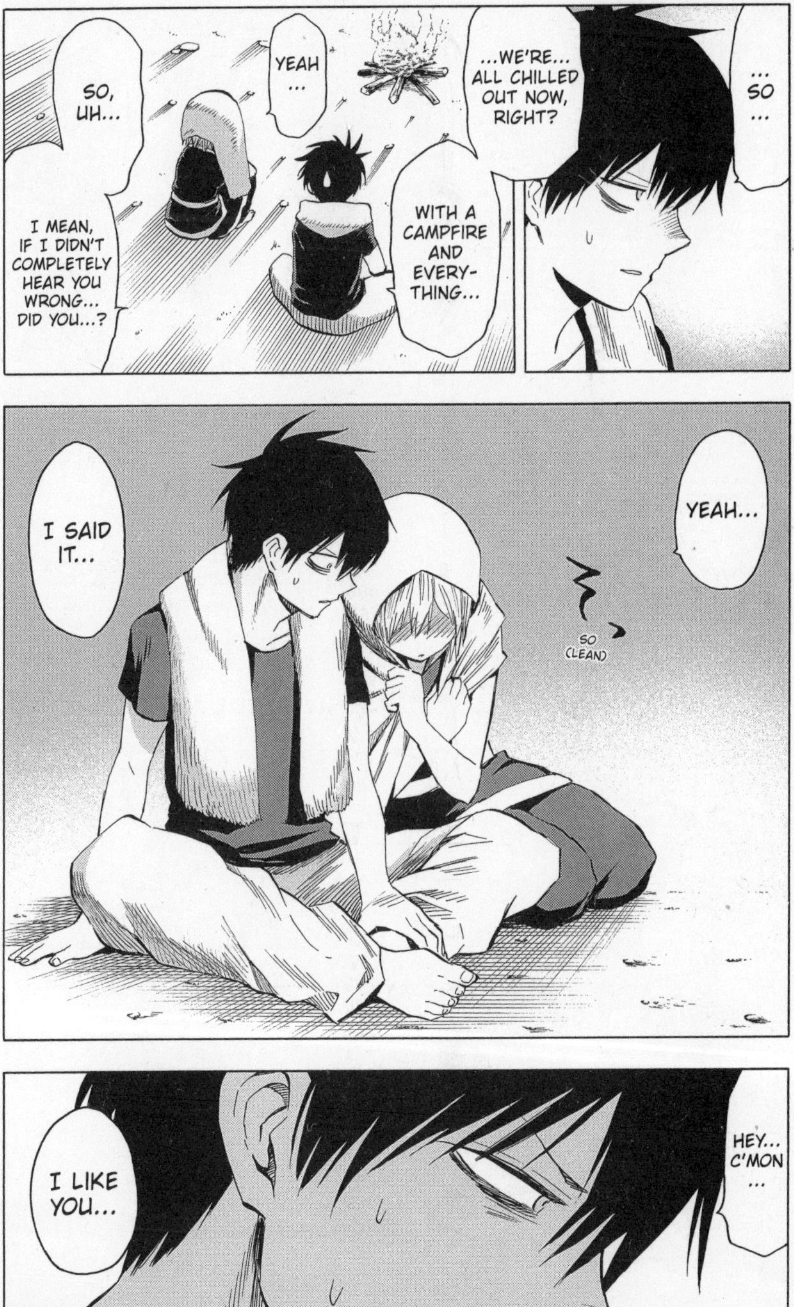
... SO ...
...WE'RE... ALL CHILLED OUT NOW, RIGHT?
WITH A CAMPFIRE AND EVERYTHING...
YEAH ...
SO, UH...
I MEAN, IF I DIDN'T COMPLETELY HEAR YOU WRONG... DID YOU...?
YEAH...
SO (LEAN)
I SAID IT...
HEY... C'MON ...
I LIKE YOU...

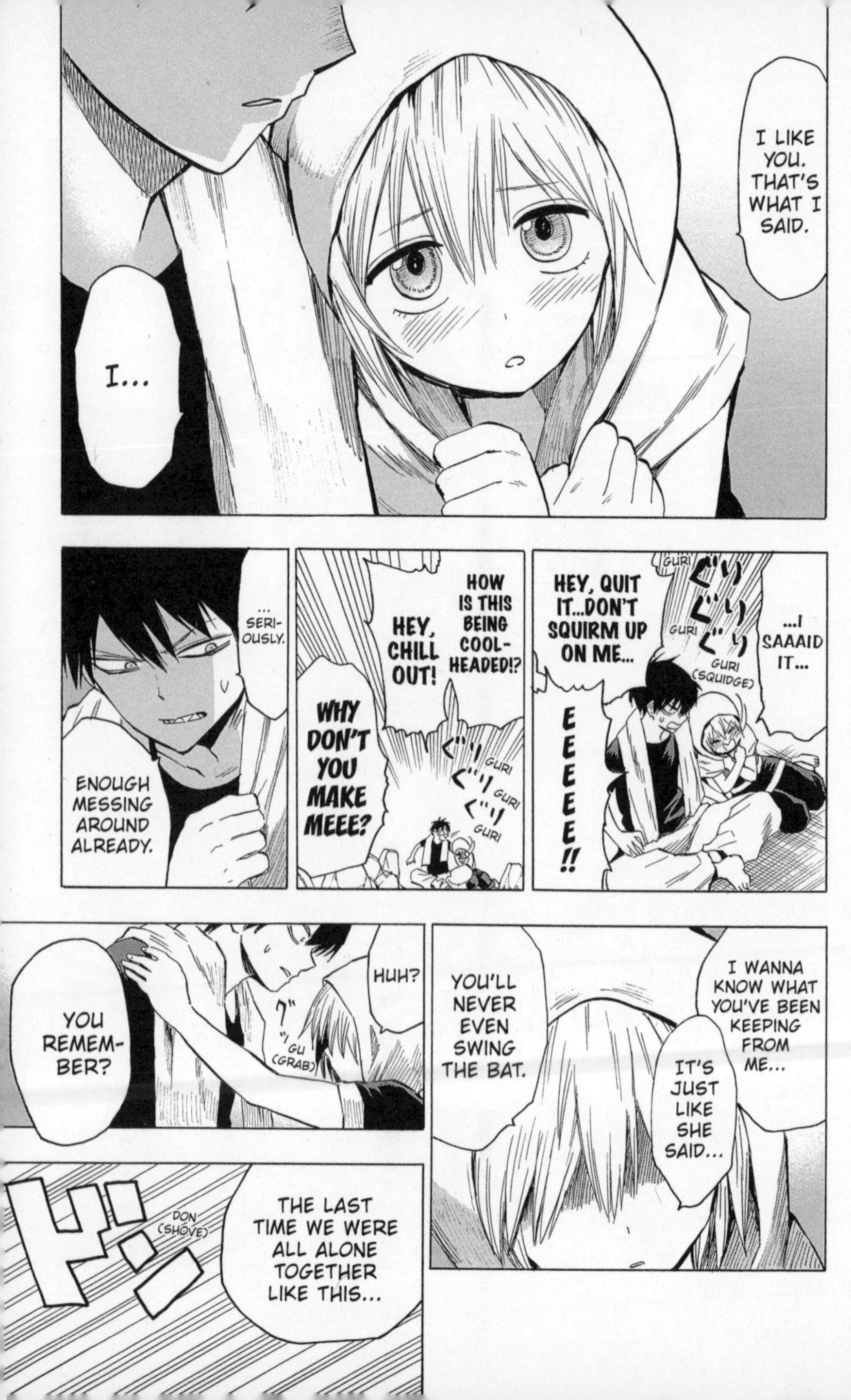
I LIKE YOU. THAT'S WHAT I SAID.
I...
...I SAAAID IT...
GURI
GURI
GURI (SQUIDGE)
HEY, QUIT IT...DON'T SQUIRM UP ON ME...
EEEEEE!!
HOW IS THIS BEING COOL-HEADED!?
HEY, CHILL OUT!
WHY DON'T YOU MAKE MEEE?
GURI
GURI
GURI
...SERI-OUSLY.
ENOUGH MESSING AROUND ALREADY.
I WANNA KNOW WHAT YOU'VE BEEN KEEPING FROM ME...
IT'S JUST LIKE SHE SAID...
YOU'LL NEVER EVEN SWING THE BAT.
HUH?
GU (GRAB)
YOU REMEM-BER?
THE LAST TIME WE WERE ALL ALONE TOGETHER LIKE THIS...
DON (SHOVE)

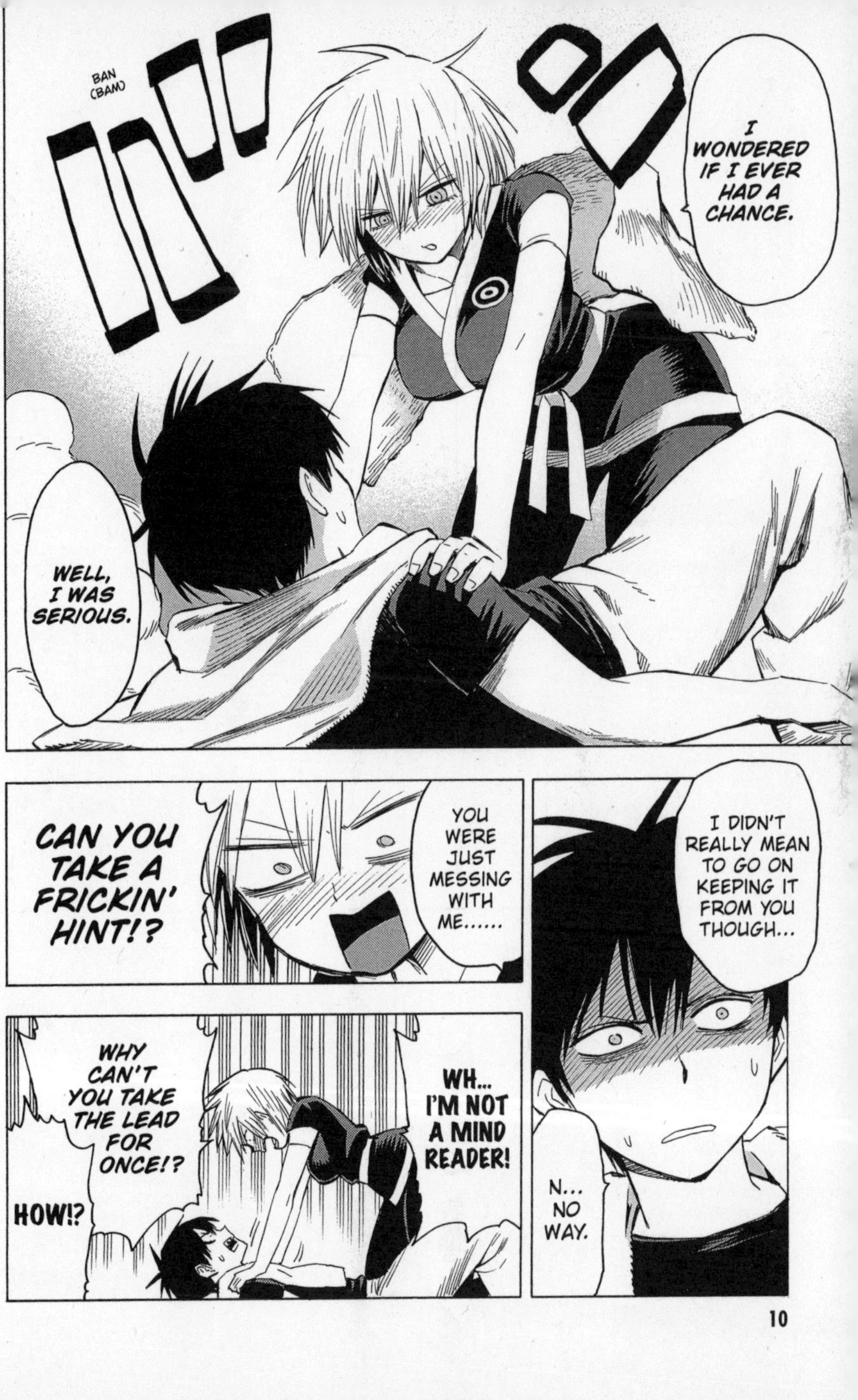
I WONDERED IF I EVER HAD A CHANCE.
BAN (BAM)
WELL, I WAS SERIOUS.
I DIDN'T REALLY MEAN TO GO ON KEEPING IT FROM YOU THOUGH...
N... NO WAY.
YOU WERE JUST MESSING WITH ME......
CAN YOU TAKE A FRICKIN' HINT!?
WH... I'M NOT A MIND READER!
WHY CAN'T YOU TAKE THE LEAD FOR ONCE!?
HOW!?

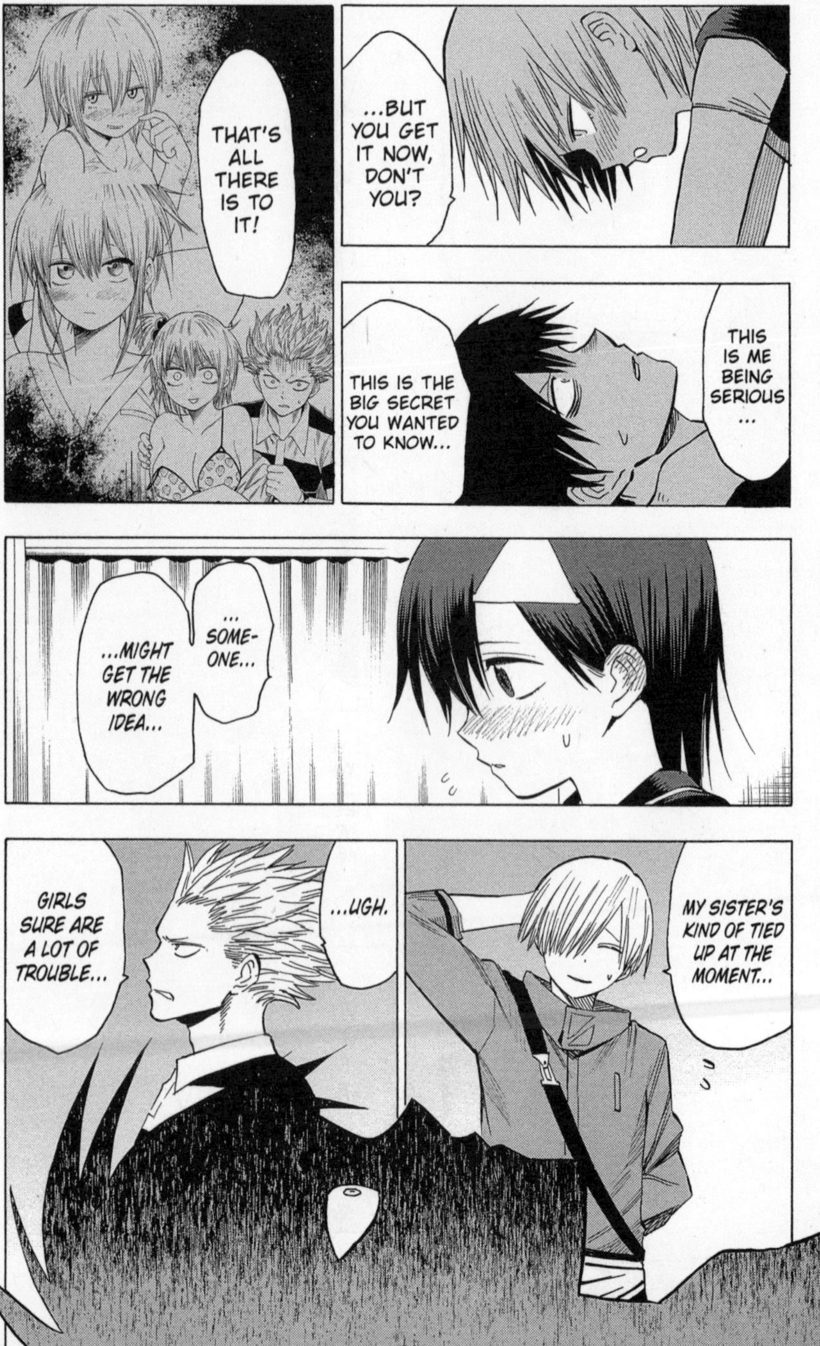
...BUT YOU GET IT NOW, DON'T YOU?
THIS IS ME BEING SERIOUS...
THIS IS THE BIG SECRET YOU WANTED TO KNOW...
THAT'S ALL THERE IS TO IT!
... SOME-ONE...
...MIGHT GET THE WRONG IDEA...
MY SISTER'S KIND OF TIED UP AT THE MOMENT...
...UGH.
GIRLS SURE ARE A LOT OF TROUBLE...

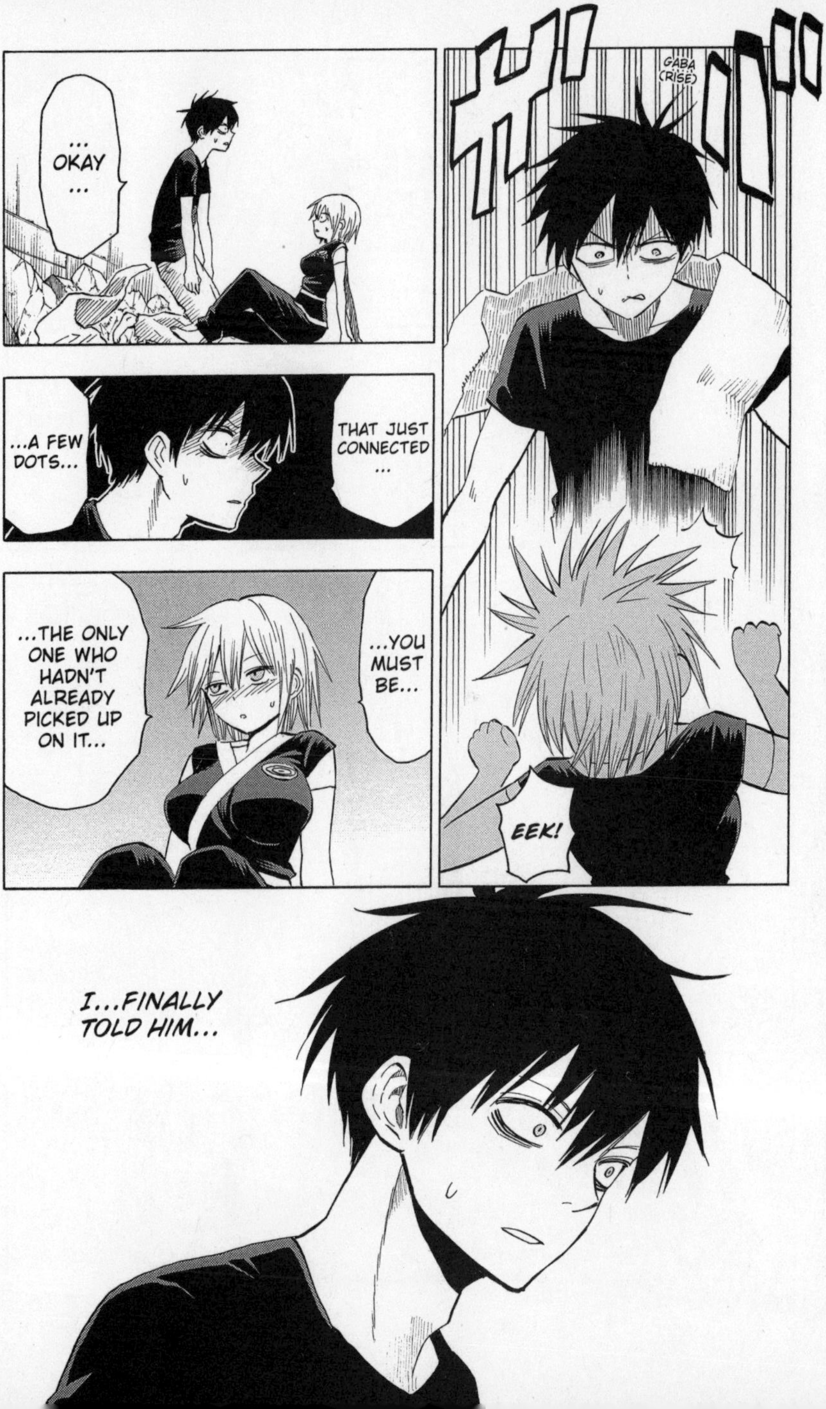
GABA (RISE)
EEK!
...OKAY...
THAT JUST CONNECTED...
...A FEW DOTS...
...YOU MUST BE...
...THE ONLY ONE WHO HADN'T ALREADY PICKED UP ON IT...
I...FINALLY TOLD HIM...

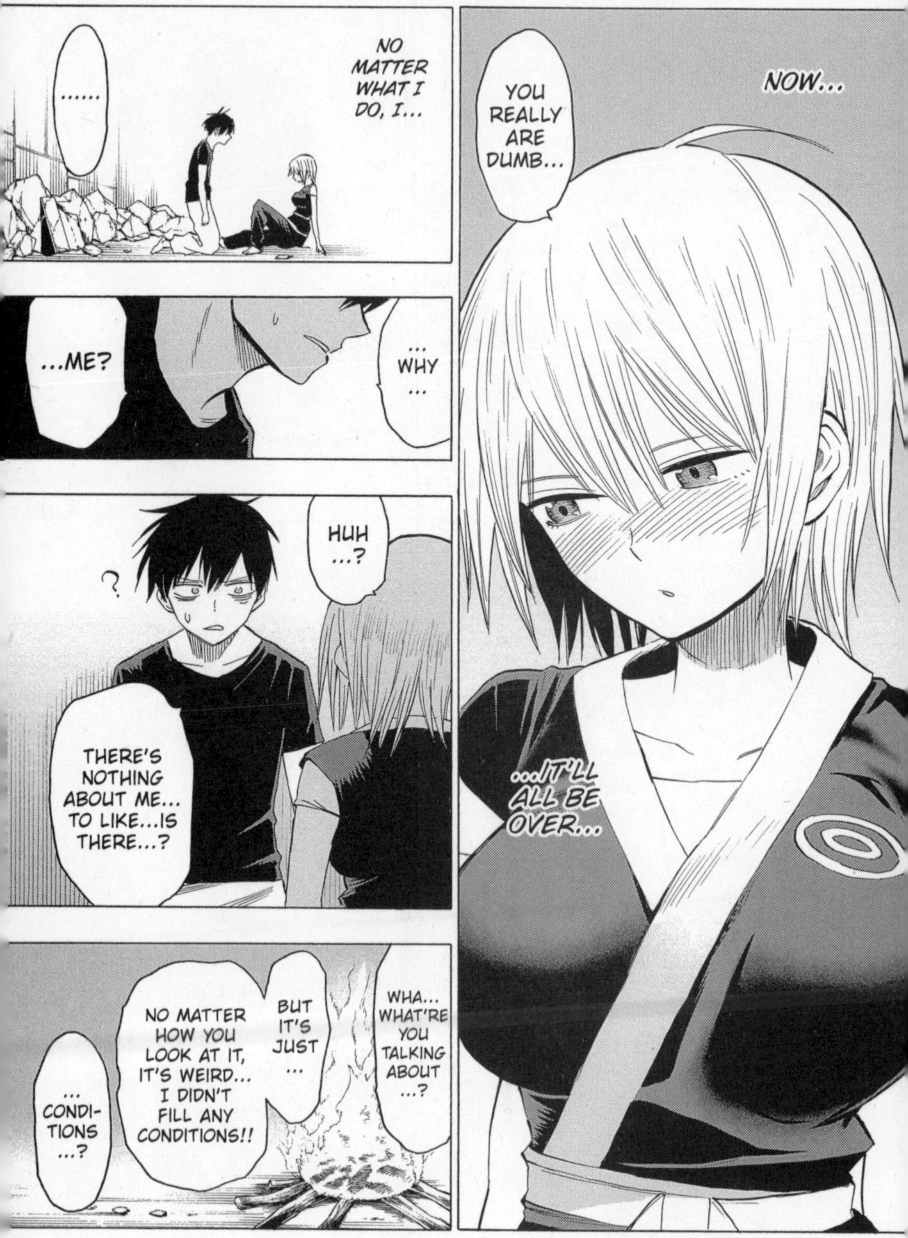
NOW...
YOU REALLY ARE DUMB...
...IT'LL ALL BE OVER...
NO MATTER WHAT I DO, I...
......
... WHY ...
...ME?
HUH ...?
?
THERE'S NOTHING ABOUT ME... TO LIKE...IS THERE...?
WHA... WHAT'RE YOU TALKING ABOUT ...?
BUT IT'S JUST ...
NO MATTER HOW YOU LOOK AT IT, IT'S WEIRD... I DIDN'T FILL ANY CONDITIONS!!
... CONDI-TIONS ...?

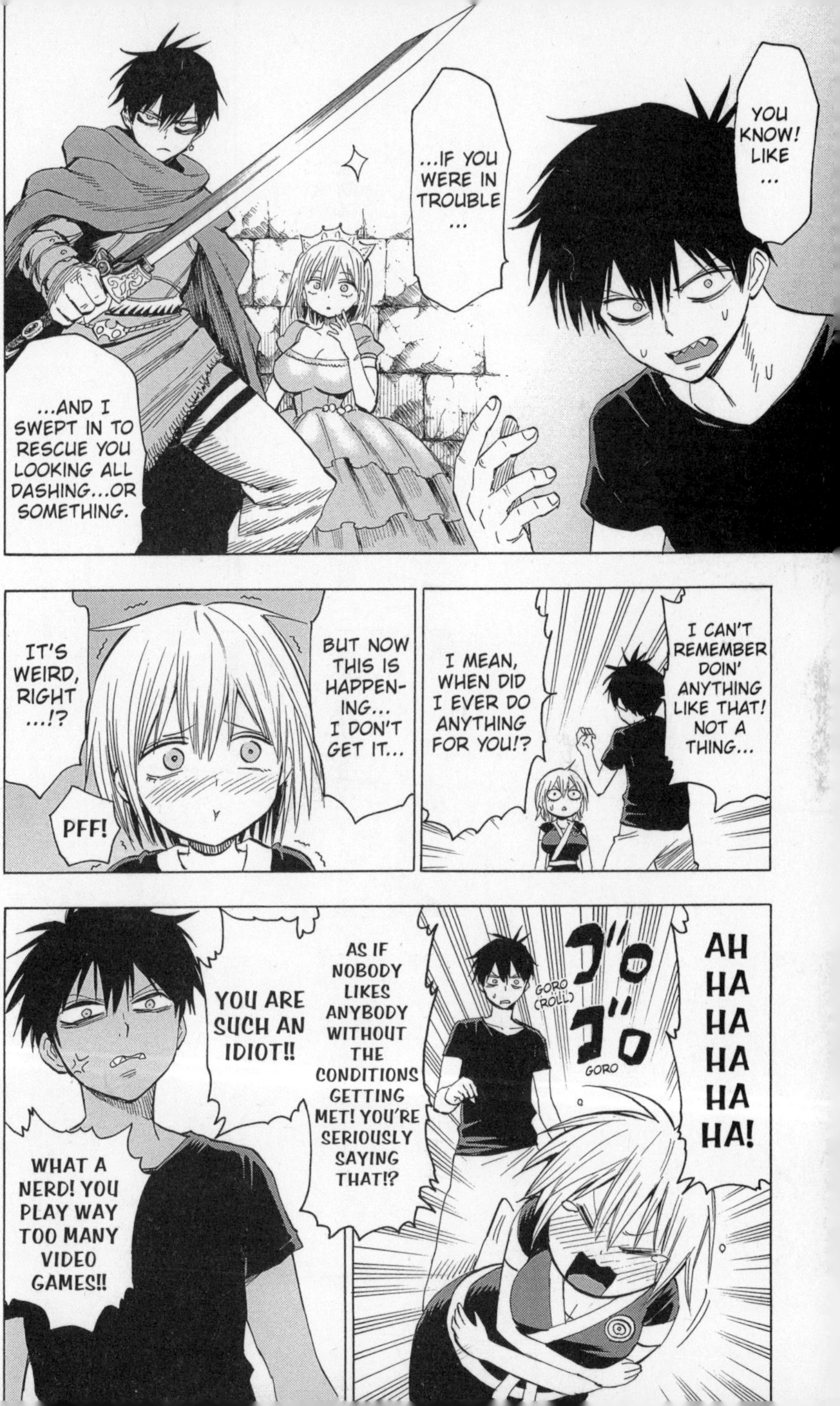
YOU KNOW! LIKE ...
...IF YOU WERE IN TROUBLE ...
...AND I SWEPT IN TO RESCUE YOU LOOKING ALL DASHING...OR SOMETHING.
I CAN'T REMEMBER DOIN' ANYTHING LIKE THAT! NOT A THING...
I MEAN, WHEN DID I EVER DO ANYTHING FOR YOU!?
BUT NOW THIS IS HAPPENING... I DON'T GET IT...
IT'S WEIRD, RIGHT ...!?
PFF!
AH HA HA HA HA HA HA!
ゴロ
GORO (ROLL)
ゴロ
GORO
AS IF NOBODY LIKES ANYBODY WITHOUT THE CONDITIONS GETTING MET! YOU'RE SERIOUSLY SAYING THAT!?
YOU ARE SUCH AN IDIOT!!
WHAT A NERD! YOU PLAY WAY TOO MANY VIDEO GAMES!!

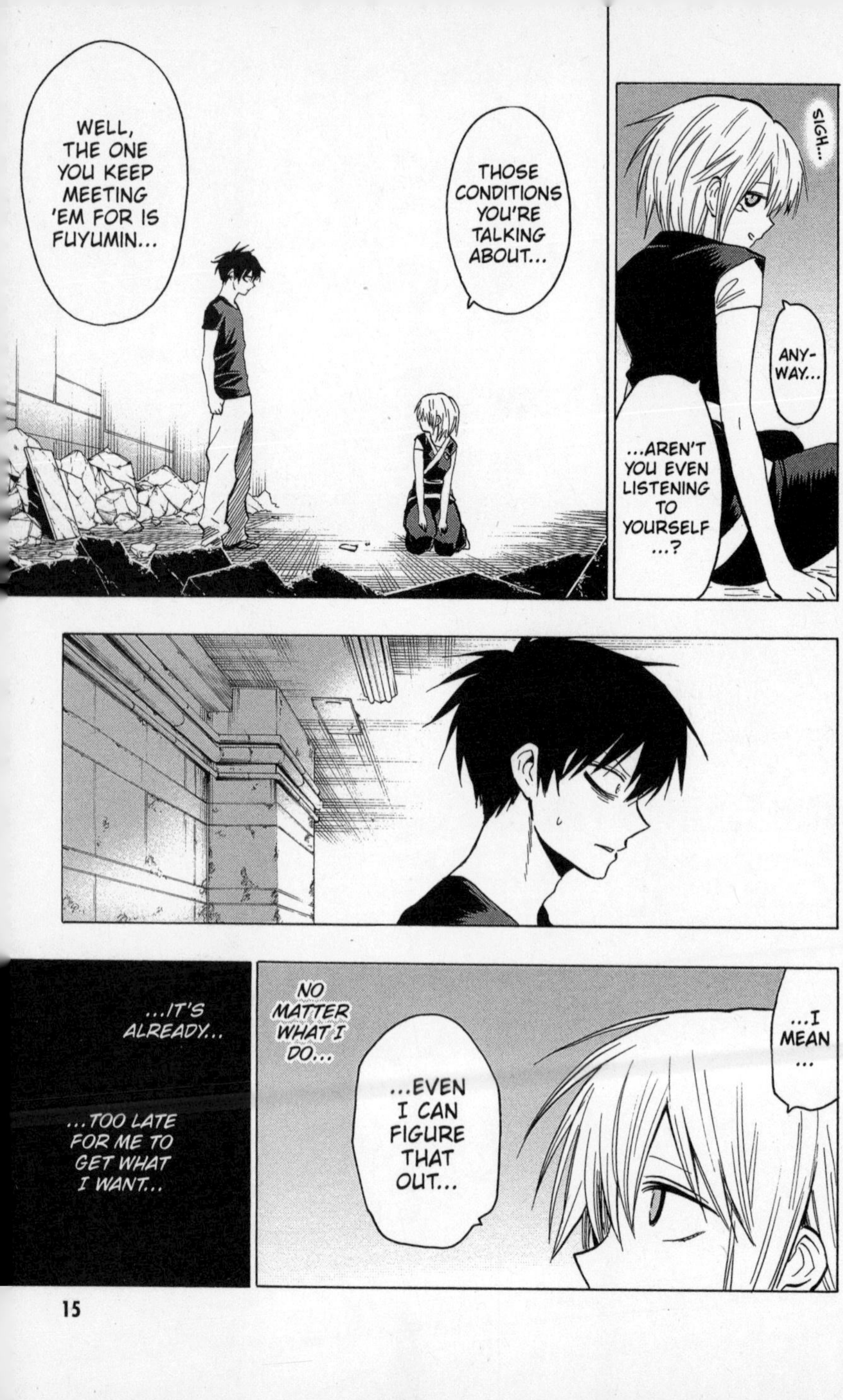
SIGH...
ANY-WAY...
...AREN'T YOU EVEN LISTENING TO YOURSELF ...?
THOSE CONDITIONS YOU'RE TALKING ABOUT...
WELL, THE ONE YOU KEEP MEETING 'EM FOR IS FUYUMIN...
...I MEAN ...
NO MATTER WHAT I DO...
...EVEN I CAN FIGURE THAT OUT...
...IT'S ALREADY...
...TOO LATE FOR ME TO GET WHAT I WANT...

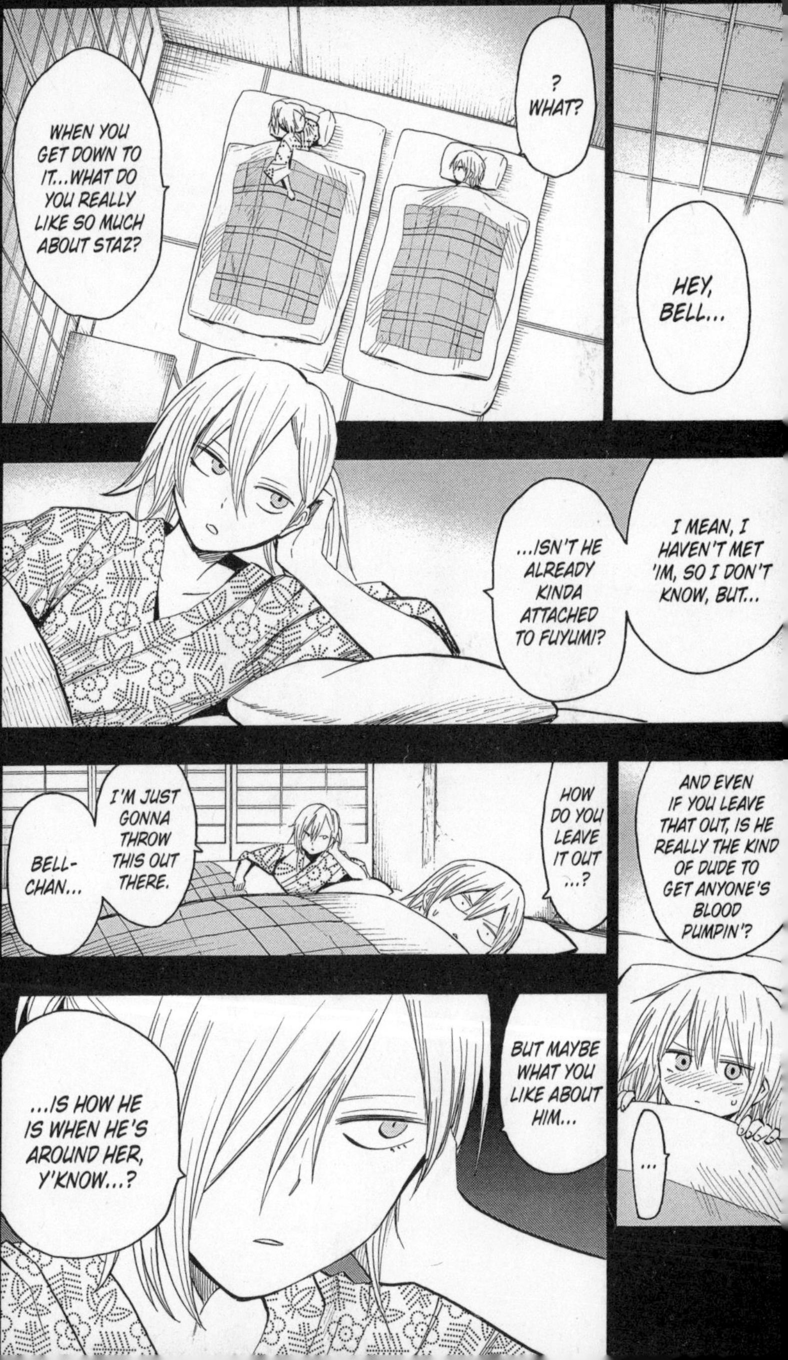
HEY, BELL...
? WHAT?
WHEN YOU GET DOWN TO IT...WHAT DO YOU REALLY LIKE SO MUCH ABOUT STAZ?
I MEAN, I HAVEN'T MET 'IM, SO I DON'T KNOW, BUT...
...ISN'T HE ALREADY KINDA ATTACHED TO FUYUMI?
AND EVEN IF YOU LEAVE THAT OUT, IS HE REALLY THE KIND OF DUDE TO GET ANYONE'S BLOOD PUMPIN'?
HOW DO YOU LEAVE IT OUT...?
I'M JUST GONNA THROW THIS OUT THERE.
BELL-CHAN...
...
BUT MAYBE WHAT YOU LIKE ABOUT HIM...
...IS HOW HE IS WHEN HE'S AROUND HER, Y'KNOW...?

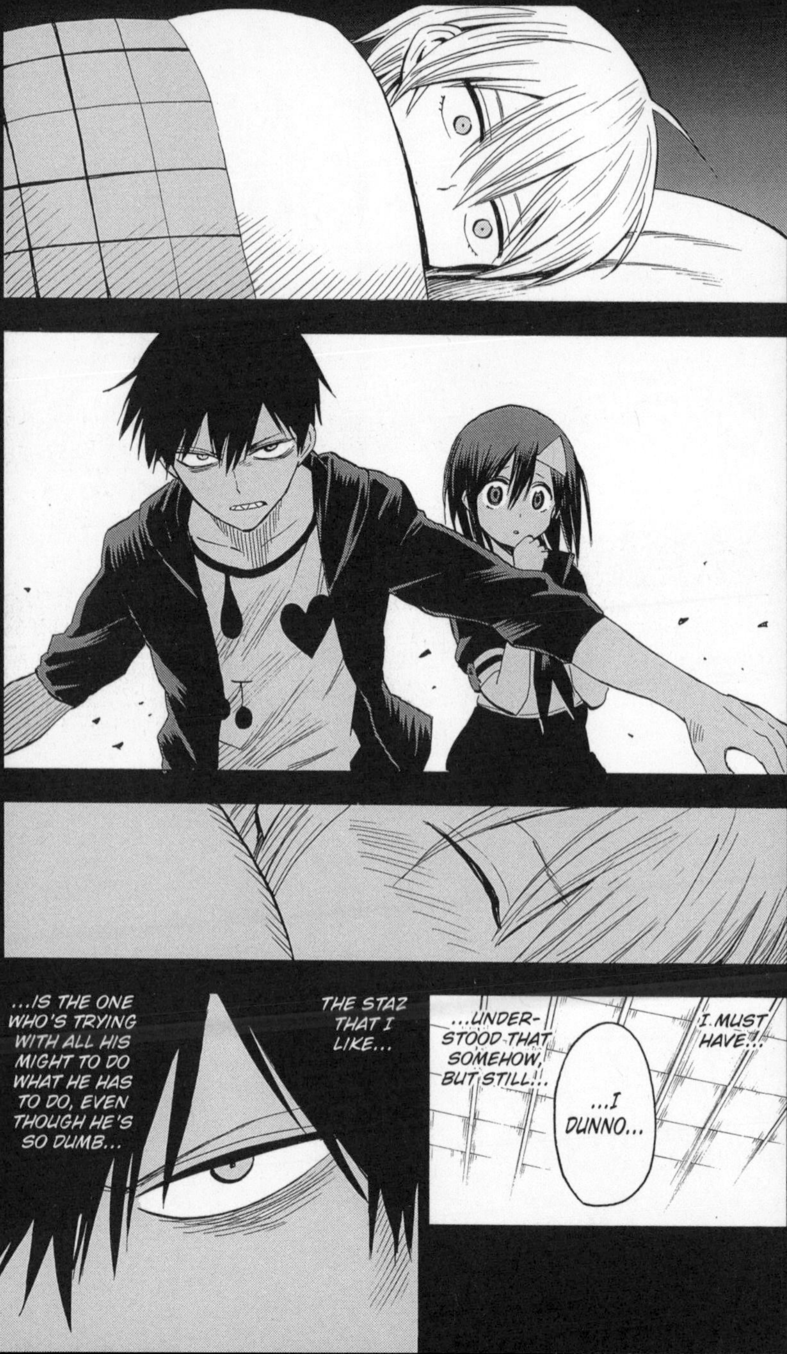
I MUST HAVE...!
...UNDER-STOOD THAT SOMEHOW, BUT STILL...
...I DUNNO...
THE STAZ THAT I LIKE...
...IS THE ONE WHO'S TRYING WITH ALL HIS MIGHT TO DO WHAT HE HAS TO DO, EVEN THOUGH HE'S SO DUMB...

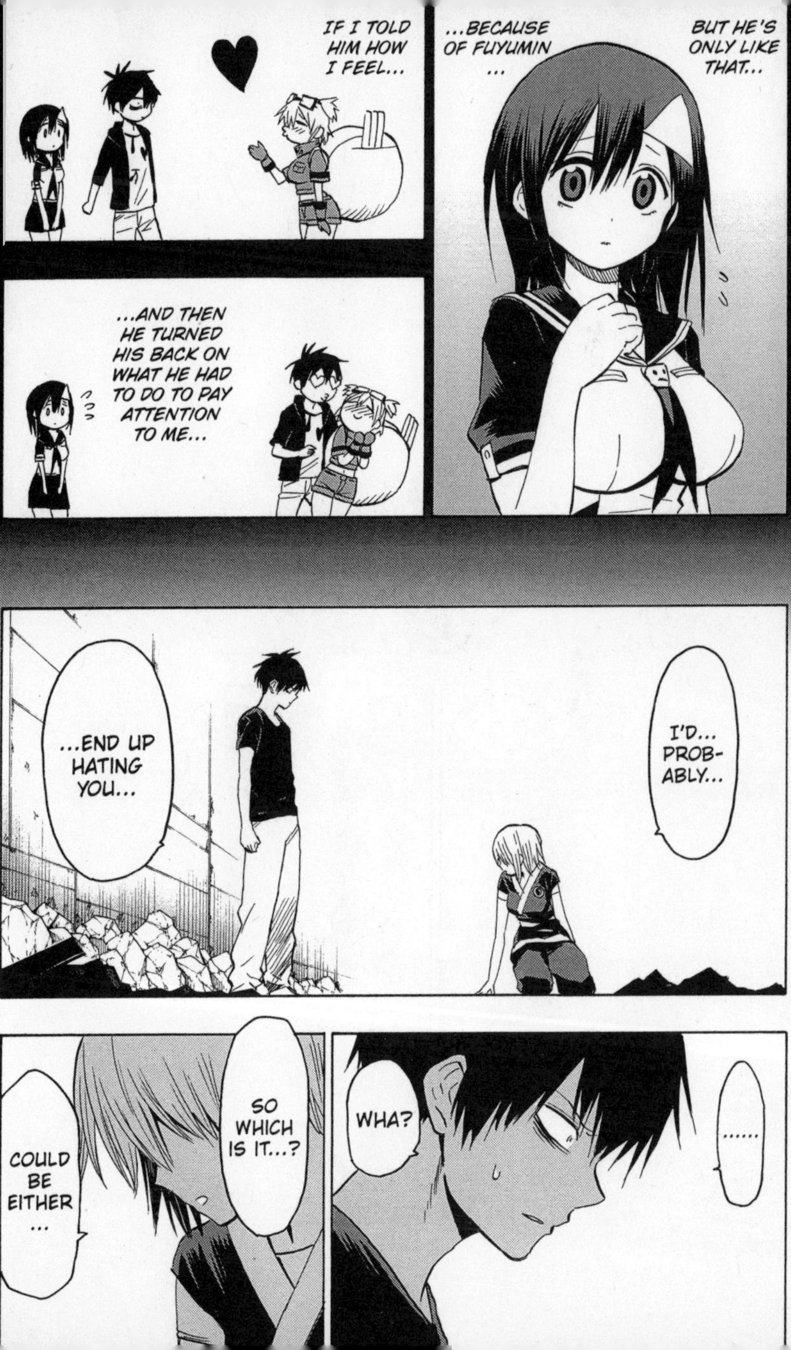
BUT HE'S ONLY LIKE THAT...
...BECAUSE OF FUYUMIN ...
IF I TOLD HIM HOW I FEEL...
...AND THEN HE TURNED HIS BACK ON WHAT HE HAD TO DO TO PAY ATTENTION TO ME...
I'D... PROBABLY...
...END UP HATING YOU...
......
WHA?
SO WHICH IS IT...?
COULD BE EITHER ...

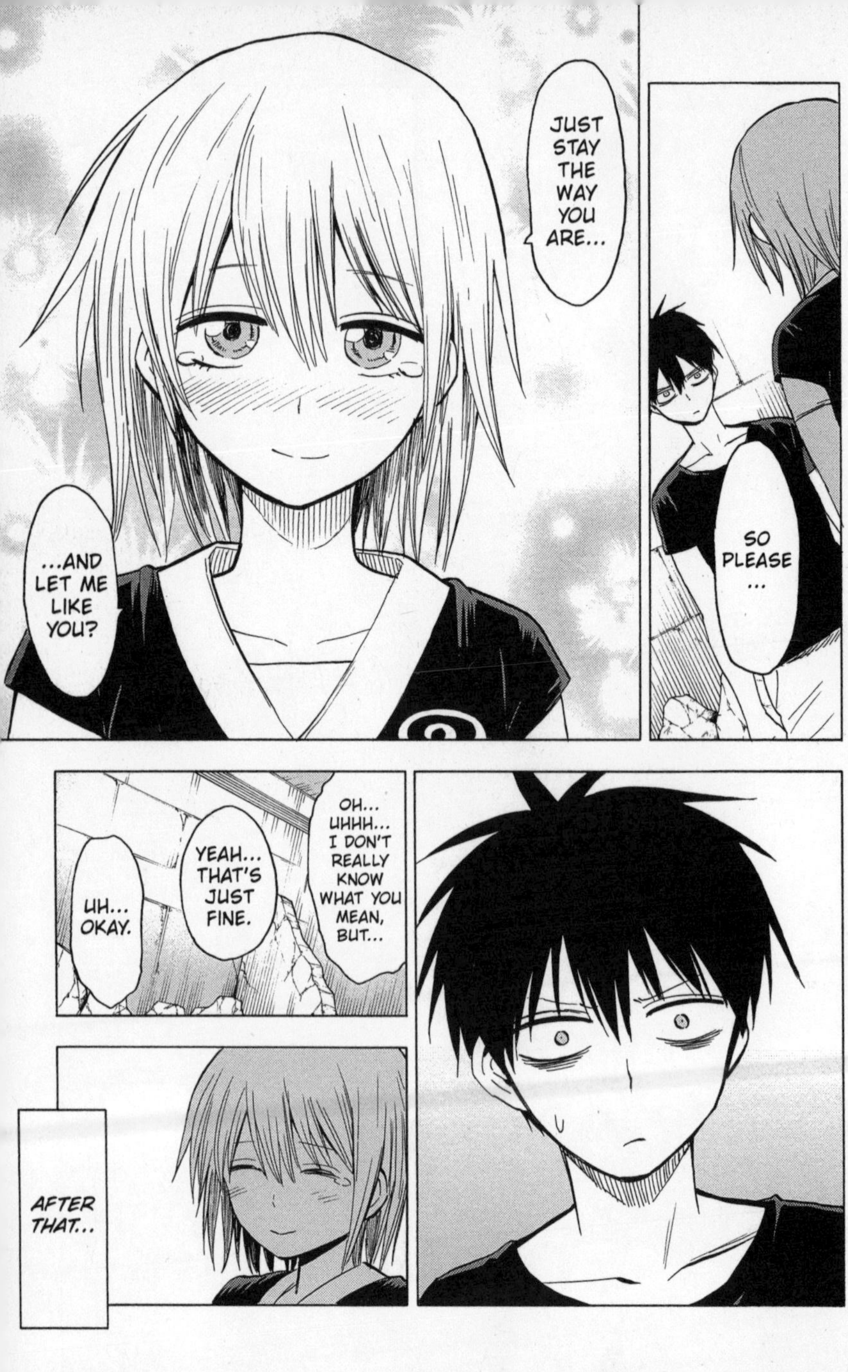
SO PLEASE ...
JUST STAY THE WAY YOU ARE...
...AND LET ME LIKE YOU?
OH... UHHH... I DON'T REALLY KNOW WHAT YOU MEAN, BUT...
YEAH... THAT'S JUST FINE.
UH... OKAY.
AFTER THAT...

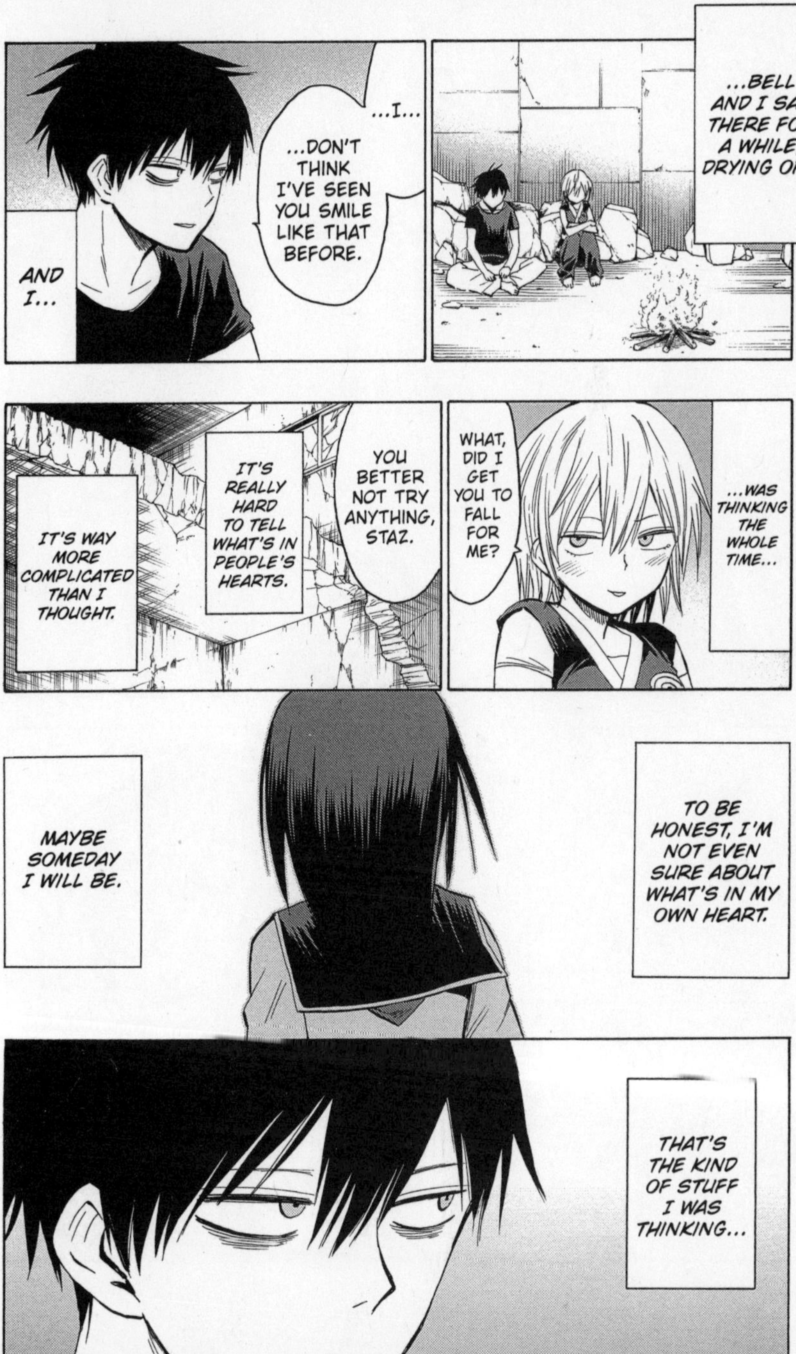
...BELL AND I SAT THERE FOR A WHILE, DRYING OFF.
...I...
...DON'T THINK I'VE SEEN YOU SMILE LIKE THAT BEFORE.
AND I...
...WAS THINKING THE WHOLE TIME...
WHAT, DID I GET YOU TO FALL FOR ME?
YOU BETTER NOT TRY ANYTHING, STAZ.
IT'S REALLY HARD TO TELL WHAT'S IN PEOPLE'S HEARTS.
IT'S WAY MORE COMPLICATED THAN I THOUGHT.
TO BE HONEST, I'M NOT EVEN SURE ABOUT WHAT'S IN MY OWN HEART.
MAYBE SOMEDAY I WILL BE.
THAT'S THE KIND OF STUFF I WAS THINKING...

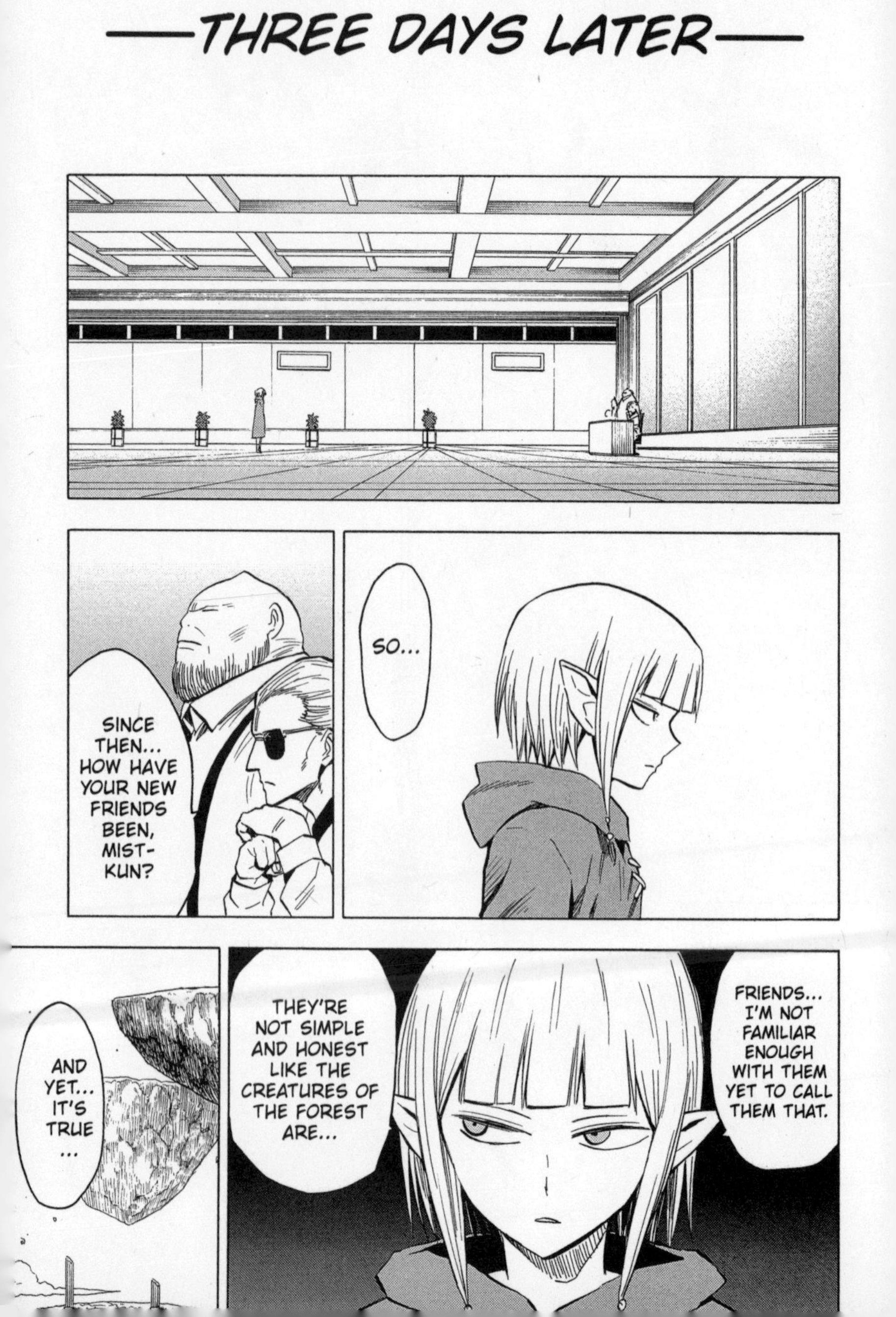
—THREE DAYS LATER—
SO...
SINCE THEN... HOW HAVE YOUR NEW FRIENDS BEEN, MIST-KUN?
FRIENDS... I'M NOT FAMILIAR ENOUGH WITH THEM YET TO CALL THEM THAT.
THEY'RE NOT SIMPLE AND HONEST LIKE THE CREATURES OF THE FOREST ARE...
AND YET... IT'S TRUE ...

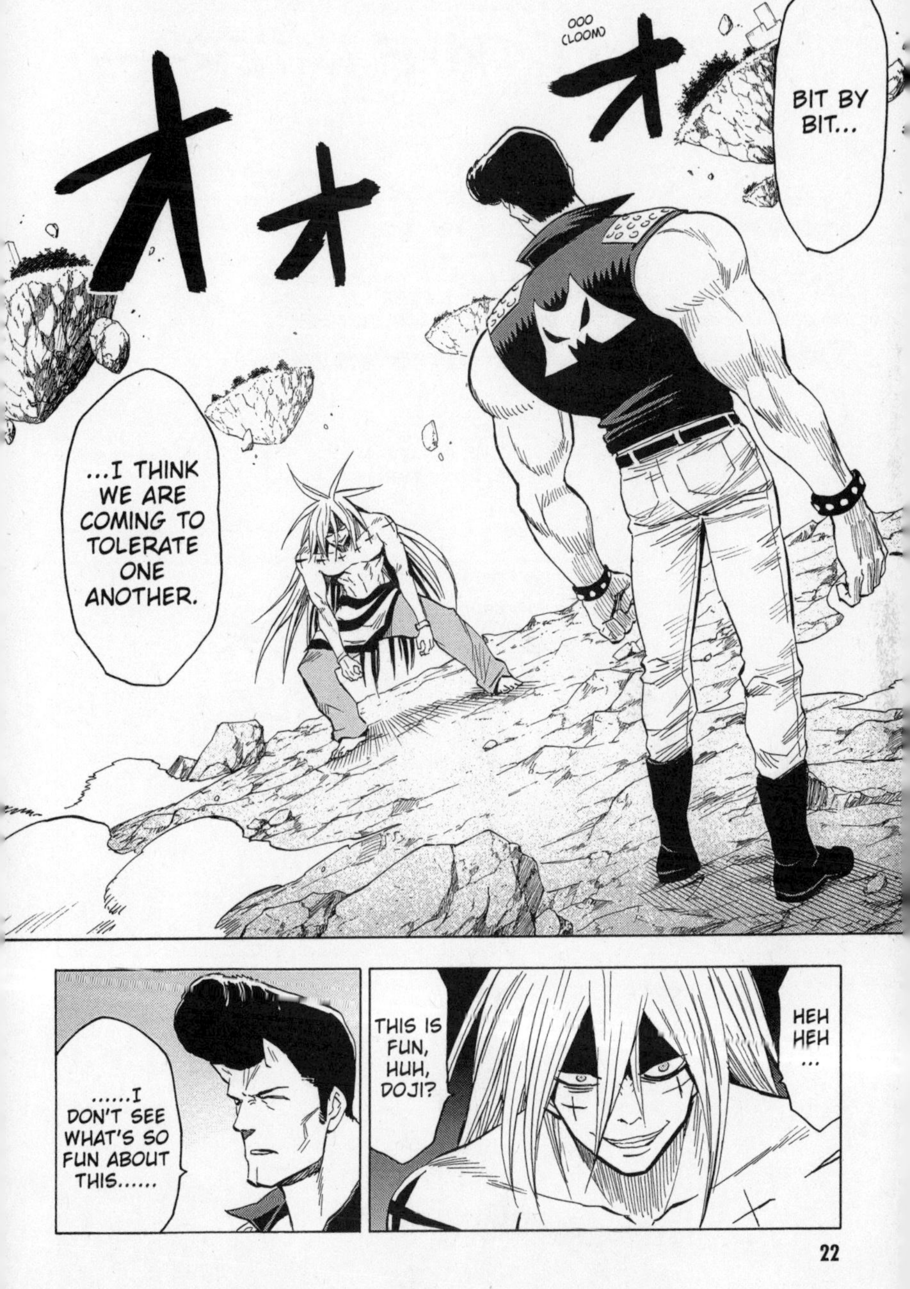
BIT BY BIT...
OOO (LOOM)
オオオ
...I THINK WE ARE COMING TO TOLERATE ONE ANOTHER.
HEH HEH ...
THIS IS FUN, HUH, DOJI?
......I DON'T SEE WHAT'S SO FUN ABOUT THIS......

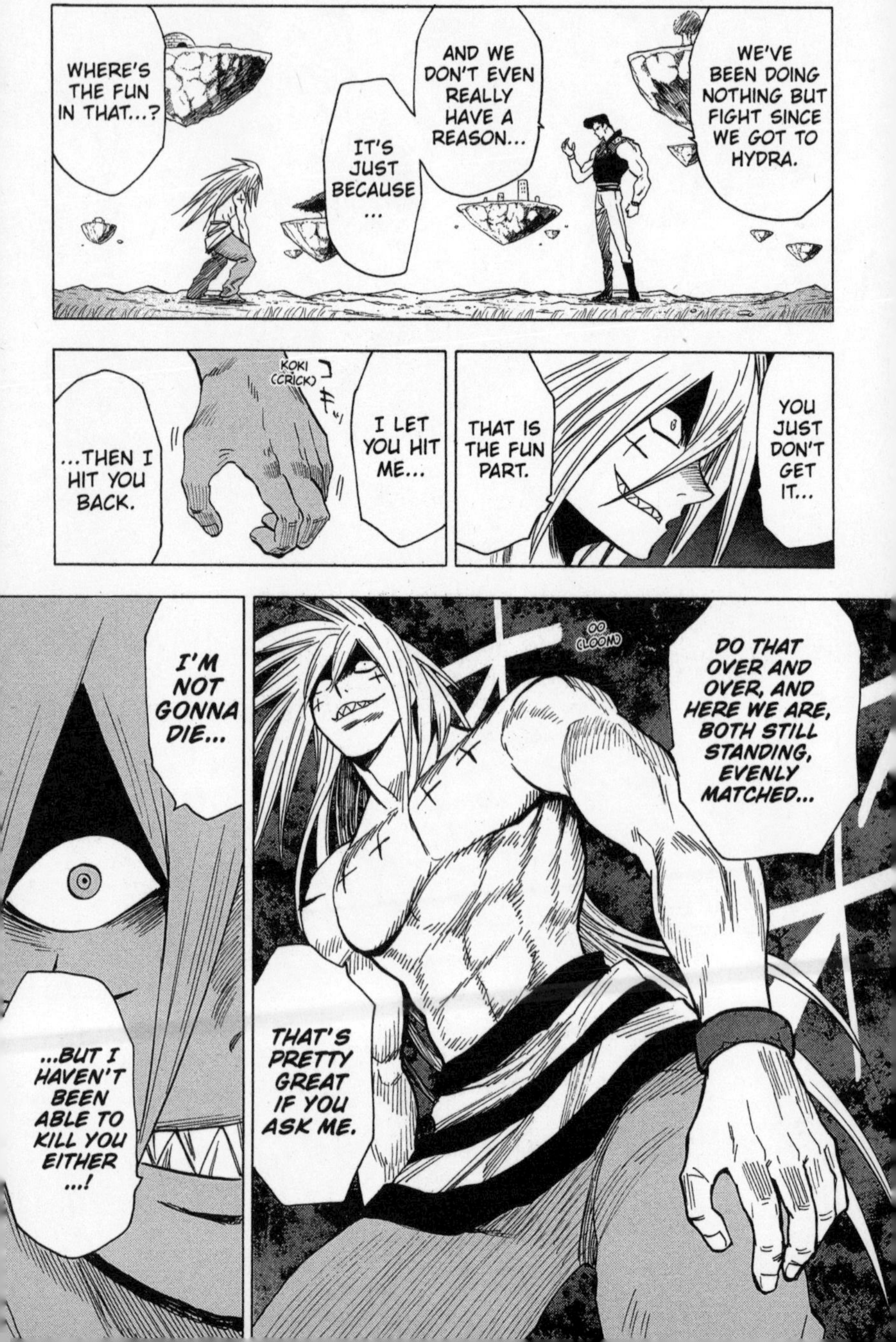
WE'VE BEEN DOING NOTHING BUT FIGHT SINCE WE GOT TO HYDRA.
AND WE DON'T EVEN REALLY HAVE A REASON...
IT'S JUST BECAUSE...
WHERE'S THE FUN IN THAT...?
YOU JUST DON'T GET IT...
THAT IS THE FUN PART.
I LET YOU HIT ME...
KOKI (CRICK)
...THEN I HIT YOU BACK.
OO (LOOM)
DO THAT OVER AND OVER, AND HERE WE ARE, BOTH STILL STANDING, EVENLY MATCHED...
THAT'S PRETTY GREAT IF YOU ASK ME.
I'M NOT GONNA DIE...
...BUT I HAVEN'T BEEN ABLE TO KILL YOU EITHER ...!

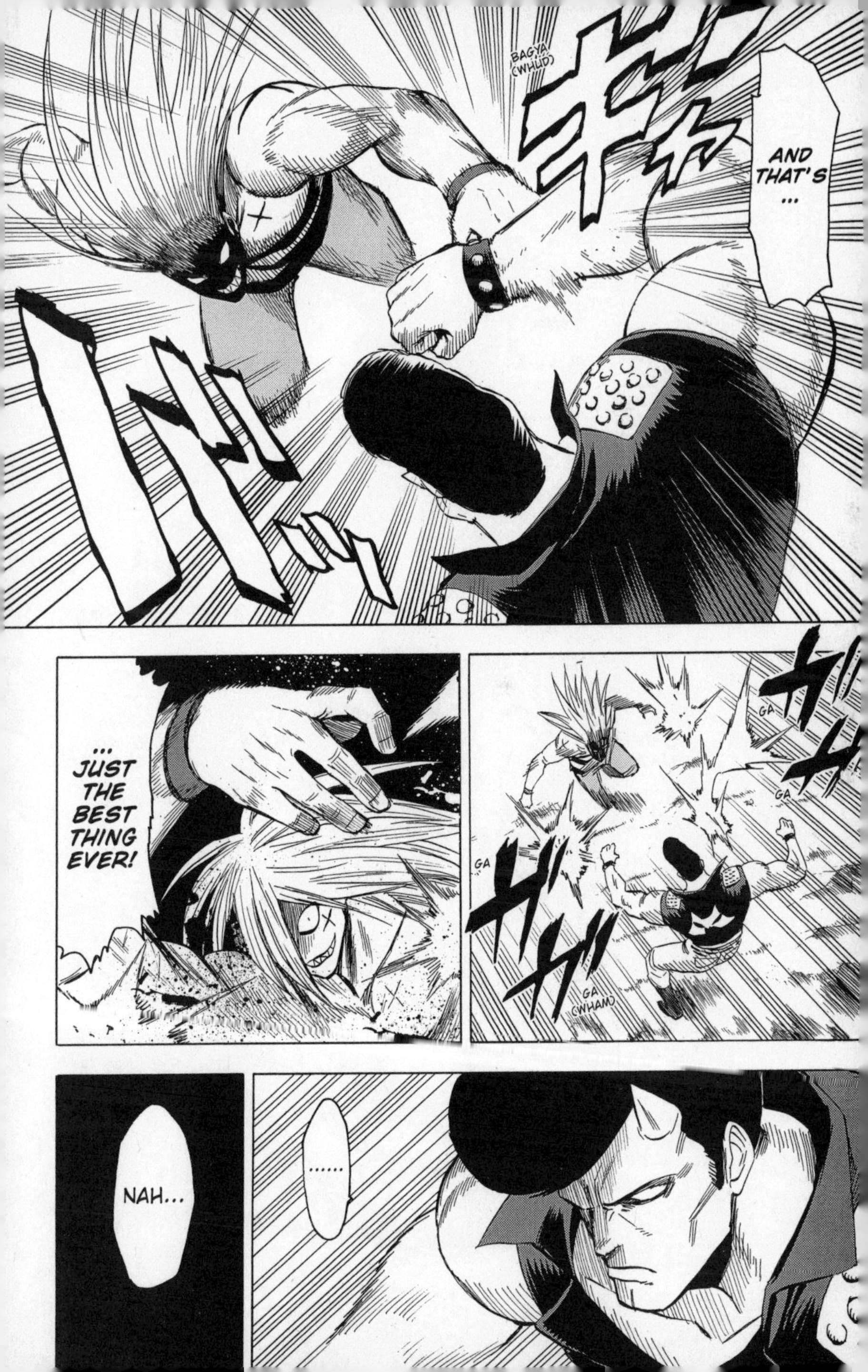
BAGYA (WHUD)
AND THAT'S ...
GA
GA
GA
GA (WHAM)
... JUST THE BEST THING EVER!
......
NAH...

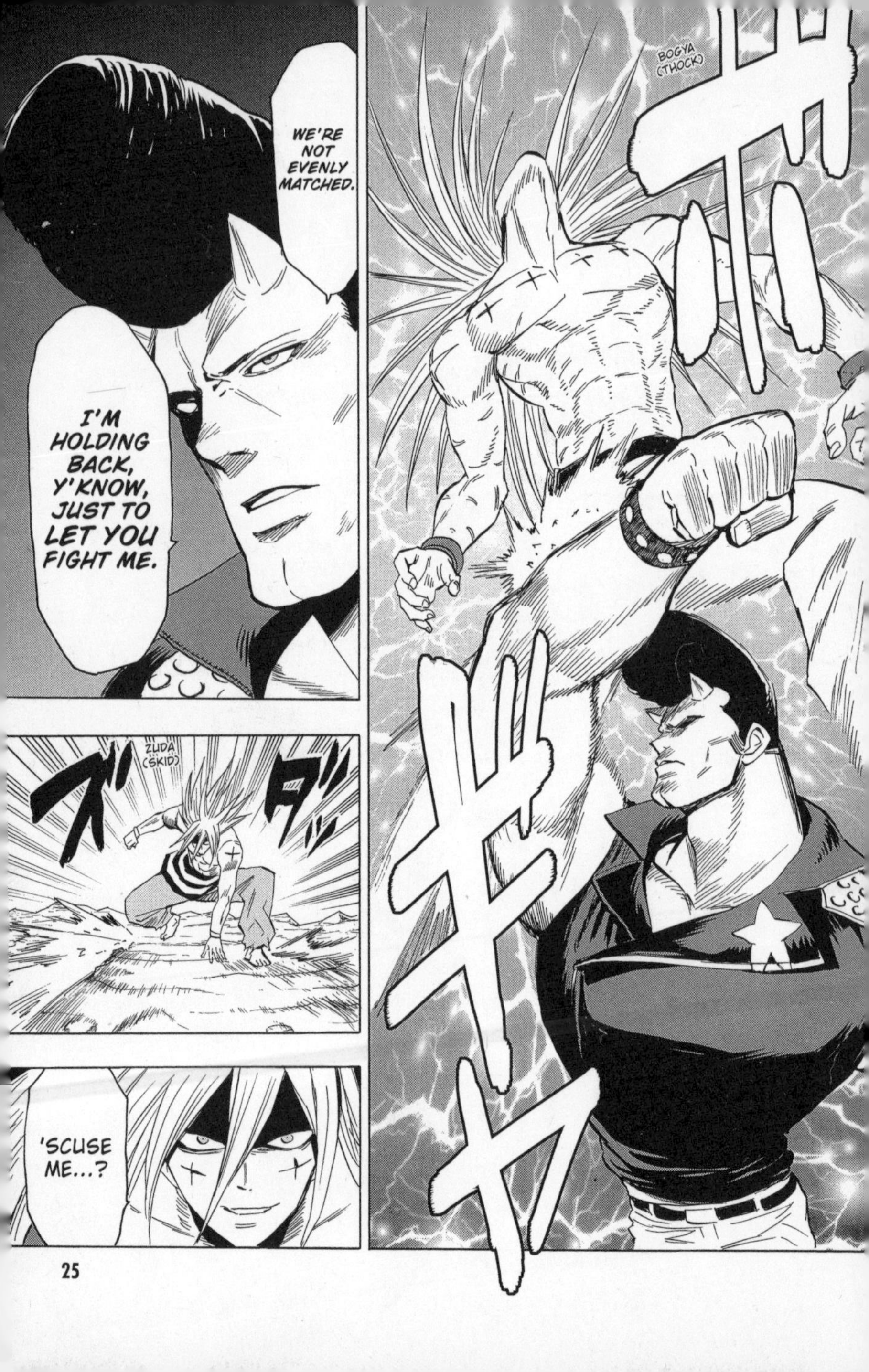
BOGYA (THOCK)
WE'RE NOT EVENLY MATCHED.
I'M HOLDING BACK, Y'KNOW, JUST TO LET YOU FIGHT ME.
ZUDA (SKID)
'SCUSE ME...?

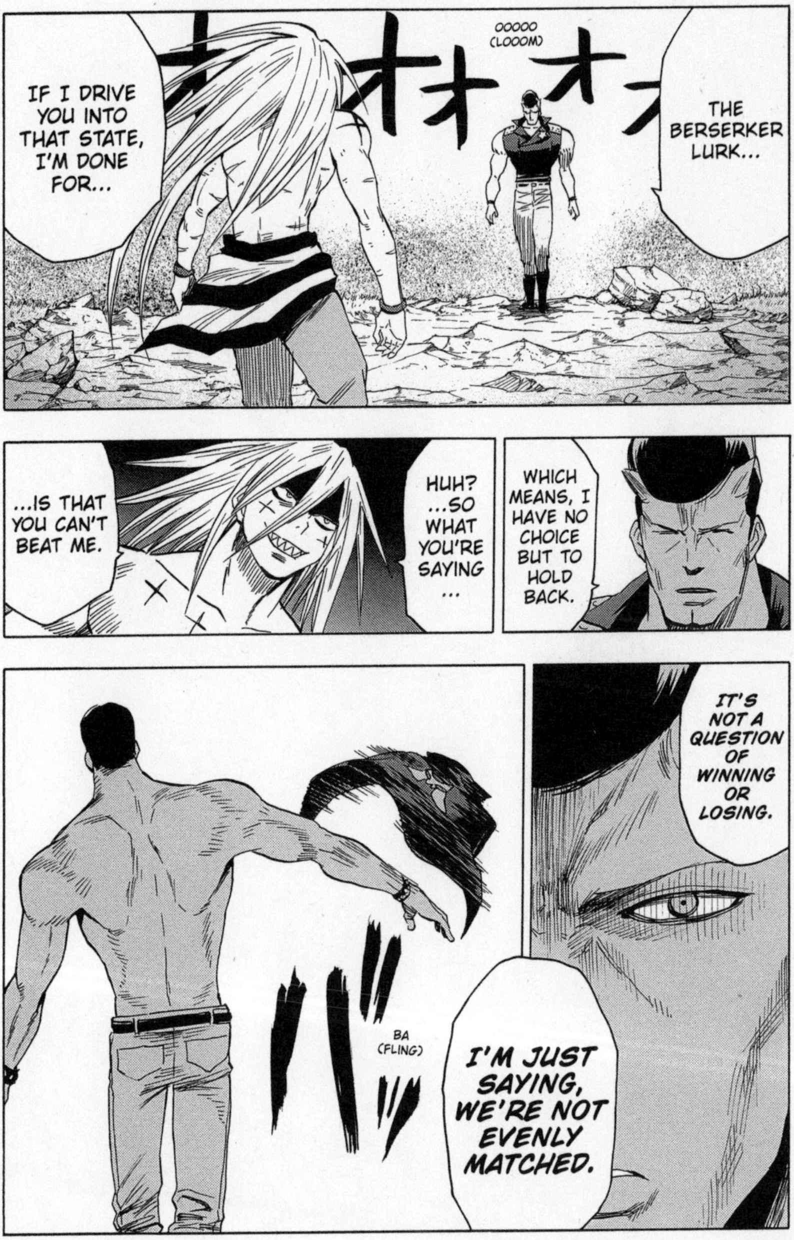
THE BERSERKER LURK...
OOOOO (LOOOM)
IF I DRIVE YOU INTO THAT STATE, I'M DONE FOR...
WHICH MEANS, I HAVE NO CHOICE BUT TO HOLD BACK.
HUH? ...SO WHAT YOU'RE SAYING ...
...IS THAT YOU CAN'T BEAT ME.
IT'S NOT A QUESTION OF WINNING OR LOSING.
I'M JUST SAYING, WE'RE NOT EVENLY MATCHED.
BA (FLING)

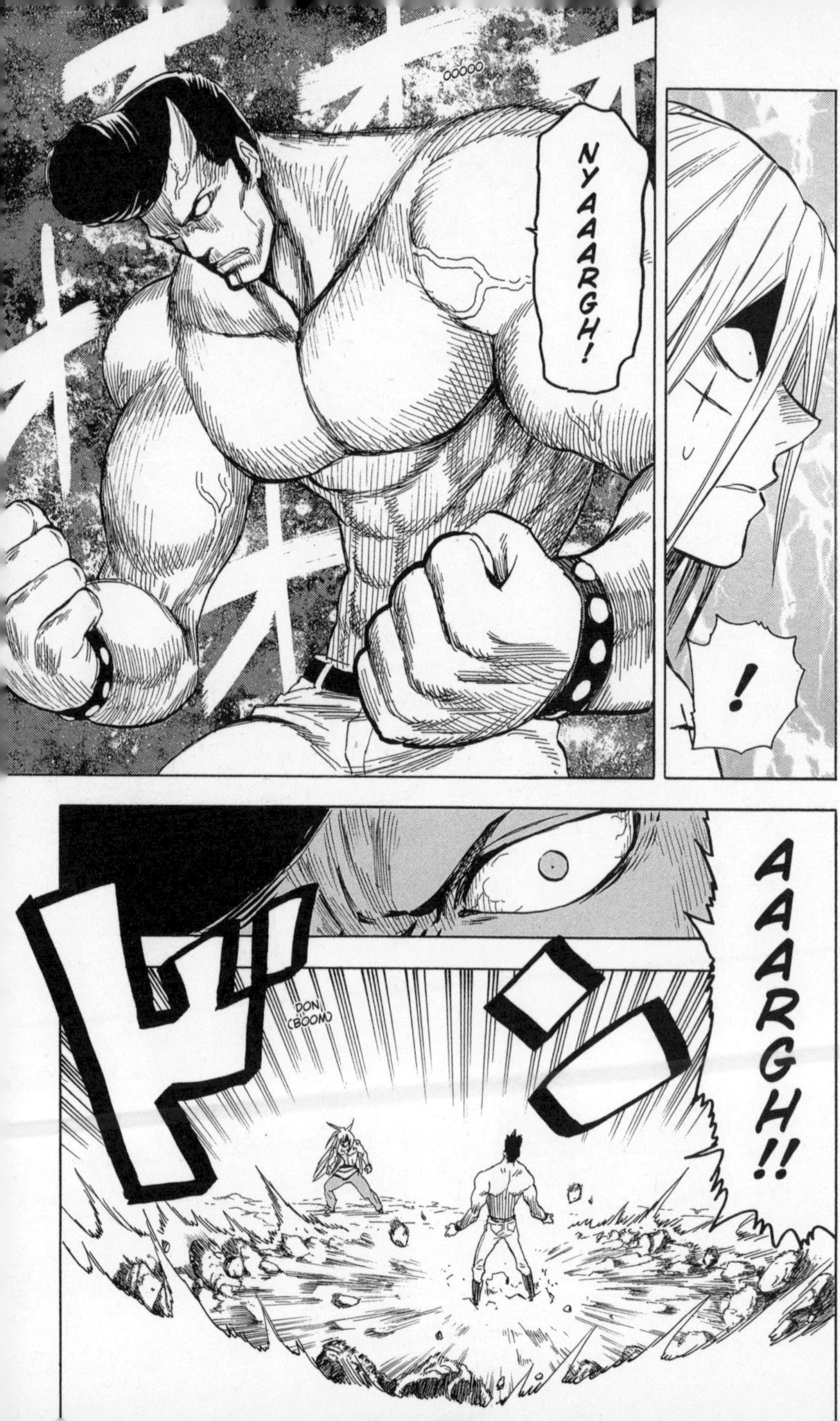
!
OOOOO
NYAAAARGH!
AAAARGH!!
DON (BOOM)

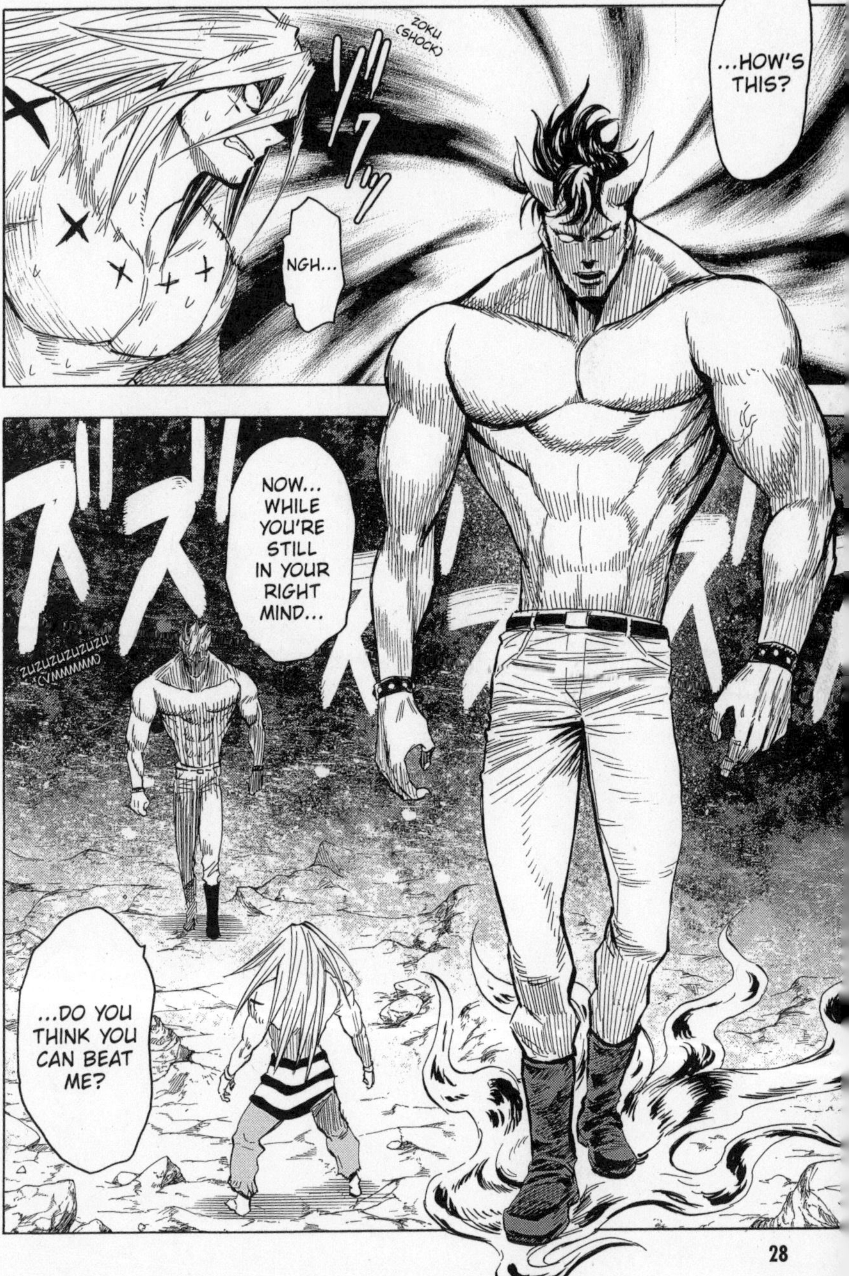
...HOW'S THIS?
ZOKU (SHOCK)
NGH...
NOW... WHILE YOU'RE STILL IN YOUR RIGHT MIND...
ZUZUZUZUZUZU (VMMMMM)
...DO YOU THINK YOU CAN BEAT ME?

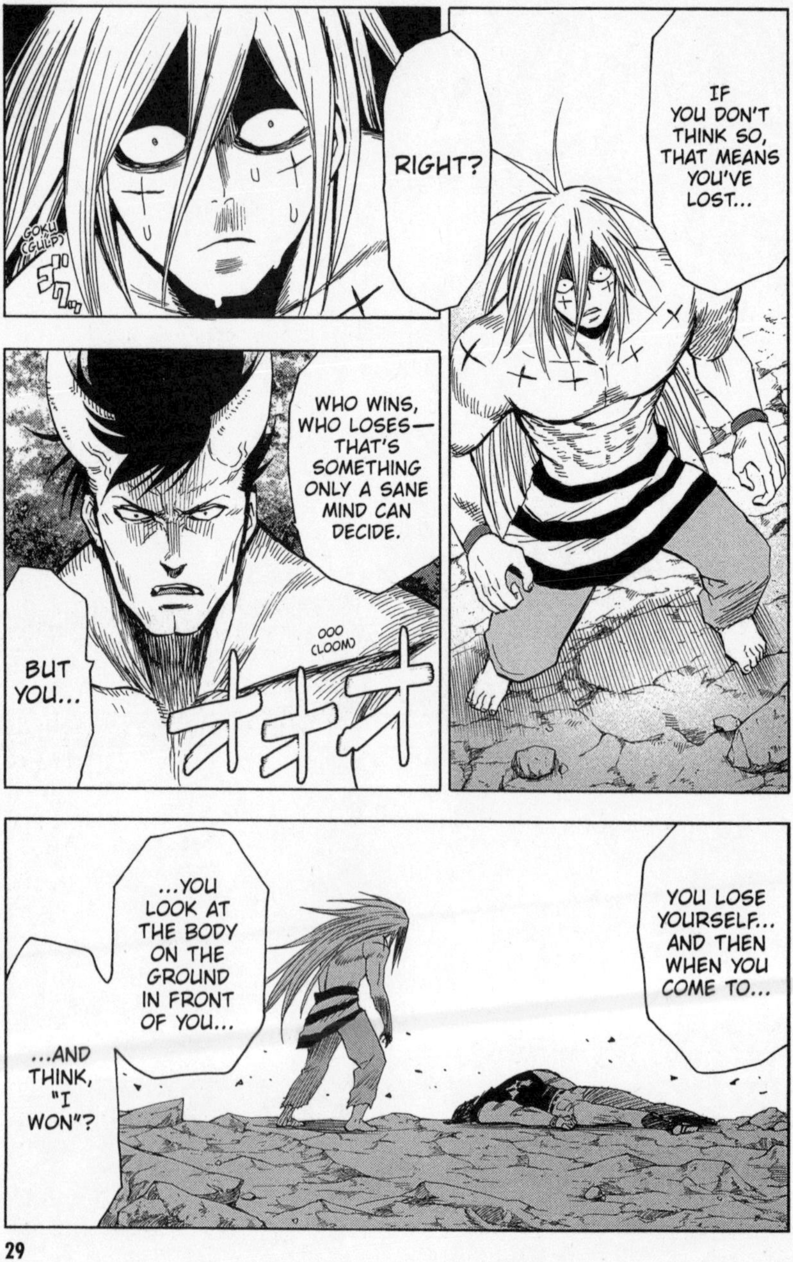
IF YOU DON'T THINK SO, THAT MEANS YOU'VE LOST...
RIGHT?
GOKU (GULP)
WHO WINS, WHO LOSES— THAT'S SOMETHING ONLY A SANE MIND CAN DECIDE.
OOO (LOOM)
BUT YOU...
YOU LOSE YOURSELF... AND THEN WHEN YOU COME TO...
...YOU LOOK AT THE BODY ON THE GROUND IN FRONT OF YOU...
...AND THINK, "I WON"?

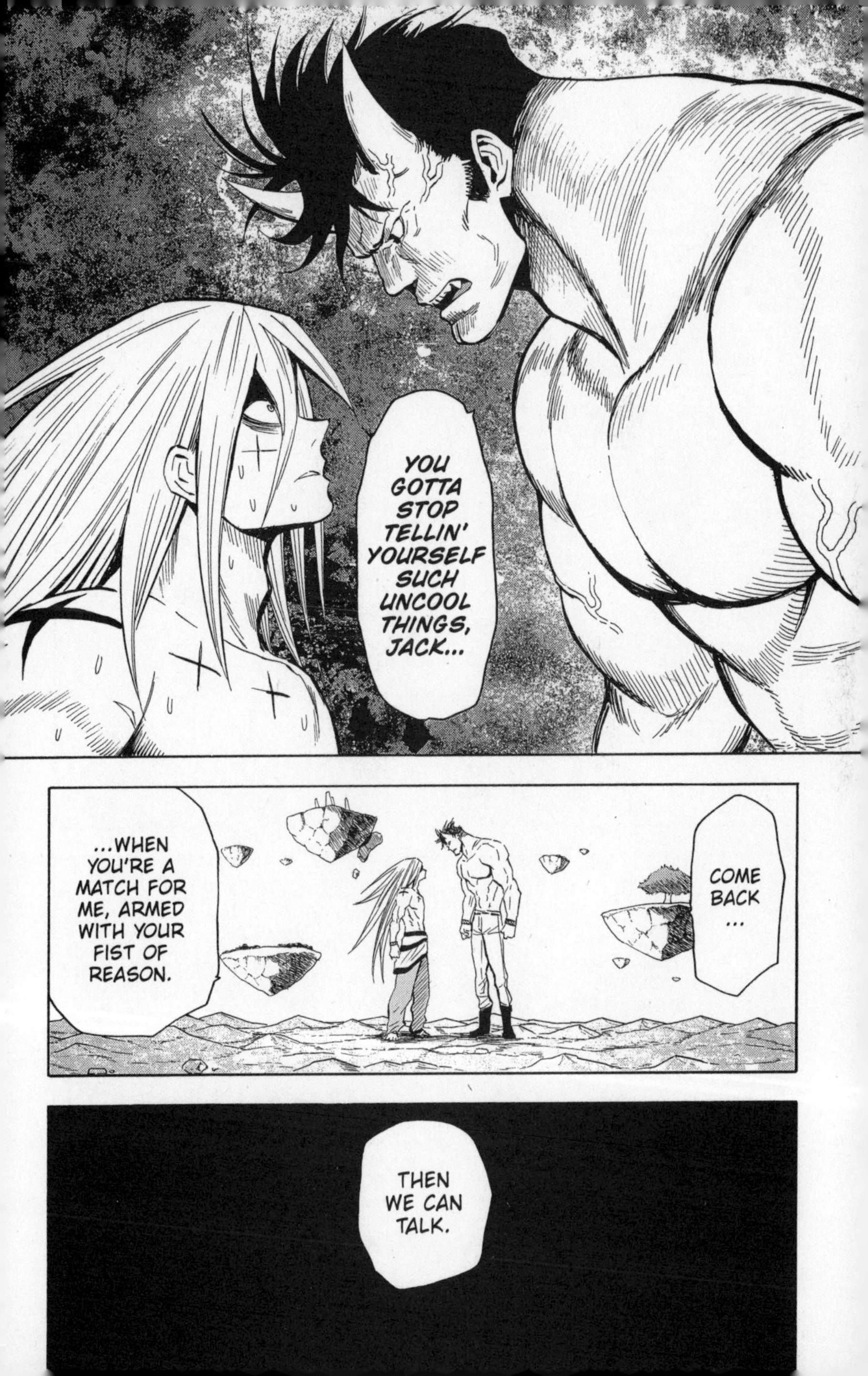
YOU GOTTA STOP TELLIN' YOURSELF SUCH UNCOOL THINGS, JACK...
COME BACK ...
...WHEN YOU'RE A MATCH FOR ME, ARMED WITH YOUR FIST OF REASON.
THEN WE CAN TALK.

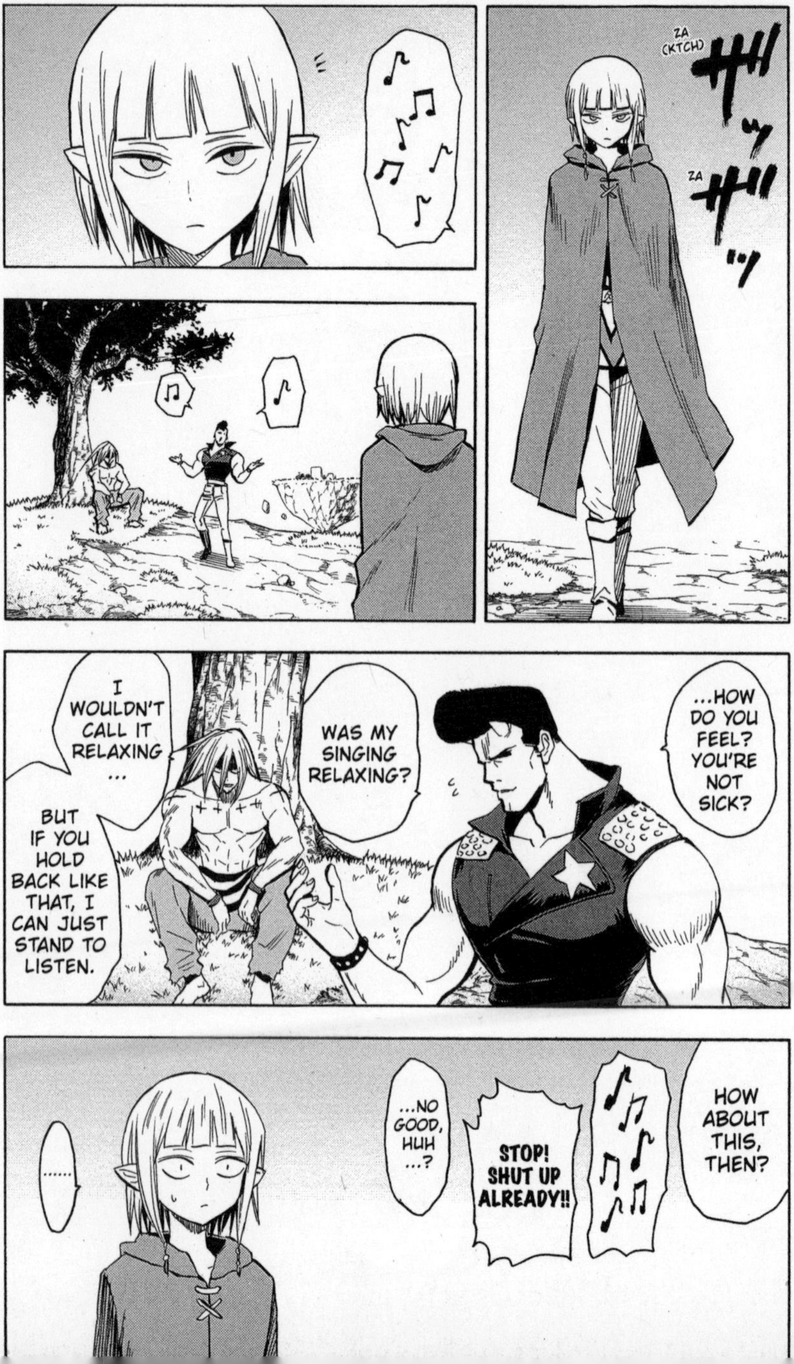
ZA (KTCH)
ZA
...HOW DO YOU FEEL? YOU'RE NOT SICK?
WAS MY SINGING RELAXING?
I WOULDN'T CALL IT RELAXING ...
BUT IF YOU HOLD BACK LIKE THAT, I CAN JUST STAND TO LISTEN.
HOW ABOUT THIS, THEN?
STOP! SHUT UP ALREADY!!
...NO GOOD, HUH ...?
......

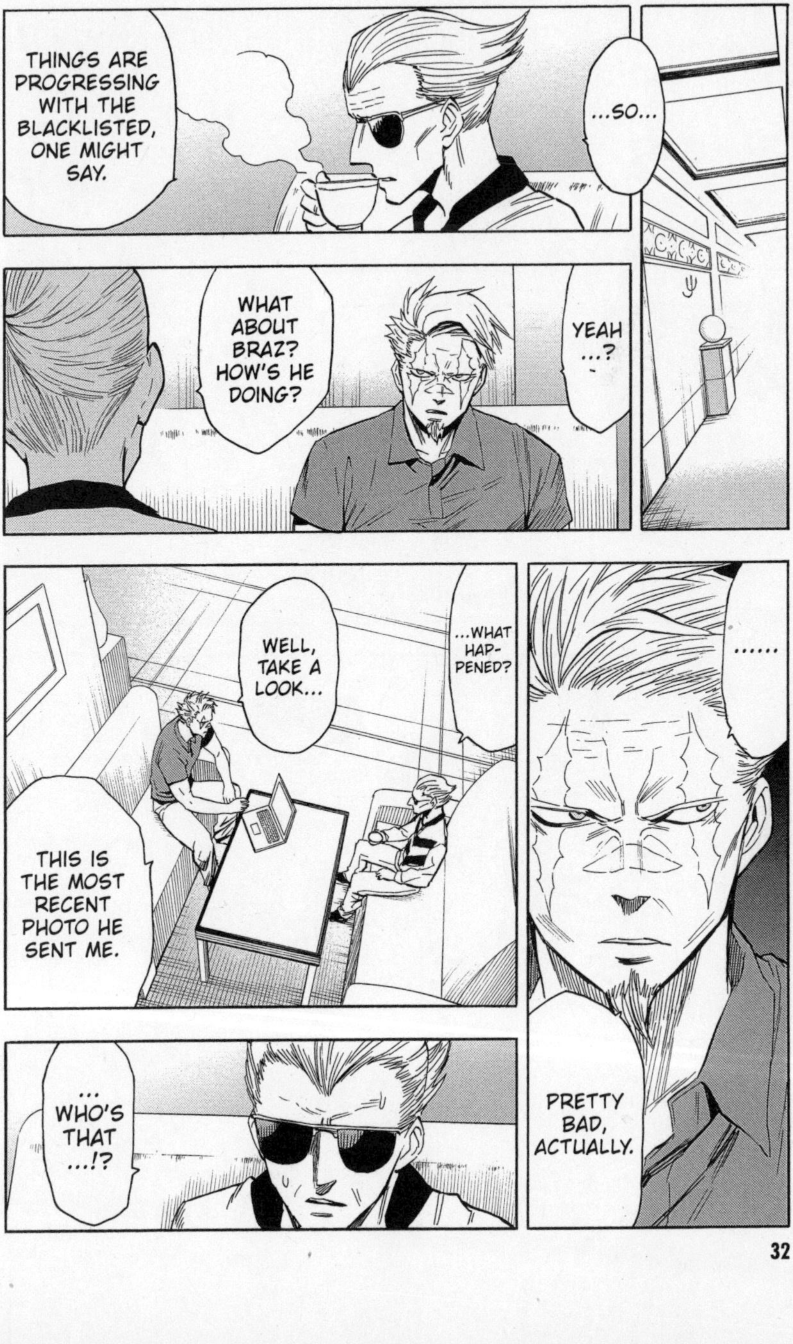
...SO...
THINGS ARE PROGRESSING WITH THE BLACKLISTED, ONE MIGHT SAY.
YEAH ...?
WHAT ABOUT BRAZ? HOW'S HE DOING?
......
PRETTY BAD, ACTUALLY.
...WHAT HAP-PENED?
WELL, TAKE A LOOK...
THIS IS THE MOST RECENT PHOTO HE SENT ME.
... WHO'S THAT ...!?

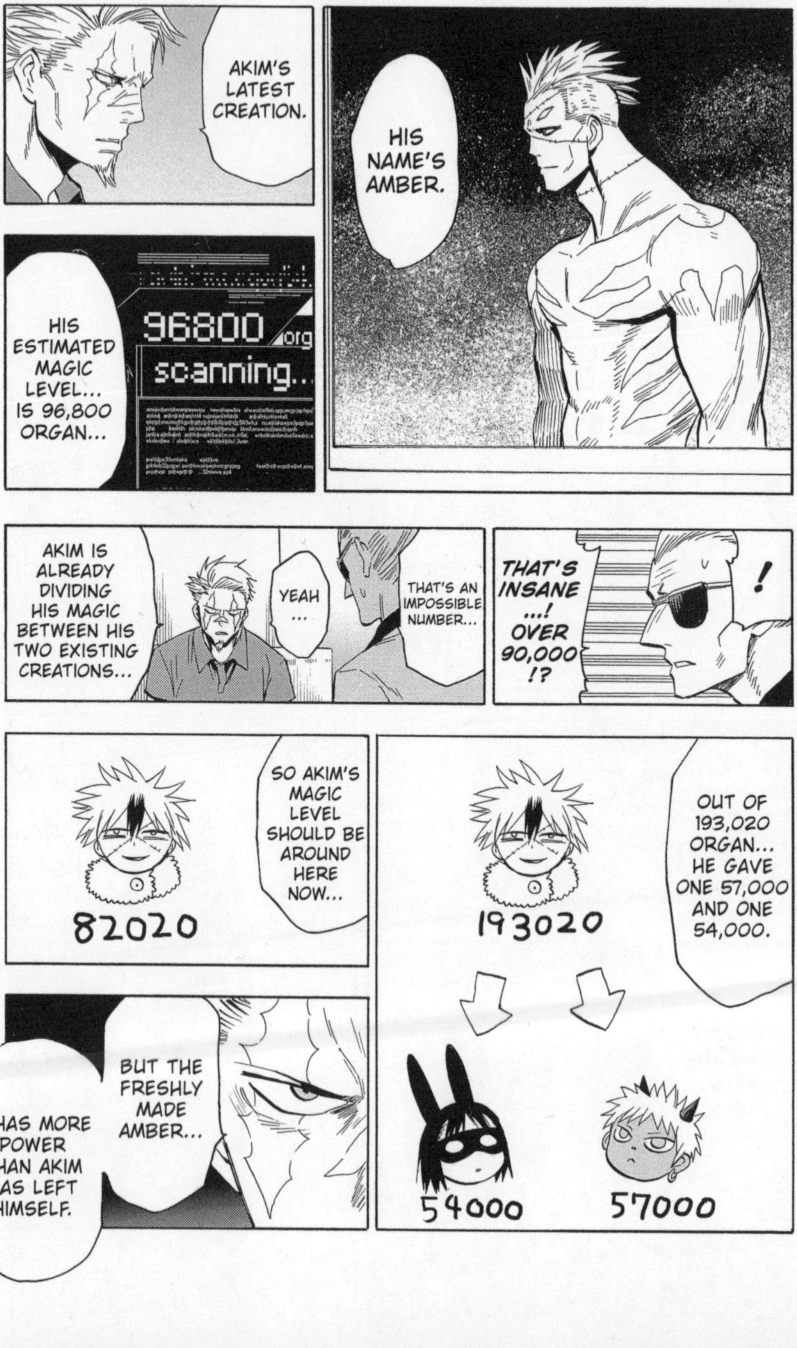

HIS NAME'S AMBER.
AKIM'S LATEST CREATION.
96800 org
scanning...
HIS ESTIMATED MAGIC LEVEL... IS 96,800 ORGAN...
!
THAT'S INSANE...! OVER 90,000!?
THAT'S AN IMPOSSIBLE NUMBER...
YEAH...
AKIM IS ALREADY DIVIDING HIS MAGIC BETWEEN HIS TWO EXISTING CREATIONS...
OUT OF 193,020 ORGAN... HE GAVE ONE 57,000 AND ONE 54,000.
193020
57000
54000
SO AKIM'S MAGIC LEVEL SHOULD BE AROUND HERE NOW...
82020
BUT THE FRESHLY MADE AMBER...
...HAS MORE POWER THAN AKIM HAS LEFT HIMSELF.

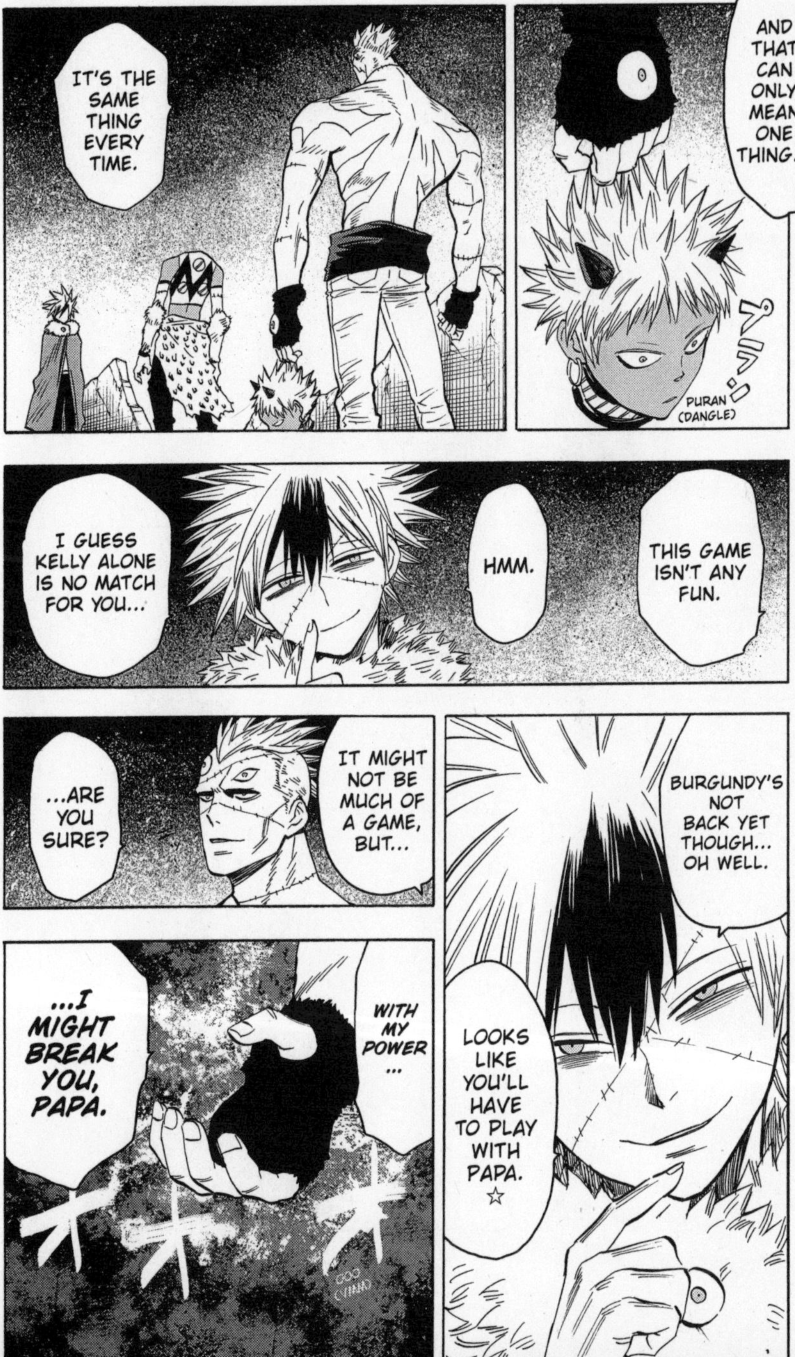
AND THAT CAN ONLY MEAN ONE THING...
PURAN (DANGLE)
IT'S THE SAME THING EVERY TIME.
THIS GAME ISN'T ANY FUN.
HMM.
I GUESS KELLY ALONE IS NO MATCH FOR YOU...
BURGUNDY'S NOT BACK YET THOUGH... OH WELL.
LOOKS LIKE YOU'LL HAVE TO PLAY WITH PAPA. ☆
IT MIGHT NOT BE MUCH OF A GAME, BUT...
...ARE YOU SURE?
WITH MY POWER...
...I MIGHT BREAK YOU, PAPA.
GOO

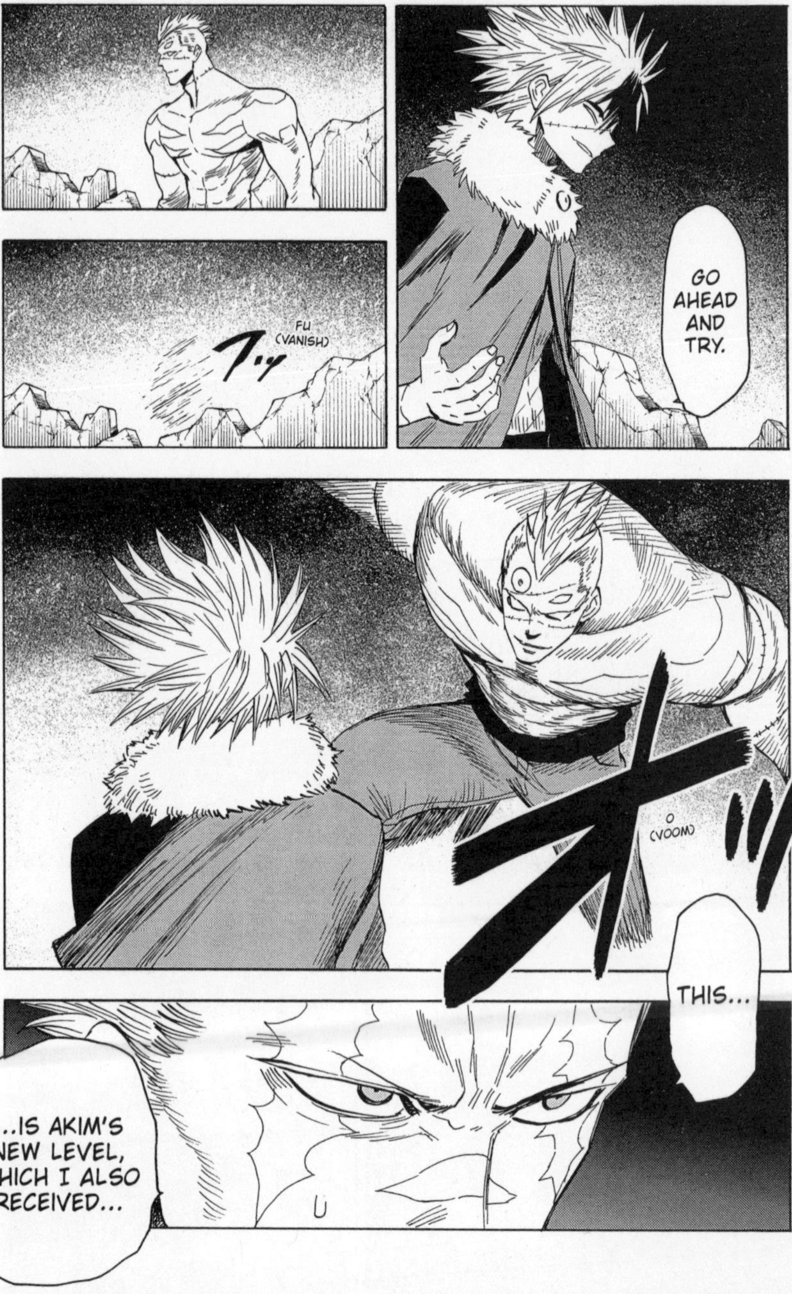
GO AHEAD AND TRY.
フッ
FU (VANISH)
オッ
O (VOOM)
THIS...
...IS AKIM'S NEW LEVEL, WHICH I ALSO RECEIVED...

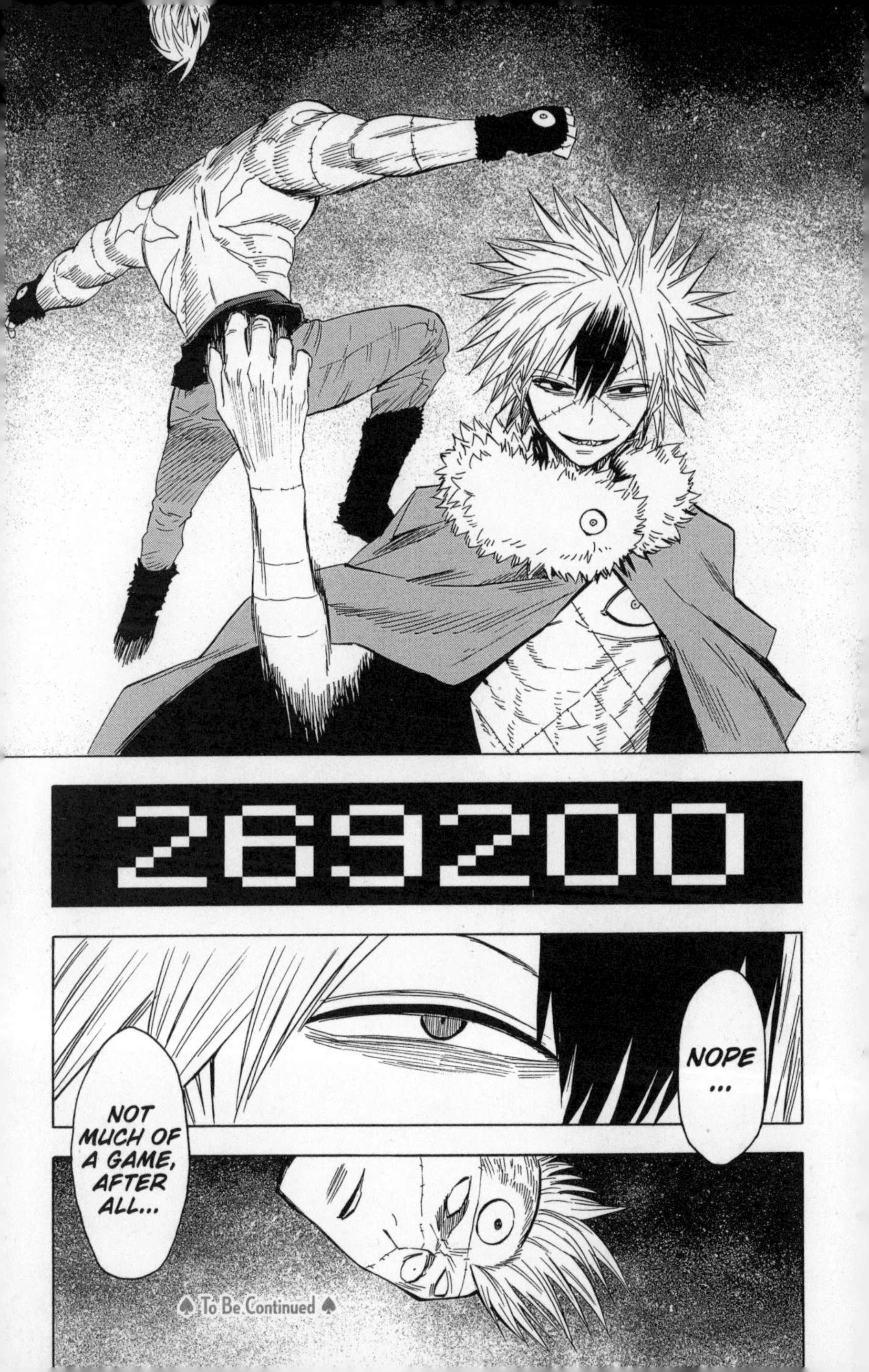
269200
NOPE ...
NOT MUCH OF A GAME, AFTER ALL...
To Be Continued

BLOOD LAD

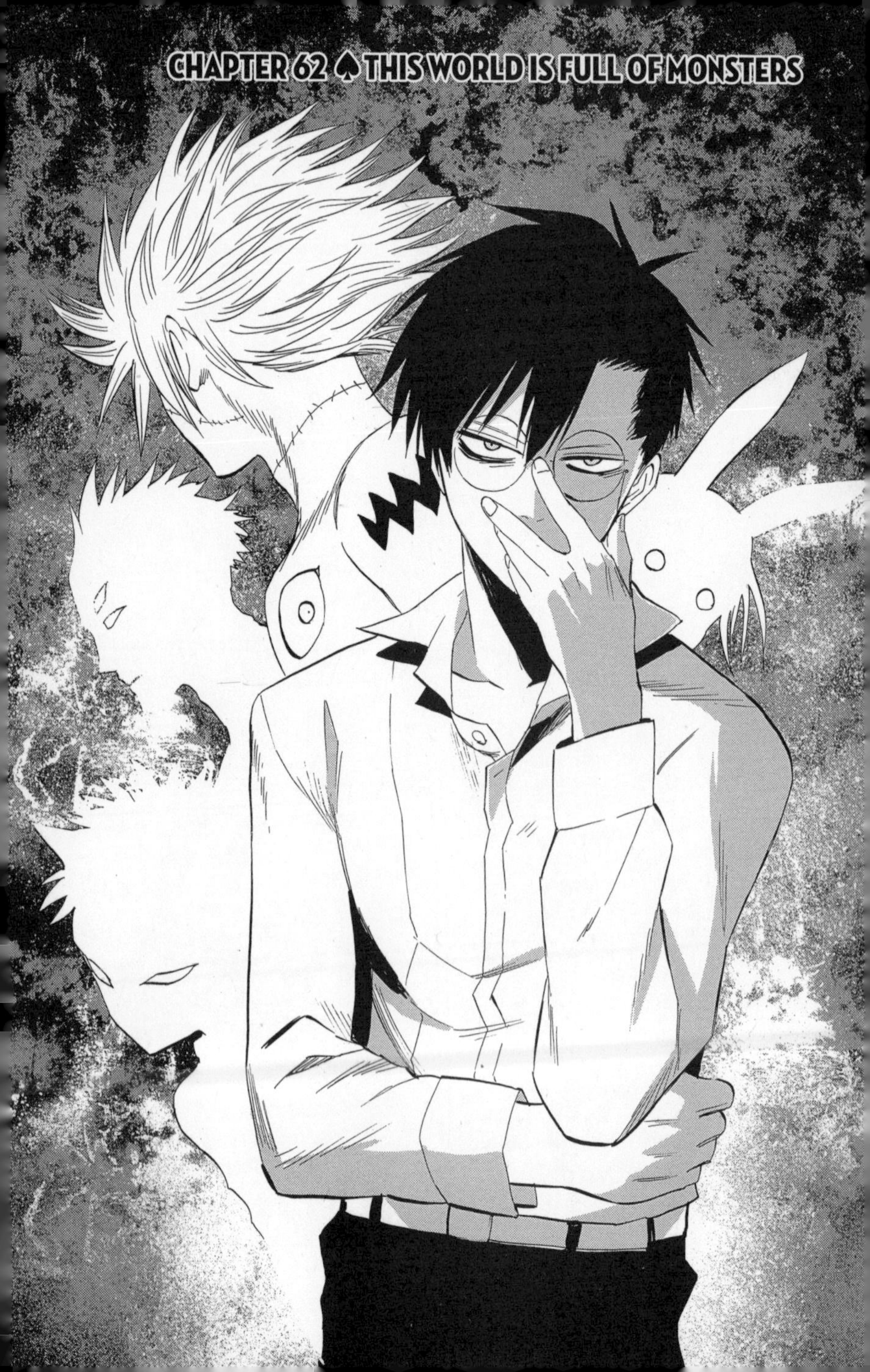
CHAPTER 62 ♠ THIS WORLD IS FULL OF MONSTERS

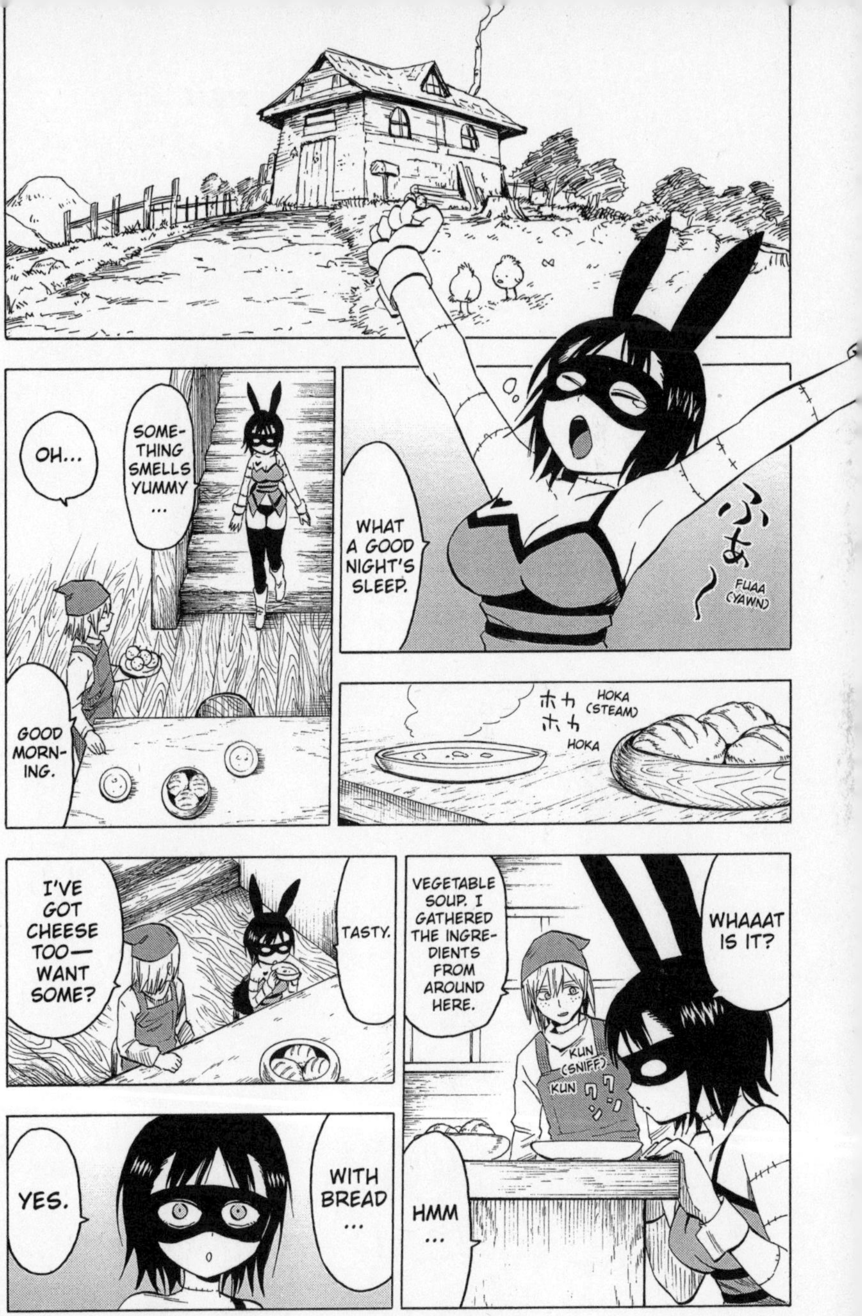
ふあ〜
FUAA (YAWN)
WHAT A GOOD NIGHT'S SLEEP.
ホカホカ
HOKA (STEAM) HOKA
SOME-THING SMELLS YUMMY ...
OH...
GOOD MORN-ING.
WHAAAT IS IT?
VEGETABLE SOUP. I GATHERED THE INGRE-DIENTS FROM AROUND HERE.
クンクン
KUN (SNIFF) KUN
HMM ...
TASTY.
I'VE GOT CHEESE TOO— WANT SOME?
WITH BREAD ...
YES.

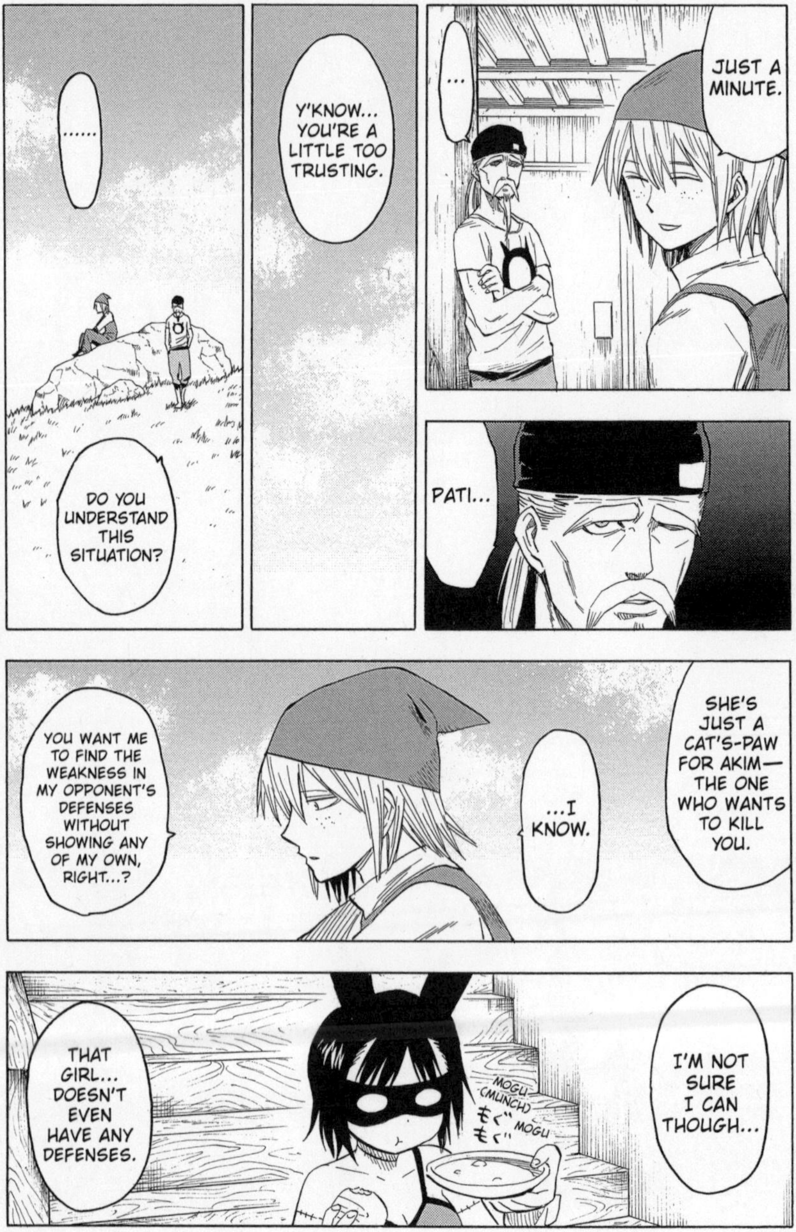
JUST A MINUTE.
...
PATI...
Y'KNOW... YOU'RE A LITTLE TOO TRUSTING.
......
DO YOU UNDERSTAND THIS SITUATION?
SHE'S JUST A CAT'S-PAW FOR AKIM— THE ONE WHO WANTS TO KILL YOU.
...I KNOW.
YOU WANT ME TO FIND THE WEAKNESS IN MY OPPONENT'S DEFENSES WITHOUT SHOWING ANY OF MY OWN, RIGHT...?
I'M NOT SURE I CAN THOUGH...
MOGU (MUNCH) もぐ
もぐ MOGU
THAT GIRL... DOESN'T EVEN HAVE ANY DEFENSES.

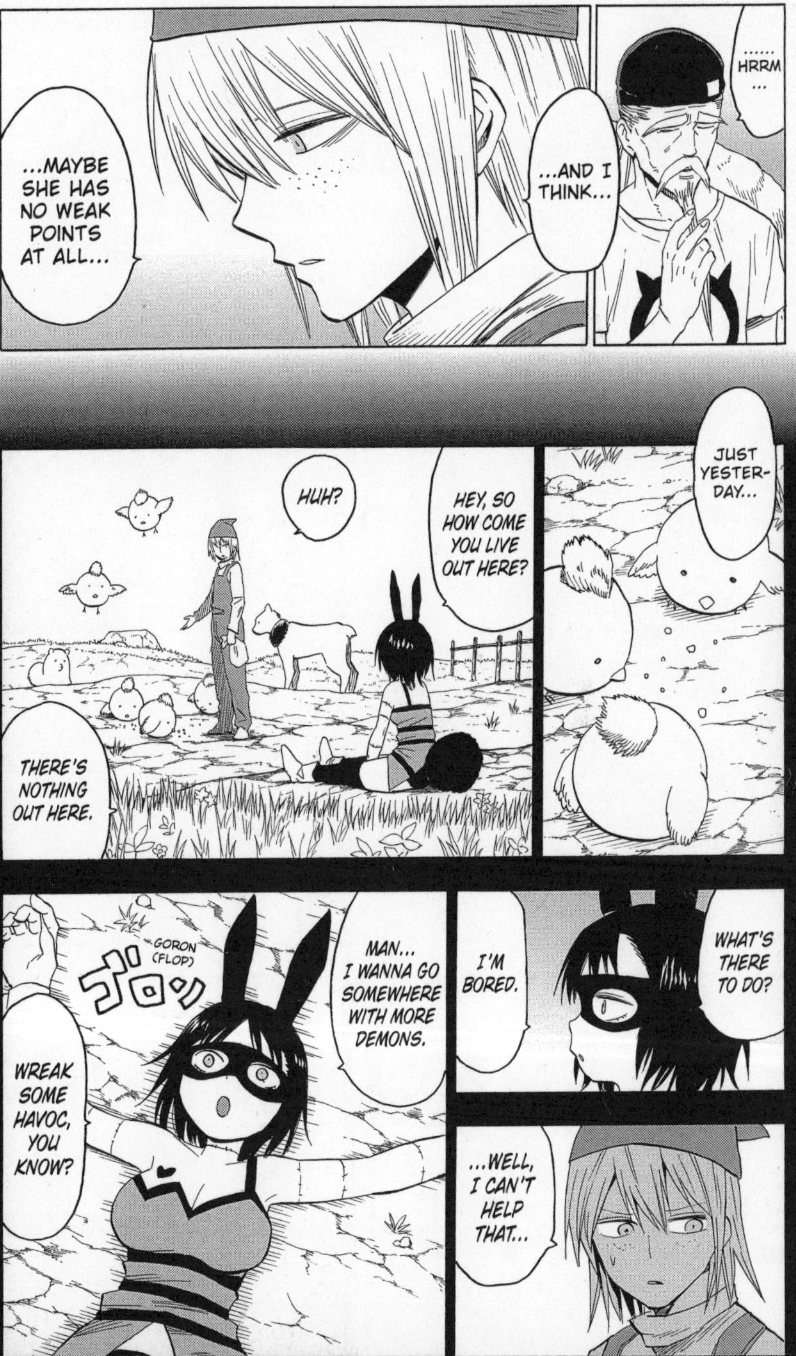
......HRRM...
...AND I THINK...
...MAYBE SHE HAS NO WEAK POINTS AT ALL...
JUST YESTER-DAY...
HEY, SO HOW COME YOU LIVE OUT HERE?
HUH?
THERE'S NOTHING OUT HERE.
WHAT'S THERE TO DO?
I'M BORED.
...WELL, I CAN'T HELP THAT...
MAN... I WANNA GO SOMEWHERE WITH MORE DEMONS.
GORON (FLOP)
ゴロッ
WREAK SOME HAVOC, YOU KNOW?

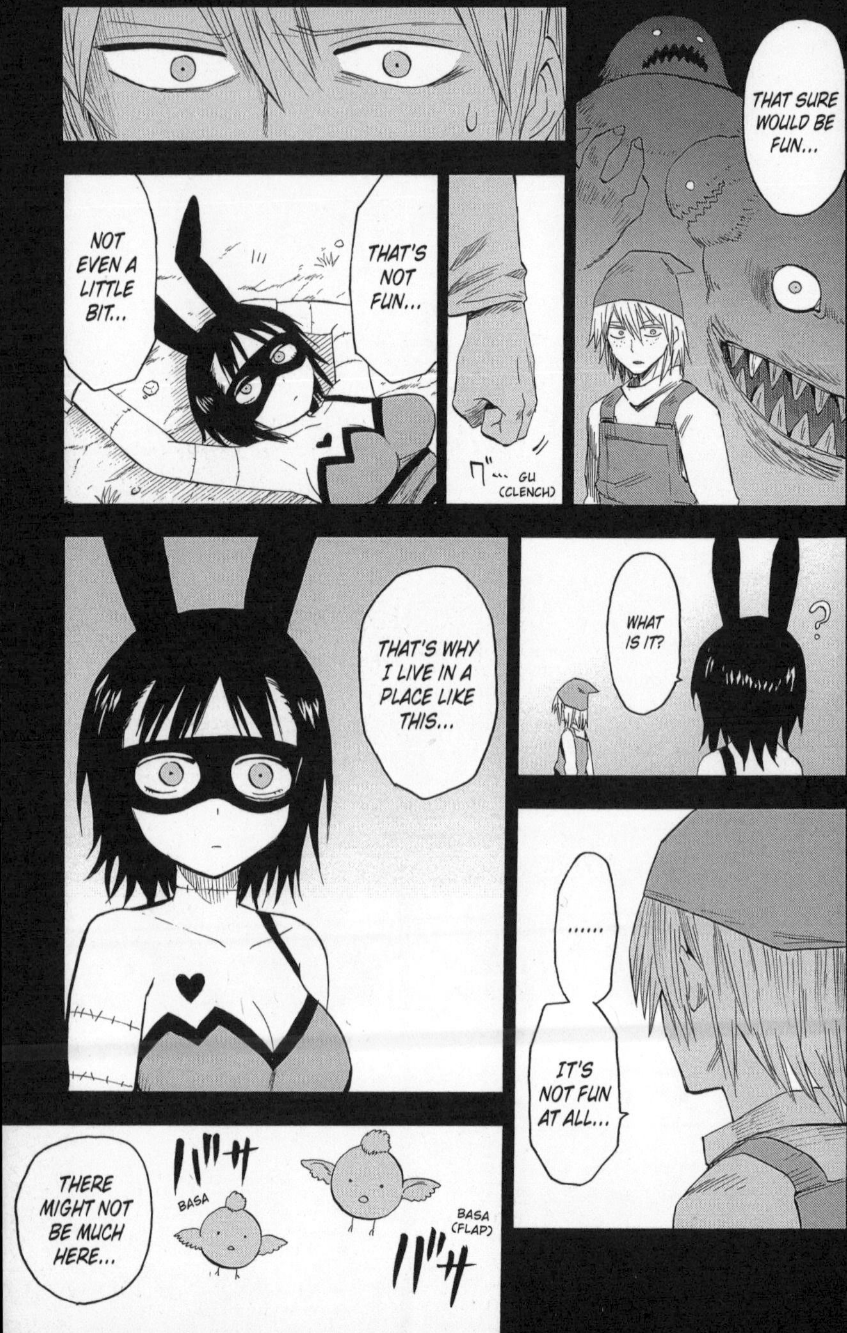
THAT SURE WOULD BE FUN...
グ…
GU (CLENCH)
THAT'S NOT FUN...
NOT EVEN A LITTLE BIT...
WHAT IS IT?
?
......
IT'S NOT FUN AT ALL...
THAT'S WHY I LIVE IN A PLACE LIKE THIS...
バサ
BASA
バサ
BASA (FLAP)
THERE MIGHT NOT BE MUCH HERE...

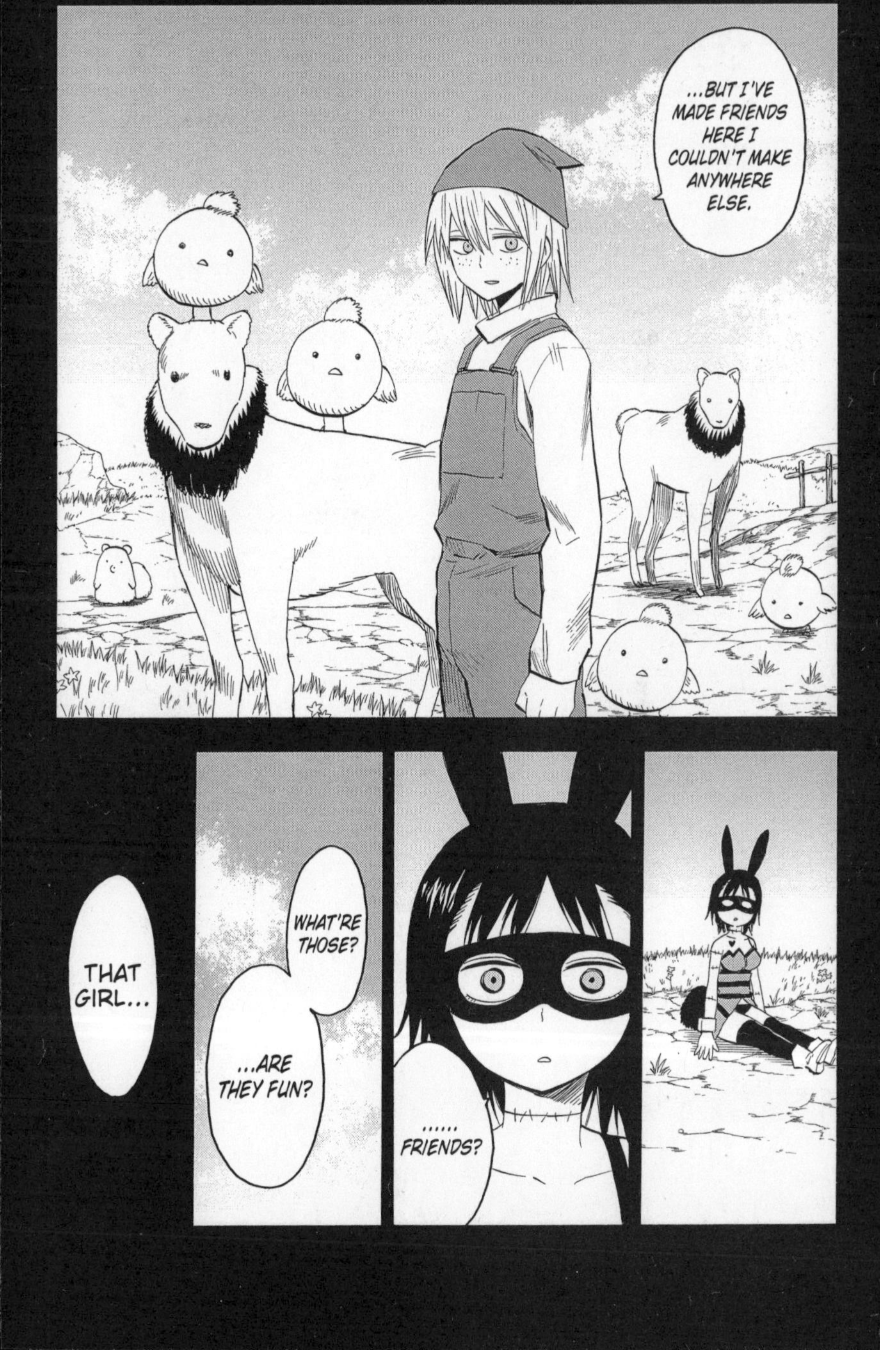
...BUT I'VE MADE FRIENDS HERE I COULDN'T MAKE ANYWHERE ELSE.
......FRIENDS?
WHAT'RE THOSE?
...ARE THEY FUN?
THAT GIRL...

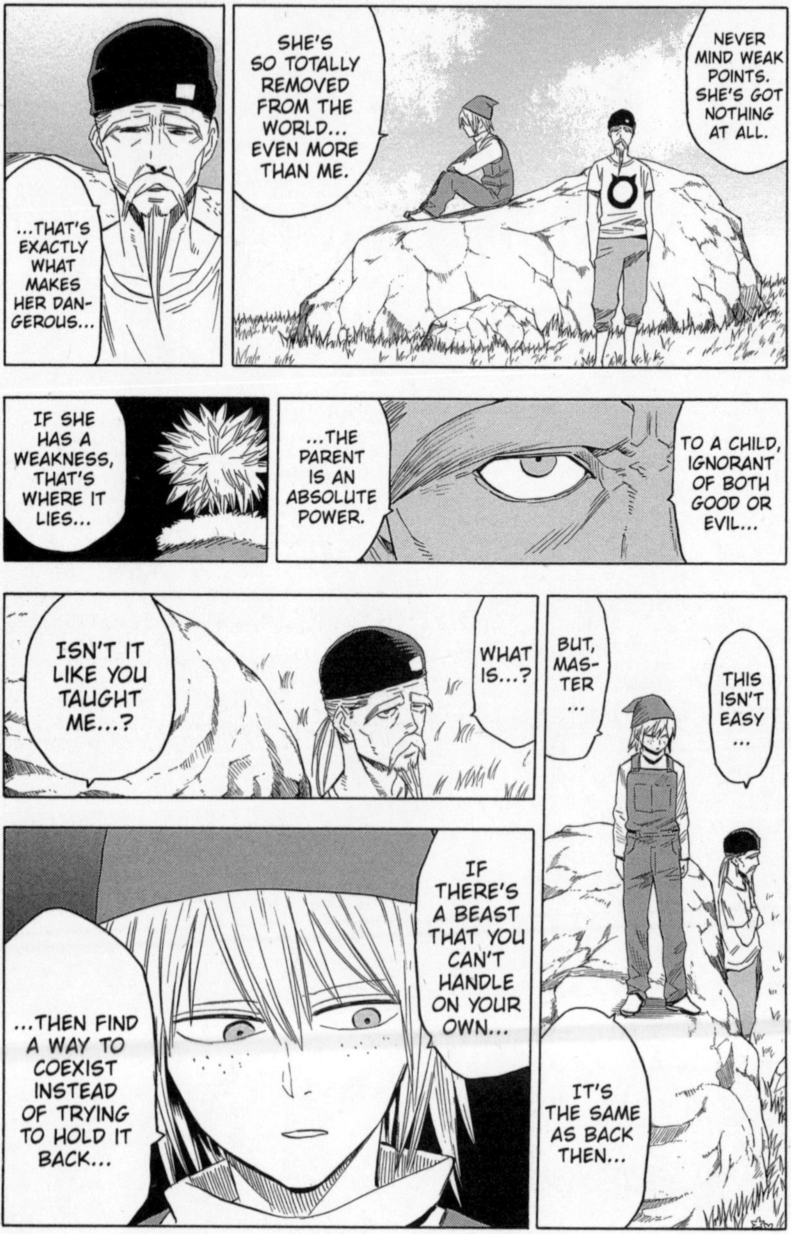
NEVER MIND WEAK POINTS. SHE'S GOT NOTHING AT ALL.
SHE'S SO TOTALLY REMOVED FROM THE WORLD... EVEN MORE THAN ME.
...THAT'S EXACTLY WHAT MAKES HER DAN-GEROUS...
TO A CHILD, IGNORANT OF BOTH GOOD OR EVIL...
...THE PARENT IS AN ABSOLUTE POWER.
IF SHE HAS A WEAKNESS, THAT'S WHERE IT LIES...
THIS ISN'T EASY...
BUT, MAS-TER...
IT'S THE SAME AS BACK THEN...
WHAT IS...?
ISN'T IT LIKE YOU TAUGHT ME...?
IF THERE'S A BEAST THAT YOU CAN'T HANDLE ON YOUR OWN...
...THEN FIND A WAY TO COEXIST INSTEAD OF TRYING TO HOLD IT BACK...

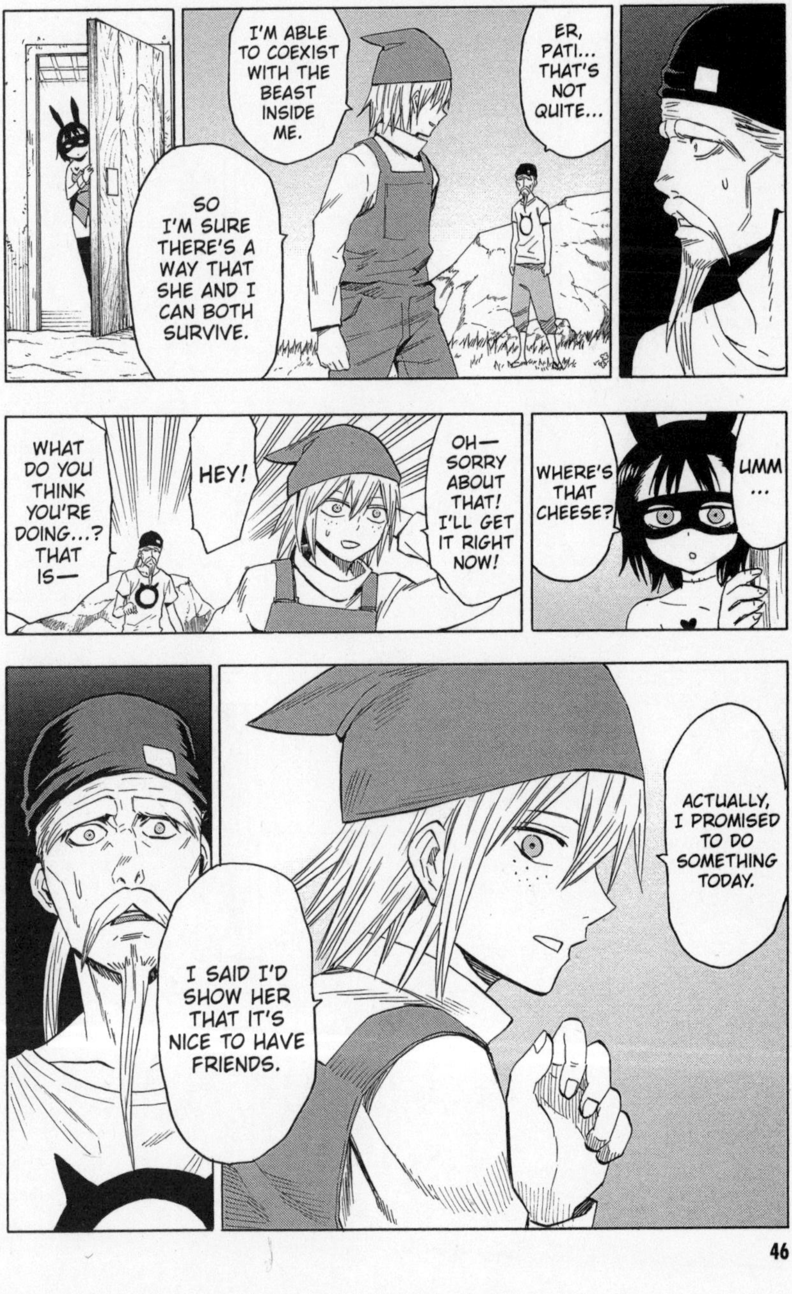
ER, PATI... THAT'S NOT QUITE...
I'M ABLE TO COEXIST WITH THE BEAST INSIDE ME.
SO I'M SURE THERE'S A WAY THAT SHE AND I CAN BOTH SURVIVE.
UMM...
WHERE'S THAT CHEESE?
OH— SORRY ABOUT THAT! I'LL GET IT RIGHT NOW!
HEY!
WHAT DO YOU THINK YOU'RE DOING...? THAT IS—
ACTUALLY, I PROMISED TO DO SOMETHING TODAY.
I SAID I'D SHOW HER THAT IT'S NICE TO HAVE FRIENDS.

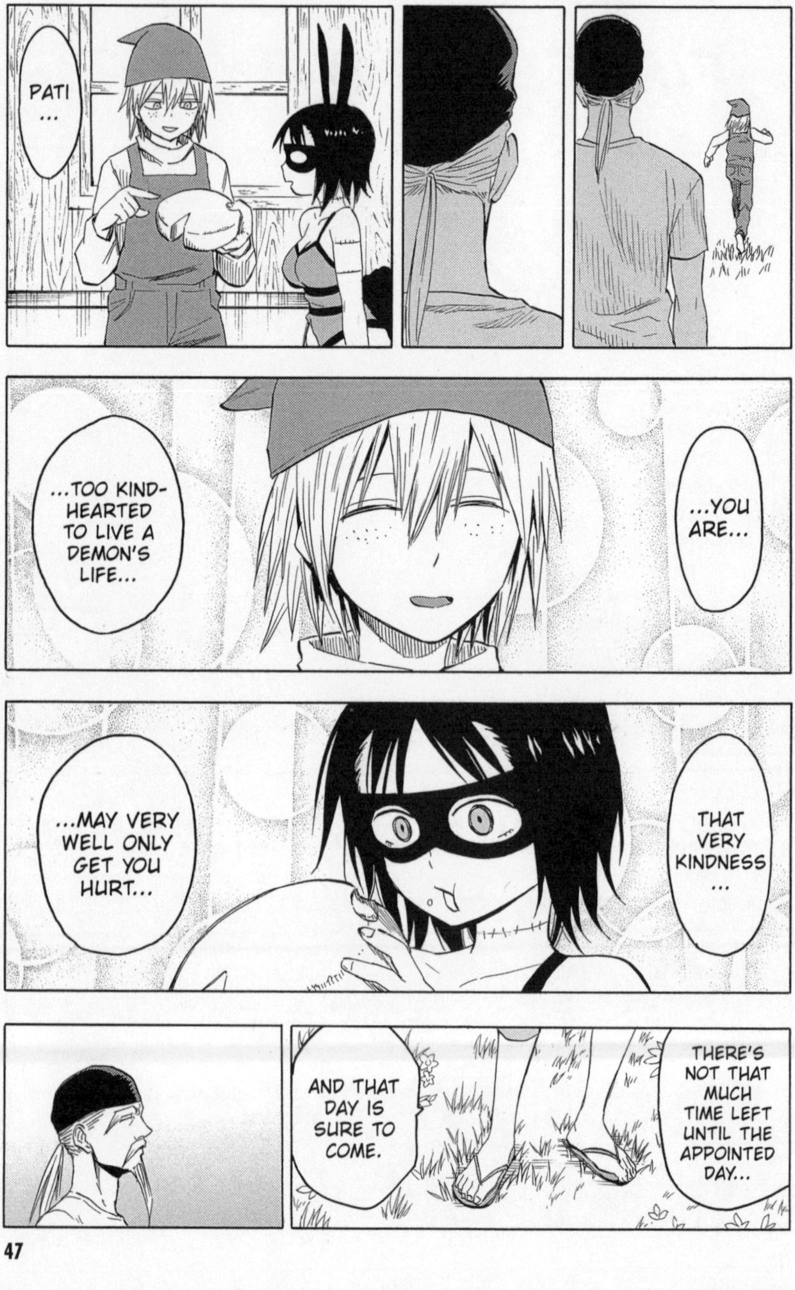
PATI ...
...YOU ARE...
...TOO KIND-HEARTED TO LIVE A DEMON'S LIFE...
THAT VERY KINDNESS ...
...MAY VERY WELL ONLY GET YOU HURT...
THERE'S NOT THAT MUCH TIME LEFT UNTIL THE APPOINTED DAY...
AND THAT DAY IS SURE TO COME.

FIFTEEN DAYS LEFT

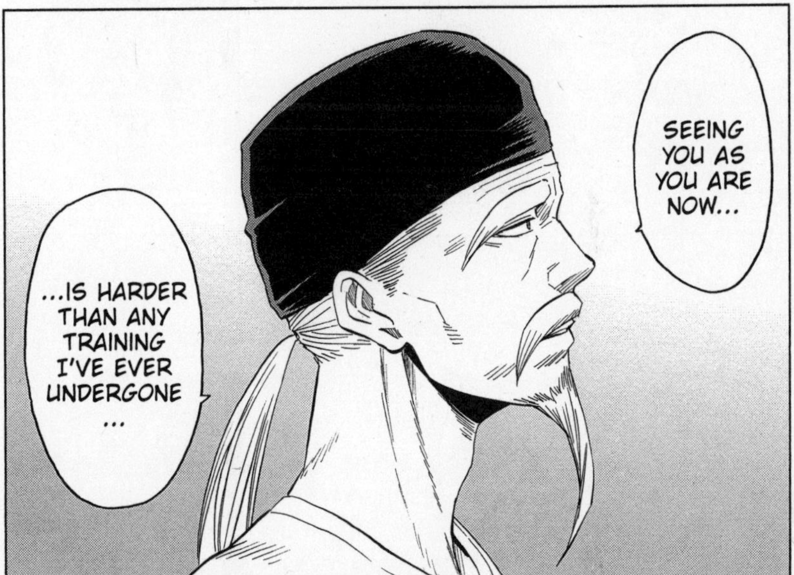
SEEING YOU AS YOU ARE NOW...
...IS HARDER THAN ANY TRAINING I'VE EVER UNDERGONE ...

LEVEL OF AKIM'S MAGIC: 278,900

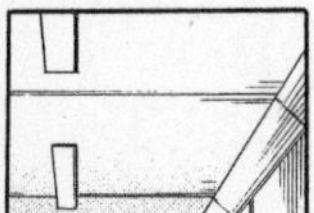

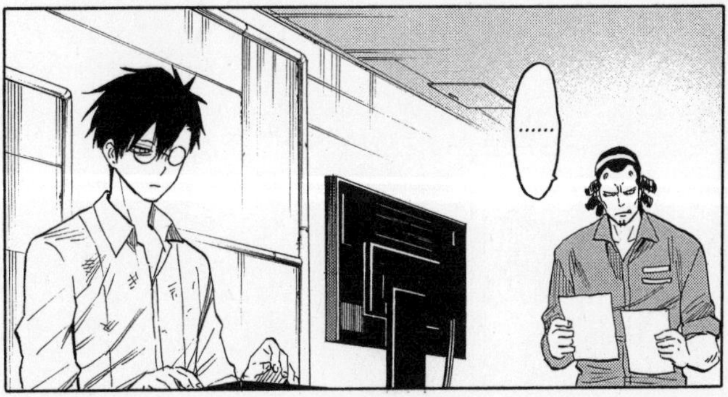
......

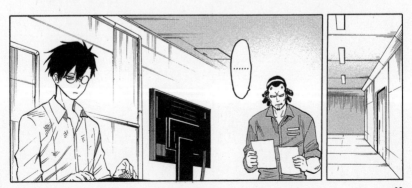

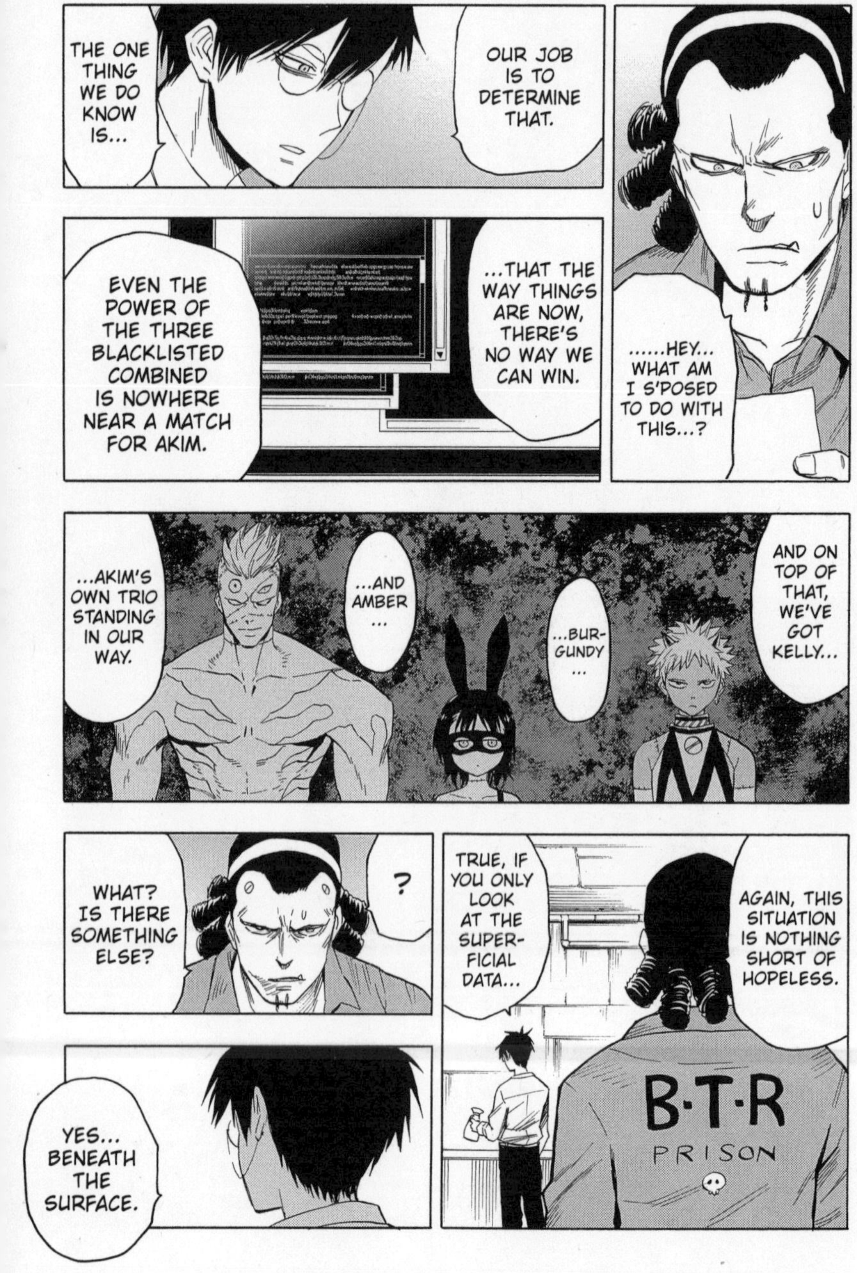
......HEY... WHAT AM I S'POSED TO DO WITH THIS...?
OUR JOB IS TO DETERMINE THAT.
THE ONE THING WE DO KNOW IS...
...THAT THE WAY THINGS ARE NOW, THERE'S NO WAY WE CAN WIN.
EVEN THE POWER OF THE THREE BLACKLISTED COMBINED IS NOWHERE NEAR A MATCH FOR AKIM.
AND ON TOP OF THAT, WE'VE GOT KELLY...
...BURGUNDY...
...AND AMBER...
...AKIM'S OWN TRIO STANDING IN OUR WAY.
AGAIN, THIS SITUATION IS NOTHING SHORT OF HOPELESS.
TRUE, IF YOU ONLY LOOK AT THE SUPERFICIAL DATA...
B·T·R
PRISON
?
WHAT? IS THERE SOMETHING ELSE?
YES... BENEATH THE SURFACE.

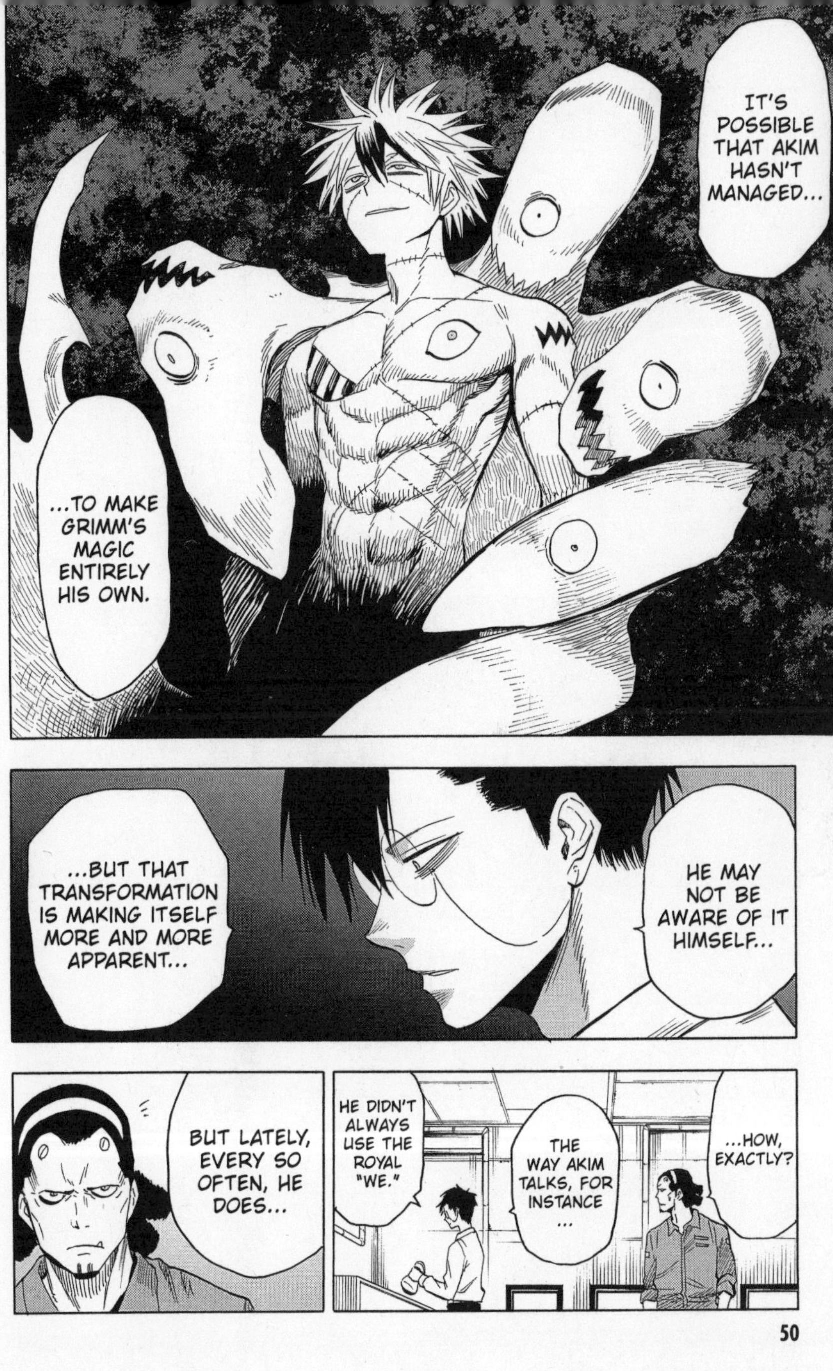
IT'S POSSIBLE THAT AKIM HASN'T MANAGED...
...TO MAKE GRIMM'S MAGIC ENTIRELY HIS OWN.
HE MAY NOT BE AWARE OF IT HIMSELF...
...BUT THAT TRANSFORMATION IS MAKING ITSELF MORE AND MORE APPARENT...
...HOW, EXACTLY?
THE WAY AKIM TALKS, FOR INSTANCE...
HE DIDN'T ALWAYS USE THE ROYAL "WE."
BUT LATELY, EVERY SO OFTEN, HE DOES...

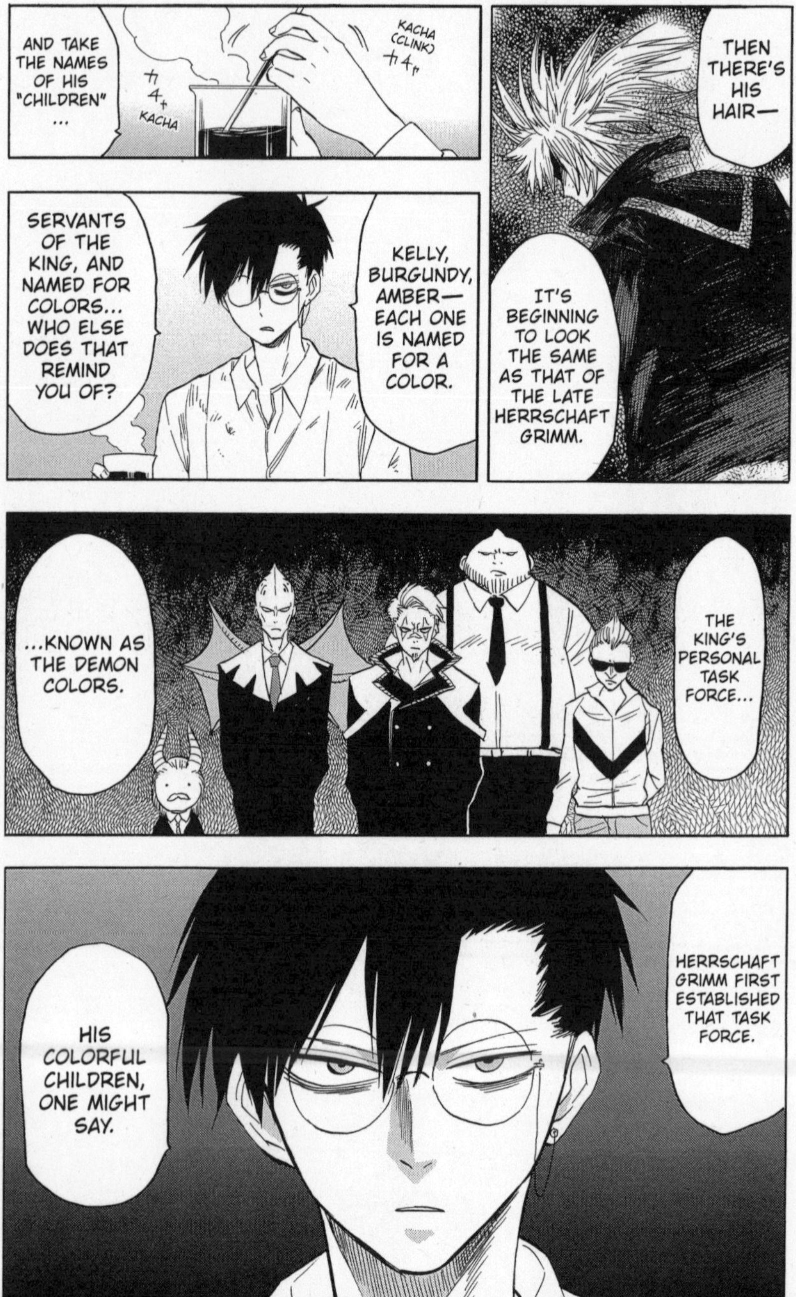
THEN THERE'S HIS HAIR—
IT'S BEGINNING TO LOOK THE SAME AS THAT OF THE LATE HERRSCHAFT GRIMM.
AND TAKE THE NAMES OF HIS "CHILDREN" ...
KACHA (CLINK)
KACHA
KELLY, BURGUNDY, AMBER— EACH ONE IS NAMED FOR A COLOR.
SERVANTS OF THE KING, AND NAMED FOR COLORS... WHO ELSE DOES THAT REMIND YOU OF?
THE KING'S PERSONAL TASK FORCE...
...KNOWN AS THE DEMON COLORS.
HERRSCHAFT GRIMM FIRST ESTABLISHED THAT TASK FORCE.
HIS COLORFUL CHILDREN, ONE MIGHT SAY.

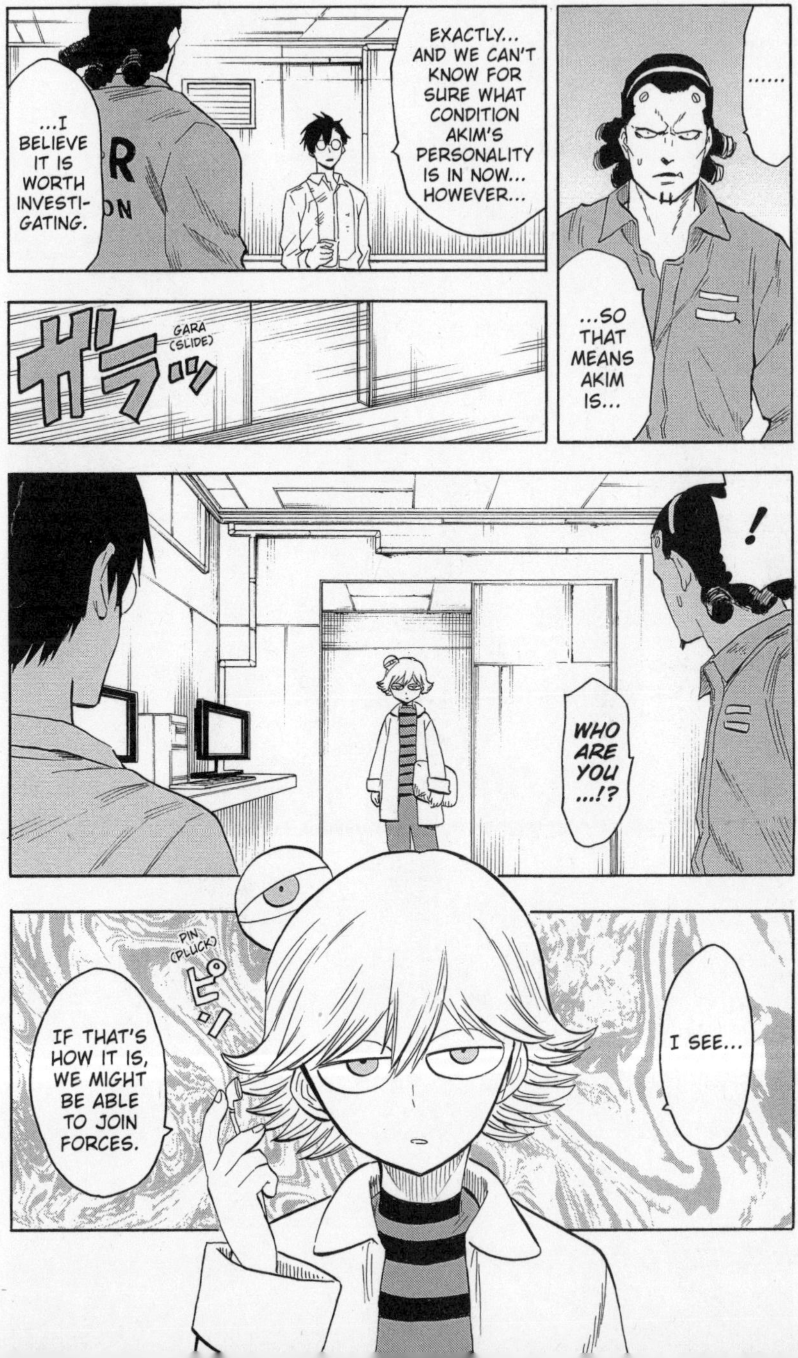
......
...SO THAT MEANS AKIM IS...
EXACTLY... AND WE CAN'T KNOW FOR SURE WHAT CONDITION AKIM'S PERSONALITY IS IN NOW... HOWEVER...
...I BELIEVE IT IS WORTH INVESTIGATING.
GARA (SLIDE)
!
WHO ARE YOU ...!?
I SEE...
PIN (PLUCK)
IF THAT'S HOW IT IS, WE MIGHT BE ABLE TO JOIN FORCES.

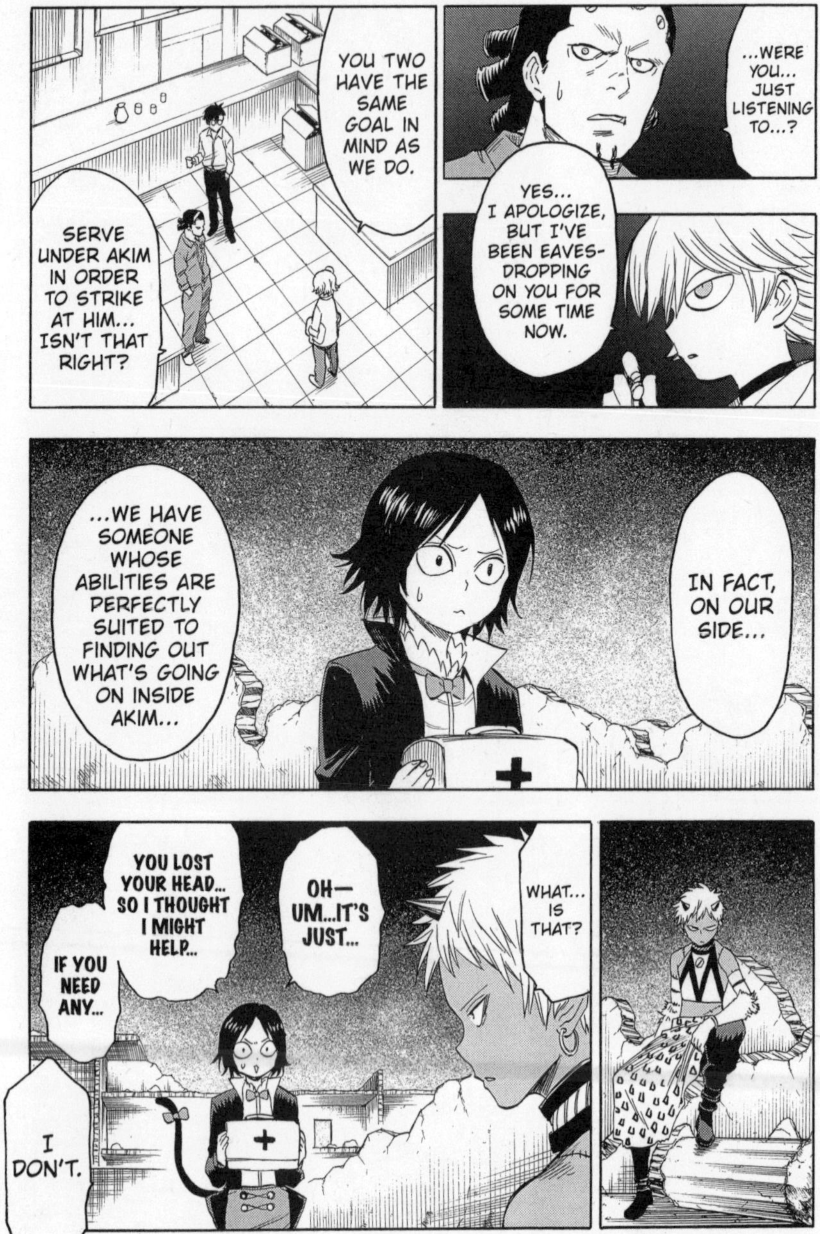
...WERE YOU... JUST LISTENING TO...?
YES... I APOLOGIZE, BUT I'VE BEEN EAVES-DROPPING ON YOU FOR SOME TIME NOW.
YOU TWO HAVE THE SAME GOAL IN MIND AS WE DO.
SERVE UNDER AKIM IN ORDER TO STRIKE AT HIM... ISN'T THAT RIGHT?
IN FACT, ON OUR SIDE...
...WE HAVE SOMEONE WHOSE ABILITIES ARE PERFECTLY SUITED TO FINDING OUT WHAT'S GOING ON INSIDE AKIM...
WHAT... IS THAT?
OH— UM...IT'S JUST...
YOU LOST YOUR HEAD... SO I THOUGHT I MIGHT HELP...
IF YOU NEED ANY...
I DON'T.

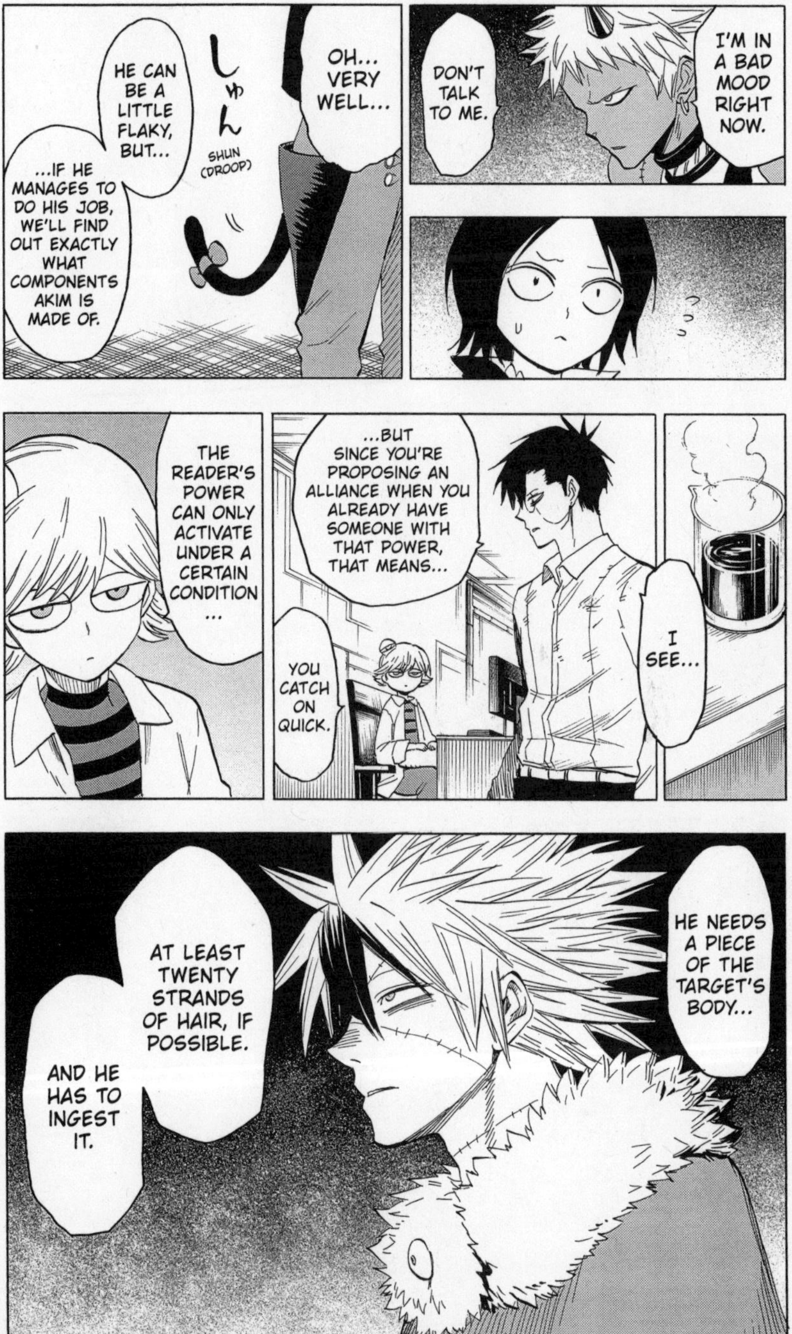
I'M IN A BAD MOOD RIGHT NOW.
DON'T TALK TO ME.
OH... VERY WELL...
しゅん
SHUN (DROOP)
HE CAN BE A LITTLE FLAKY, BUT...
...IF HE MANAGES TO DO HIS JOB, WE'LL FIND OUT EXACTLY WHAT COMPONENTS AKIM IS MADE OF.
I SEE...
...BUT SINCE YOU'RE PROPOSING AN ALLIANCE WHEN YOU ALREADY HAVE SOMEONE WITH THAT POWER, THAT MEANS...
YOU CATCH ON QUICK.
THE READER'S POWER CAN ONLY ACTIVATE UNDER A CERTAIN CONDITION...
HE NEEDS A PIECE OF THE TARGET'S BODY...
AT LEAST TWENTY STRANDS OF HAIR, IF POSSIBLE.
AND HE HAS TO INGEST IT.

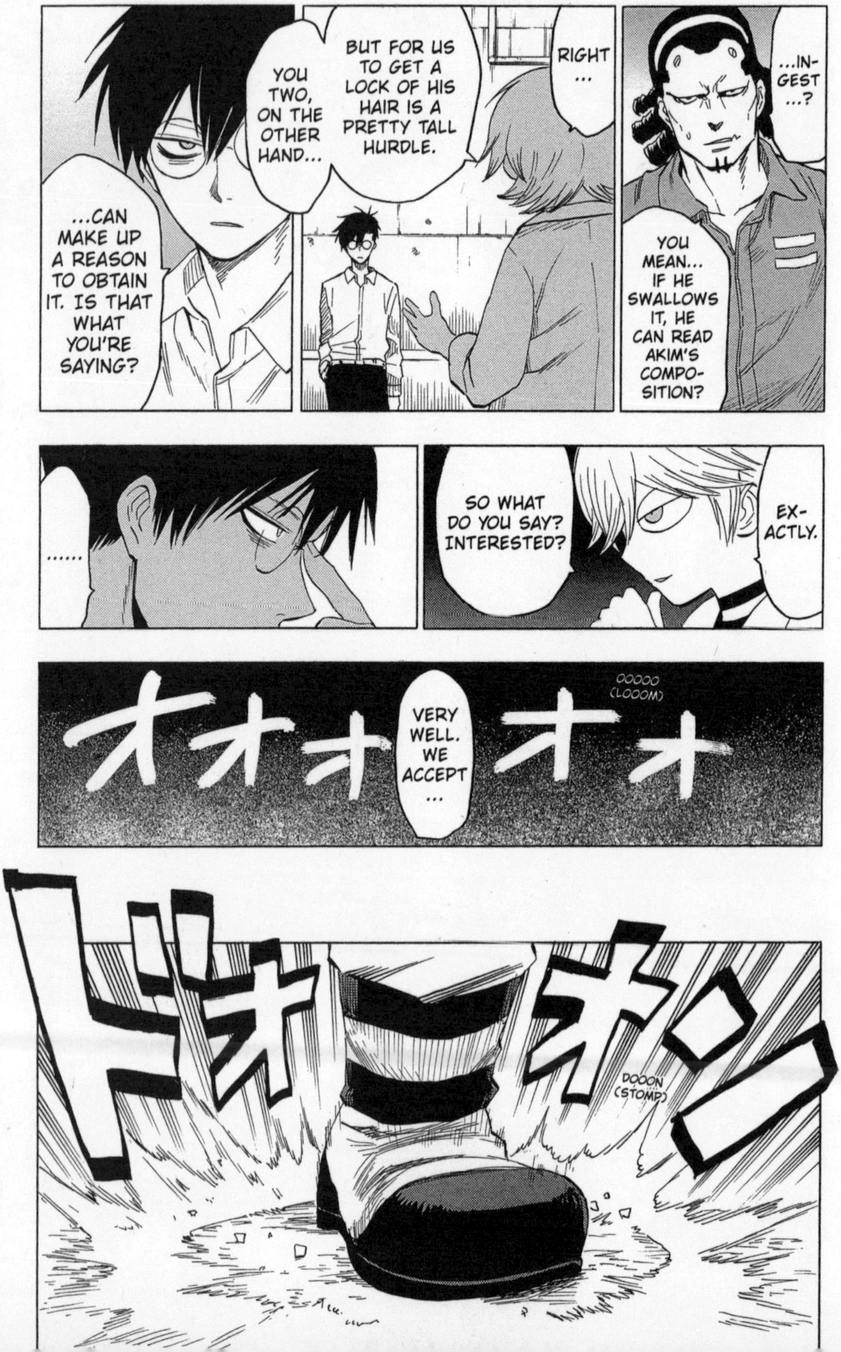
...IN-GEST...?
YOU MEAN... IF HE SWALLOWS IT, HE CAN READ AKIM'S COMPOSITION?
RIGHT...
BUT FOR US TO GET A LOCK OF HIS HAIR IS A PRETTY TALL HURDLE.
YOU TWO, ON THE OTHER HAND...
...CAN MAKE UP A REASON TO OBTAIN IT. IS THAT WHAT YOU'RE SAYING?
EX-ACTLY.
SO WHAT DO YOU SAY? INTERESTED?
......
OOOOO (LOOOM)
VERY WELL. WE ACCEPT...
DOOON (STOMP)

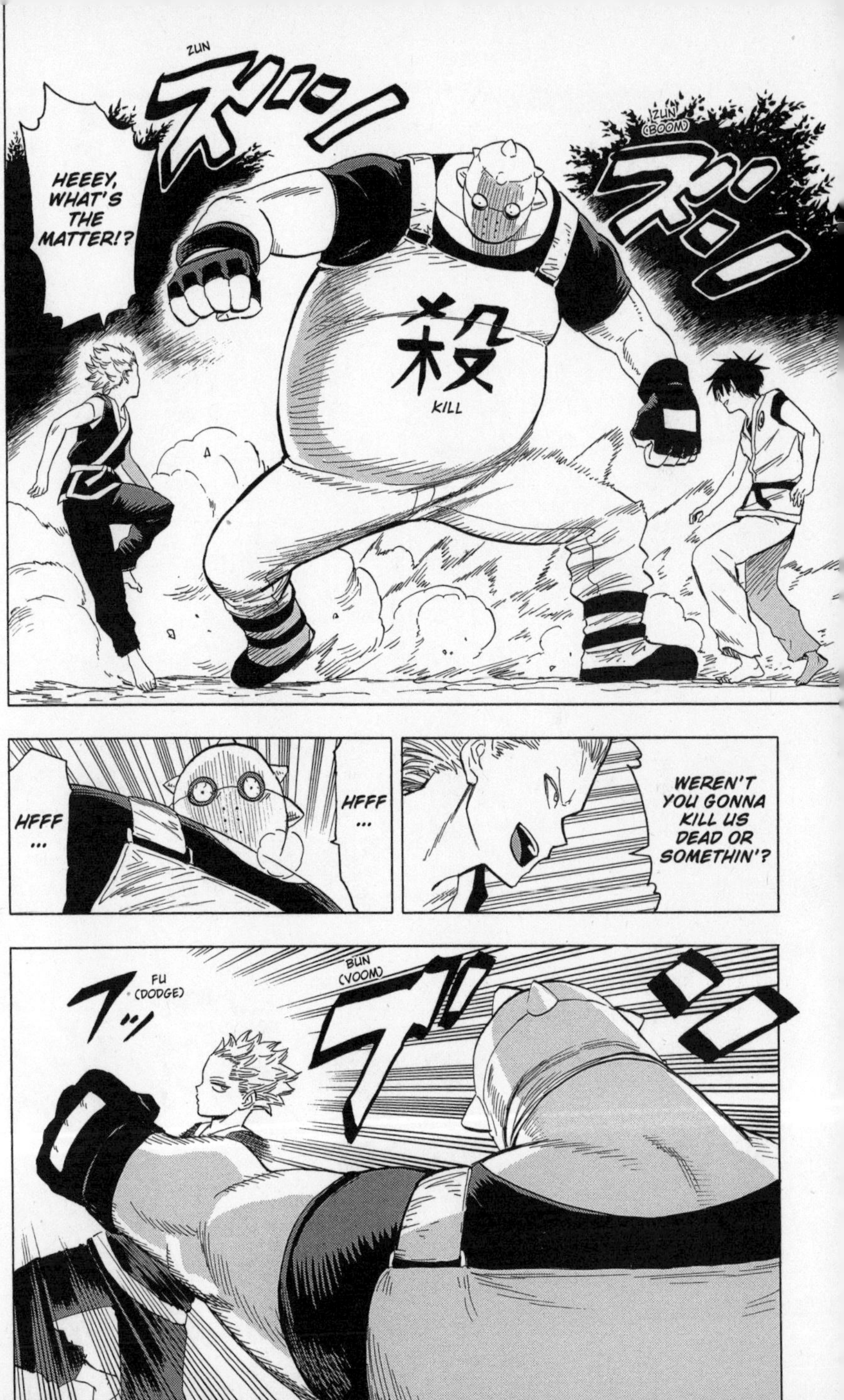
ZUN
(BOOM)
ZUN
HEEEY, WHAT'S THE MATTER!?
KILL
WEREN'T YOU GONNA KILL US DEAD OR SOMETHIN'?
HFFF ...
HFFF ...
BUN
(VOOM)
FU
(DODGE)

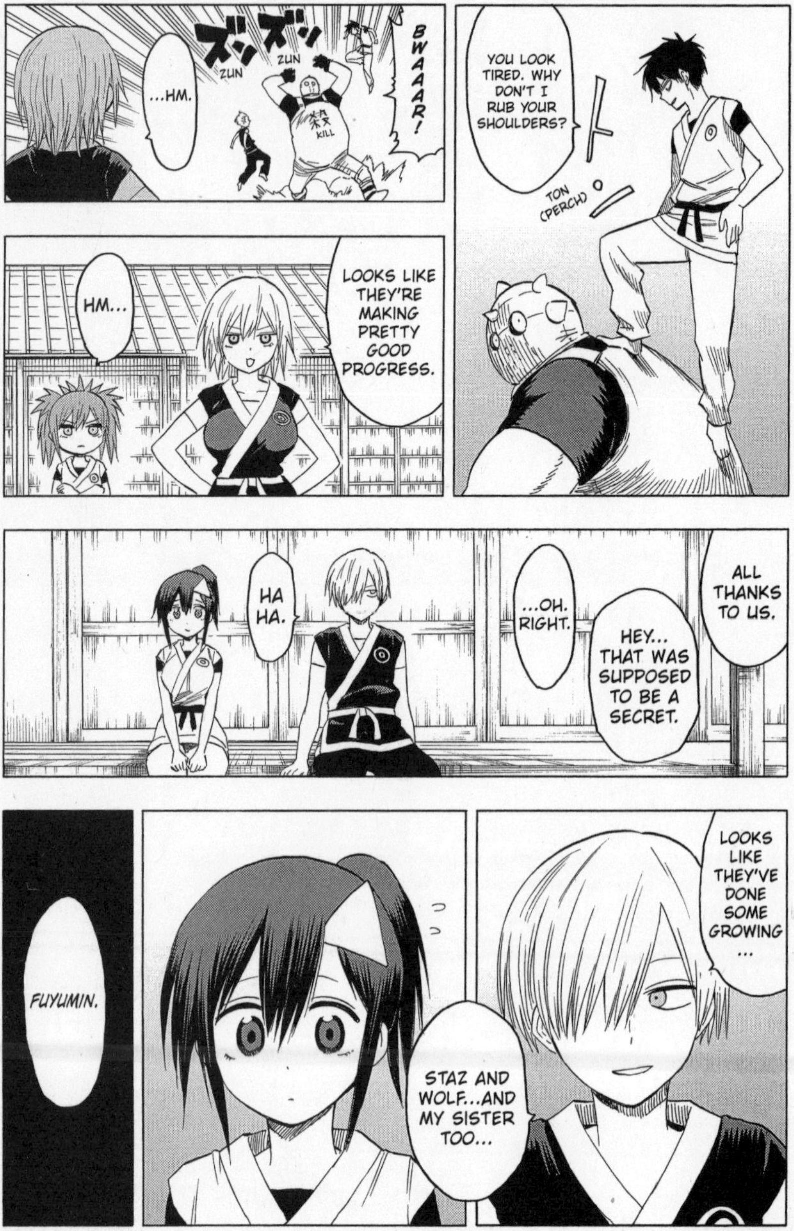
YOU LOOK TIRED. WHY DON'T I RUB YOUR SHOULDERS?
TON (PERCH)
BWAAAR!
ズッズッ
ZUN ZUN
殺
KILL
...HM.
LOOKS LIKE THEY'RE MAKING PRETTY GOOD PROGRESS.
HM...
ALL THANKS TO US.
HEY... THAT WAS SUPPOSED TO BE A SECRET.
...OH. RIGHT.
HA HA.
LOOKS LIKE THEY'VE DONE SOME GROWING...
STAZ AND WOLF...AND MY SISTER TOO...
FUYUMIN.

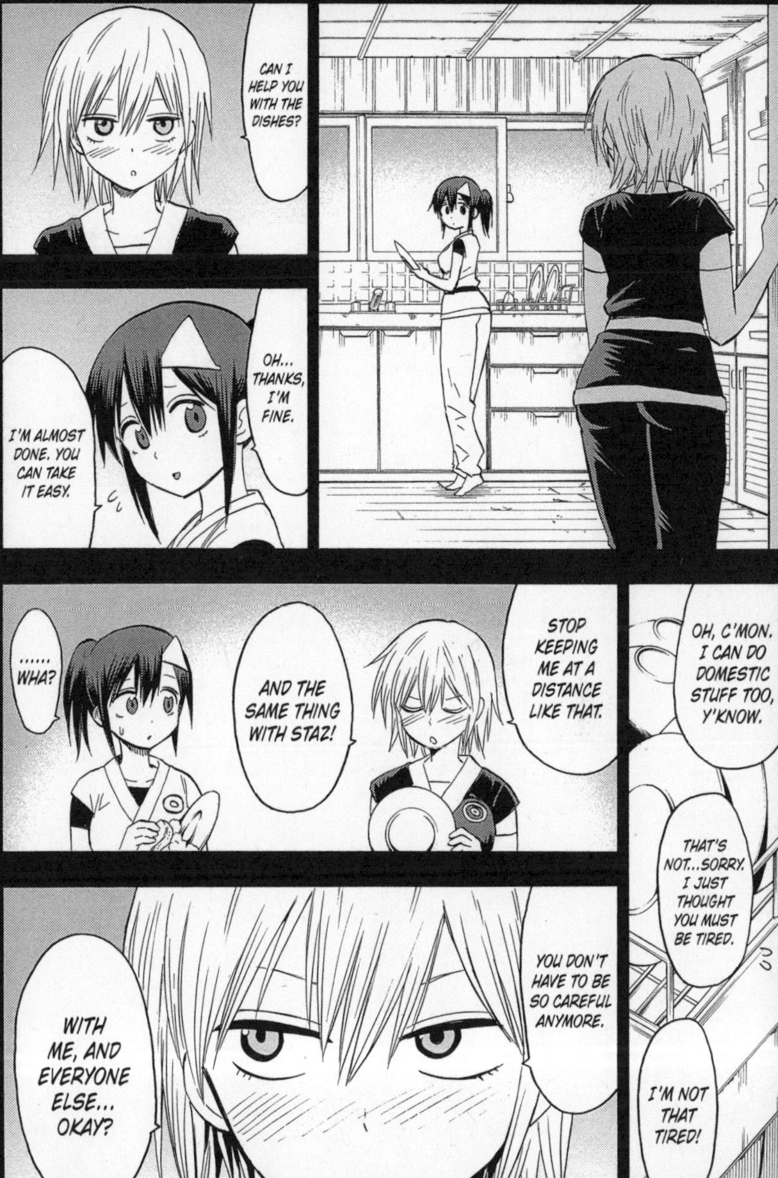
CAN I HELP YOU WITH THE DISHES?
OH... THANKS, I'M FINE.
I'M ALMOST DONE. YOU CAN TAKE IT EASY.
OH, C'MON. I CAN DO DOMESTIC STUFF TOO, Y'KNOW.
THAT'S NOT...SORRY. I JUST THOUGHT YOU MUST BE TIRED.
I'M NOT THAT TIRED!
STOP KEEPING ME AT A DISTANCE LIKE THAT.
AND THE SAME THING WITH STAZ!
......WHA?
YOU DON'T HAVE TO BE SO CAREFUL ANYMORE.
WITH ME, AND EVERYONE ELSE... OKAY?

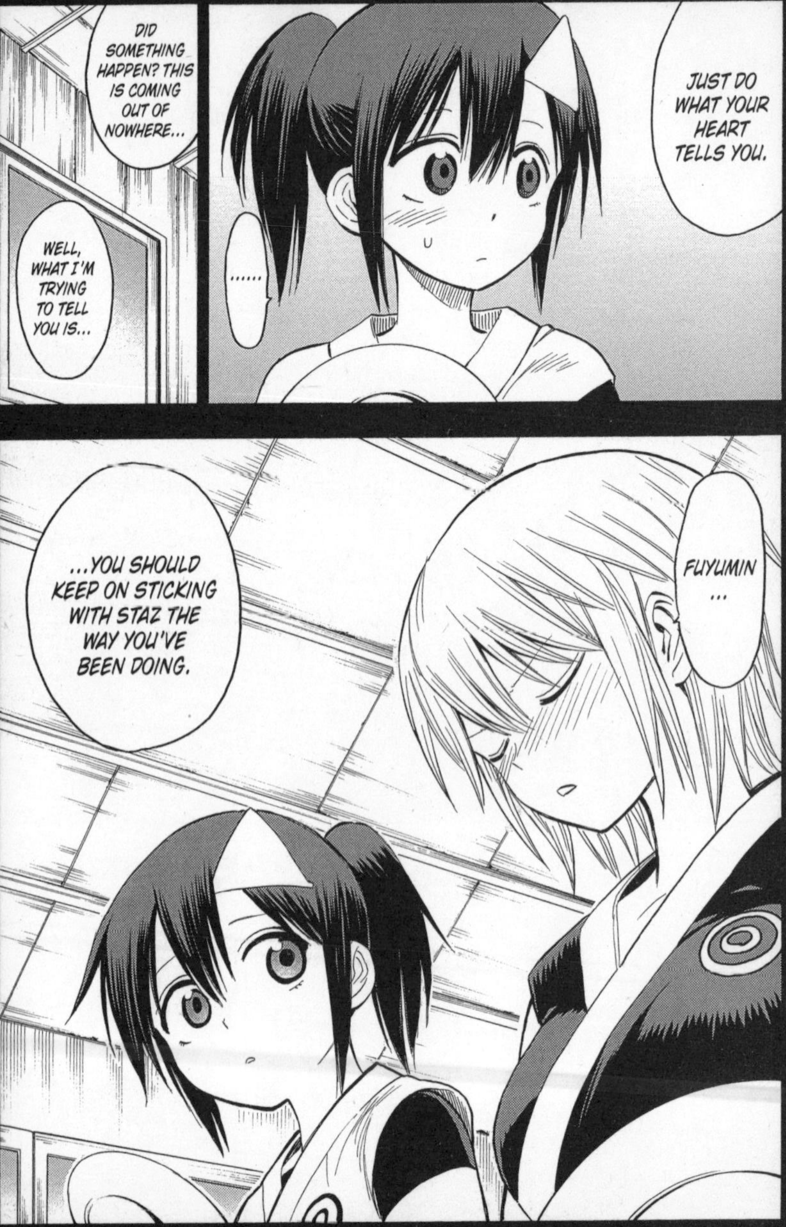
JUST DO WHAT YOUR HEART TELLS YOU.
......
DID SOMETHING HAPPEN? THIS IS COMING OUT OF NOWHERE...
WELL, WHAT I'M TRYING TO TELL YOU IS...
FUYUMIN ...
...YOU SHOULD KEEP ON STICKING WITH STAZ THE WAY YOU'VE BEEN DOING.

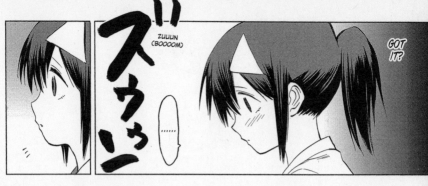

GOT IT?
ZUUUN (BOOOOM)
......
FUU
FUU (HFF)
TIME... ...IS... ...UP...
FUU
FUU
WHAT, WE'RE DONE ALREADY?
CAN WE GET AN EXTENSION?
MONSTERS...
FUU
FUU
JUST MESSING WITH YOU.
IT'S ABOUT TIME WE GOT GOING.
BASA (FLAP)
BASA
BASA
BASA
HUH?

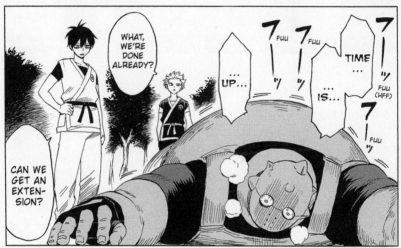

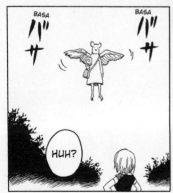

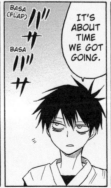

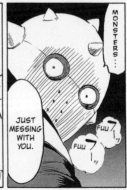

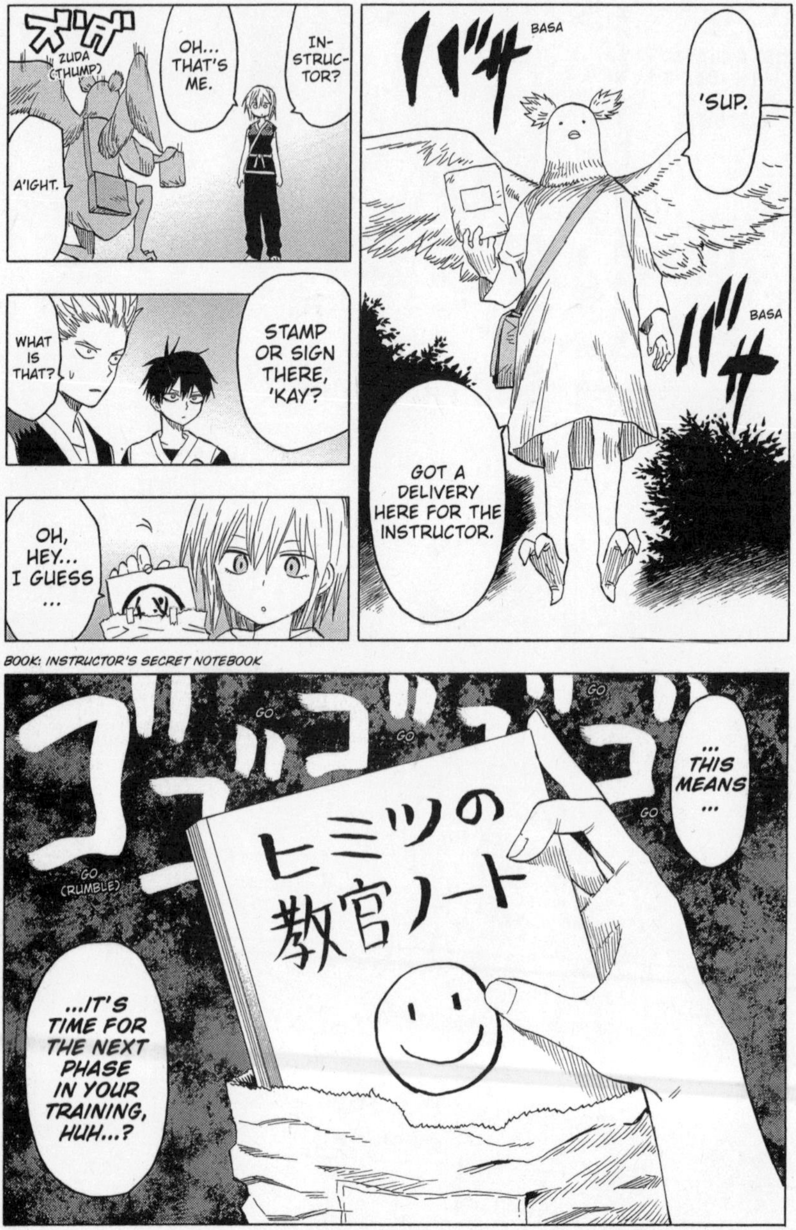
BASA
'SUP.
BASA
GOT A DELIVERY HERE FOR THE INSTRUCTOR.
ZUDA (THUMP)
IN-STRUC-TOR?
OH... THAT'S ME.
A'IGHT.
STAMP OR SIGN THERE, 'KAY?
WHAT IS THAT?
OH, HEY... I GUESS...
BOOK: INSTRUCTOR'S SECRET NOTEBOOK
ヒミツの教官ノート
GO GO GO GO GO (RUMBLE)
...THIS MEANS...
...IT'S TIME FOR THE NEXT PHASE IN YOUR TRAINING, HUH...?

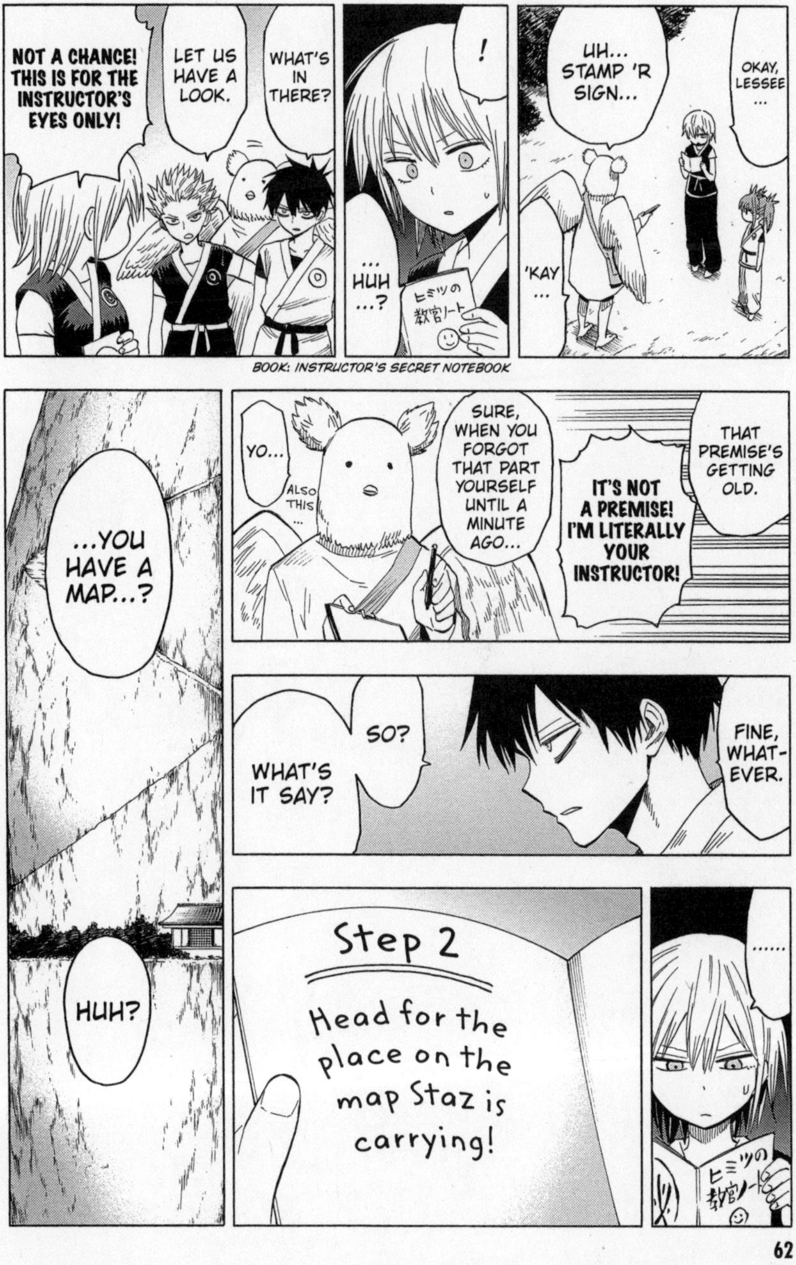
OKAY, LESSEE...
UH... STAMP 'R SIGN...
'KAY...
!
...HUH...?
ヒミツの教官ノート
WHAT'S IN THERE?
LET US HAVE A LOOK.
NOT A CHANCE! THIS IS FOR THE INSTRUCTOR'S EYES ONLY!
BOOK: INSTRUCTOR'S SECRET NOTEBOOK
THAT PREMISE'S GETTING OLD.
IT'S NOT A PREMISE! I'M LITERALLY YOUR INSTRUCTOR!
SURE, WHEN YOU FORGOT THAT PART YOURSELF UNTIL A MINUTE AGO...
YO...
ALSO THIS...
FINE, WHATEVER.
SO?
WHAT'S IT SAY?
......
ヒミツの教官ノート
Step 2
Head for the place on the map Staz is carrying!
...YOU HAVE A MAP...?
HUH?

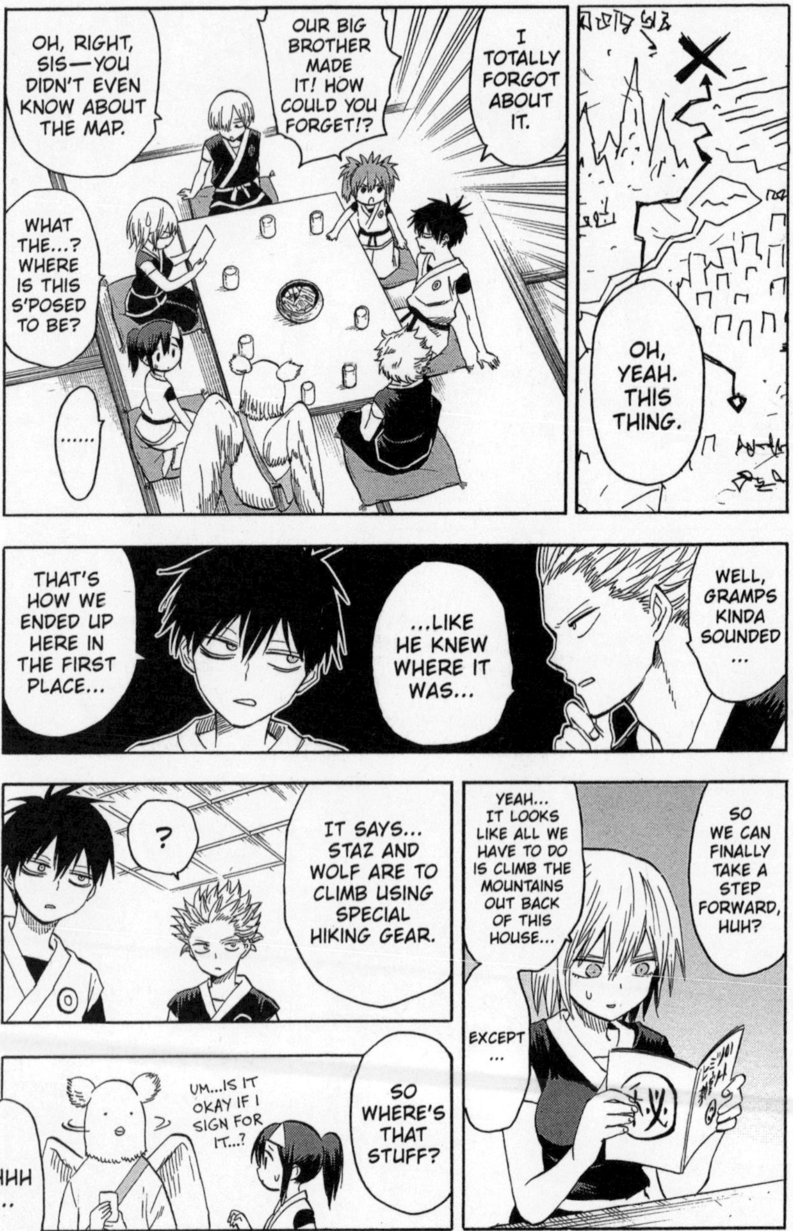
OH, YEAH. THIS THING.
I TOTALLY FORGOT ABOUT IT.
OUR BIG BROTHER MADE IT! HOW COULD YOU FORGET!?
OH, RIGHT, SIS—YOU DIDN'T EVEN KNOW ABOUT THE MAP.
WHAT THE...? WHERE IS THIS S'POSED TO BE?
......
WELL, GRAMPS KINDA SOUNDED ...
...LIKE HE KNEW WHERE IT WAS...
THAT'S HOW WE ENDED UP HERE IN THE FIRST PLACE...
SO WE CAN FINALLY TAKE A STEP FORWARD, HUH?
YEAH... IT LOOKS LIKE ALL WE HAVE TO DO IS CLIMB THE MOUNTAINS OUT BACK OF THIS HOUSE...
EXCEPT ...
IT SAYS... STAZ AND WOLF ARE TO CLIMB USING SPECIAL HIKING GEAR.
?
SO WHERE'S THAT STUFF?
UM...IS IT OKAY IF I SIGN FOR IT...?
UHHH ...

BOOK: TOP SECRET

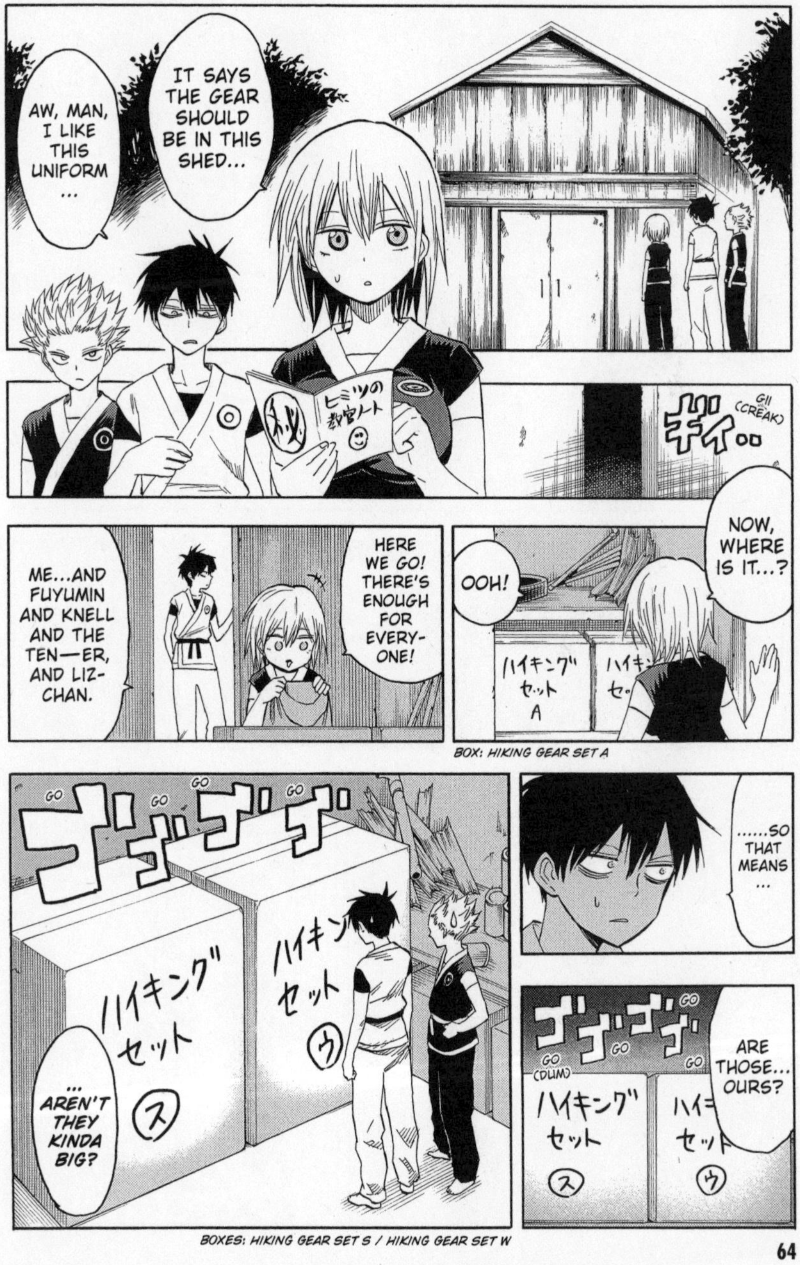
IT SAYS THE GEAR SHOULD BE IN THIS SHED...
AW, MAN, I LIKE THIS UNIFORM...
GII (CREAK)
ギィ
ヒミツの教官ノート
NOW, WHERE IS IT...?
OOH!
ハイキングセット A
ハイキン セッ
HERE WE GO! THERE'S ENOUGH FOR EVERY-ONE!
ME...AND FUYUMIN AND KNELL AND THE TEN—ER, AND LIZ-CHAN.
......SO THAT MEANS...
GO GO GO GO (DUM)
ARE THOSE... OURS?
ハイキングセット ス
ハイ セット ウ
GO GO GO GO
ハイキングセット ス
ハイキン セット ウ
... AREN'T THEY KINDA BIG?

BOX: HIKING GEAR SET A

BOXES: HIKING GEAR SET S / HIKING GEAR SET W

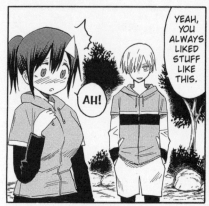

AHHH! ♡
PAAA (GLOW)
IT'S SO EASY TO MOVE IN!
YEAH, YOU ALWAYS LIKED STUFF LIKE THIS.
AH!
LIZ-CHAN, YOU LOOK SOOO CUTE!!
......
IT'S JUST THE SAME AS YOURS, FUYUMI.
IT'S A BIT BIG FOR ME.
KYA (SQUEAL)
THAT'S WHAT MAKES IT SO CUTE!
RIGHT !?
KYA
ZUN (STOMP)
...HEY.

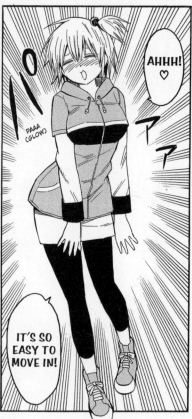

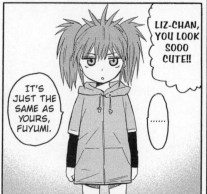

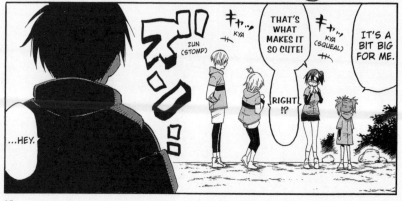

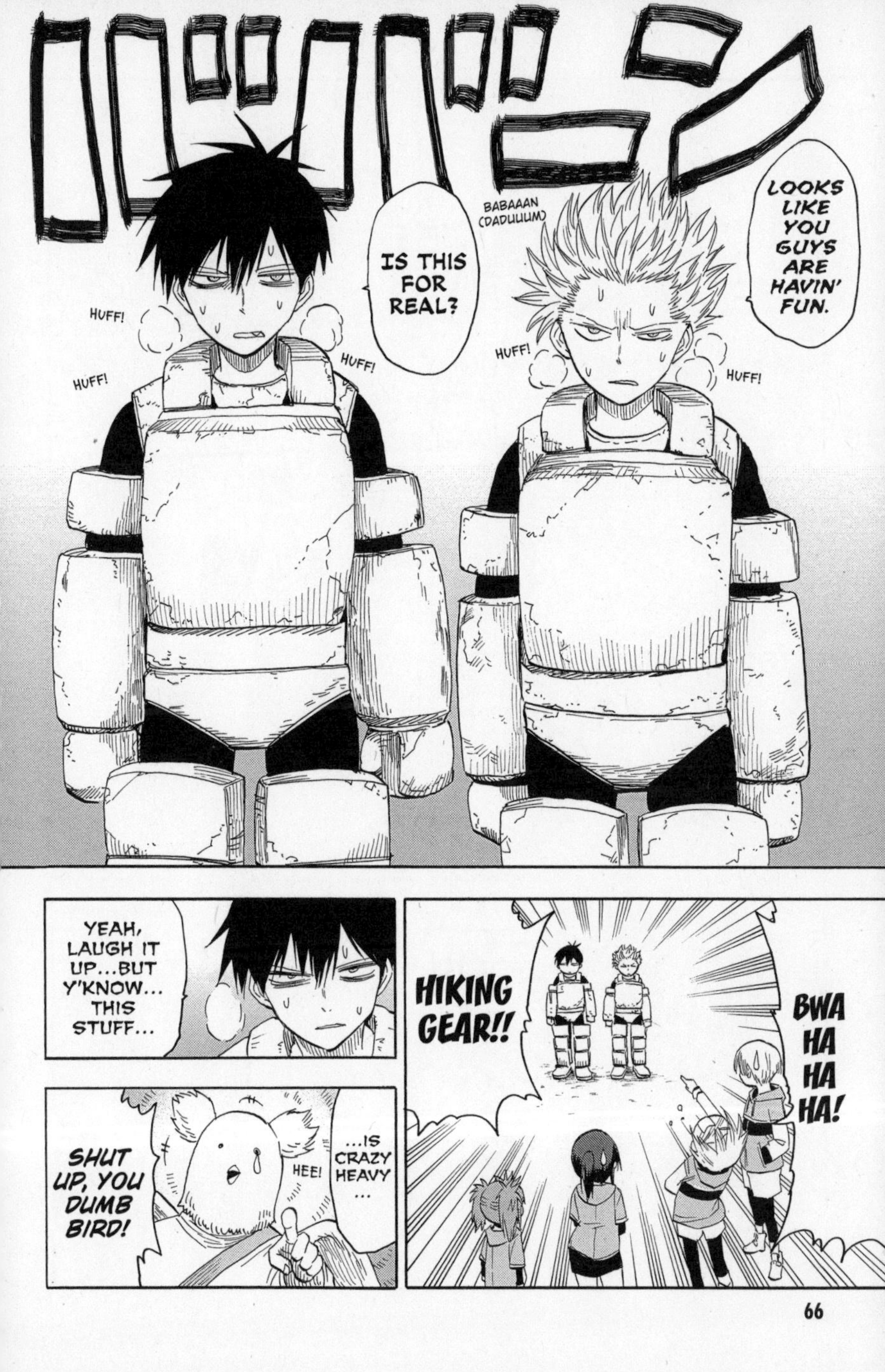
LOOKS LIKE YOU GUYS ARE HAVIN' FUN.
BABAAAN (DADUUUM)
HUFF!
HUFF!
IS THIS FOR REAL?
HUFF!
HUFF!
HUFF!
BWA HA HA HA!
HIKING GEAR!!
YEAH, LAUGH IT UP...BUT Y'KNOW... THIS STUFF...
...IS CRAZY HEAVY ...
HEE!
SHUT UP, YOU DUMB BIRD!

SFX: GERA (CHORTLE) GERA

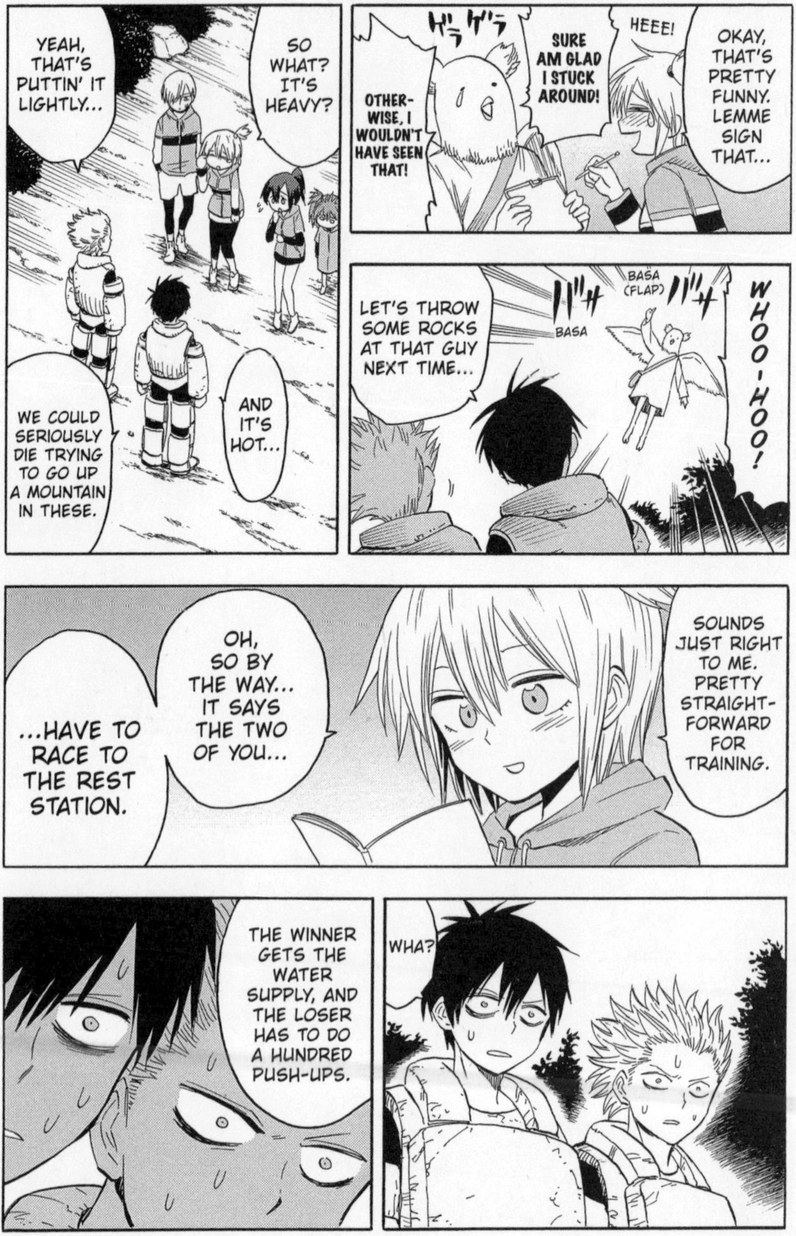
OKAY, THAT'S PRETTY FUNNY. LEMME SIGN THAT...
HEEE!
SURE AM GLAD I STUCK AROUND!
ゲラゲラ
OTHER-WISE, I WOULDN'T HAVE SEEN THAT!
WHOO-HOO!
BASA (FLAP)
BASA
LET'S THROW SOME ROCKS AT THAT GUY NEXT TIME...
SO WHAT? IT'S HEAVY?
YEAH, THAT'S PUTTIN' IT LIGHTLY...
AND IT'S HOT...
WE COULD SERIOUSLY DIE TRYING TO GO UP A MOUNTAIN IN THESE.
SOUNDS JUST RIGHT TO ME. PRETTY STRAIGHT-FORWARD FOR TRAINING.
OH, SO BY THE WAY... IT SAYS THE TWO OF YOU...
...HAVE TO RACE TO THE REST STATION.
WHA?
THE WINNER GETS THE WATER SUPPLY, AND THE LOSER HAS TO DO A HUNDRED PUSH-UPS.

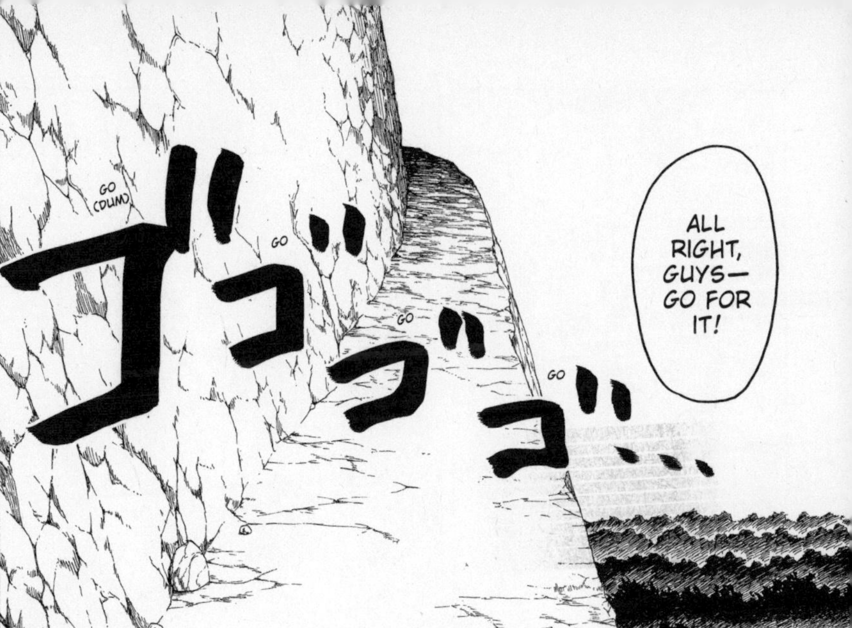
ALL RIGHT, GUYS— GO FOR IT!
GO (DUM)
GO
GO
GO

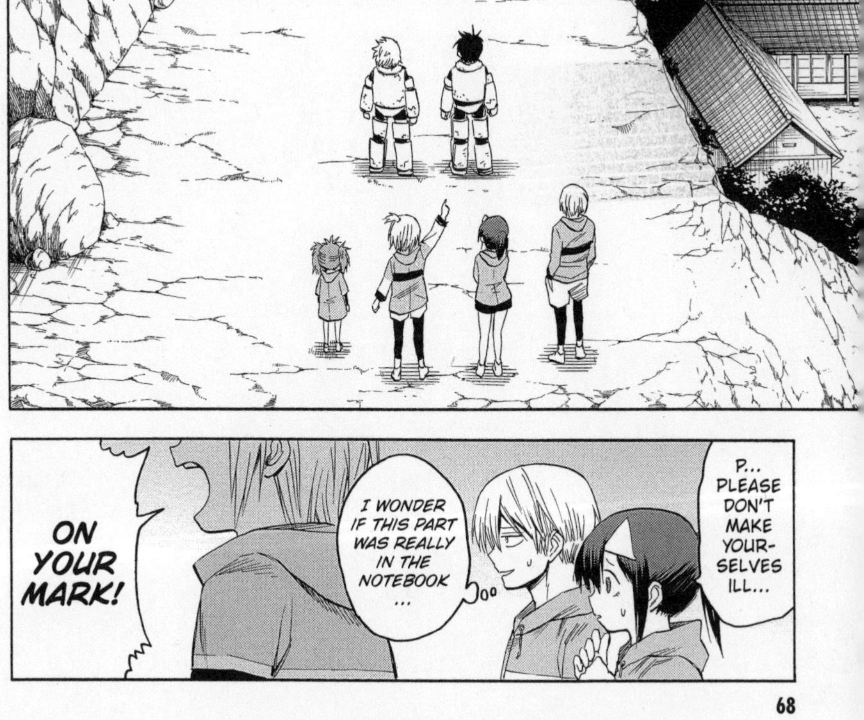
P... PLEASE DON'T MAKE YOUR-SELVES ILL...
I WONDER IF THIS PART WAS REALLY IN THE NOTEBOOK ...
ON YOUR MARK!

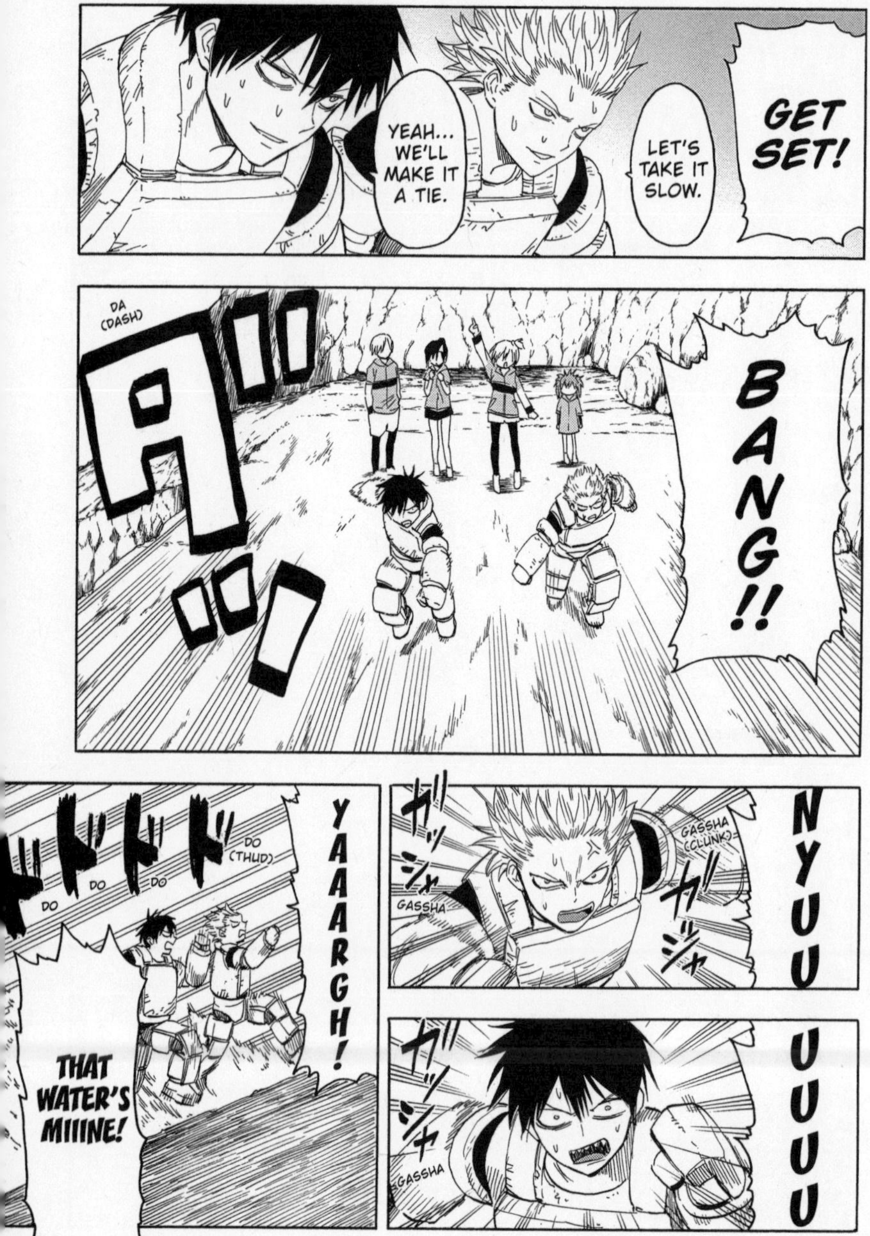
GET SET!
LET'S TAKE IT SLOW.
YEAH... WE'LL MAKE IT A TIE.
BANG!!
DA (DASH)
NYUUUUUUUU
GASSHA (CLUNK)
GASSHA
GASSHA
YAAAARGH!
DO (THUD)
DO DO DO
THAT WATER'S MIIINE!

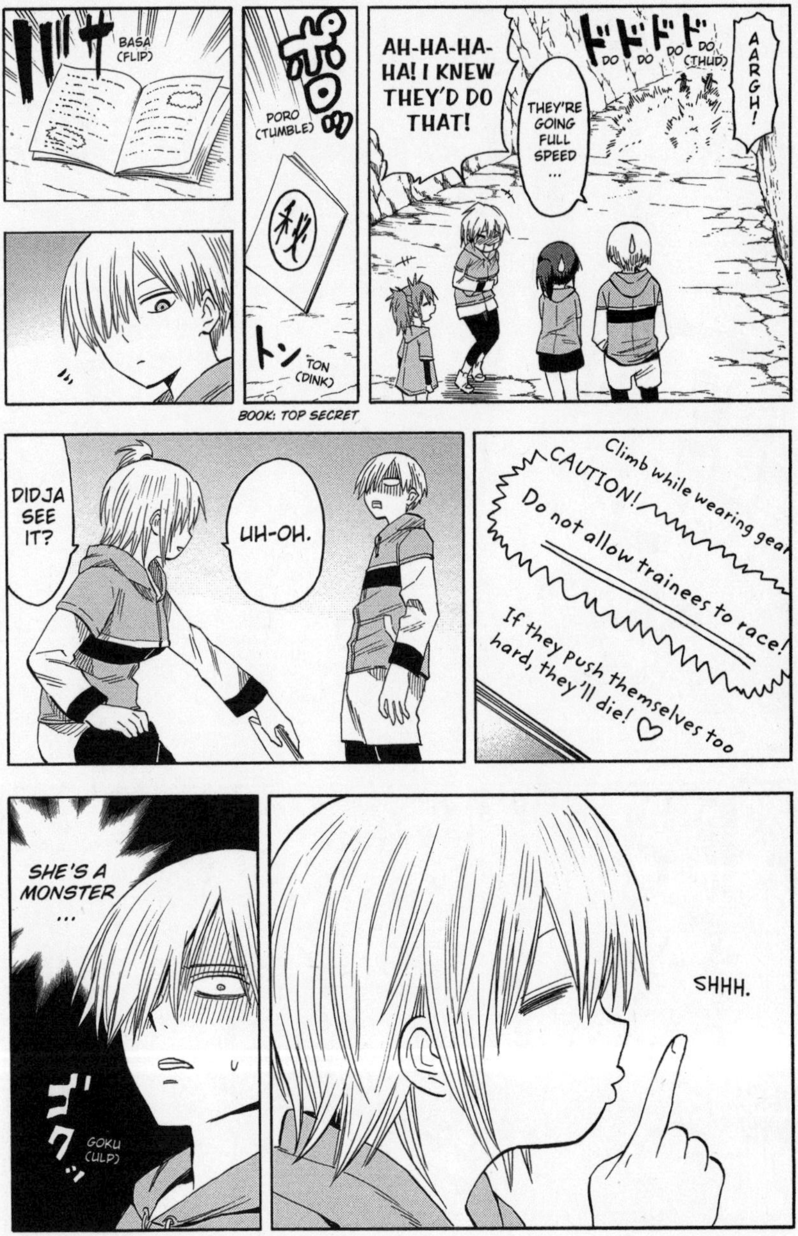
AARGH!
ドドドド DO DO DO DO (THUD)
AH-HA-HA-HA! I KNEW THEY'D DO THAT!
THEY'RE GOING FULL SPEED ...
ポロッ PORO (TUMBLE)
秘
トン TON (DINK)
バサ BASA (FLIP)
BOOK: TOP SECRET
Climb while wearing gear
CAUTION!
Do not allow trainees to race!
If they push themselves too hard, they'll die! ♡
UH-OH.
DIDJA SEE IT?
SHHH.
SHE'S A MONSTER ...
ゴクッ GOKU (ULP)

♠ To Be Continued ♠

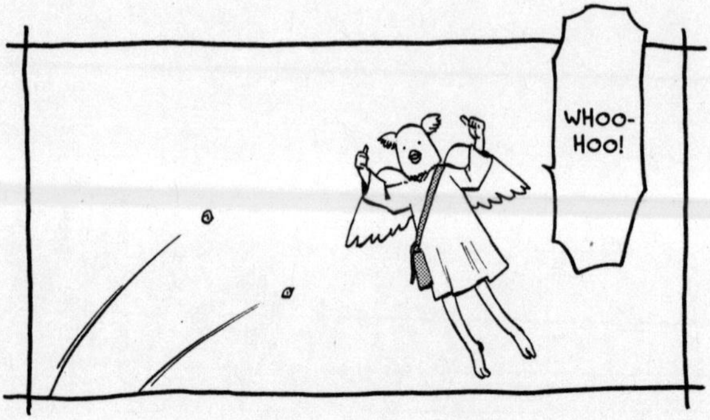
WHOO-HOO!

BLOOD LAD

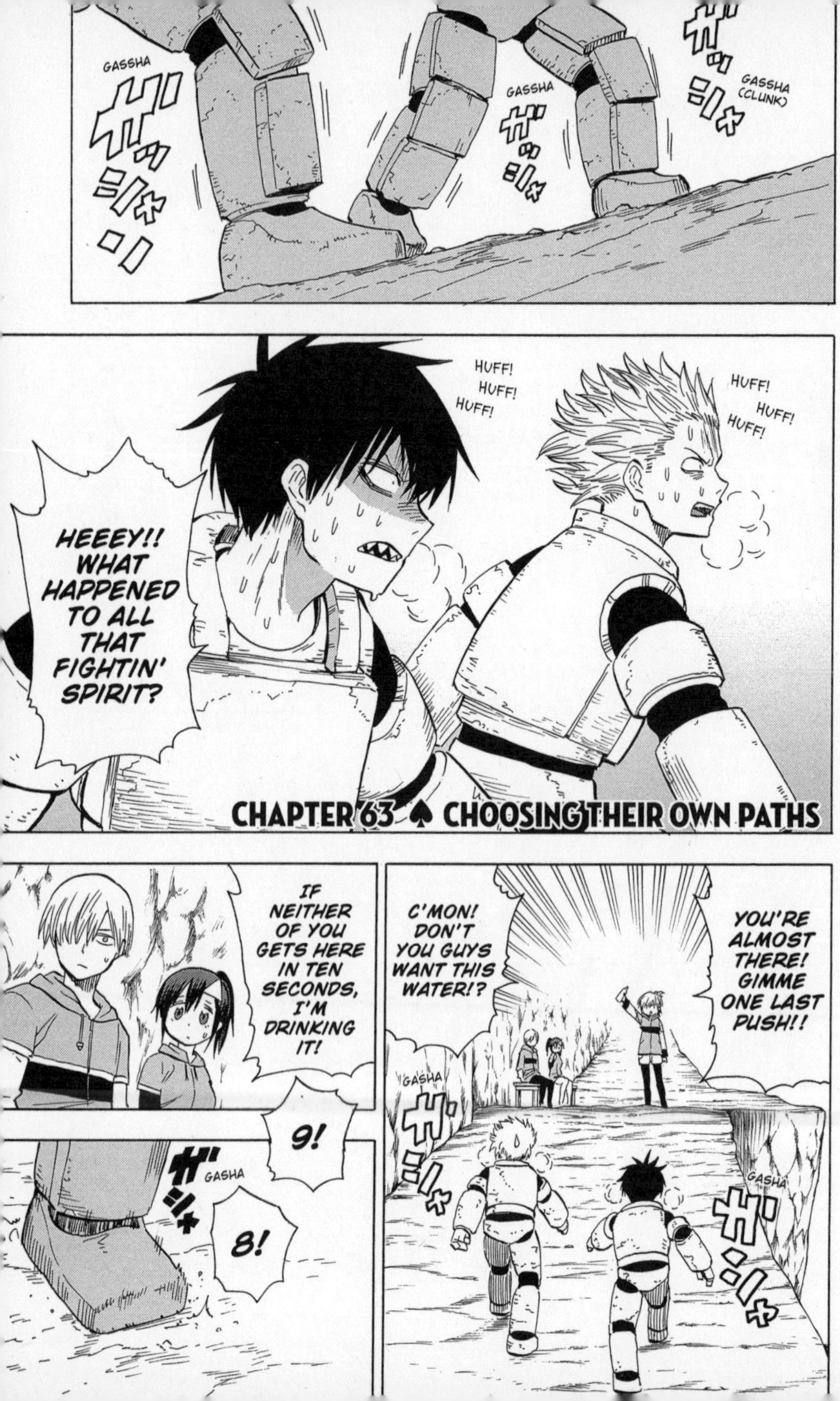
GASSHA (CLUNK)
GASSHA
GASSHA
HUFF! HUFF! HUFF!
HUFF! HUFF! HUFF!
HEEEY!! WHAT HAPPENED TO ALL THAT FIGHTIN' SPIRIT?
CHAPTER 63 ♠ CHOOSING THEIR OWN PATHS
YOU'RE ALMOST THERE! GIMME ONE LAST PUSH!!
C'MON! DON'T YOU GUYS WANT THIS WATER!?
GASHA
GASHA
IF NEITHER OF YOU GETS HERE IN TEN SECONDS, I'M DRINKING IT!
9!
GASHA
8!

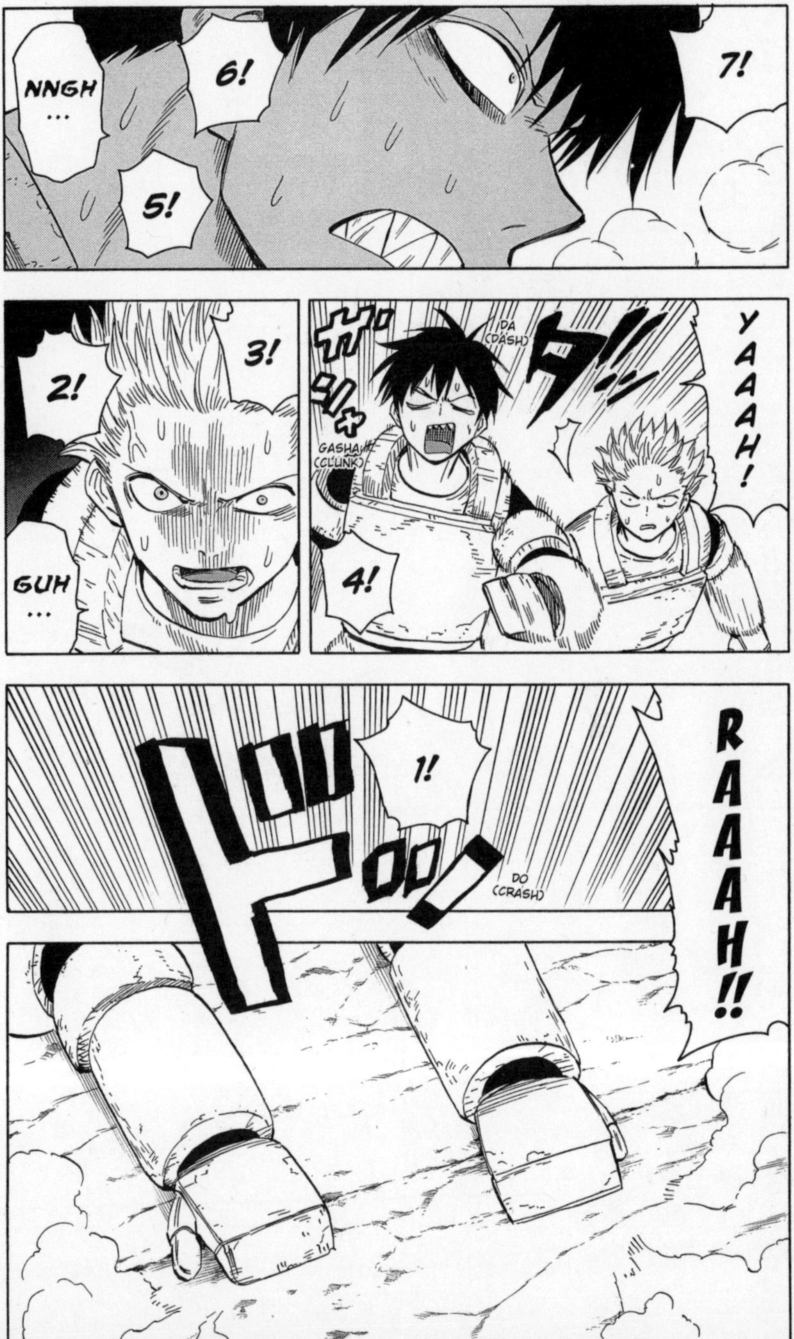
7!
6!
NNGH ...
5!
YAAAAH!
DA (DASH)
GASHA (CLUNK)
4!
3!
2!
GUH ...
RAAAAH!!
1!
DO (CRASH)

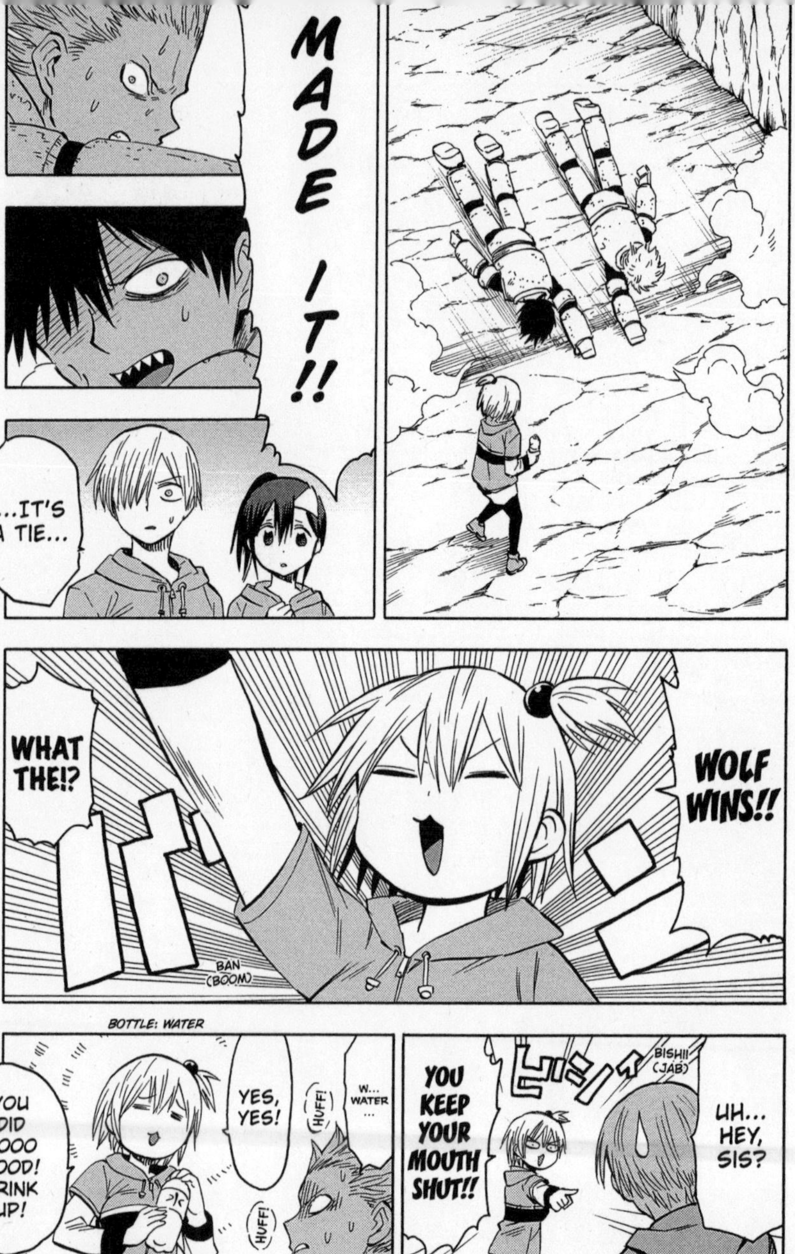
MADE IT!!
...IT'S A TIE...
WOLF WINS!!
WHAT THE!?
BAN (BOOM)
UH... HEY, SIS?
BISHI! (JAB)
YOU KEEP YOUR MOUTH SHUT!!
W... WATER...
(HUFF!)
YES, YES!
YOU DID SOOO GOOD! DRINK UP!
(HUFF!)
BOTTLE: WATER

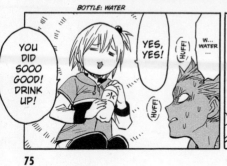

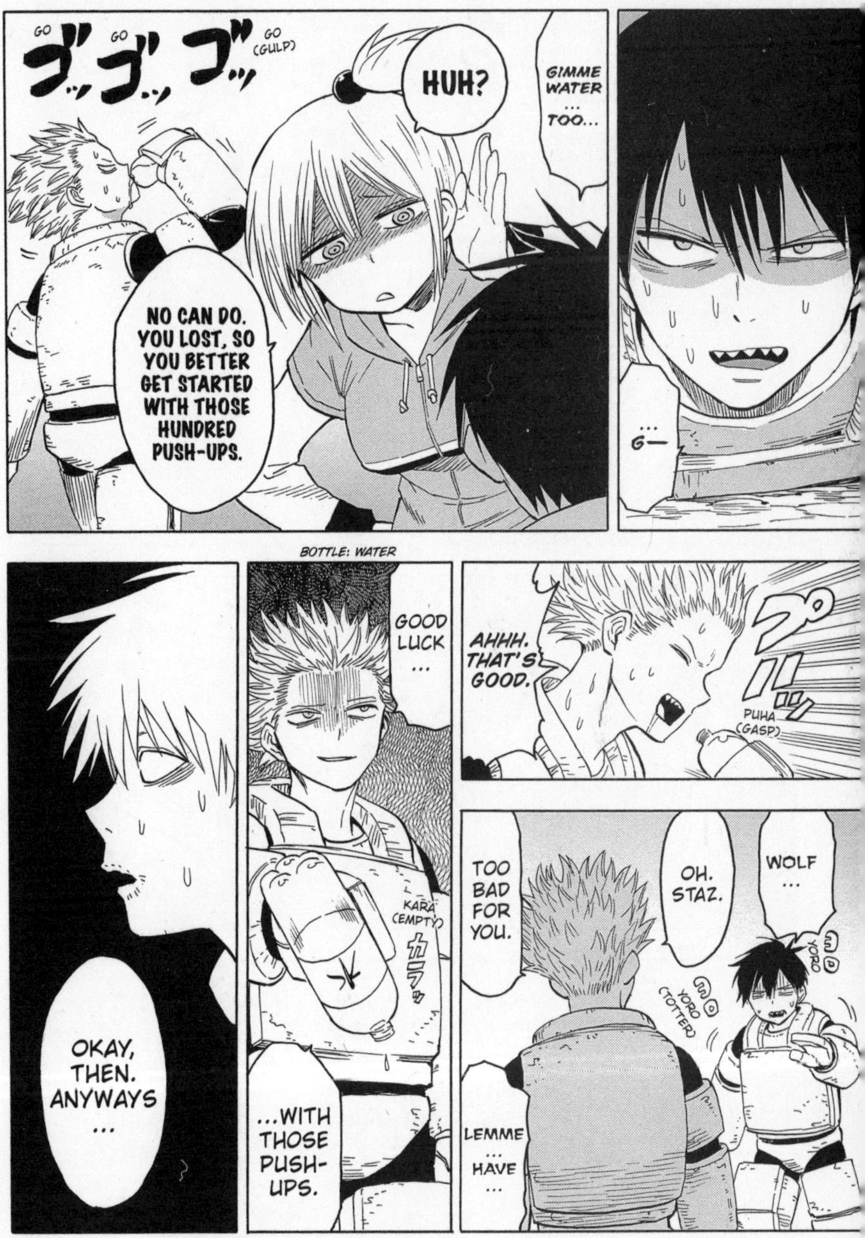
GIMME WATER ... TOO...
... G—
HUH?
GO GO GO (GULP)
NO CAN DO. YOU LOST, SO YOU BETTER GET STARTED WITH THOSE HUNDRED PUSH-UPS.
BOTTLE: WATER
AHHH. THAT'S GOOD.
PUHA (GASP)
WOLF ...
OH. STAZ.
TOO BAD FOR YOU.
YORO YORO (TOTTER)
LEMME ... HAVE ...
GOOD LUCK ...
KARA (EMPTY)
...WITH THOSE PUSH-UPS.
OKAY, THEN. ANYWAYS ...

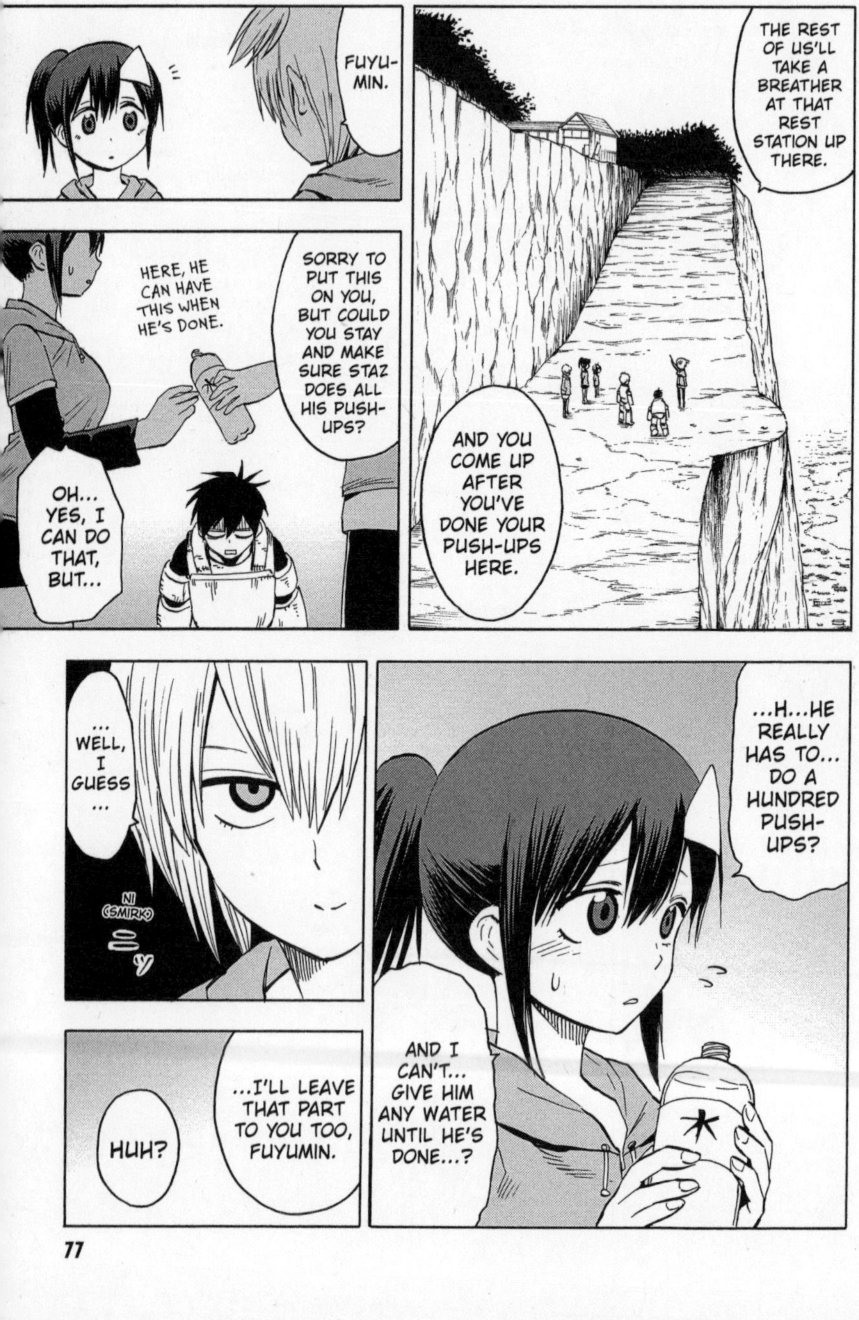
THE REST OF US'LL TAKE A BREATHER AT THAT REST STATION UP THERE.
AND YOU COME UP AFTER YOU'VE DONE YOUR PUSH-UPS HERE.
FUYU-MIN.
SORRY TO PUT THIS ON YOU, BUT COULD YOU STAY AND MAKE SURE STAZ DOES ALL HIS PUSH-UPS?
HERE, HE CAN HAVE THIS WHEN HE'S DONE.
OH... YES, I CAN DO THAT, BUT...
...H...HE REALLY HAS TO... DO A HUNDRED PUSH-UPS?
AND I CAN'T... GIVE HIM ANY WATER UNTIL HE'S DONE...?
... WELL, I GUESS ...
NI (SMIRK)
...I'LL LEAVE THAT PART TO YOU TOO, FUYUMIN.
HUH?

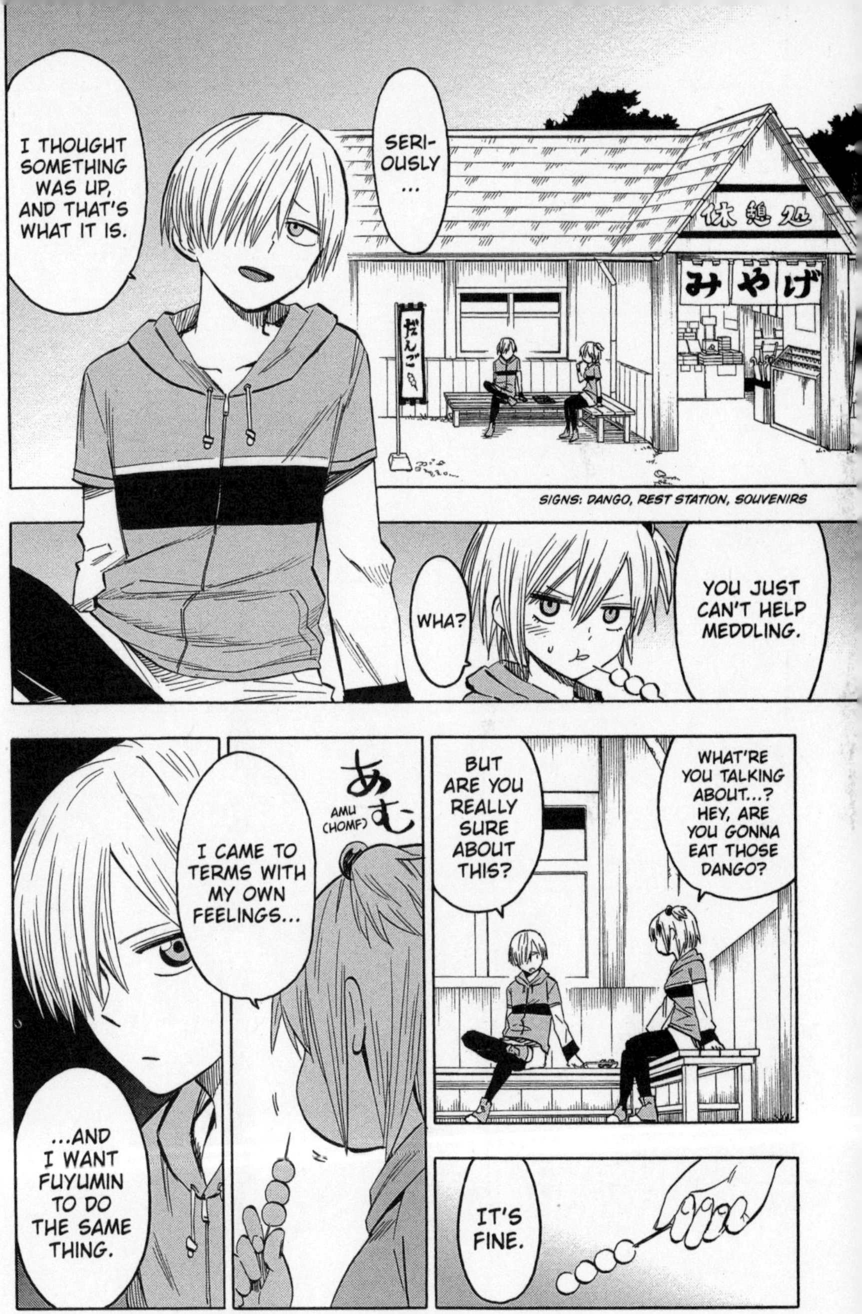
SERI-OUSLY...
I THOUGHT SOMETHING WAS UP, AND THAT'S WHAT IT IS.
休憩処
みやげ
だんご
SIGNS: DANGO, REST STATION, SOUVENIRS
YOU JUST CAN'T HELP MEDDLING.
WHA?
WHAT'RE YOU TALKING ABOUT...? HEY, ARE YOU GONNA EAT THOSE DANGO?
BUT ARE YOU REALLY SURE ABOUT THIS?
IT'S FINE.
あむ
AMU (HOMF)
I CAME TO TERMS WITH MY OWN FEELINGS...
...AND I WANT FUYUMIN TO DO THE SAME THING.

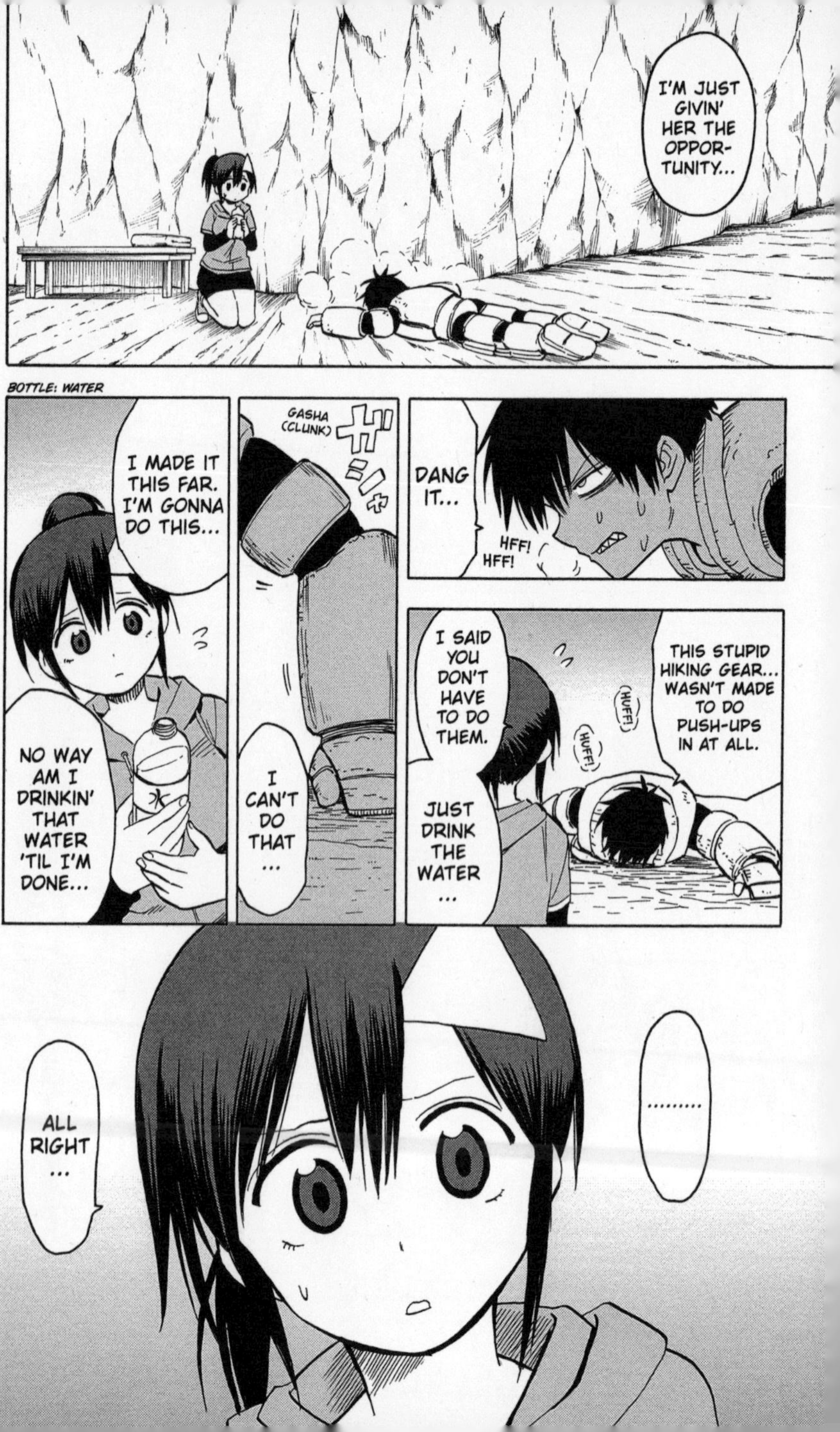
I'M JUST GIVIN' HER THE OPPORTUNITY...
BOTTLE: WATER
DANG IT...
HFF! HFF!
THIS STUPID HIKING GEAR... WASN'T MADE TO DO PUSH-UPS IN AT ALL.
(HUFF!)
(HUFF!)
I SAID YOU DON'T HAVE TO DO THEM.
JUST DRINK THE WATER ...
GASHA (CLUNK)
I CAN'T DO THAT ...
I MADE IT THIS FAR. I'M GONNA DO THIS...
NO WAY AM I DRINKIN' THAT WATER 'TIL I'M DONE...
....
ALL RIGHT ...

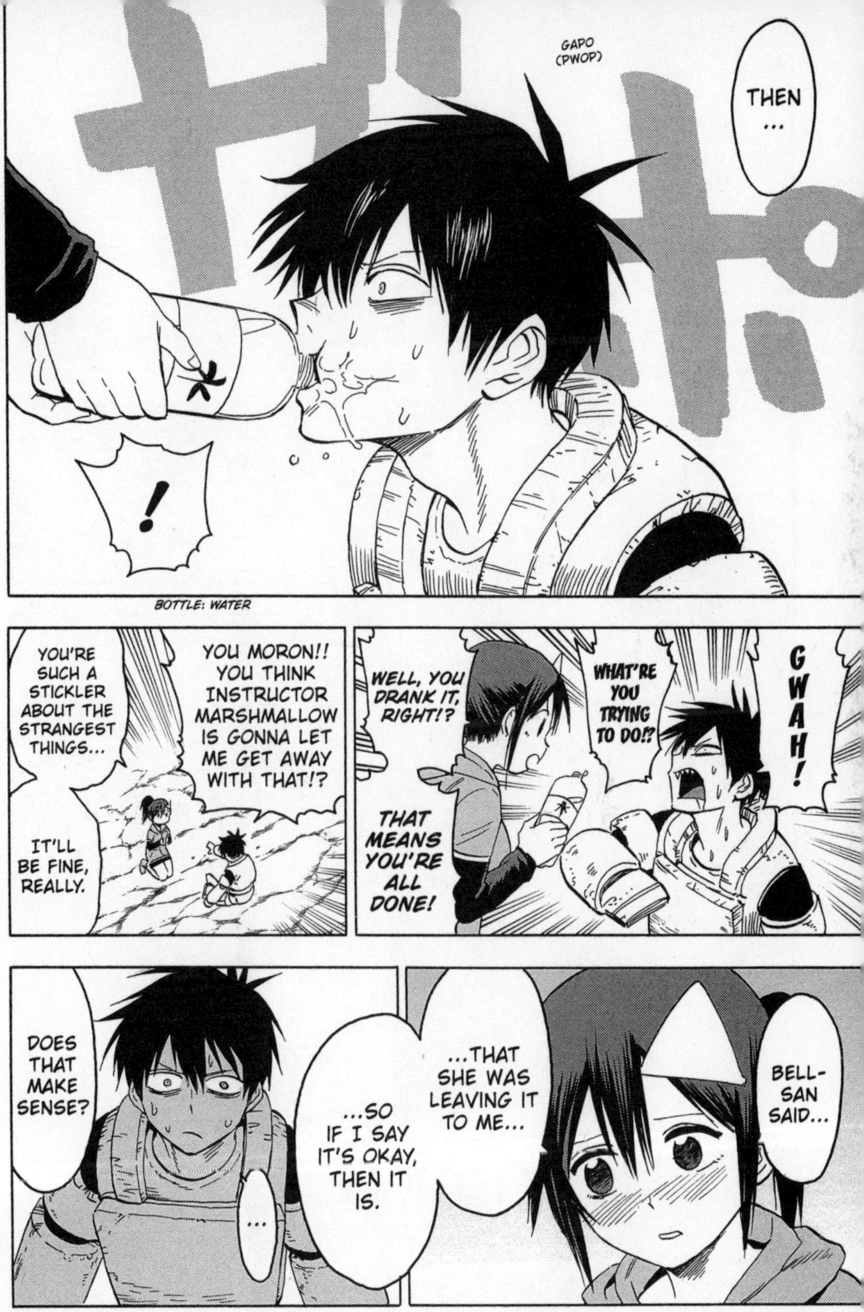
THEN...
GAPO (PWOP)
!
BOTTLE: WATER
GWAH!
WHAT'RE YOU TRYING TO DO!?
WELL, YOU DRANK IT, RIGHT!?
THAT MEANS YOU'RE ALL DONE!
YOU MORON!! YOU THINK INSTRUCTOR MARSHMALLOW IS GONNA LET ME GET AWAY WITH THAT!?
YOU'RE SUCH A STICKLER ABOUT THE STRANGEST THINGS...
IT'LL BE FINE, REALLY.
BELL-SAN SAID...
...THAT SHE WAS LEAVING IT TO ME...
...SO IF I SAY IT'S OKAY, THEN IT IS.
...
DOES THAT MAKE SENSE?

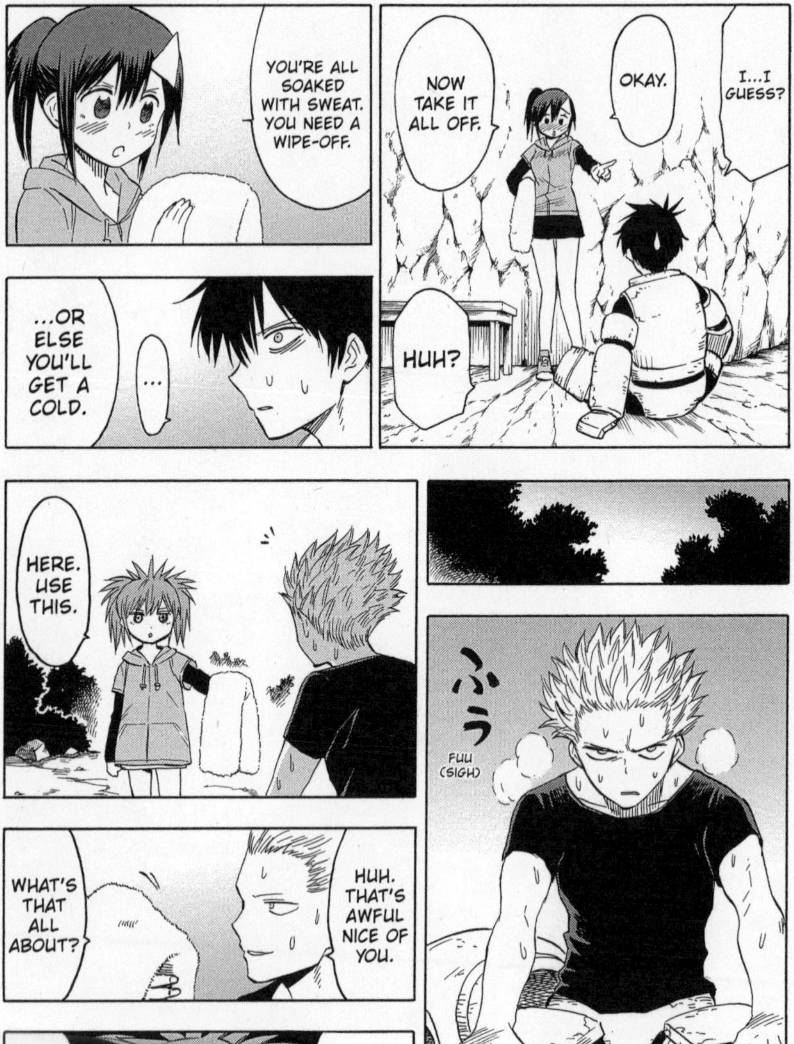
I...I GUESS?
OKAY.
NOW TAKE IT ALL OFF.
HUH?
YOU'RE ALL SOAKED WITH SWEAT. YOU NEED A WIPE-OFF.
...OR ELSE YOU'LL GET A COLD.
...
ふう
FUU (SIGH)
HERE. USE THIS.
HUH. THAT'S AWFUL NICE OF YOU.
WHAT'S THAT ALL ABOUT?
YOU'RE TINY, BUT YOU'RE WORKING AS HARD AS YOU CAN.
I THINK BETTER OF YOU NOW.

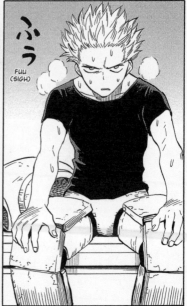

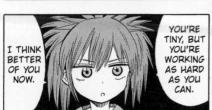

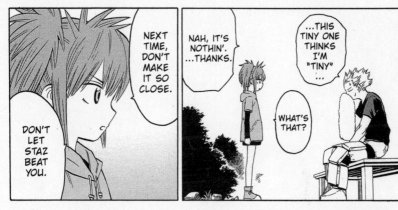

...THIS TINY ONE THINKS I'M "TINY"...
WHAT'S THAT?
NAH, IT'S NOTHIN'. ...THANKS.
NEXT TIME, DON'T MAKE IT SO CLOSE.
DON'T LET STAZ BEAT YOU.
......YOU DON'T HAVE TO TELL ME THAT.
OOOH.
LOOKS LIKE THE LITTLE INSTRUCTOR IS TURNING INTO A WOLF TAMER.
PER- FECT...
HEE HEE.
SHE'S UP TO SOME- THING AGAIN...
GASHA (CLUNK)

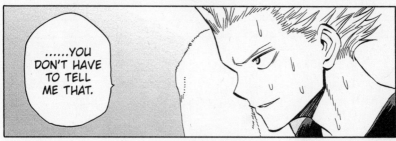

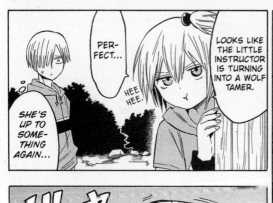

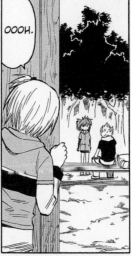

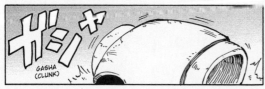

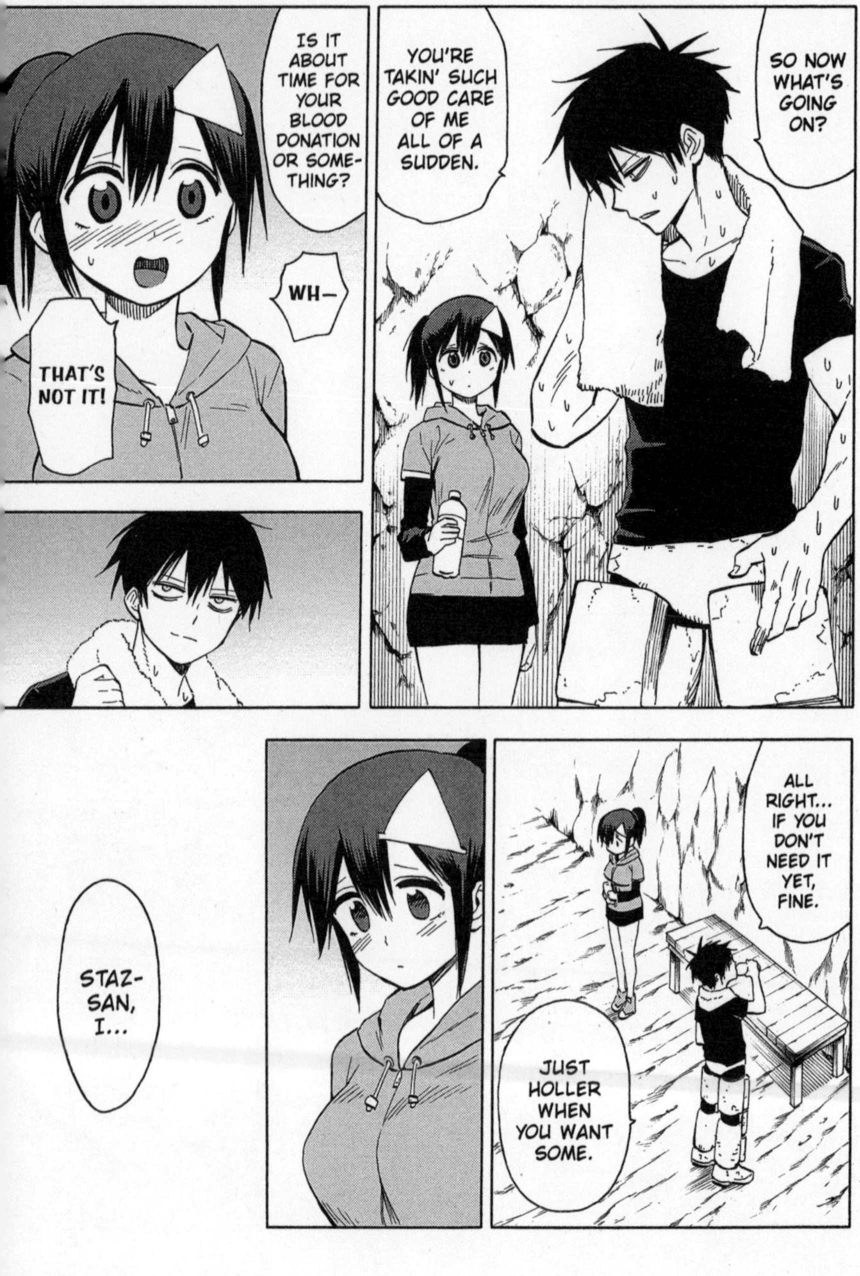
SO NOW WHAT'S GOING ON?
YOU'RE TAKIN' SUCH GOOD CARE OF ME ALL OF A SUDDEN.
IS IT ABOUT TIME FOR YOUR BLOOD DONATION OR SOME-THING?
WH—
THAT'S NOT IT!
ALL RIGHT... IF YOU DON'T NEED IT YET, FINE.
JUST HOLLER WHEN YOU WANT SOME.
STAZ-SAN, I...

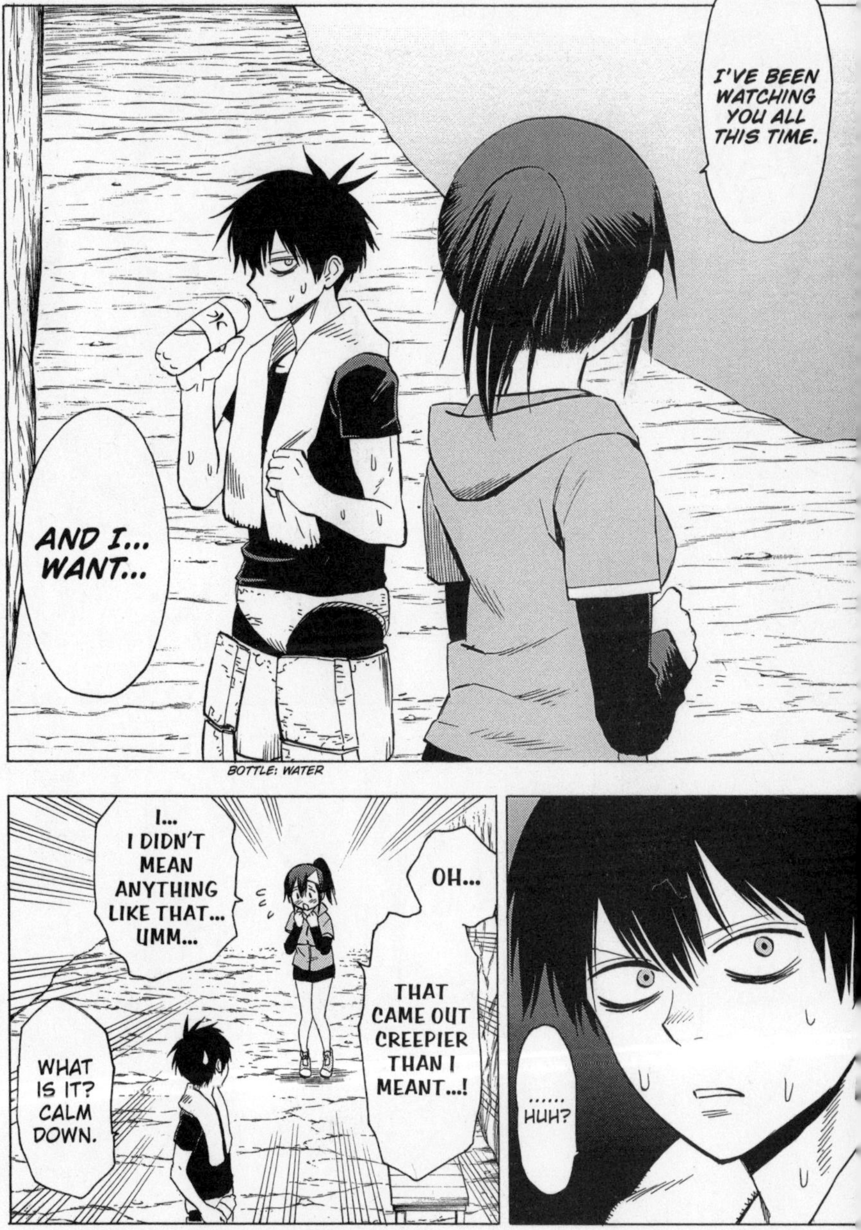
I'VE BEEN WATCHING YOU ALL THIS TIME.
AND I... WANT...
BOTTLE: WATER
......HUH?
OH...
THAT CAME OUT CREEPIER THAN I MEANT...!
I... I DIDN'T MEAN ANYTHING LIKE THAT... UMM...
WHAT IS IT? CALM DOWN.

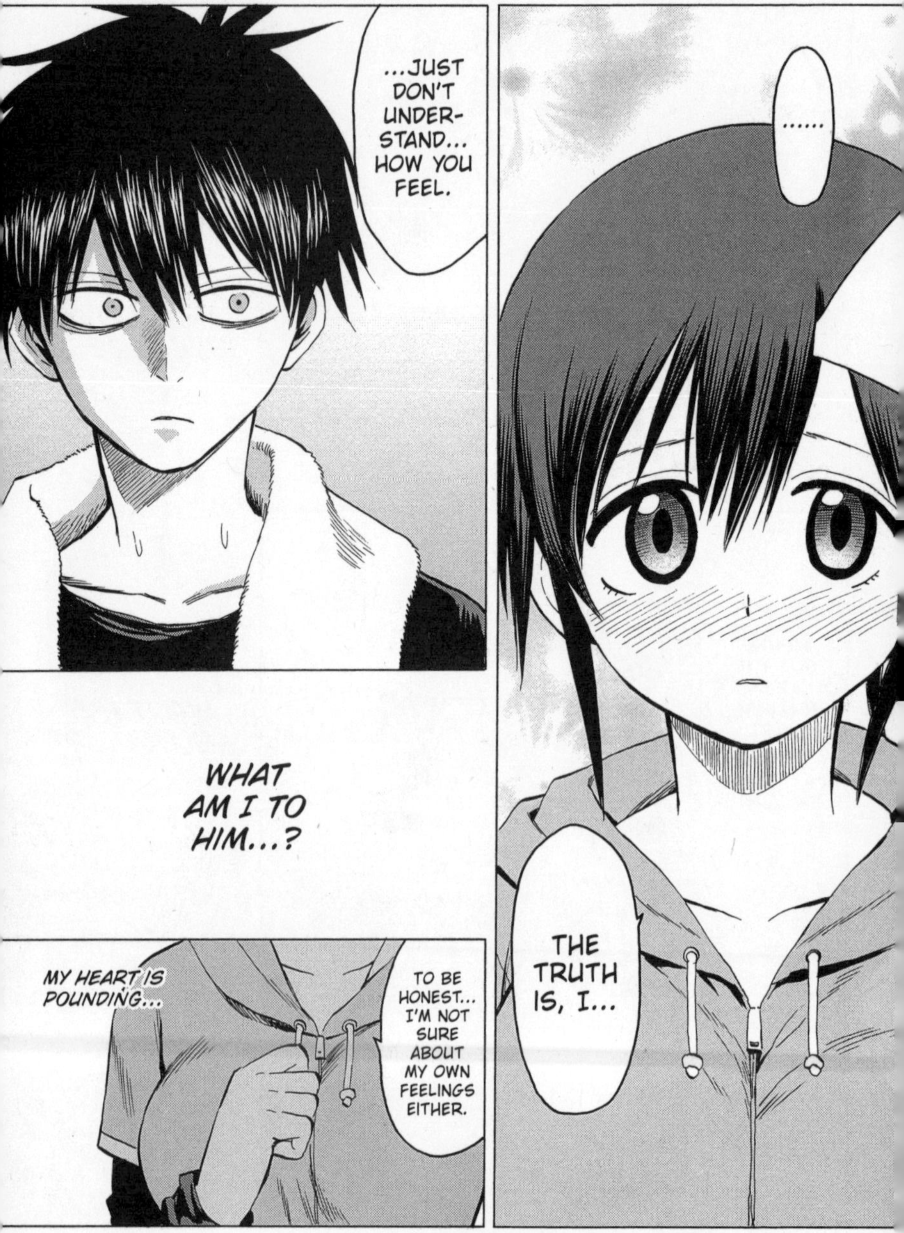
......
THE TRUTH IS, I...
...JUST DON'T UNDERSTAND... HOW YOU FEEL.
WHAT AM I TO HIM...?
TO BE HONEST... I'M NOT SURE ABOUT MY OWN FEELINGS EITHER.
MY HEART IS POUNDING...

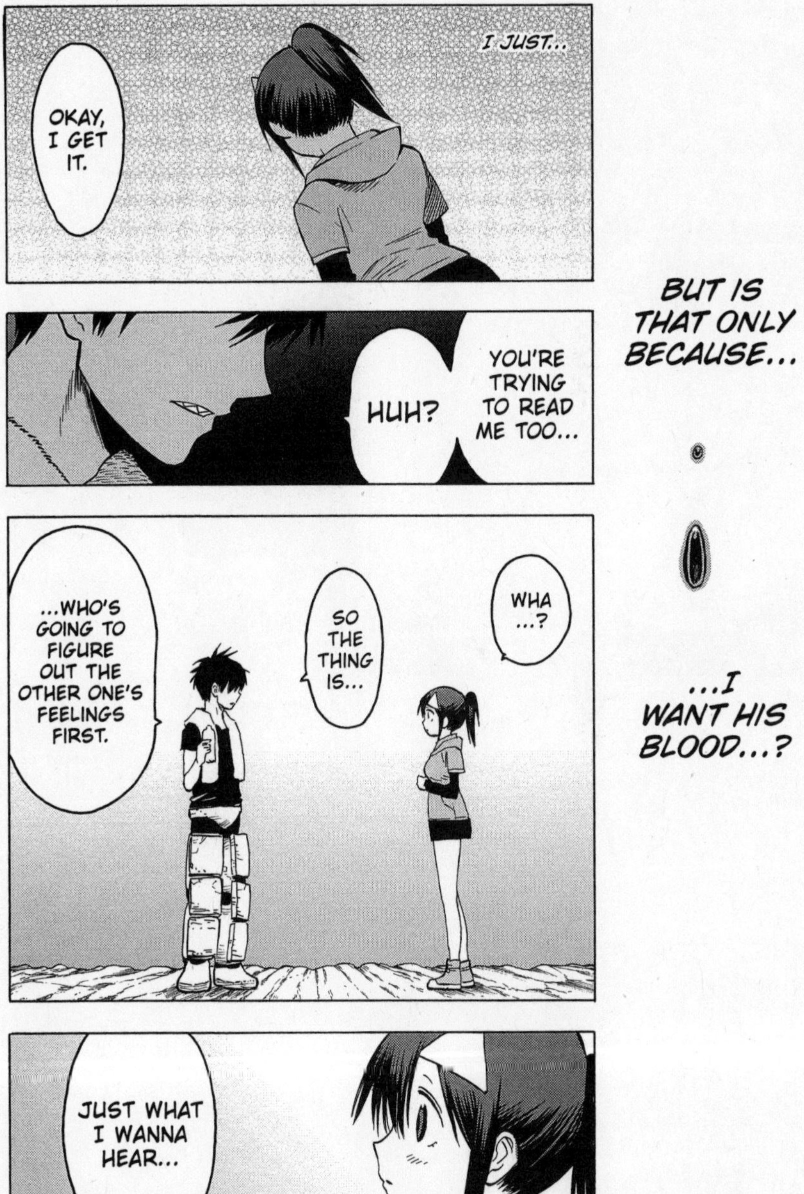
I JUST...
OKAY, I GET IT.
BUT IS THAT ONLY BECAUSE...
YOU'RE TRYING TO READ ME TOO...
HUH?
...I WANT HIS BLOOD...?
WHA...?
SO THE THING IS...
...WHO'S GOING TO FIGURE OUT THE OTHER ONE'S FEELINGS FIRST.
JUST WHAT I WANNA HEAR...

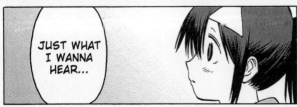

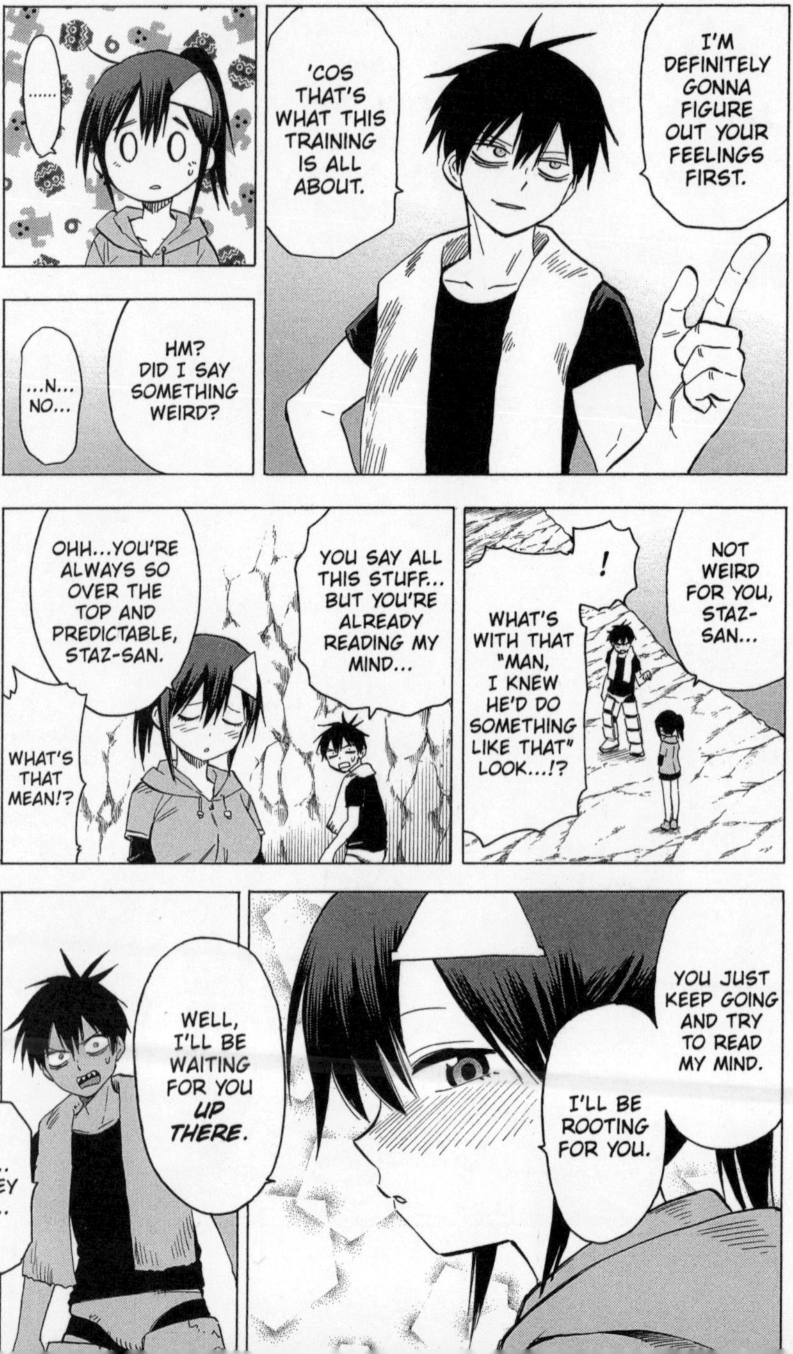
I'M DEFINITELY GONNA FIGURE OUT YOUR FEELINGS FIRST.
'COS THAT'S WHAT THIS TRAINING IS ALL ABOUT.
......
HM? DID I SAY SOMETHING WEIRD?
...N... NO...
NOT WEIRD FOR YOU, STAZ-SAN...
!
WHAT'S WITH THAT "MAN, I KNEW HE'D DO SOMETHING LIKE THAT" LOOK...!?
YOU SAY ALL THIS STUFF... BUT YOU'RE ALREADY READING MY MIND...
OHH...YOU'RE ALWAYS SO OVER THE TOP AND PREDICTABLE, STAZ-SAN.
WHAT'S THAT MEAN!?
YOU JUST KEEP GOING AND TRY TO READ MY MIND.
I'LL BE ROOTING FOR YOU.
WELL, I'LL BE WAITING FOR YOU *UP THERE*.
...HEY...

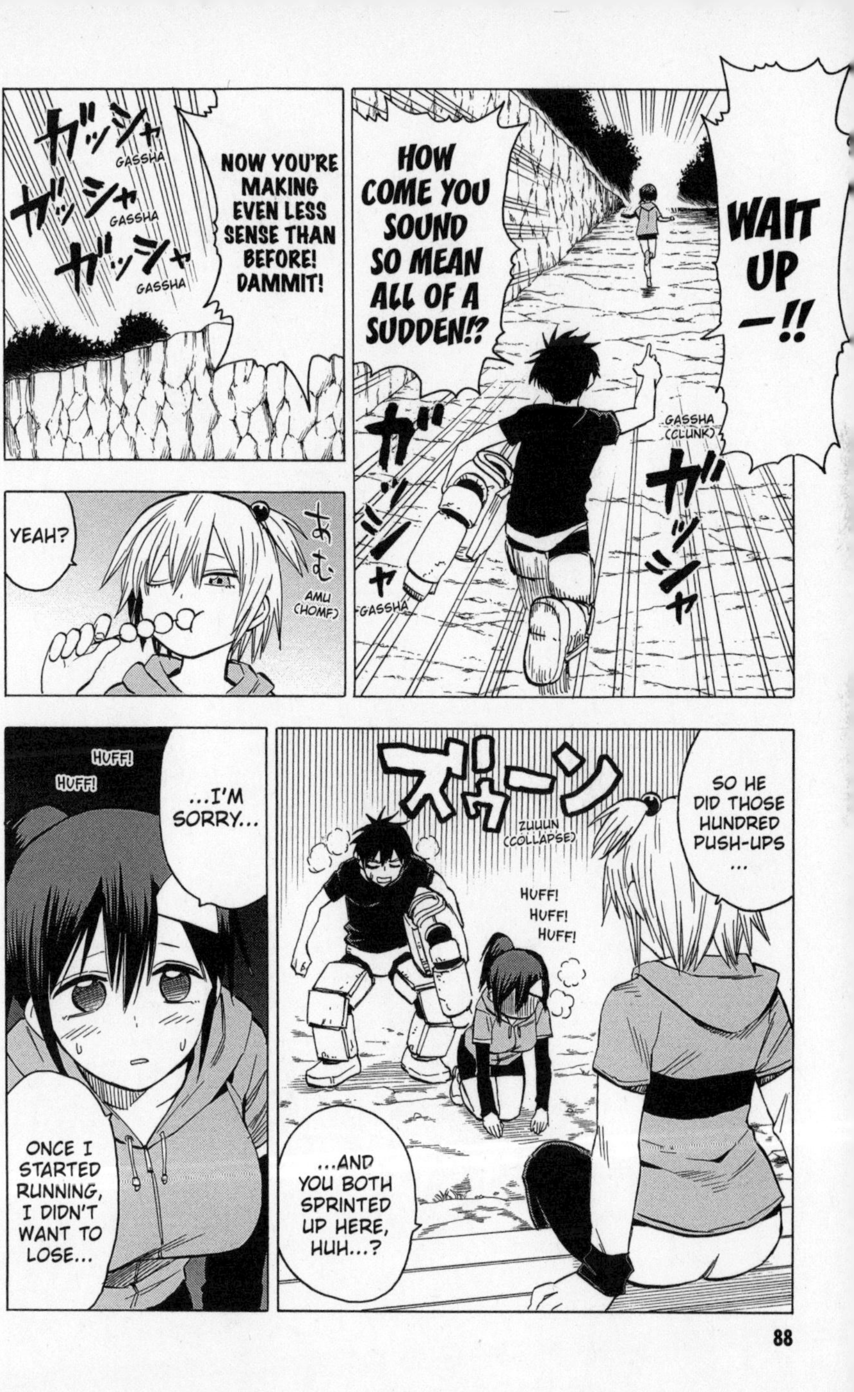
WAIT UP—!!
HOW COME YOU SOUND SO MEAN ALL OF A SUDDEN!?
GASSHA (CLUNK)
GASSHA
NOW YOU'RE MAKING EVEN LESS SENSE THAN BEFORE! DAMMIT!
GASSHA
GASSHA
GASSHA
YEAH?
AMU (HOMF)
SO HE DID THOSE HUNDRED PUSH-UPS ...
ZUUUN (COLLAPSE)
HUFF! HUFF! HUFF!
...AND YOU BOTH SPRINTED UP HERE, HUH...?
HUFF! HUFF!
...I'M SORRY...
ONCE I STARTED RUNNING, I DIDN'T WANT TO LOSE...

BOOK: INSTRUCTOR'S SECRET NOTEBOOK

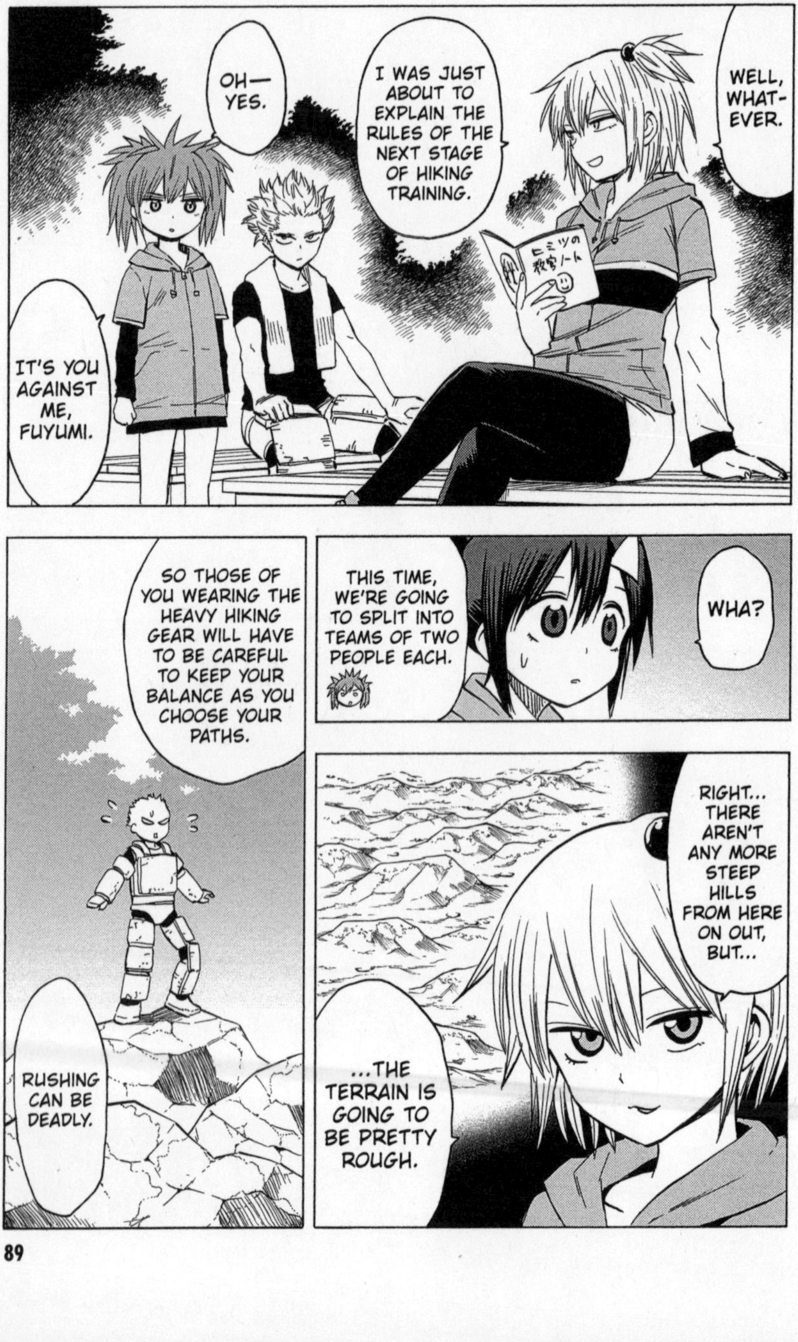
WELL, WHAT-EVER.
I WAS JUST ABOUT TO EXPLAIN THE RULES OF THE NEXT STAGE OF HIKING TRAINING.
ヒミツの教官ノート
OH— YES.
IT'S YOU AGAINST ME, FUYUMI.
WHA?
THIS TIME, WE'RE GOING TO SPLIT INTO TEAMS OF TWO PEOPLE EACH.
RIGHT... THERE AREN'T ANY MORE STEEP HILLS FROM HERE ON OUT, BUT...
...THE TERRAIN IS GOING TO BE PRETTY ROUGH.
SO THOSE OF YOU WEARING THE HEAVY HIKING GEAR WILL HAVE TO BE CAREFUL TO KEEP YOUR BALANCE AS YOU CHOOSE YOUR PATHS.
RUSHING CAN BE DEADLY.

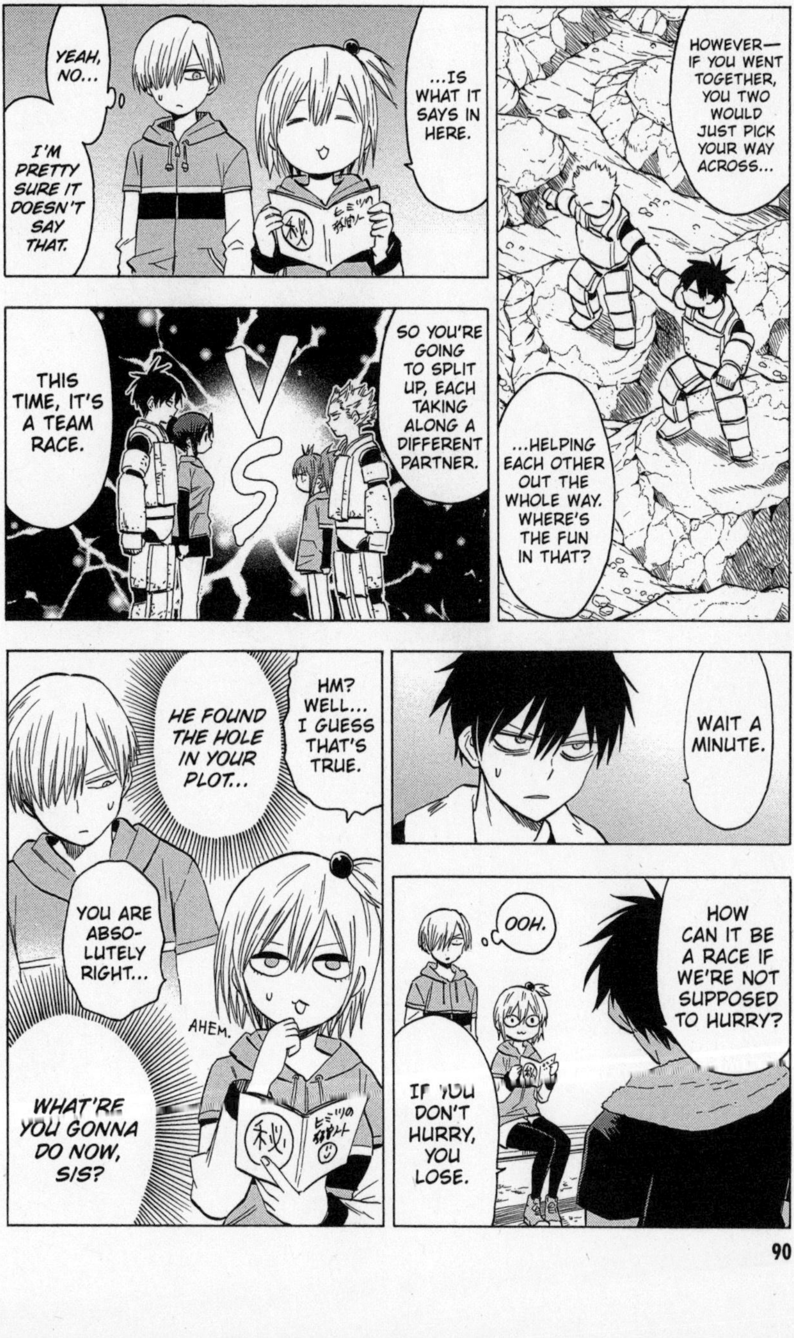
HOWEVER— IF YOU WENT TOGETHER, YOU TWO WOULD JUST PICK YOUR WAY ACROSS...
...HELPING EACH OTHER OUT THE WHOLE WAY. WHERE'S THE FUN IN THAT?
...IS WHAT IT SAYS IN HERE.
YEAH, NO...
I'M PRETTY SURE IT DOESN'T SAY THAT.
SO YOU'RE GOING TO SPLIT UP, EACH TAKING ALONG A DIFFERENT PARTNER.
THIS TIME, IT'S A TEAM RACE.
VS
WAIT A MINUTE.
HOW CAN IT BE A RACE IF WE'RE NOT SUPPOSED TO HURRY?
OOH.
IF YOU DON'T HURRY, YOU LOSE.
HM? WELL... I GUESS THAT'S TRUE.
HE FOUND THE HOLE IN YOUR PLOT...
YOU ARE ABSO-LUTELY RIGHT...
AHEM.
WHAT'RE YOU GONNA DO NOW, SIS?

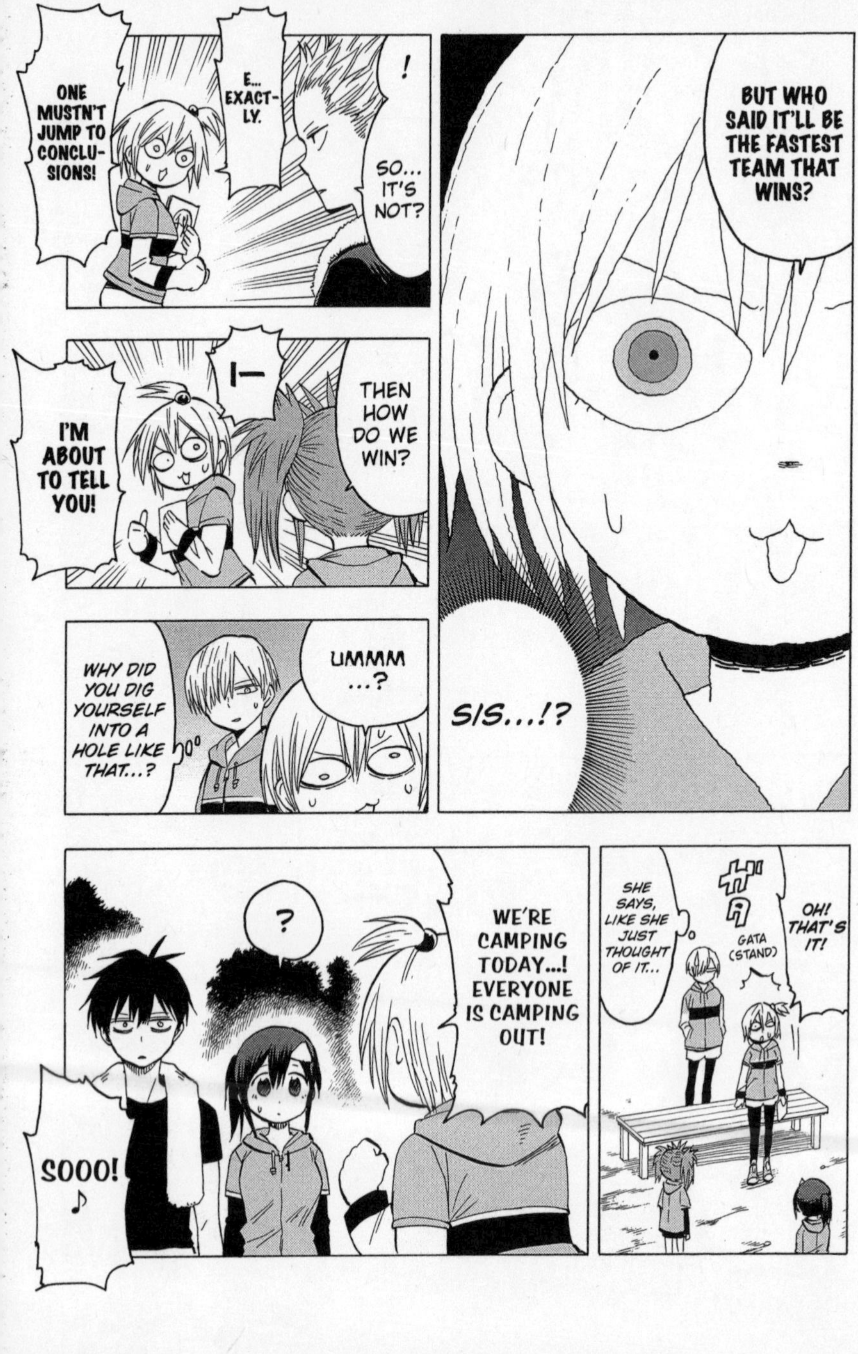
BUT WHO SAID IT'LL BE THE FASTEST TEAM THAT WINS?
SIS...!?
!
SO... IT'S NOT?
E... EXACT-LY.
ONE MUSTN'T JUMP TO CONCLU-SIONS!
THEN HOW DO WE WIN?
I—
I'M ABOUT TO TELL YOU!
UMMM ...?
WHY DID YOU DIG YOURSELF INTO A HOLE LIKE THAT...?
OH! THAT'S IT!
ガタ
GATA (STAND)
SHE SAYS, LIKE SHE JUST THOUGHT OF IT...
WE'RE CAMPING TODAY...! EVERYONE IS CAMPING OUT!
?
SOOO! ♪

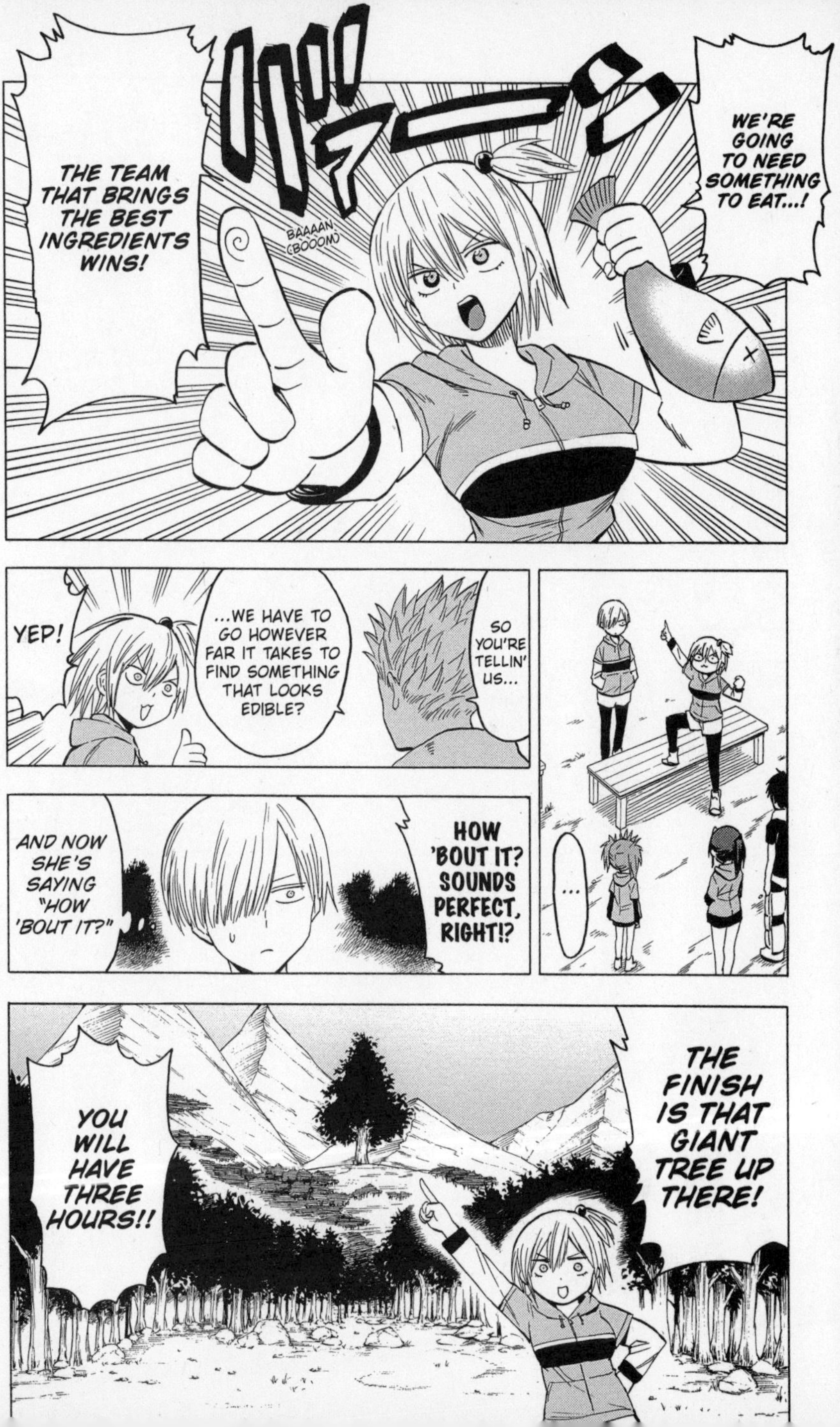
WE'RE GOING TO NEED SOMETHING TO EAT...!
BAAAAN (BOOOM)
THE TEAM THAT BRINGS THE BEST INGREDIENTS WINS!
...
SO YOU'RE TELLIN' US...
...WE HAVE TO GO HOWEVER FAR IT TAKES TO FIND SOMETHING THAT LOOKS EDIBLE?
YEP!
HOW 'BOUT IT? SOUNDS PERFECT, RIGHT!?
AND NOW SHE'S SAYING "HOW 'BOUT IT?"
THE FINISH IS THAT GIANT TREE UP THERE!
YOU WILL HAVE THREE HOURS!!

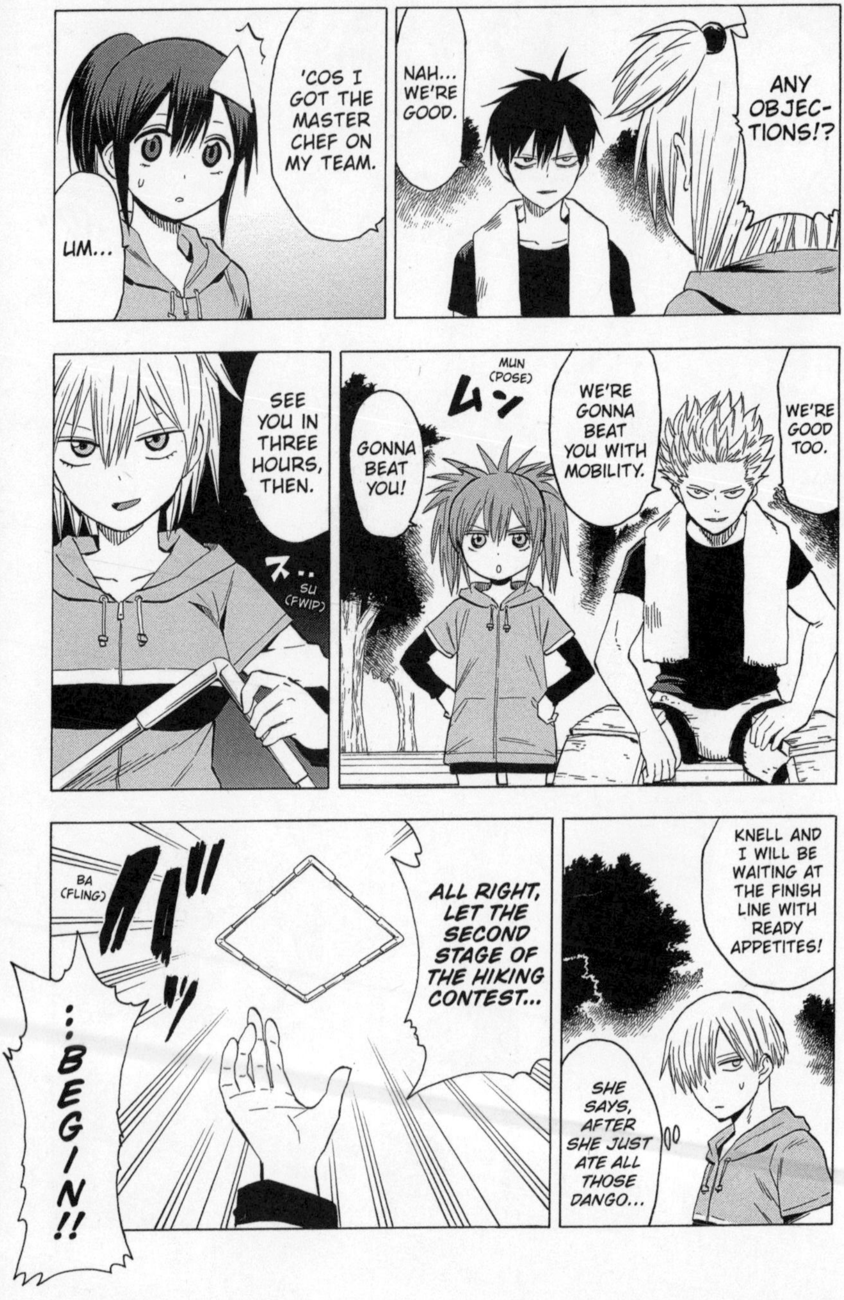
ANY OBJECTIONS!?
NAH... WE'RE GOOD.
'COS I GOT THE MASTER CHEF ON MY TEAM.
UM...
WE'RE GOOD TOO.
WE'RE GONNA BEAT YOU WITH MOBILITY.
ムン
MUN (POSE)
GONNA BEAT YOU!
SEE YOU IN THREE HOURS, THEN.
ス..
SU (FWIP)
KNELL AND I WILL BE WAITING AT THE FINISH LINE WITH READY APPETITES!
SHE SAYS, AFTER SHE JUST ATE ALL THOSE DANGO...
BA (FLING)
ALL RIGHT, LET THE SECOND STAGE OF THE HIKING CONTEST...
...BEGIN!!

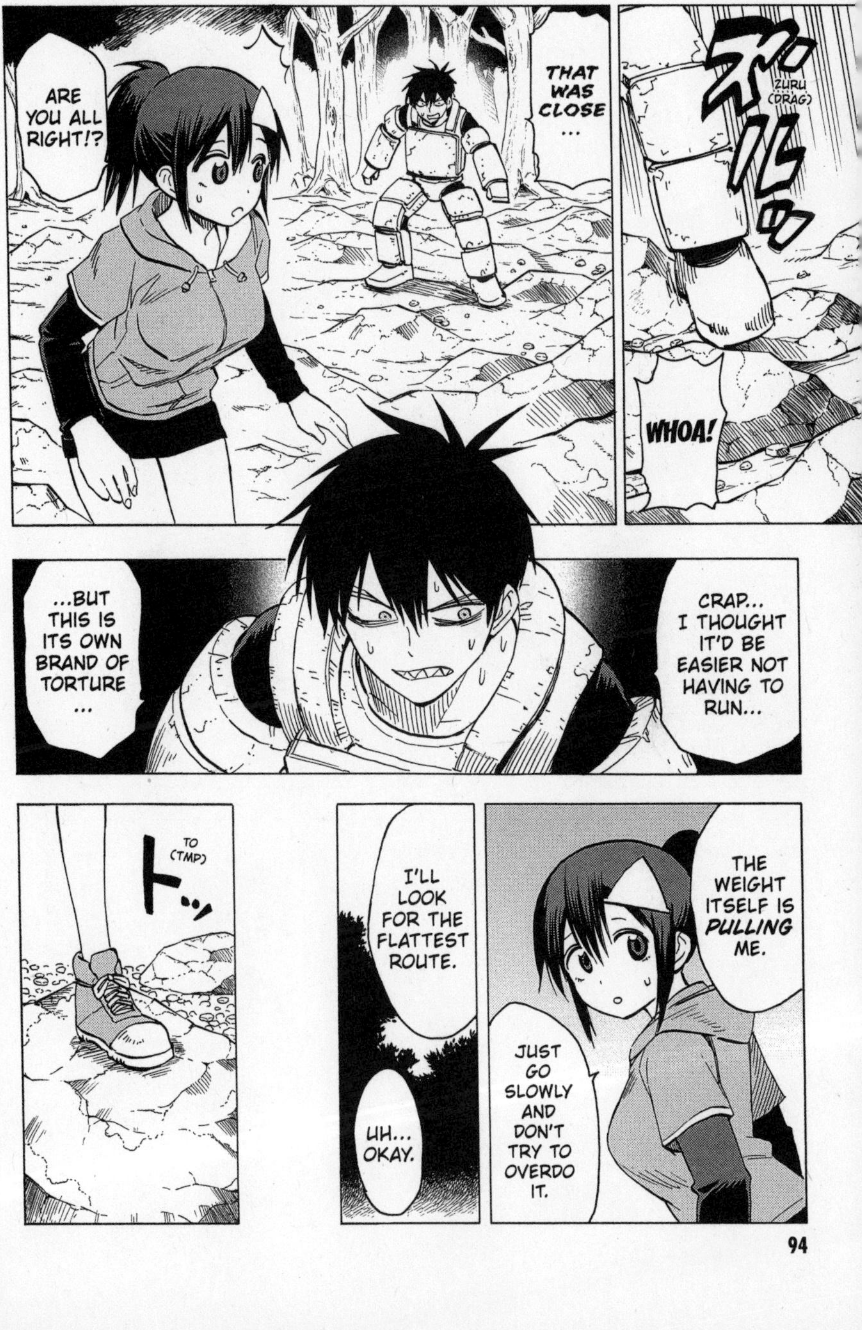
ズルッ
ZURU (DRAG)
WHOA!
THAT WAS CLOSE ...
ARE YOU ALL RIGHT!?
CRAP... I THOUGHT IT'D BE EASIER NOT HAVING TO RUN...
...BUT THIS IS ITS OWN BRAND OF TORTURE ...
THE WEIGHT ITSELF IS *PULLING* ME.
JUST GO SLOWLY AND DON'T TRY TO OVERDO IT.
I'LL LOOK FOR THE FLATTEST ROUTE.
UH... OKAY.
トッ
TO (TMP)

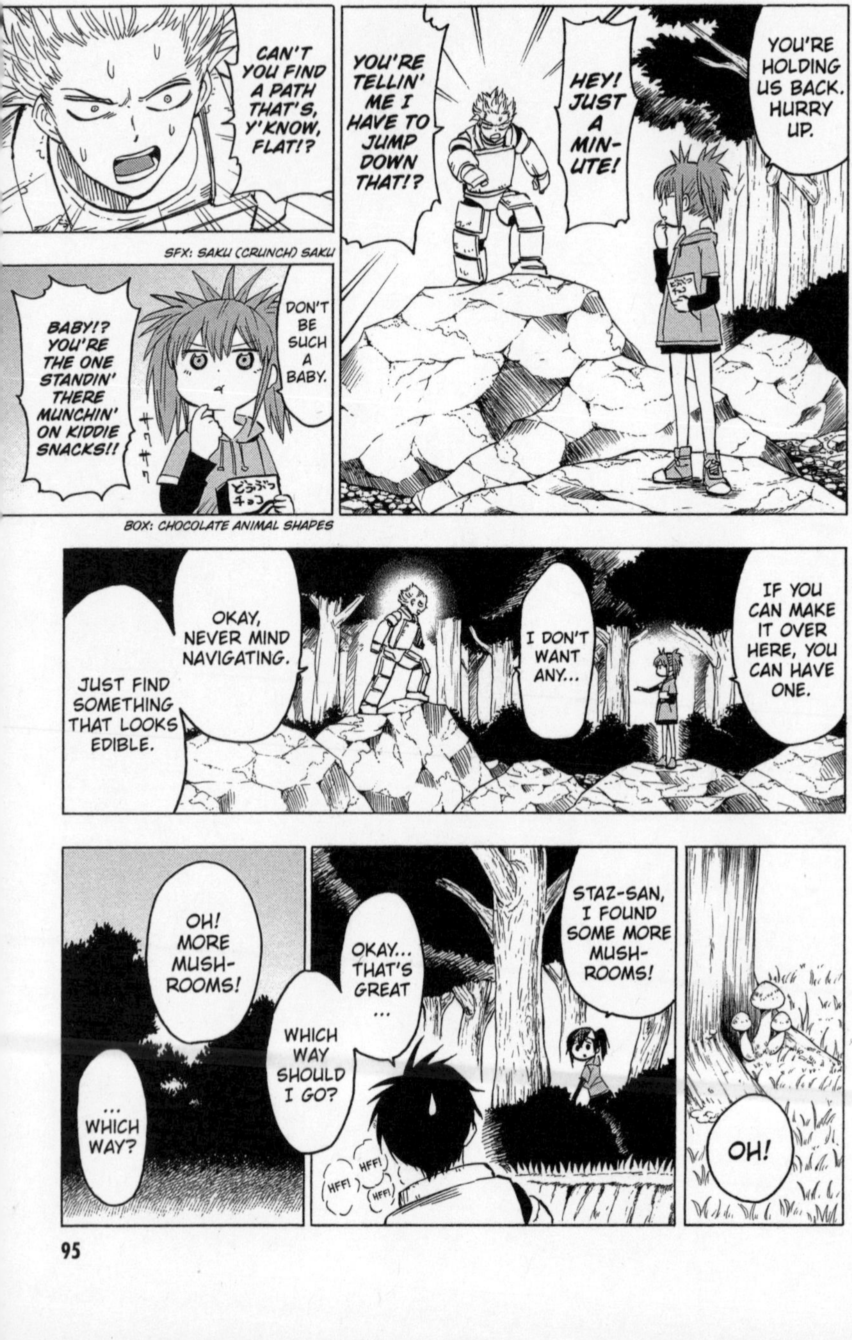
YOU'RE HOLDING US BACK. HURRY UP.
HEY! JUST A MIN-UTE!
YOU'RE TELLIN' ME I HAVE TO JUMP DOWN THAT!?
CAN'T YOU FIND A PATH THAT'S, Y'KNOW, FLAT!?
DON'T BE SUCH A BABY.
BABY!? YOU'RE THE ONE STANDIN' THERE MUNCHIN' ON KIDDIE SNACKS!!
サクサク
どうぶつチョコ
IF YOU CAN MAKE IT OVER HERE, YOU CAN HAVE ONE.
I DON'T WANT ANY...
OKAY, NEVER MIND NAVIGATING.
JUST FIND SOMETHING THAT LOOKS EDIBLE.
OH!
STAZ-SAN, I FOUND SOME MORE MUSH-ROOMS!
OKAY... THAT'S GREAT ...
WHICH WAY SHOULD I GO?
HFF! HFF! HFF! HFF!
OH! MORE MUSH-ROOMS!
... WHICH WAY?

SFX: SAKU (CRUNCH) SAKU

BOX: CHOCOLATE ANIMAL SHAPES

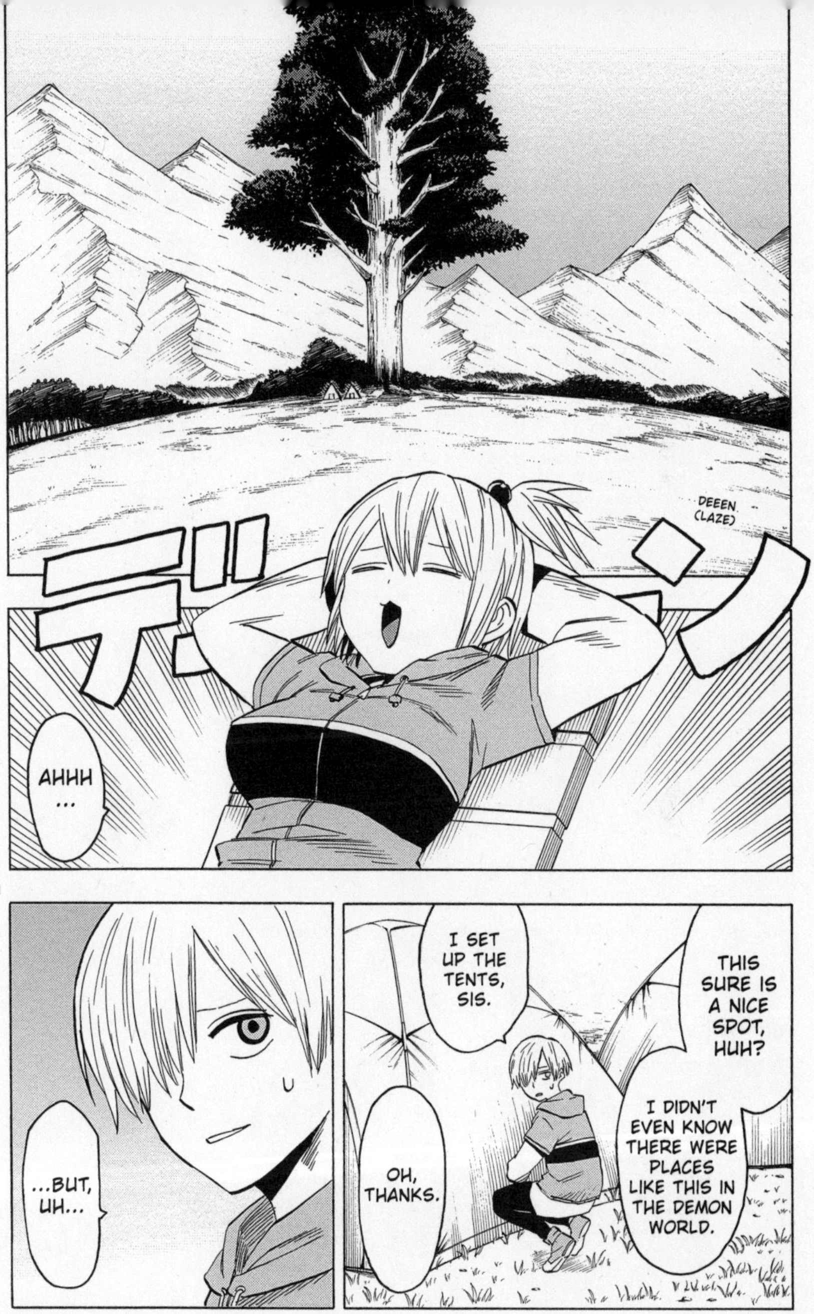
DEEEN. (LAZE)
AHHH ...
THIS SURE IS A NICE SPOT, HUH?
I DIDN'T EVEN KNOW THERE WERE PLACES LIKE THIS IN THE DEMON WORLD.
I SET UP THE TENTS, SIS.
OH, THANKS.
...BUT, UH...

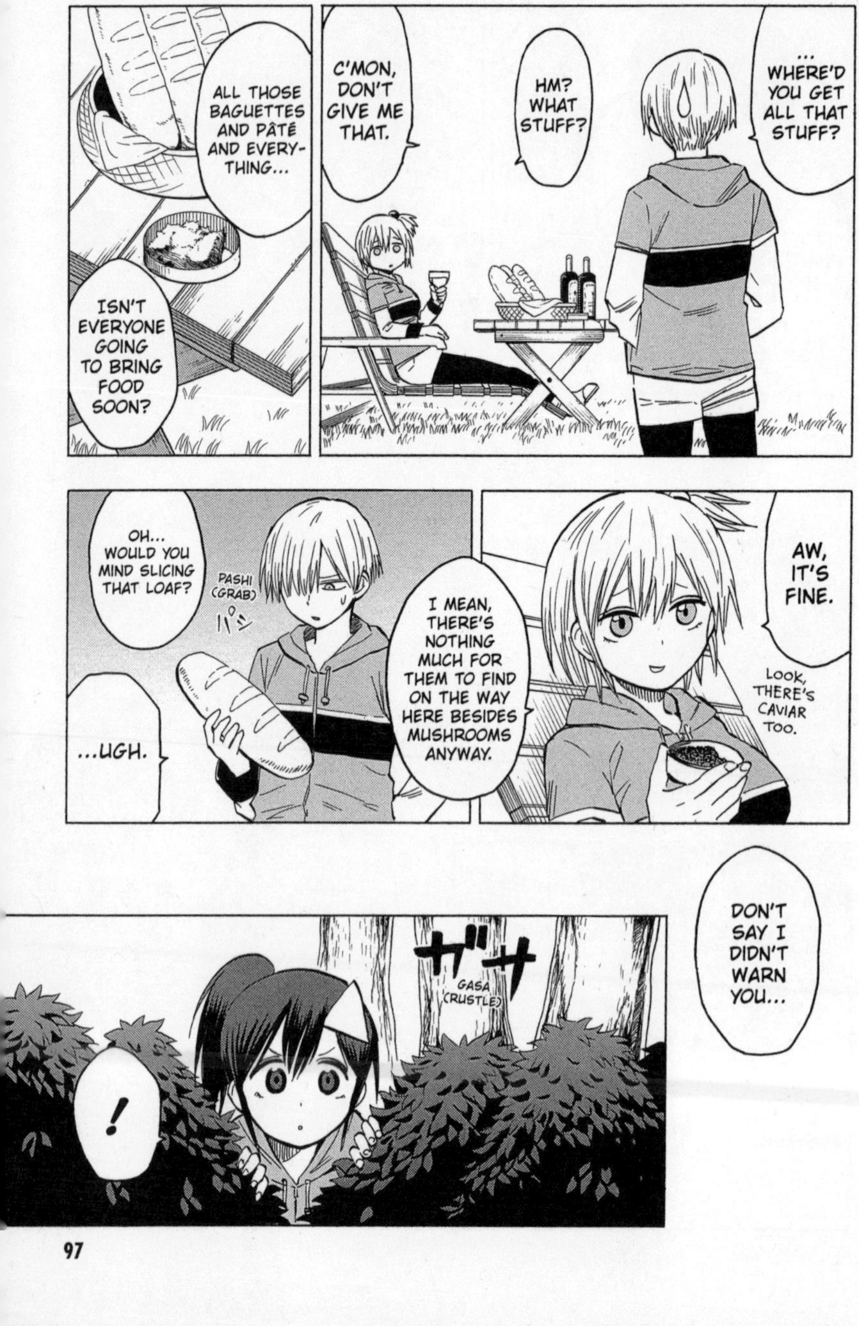

... WHERE'D YOU GET ALL THAT STUFF?
HM? WHAT STUFF?
C'MON, DON'T GIVE ME THAT.
ALL THOSE BAGUETTES AND PÂTÉ AND EVERY-THING...
ISN'T EVERYONE GOING TO BRING FOOD SOON?
AW, IT'S FINE.
LOOK, THERE'S CAVIAR TOO.
I MEAN, THERE'S NOTHING MUCH FOR THEM TO FIND ON THE WAY HERE BESIDES MUSHROOMS ANYWAY.
PASHI (GRAB)
パシ
OH... WOULD YOU MIND SLICING THAT LOAF?
...UGH.
DON'T SAY I DIDN'T WARN YOU...
ガサ
GASA (CRUSTLE)
!

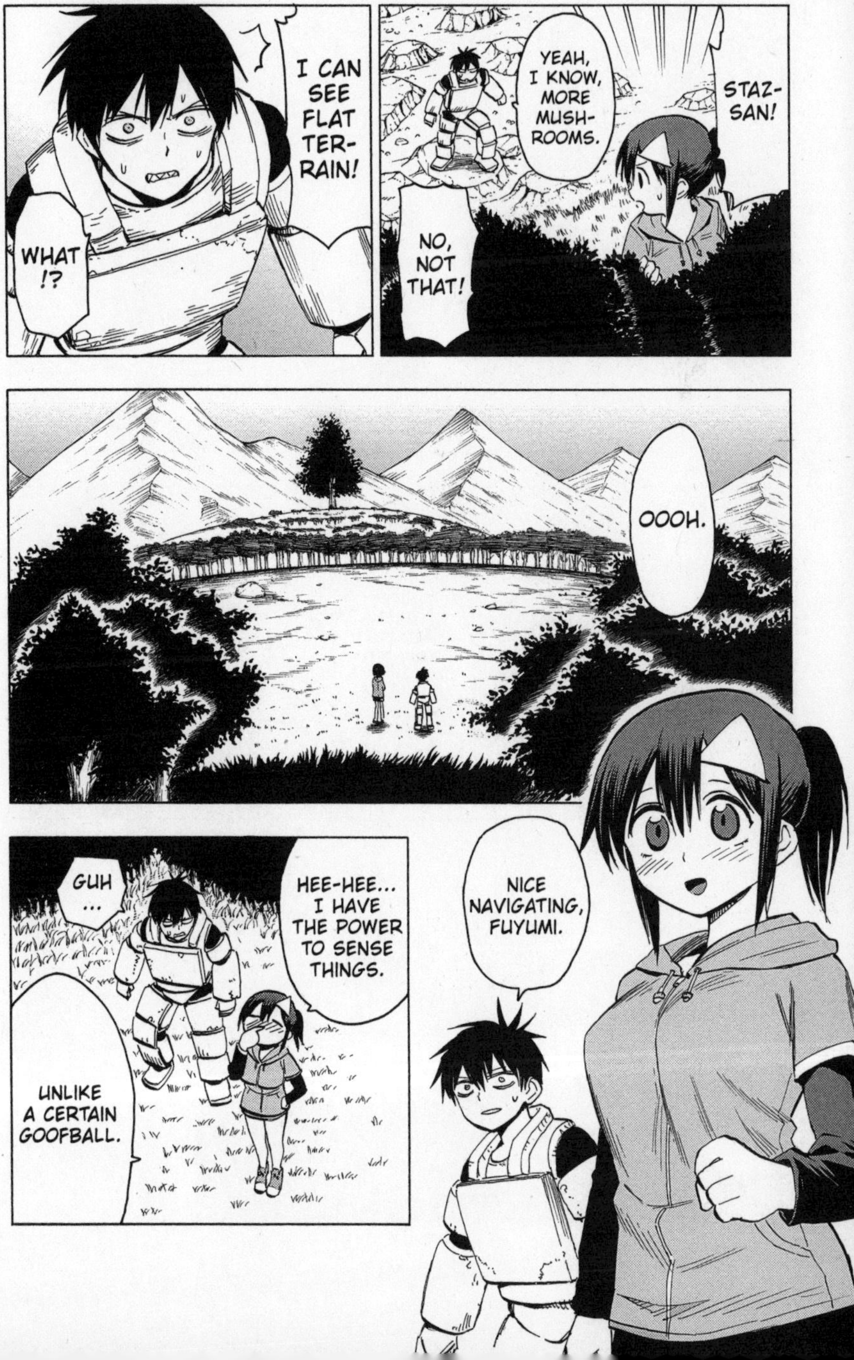
STAZ-SAN!
YEAH, I KNOW, MORE MUSH-ROOMS.
NO, NOT THAT!
I CAN SEE FLAT TER-RAIN!
WHAT!?
OOOH.
NICE NAVIGATING, FUYUMI.
HEE-HEE... I HAVE THE POWER TO SENSE THINGS.
GUH ...
UNLIKE A CERTAIN GOOFBALL.

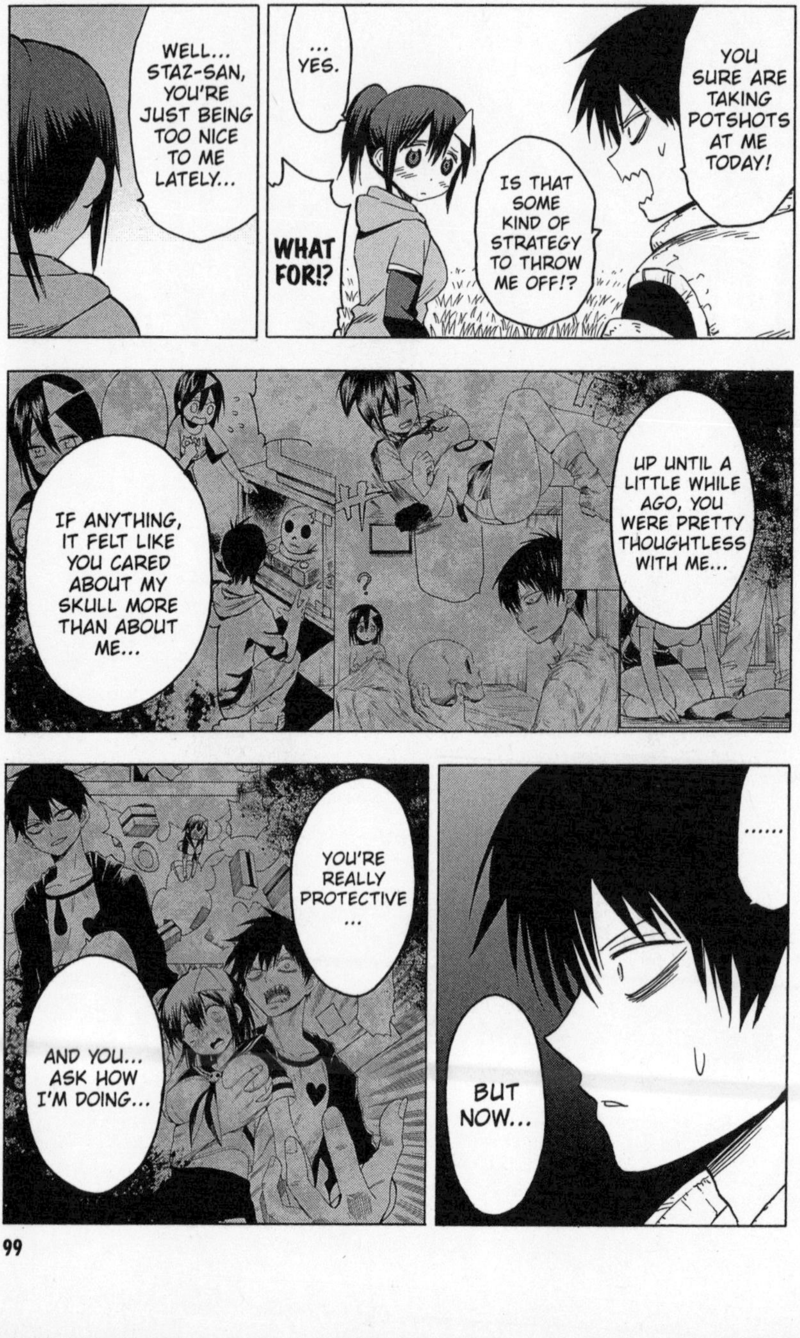
YOU SURE ARE TAKING POTSHOTS AT ME TODAY!
IS THAT SOME KIND OF STRATEGY TO THROW ME OFF!?
... YES.
WHAT FOR!?
WELL... STAZ-SAN, YOU'RE JUST BEING TOO NICE TO ME LATELY...
UP UNTIL A LITTLE WHILE AGO, YOU WERE PRETTY THOUGHTLESS WITH ME...
IF ANYTHING, IT FELT LIKE YOU CARED ABOUT MY SKULL MORE THAN ABOUT ME...
......
BUT NOW...
YOU'RE REALLY PROTECTIVE ...
AND YOU... ASK HOW I'M DOING...

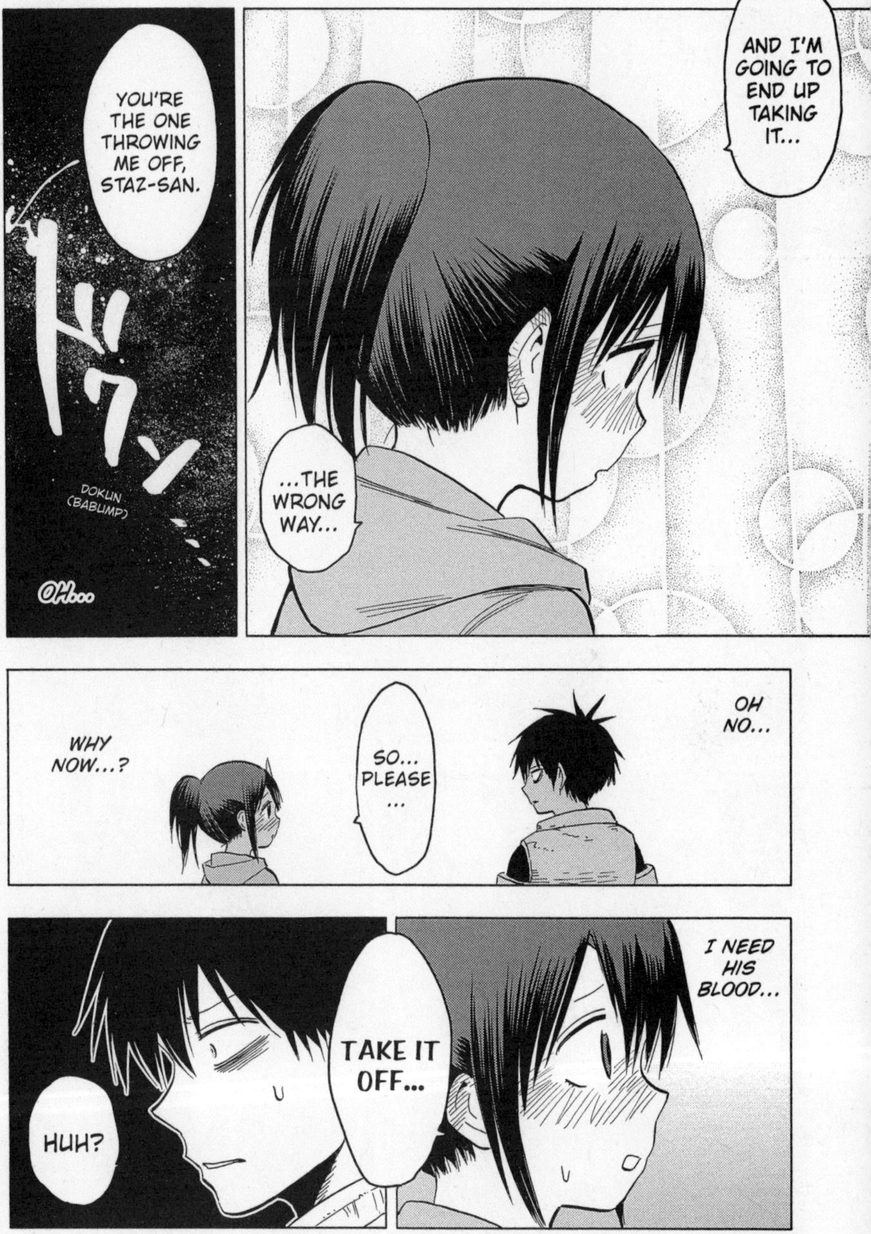
AND I'M GOING TO END UP TAKING IT...
...THE WRONG WAY...
YOU'RE THE ONE THROWING ME OFF, STAZ-SAN.
ドクン
DOKUN (BABUMP)
Oh...
OH NO...
SO... PLEASE ...
WHY NOW...?
I NEED HIS BLOOD...
TAKE IT OFF...
HUH?

スウ
(VANISH)

WHA
...?

ドサ
DOSA
(WHUMP)

SERI-
OUSLY!?

!

HEY!?

I'M
SORRY...

OHH...

YOU...
HAVE
THE
WORST
TIMING
...

ガッシャ
GASSHA
(KACLUNK)

DO
YOU...

...EVEN
REALIZE IT
YOURSELF
...?

HOLD
ON, I'LL
GIVE YOU
SOME.

...STAZ-
SAN...

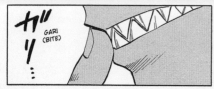
ガリ
GARI
(BITE)

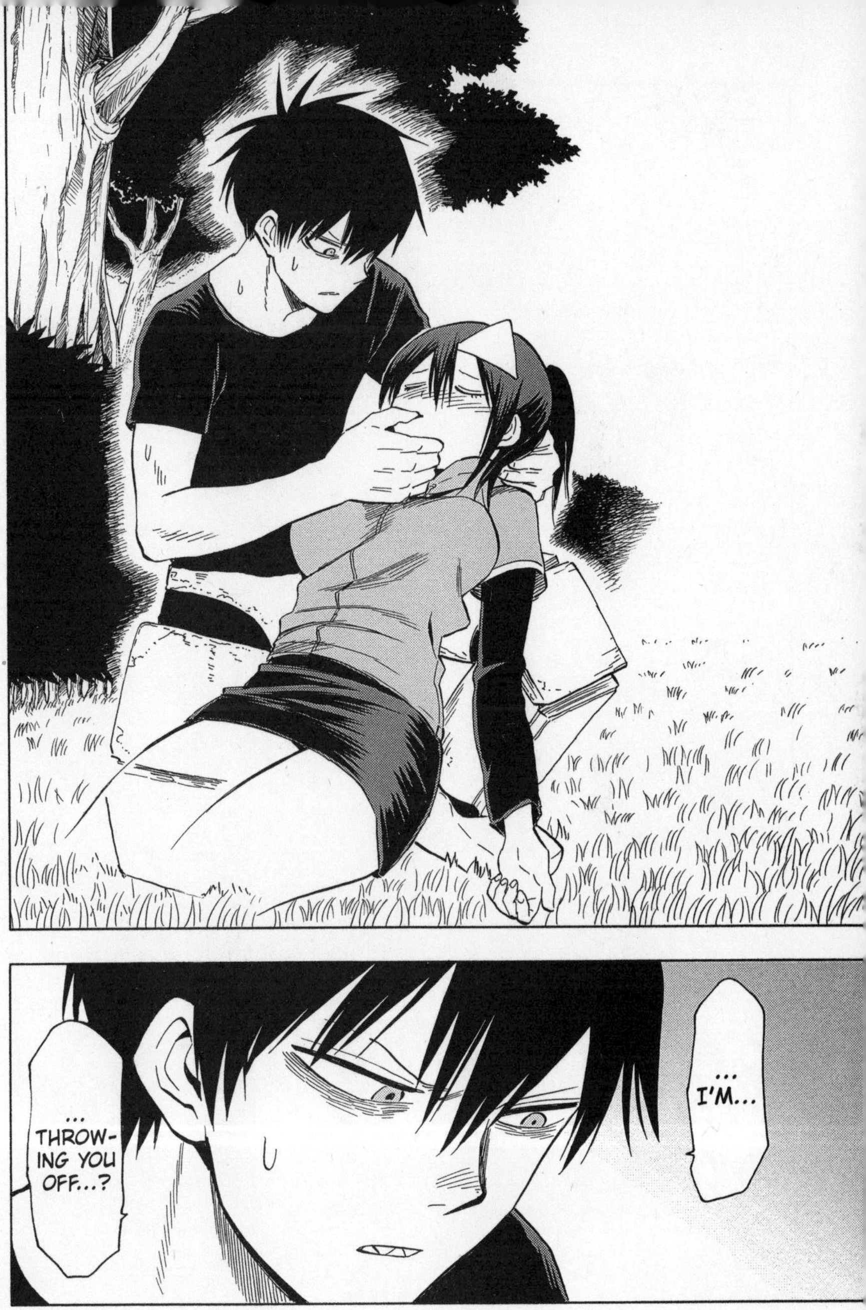
... I'M...
... THROWING YOU OFF...?

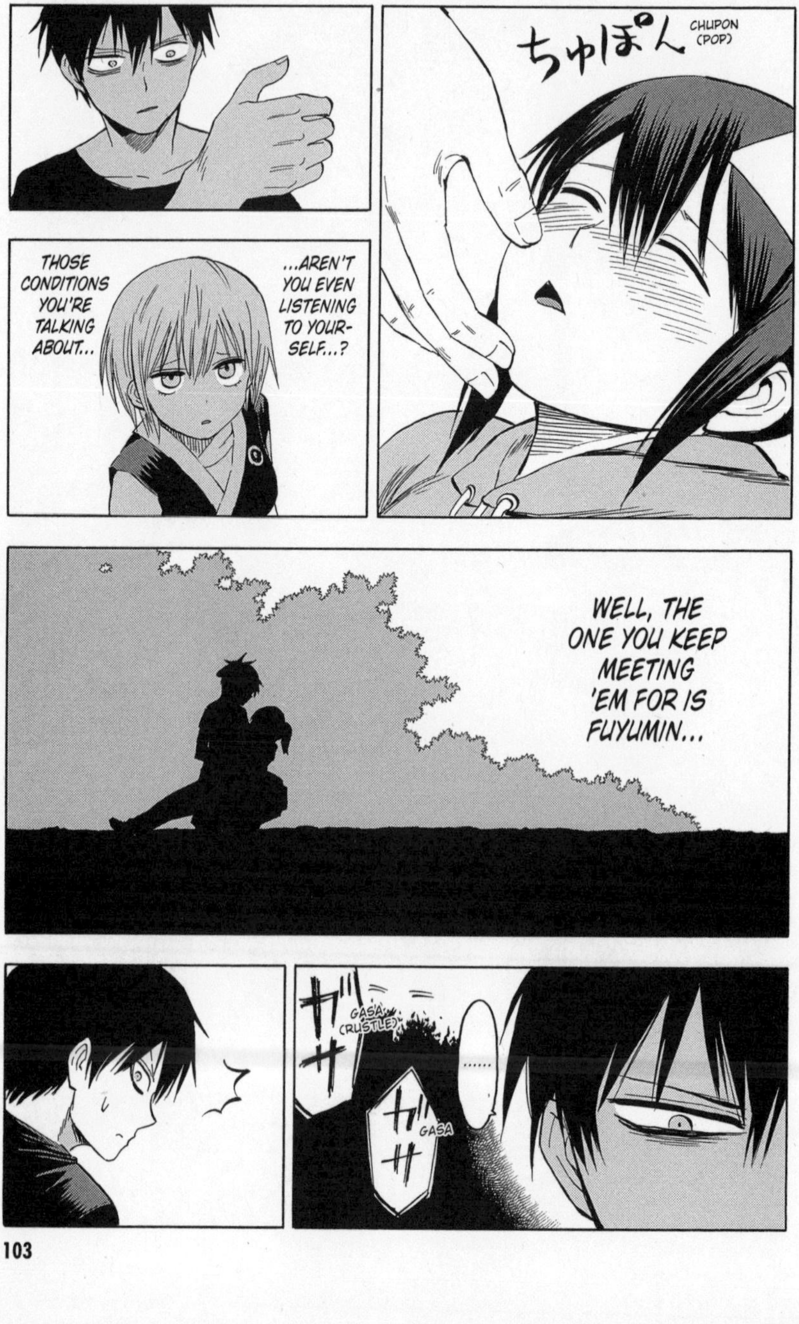
ちゅぽん
CHUPON (POP)
THOSE CONDITIONS YOU'RE TALKING ABOUT...
...AREN'T YOU EVEN LISTENING TO YOURSELF...?
WELL, THE ONE YOU KEEP MEETING 'EM FOR IS FUYUMIN...
......
ガサ
GASA (RUSTLE)
ガサ
GASA

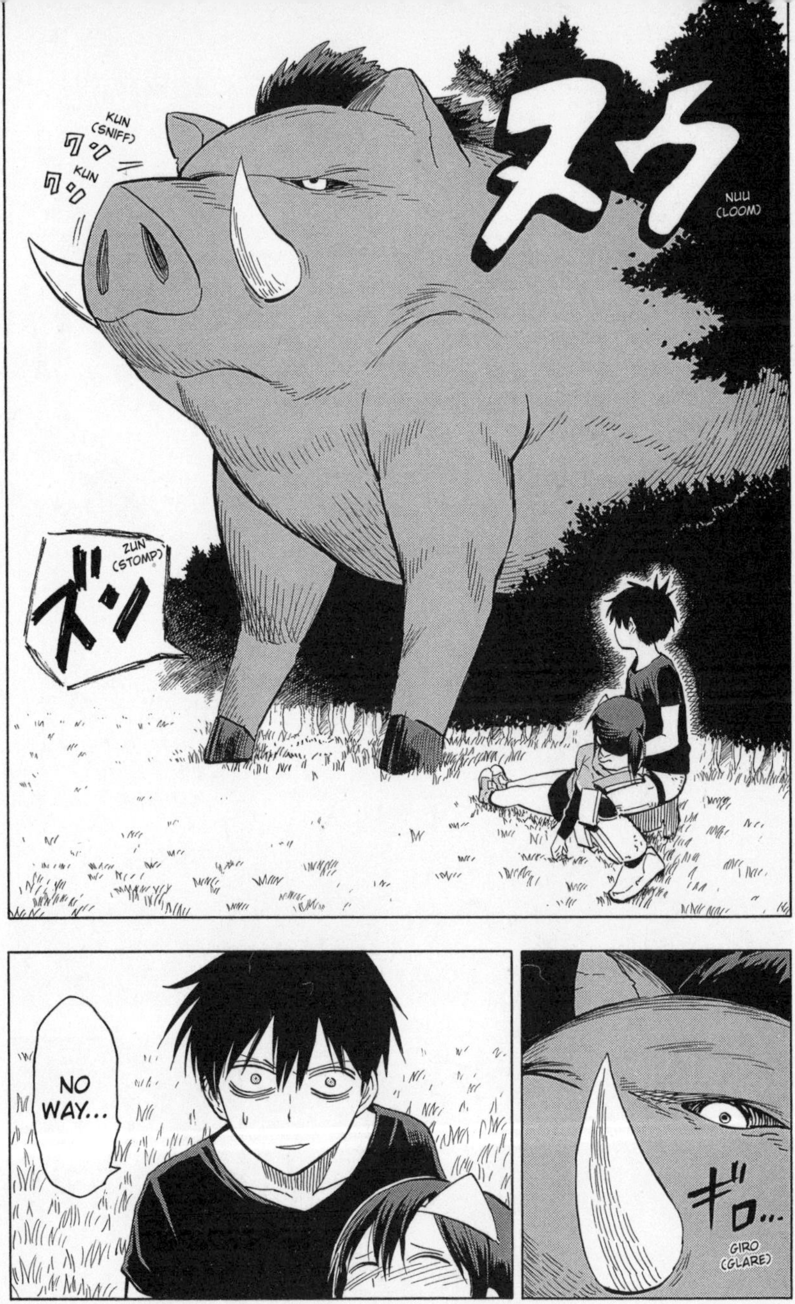
NUU (LOOM)
KUN (SNIFF)
KUN
ZUN (STOMP)
GIRO (GLARE)
NO WAY...

♠ To Be Continued ♠

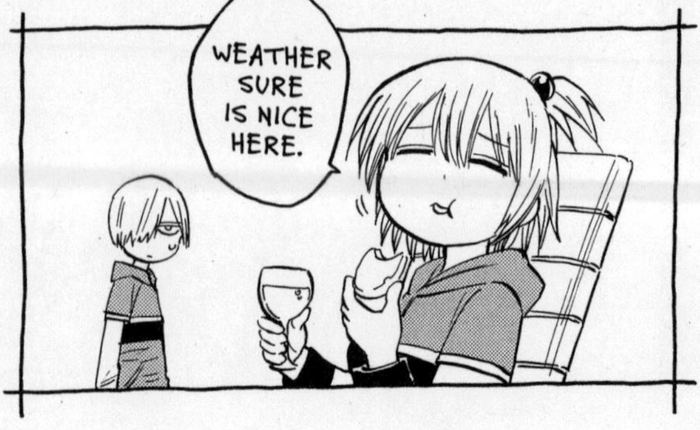
WEATHER SURE IS NICE HERE.

BLOOD LAD

CHAPTER 64 ♠ THE WORLD OF THE WEAK

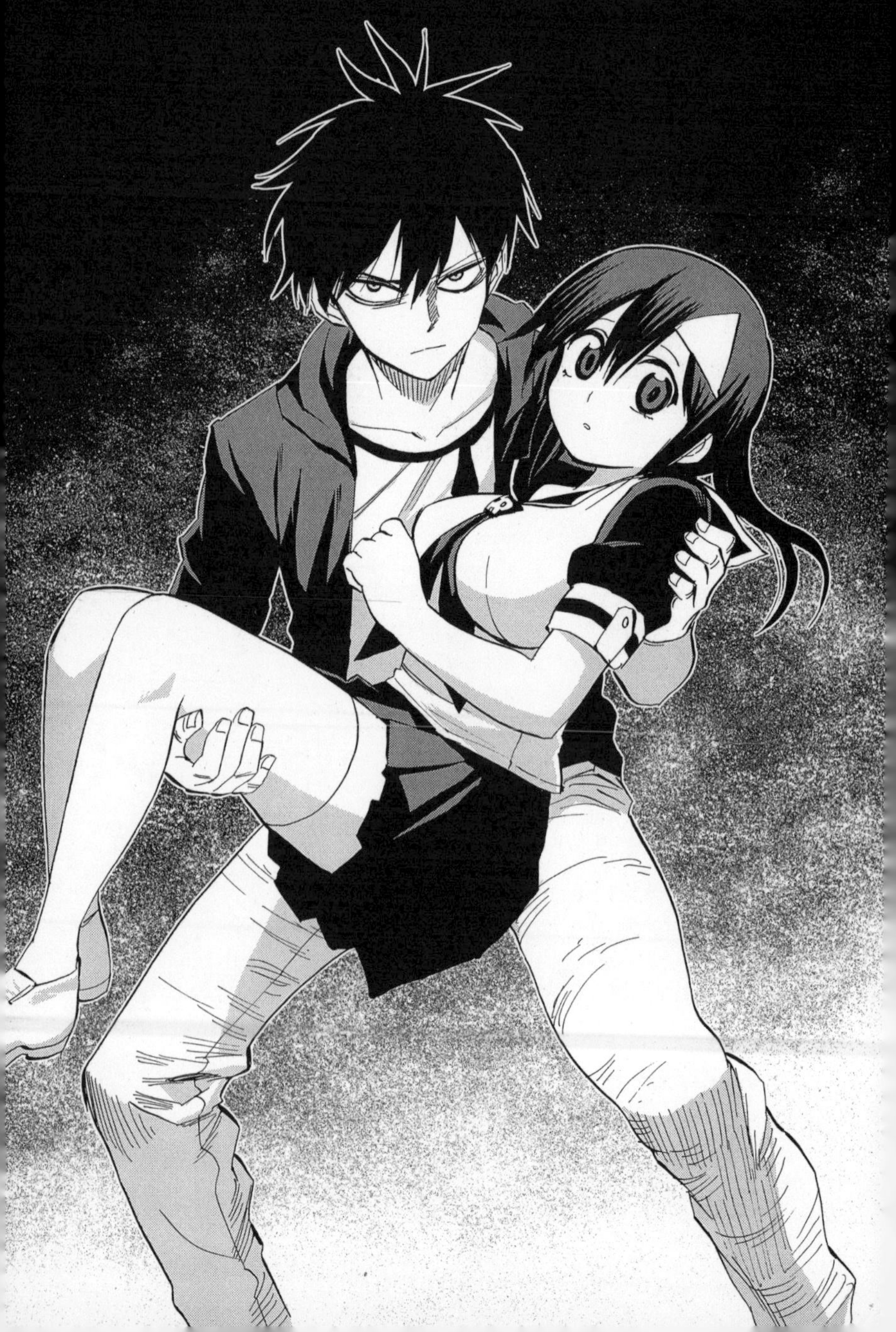

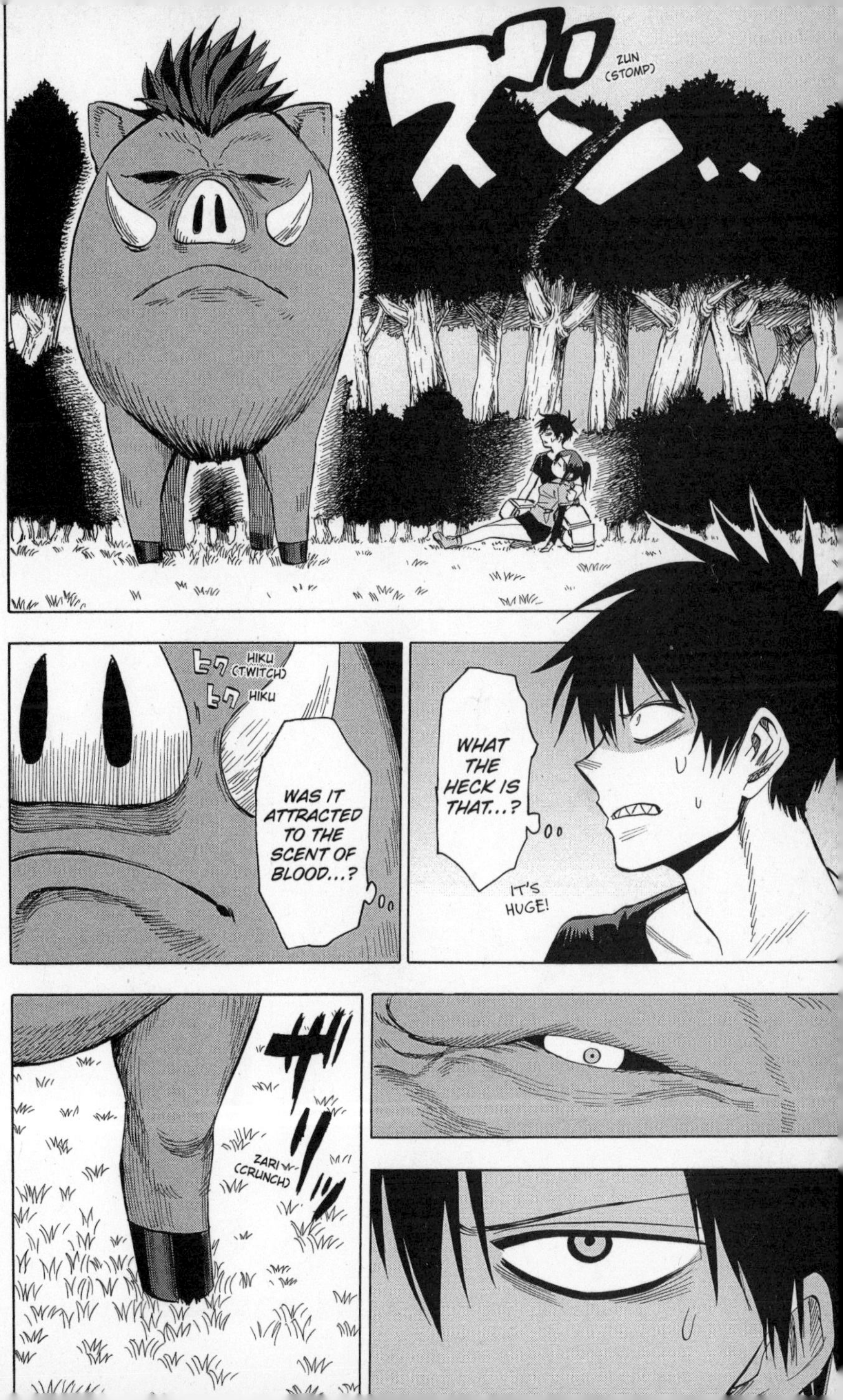
ズン..
ZUN (STOMP)
WHAT THE HECK IS THAT...?
IT'S HUGE!
ヒク HIKU (TWITCH)
ヒク HIKU
WAS IT ATTRACTED TO THE SCENT OF BLOOD...?
ZARI (CRUNCH)

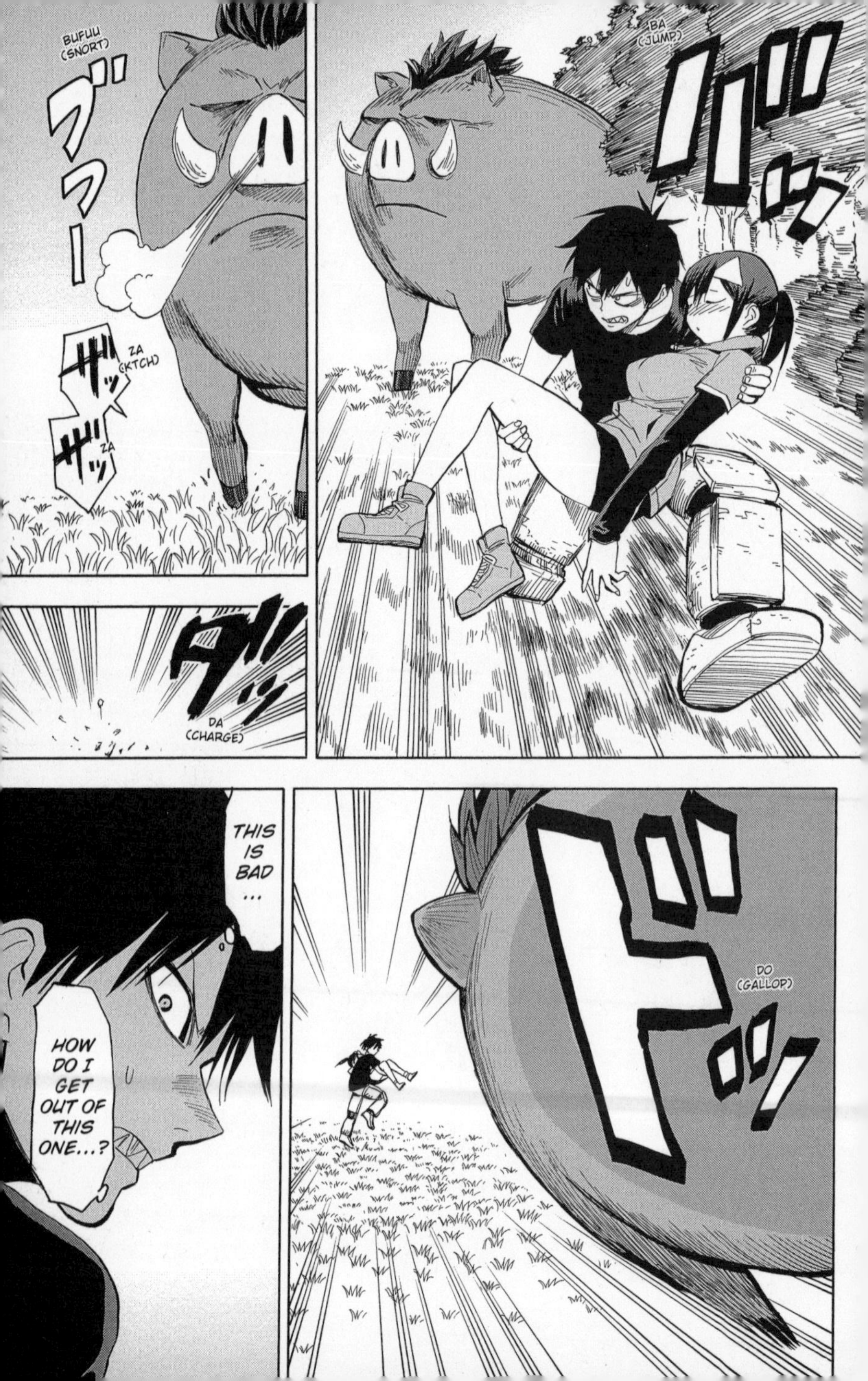
BA
(JUMP)
BUFUU
(SNORT)
ブフー
ZA
(KTCH)
ザッ
ZA
ザッ
DA
(CHARGE)
DO
(GALLOP)
THIS IS BAD...
HOW DO I GET OUT OF THIS ONE...?

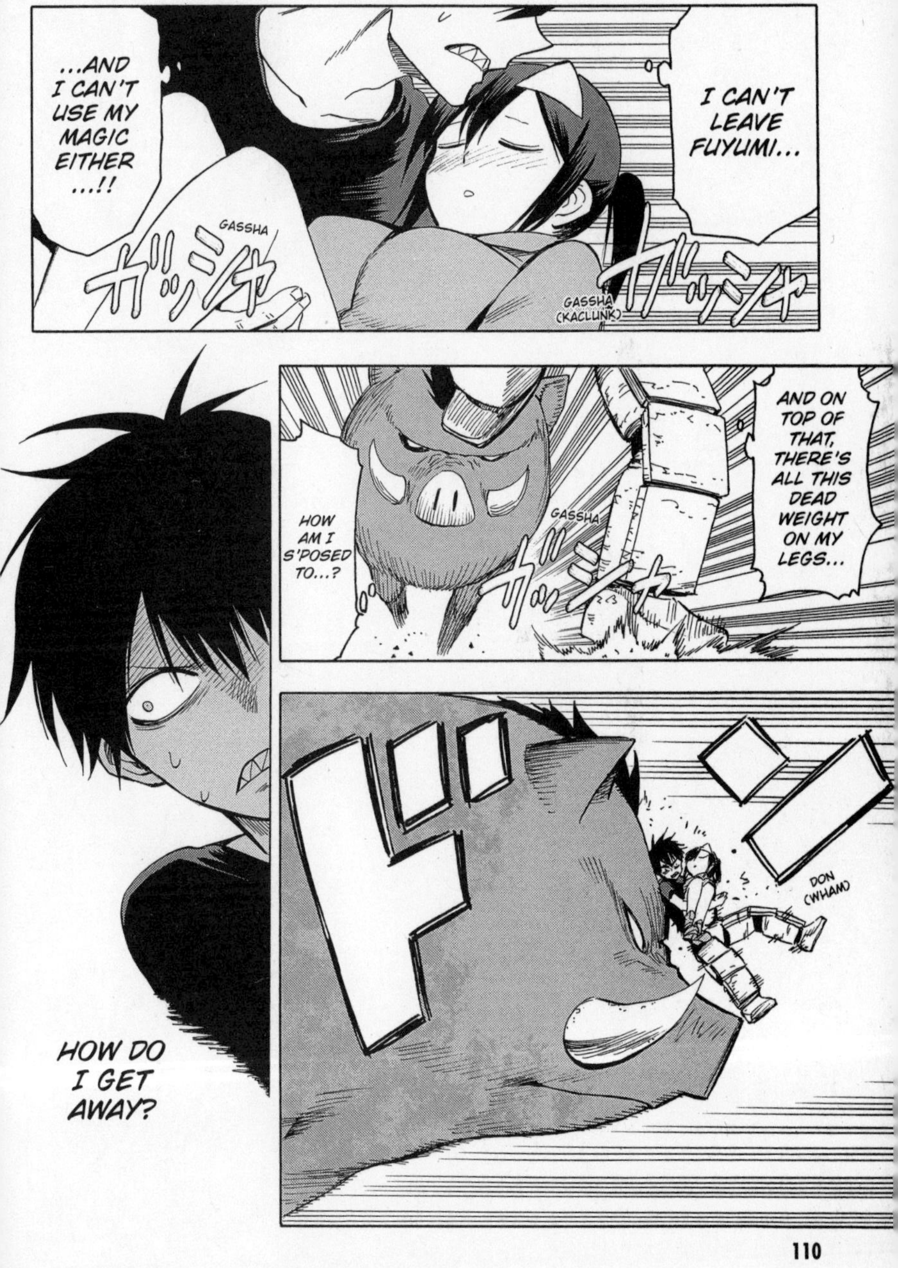
I CAN'T LEAVE FUYUMI...
GASSHA (KACLUNK)
...AND I CAN'T USE MY MAGIC EITHER ...!!
GASSHA
AND ON TOP OF THAT, THERE'S ALL THIS DEAD WEIGHT ON MY LEGS...
GASSHA
HOW AM I S'POSED TO...?
DON (WHAM)
HOW DO I GET AWAY?

GUA
(LIFT)

DOSA
(THUD)

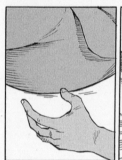

KUH!

ZUN
(STOMP)

DO
(THUMP)

FUYU-MI!!

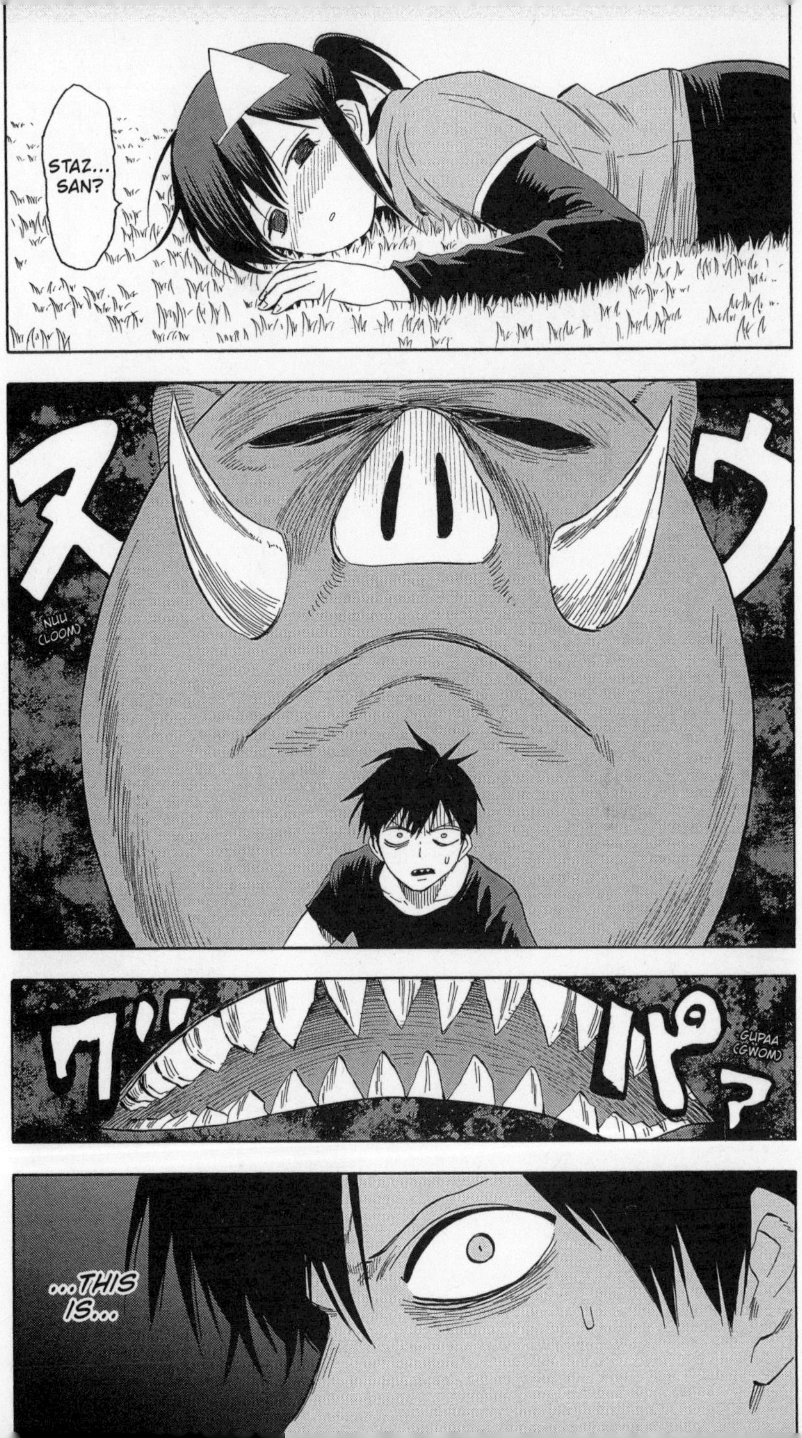
STAZ... SAN?
NUU (LOOM)
GUPAA (GWOM)
...THIS IS...

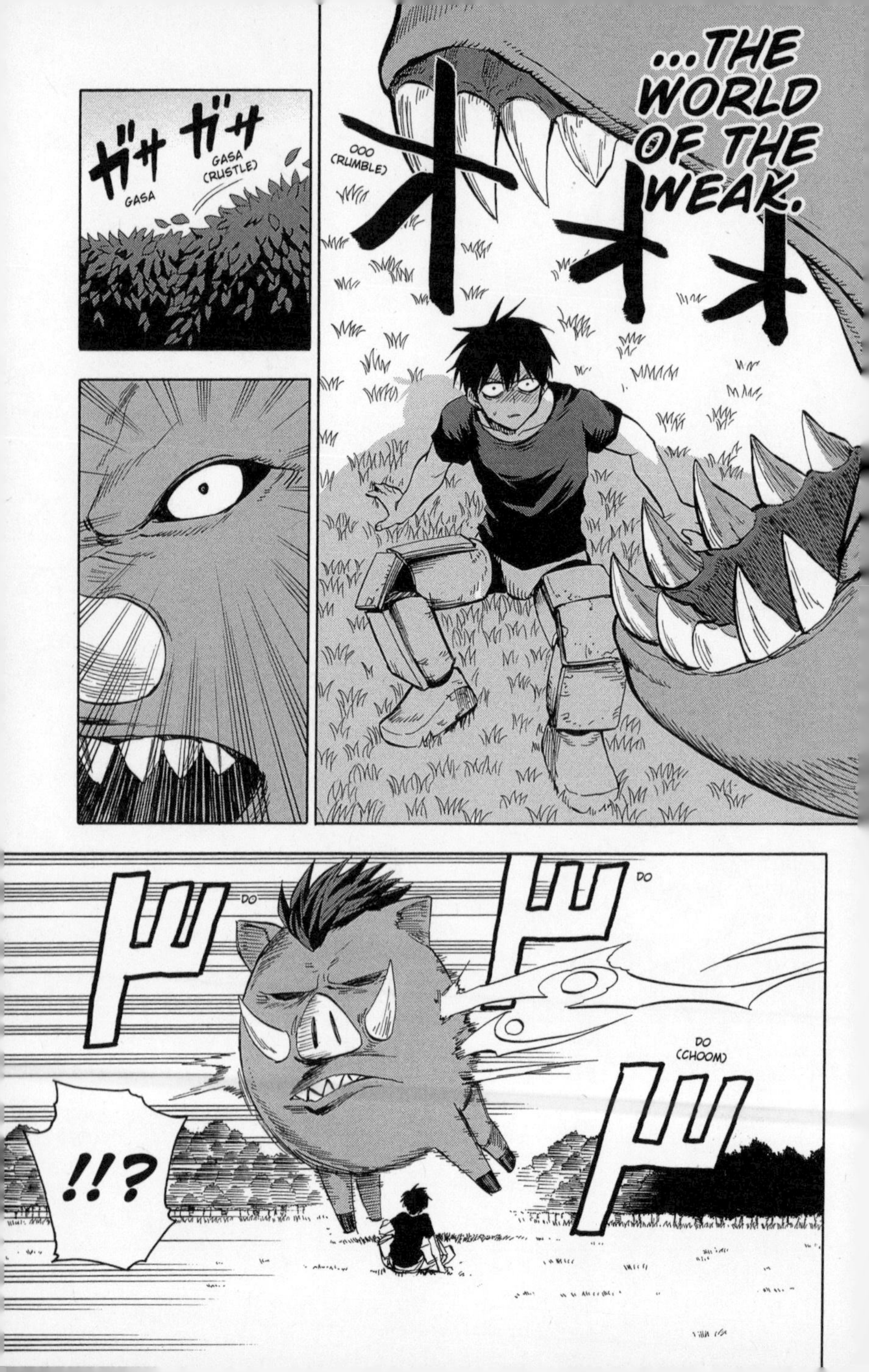
...THE WORLD OF THE WEAK.
OOO (RUMBLE)
GASA (RUSTLE)
GASA
DO
DO
DO (CHOOM)
!!?

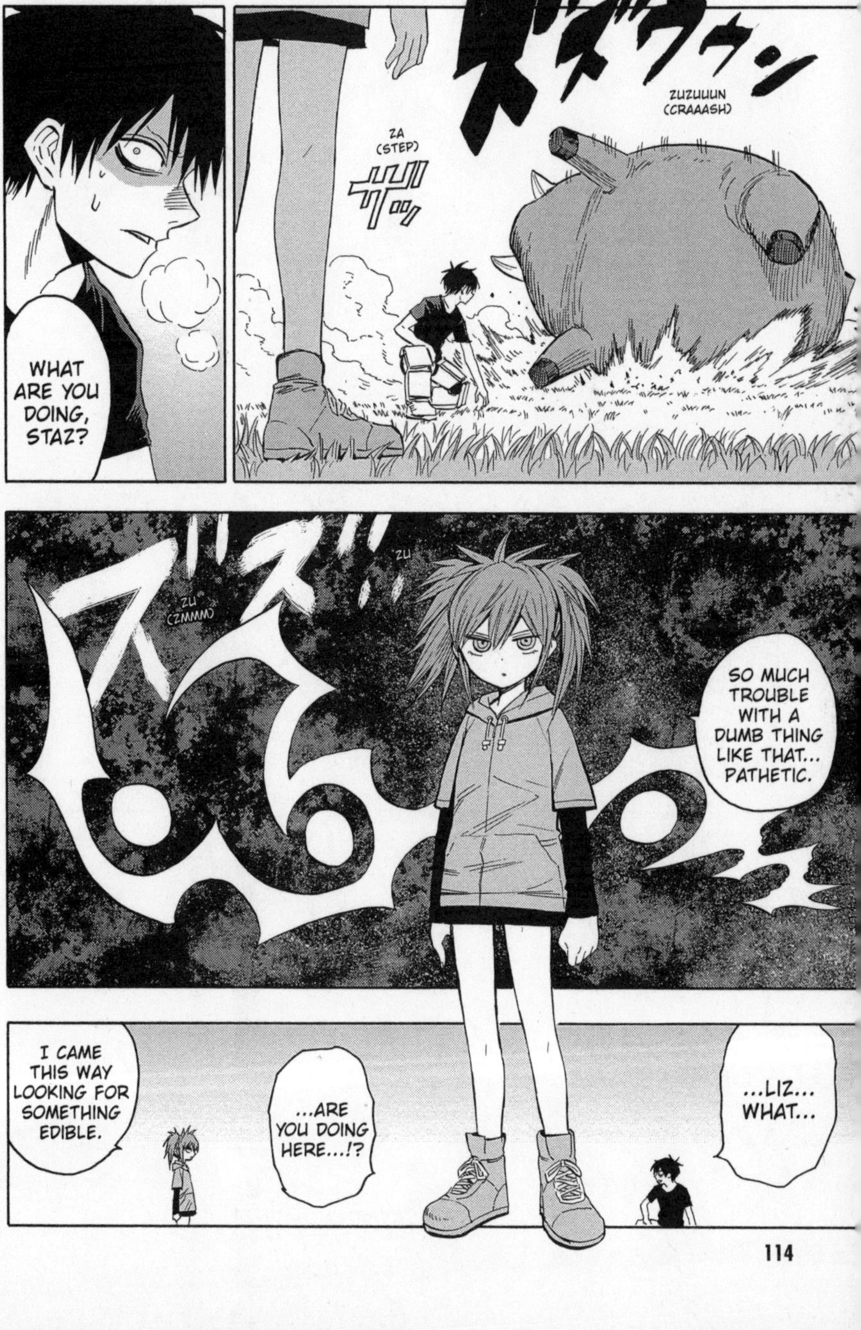
ZUZUUUN (CRAAASH)
ZA (STEP)
WHAT ARE YOU DOING, STAZ?
ZU
ZU (ZMMM)
SO MUCH TROUBLE WITH A DUMB THING LIKE THAT... PATHETIC.
...LIZ... WHAT...
...ARE YOU DOING HERE...!?
I CAME THIS WAY LOOKING FOR SOMETHING EDIBLE.

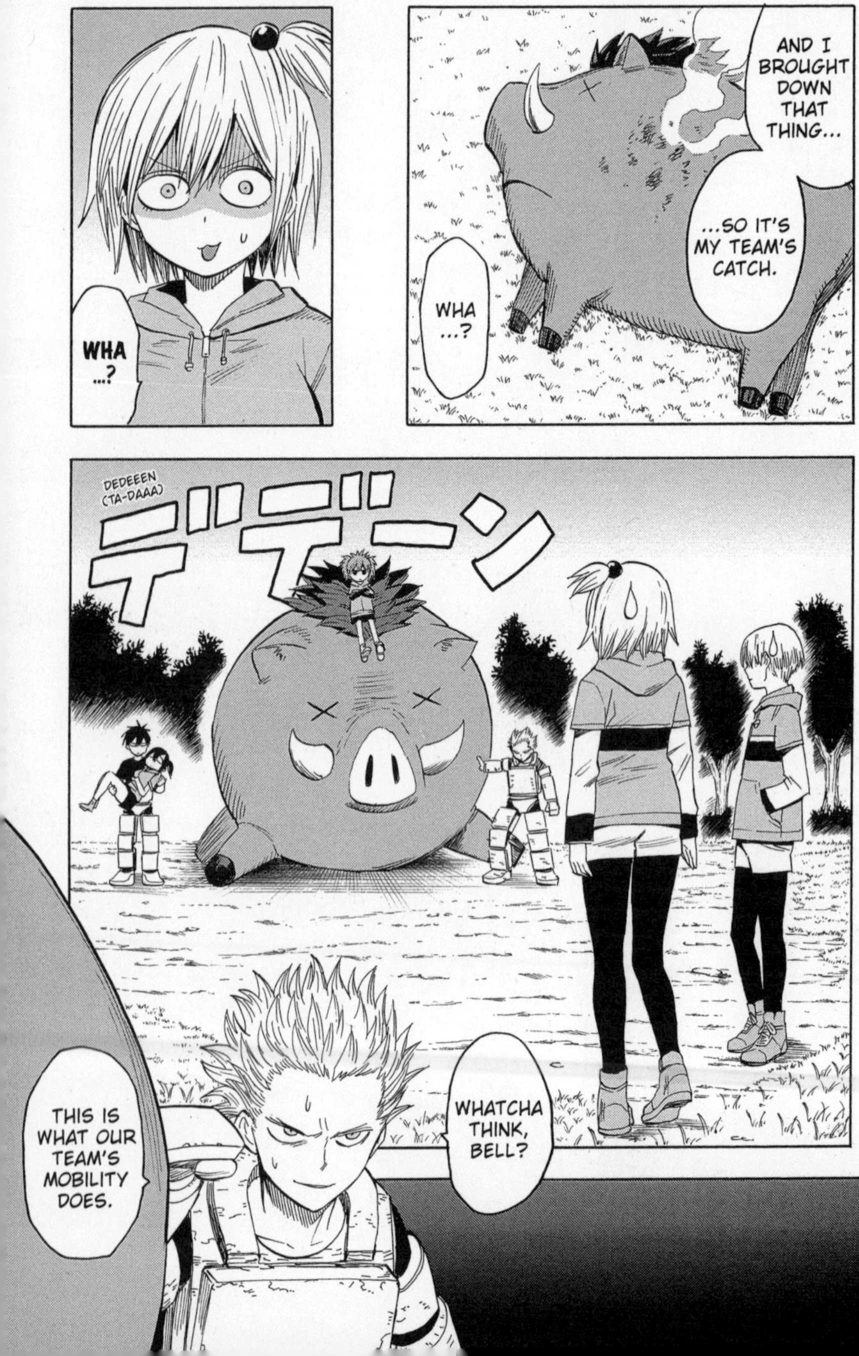
AND I BROUGHT DOWN THAT THING...
...SO IT'S MY TEAM'S CATCH.
WHA ...?
WHA ...?
DEDEEEN (TA-DAAA)
WHATCHA THINK, BELL?
THIS IS WHAT OUR TEAM'S MOBILITY DOES.

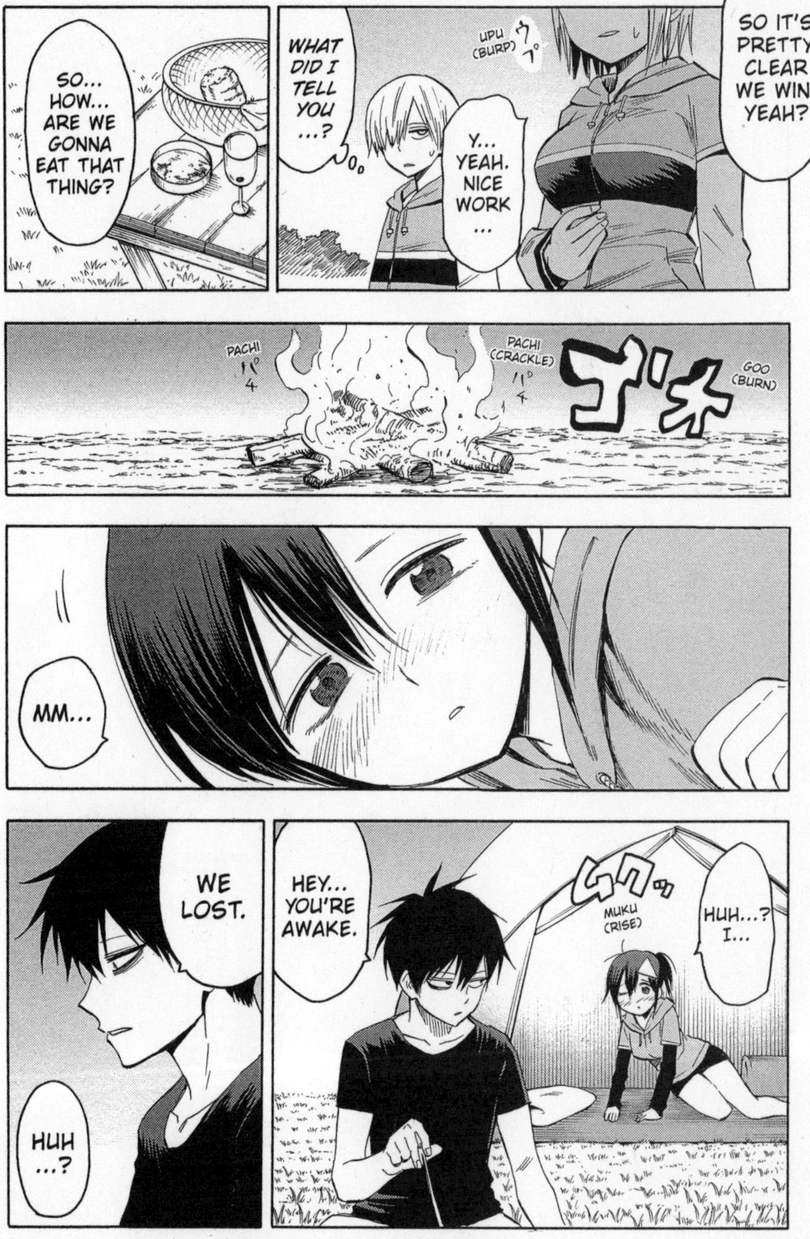
SO IT'S PRETTY CLEAR WE WIN, YEAH?
UPU (BURP) ウプ
Y... YEAH. NICE WORK ...
WHAT DID I TELL YOU ...?
SO... HOW... ARE WE GONNA EAT THAT THING?
GOO (BURN) ゴオ
PACHI (CRACKLE) パチ
PACHI パチ
MM...
HUH...? I...
MUKU (RISE) ムクッ
HEY... YOU'RE AWAKE.
WE LOST.
HUH ...?

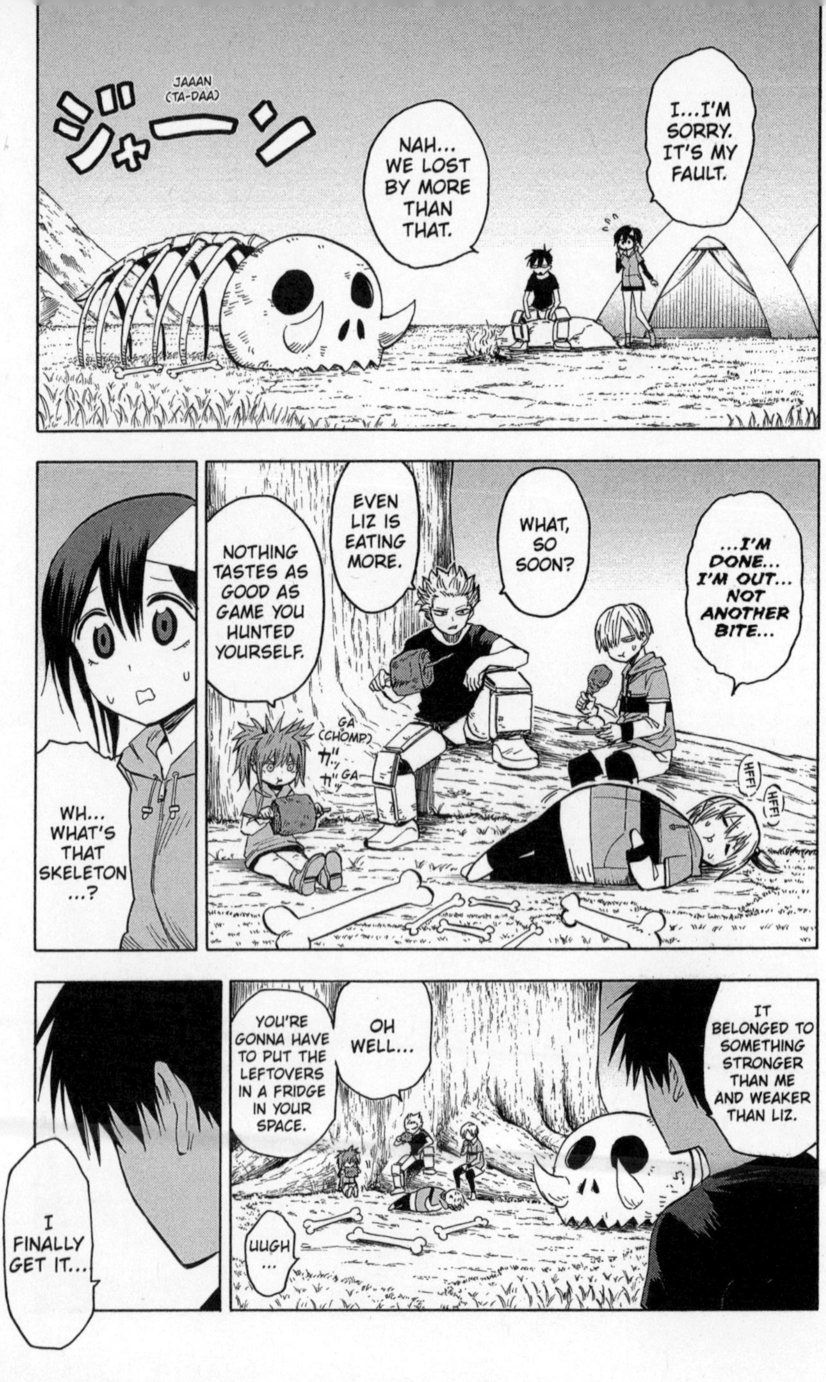
I...I'M SORRY. IT'S MY FAULT.
NAH... WE LOST BY MORE THAN THAT.
ジャーン
JAAAN (TA-DAA)
...I'M DONE... I'M OUT... NOT ANOTHER BITE...
WHAT, SO SOON?
EVEN LIZ IS EATING MORE.
NOTHING TASTES AS GOOD AS GAME YOU HUNTED YOURSELF.
HFF!
HFF!
ガッ ガッ
GA GA (CHOMP)
WH... WHAT'S THAT SKELETON ...?
IT BELONGED TO SOMETHING STRONGER THAN ME AND WEAKER THAN LIZ.
OH WELL...
YOU'RE GONNA HAVE TO PUT THE LEFTOVERS IN A FRIDGE IN YOUR SPACE.
UUGH ...
I FINALLY GET IT...

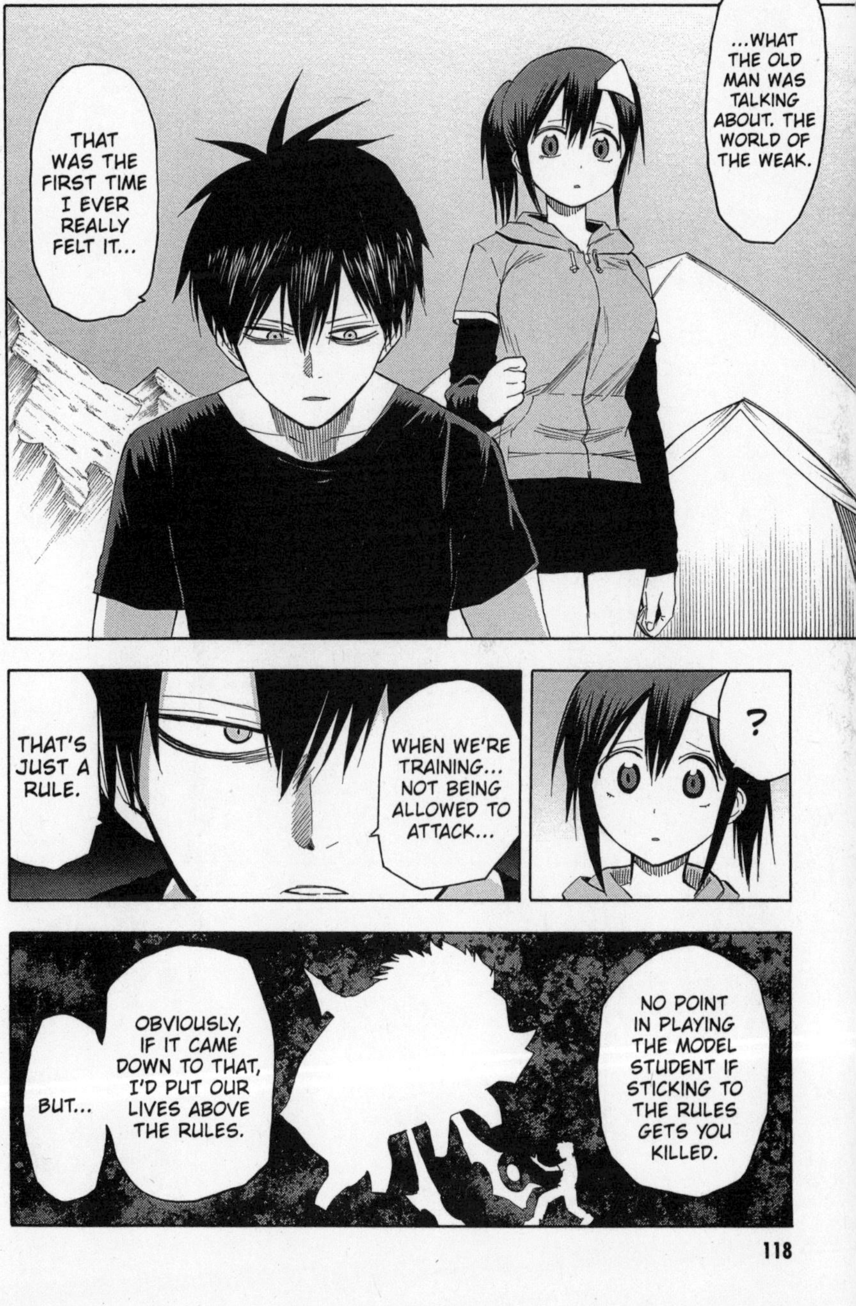
...WHAT THE OLD MAN WAS TALKING ABOUT. THE WORLD OF THE WEAK.
THAT WAS THE FIRST TIME I EVER REALLY FELT IT...
?
WHEN WE'RE TRAINING... NOT BEING ALLOWED TO ATTACK...
THAT'S JUST A RULE.
NO POINT IN PLAYING THE MODEL STUDENT IF STICKING TO THE RULES GETS YOU KILLED.
OBVIOUSLY, IF IT CAME DOWN TO THAT, I'D PUT OUR LIVES ABOVE THE RULES.
BUT...

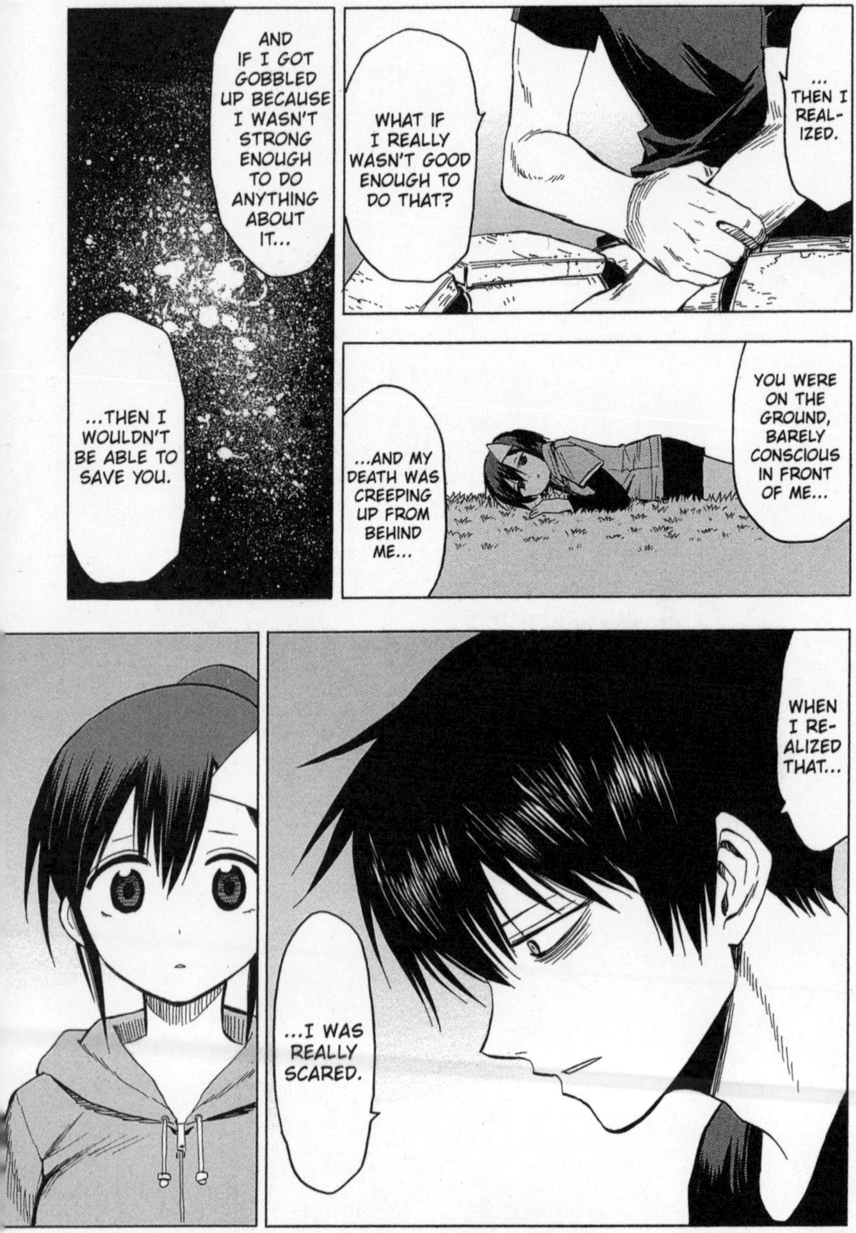
...THEN I REALIZED.
WHAT IF I REALLY WASN'T GOOD ENOUGH TO DO THAT?
YOU WERE ON THE GROUND, BARELY CONSCIOUS IN FRONT OF ME...
...AND MY DEATH WAS CREEPING UP FROM BEHIND ME...
AND IF I GOT GOBBLED UP BECAUSE I WASN'T STRONG ENOUGH TO DO ANYTHING ABOUT IT...
...THEN I WOULDN'T BE ABLE TO SAVE YOU.
WHEN I REALIZED THAT...
...I WAS REALLY SCARED.

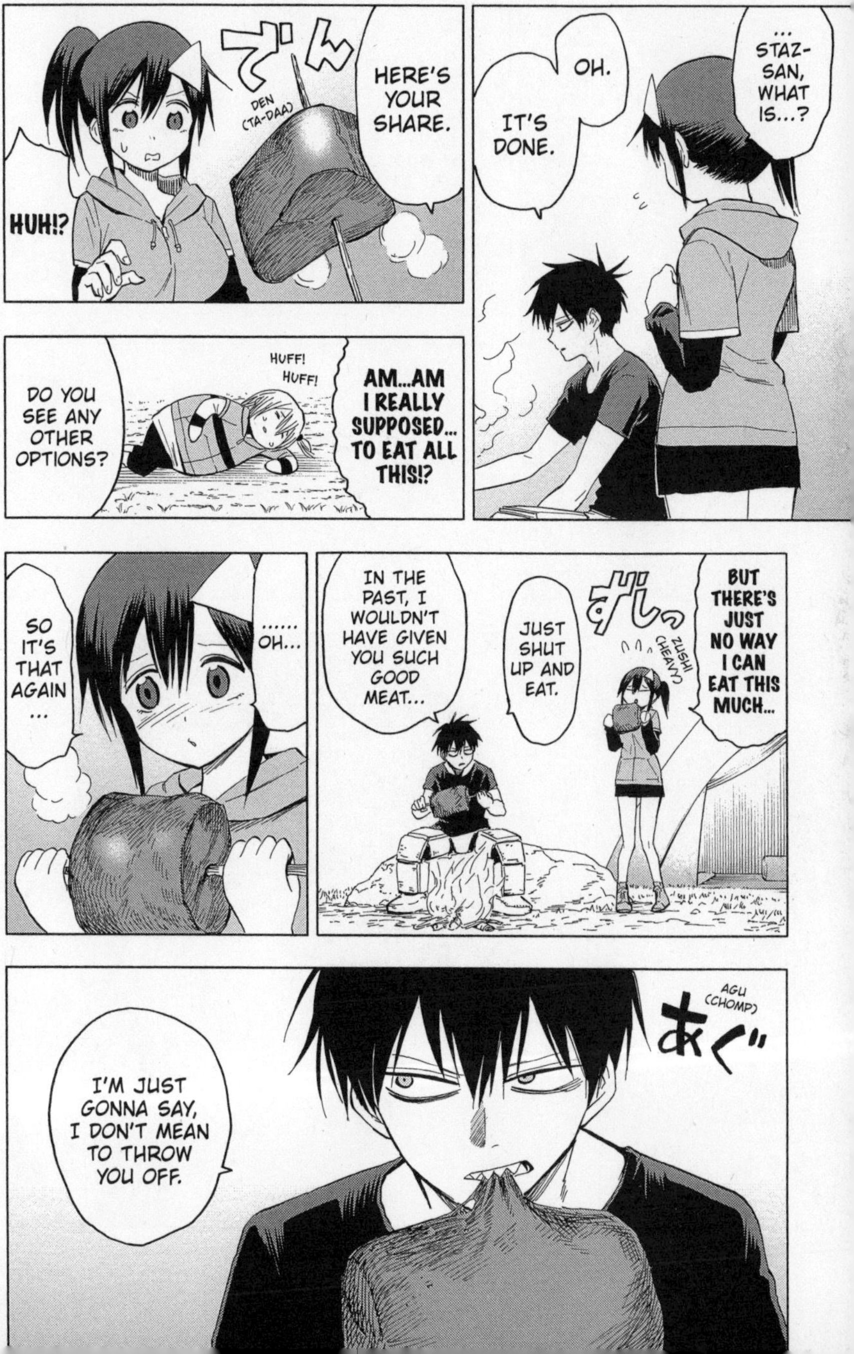
...STAZ-SAN, WHAT IS...?
OH.
IT'S DONE.
HERE'S YOUR SHARE.
でん
DEN (TA-DAA)
HUH!?
AM...AM I REALLY SUPPOSED... TO EAT ALL THIS!?
HUFF! HUFF!
DO YOU SEE ANY OTHER OPTIONS?
BUT THERE'S JUST NO WAY I CAN EAT THIS MUCH...
ずしっ
ZUSHI (HEAVY)
JUST SHUT UP AND EAT.
IN THE PAST, I WOULDN'T HAVE GIVEN YOU SUCH GOOD MEAT...
......OH...
SO IT'S THAT AGAIN...
あぐ
AGU (CHOMP)
I'M JUST GONNA SAY, I DON'T MEAN TO THROW YOU OFF.

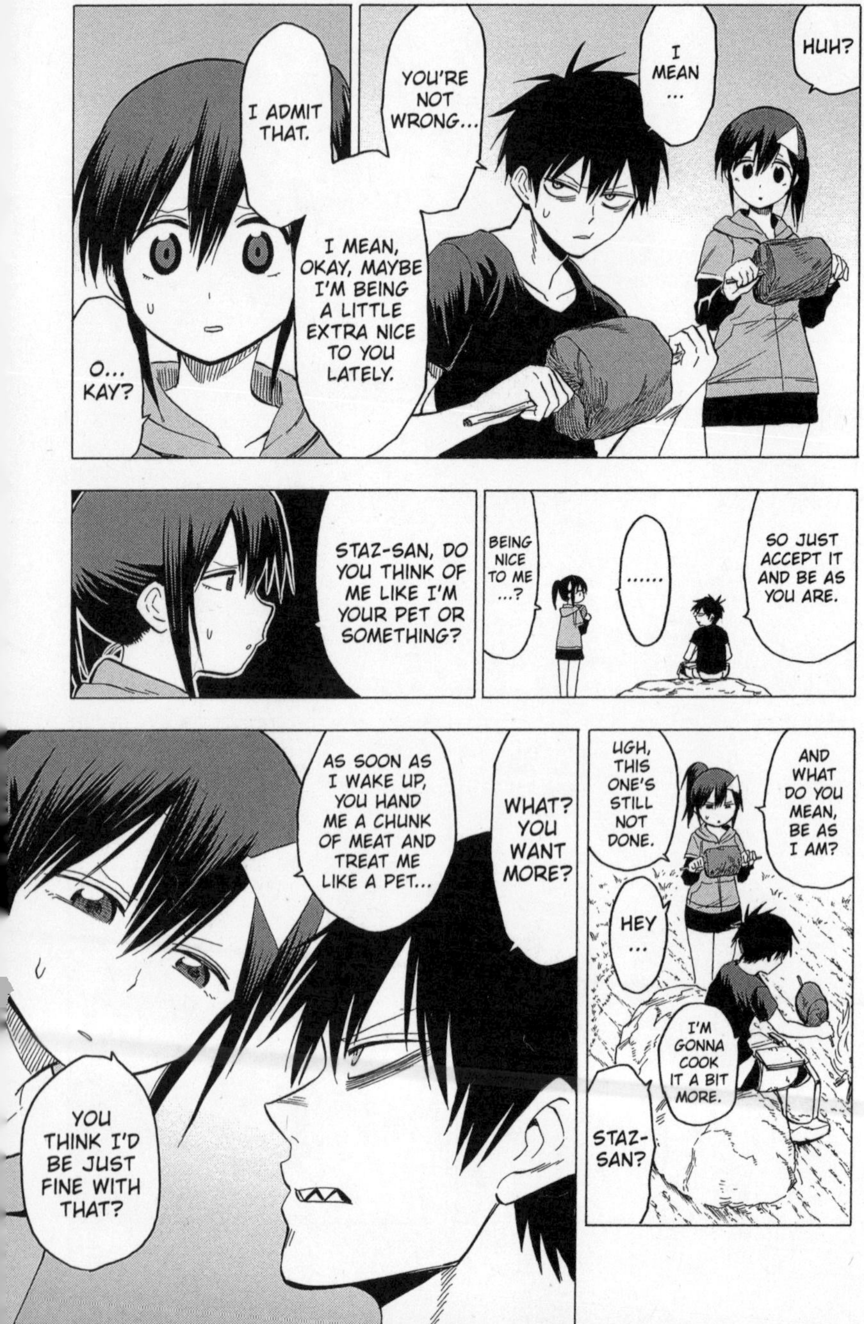
HUH?
I MEAN ...
YOU'RE NOT WRONG...
I ADMIT THAT.
I MEAN, OKAY, MAYBE I'M BEING A LITTLE EXTRA NICE TO YOU LATELY.
O... KAY?
SO JUST ACCEPT IT AND BE AS YOU ARE.
......
BEING NICE TO ME ...?
STAZ-SAN, DO YOU THINK OF ME LIKE I'M YOUR PET OR SOMETHING?
AND WHAT DO YOU MEAN, BE AS I AM?
UGH, THIS ONE'S STILL NOT DONE.
HEY ...
I'M GONNA COOK IT A BIT MORE.
STAZ-SAN?
WHAT? YOU WANT MORE?
AS SOON AS I WAKE UP, YOU HAND ME A CHUNK OF MEAT AND TREAT ME LIKE A PET...
YOU THINK I'D BE JUST FINE WITH THAT?

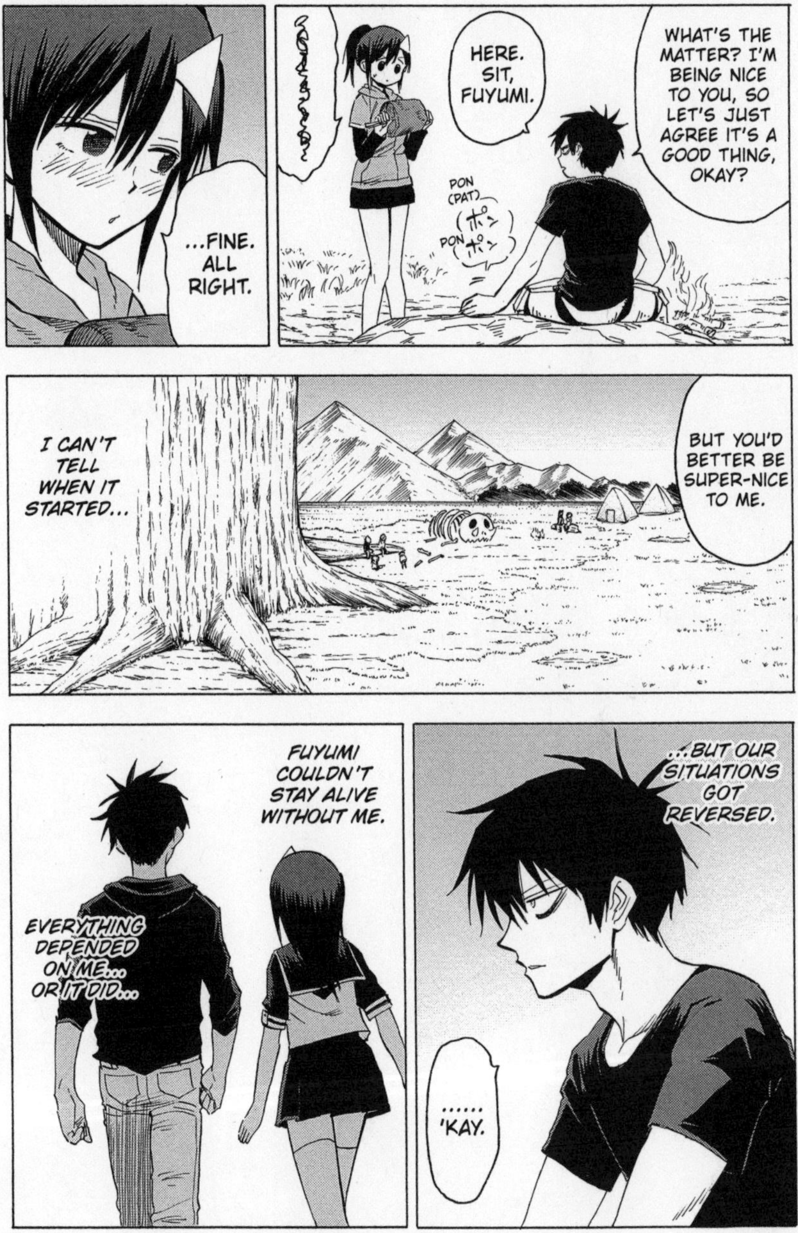
WHAT'S THE MATTER? I'M BEING NICE TO YOU, SO LET'S JUST AGREE IT'S A GOOD THING, OKAY?
HERE. SIT, FUYUMI.
PON (PAT)
PON
...FINE. ALL RIGHT.
BUT YOU'D BETTER BE SUPER-NICE TO ME.
I CAN'T TELL WHEN IT STARTED...
...BUT OUR SITUATIONS GOT REVERSED.
...... 'KAY.
FUYUMI COULDN'T STAY ALIVE WITHOUT ME.
EVERYTHING DEPENDED ON ME... OR IT DID...

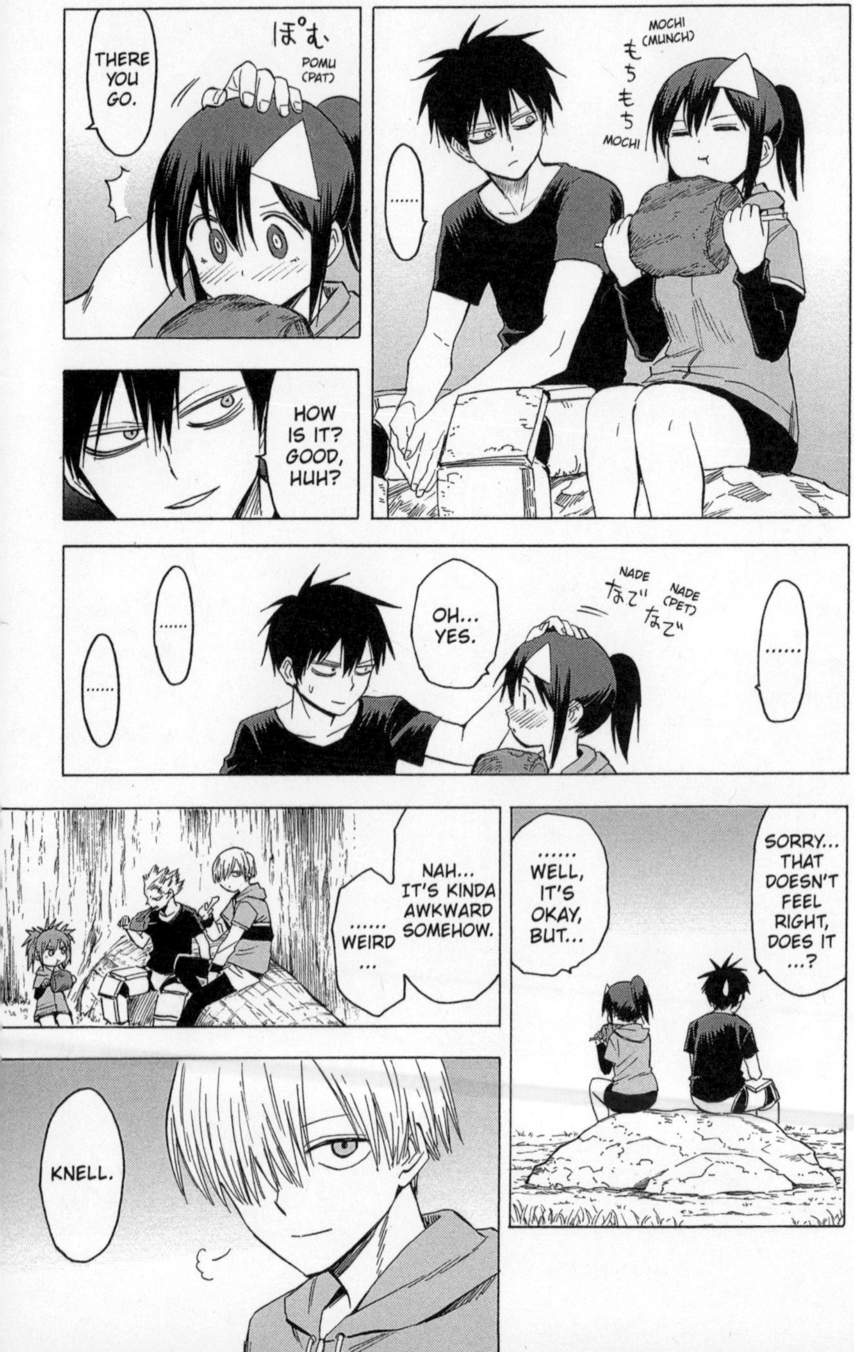
MOCHI (MUNCH)
もちもち
MOCHI
......
ぽむ
POMU (PAT)
THERE YOU GO.
HOW IS IT? GOOD, HUH?
......
NADE
なで
NADE (PET)
なで
OH... YES.
......
......
SORRY... THAT DOESN'T FEEL RIGHT, DOES IT ...?
...... WELL, IT'S OKAY, BUT...
NAH... IT'S KINDA AWKWARD SOMEHOW.
...... WEIRD ...
KNELL.

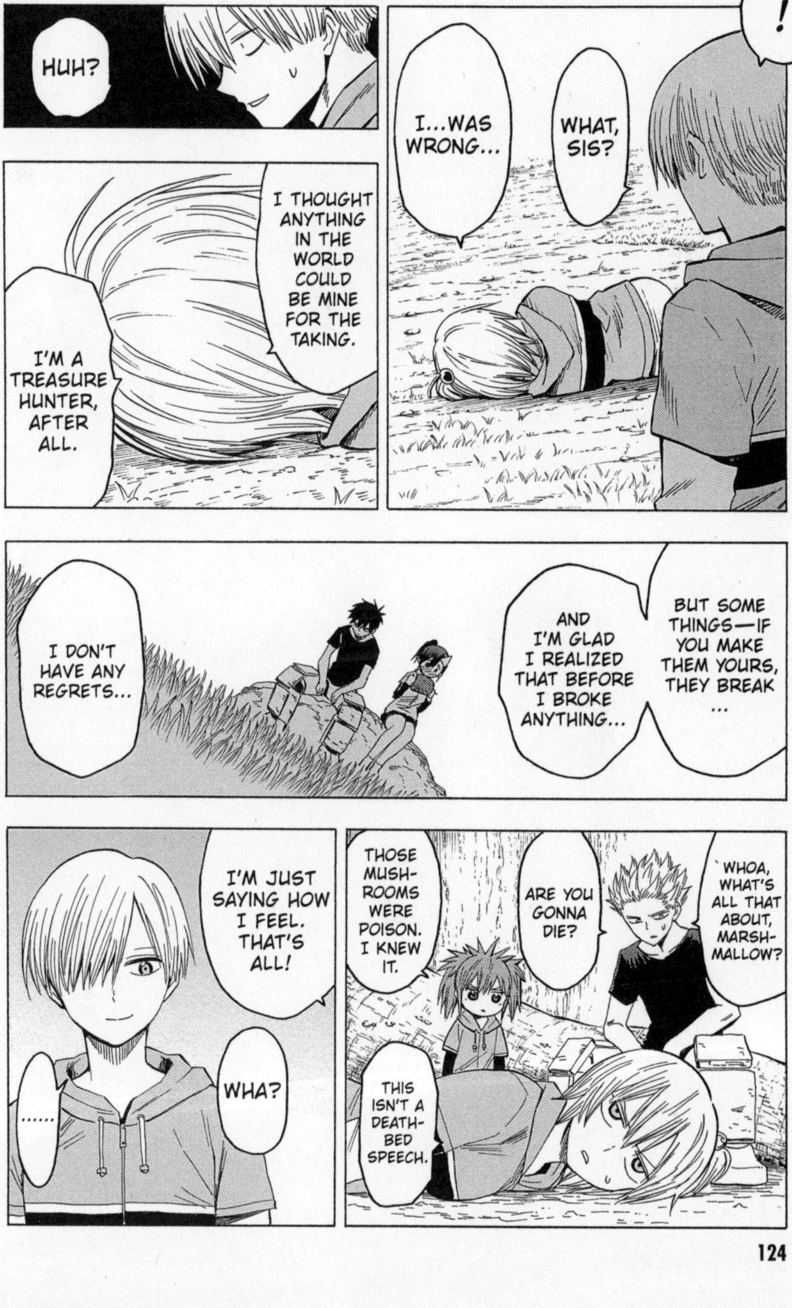
!
WHAT, SIS?
I...WAS WRONG...
HUH?
I THOUGHT ANYTHING IN THE WORLD COULD BE MINE FOR THE TAKING.
I'M A TREASURE HUNTER, AFTER ALL.
BUT SOME THINGS—IF YOU MAKE THEM YOURS, THEY BREAK ...
AND I'M GLAD I REALIZED THAT BEFORE I BROKE ANYTHING...
I DON'T HAVE ANY REGRETS...
WHOA, WHAT'S ALL THAT ABOUT, MARSHMALLOW?
ARE YOU GONNA DIE?
THOSE MUSHROOMS WERE POISON. I KNEW IT.
THIS ISN'T A DEATHBED SPEECH.
I'M JUST SAYING HOW I FEEL. THAT'S ALL!
WHA?
......

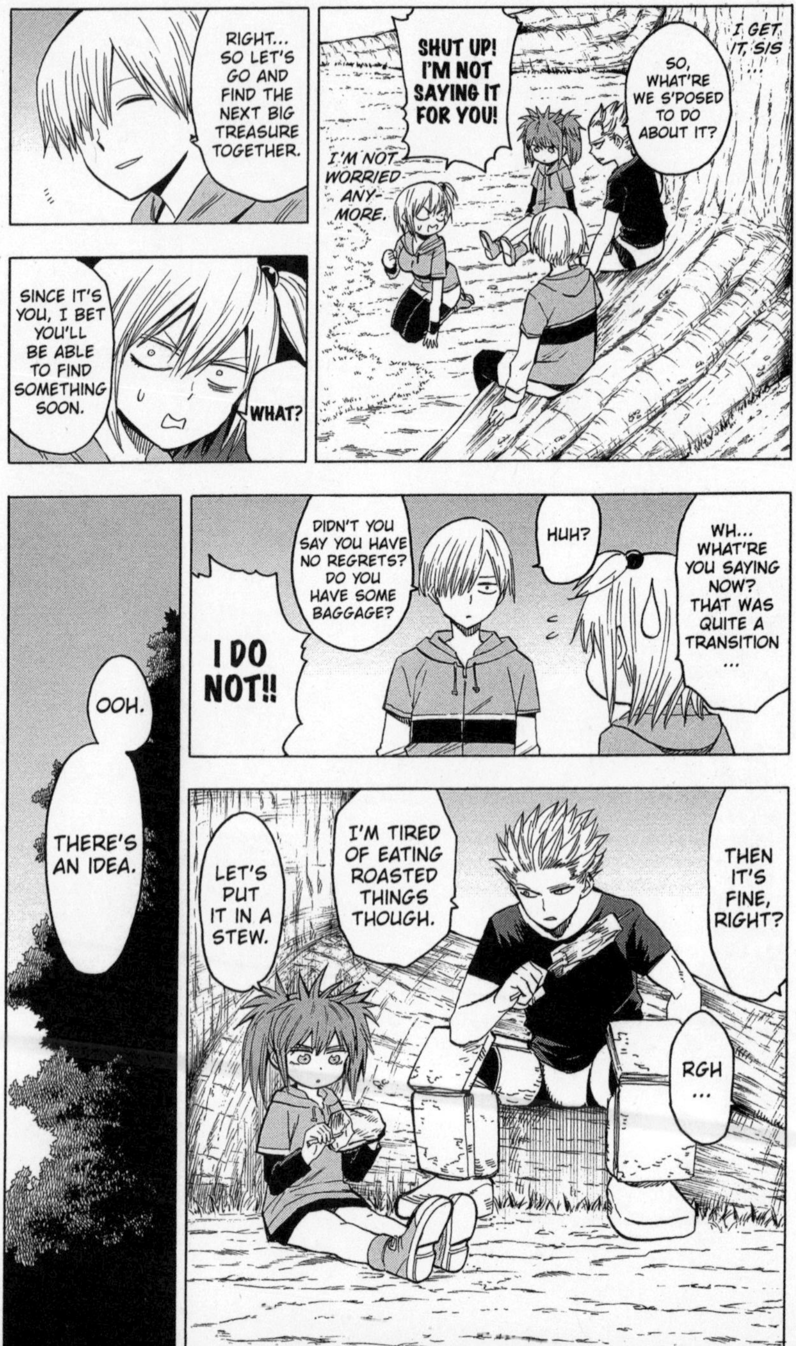
I GET IT, SIS...
SO, WHAT'RE WE S'POSED TO DO ABOUT IT?
SHUT UP! I'M NOT SAYING IT FOR YOU!
I'M NOT WORRIED ANY-MORE.
RIGHT... SO LET'S GO AND FIND THE NEXT BIG TREASURE TOGETHER.
SINCE IT'S YOU, I BET YOU'LL BE ABLE TO FIND SOMETHING SOON.
WHAT?
WH... WHAT'RE YOU SAYING NOW? THAT WAS QUITE A TRANSITION...
HUH?
DIDN'T YOU SAY YOU HAVE NO REGRETS? DO YOU HAVE SOME BAGGAGE?
I DO NOT!!
THEN IT'S FINE, RIGHT?
RGH...
I'M TIRED OF EATING ROASTED THINGS THOUGH.
LET'S PUT IT IN A STEW.
OOH.
THERE'S AN IDEA.

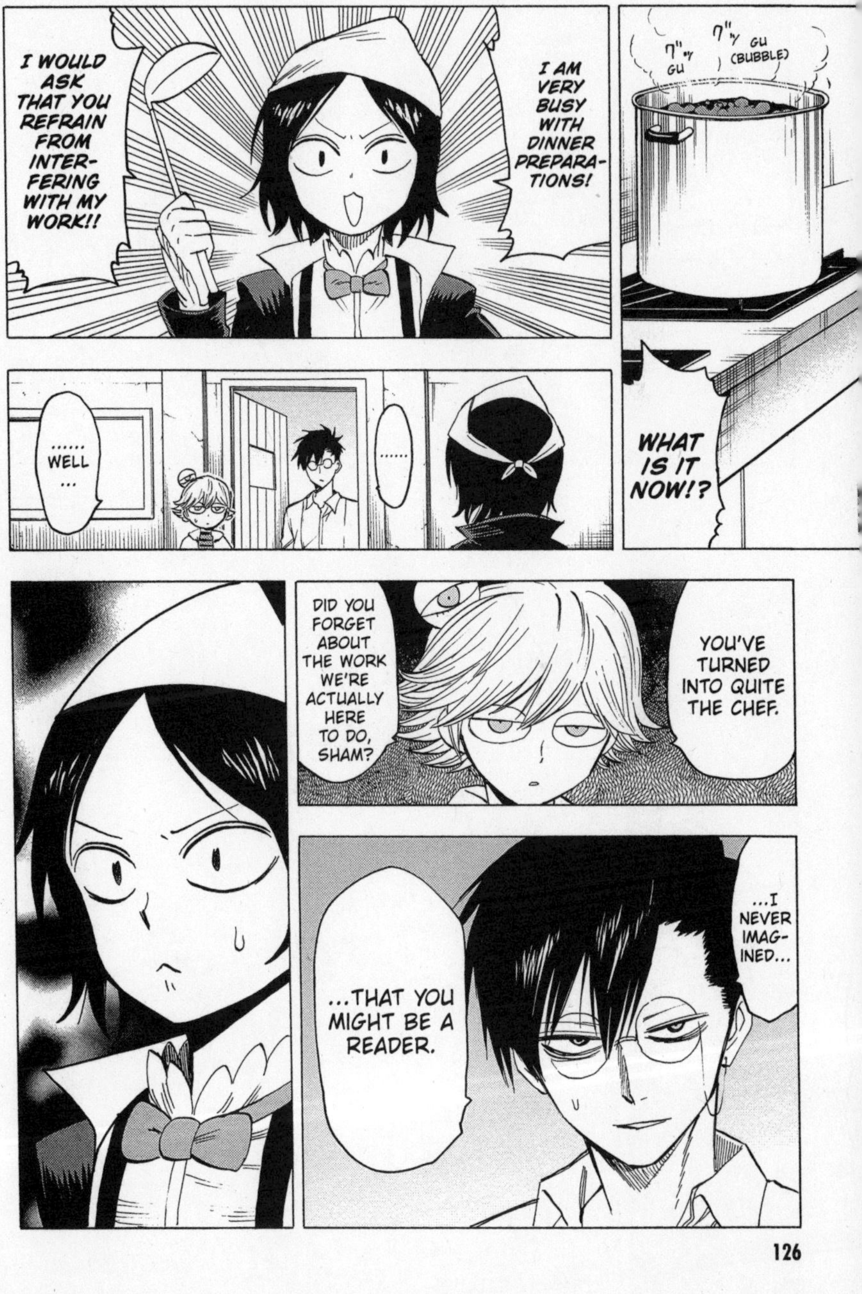
グッ GU (BUBBLE)
グッ GU
WHAT IS IT NOW!?
I AM VERY BUSY WITH DINNER PREPARA-TIONS!
I WOULD ASK THAT YOU REFRAIN FROM INTER-FERING WITH MY WORK!!
......
...... WELL ...
YOU'VE TURNED INTO QUITE THE CHEF.
DID YOU FORGET ABOUT THE WORK WE'RE ACTUALLY HERE TO DO, SHAM?
...I NEVER IMAG-INED...
...THAT YOU MIGHT BE A READER.

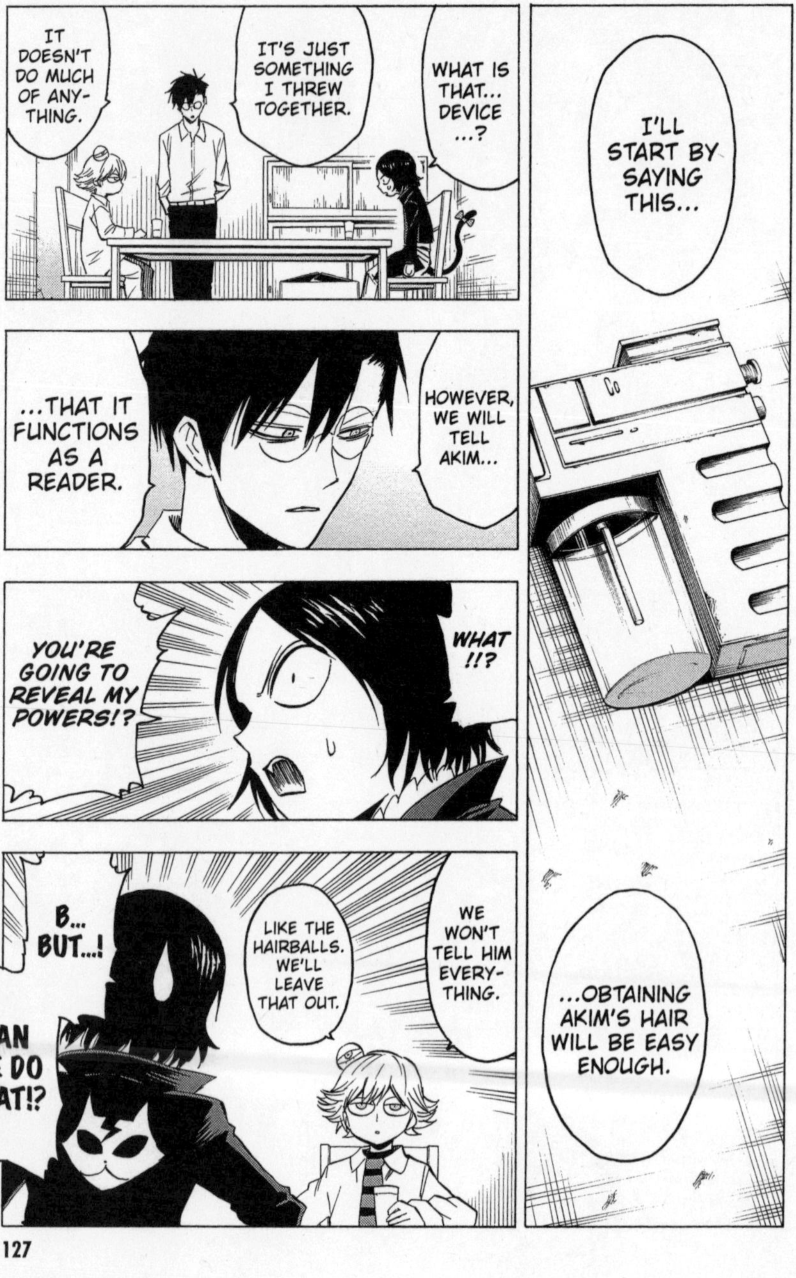
I'LL START BY SAYING THIS...
...OBTAINING AKIM'S HAIR WILL BE EASY ENOUGH.
WHAT IS THAT... DEVICE ...?
IT'S JUST SOMETHING I THREW TOGETHER.
IT DOESN'T DO MUCH OF ANY-THING.
HOWEVER, WE WILL TELL AKIM...
...THAT IT FUNCTIONS AS A READER.
WHAT !!?
YOU'RE GOING TO REVEAL MY POWERS!?
WE WON'T TELL HIM EVERY-THING.
LIKE THE HAIRBALLS. WE'LL LEAVE THAT OUT.
B... BUT...!
CAN WE DO THAT!?

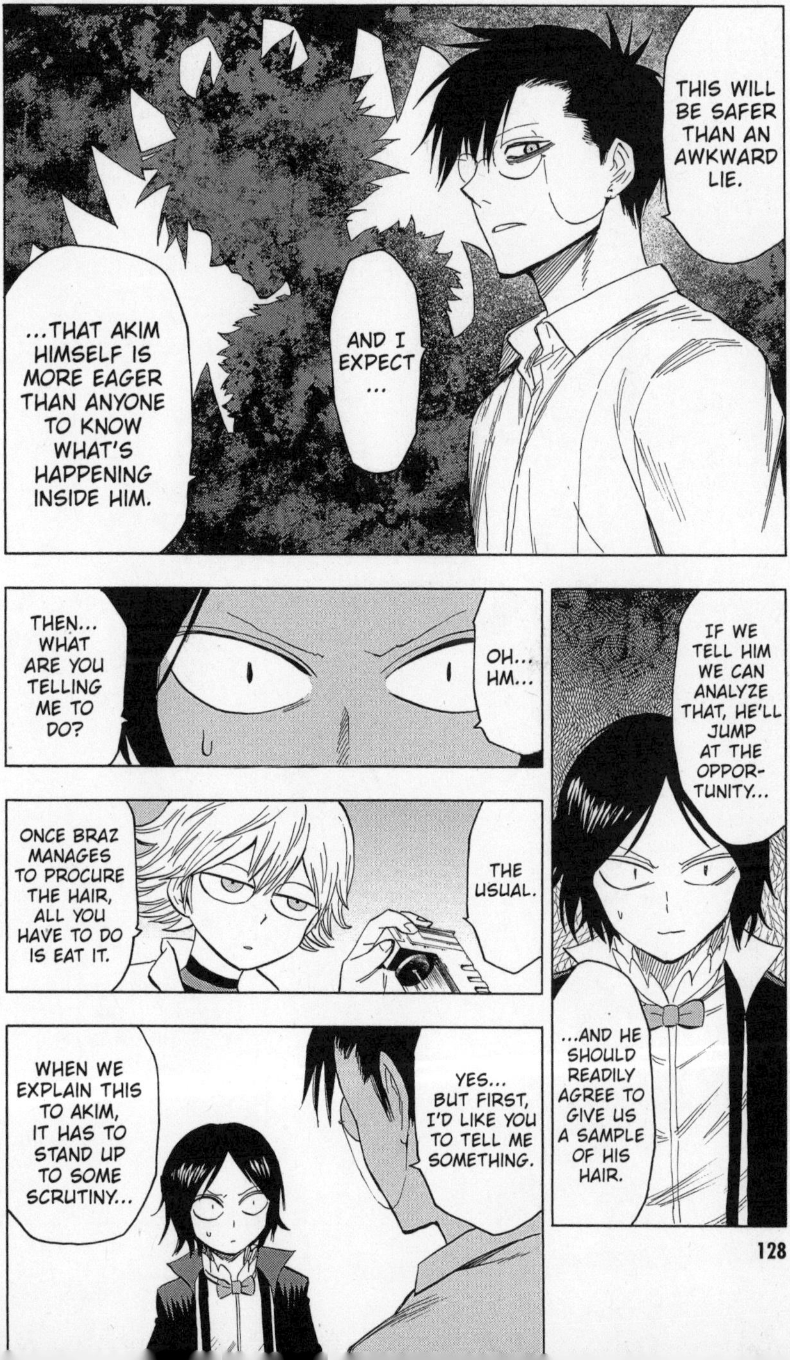
THIS WILL BE SAFER THAN AN AWKWARD LIE.
AND I EXPECT ...
...THAT AKIM HIMSELF IS MORE EAGER THAN ANYONE TO KNOW WHAT'S HAPPENING INSIDE HIM.
IF WE TELL HIM WE CAN ANALYZE THAT, HE'LL JUMP AT THE OPPOR-TUNITY...
...AND HE SHOULD READILY AGREE TO GIVE US A SAMPLE OF HIS HAIR.
OH... HM...
THEN... WHAT ARE YOU TELLING ME TO DO?
THE USUAL.
ONCE BRAZ MANAGES TO PROCURE THE HAIR, ALL YOU HAVE TO DO IS EAT IT.
YES... BUT FIRST, I'D LIKE YOU TO TELL ME SOMETHING.
WHEN WE EXPLAIN THIS TO AKIM, IT HAS TO STAND UP TO SOME SCRUTINY...

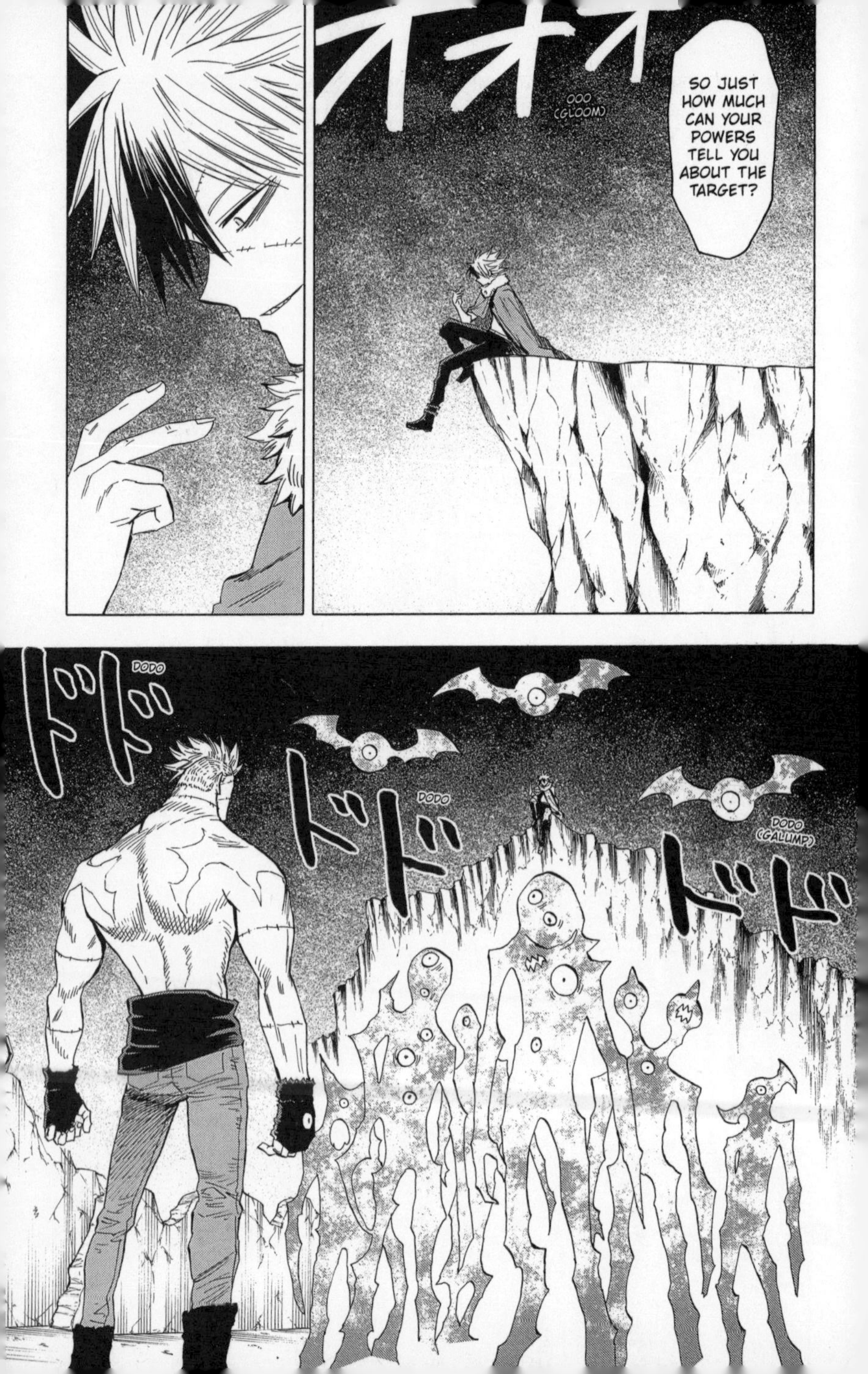
SO JUST HOW MUCH CAN YOUR POWERS TELL YOU ABOUT THE TARGET?
オオオ
OOO (GLOOM)
ドドド
DODO (GALUMP)
ドド
DODO
ドド
DODO

BYU
(LUNGE)

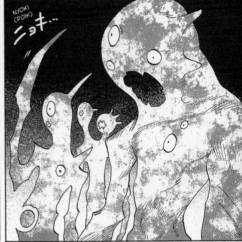

NYOKI
(POIK)

BO
(BOMF)

SU
(DODGE)

BAO
(VOOM)

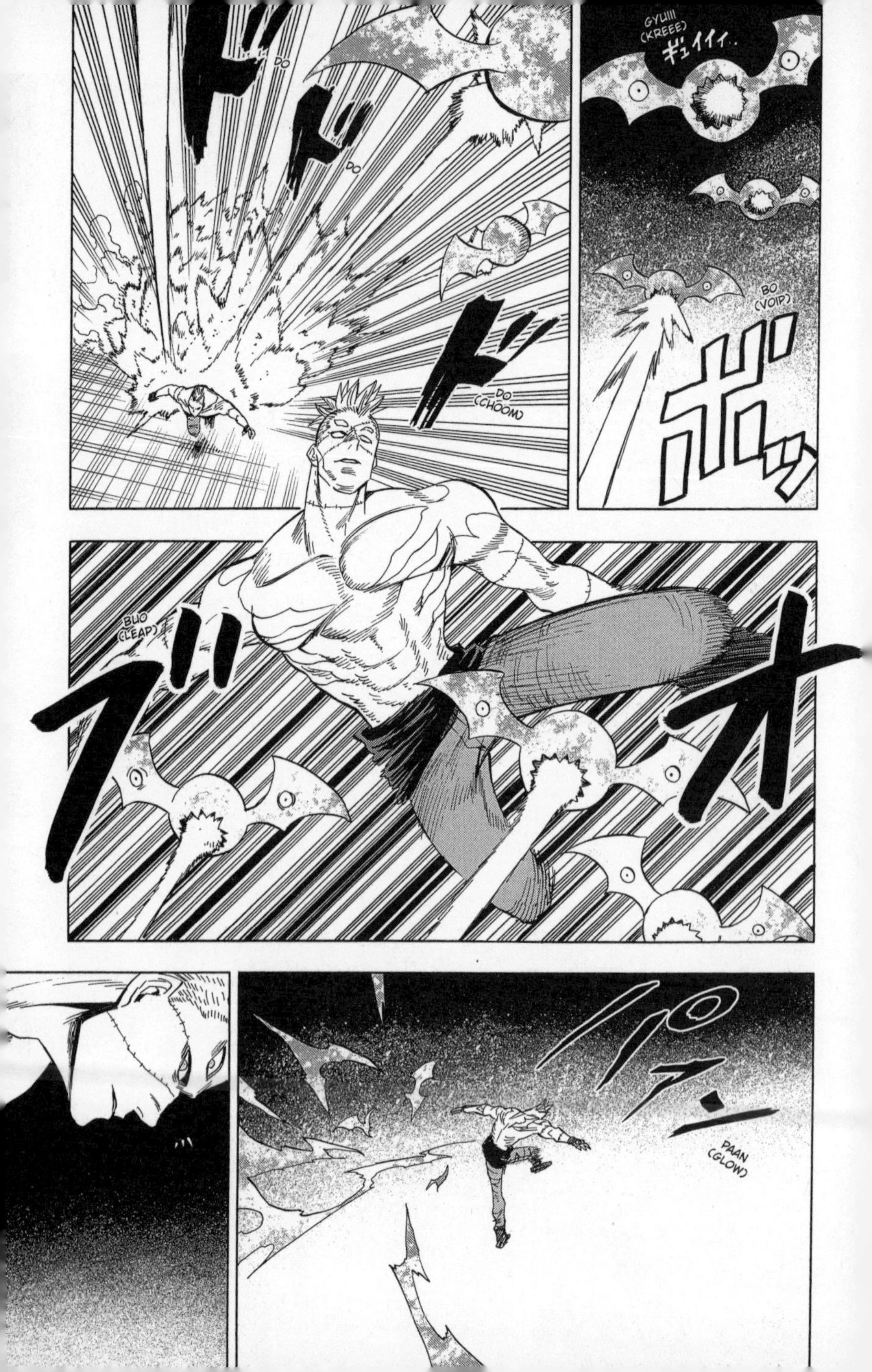
GYUIII (KREEE)
ギュイイイ..
BO (VOIP)
ボッ
DO
DO
DO (CHOOM)
BUO (LEAP)
PAAN (GLOW)

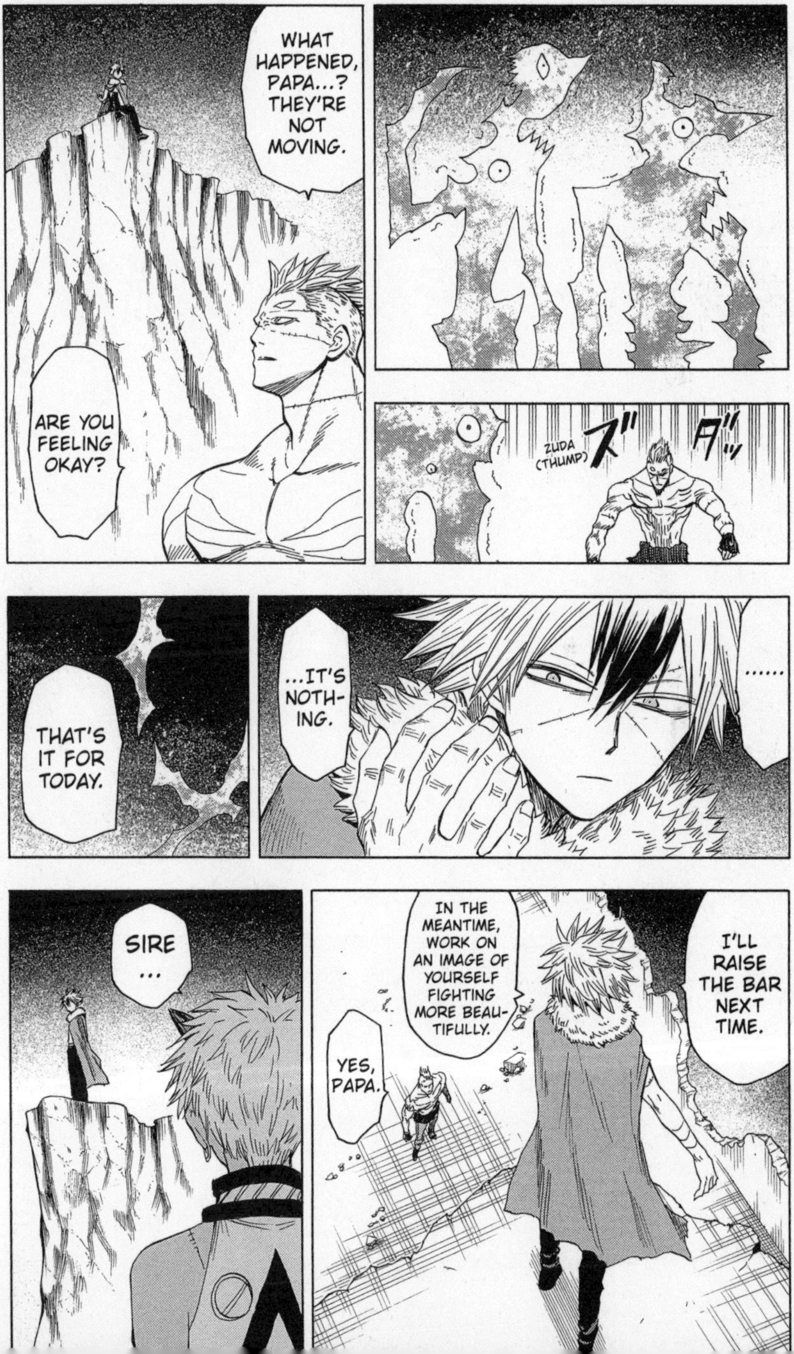
ズダッ
ZUDA (THUMP)
WHAT HAPPENED, PAPA...? THEY'RE NOT MOVING.
ARE YOU FEELING OKAY?
......
...IT'S NOTH-ING.
THAT'S IT FOR TODAY.
I'LL RAISE THE BAR NEXT TIME.
IN THE MEANTIME, WORK ON AN IMAGE OF YOURSELF FIGHTING MORE BEAU-TIFULLY.
YES, PAPA.
SIRE ...

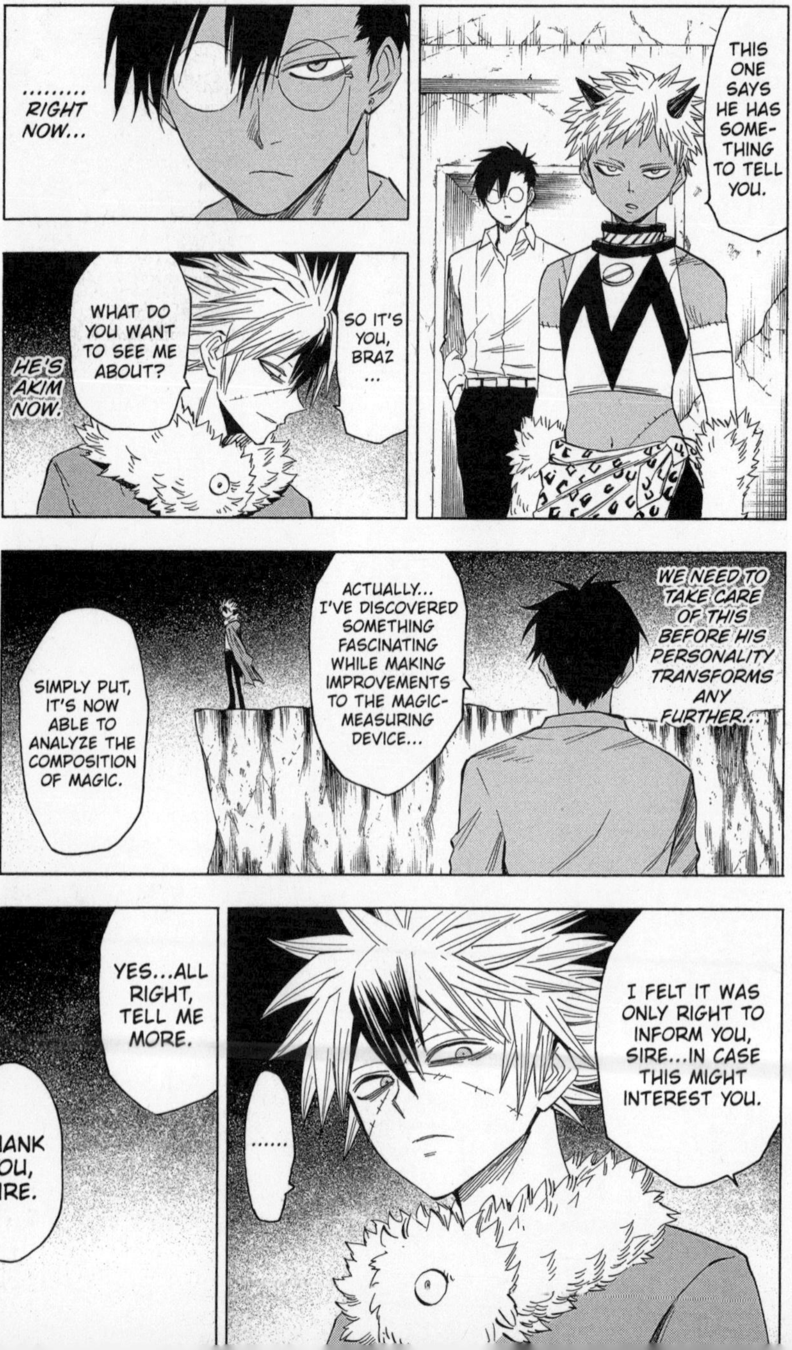
THIS ONE SAYS HE HAS SOMETHING TO TELL YOU.
.... RIGHT NOW...
SO IT'S YOU, BRAZ ...
WHAT DO YOU WANT TO SEE ME ABOUT?
HE'S AKIM NOW.
WE NEED TO TAKE CARE OF THIS BEFORE HIS PERSONALITY TRANSFORMS ANY FURTHER...
ACTUALLY... I'VE DISCOVERED SOMETHING FASCINATING WHILE MAKING IMPROVEMENTS TO THE MAGIC-MEASURING DEVICE...
SIMPLY PUT, IT'S NOW ABLE TO ANALYZE THE COMPOSITION OF MAGIC.
I FELT IT WAS ONLY RIGHT TO INFORM YOU, SIRE...IN CASE THIS MIGHT INTEREST YOU.
......
YES...ALL RIGHT, TELL ME MORE.
THANK YOU, SIRE.

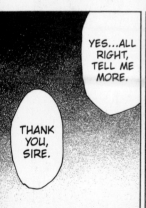

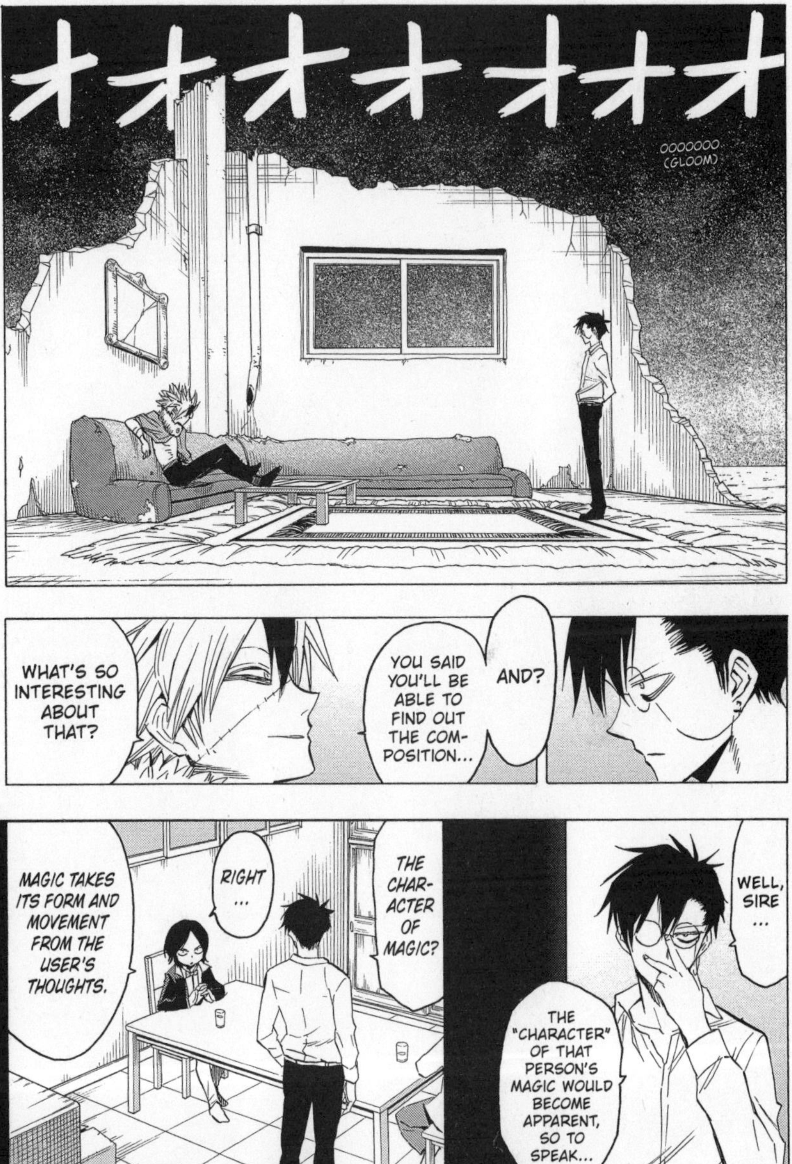
オオオオオオオ
OOOOOOO (GLOOM)
AND?
YOU SAID YOU'LL BE ABLE TO FIND OUT THE COMPOSITION...
WHAT'S SO INTERESTING ABOUT THAT?
WELL, SIRE ...
THE "CHARACTER" OF THAT PERSON'S MAGIC WOULD BECOME APPARENT, SO TO SPEAK...
THE CHARACTER OF MAGIC?
RIGHT ...
MAGIC TAKES ITS FORM AND MOVEMENT FROM THE USER'S THOUGHTS.

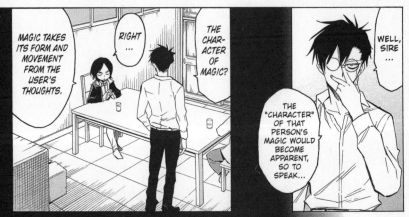

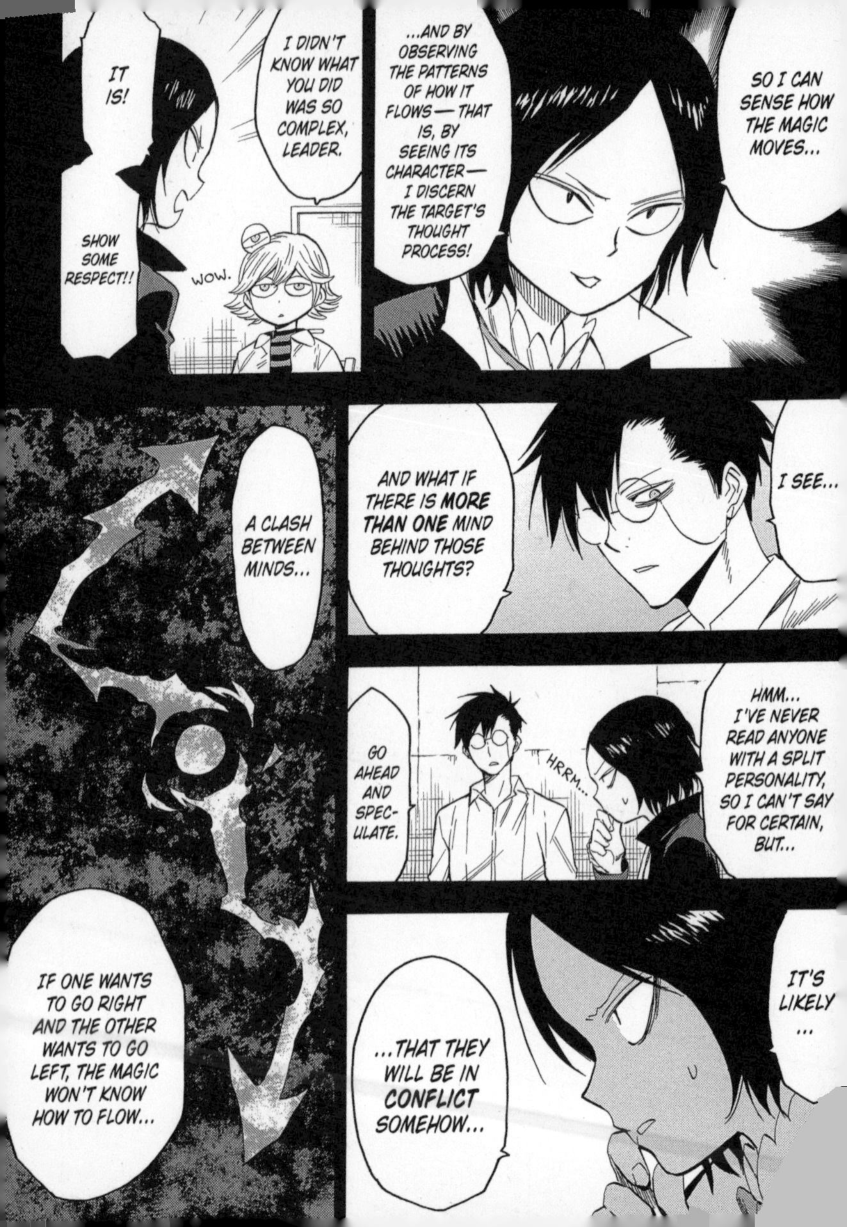
SO I CAN SENSE HOW THE MAGIC MOVES...
...AND BY OBSERVING THE PATTERNS OF HOW IT FLOWS—THAT IS, BY SEEING ITS CHARACTER—I DISCERN THE TARGET'S THOUGHT PROCESS!
I DIDN'T KNOW WHAT YOU DID WAS SO COMPLEX, LEADER.
IT IS!
SHOW SOME RESPECT!!
WOW.
I SEE...
AND WHAT IF THERE IS MORE THAN ONE MIND BEHIND THOSE THOUGHTS?
HMM... I'VE NEVER READ ANYONE WITH A SPLIT PERSONALITY, SO I CAN'T SAY FOR CERTAIN, BUT...
HRRM...
GO AHEAD AND SPEC-ULATE.
IT'S LIKELY ...
...THAT THEY WILL BE IN CONFLICT SOMEHOW...
A CLASH BETWEEN MINDS...
IF ONE WANTS TO GO RIGHT AND THE OTHER WANTS TO GO LEFT, THE MAGIC WON'T KNOW HOW TO FLOW...

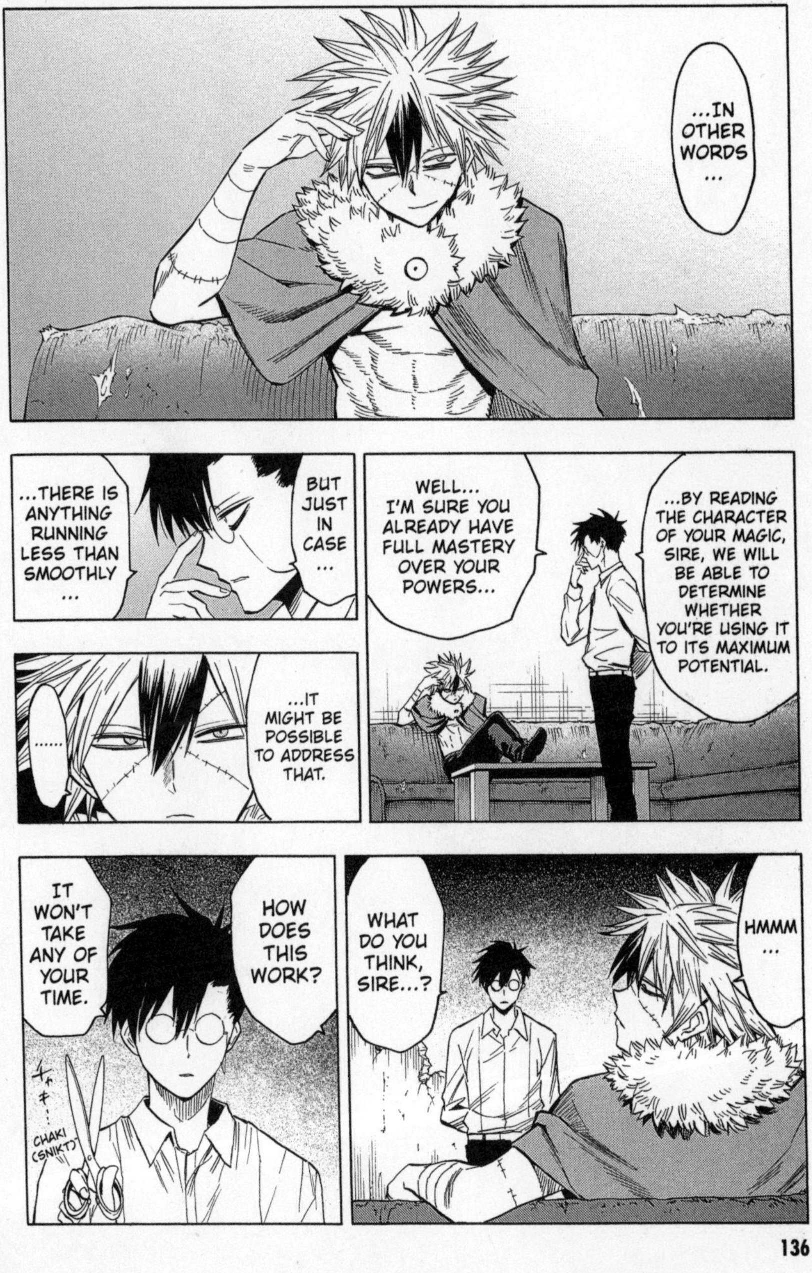
...IN OTHER WORDS ...
...BY READING THE CHARACTER OF YOUR MAGIC, SIRE, WE WILL BE ABLE TO DETERMINE WHETHER YOU'RE USING IT TO ITS MAXIMUM POTENTIAL.
WELL... I'M SURE YOU ALREADY HAVE FULL MASTERY OVER YOUR POWERS...
BUT JUST IN CASE ...
...THERE IS ANYTHING RUNNING LESS THAN SMOOTHLY ...
...IT MIGHT BE POSSIBLE TO ADDRESS THAT.
......
HMMM ...
WHAT DO YOU THINK, SIRE...?
HOW DOES THIS WORK?
IT WON'T TAKE ANY OF YOUR TIME.
CHAKI (SNIKT)

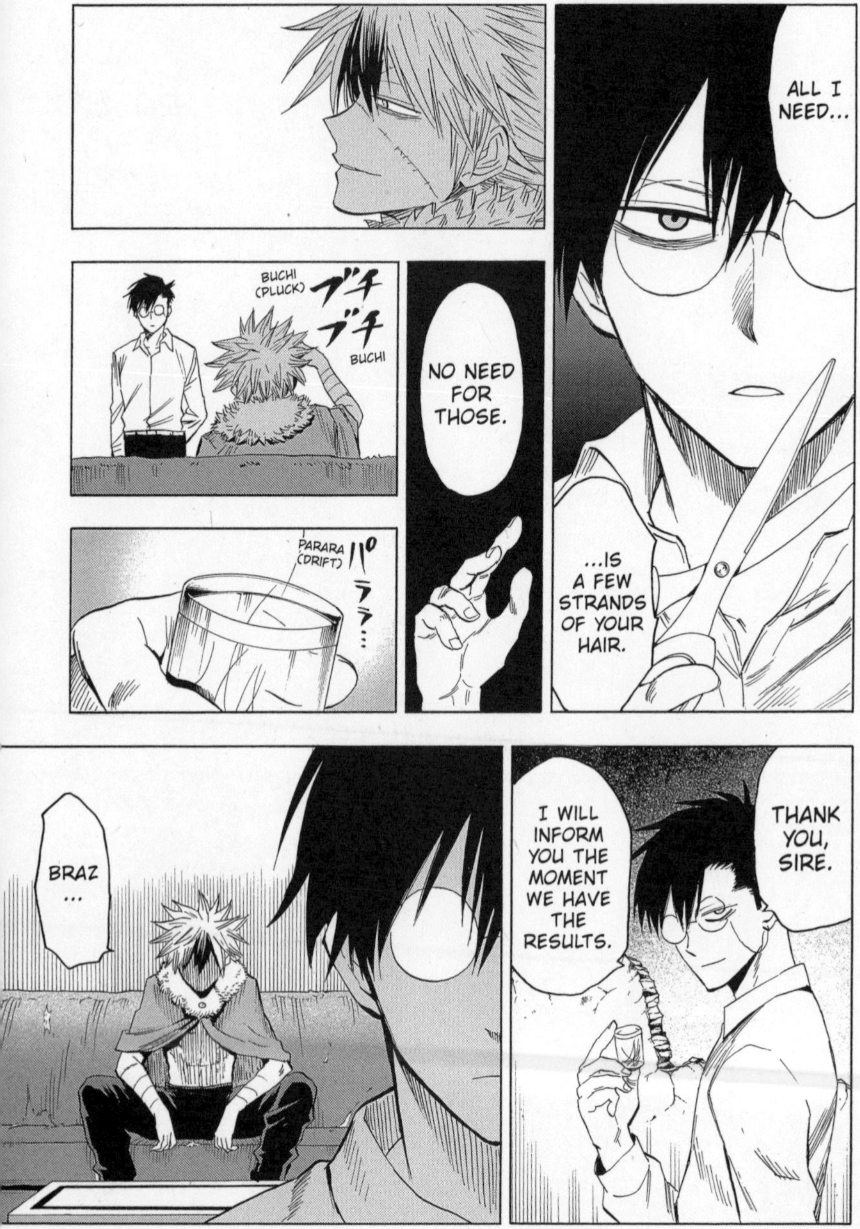
ALL I NEED...
...IS A FEW STRANDS OF YOUR HAIR.
NO NEED FOR THOSE.
ブチ
BUCHI (PLUCK)
ブチ
BUCHI
パラ ラ…
PARARA (DRIFT)
THANK YOU, SIRE.
I WILL INFORM YOU THE MOMENT WE HAVE THE RESULTS.
BRAZ ...

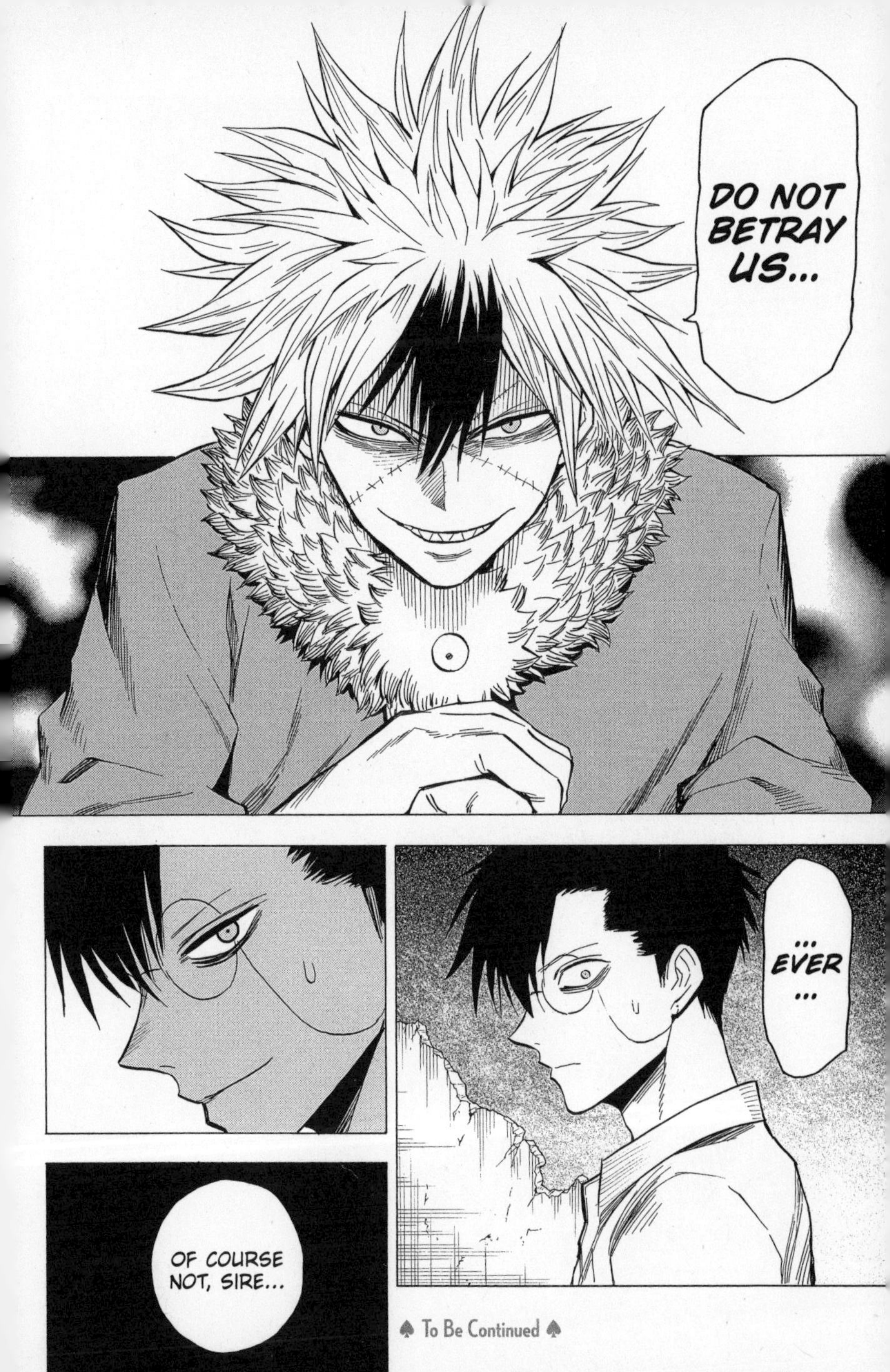
DO NOT BETRAY US...
... EVER ...
OF COURSE NOT, SIRE...
♠ To Be Continued ♠

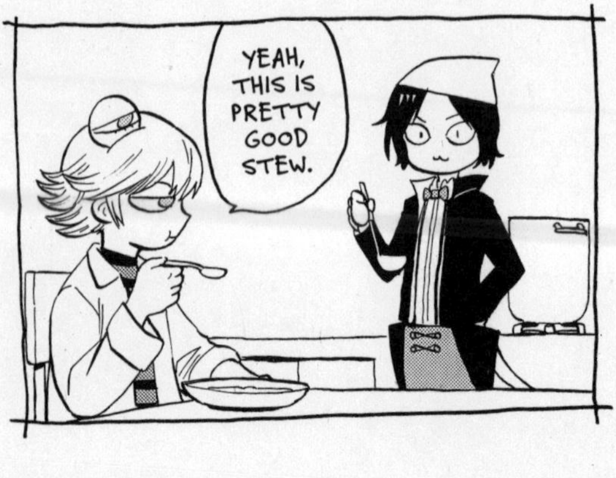
YEAH, THIS IS PRETTY GOOD STEW.

BLOOD LAD

SCREEN: DEMONTV

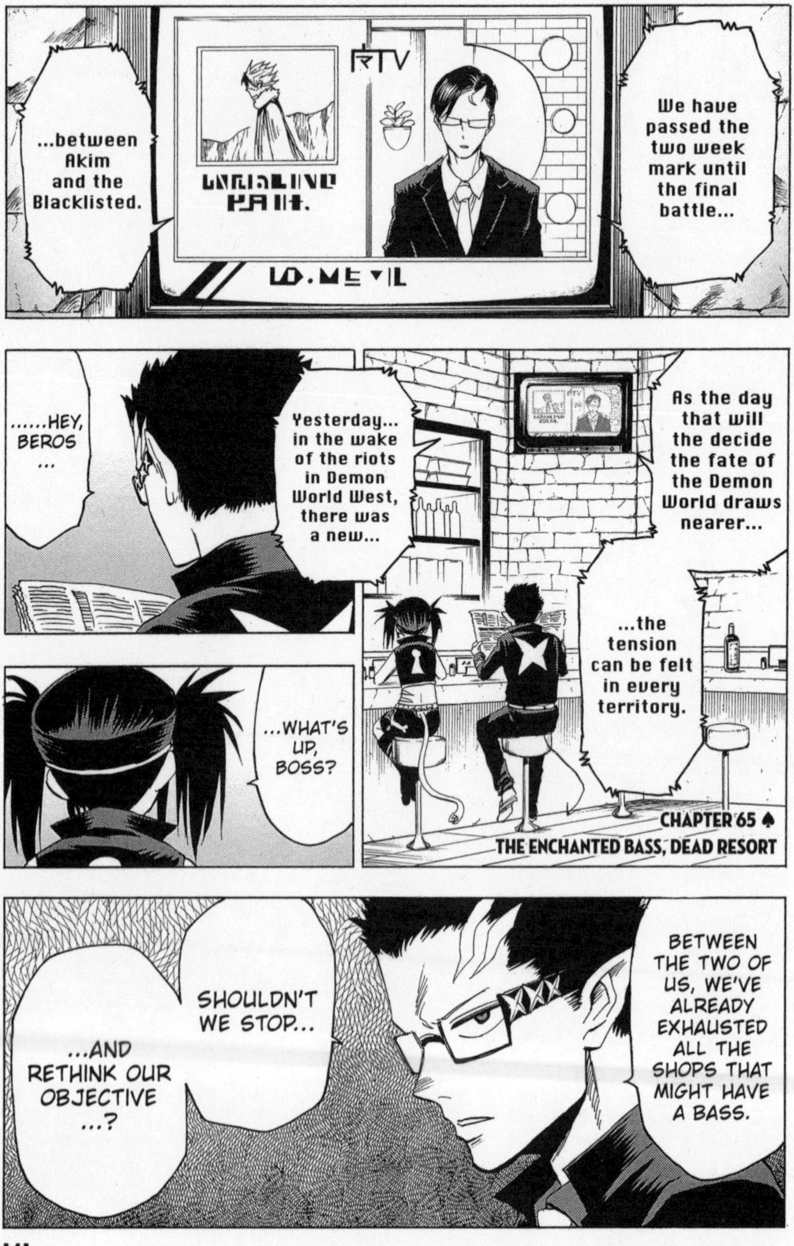
We have passed the two week mark until the final battle...
...between Akim and the Blacklisted.
As the day that will the decide the fate of the Demon World draws nearer...
Yesterday... in the wake of the riots in Demon World West, there was a new...
...the tension can be felt in every territory.
CHAPTER 65
THE ENCHANTED BASS, DEAD RESORT
......HEY, BEROS ...
...WHAT'S UP, BOSS?
BETWEEN THE TWO OF US, WE'VE ALREADY EXHAUSTED ALL THE SHOPS THAT MIGHT HAVE A BASS.
SHOULDN'T WE STOP...
...AND RETHINK OUR OBJECTIVE ...?

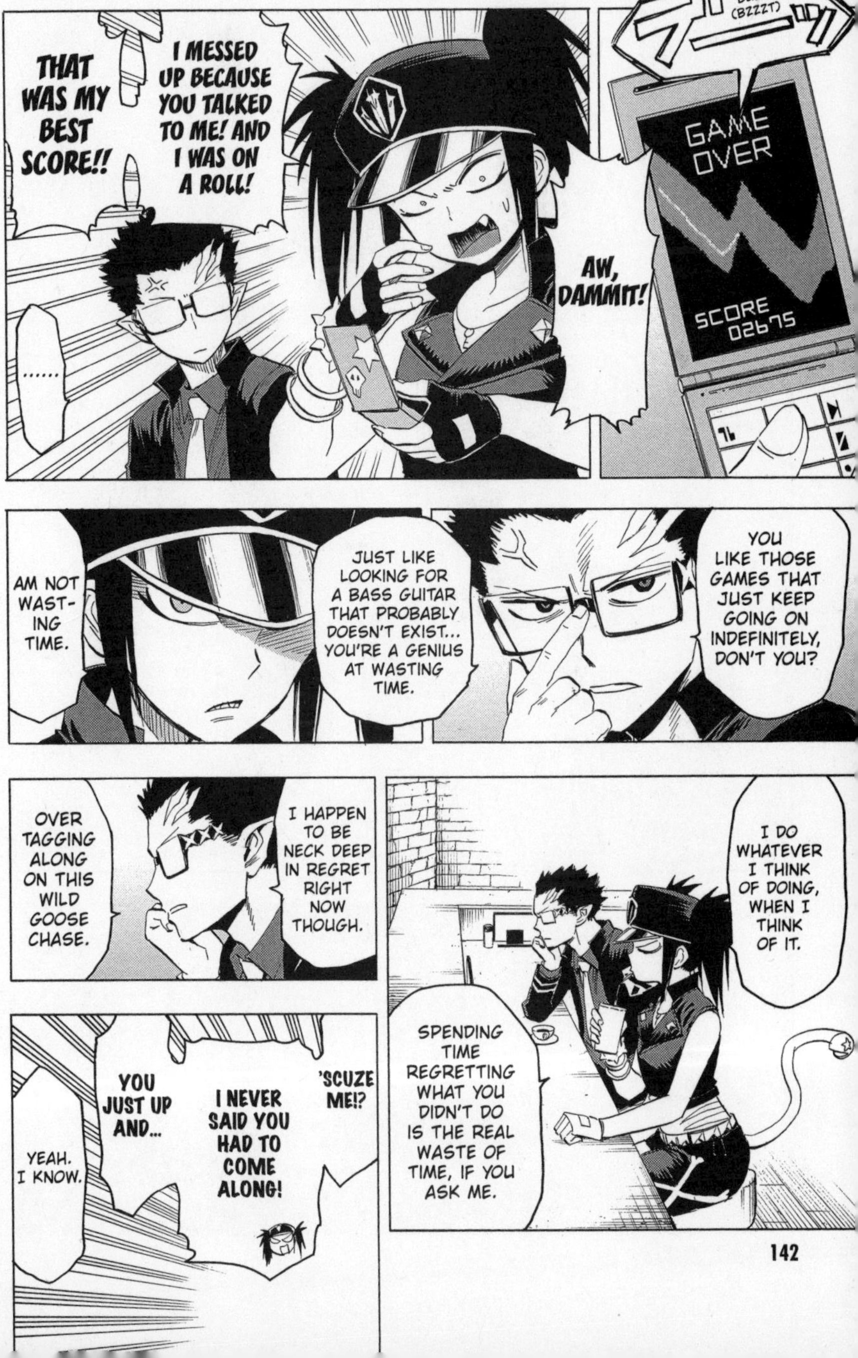
BUUU (BZZZT)
GAME OVER
SCORE 02675
AW, DAMMIT!
I MESSED UP BECAUSE YOU TALKED TO ME! AND I WAS ON A ROLL!
THAT WAS MY BEST SCORE!!
......
YOU LIKE THOSE GAMES THAT JUST KEEP GOING ON INDEFINITELY, DON'T YOU?
JUST LIKE LOOKING FOR A BASS GUITAR THAT PROBABLY DOESN'T EXIST... YOU'RE A GENIUS AT WASTING TIME.
AM NOT WAST-ING TIME.
I DO WHATEVER I THINK OF DOING, WHEN I THINK OF IT.
SPENDING TIME REGRETTING WHAT YOU DIDN'T DO IS THE REAL WASTE OF TIME, IF YOU ASK ME.
I HAPPEN TO BE NECK DEEP IN REGRET RIGHT NOW THOUGH.
OVER TAGGING ALONG ON THIS WILD GOOSE CHASE.
'SCUZE ME!?
I NEVER SAID YOU HAD TO COME ALONG!
YOU JUST UP AND...
YEAH. I KNOW.

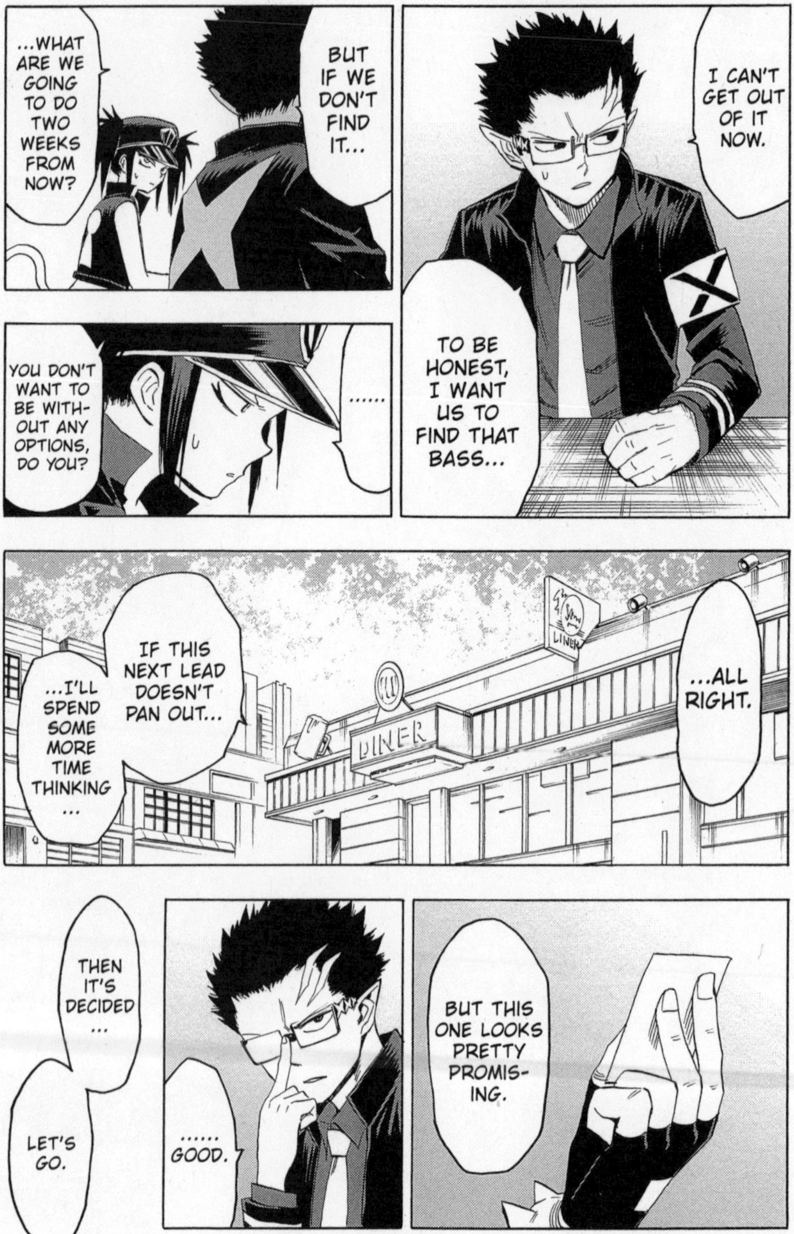
I CAN'T GET OUT OF IT NOW.
TO BE HONEST, I WANT US TO FIND THAT BASS...
BUT IF WE DON'T FIND IT...
...WHAT ARE WE GOING TO DO TWO WEEKS FROM NOW?
......
YOU DON'T WANT TO BE WITHOUT ANY OPTIONS, DO YOU?
...ALL RIGHT.
LINER
DINER
IF THIS NEXT LEAD DOESN'T PAN OUT...
...I'LL SPEND SOME MORE TIME THINKING ...
BUT THIS ONE LOOKS PRETTY PROMISING.
......GOOD.
THEN IT'S DECIDED ...
LET'S GO.

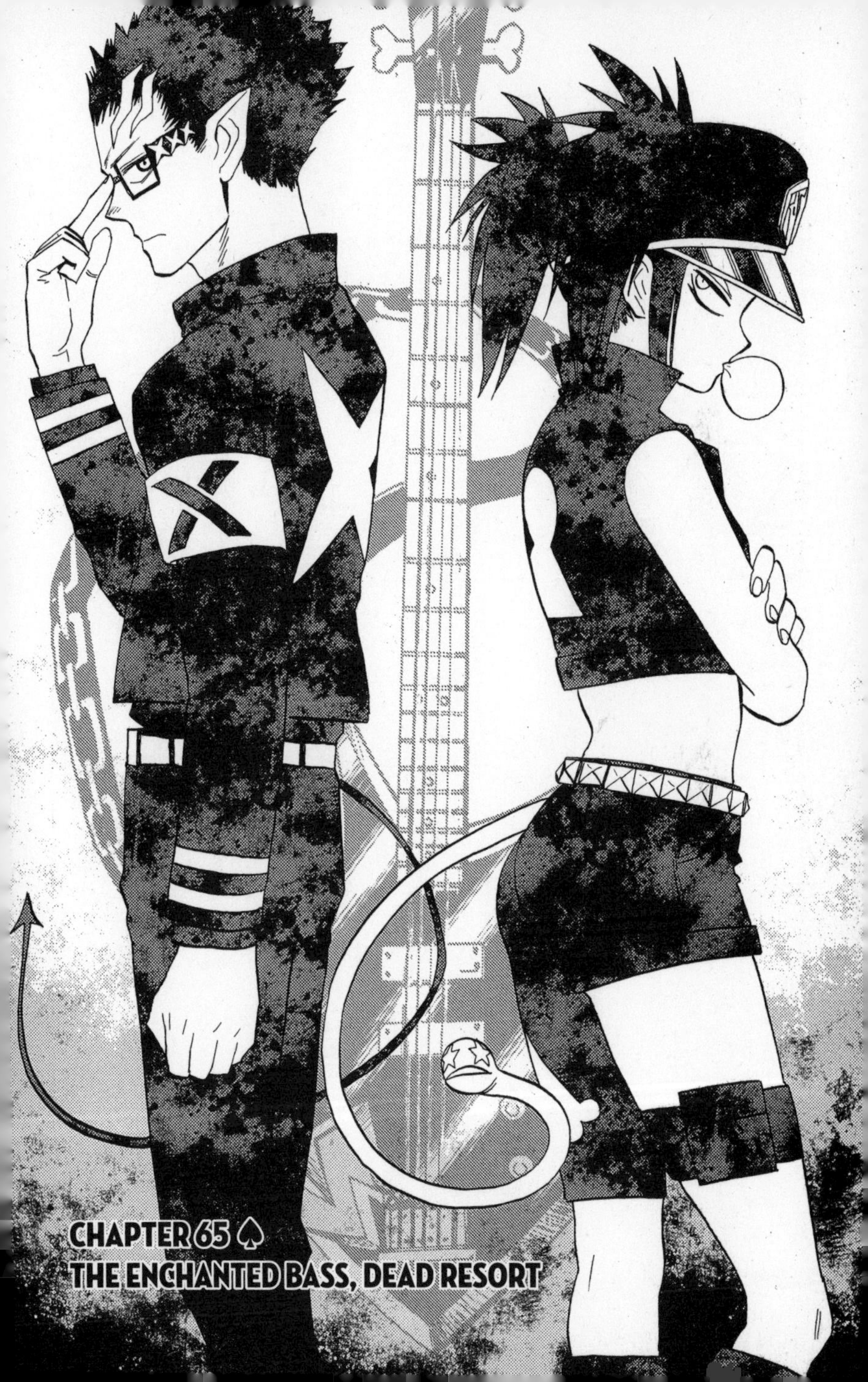

CHAPTER 65 ♠
THE ENCHANTED BASS, DEAD RESORT

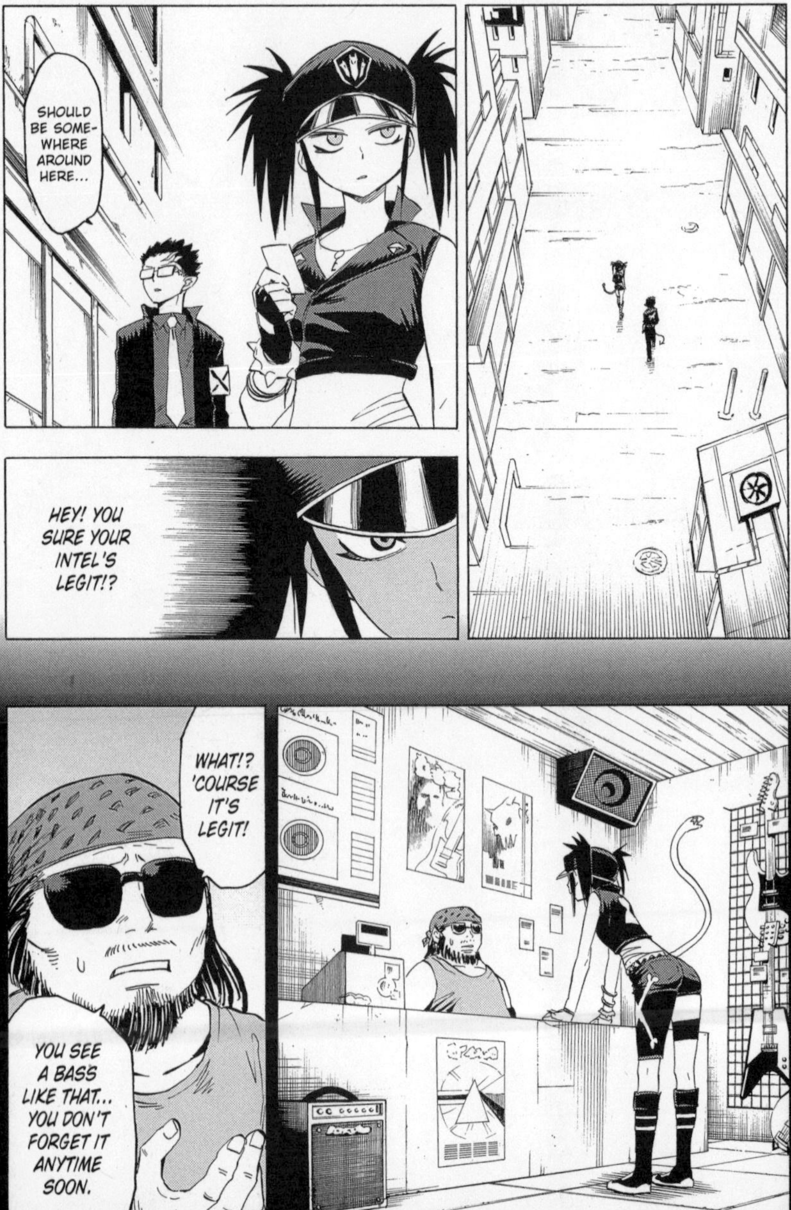
SHOULD BE SOME-WHERE AROUND HERE...
HEY! YOU SURE YOUR INTEL'S LEGIT!?
WHAT!? 'COURSE IT'S LEGIT!
YOU SEE A BASS LIKE THAT... YOU DON'T FORGET IT ANYTIME SOON.

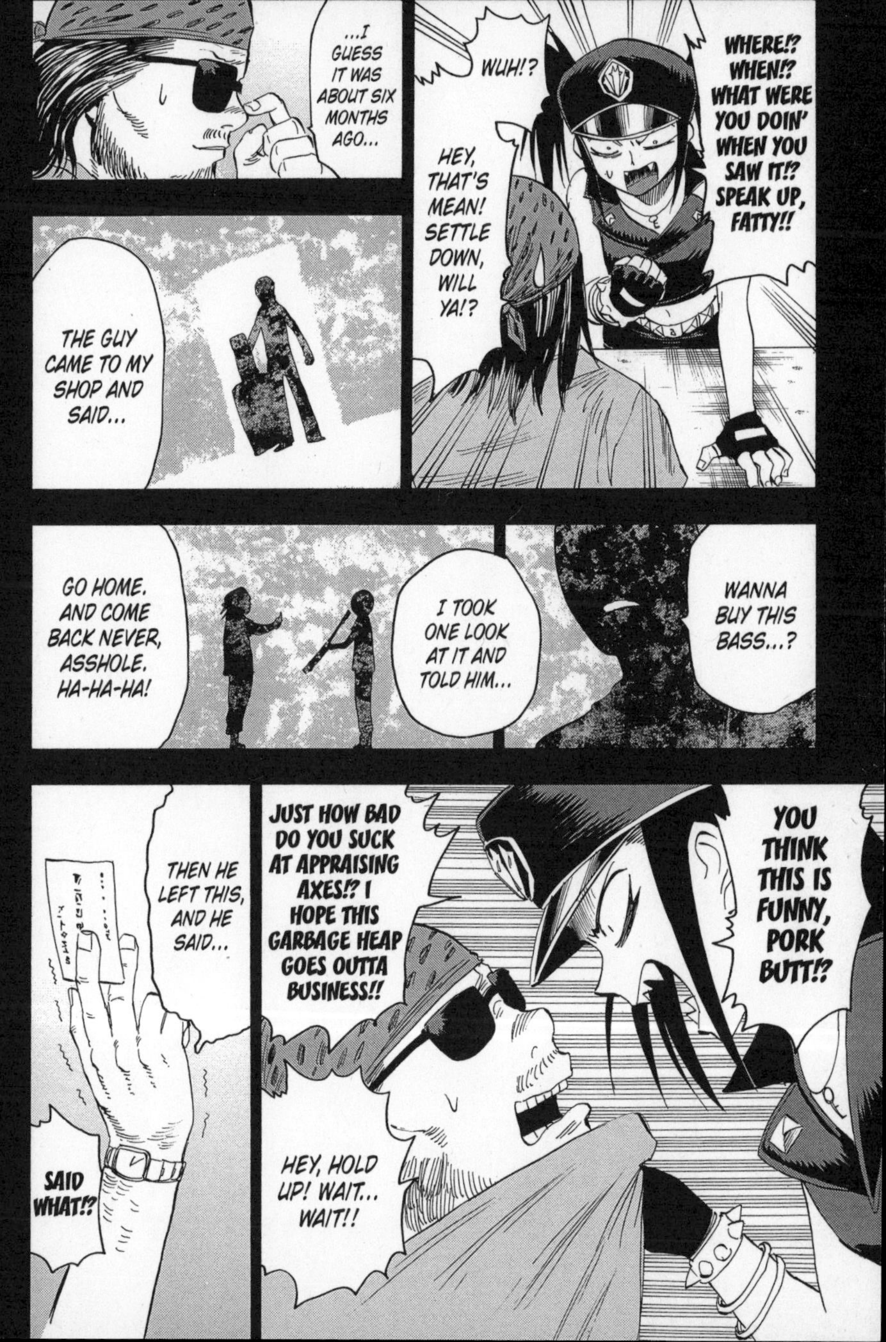
WHERE!? WHEN!? WHAT WERE YOU DOIN' WHEN YOU SAW IT!? SPEAK UP, FATTY!!
WUH!?
HEY, THAT'S MEAN! SETTLE DOWN, WILL YA!?
...I GUESS IT WAS ABOUT SIX MONTHS AGO...
THE GUY CAME TO MY SHOP AND SAID...
WANNA BUY THIS BASS...?
I TOOK ONE LOOK AT IT AND TOLD HIM...
GO HOME. AND COME BACK NEVER, ASSHOLE. HA-HA-HA!
YOU THINK THIS IS FUNNY, PORK BUTT!?
JUST HOW BAD DO YOU SUCK AT APPRAISING AXES!? I HOPE THIS GARBAGE HEAP GOES OUTTA BUSINESS!!
HEY, HOLD UP! WAIT... WAIT!!
THEN HE LEFT THIS, AND HE SAID...
SAID WHAT!?

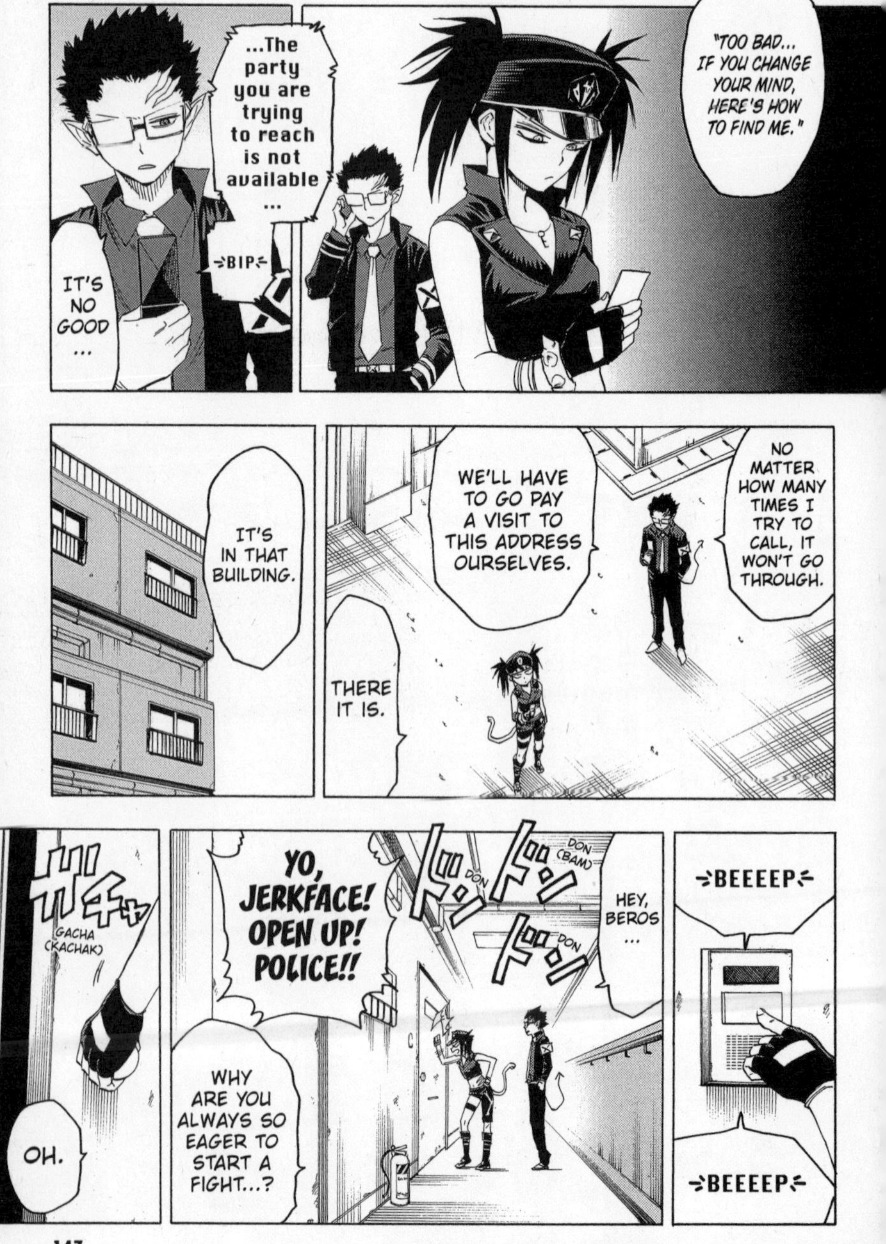
"TOO BAD... IF YOU CHANGE YOUR MIND, HERE'S HOW TO FIND ME."
...The party you are trying to reach is not available...
BIP
IT'S NO GOOD...
NO MATTER HOW MANY TIMES I TRY TO CALL, IT WON'T GO THROUGH.
WE'LL HAVE TO GO PAY A VISIT TO THIS ADDRESS OURSELVES.
THERE IT IS.
IT'S IN THAT BUILDING.
BEEEEP
BEEEEP
DON (BAM)
DON
DON
HEY, BEROS...
YO, JERKFACE! OPEN UP! POLICE!!
WHY ARE YOU ALWAYS SO EAGER TO START A FIGHT...?
GACHA (KACHAK)
OH.

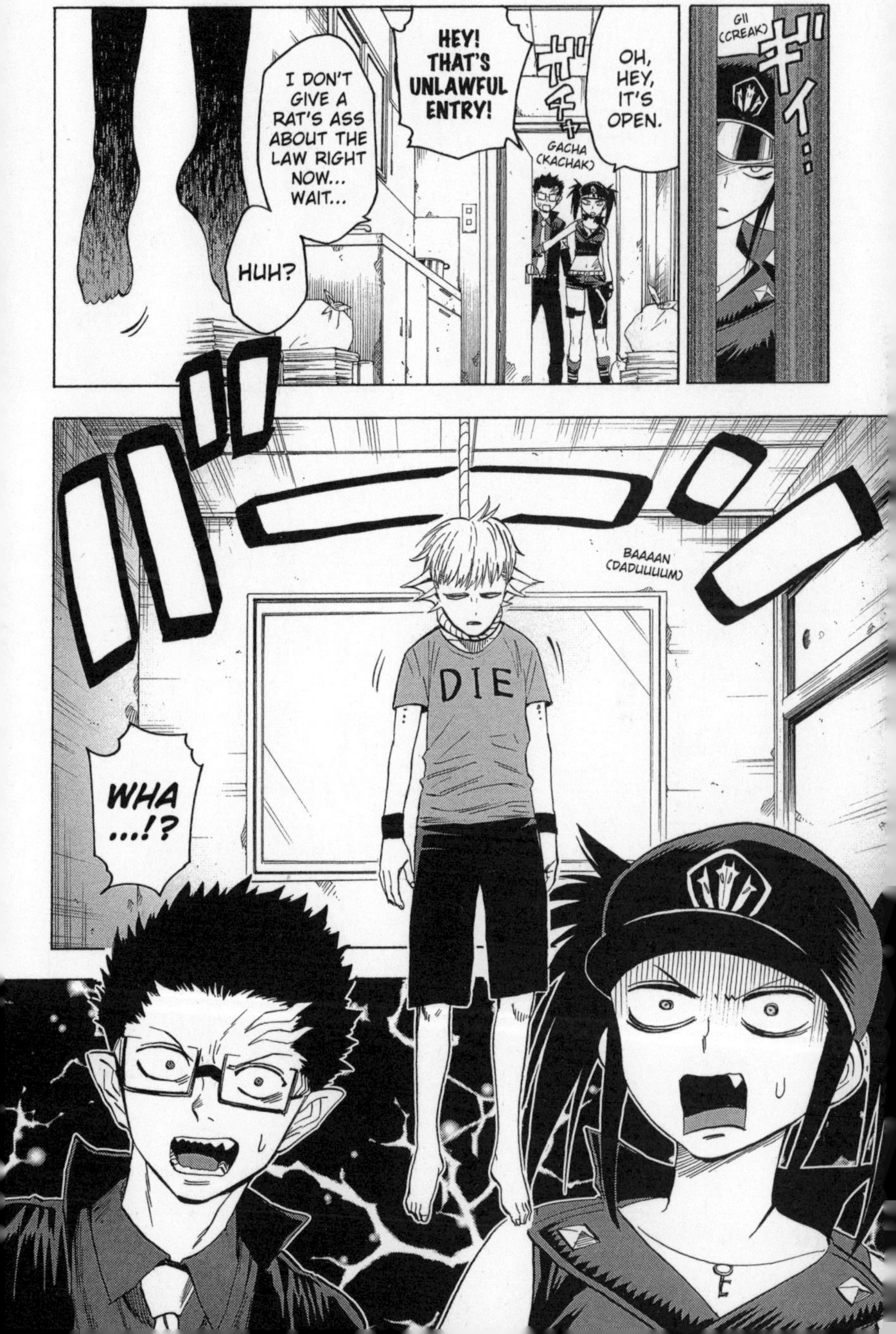
GII (CREAK)
OH, HEY, IT'S OPEN.
GACHA (KACHAK)
HEY! THAT'S UNLAWFUL ENTRY!
I DON'T GIVE A RAT'S ASS ABOUT THE LAW RIGHT NOW... WAIT...
HUH?
BAAAAN (DADUUUUM)
DIE
WHA ...!?

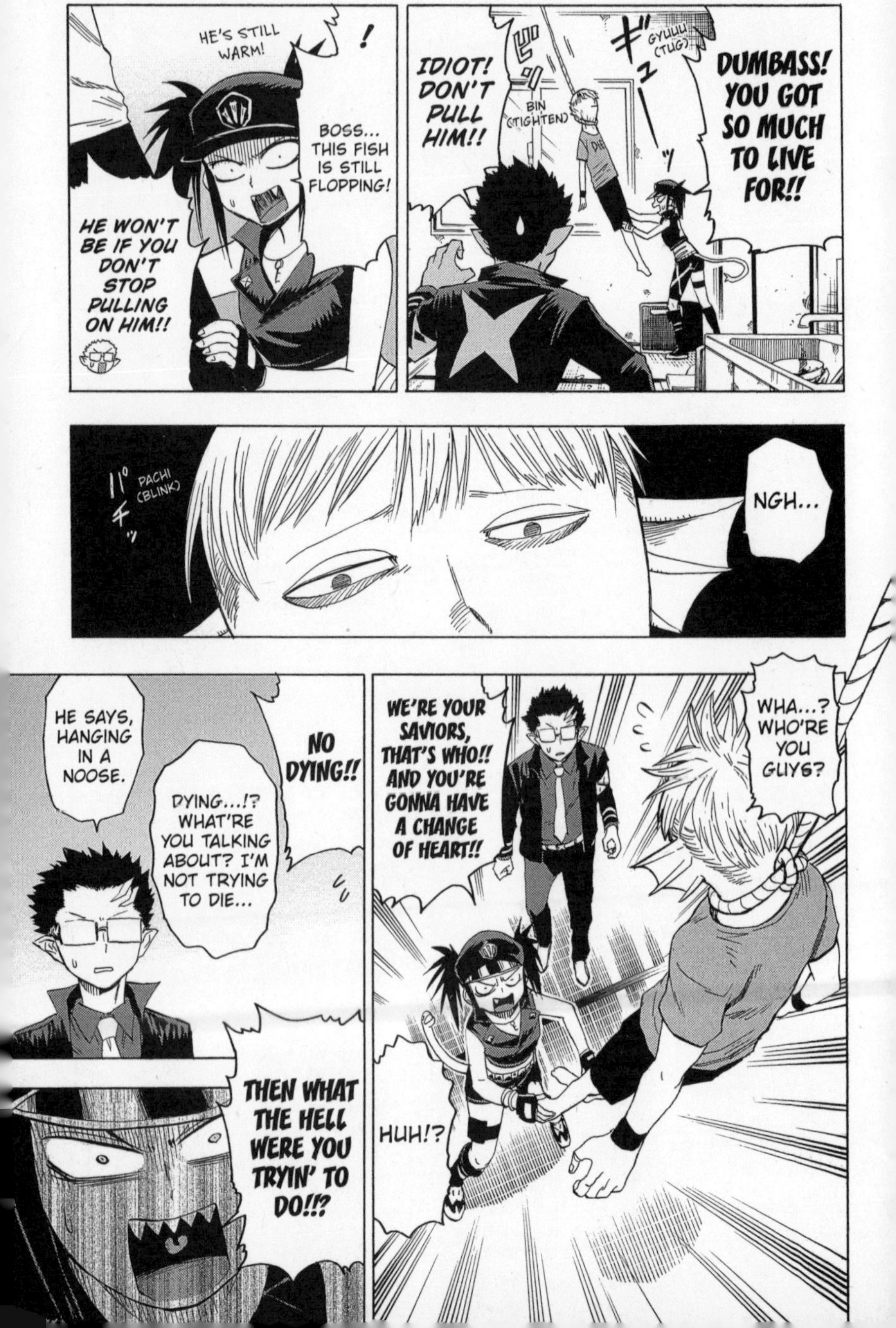
DUMBASS! YOU GOT SO MUCH TO LIVE FOR!!
GYUUU (TUG)
BIN (TIGHTEN)
IDIOT! DON'T PULL HIM!!
!
HE'S STILL WARM!
BOSS... THIS FISH IS STILL FLOPPING!
HE WON'T BE IF YOU DON'T STOP PULLING ON HIM!!
NGH...
PACHI (BLINK)
WHA...? WHO'RE YOU GUYS?
WE'RE YOUR SAVIORS, THAT'S WHO!! AND YOU'RE GONNA HAVE A CHANGE OF HEART!!
HUH!?
NO DYING!!
HE SAYS, HANGING IN A NOOSE.
DYING...!? WHAT'RE YOU TALKING ABOUT? I'M NOT TRYING TO DIE...
THEN WHAT THE HELL WERE YOU TRYIN' TO DO!!?

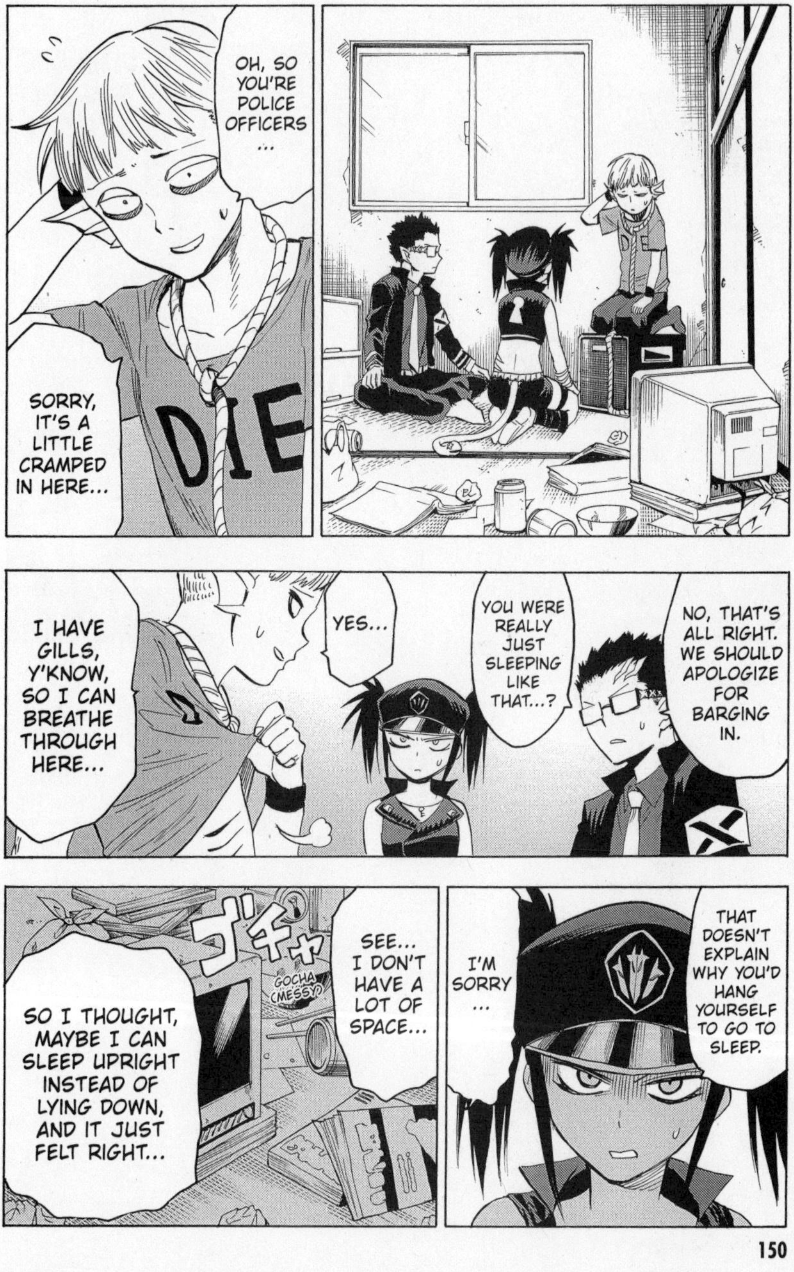
OH, SO YOU'RE POLICE OFFICERS ...
SORRY, IT'S A LITTLE CRAMPED IN HERE...
NO, THAT'S ALL RIGHT. WE SHOULD APOLOGIZE FOR BARGING IN.
YOU WERE REALLY JUST SLEEPING LIKE THAT...?
YES...
I HAVE GILLS, Y'KNOW, SO I CAN BREATHE THROUGH HERE...
THAT DOESN'T EXPLAIN WHY YOU'D HANG YOURSELF TO GO TO SLEEP.
I'M SORRY ...
SEE... I DON'T HAVE A LOT OF SPACE...
GOCHA (MESSY)
SO I THOUGHT, MAYBE I CAN SLEEP UPRIGHT INSTEAD OF LYING DOWN, AND IT JUST FELT RIGHT...

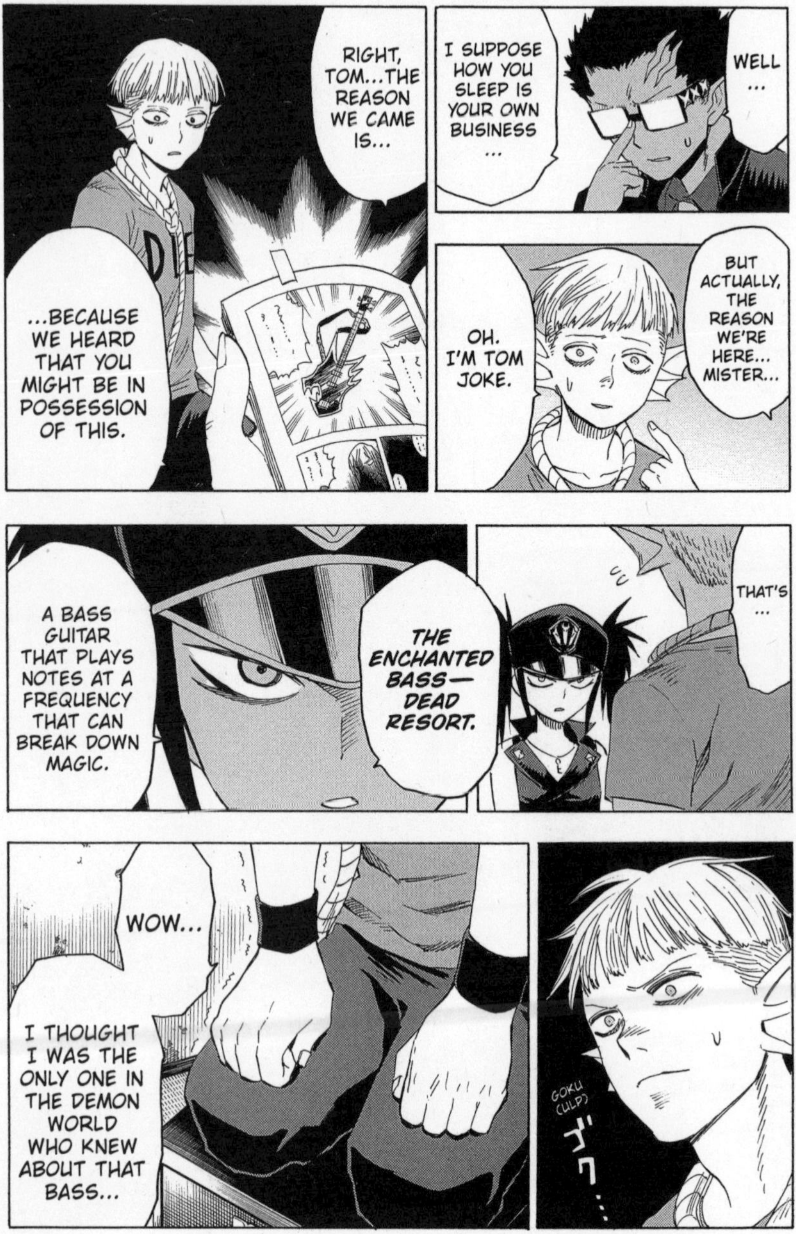
WELL ...
I SUPPOSE HOW YOU SLEEP IS YOUR OWN BUSINESS ...
BUT ACTUALLY, THE REASON WE'RE HERE... MISTER...
OH. I'M TOM JOKE.
RIGHT, TOM...THE REASON WE CAME IS...
...BECAUSE WE HEARD THAT YOU MIGHT BE IN POSSESSION OF THIS.
THAT'S ...
THE ENCHANTED BASS—DEAD RESORT.
A BASS GUITAR THAT PLAYS NOTES AT A FREQUENCY THAT CAN BREAK DOWN MAGIC.
GOKU (ULP)
WOW...
I THOUGHT I WAS THE ONLY ONE IN THE DEMON WORLD WHO KNEW ABOUT THAT BASS...

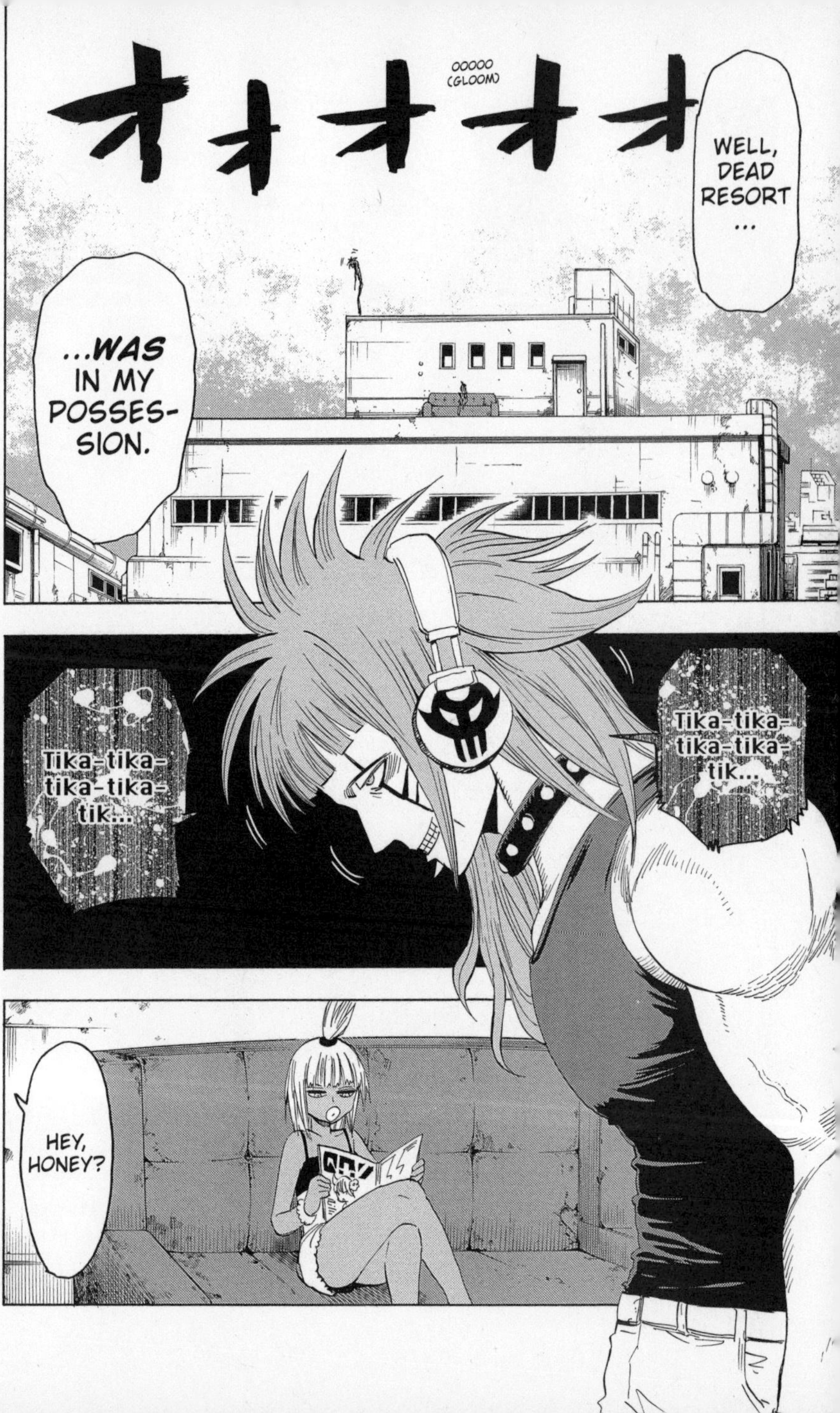
オオオオオ
OOOOO (GLOOM)
WELL, DEAD RESORT ...
...WAS IN MY POSSES-SION.
Tika-tika-tika-tika-tik...
Tika-tika-tika-tika-tik...
HEY, HONEY?

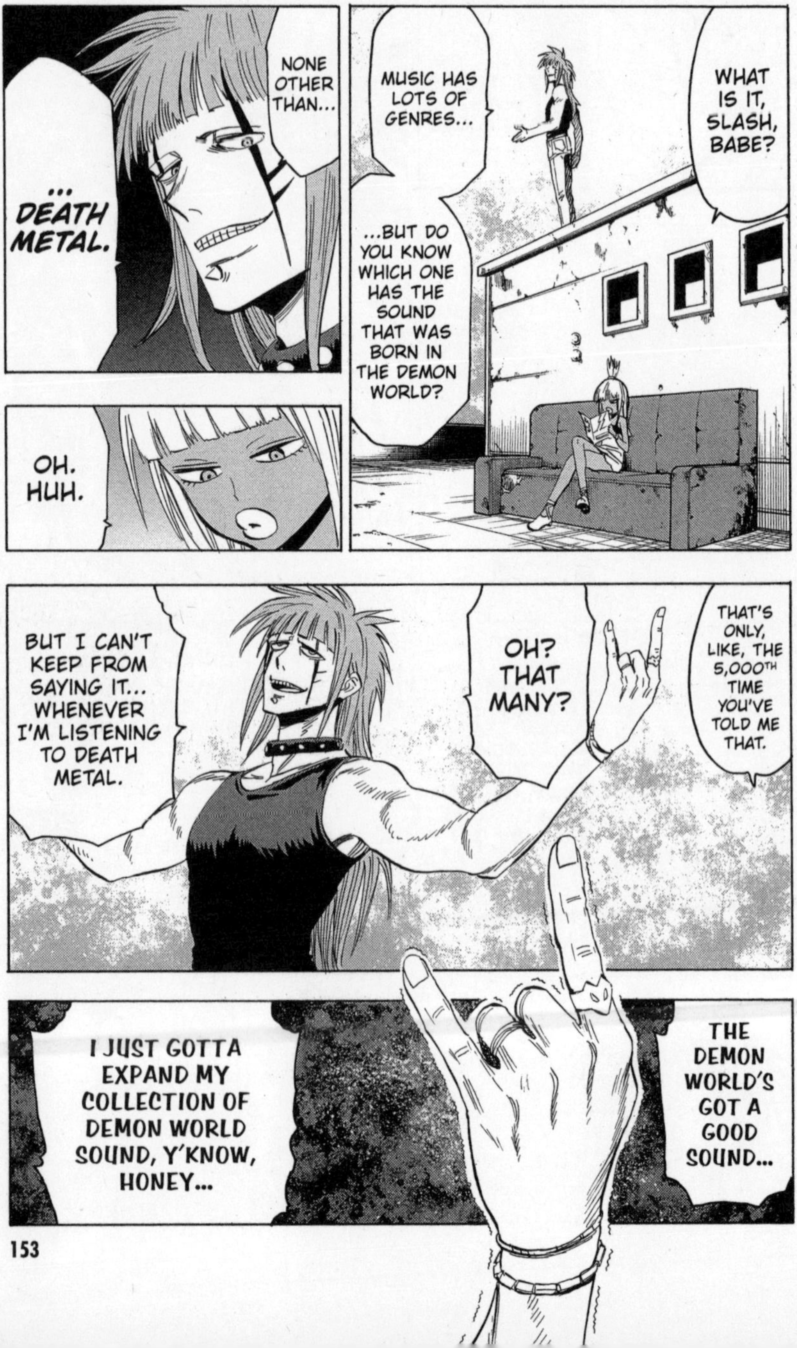
WHAT IS IT, SLASH, BABE?
MUSIC HAS LOTS OF GENRES...
...BUT DO YOU KNOW WHICH ONE HAS THE SOUND THAT WAS BORN IN THE DEMON WORLD?
NONE OTHER THAN...
...DEATH METAL.
OH. HUH.
THAT'S ONLY, LIKE, THE 5,000TH TIME YOU'VE TOLD ME THAT.
OH? THAT MANY?
BUT I CAN'T KEEP FROM SAYING IT... WHENEVER I'M LISTENING TO DEATH METAL.
THE DEMON WORLD'S GOT A GOOD SOUND...
I JUST GOTTA EXPAND MY COLLECTION OF DEMON WORLD SOUND, Y'KNOW, HONEY...

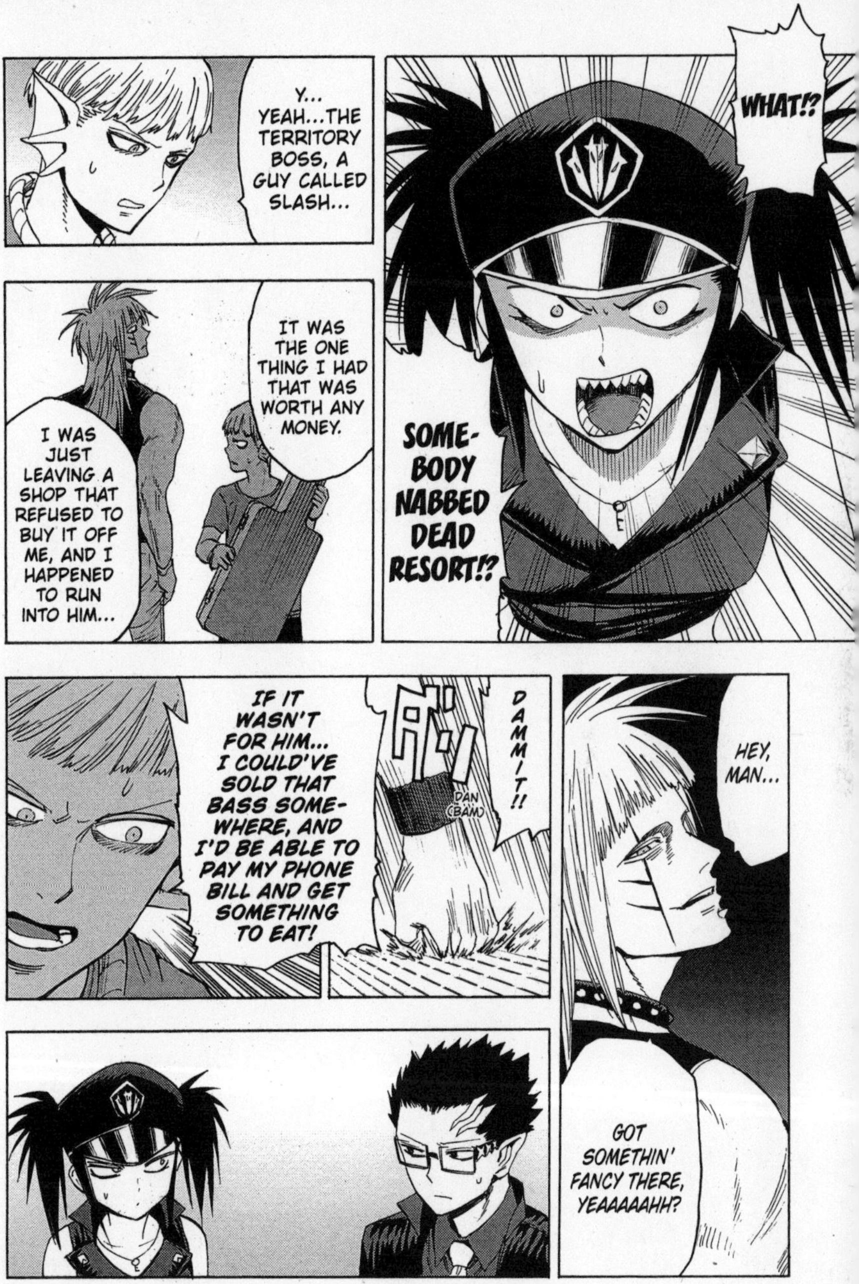
WHAT!?
SOME-BODY NABBED DEAD RESORT!?
Y... YEAH...THE TERRITORY BOSS, A GUY CALLED SLASH...
IT WAS THE ONE THING I HAD THAT WAS WORTH ANY MONEY.
I WAS JUST LEAVING A SHOP THAT REFUSED TO BUY IT OFF ME, AND I HAPPENED TO RUN INTO HIM...
HEY, MAN...
GOT SOMETHIN' FANCY THERE, YEAAAAAHH?
DAMMIT!!
DAN (BAM)
IF IT WASN'T FOR HIM... I COULD'VE SOLD THAT BASS SOME-WHERE, AND I'D BE ABLE TO PAY MY PHONE BILL AND GET SOMETHING TO EAT!

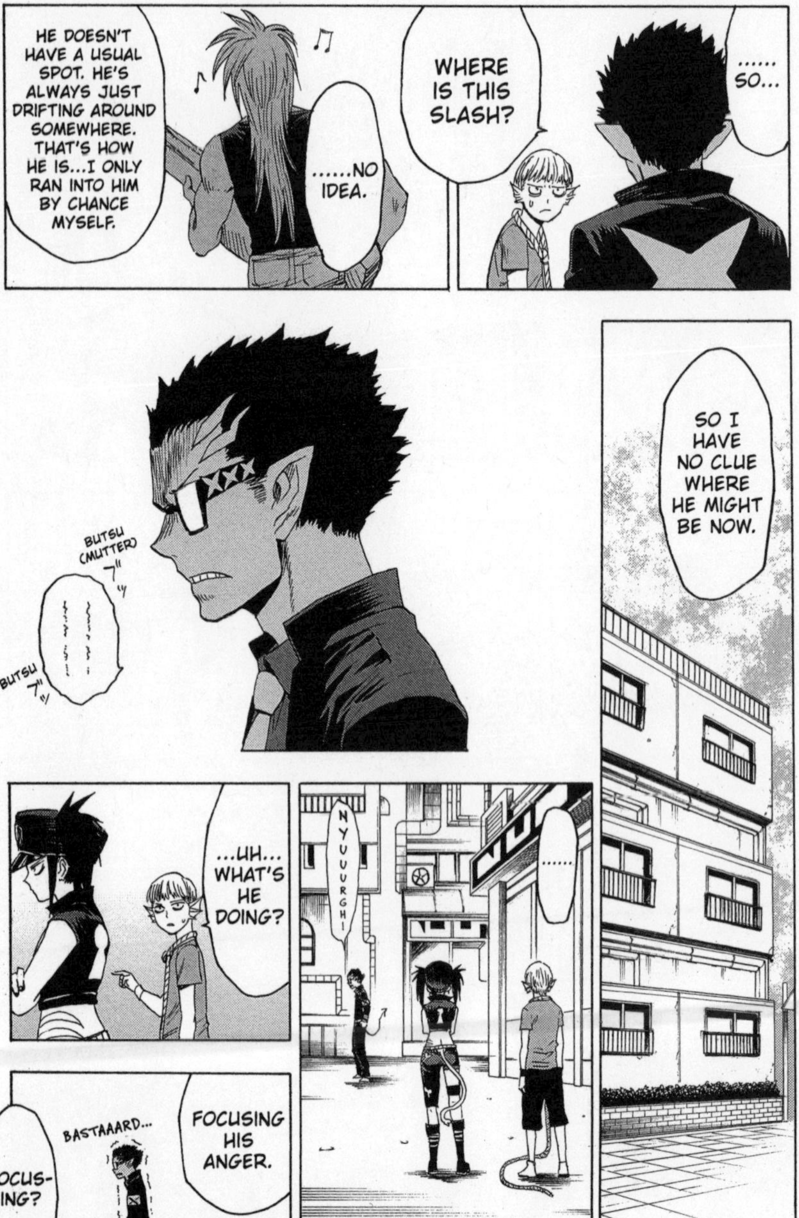
......SO...
WHERE IS THIS SLASH?
......NO IDEA.
HE DOESN'T HAVE A USUAL SPOT. HE'S ALWAYS JUST DRIFTING AROUND SOMEWHERE. THAT'S HOW HE IS...I ONLY RAN INTO HIM BY CHANCE MYSELF.
SO I HAVE NO CLUE WHERE HE MIGHT BE NOW.
BUTSU (MUTTER)
BUTSU
......
NYUUURGH!
...UH... WHAT'S HE DOING?
FOCUSING HIS ANGER.
BASTAAARD...
FOCUS-ING?

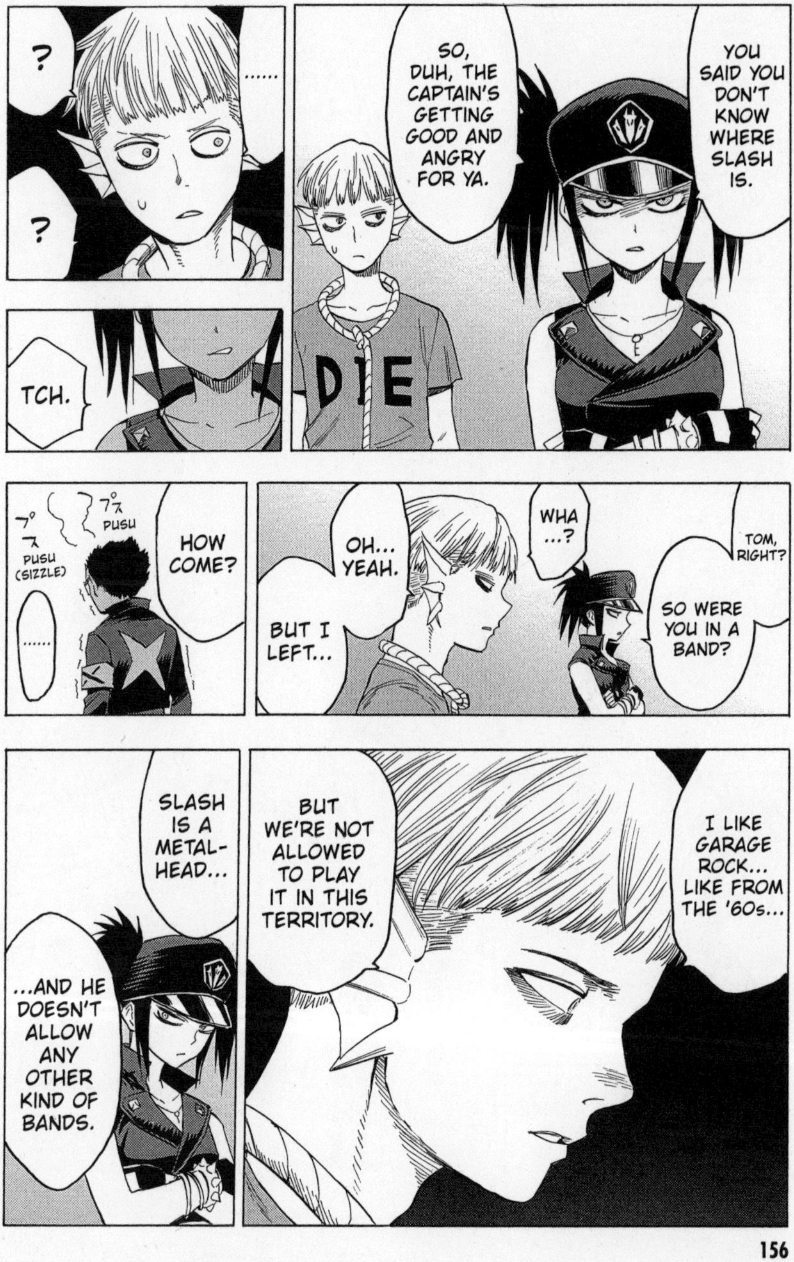
YOU SAID YOU DON'T KNOW WHERE SLASH IS.
SO, DUH, THE CAPTAIN'S GETTING GOOD AND ANGRY FOR YA.
DIE
......
?
?
TCH.
TOM, RIGHT?
SO WERE YOU IN A BAND?
WHA ...?
OH... YEAH.
BUT I LEFT...
HOW COME?
プス PUSU
プス PUSU (SIZZLE)
......
I LIKE GARAGE ROCK... LIKE FROM THE '60s...
BUT WE'RE NOT ALLOWED TO PLAY IT IN THIS TERRITORY.
SLASH IS A METAL-HEAD...
...AND HE DOESN'T ALLOW ANY OTHER KIND OF BANDS.

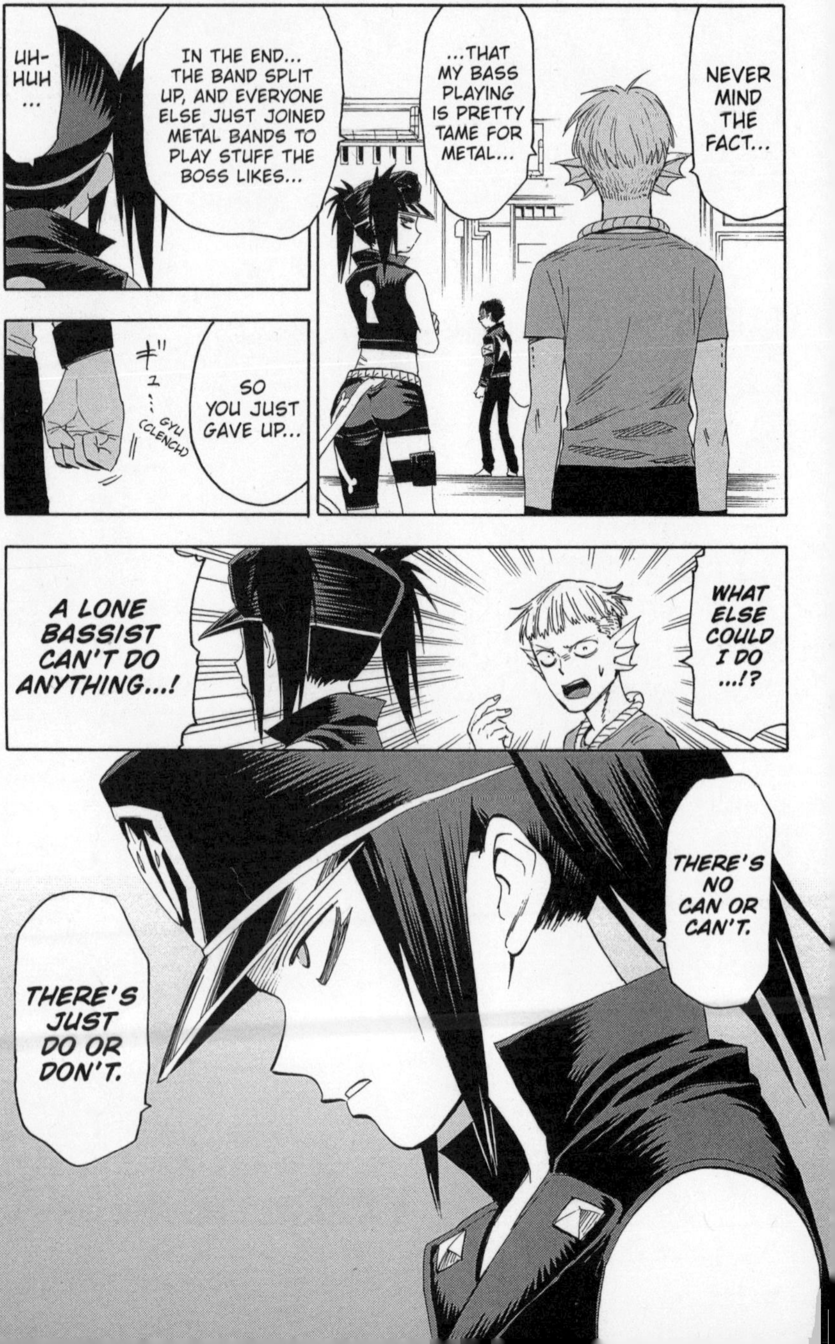
NEVER MIND THE FACT...
...THAT MY BASS PLAYING IS PRETTY TAME FOR METAL...
IN THE END... THE BAND SPLIT UP, AND EVERYONE ELSE JUST JOINED METAL BANDS TO PLAY STUFF THE BOSS LIKES...
UH-HUH...
SO YOU JUST GAVE UP...
ギュ
GYU (CLENCH)
WHAT ELSE COULD I DO ...!?
A LONE BASSIST CAN'T DO ANYTHING...!
THERE'S NO CAN OR CAN'T.
THERE'S JUST DO OR DON'T.

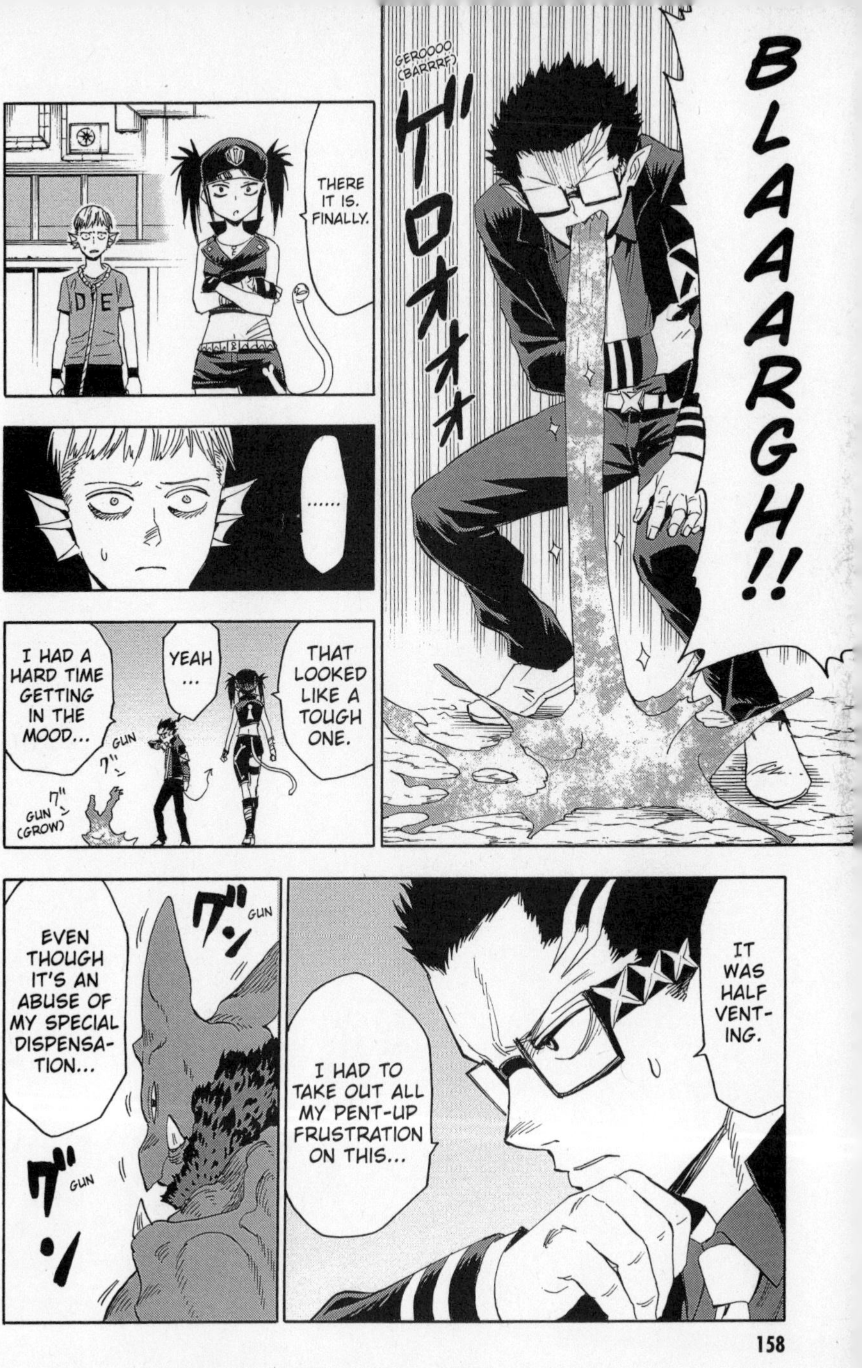
BLAAARGH!!
GEROOOO (BARRRF)
THERE IT IS. FINALLY.
......
THAT LOOKED LIKE A TOUGH ONE.
YEAH ...
I HAD A HARD TIME GETTING IN THE MOOD...
GUN
GUN (GROW)
IT WAS HALF VENTING.
I HAD TO TAKE OUT ALL MY PENT-UP FRUSTRATION ON THIS...
GUN
EVEN THOUGH IT'S AN ABUSE OF MY SPECIAL DISPENSATION...
GUN

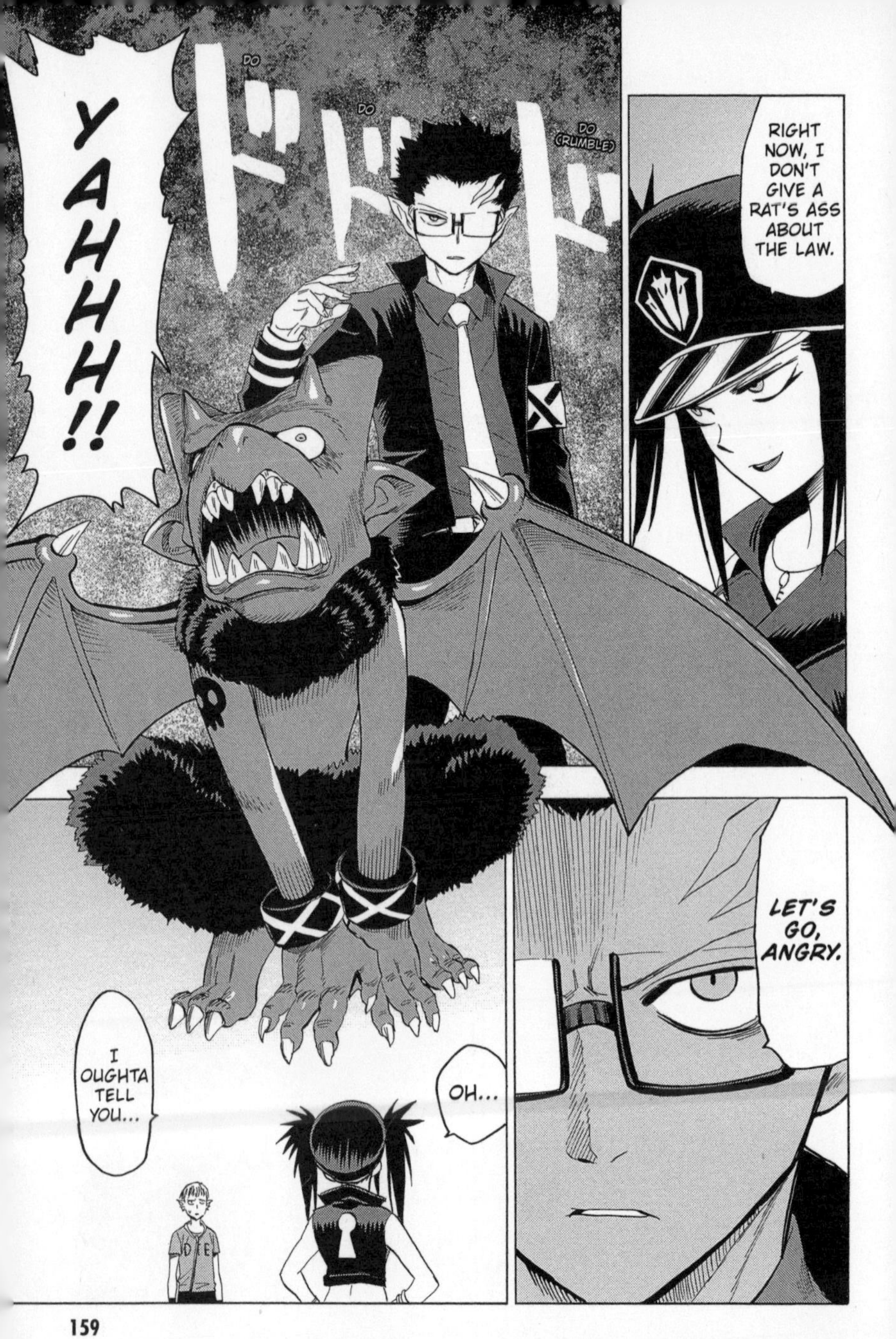
RIGHT NOW, I DON'T GIVE A RAT'S ASS ABOUT THE LAW.
LET'S GO, ANGRY.
YAHHHH!!
DO
DO
DO (RUMBLE)
OH...
I OUGHTA TELL YOU...

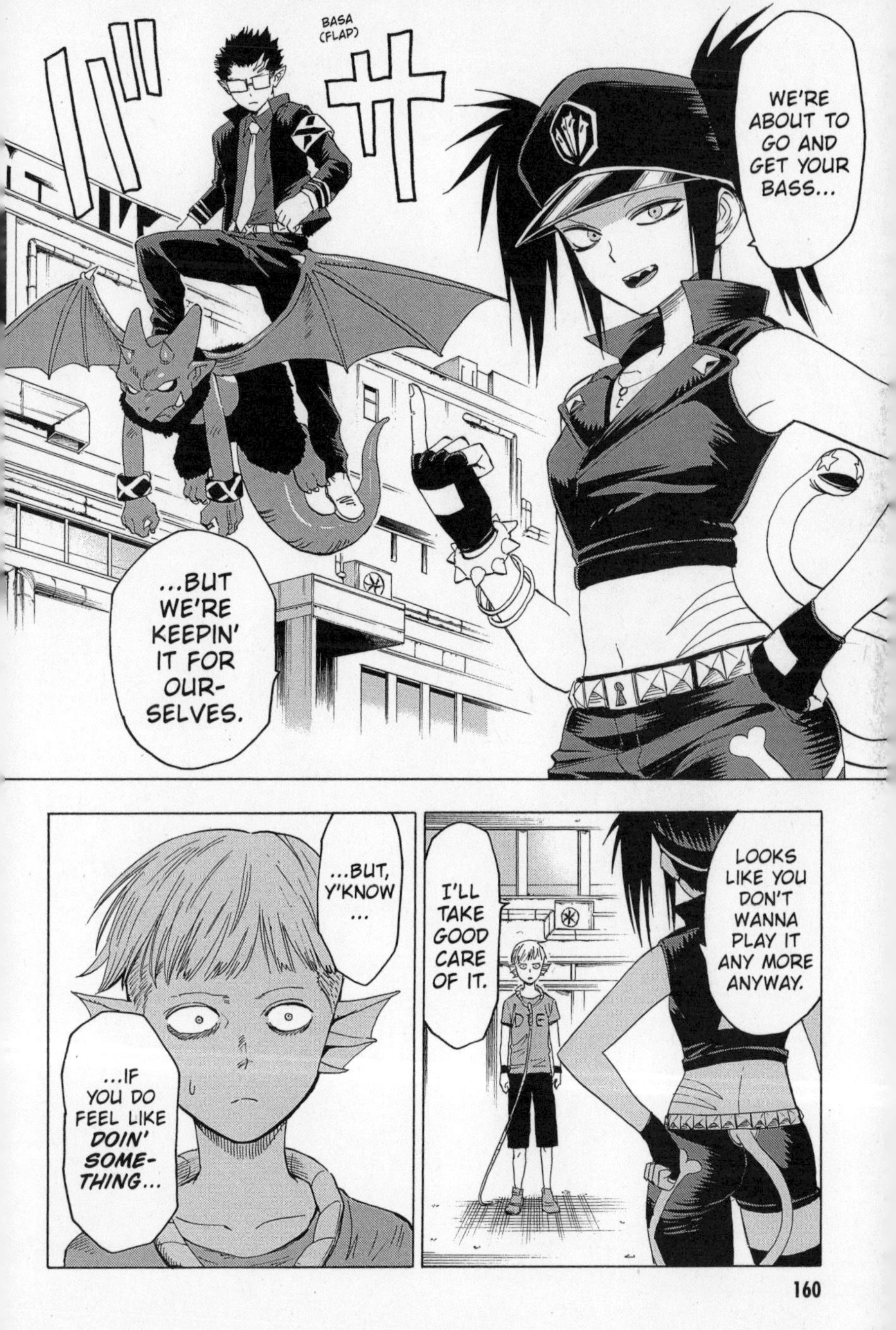
BASA (FLAP)
WE'RE ABOUT TO GO AND GET YOUR BASS...
...BUT WE'RE KEEPIN' IT FOR OUR-SELVES.
LOOKS LIKE YOU DON'T WANNA PLAY IT ANY MORE ANYWAY.
I'LL TAKE GOOD CARE OF IT.
...BUT, Y'KNOW ...
...IF YOU DO FEEL LIKE *DOIN' SOMETHING*...

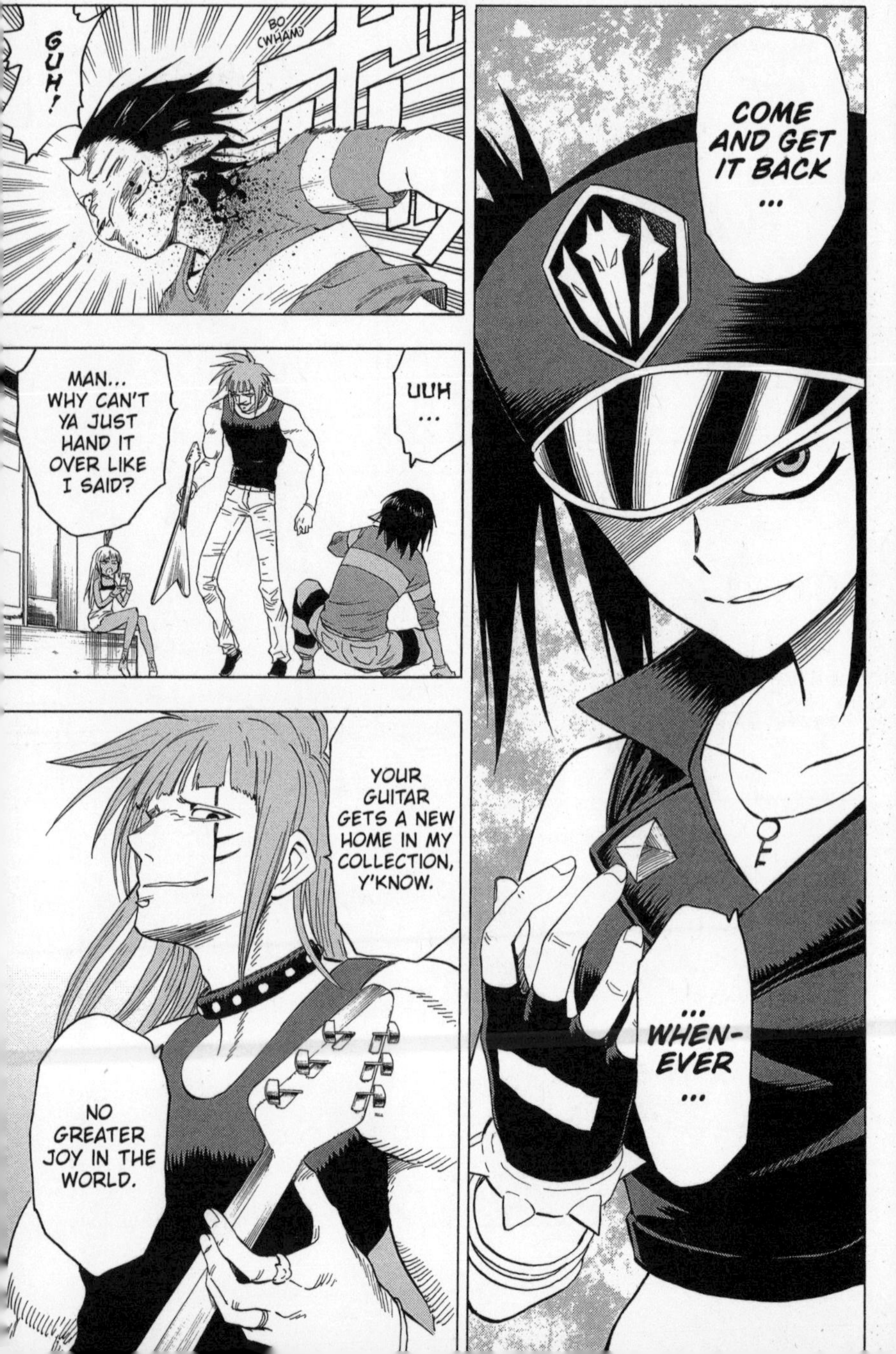
COME AND GET IT BACK ...
... WHEN-EVER ...
BO (WHAM)
GUH!
UUH ...
MAN... WHY CAN'T YA JUST HAND IT OVER LIKE I SAID?
YOUR GUITAR GETS A NEW HOME IN MY COLLECTION, Y'KNOW.
NO GREATER JOY IN THE WORLD.

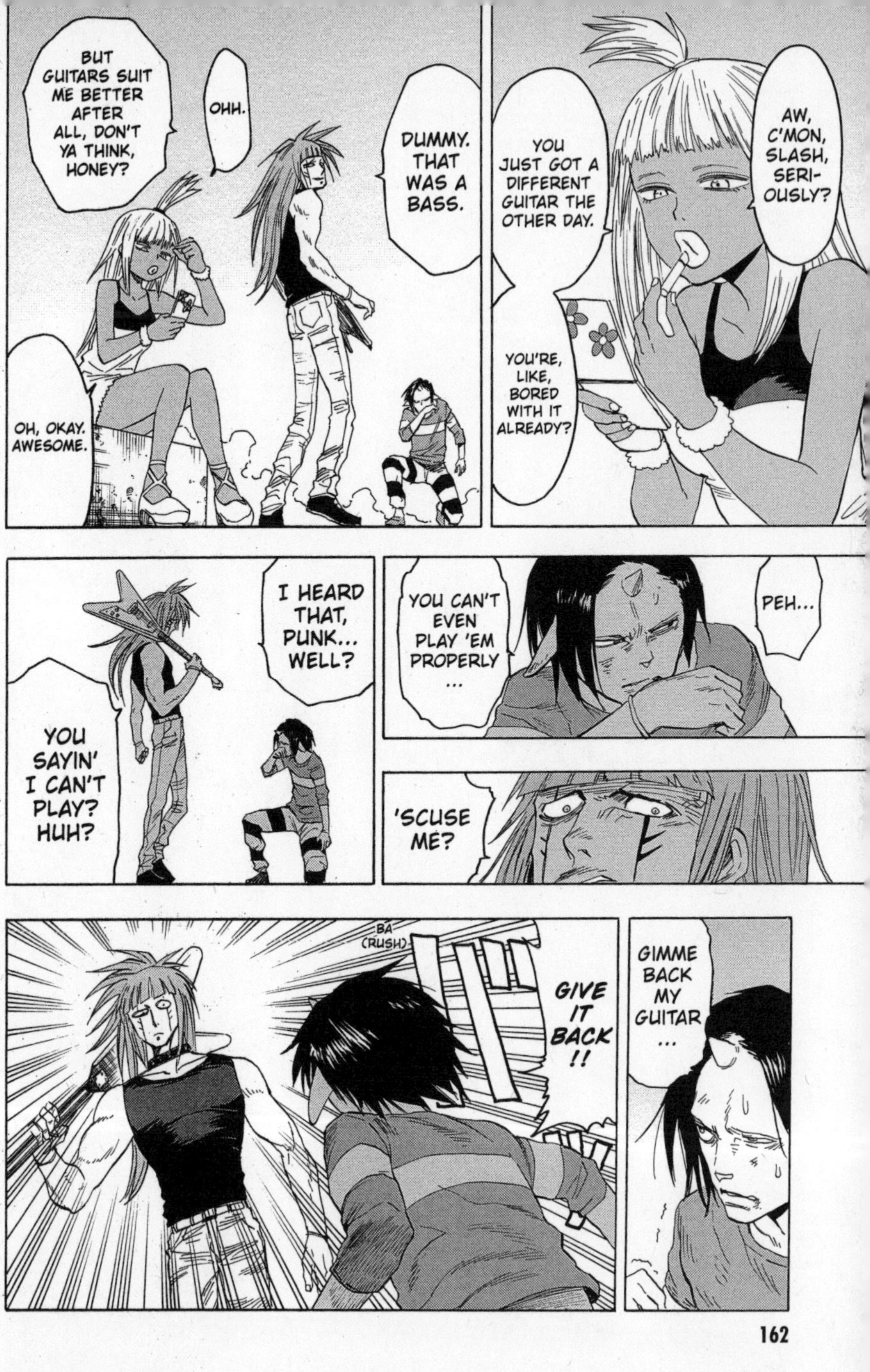
AW, C'MON, SLASH, SERI-OUSLY?
YOU JUST GOT A DIFFERENT GUITAR THE OTHER DAY.
YOU'RE, LIKE, BORED WITH IT ALREADY?
DUMMY. THAT WAS A BASS.
OHH.
BUT GUITARS SUIT ME BETTER AFTER ALL, DON'T YA THINK, HONEY?
OH, OKAY. AWESOME.
PEH...
YOU CAN'T EVEN PLAY 'EM PROPERLY ...
'SCUSE ME?
I HEARD THAT, PUNK... WELL?
YOU SAYIN' I CAN'T PLAY? HUH?
GIMME BACK MY GUITAR ...
GIVE IT BACK !!
BA (RUSH)

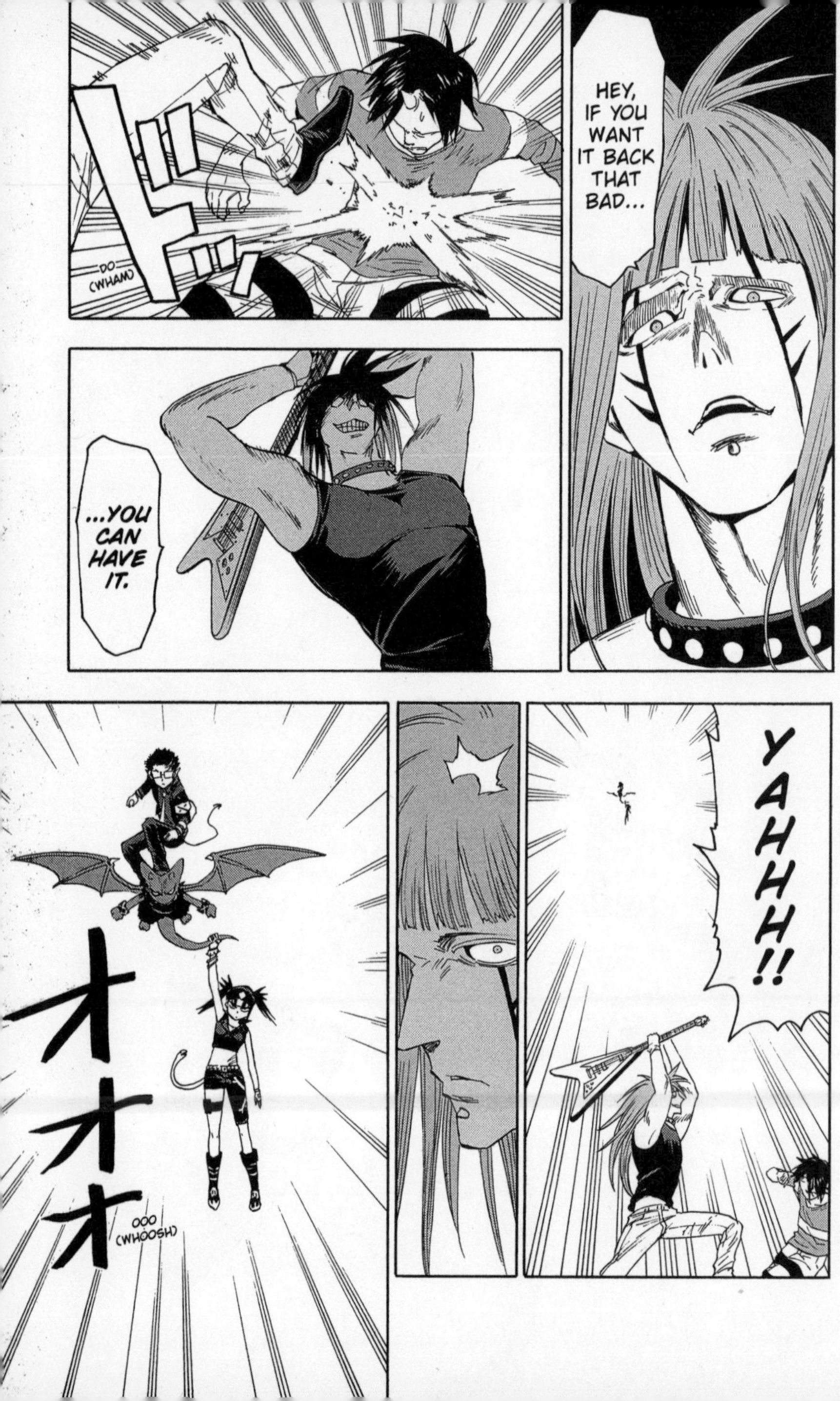
HEY, IF YOU WANT IT BACK THAT BAD...
ドッ
DO (WHAM)
...YOU CAN HAVE IT.
YAHHHH!!
オオオ
OOO (WHOOSH)

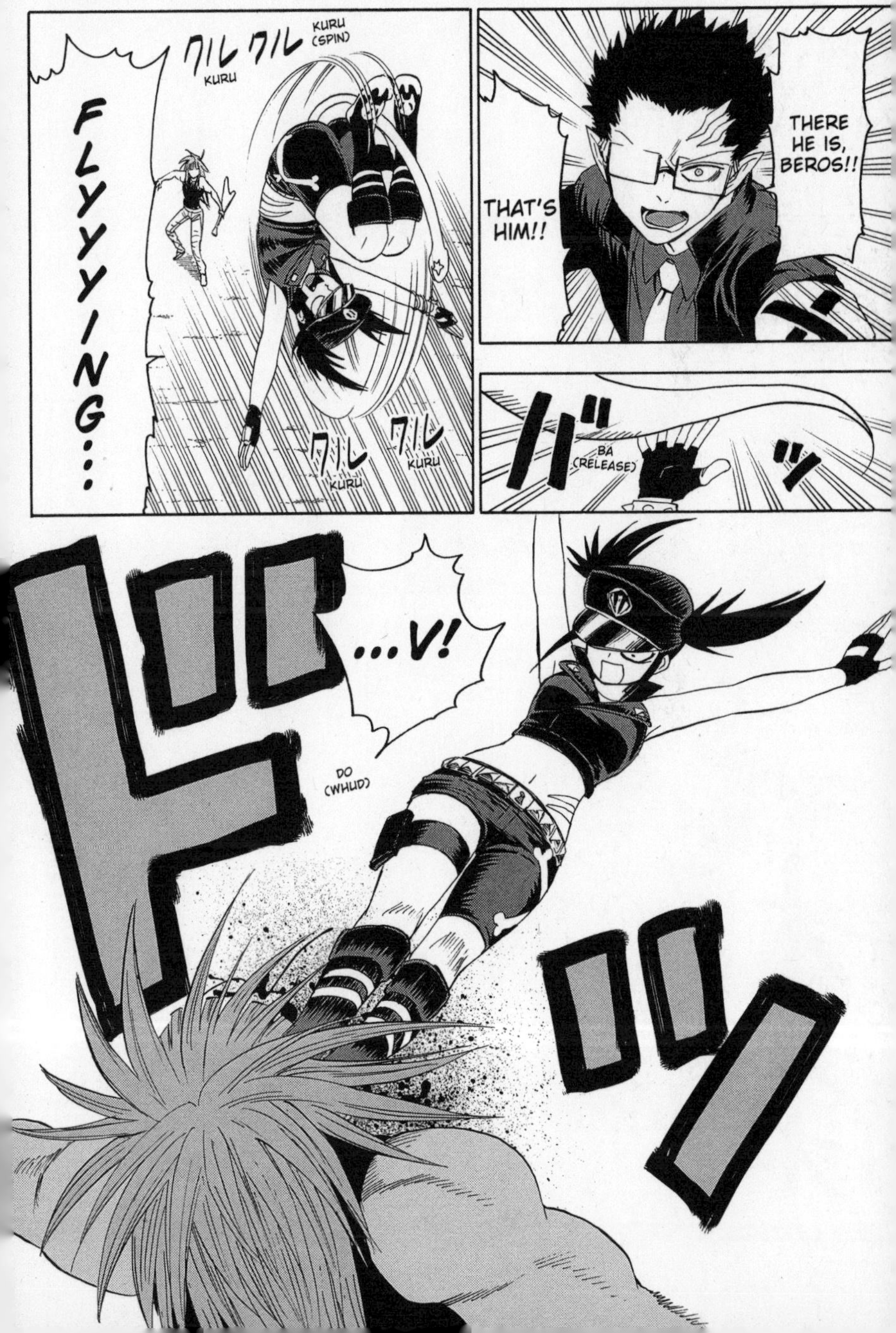
THERE HE IS, BEROS!!
THAT'S HIM!!
BA (RELEASE)
KURU (SPIN)
KURU
FLYYYYING...
KURU
KURU
...V!
DO (WHUD)

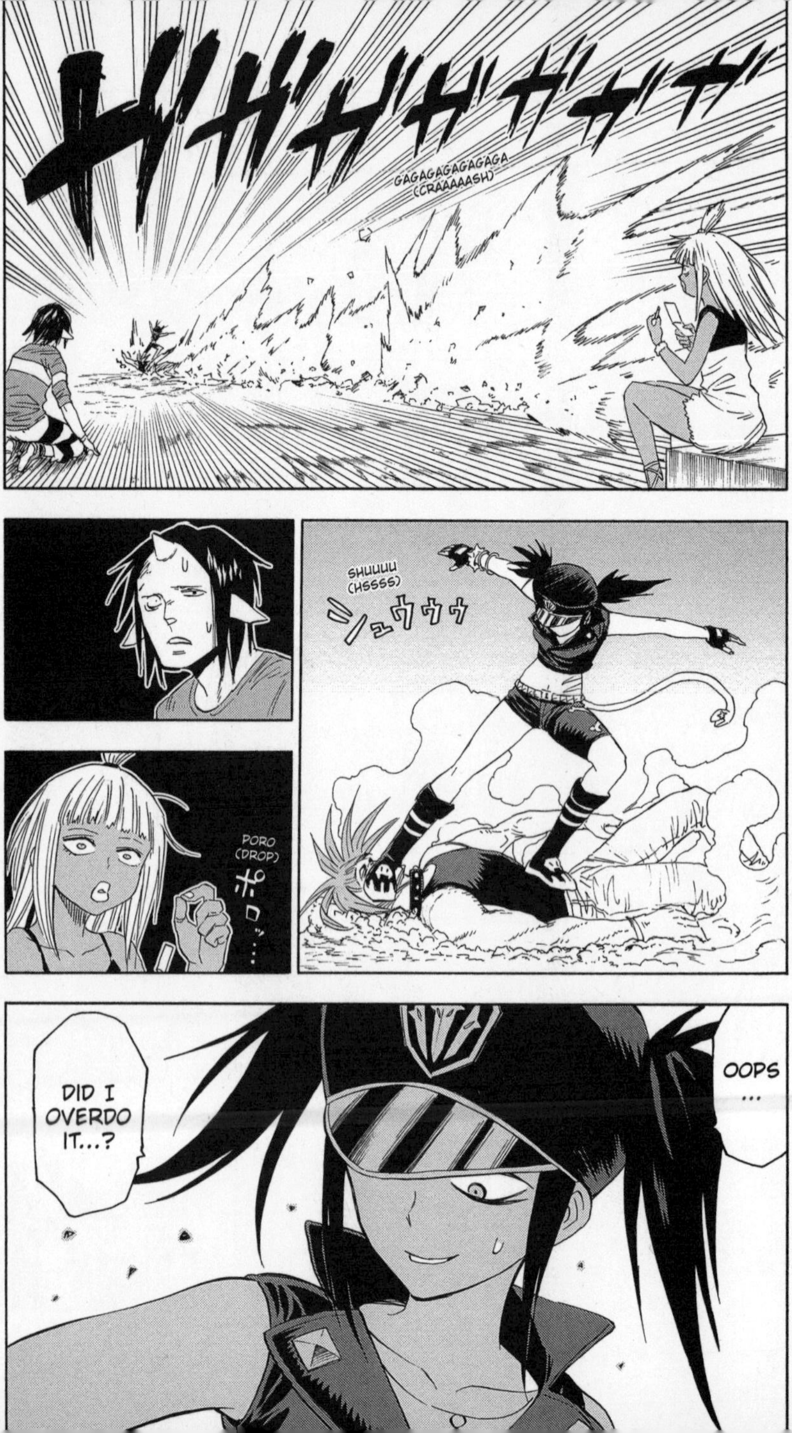
GAGAGAGAGAGAGA
(CRAAAAASH)
SHUUUU
(HSSSS)
シュウウウ
PORO
(DROP)
ポロッ…
OOPS
...
DID I OVERDO IT...?

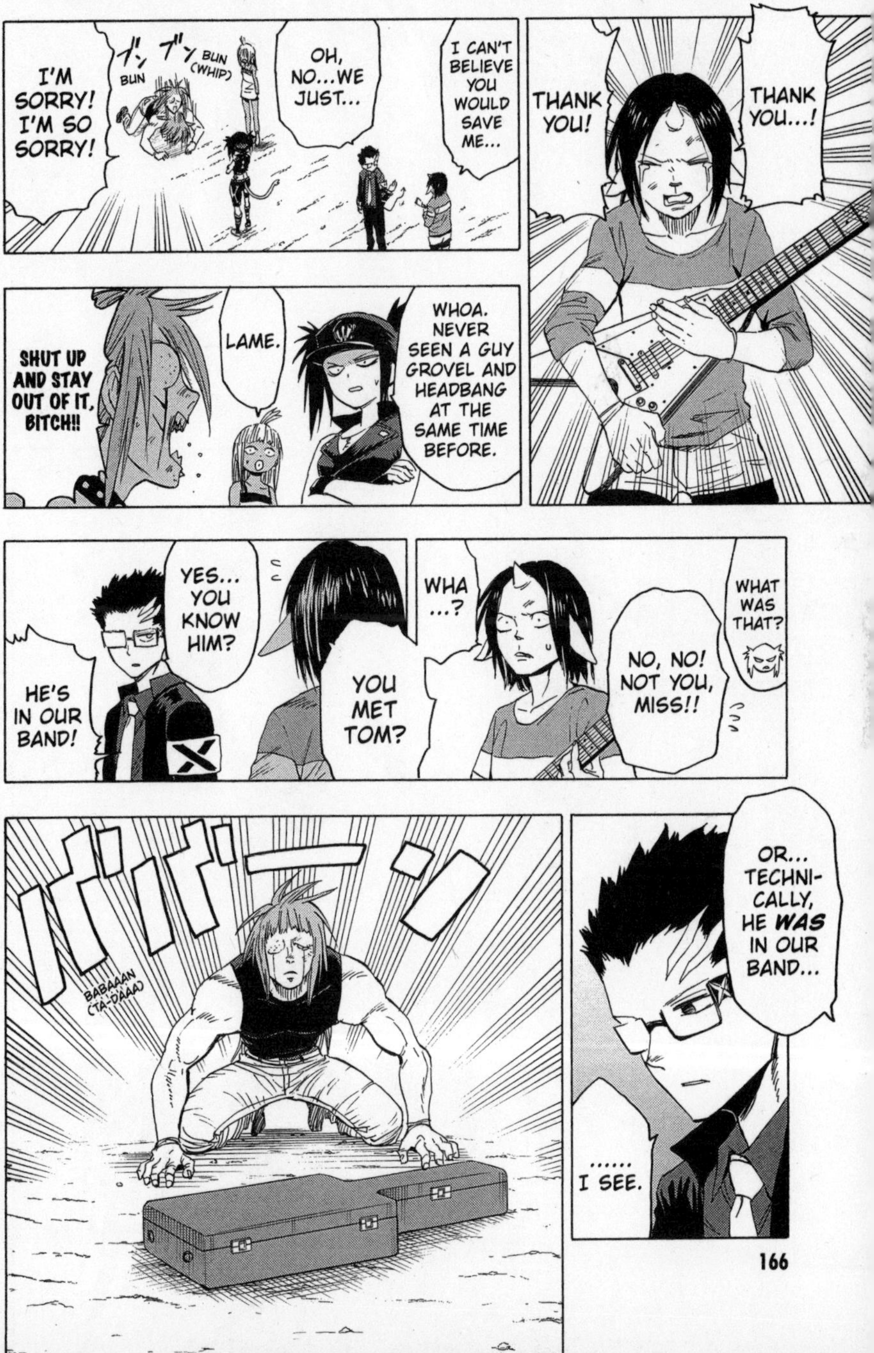
THANK YOU...!
THANK YOU!
I CAN'T BELIEVE YOU WOULD SAVE ME...
OH, NO...WE JUST...
BUN (WHIP)
BUN
I'M SORRY! I'M SO SORRY!
WHOA. NEVER SEEN A GUY GROVEL AND HEADBANG AT THE SAME TIME BEFORE.
LAME.
SHUT UP AND STAY OUT OF IT, BITCH!!
WHAT WAS THAT?
NO, NO! NOT YOU, MISS!!
WHA ...?
YOU MET TOM?
YES... YOU KNOW HIM?
HE'S IN OUR BAND!
OR... TECHNICALLY, HE *WAS* IN OUR BAND...
...... I SEE.
BABAAAN (TA-DAAA)

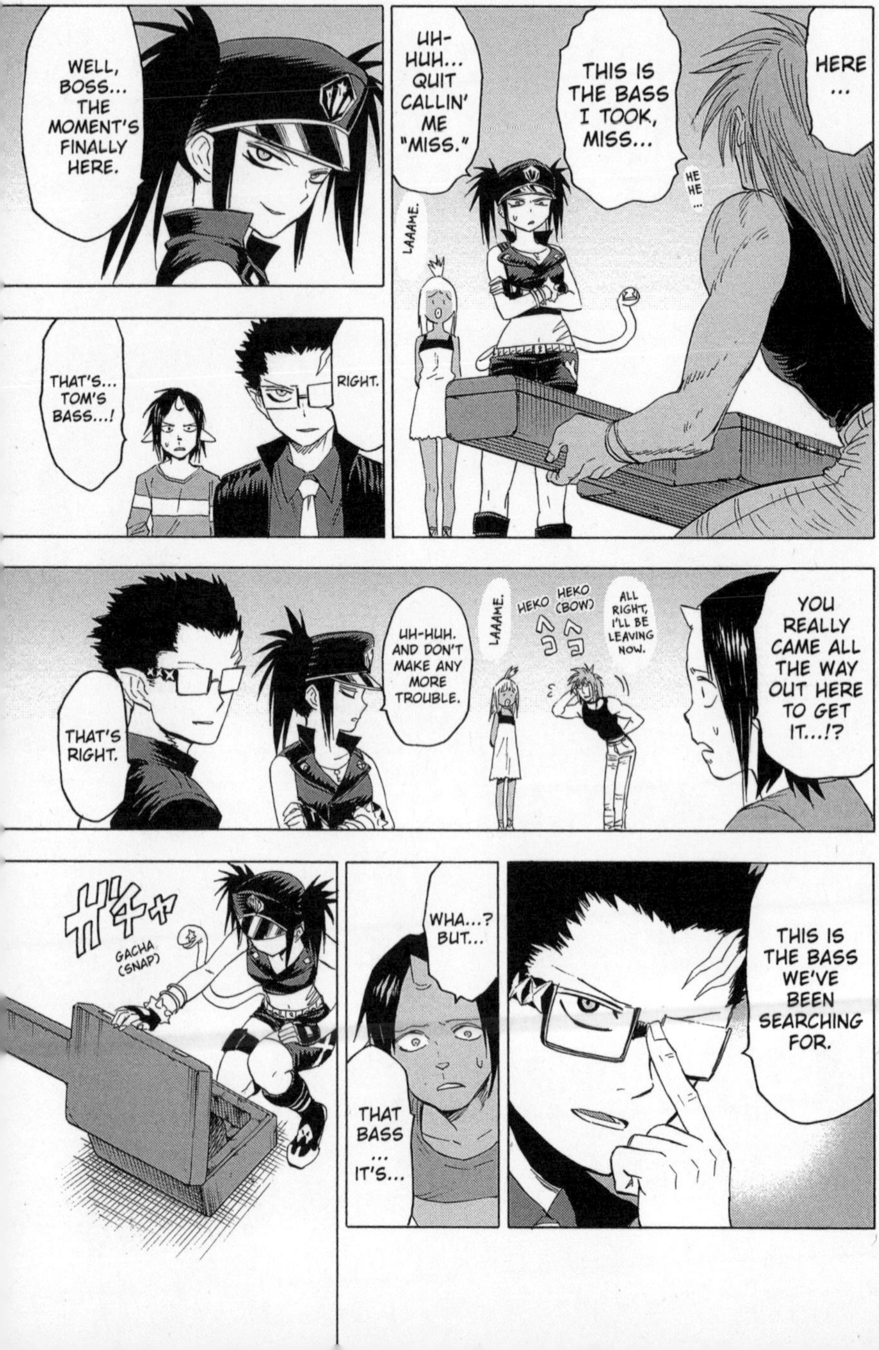
HERE ...
THIS IS THE BASS I TOOK, MISS...
HE HE ...
UH-HUH... QUIT CALLIN' ME "MISS."
LAAAME.
WELL, BOSS... THE MOMENT'S FINALLY HERE.
RIGHT.
THAT'S... TOM'S BASS...!
YOU REALLY CAME ALL THE WAY OUT HERE TO GET IT...!?
ALL RIGHT, I'LL BE LEAVING NOW.
HEKO HEKO (BOW)
LAAAME.
UH-HUH. AND DON'T MAKE ANY MORE TROUBLE.
THAT'S RIGHT.
THIS IS THE BASS WE'VE BEEN SEARCHING FOR.
WHA...? BUT...
THAT BASS ... IT'S...
ガチャ
GACHA (SNAP)

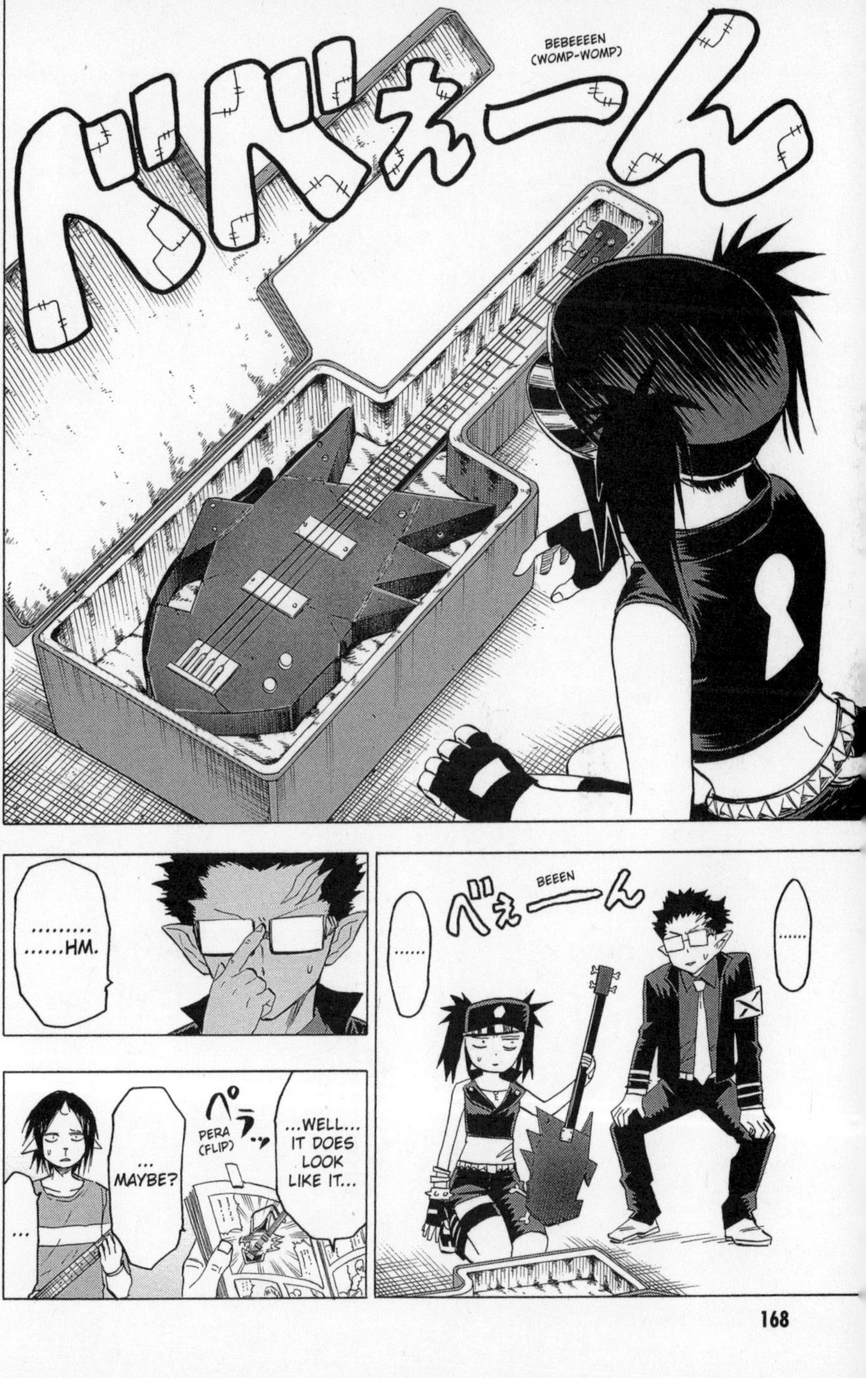
べべぇーん
BEBEEEEN (WOMP-WOMP)
......
べぇーん
BEEEN
......
....
......HM.
...WELL... IT DOES LOOK LIKE IT...
ペラ
PERA (FLIP)
... MAYBE?
...

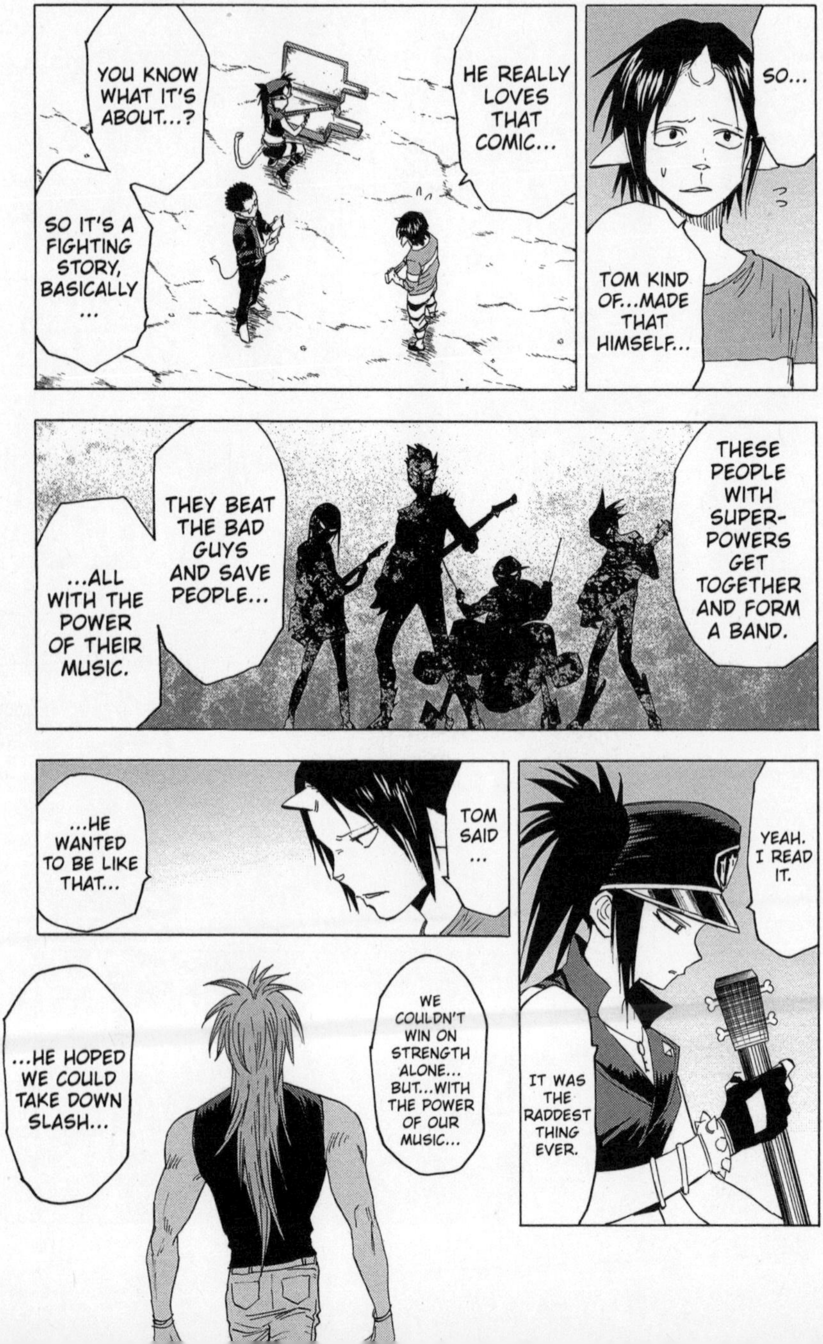
SO...
TOM KIND OF...MADE THAT HIMSELF...
HE REALLY LOVES THAT COMIC...
YOU KNOW WHAT IT'S ABOUT...?
SO IT'S A FIGHTING STORY, BASICALLY ...
THESE PEOPLE WITH SUPER-POWERS GET TOGETHER AND FORM A BAND.
THEY BEAT THE BAD GUYS AND SAVE PEOPLE...
...ALL WITH THE POWER OF THEIR MUSIC.
YEAH. I READ IT.
IT WAS THE RADDEST THING EVER.
TOM SAID ...
...HE WANTED TO BE LIKE THAT...
WE COULDN'T WIN ON STRENGTH ALONE... BUT...WITH THE POWER OF OUR MUSIC...
...HE HOPED WE COULD TAKE DOWN SLASH...

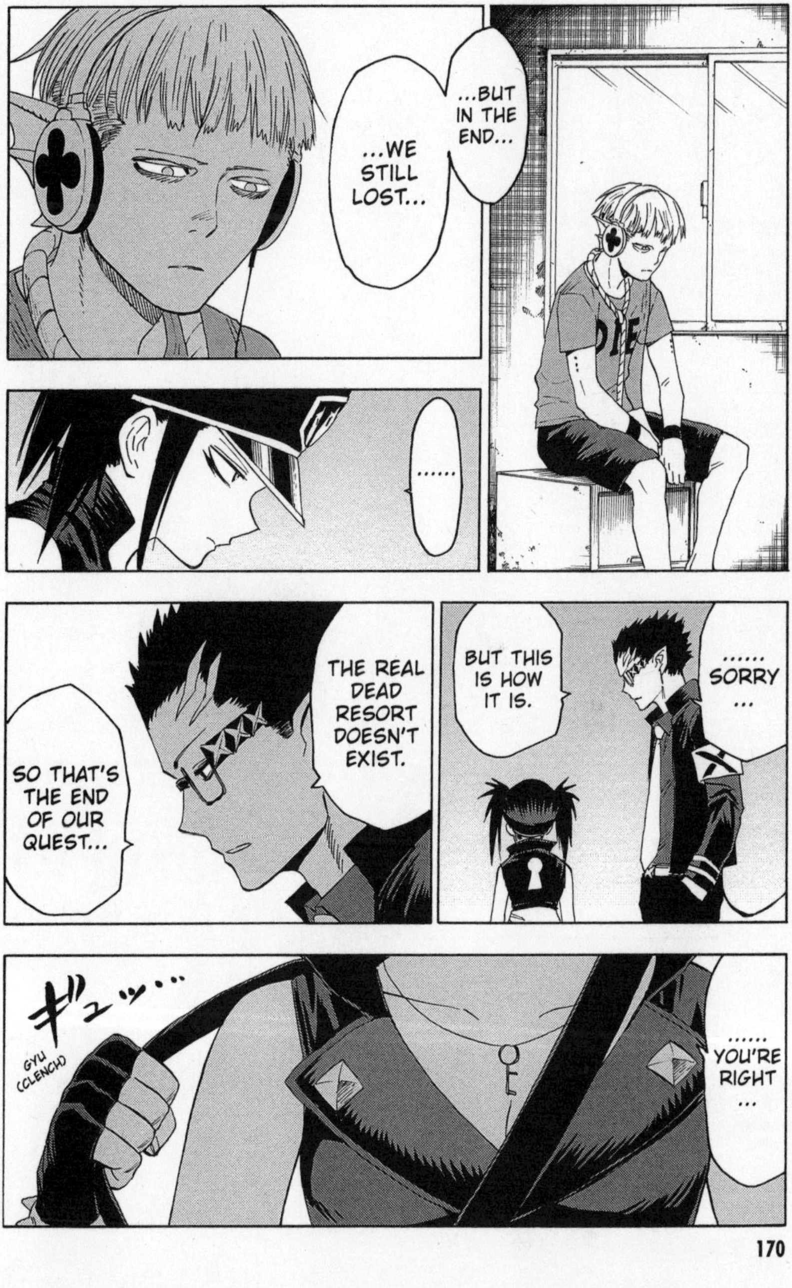
...BUT IN THE END...
...WE STILL LOST...
......
......SORRY...
BUT THIS IS HOW IT IS.
THE REAL DEAD RESORT DOESN'T EXIST.
SO THAT'S THE END OF OUR QUEST...
......YOU'RE RIGHT...
ギュッ...
GYU (CLENCH)

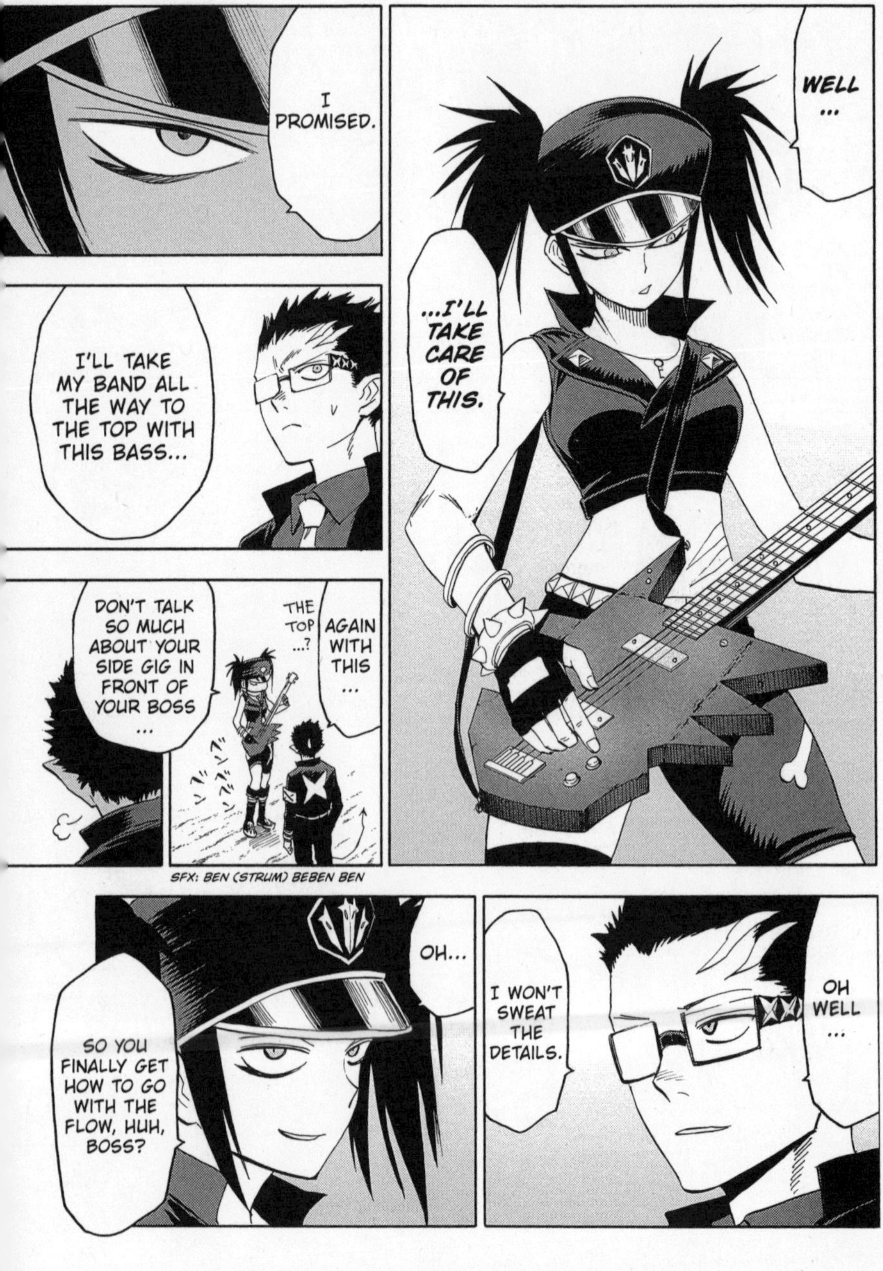
WELL...
...I'LL TAKE CARE OF THIS.
I PROMISED.
I'LL TAKE MY BAND ALL THE WAY TO THE TOP WITH THIS BASS...
AGAIN WITH THIS...
THE TOP...?
DON'T TALK SO MUCH ABOUT YOUR SIDE GIG IN FRONT OF YOUR BOSS...
SFX: BEN (STRUM) BEBEN BEN
OH WELL...
I WON'T SWEAT THE DETAILS.
OH...
SO YOU FINALLY GET HOW TO GO WITH THE FLOW, HUH, BOSS?

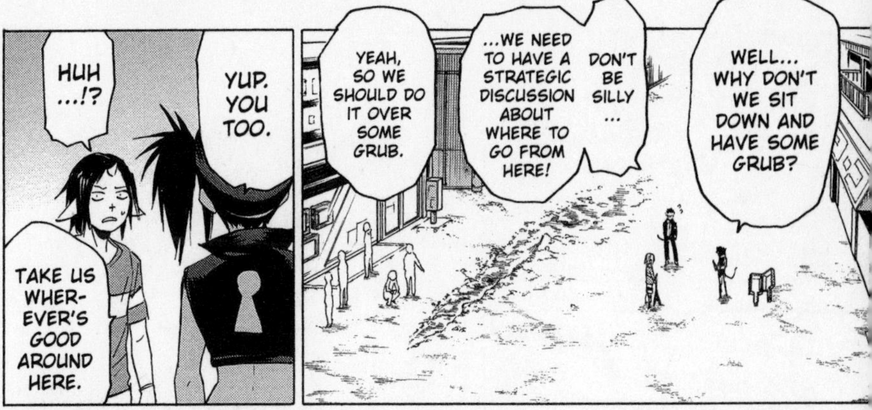
WELL... WHY DON'T WE SIT DOWN AND HAVE SOME GRUB?
DON'T BE SILLY ...
...WE NEED TO HAVE A STRATEGIC DISCUSSION ABOUT WHERE TO GO FROM HERE!
YEAH, SO WE SHOULD DO IT OVER SOME GRUB.
YUP. YOU TOO.
HUH ...!?
TAKE US WHEREVER'S GOOD AROUND HERE.

SCREEN: DEMONTV

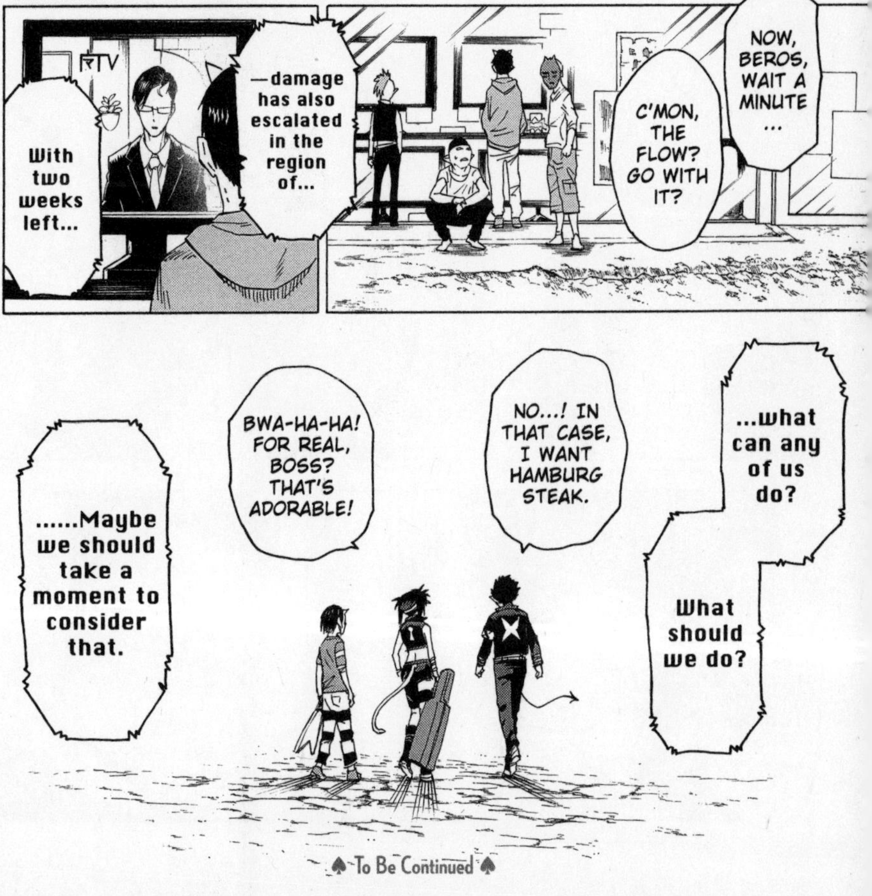
NOW, BEROS, WAIT A MINUTE ...
C'MON, THE FLOW? GO WITH IT?
RTV
—damage has also escalated in the region of...
With two weeks left...
...what can any of us do?
What should we do?
NO...! IN THAT CASE, I WANT HAMBURG STEAK.
BWA-HA-HA! FOR REAL, BOSS? THAT'S ADORABLE!
......Maybe we should take a moment to consider that.

♠ To Be Continued ♠

To Be Continued

BLOOD LAD

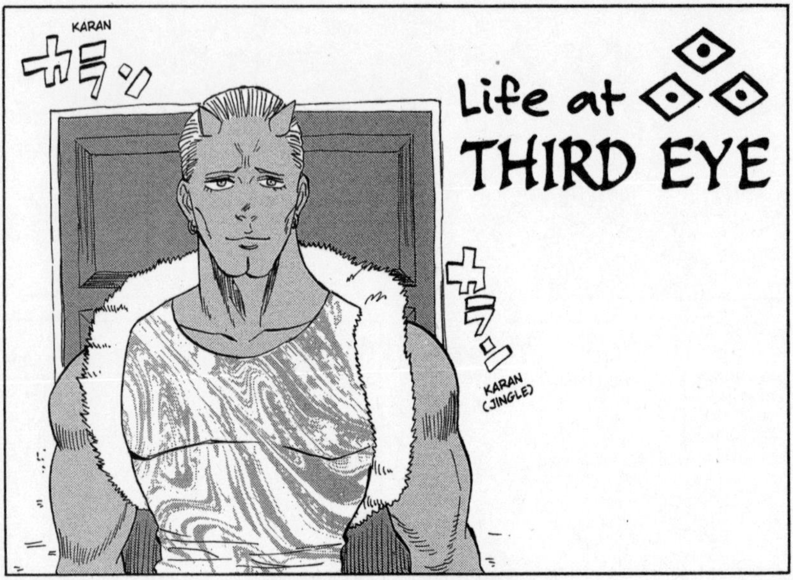
KARAN
カラン
Life at THIRD EYE
カラン
KARAN (JINGLE)

AN OGRE ARRIVES

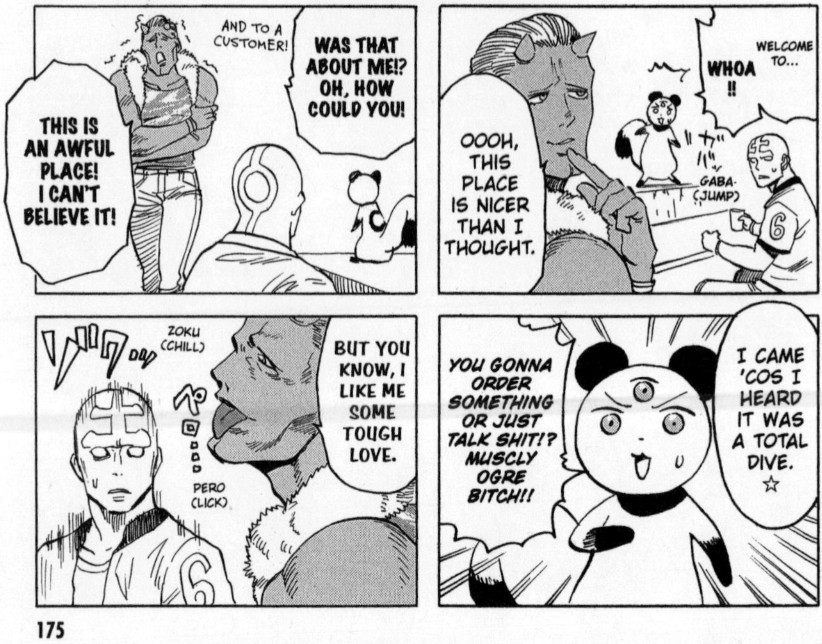
WELCOME TO...
WHOA !!
GABA (JUMP)
OOOH, THIS PLACE IS NICER THAN I THOUGHT.
WAS THAT ABOUT ME!? OH, HOW COULD YOU!
AND TO A CUSTOMER!
THIS IS AN AWFUL PLACE! I CAN'T BELIEVE IT!
I CAME 'COS I HEARD IT WAS A TOTAL DIVE. ☆
YOU GONNA ORDER SOMETHING OR JUST TALK SHIT!? MUSCLY OGRE BITCH!!
BUT YOU KNOW, I LIKE ME SOME TOUGH LOVE.
ZOKU (CHILL)
PERO (LICK)

THE OGRE LIKES IT

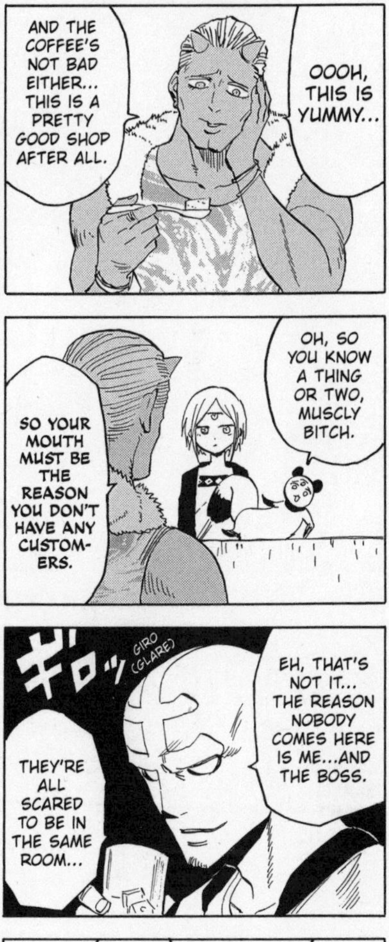
OOOH, THIS IS YUMMY...
AND THE COFFEE'S NOT BAD EITHER... THIS IS A PRETTY GOOD SHOP AFTER ALL.
OH, SO YOU KNOW A THING OR TWO, MUSCLY BITCH.
SO YOUR MOUTH MUST BE THE REASON YOU DON'T HAVE ANY CUSTOM-ERS.
EH, THAT'S NOT IT... THE REASON NOBODY COMES HERE IS ME...AND THE BOSS.
GIRO (GLARE)
THEY'RE ALL SCARED TO BE IN THE SAME ROOM...
HMM... I'M NOT SCARED.
BACCHIN (WINK)
IN FACT... YOU JUST HAPPEN TO BE MY TYPE.
ZO (SHIVER)
ZO
ZO

THE OGRE ATTACKS (PHYSICAL)

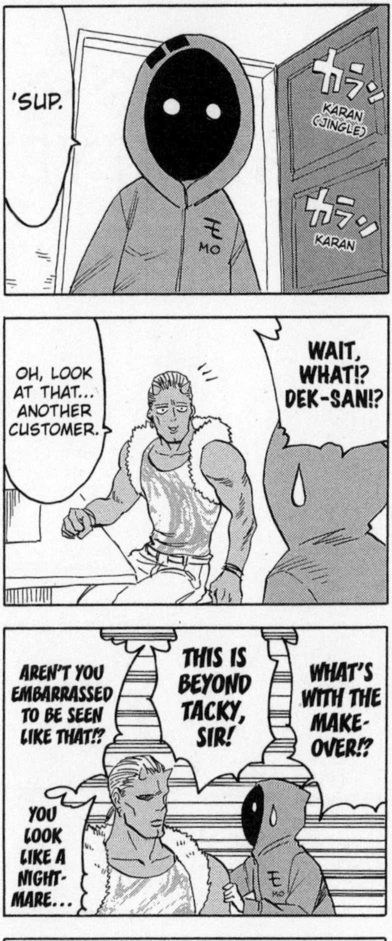
KARAN (JINGLE)
KARAN
MO
'SUP.
WAIT, WHAT!? DEK-SAN!?
OH, LOOK AT THAT... ANOTHER CUSTOMER.
WHAT'S WITH THE MAKE-OVER!?
THIS IS BEYOND TACKY, SIR!
AREN'T YOU EMBARRASSED TO BE SEEN LIKE THAT!?
YOU LOOK LIKE A NIGHT-MARE...
MO
ZURU (SLIDE)
GAKU (SHAKE)
GAKU

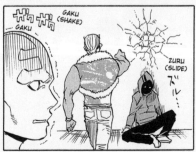

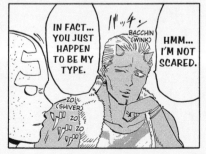

THE OGRE ATTACKS (MENTAL)

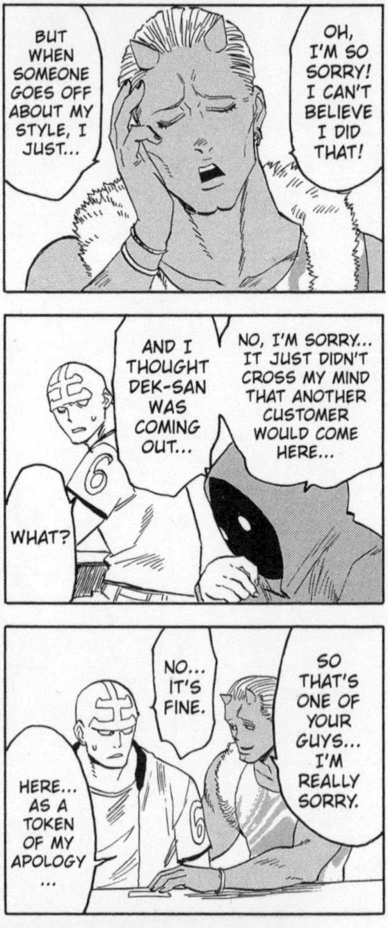
OH, I'M SO SORRY! I CAN'T BELIEVE I DID THAT!
BUT WHEN SOMEONE GOES OFF ABOUT MY STYLE, I JUST...
NO, I'M SORRY... IT JUST DIDN'T CROSS MY MIND THAT ANOTHER CUSTOMER WOULD COME HERE...
AND I THOUGHT DEK-SAN WAS COMING OUT...
WHAT?
SO THAT'S ONE OF YOUR GUYS... I'M REALLY SORRY.
NO... IT'S FINE.
HERE... AS A TOKEN OF MY APOLOGY ...
DAKU ダクダク
DAKU (SWEAT)
MY PHONE NUMBER. ♥

EVERYONE IS AN OGRE

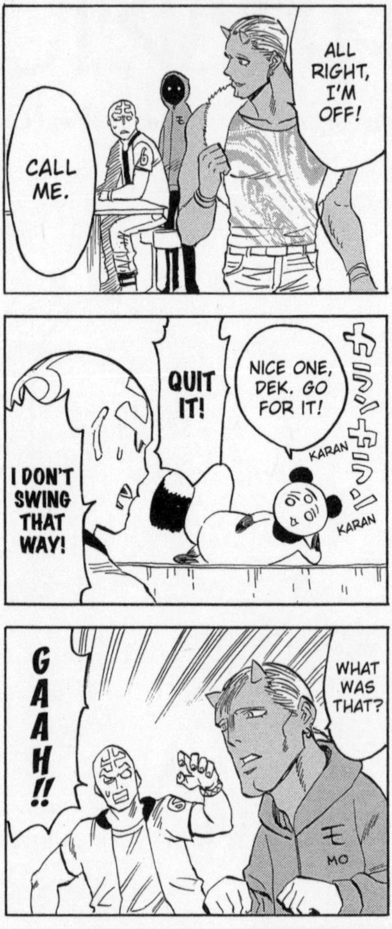
ALL RIGHT, I'M OFF!
CALL ME.
カランカラン
KARAN
KARAN
NICE ONE, DEK. GO FOR IT!
QUIT IT!
I DON'T SWING THAT WAY!
WHAT WAS THAT?
GAAH!!
モ
MO
AH-HA-HA-HA!! I'VE DISCOVERED YOUR WEAKNESS, DEK-SAN!!
LET'S SEND HIM A TEXT FROM DEK.
YO-SHIDA... WHY YOU!!

END

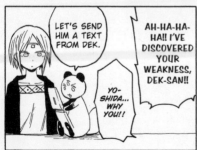

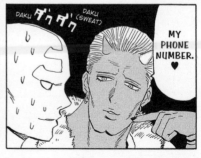

BLOOD LAD 13

These images appeared under the jacket of the original edition of *Blood Lad*!

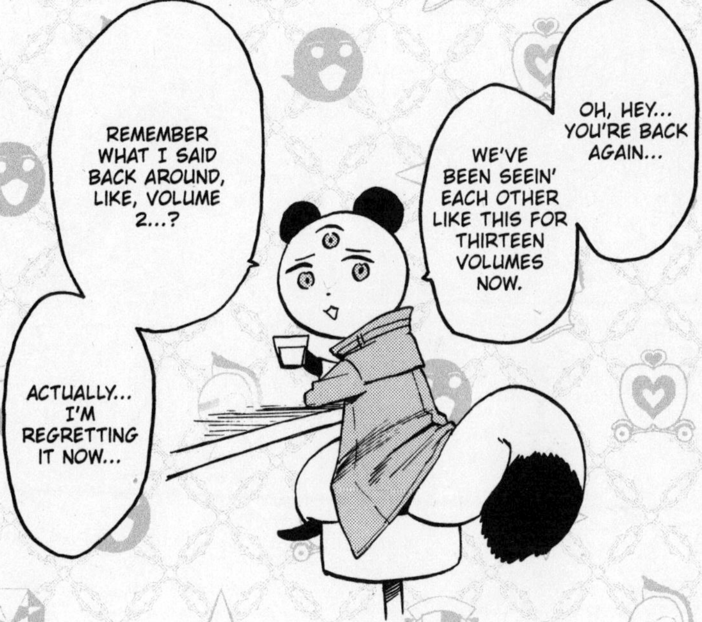
OH, HEY... YOU'RE BACK AGAIN...
WE'VE BEEN SEEIN' EACH OTHER LIKE THIS FOR THIRTEEN VOLUMES NOW.
REMEMBER WHAT I SAID BACK AROUND, LIKE, VOLUME 2...?
ACTUALLY... I'M REGRETTING IT NOW...

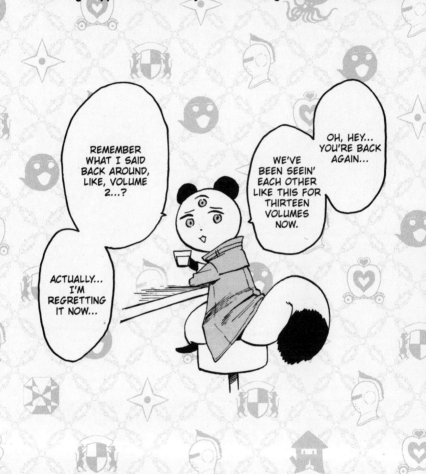

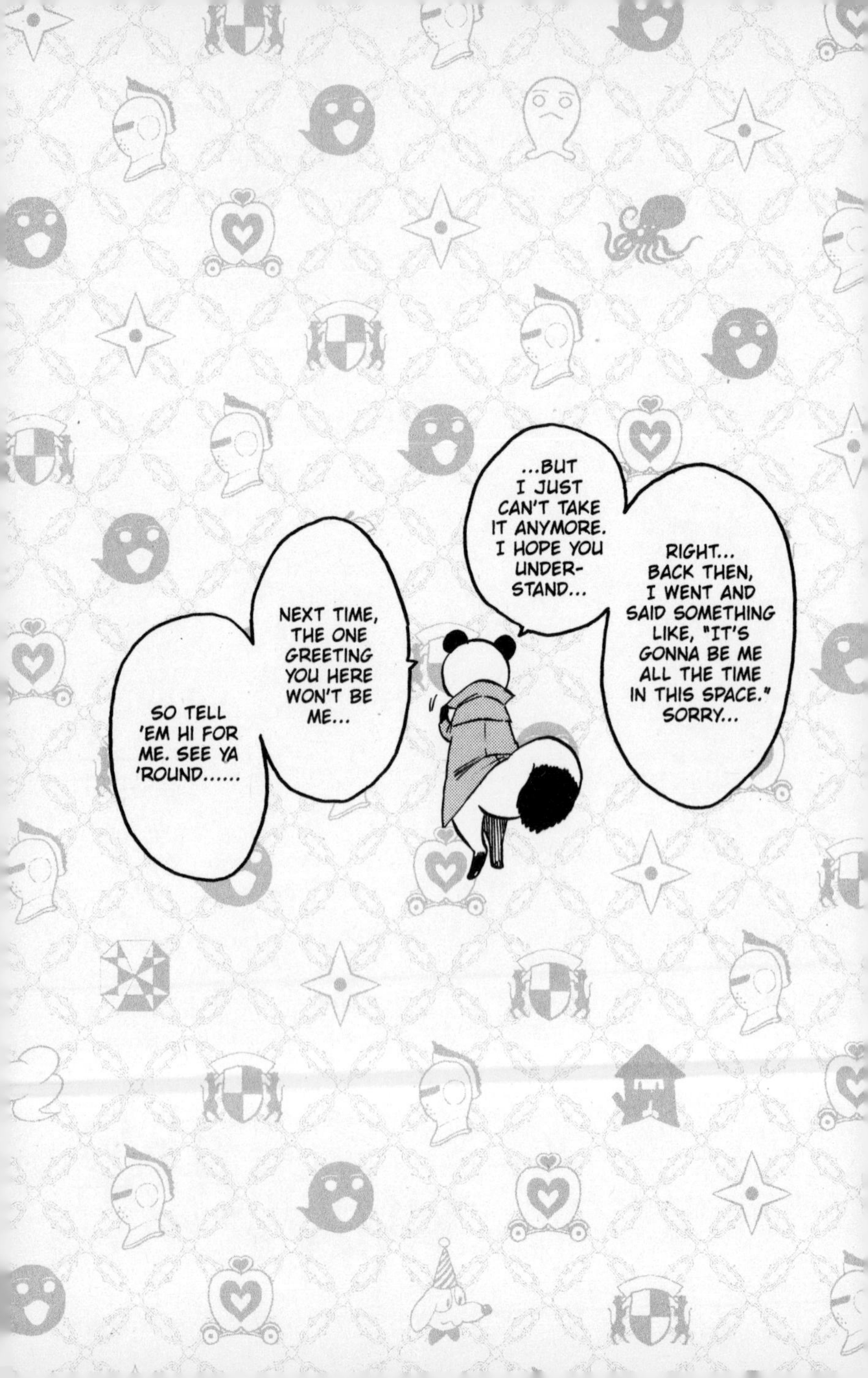
RIGHT... BACK THEN, I WENT AND SAID SOMETHING LIKE, "IT'S GONNA BE ME ALL THE TIME IN THIS SPACE." SORRY...
...BUT I JUST CAN'T TAKE IT ANYMORE. I HOPE YOU UNDER-STAND...
NEXT TIME, THE ONE GREETING YOU HERE WON'T BE ME...
SO TELL 'EM HI FOR ME. SEE YA 'ROUND......

BLOOD LAD

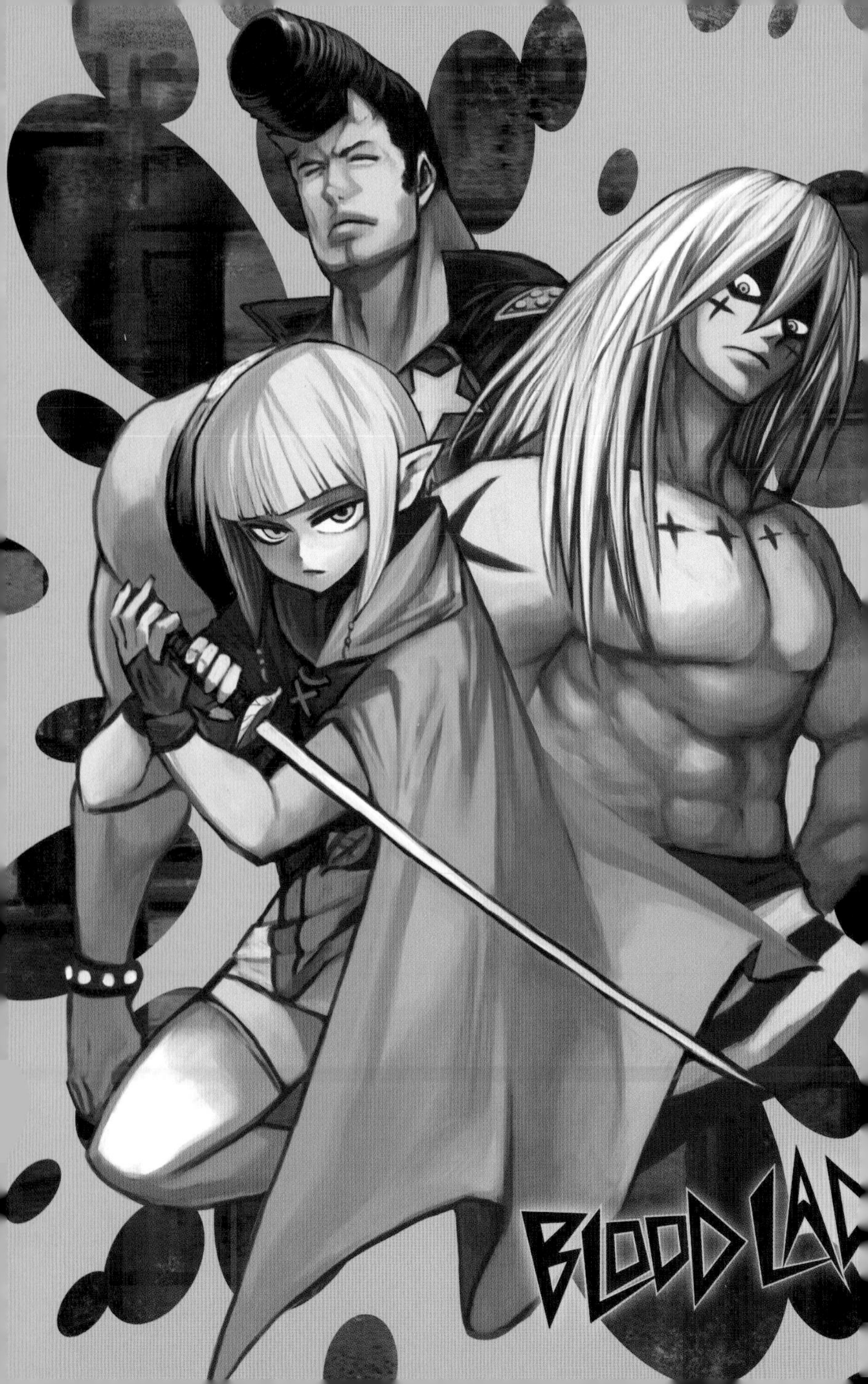
BLOOD LAD

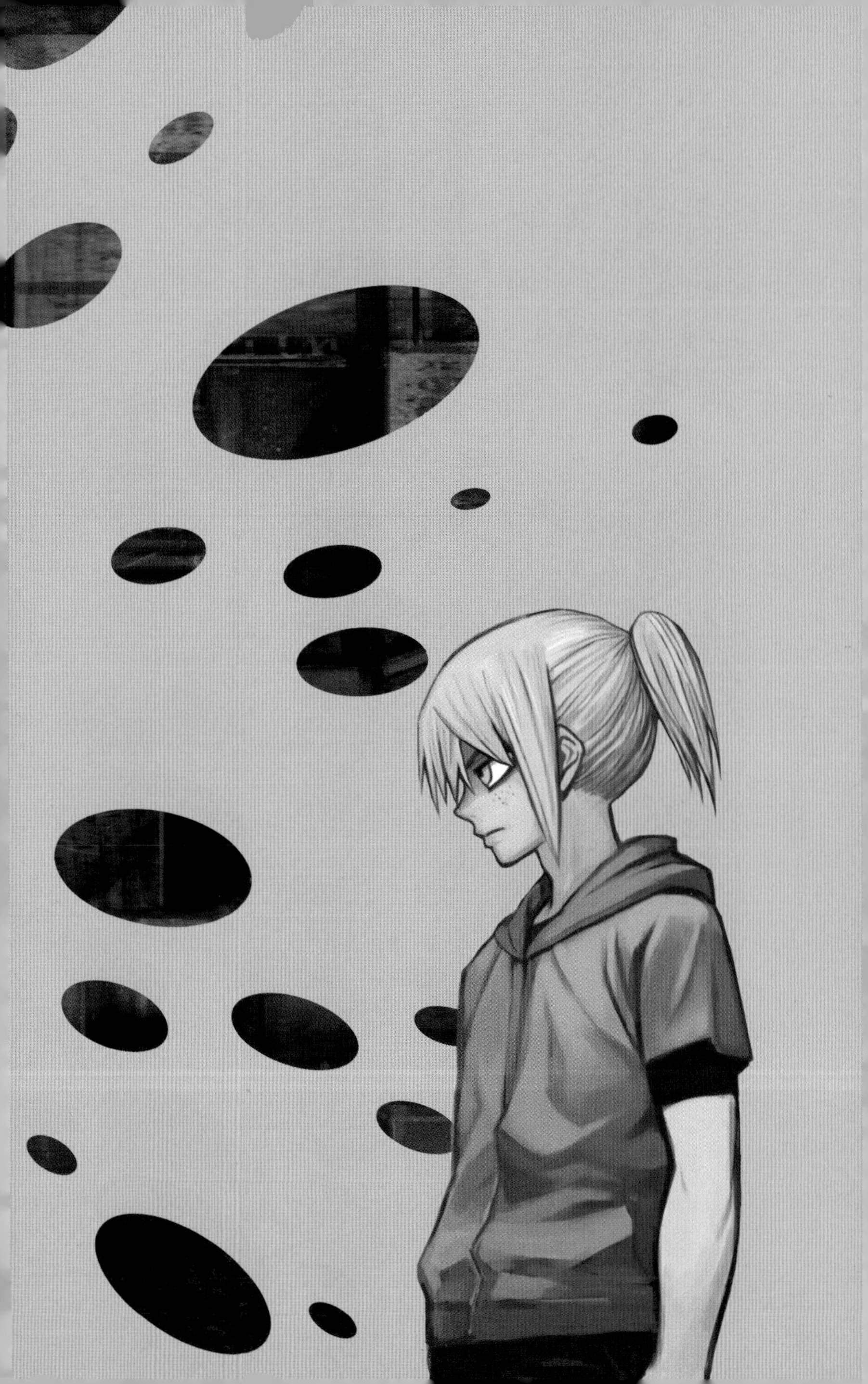

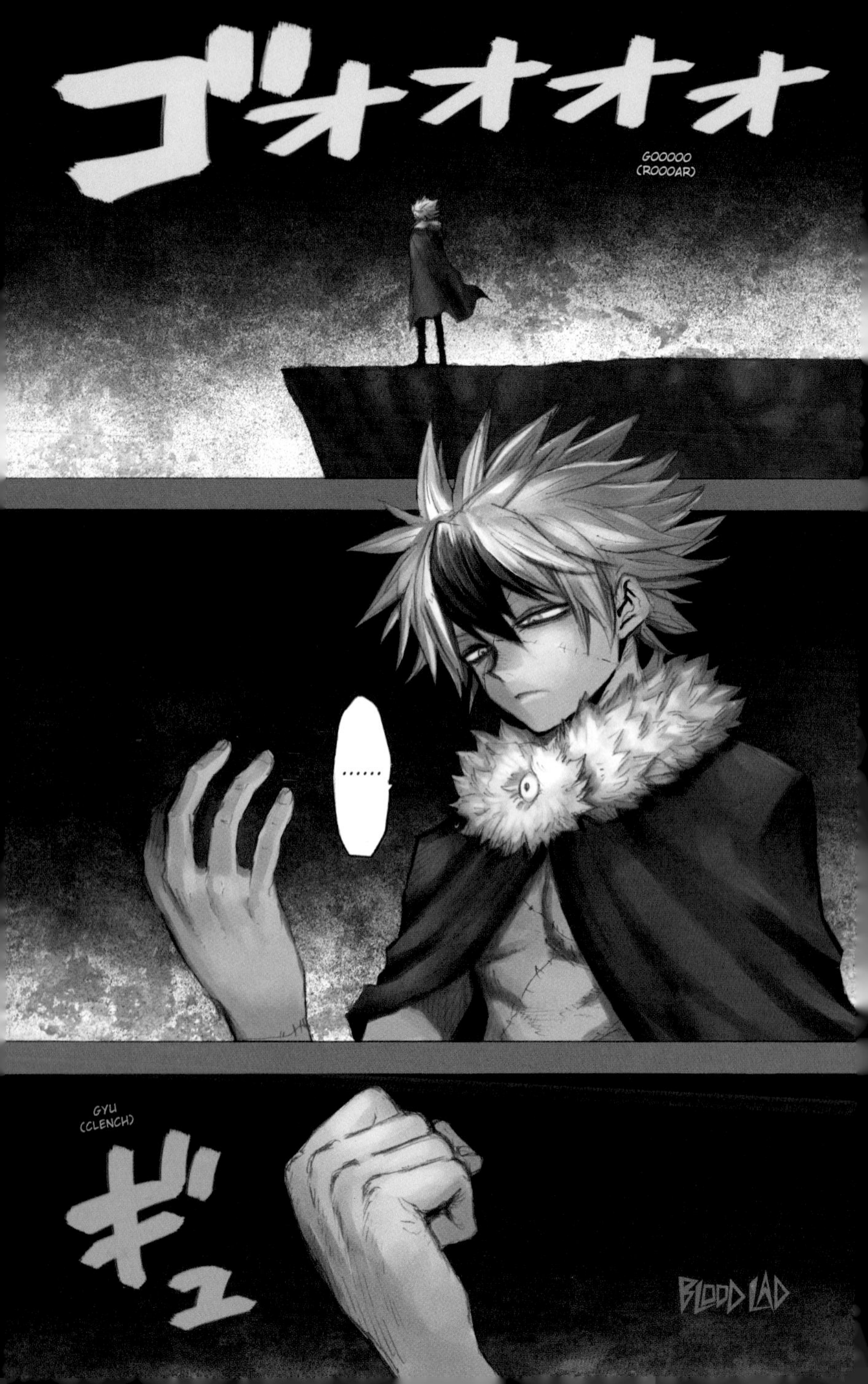
ゴオオオオオ
GOOOOO (ROOOAR)
......
GYU (CLENCH)
ギュ
BLOOD LAD

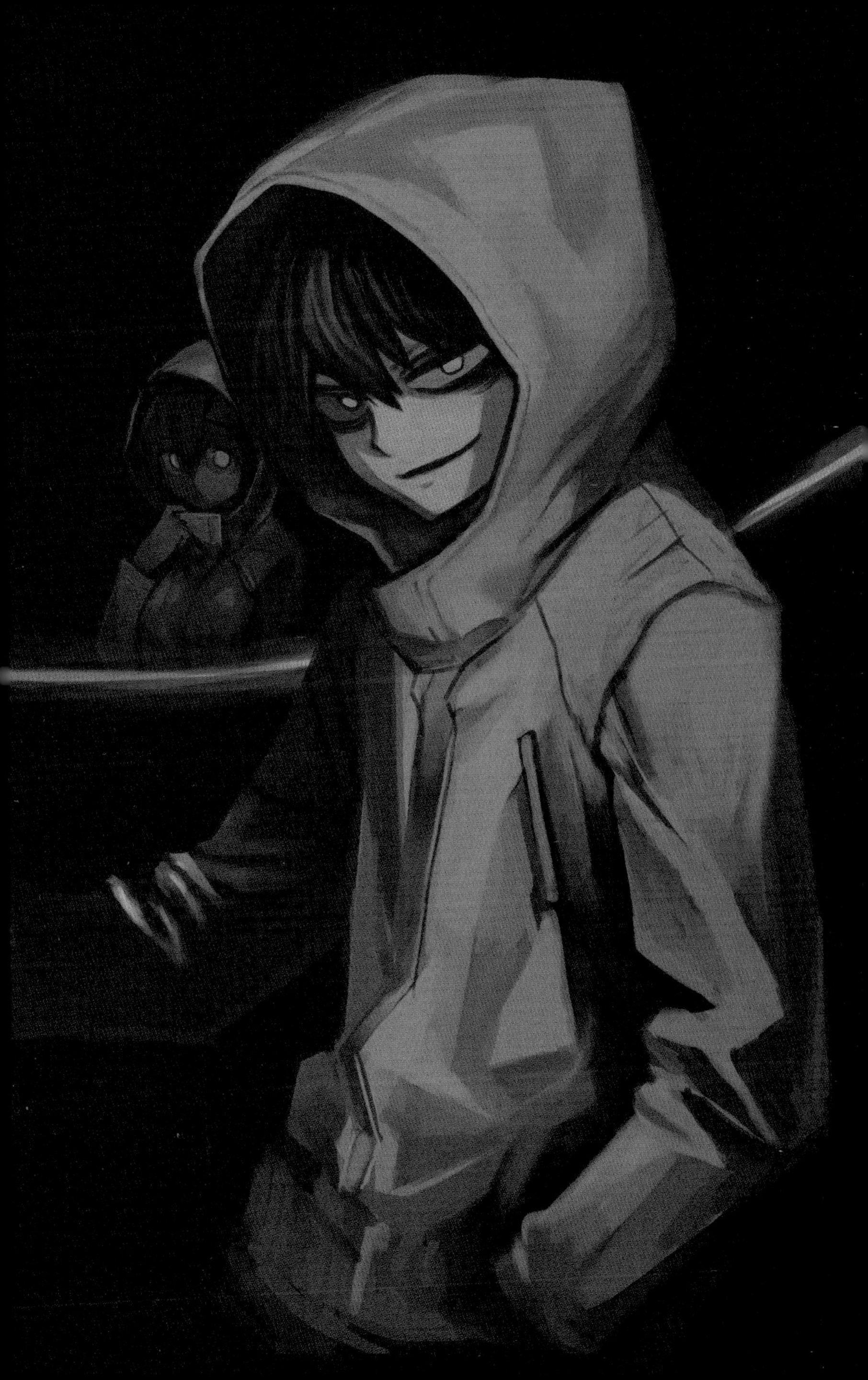

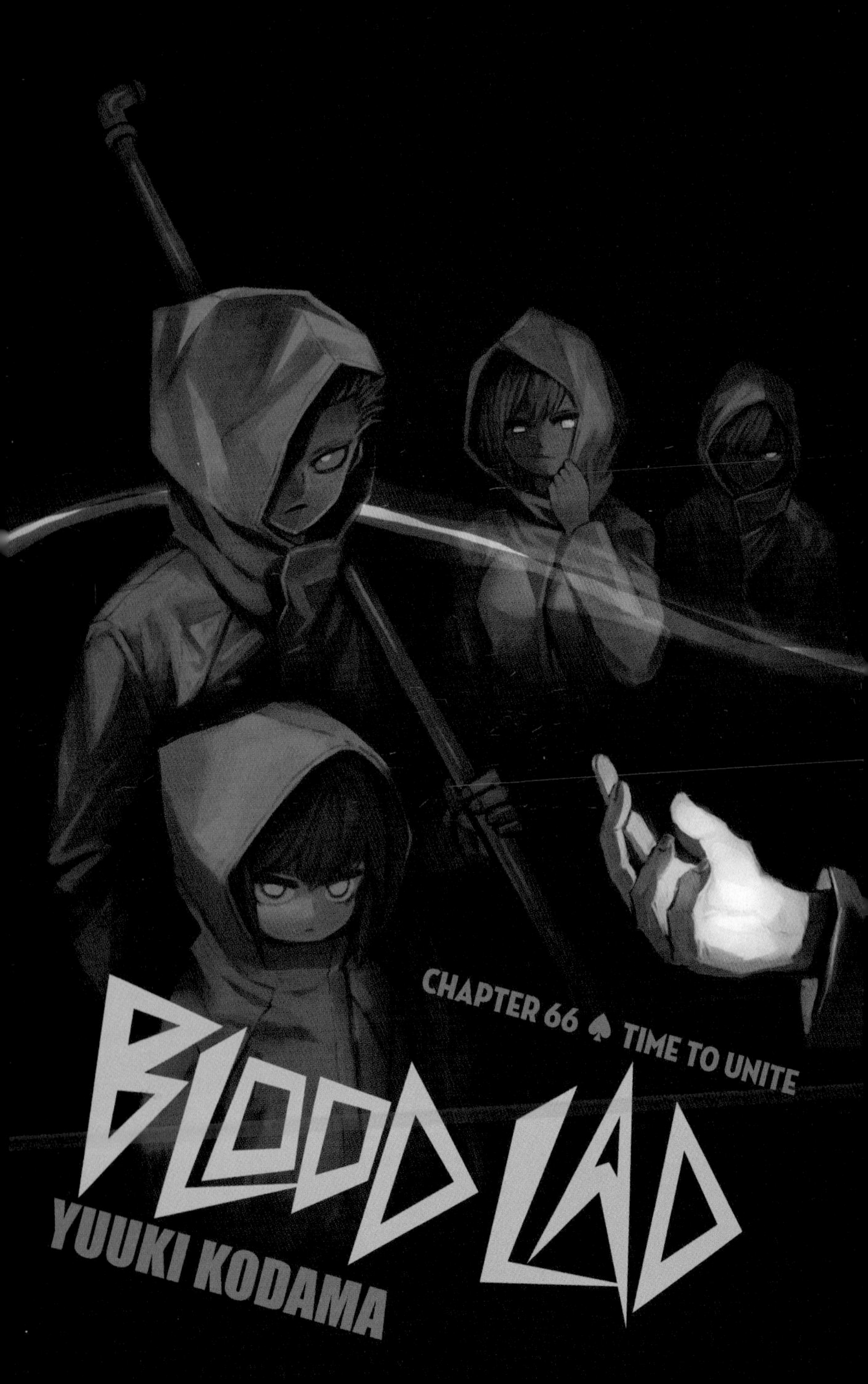
CHAPTER 66 ♠ TIME TO UNITE
BLOOD LAD
YUUKI KODAMA

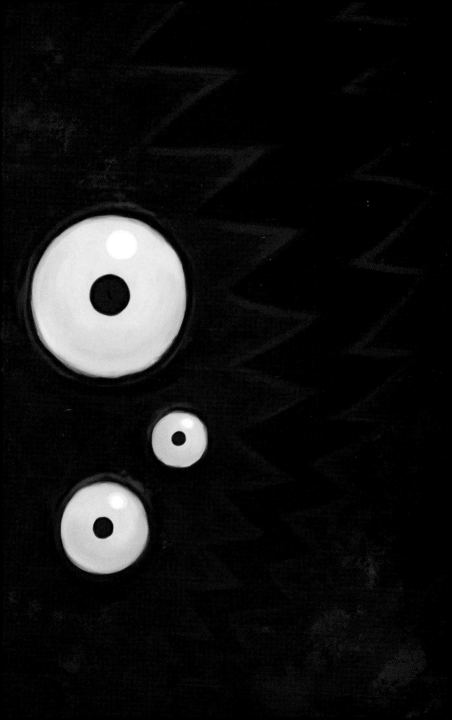

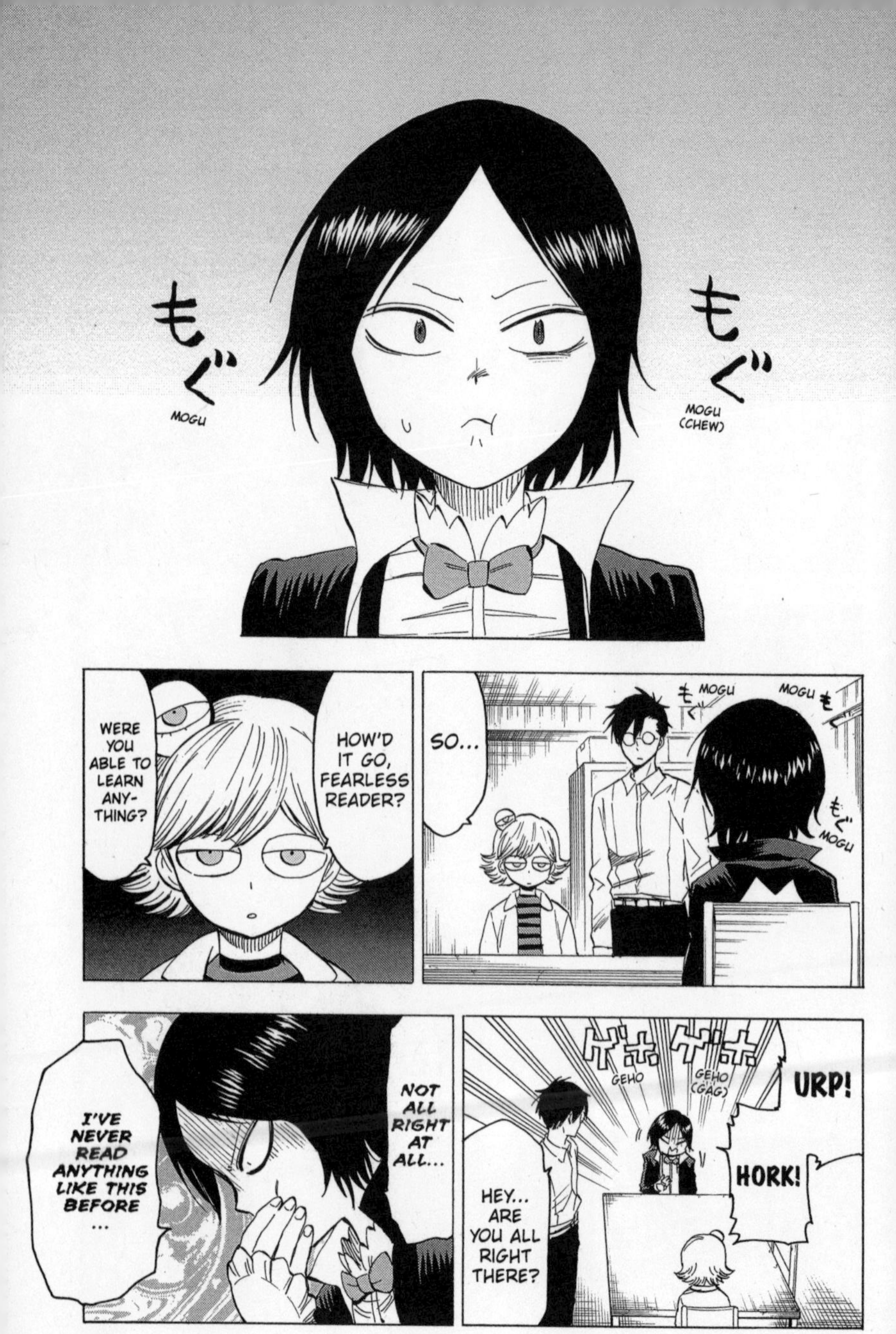
もぐ
MOGU (CHEW)
もぐ
MOGU
SO...
もぐ MOGU
もぐ MOGU
もぐ MOGU
HOW'D IT GO, FEARLESS READER?
WERE YOU ABLE TO LEARN ANYTHING?
URP!
HORK!
ゲホ GEHO (GAG)
ゲホ GEHO
HEY... ARE YOU ALL RIGHT THERE?
NOT ALL RIGHT AT ALL...
I'VE NEVER READ ANYTHING LIKE THIS BEFORE...

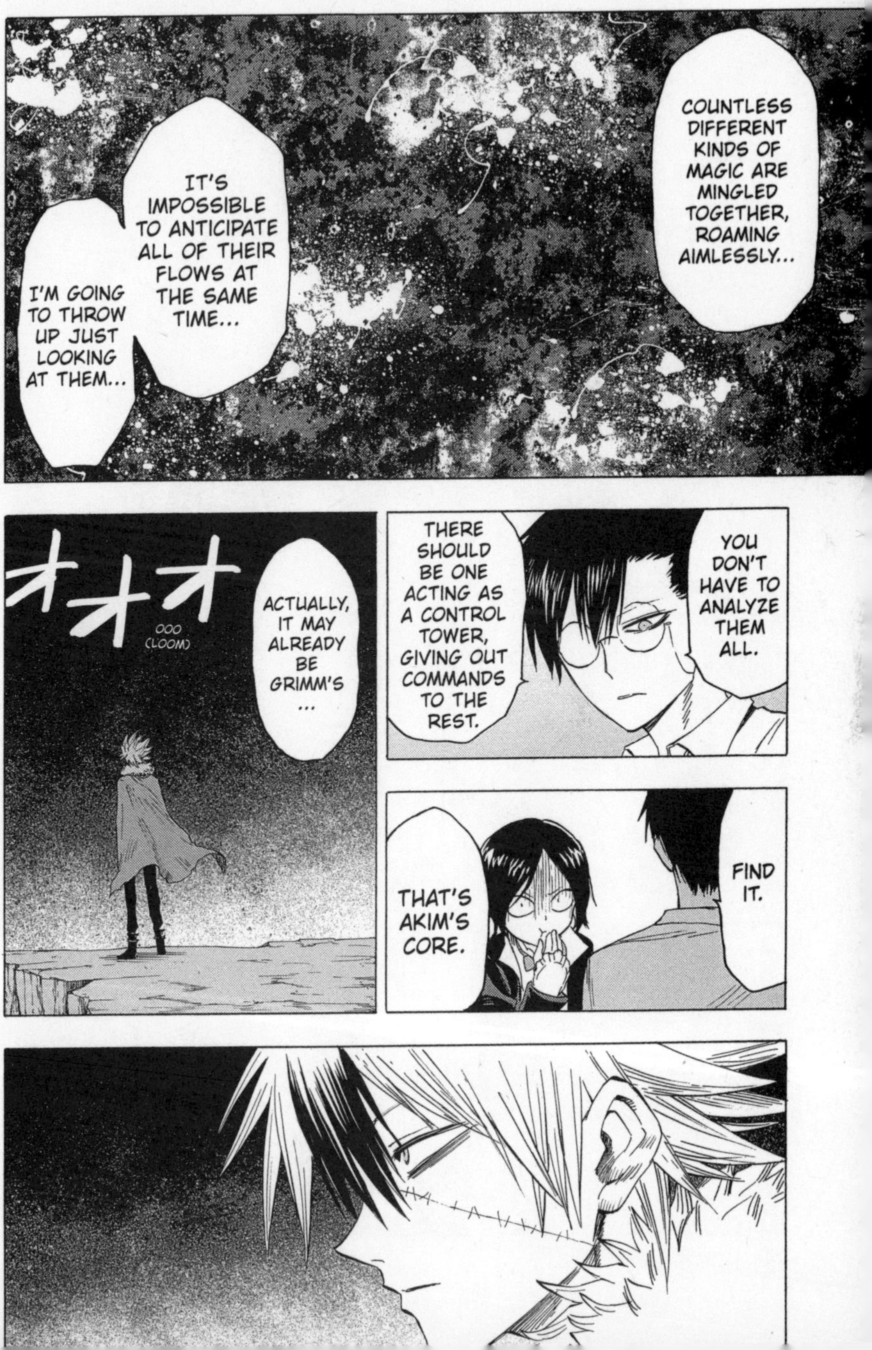
COUNTLESS DIFFERENT KINDS OF MAGIC ARE MINGLED TOGETHER, ROAMING AIMLESSLY...
IT'S IMPOSSIBLE TO ANTICIPATE ALL OF THEIR FLOWS AT THE SAME TIME...
I'M GOING TO THROW UP JUST LOOKING AT THEM...
YOU DON'T HAVE TO ANALYZE THEM ALL.
THERE SHOULD BE ONE ACTING AS A CONTROL TOWER, GIVING OUT COMMANDS TO THE REST.
FIND IT.
THAT'S AKIM'S CORE.
オオオ
OOO (LOOM)
ACTUALLY, IT MAY ALREADY BE GRIMM'S...

GOOOO
(ROOOAR)

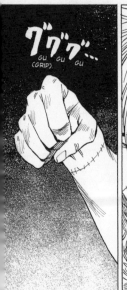

グググ..
GU GU GU
(GRIP)

ス..
SU
(LIFT)

BOKO
(GLOP)
BOKO

189

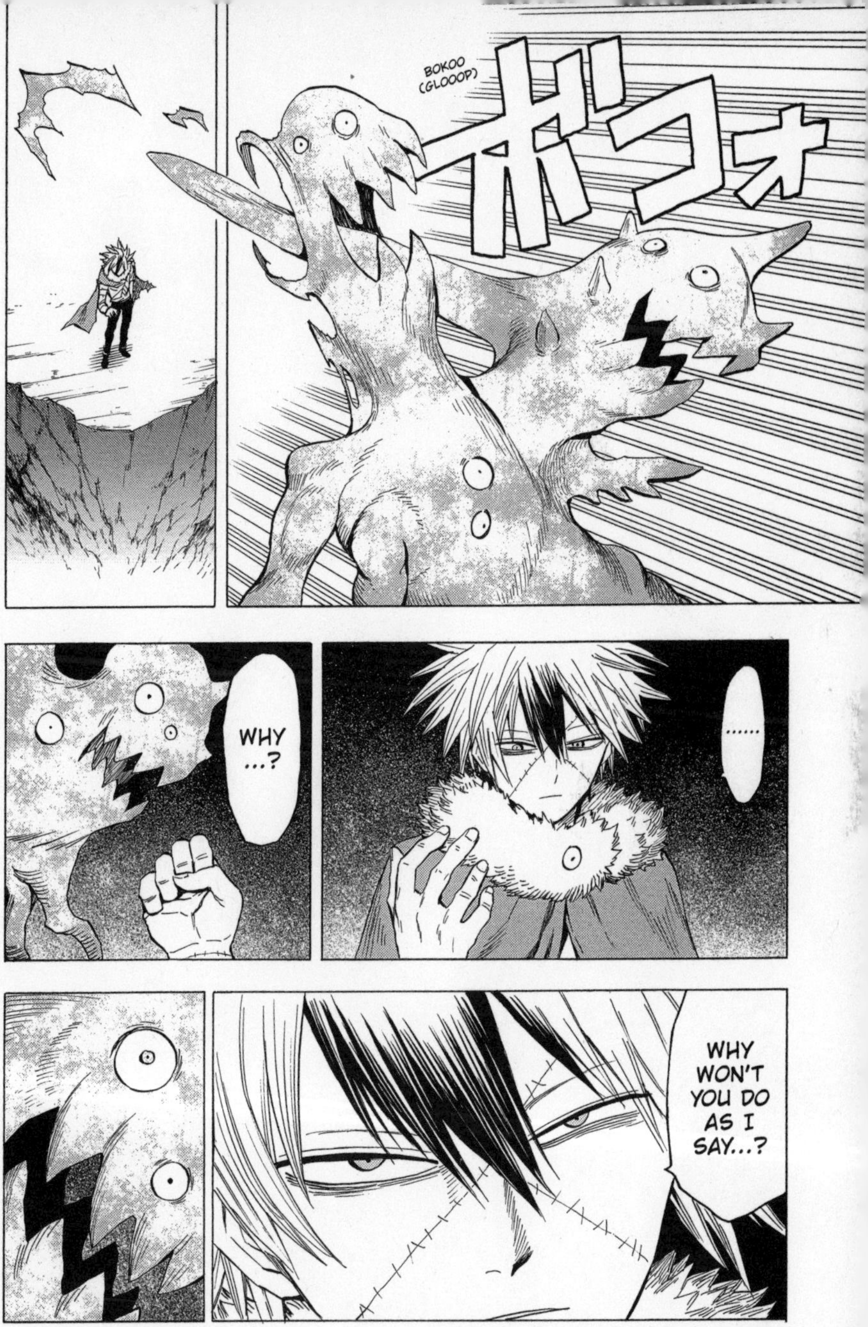
ボコォ
BOKOO (GLOOOP)
……
WHY …?
WHY WON'T YOU DO AS I SAY…?

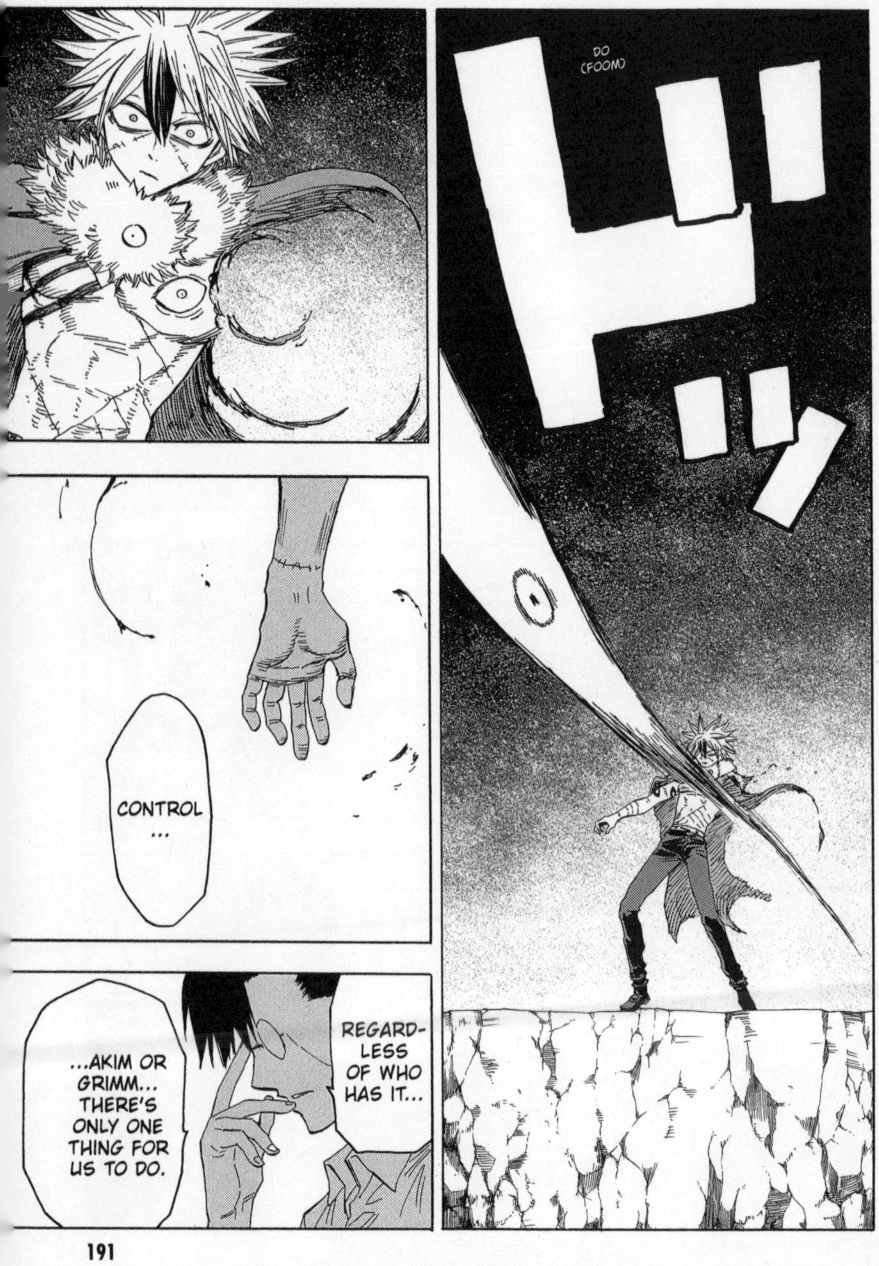
DO (FOOM)
CONTROL ...
REGARDLESS OF WHO HAS IT...
...AKIM OR GRIMM... THERE'S ONLY ONE THING FOR US TO DO.

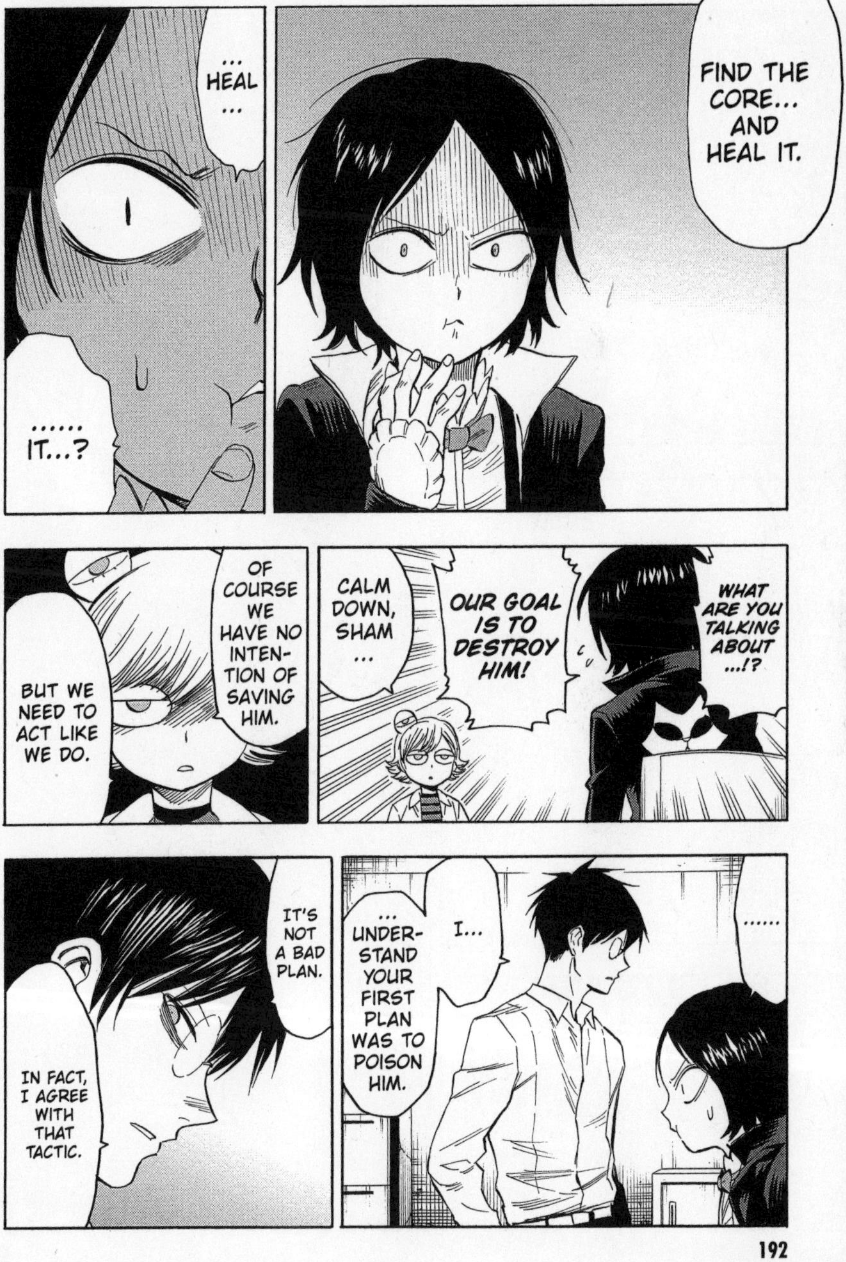
FIND THE CORE... AND HEAL IT.
... HEAL ...
...... IT...?
WHAT ARE YOU TALKING ABOUT ...!?
OUR GOAL IS TO DESTROY HIM!
CALM DOWN, SHAM ...
OF COURSE WE HAVE NO INTEN- TION OF SAVING HIM.
BUT WE NEED TO ACT LIKE WE DO.
......
I...
... UNDER- STAND YOUR FIRST PLAN WAS TO POISON HIM.
IT'S NOT A BAD PLAN.
IN FACT, I AGREE WITH THAT TACTIC.

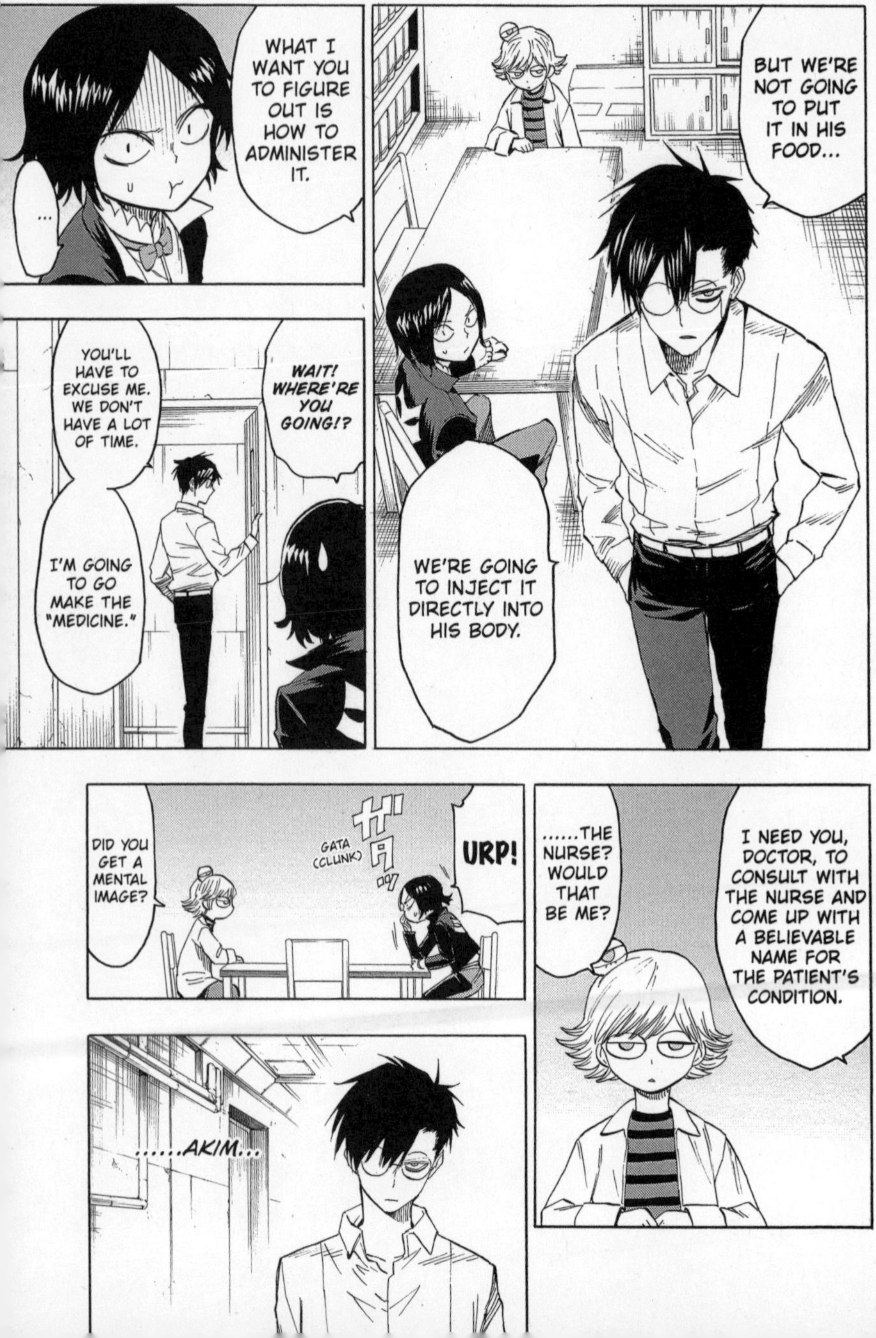
BUT WE'RE NOT GOING TO PUT IT IN HIS FOOD...
WE'RE GOING TO INJECT IT DIRECTLY INTO HIS BODY.
WHAT I WANT YOU TO FIGURE OUT IS HOW TO ADMINISTER IT.
...
WAIT! WHERE'RE YOU GOING!?
YOU'LL HAVE TO EXCUSE ME. WE DON'T HAVE A LOT OF TIME.
I'M GOING TO GO MAKE THE "MEDICINE."
I NEED YOU, DOCTOR, TO CONSULT WITH THE NURSE AND COME UP WITH A BELIEVABLE NAME FOR THE PATIENT'S CONDITION.
......THE NURSE? WOULD THAT BE ME?
URP!
GATA (CLUNK)
DID YOU GET A MENTAL IMAGE?
......AKIM...

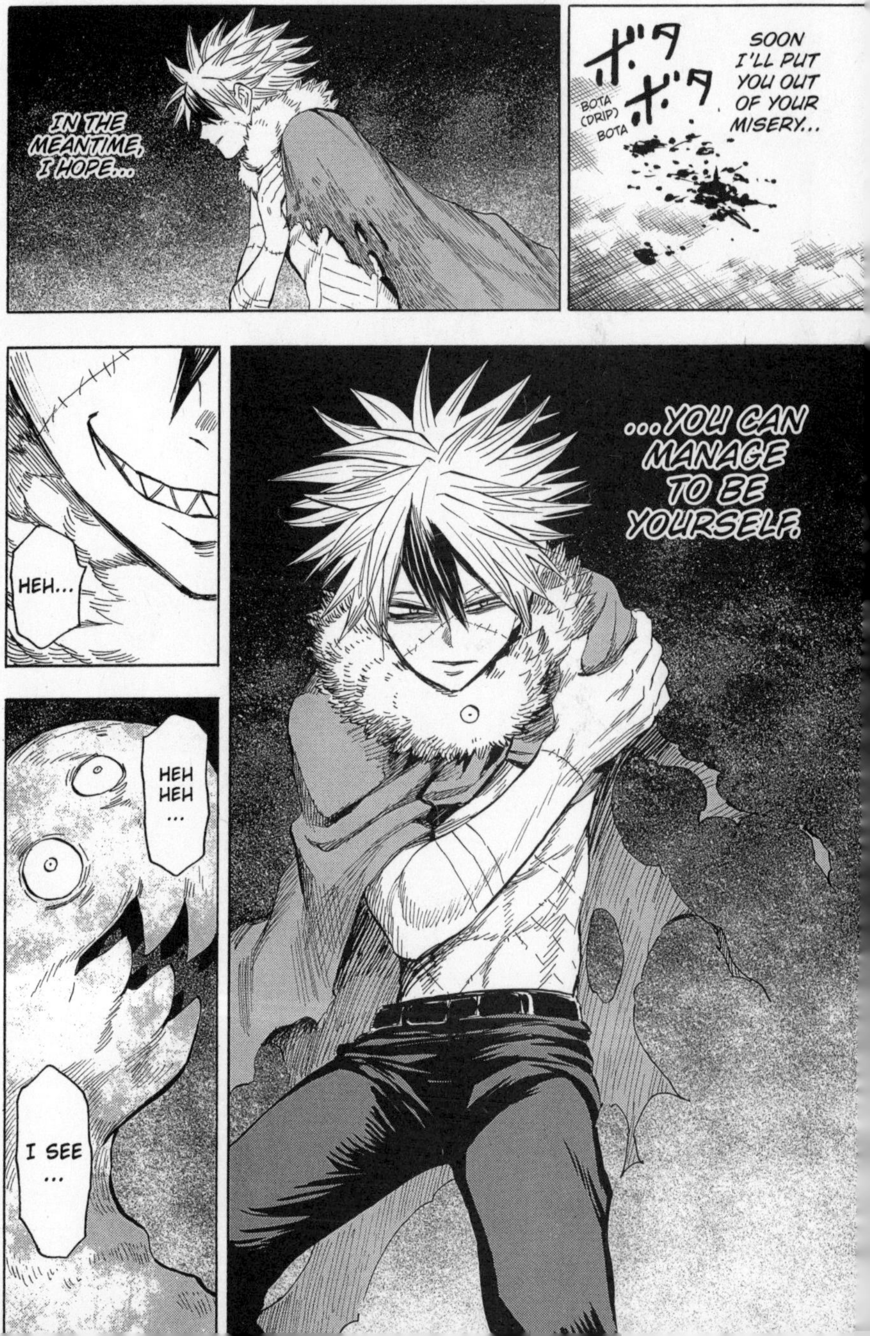
SOON I'LL PUT YOU OUT OF YOUR MISERY...
ボタ ボタ
BOTA (DRIP) BOTA
IN THE MEANTIME, I HOPE...
...YOU CAN MANAGE TO BE YOURSELF.
HEH...
HEH HEH ...
I SEE ...

BUT...

JIGU
(CREAK)

SO YOU DON'T LIKE...

...THE LEFT ARM I HAVE.

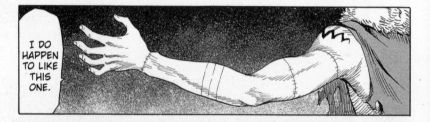

I DO HAPPEN TO LIKE THIS ONE.

YOU WILL OBEY ME...

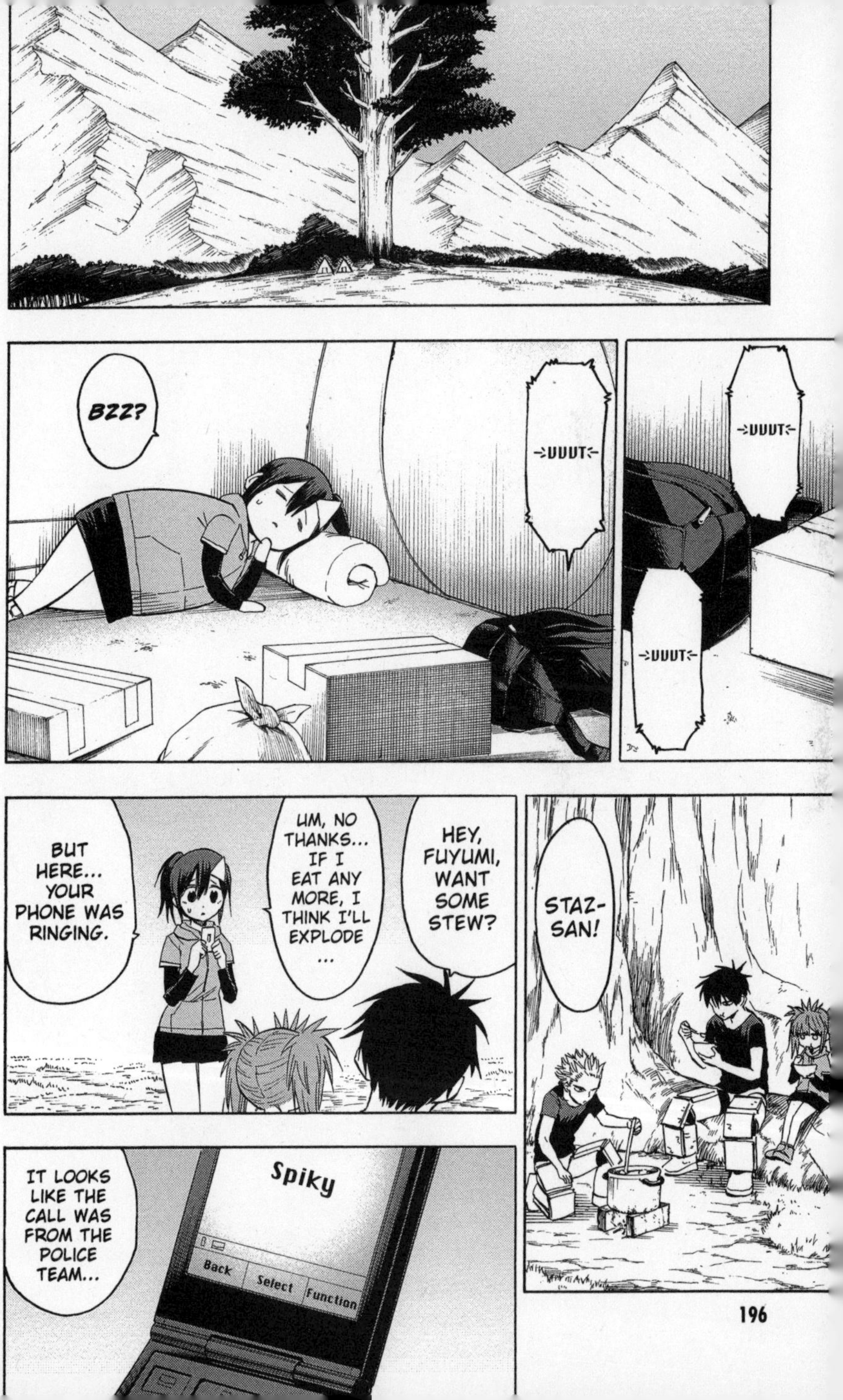
VUUT
VUUT
VUUT
BZZ?
STAZ-SAN!
HEY, FUYUMI, WANT SOME STEW?
UM, NO THANKS... IF I EAT ANY MORE, I THINK I'LL EXPLODE ...
BUT HERE... YOUR PHONE WAS RINGING.
IT LOOKS LIKE THE CALL WAS FROM THE POLICE TEAM...
Spiky
Back
Select
Function

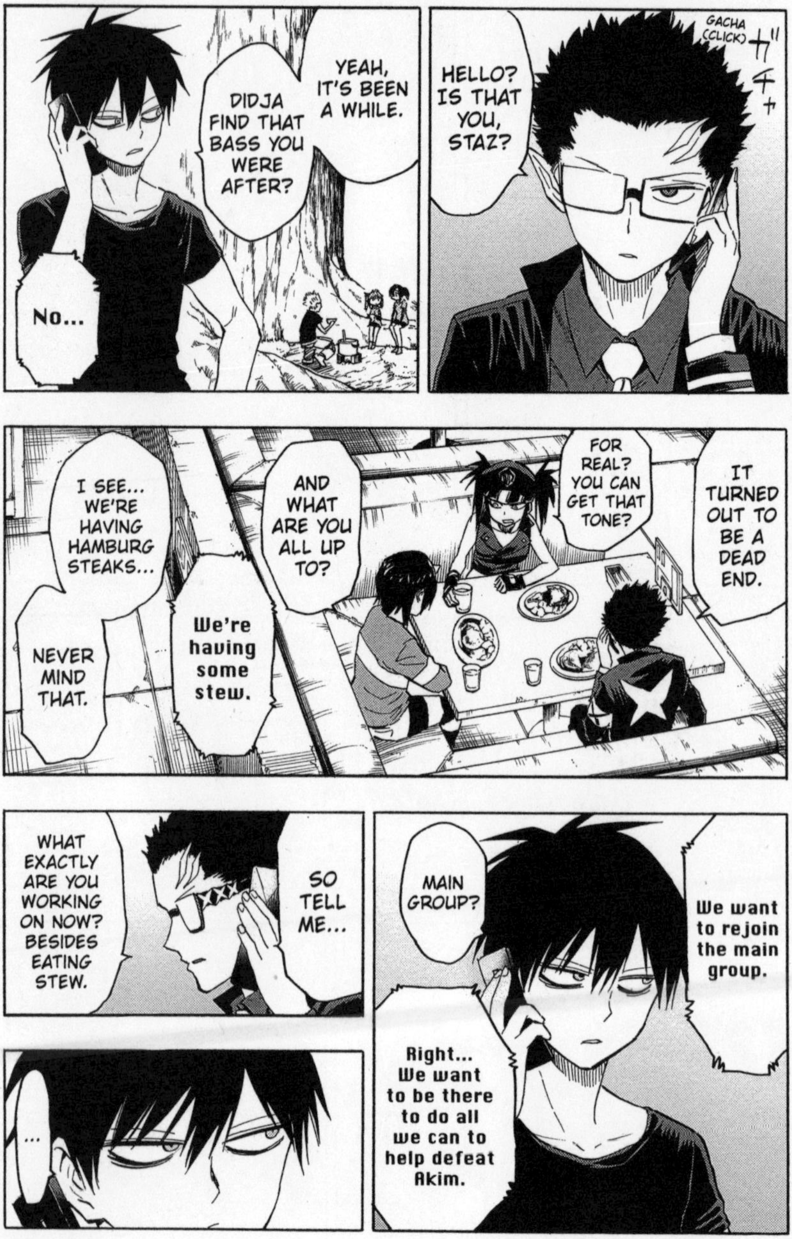
GACHA (CLICK)
ガチャ
HELLO? IS THAT YOU, STAZ?
YEAH, IT'S BEEN A WHILE.
DIDJA FIND THAT BASS YOU WERE AFTER?
No...
IT TURNED OUT TO BE A DEAD END.
FOR REAL? YOU CAN GET THAT TONE?
AND WHAT ARE YOU ALL UP TO?
We're having some stew.
I SEE... WE'RE HAVING HAMBURG STEAKS...
NEVER MIND THAT.
We want to rejoin the main group.
MAIN GROUP?
Right... We want to be there to do all we can to help defeat Akim.
SO TELL ME...
WHAT EXACTLY ARE YOU WORKING ON NOW? BESIDES EATING STEW.
...

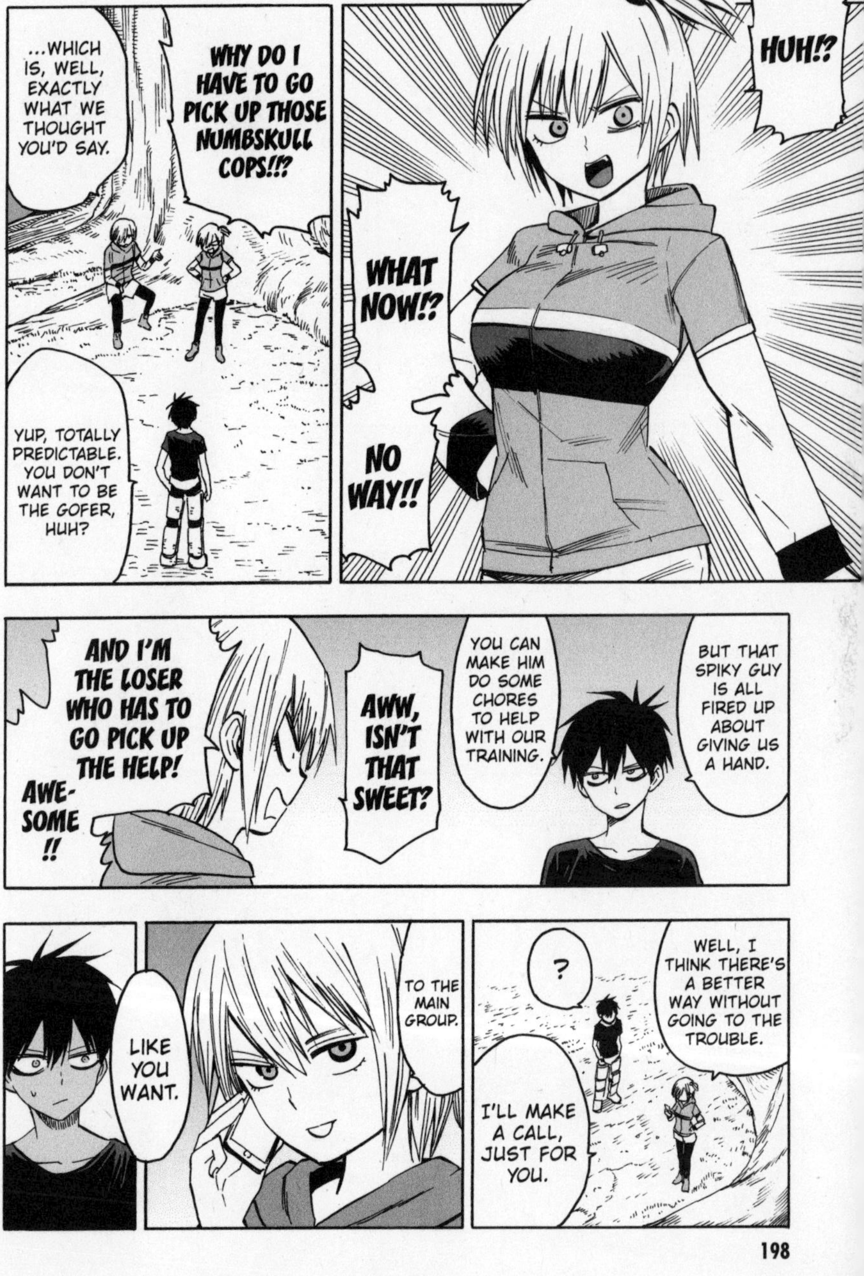
HUH!?
WHAT NOW!?
NO WAY!!
WHY DO I HAVE TO GO PICK UP THOSE NUMBSKULL COPS!!?
...WHICH IS, WELL, EXACTLY WHAT WE THOUGHT YOU'D SAY.
YUP, TOTALLY PREDICTABLE. YOU DON'T WANT TO BE THE GOFER, HUH?
BUT THAT SPIKY GUY IS ALL FIRED UP ABOUT GIVING US A HAND.
YOU CAN MAKE HIM DO SOME CHORES TO HELP WITH OUR TRAINING.
AWW, ISN'T THAT SWEET?
AND I'M THE LOSER WHO HAS TO GO PICK UP THE HELP!
AWESOME!!
WELL, I THINK THERE'S A BETTER WAY WITHOUT GOING TO THE TROUBLE.
?
I'LL MAKE A CALL, JUST FOR YOU.
TO THE MAIN GROUP.
LIKE YOU WANT.

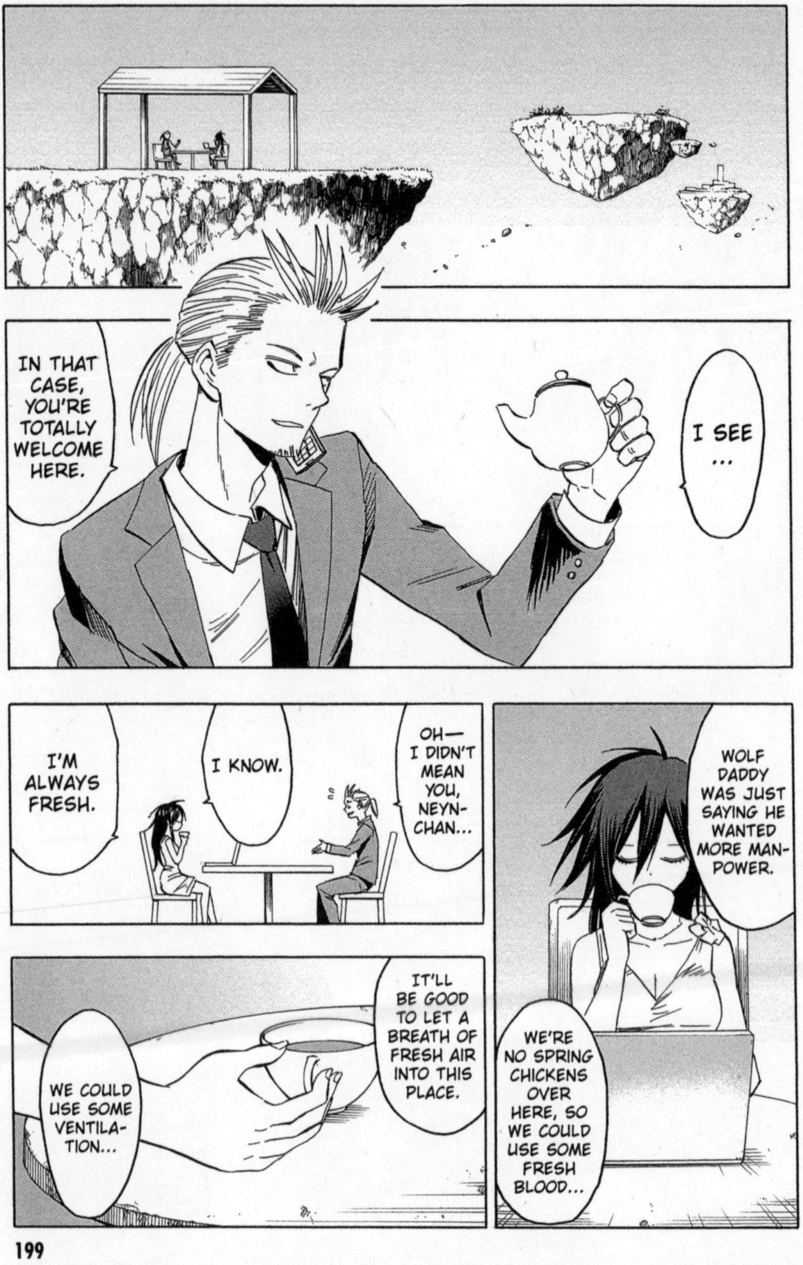
I SEE ...
IN THAT CASE, YOU'RE TOTALLY WELCOME HERE.
WOLF DADDY WAS JUST SAYING HE WANTED MORE MAN-POWER.
WE'RE NO SPRING CHICKENS OVER HERE, SO WE COULD USE SOME FRESH BLOOD...
OH— I DIDN'T MEAN YOU, NEYN-CHAN...
I KNOW.
I'M ALWAYS FRESH.
IT'LL BE GOOD TO LET A BREATH OF FRESH AIR INTO THIS PLACE.
WE COULD USE SOME VENTILA-TION...

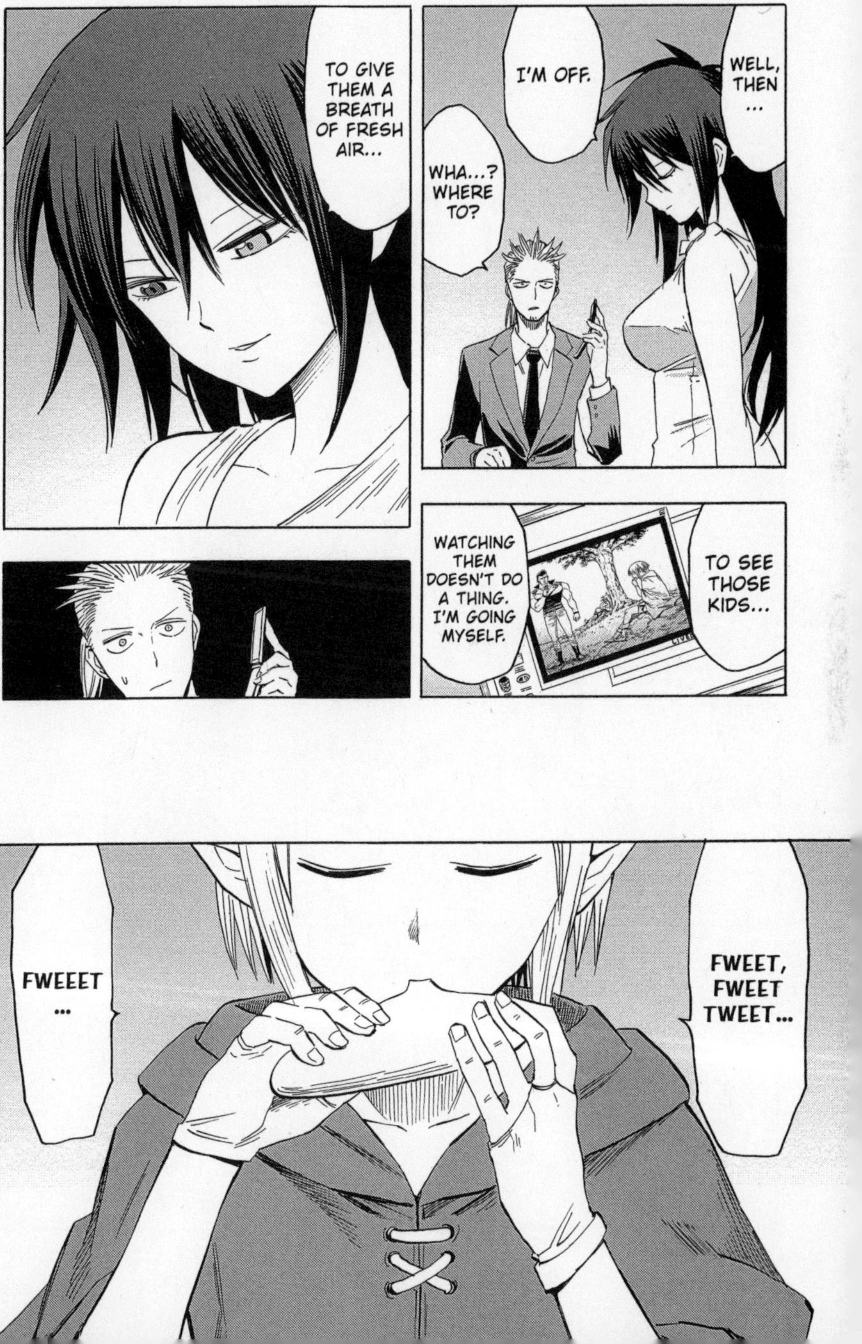
WELL, THEN ...
I'M OFF.
WHA...? WHERE TO?
TO GIVE THEM A BREATH OF FRESH AIR...
TO SEE THOSE KIDS...
WATCHING THEM DOESN'T DO A THING. I'M GOING MYSELF.
FWEET, FWEET TWEET...
FWEEET ...

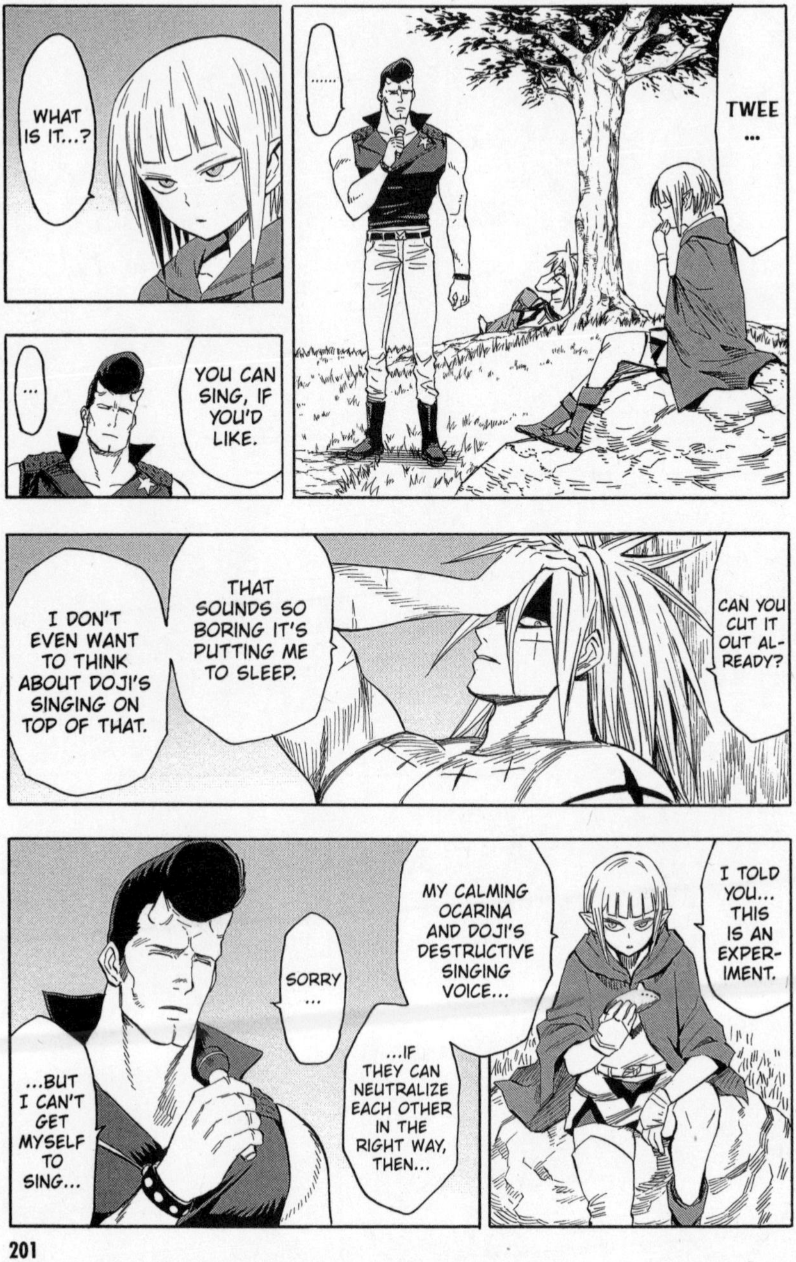
TWEE ...
......
WHAT IS IT...?
YOU CAN SING, IF YOU'D LIKE.
...
CAN YOU CUT IT OUT AL-READY?
THAT SOUNDS SO BORING IT'S PUTTING ME TO SLEEP.
I DON'T EVEN WANT TO THINK ABOUT DOJI'S SINGING ON TOP OF THAT.
I TOLD YOU... THIS IS AN EXPER-IMENT.
MY CALMING OCARINA AND DOJI'S DESTRUCTIVE SINGING VOICE...
...IF THEY CAN NEUTRALIZE EACH OTHER IN THE RIGHT WAY, THEN...
SORRY ...
...BUT I CAN'T GET MYSELF TO SING...

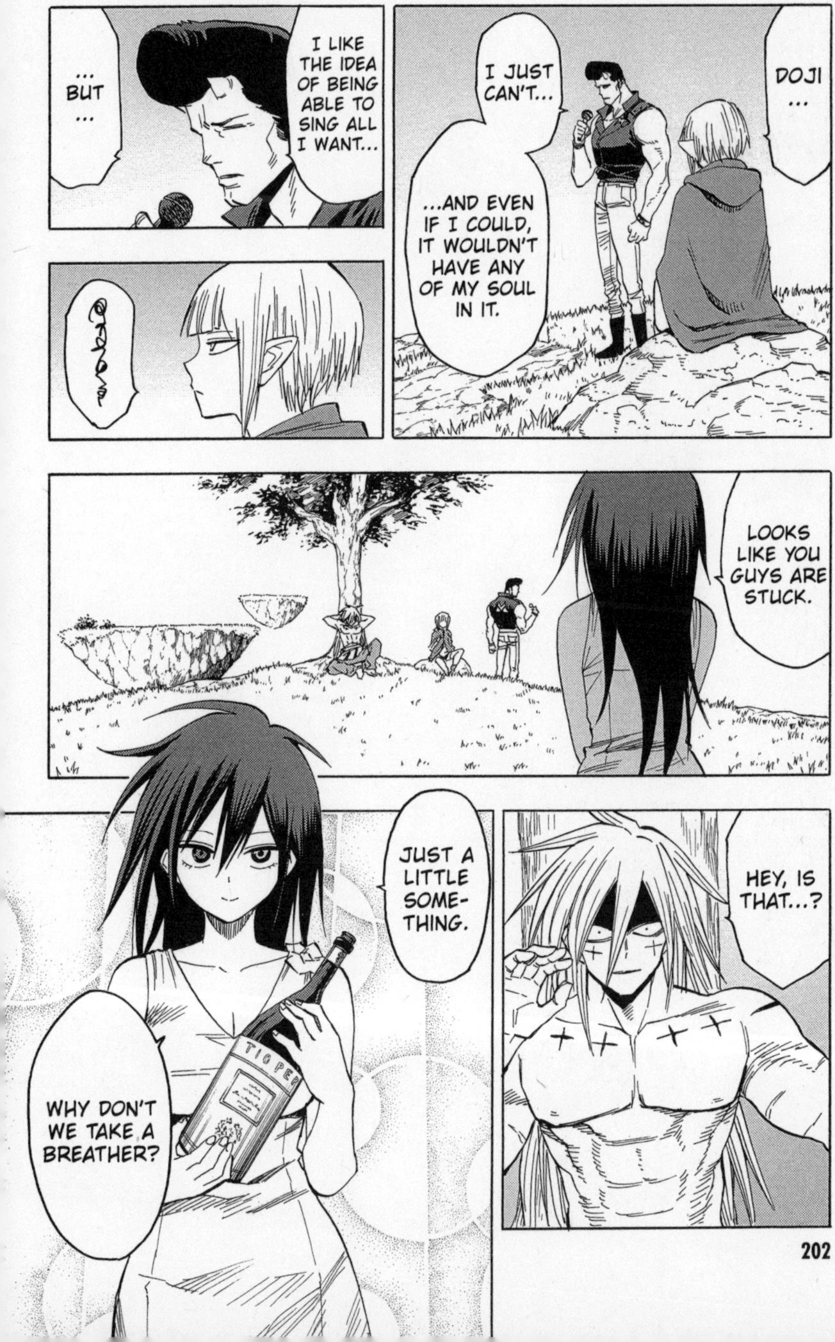
DOJI ...
I JUST CAN'T...
...AND EVEN IF I COULD, IT WOULDN'T HAVE ANY OF MY SOUL IN IT.
I LIKE THE IDEA OF BEING ABLE TO SING ALL I WANT...
... BUT ...
LOOKS LIKE YOU GUYS ARE STUCK.
HEY, IS THAT...?
JUST A LITTLE SOME-THING.
WHY DON'T WE TAKE A BREATHER?

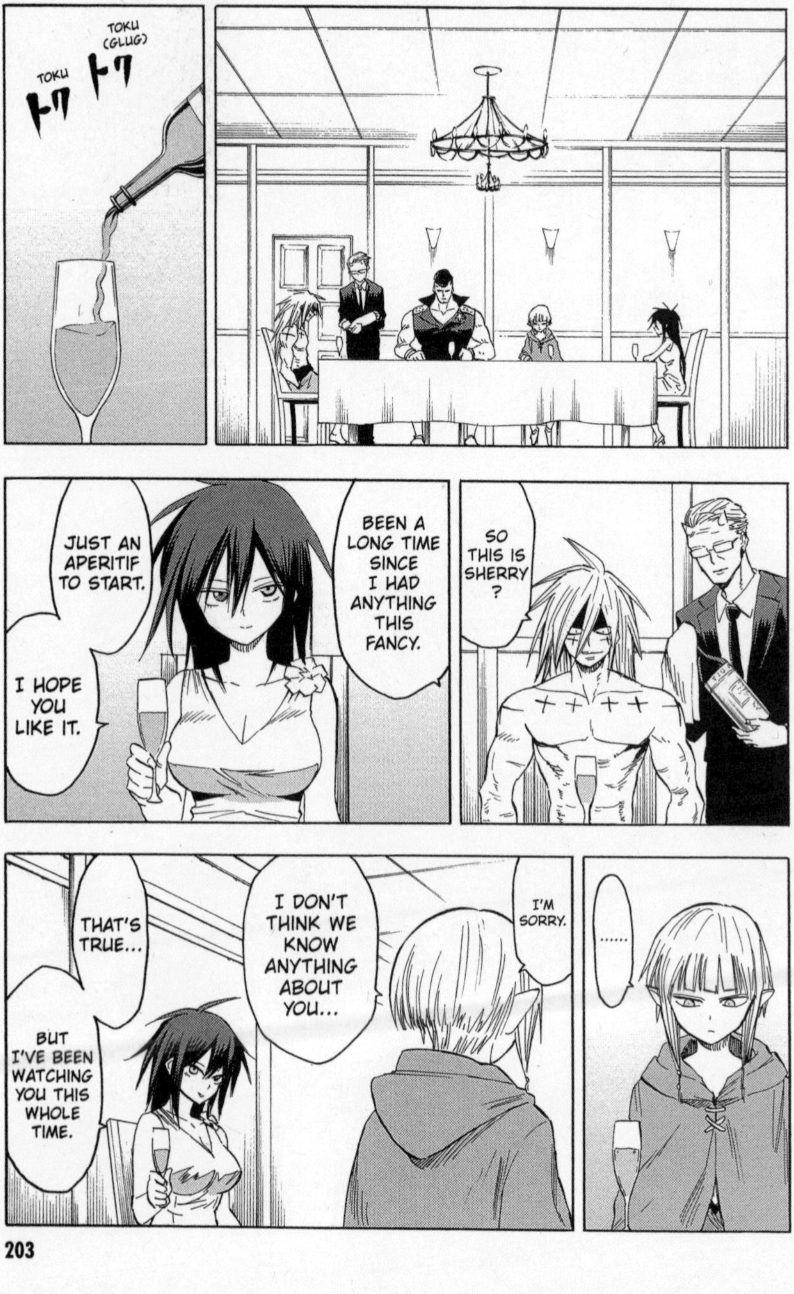
TOKU (GLUG)
トク
TOKU
トク
SO THIS IS SHERRY?
BEEN A LONG TIME SINCE I HAD ANYTHING THIS FANCY.
JUST AN APERITIF TO START.
I HOPE YOU LIKE IT.
......
I'M SORRY.
I DON'T THINK WE KNOW ANYTHING ABOUT YOU...
THAT'S TRUE...
BUT I'VE BEEN WATCHING YOU THIS WHOLE TIME.

JUST WHO ARE YOU?
NO NEED TO RUSH.
LET'S HAVE OUR APPETIZER FIRST.
I HAVE NO INTENTION OF ACCEPTING HOSPITALITY FROM A COMPLETE STRANGER.
MIST... RIGHT, THIS IS HOW YOU ARE.
SO CAUTIOUS—FITTING FOR THE GUARDIAN SPIRIT OF THE FOREST...
ALWAYS KEEPING A CLOSE EYE ON YOUR SURROUND-INGS.
BUT IF YOU ASK ME, YOU'RE RATHER CONSER-VATIVE...
...AND LACKING IN AUDACITY.
YOU WERE TRYING TO CONTAIN DOJI'S SONG...
YOU'RE SEEKING TO SOFTEN THE SHARP EDGES THAT MAKE EACH OF YOU UNIQUE.
THAT'S NOT GOING TO WORK.

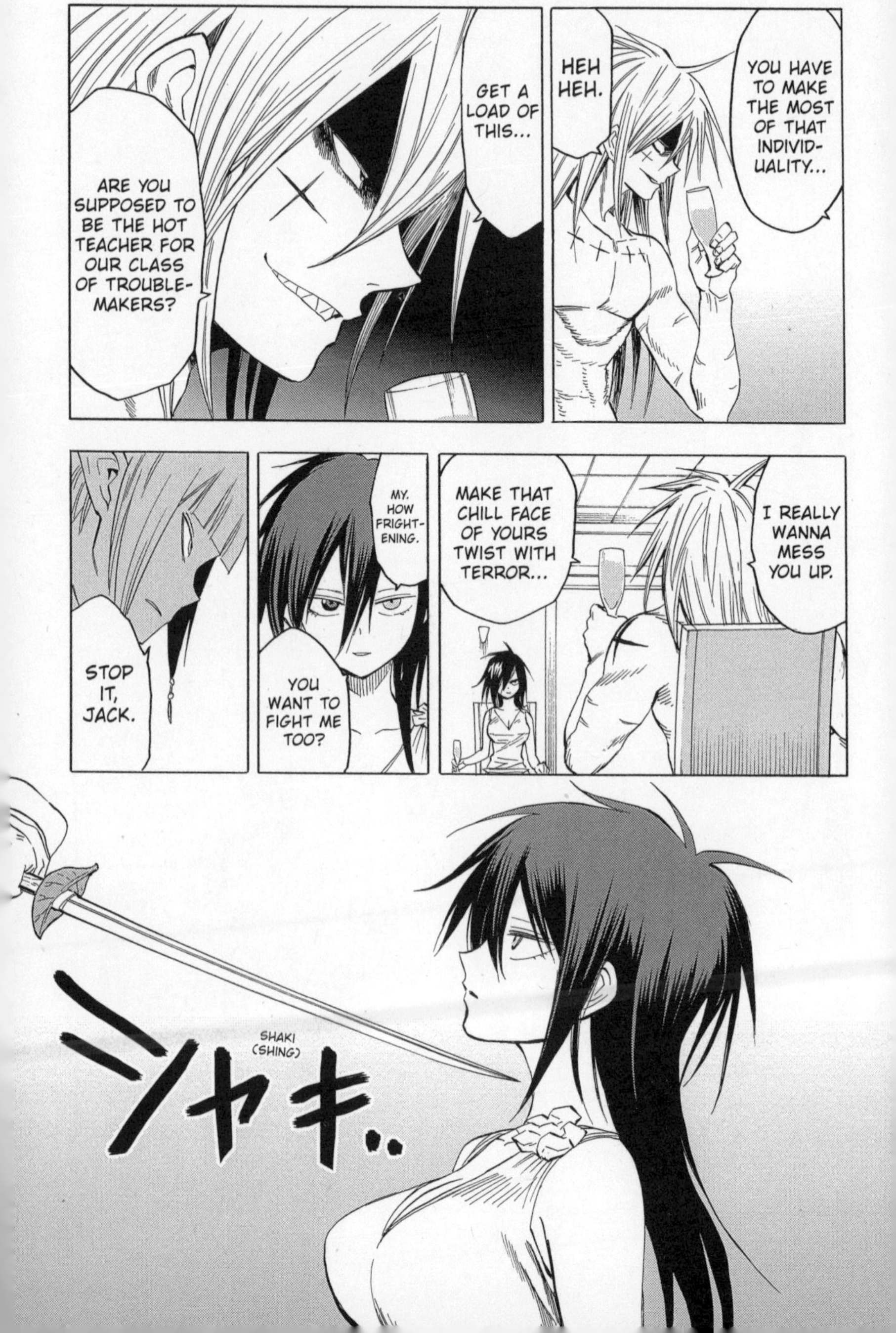
YOU HAVE TO MAKE THE MOST OF THAT INDIVIDUALITY...
HEH HEH.
GET A LOAD OF THIS...
ARE YOU SUPPOSED TO BE THE HOT TEACHER FOR OUR CLASS OF TROUBLE-MAKERS?
I REALLY WANNA MESS YOU UP.
MAKE THAT CHILL FACE OF YOURS TWIST WITH TERROR...
MY. HOW FRIGHTENING.
YOU WANT TO FIGHT ME TOO?
STOP IT, JACK.
シャキ..
SHAKI (SHING)

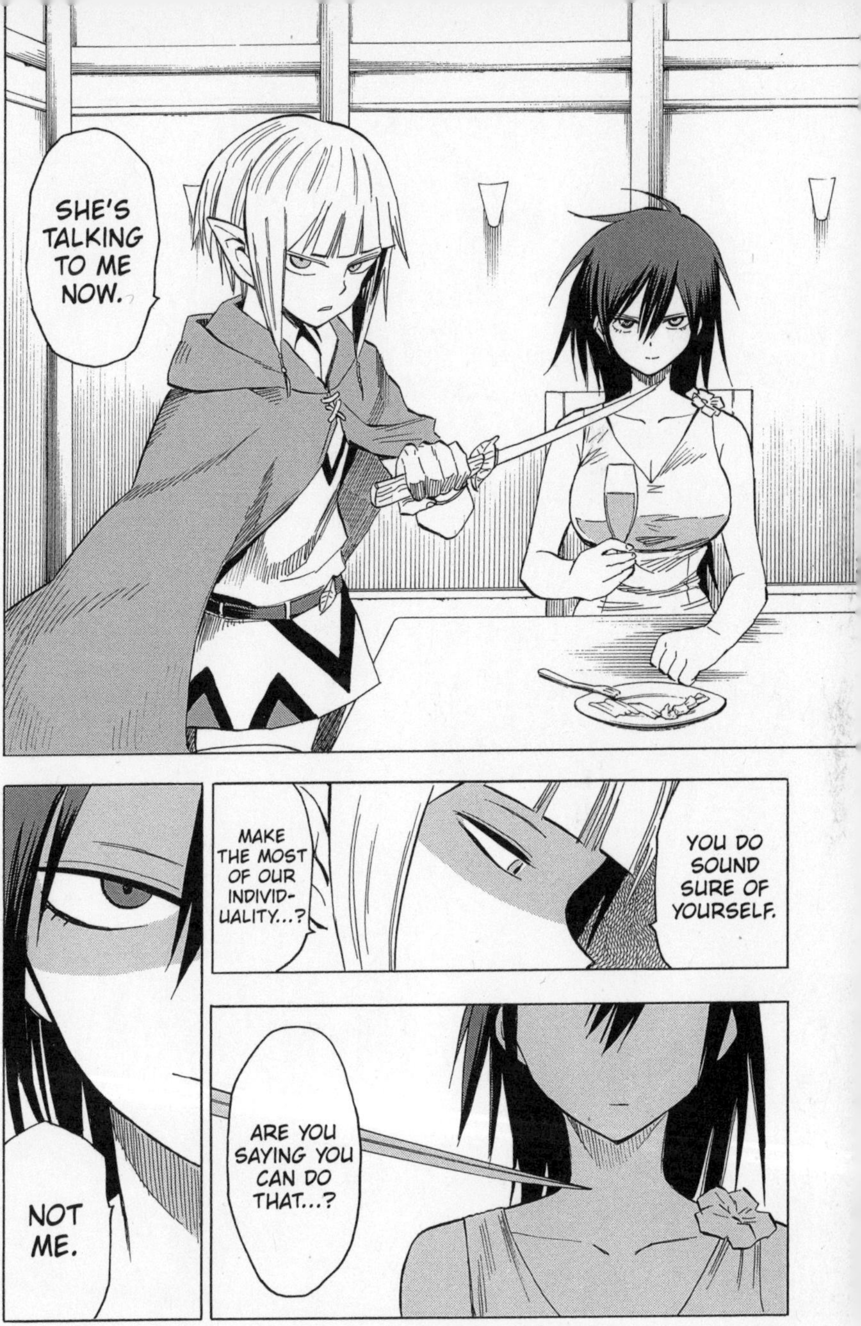
SHE'S TALKING TO ME NOW.
YOU DO SOUND SURE OF YOURSELF.
MAKE THE MOST OF OUR INDIVID-UALITY...?
ARE YOU SAYING YOU CAN DO THAT...?
NOT ME.

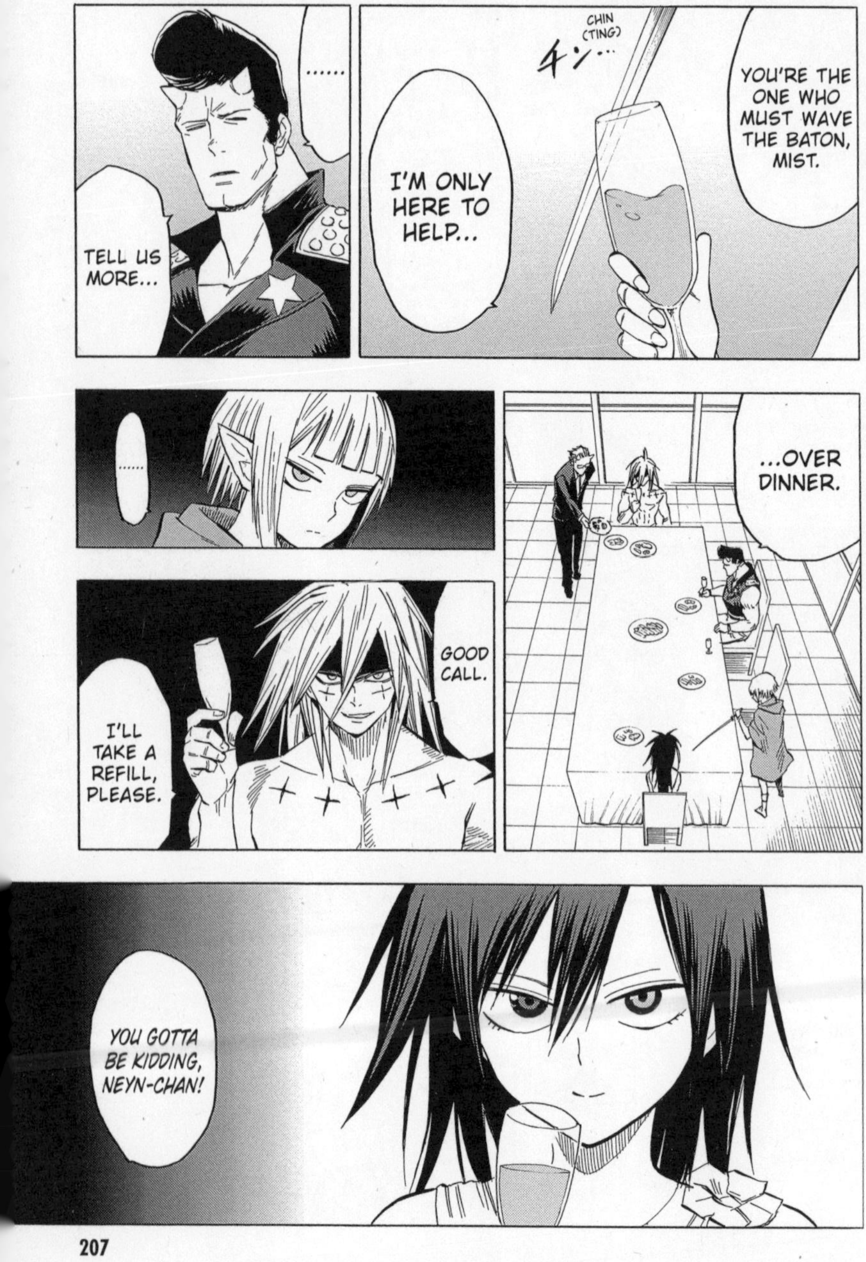
CHIN (TING)
チン…
YOU'RE THE ONE WHO MUST WAVE THE BATON, MIST.
I'M ONLY HERE TO HELP...
......
TELL US MORE...
...OVER DINNER.
......
GOOD CALL.
I'LL TAKE A REFILL, PLEASE.
YOU GOTTA BE KIDDING, NEYN-CHAN!

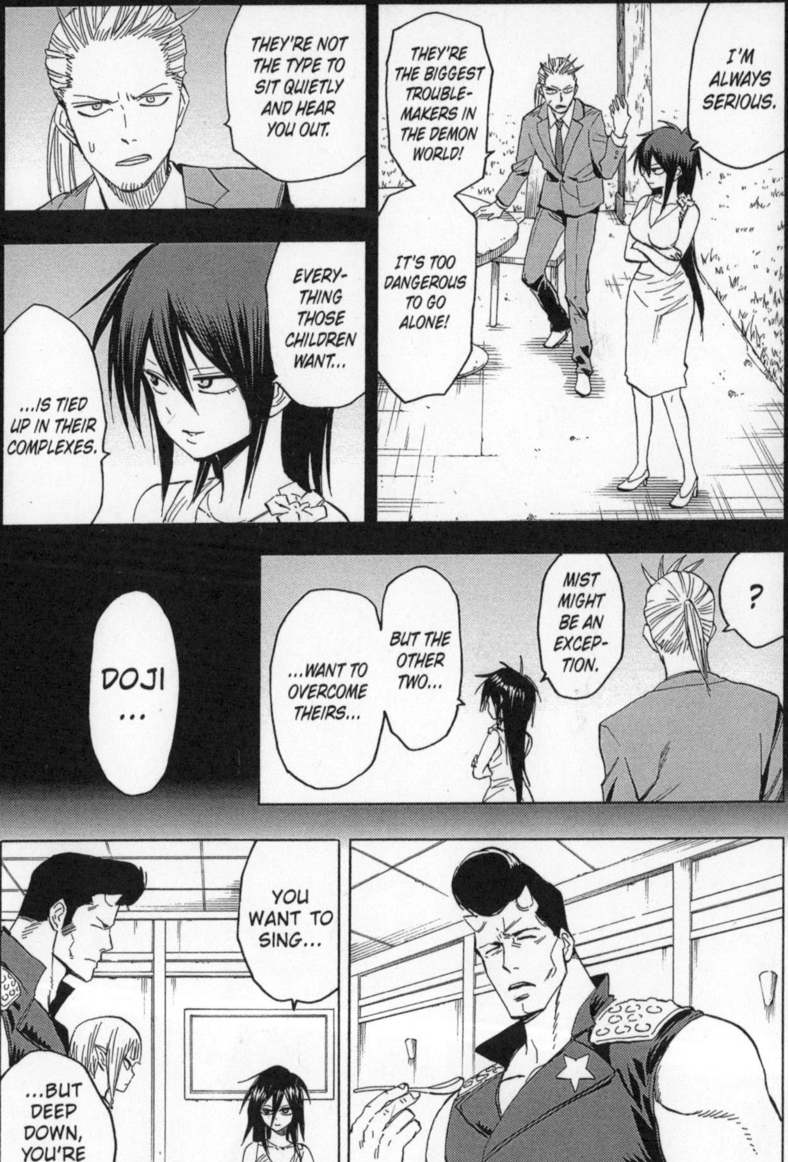
I'M ALWAYS SERIOUS.
THEY'RE THE BIGGEST TROUBLE-MAKERS IN THE DEMON WORLD!
IT'S TOO DANGEROUS TO GO ALONE!
THEY'RE NOT THE TYPE TO SIT QUIETLY AND HEAR YOU OUT.
EVERY-THING THOSE CHILDREN WANT...
...IS TIED UP IN THEIR COMPLEXES.
?
MIST MIGHT BE AN EXCEP-TION.
BUT THE OTHER TWO...
...WANT TO OVERCOME THEIRS...
DOJI ...
YOU WANT TO SING...
...BUT DEEP DOWN, YOU'RE AFRAID TO.

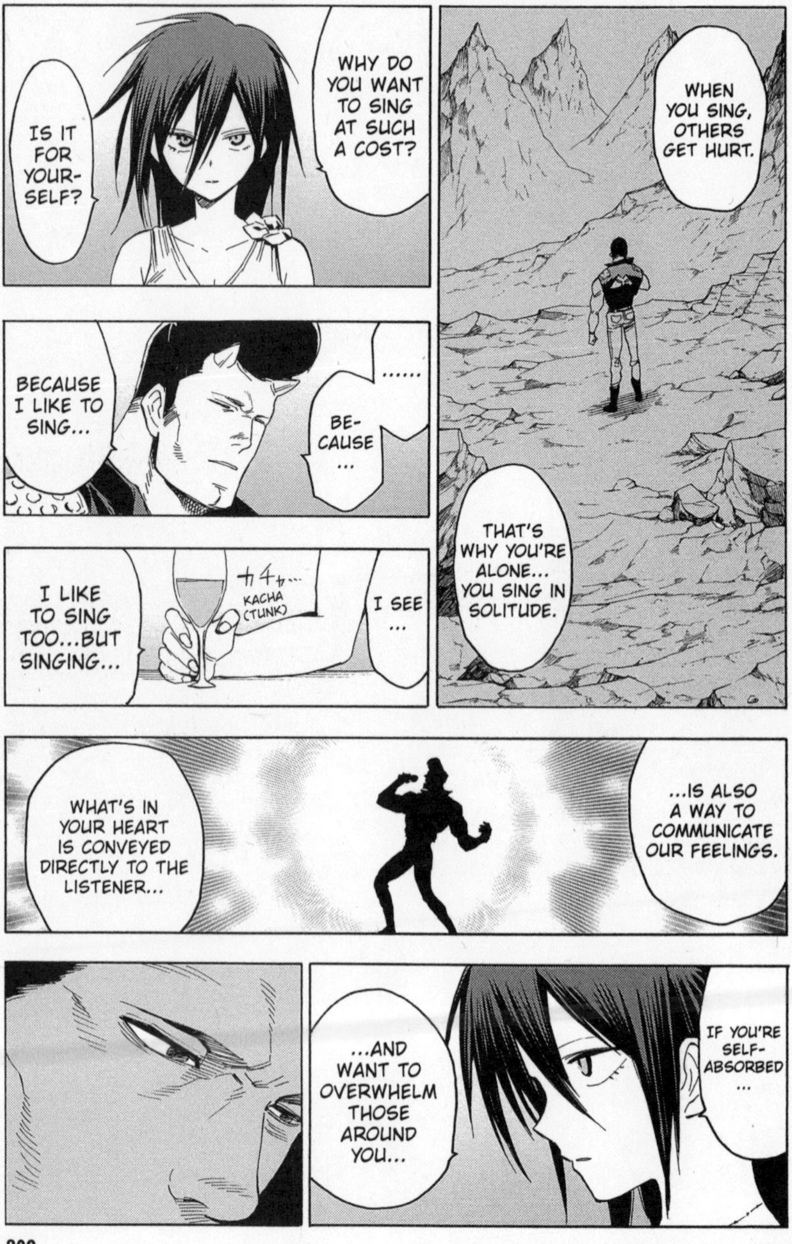
WHEN YOU SING, OTHERS GET HURT.
THAT'S WHY YOU'RE ALONE... YOU SING IN SOLITUDE.
WHY DO YOU WANT TO SING AT SUCH A COST?
IS IT FOR YOURSELF?
......
BE-CAUSE ...
BECAUSE I LIKE TO SING...
I SEE ...
カチャ...
KACHA (TUNK)
I LIKE TO SING TOO...BUT SINGING...
...IS ALSO A WAY TO COMMUNICATE OUR FEELINGS.
WHAT'S IN YOUR HEART IS CONVEYED DIRECTLY TO THE LISTENER...
IF YOU'RE SELF-ABSORBED ...
...AND WANT TO OVERWHELM THOSE AROUND YOU...

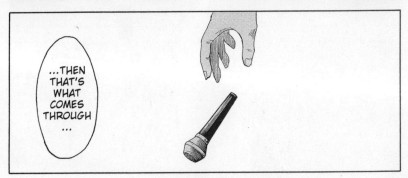

...THEN
THAT'S
WHAT
COMES
THROUGH
...

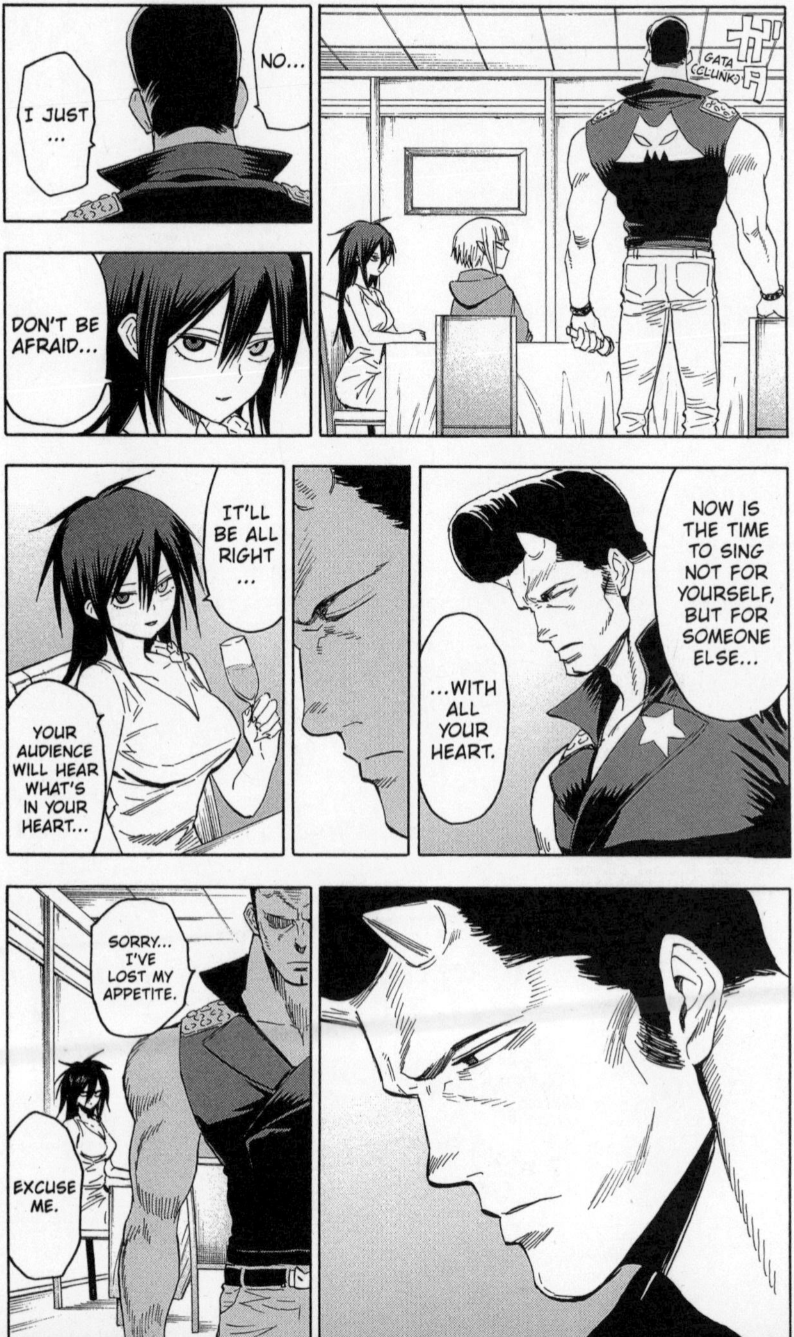
GATA (CLUNK)
NO...
I JUST ...
DON'T BE AFRAID...
NOW IS THE TIME TO SING NOT FOR YOURSELF, BUT FOR SOMEONE ELSE...
...WITH ALL YOUR HEART.
IT'LL BE ALL RIGHT ...
YOUR AUDIENCE WILL HEAR WHAT'S IN YOUR HEART...
SORRY... I'VE LOST MY APPETITE.
EXCUSE ME.

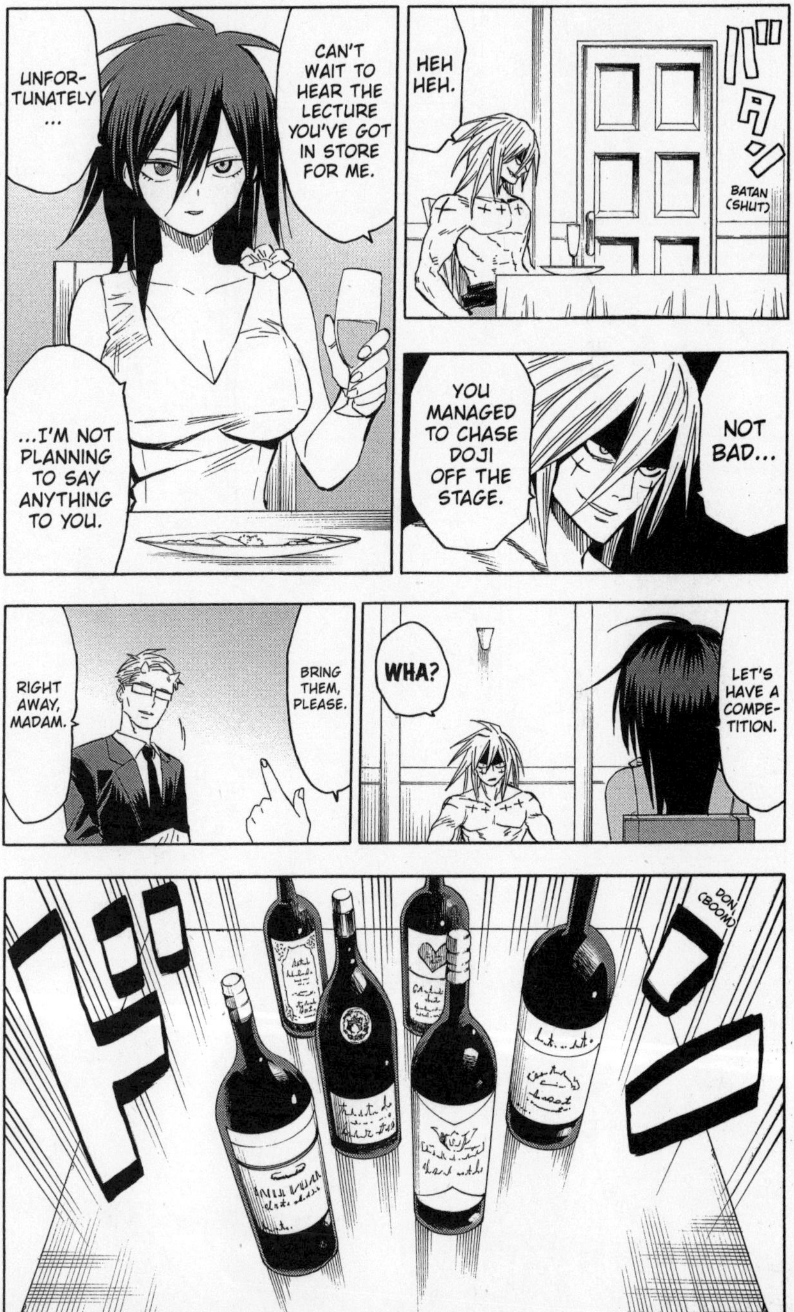
バタン
BATAN (SHUT)
HEH HEH.
NOT BAD...
YOU MANAGED TO CHASE DOJI OFF THE STAGE.
CAN'T WAIT TO HEAR THE LECTURE YOU'VE GOT IN STORE FOR ME.
UNFORTUNATELY...
...I'M NOT PLANNING TO SAY ANYTHING TO YOU.
LET'S HAVE A COMPETITION.
WHA?
BRING THEM, PLEASE.
RIGHT AWAY, MADAM.
ドン
DON (BOOM)

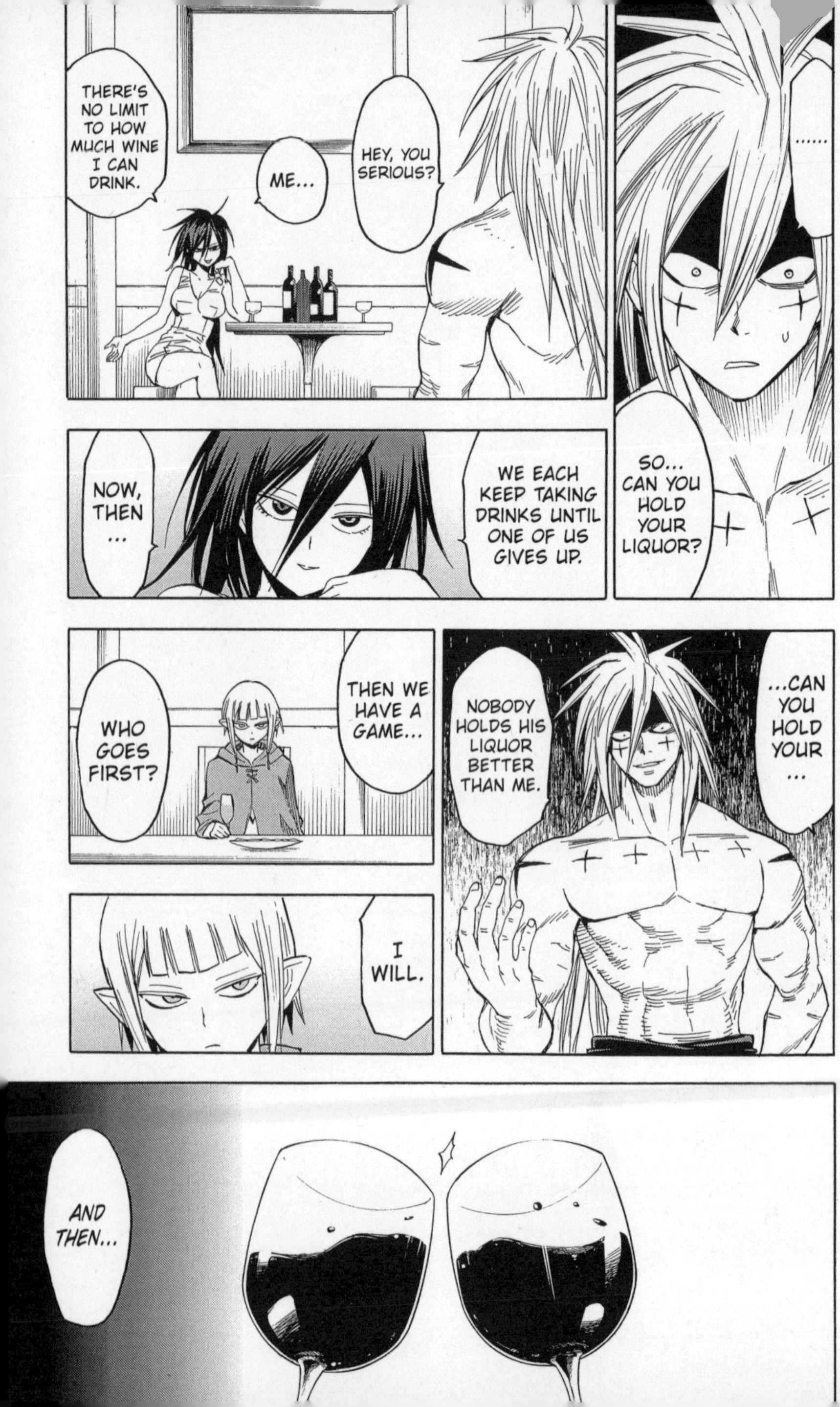
......
SO... CAN YOU HOLD YOUR LIQUOR?
HEY, YOU SERIOUS?
ME...
THERE'S NO LIMIT TO HOW MUCH WINE I CAN DRINK.
WE EACH KEEP TAKING DRINKS UNTIL ONE OF US GIVES UP.
NOW, THEN ...
...CAN YOU HOLD YOUR ...
NOBODY HOLDS HIS LIQUOR BETTER THAN ME.
THEN WE HAVE A GAME...
WHO GOES FIRST?
I WILL.
AND THEN...

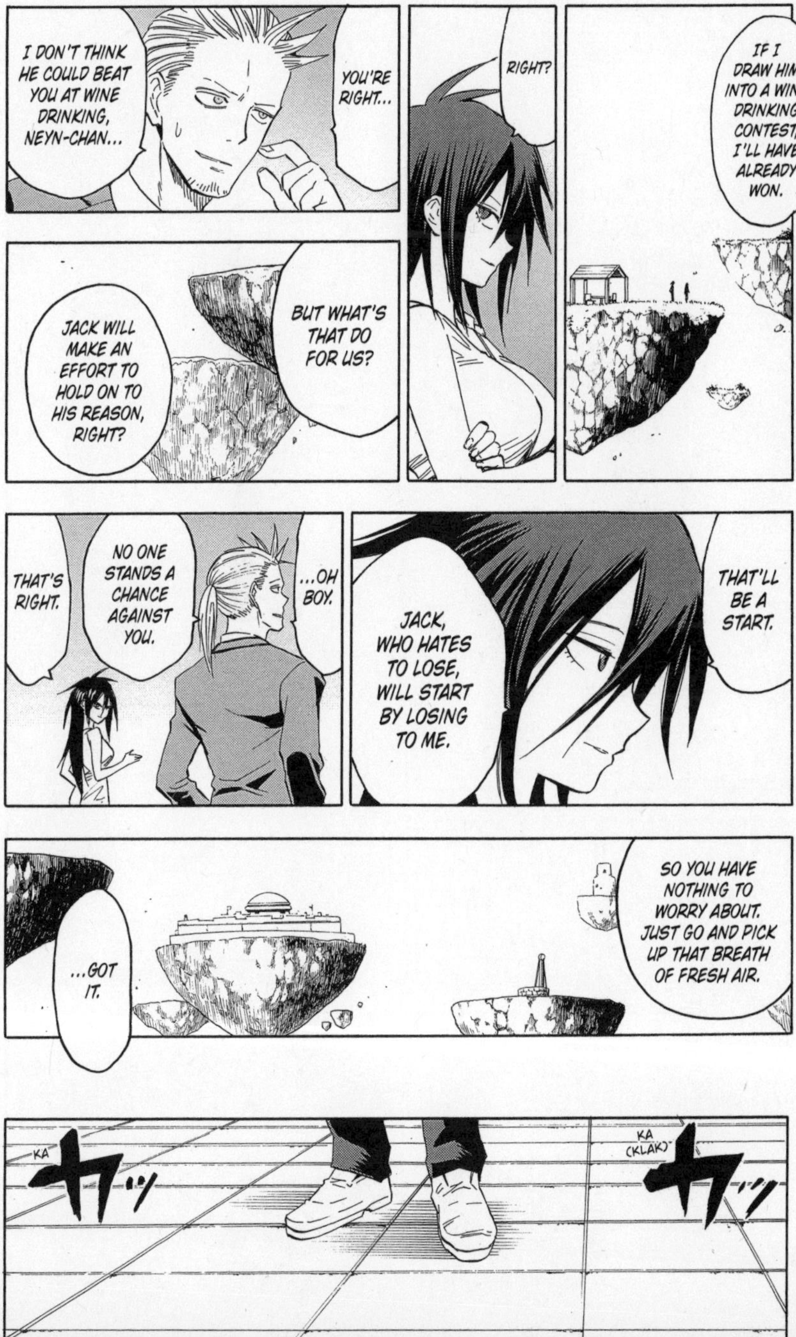
IF I DRAW HIM INTO A WINE DRINKING CONTEST, I'LL HAVE ALREADY WON.
RIGHT?
YOU'RE RIGHT...
I DON'T THINK HE COULD BEAT YOU AT WINE DRINKING, NEYN-CHAN...
BUT WHAT'S THAT DO FOR US?
JACK WILL MAKE AN EFFORT TO HOLD ON TO HIS REASON, RIGHT?
THAT'LL BE A START.
JACK, WHO HATES TO LOSE, WILL START BY LOSING TO ME.
...OH BOY.
NO ONE STANDS A CHANCE AGAINST YOU.
THAT'S RIGHT.
SO YOU HAVE NOTHING TO WORRY ABOUT. JUST GO AND PICK UP THAT BREATH OF FRESH AIR.
...GOT IT.
KA (KLAK)
カッ
KA
カッ

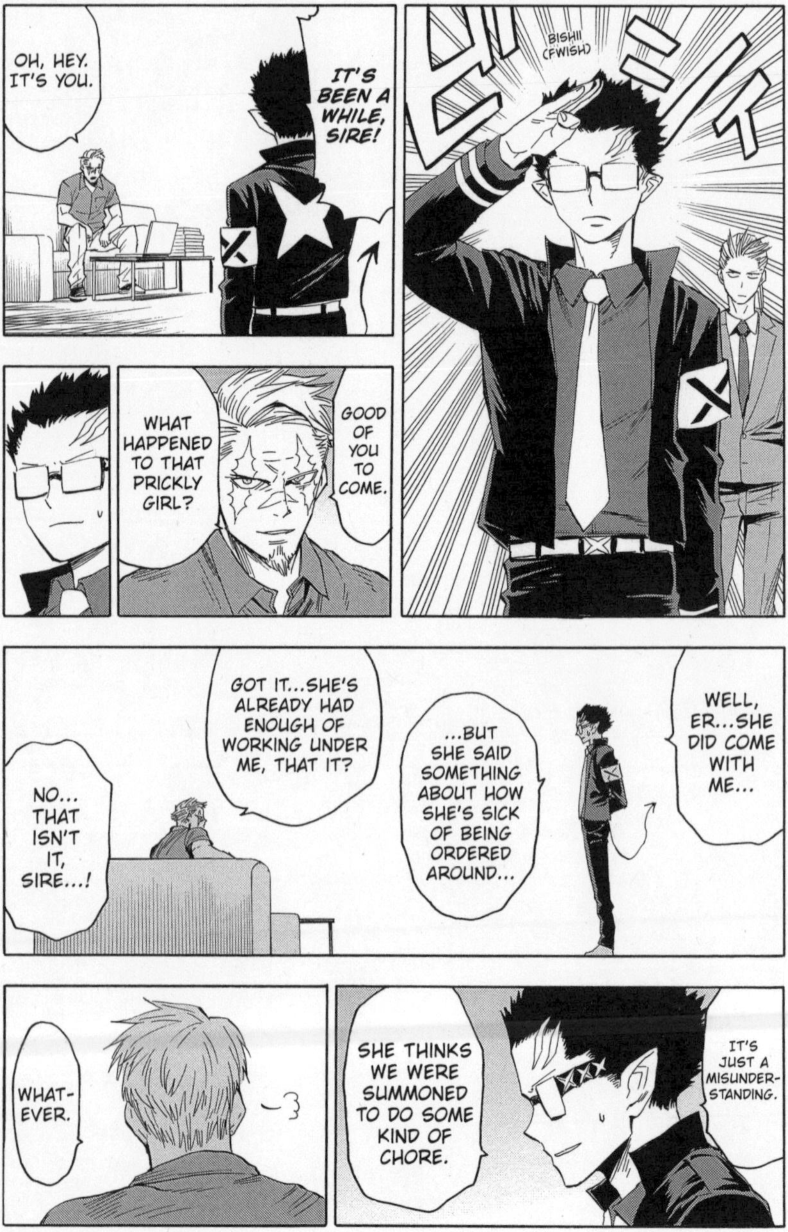
BISHII
(FWISH)
IT'S BEEN A WHILE, SIRE!
OH, HEY. IT'S YOU.
GOOD OF YOU TO COME.
WHAT HAPPENED TO THAT PRICKLY GIRL?
WELL, ER...SHE DID COME WITH ME...
...BUT SHE SAID SOMETHING ABOUT HOW SHE'S SICK OF BEING ORDERED AROUND...
GOT IT...SHE'S ALREADY HAD ENOUGH OF WORKING UNDER ME, THAT IT?
NO... THAT ISN'T IT, SIRE...!
IT'S JUST A MISUNDER-STANDING.
SHE THINKS WE WERE SUMMONED TO DO SOME KIND OF CHORE.
WHAT-EVER.

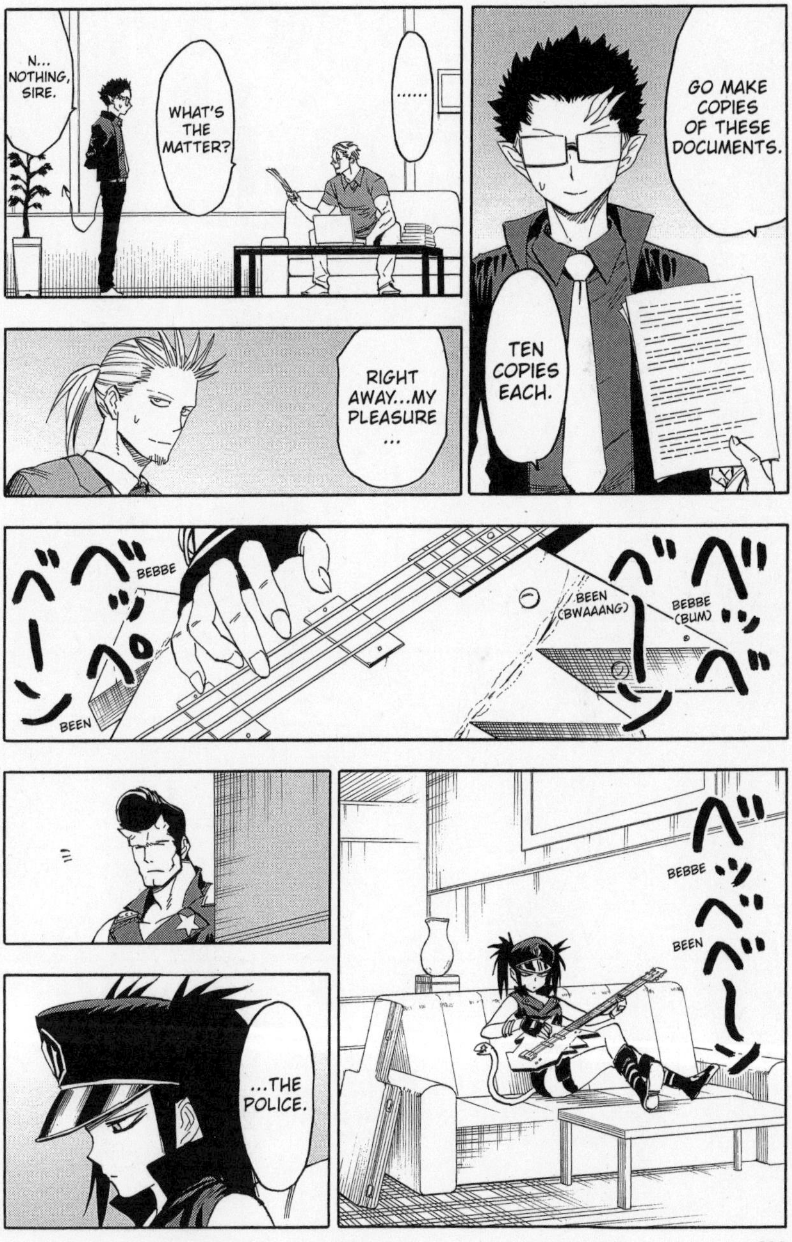
GO MAKE COPIES OF THESE DOCUMENTS.
TEN COPIES EACH.
......
WHAT'S THE MATTER?
N... NOTHING, SIRE.
RIGHT AWAY...MY PLEASURE...
BEBBE (BUM)
BEEN (BWAAANG)
BEBBE
BEEN
BEBBE
BEEN
...THE POLICE.

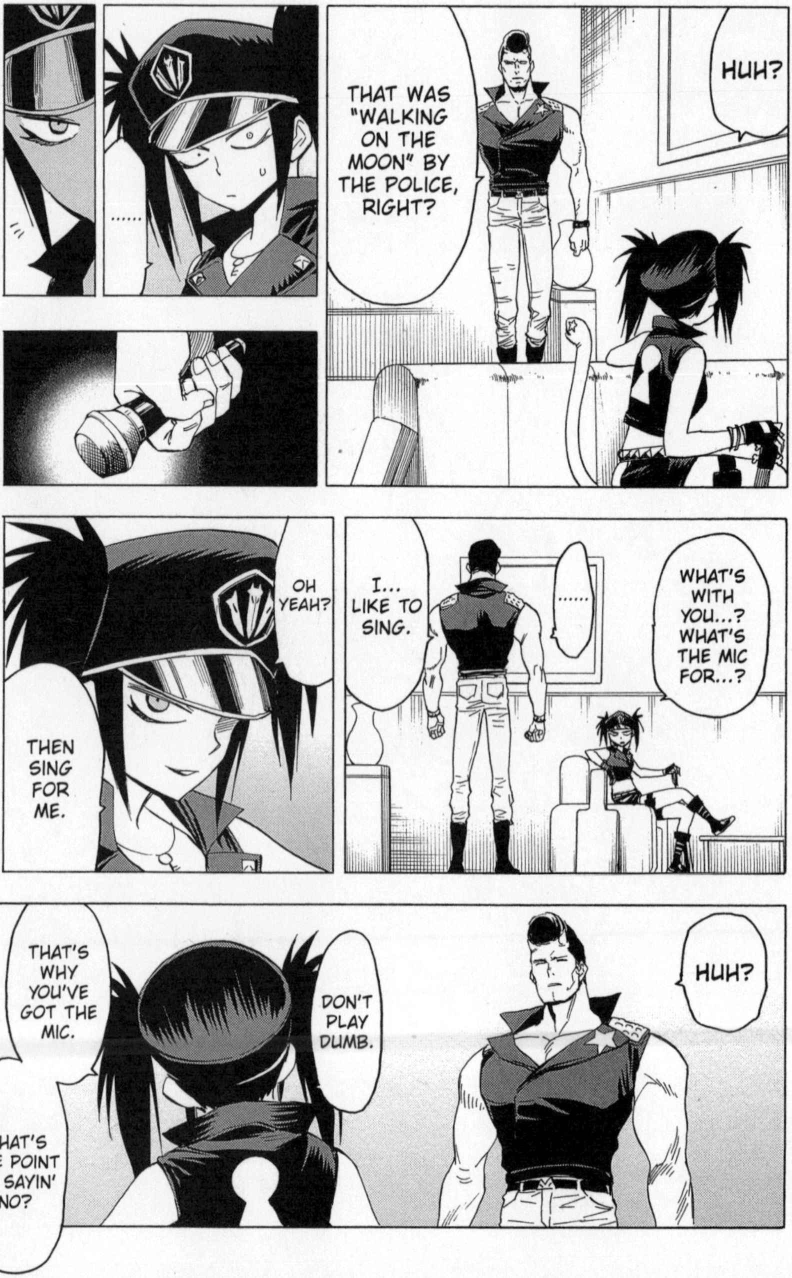
HUH?
THAT WAS "WALKING ON THE MOON" BY THE POLICE, RIGHT?
......
WHAT'S WITH YOU...? WHAT'S THE MIC FOR...?
......
I... LIKE TO SING.
OH YEAH?
THEN SING FOR ME.
HUH?
DON'T PLAY DUMB.
THAT'S WHY YOU'VE GOT THE MIC.
WHAT'S THE POINT OF SAYIN' NO?

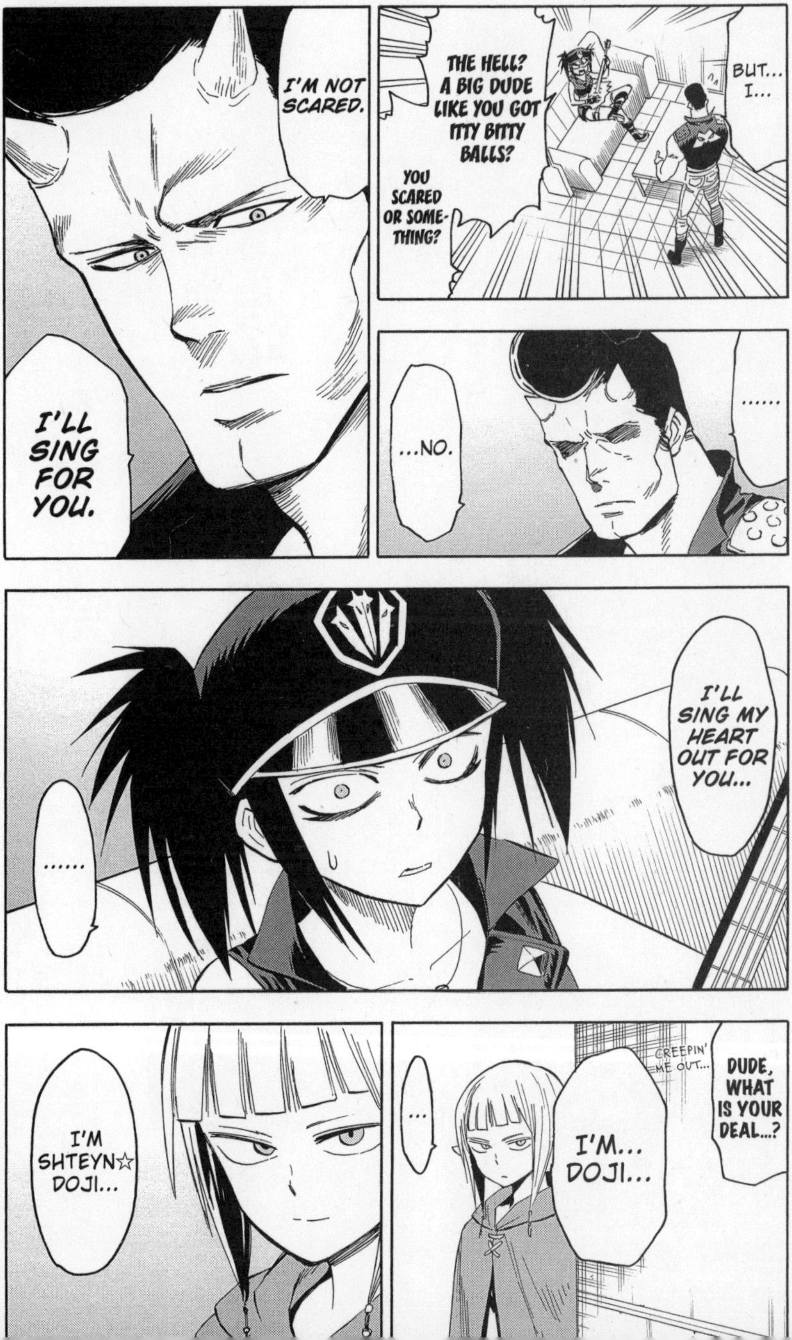
THE HELL? A BIG DUDE LIKE YOU GOT ITTY BITTY BALLS?
YOU SCARED OR SOME-THING?
BUT... I...
......
...NO.
I'M NOT SCARED.
I'LL SING FOR YOU.
I'LL SING MY HEART OUT FOR YOU...
......
DUDE, WHAT IS YOUR DEAL...?
CREEPIN' ME OUT...
I'M... DOJI...
...
I'M SHTEYN☆ DOJI...

♠ To Be Continued ♠

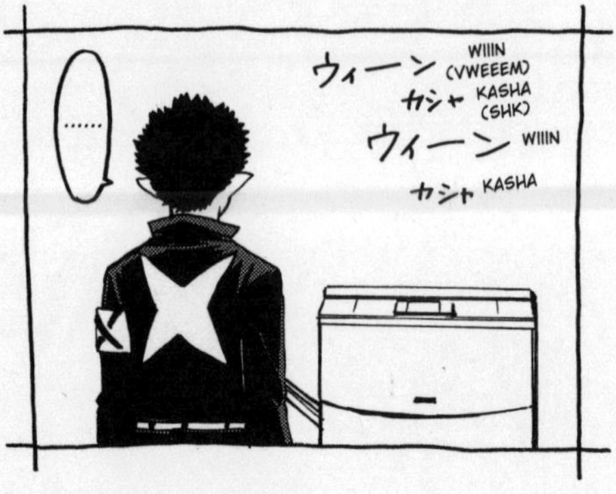
ウィーン WIIIN (VWEEEM)
カシャ KASHA (SHK)
ウィーン WIIIN
カシャ KASHA
......

BLOOD LAD

FIVE DAYS LEFT

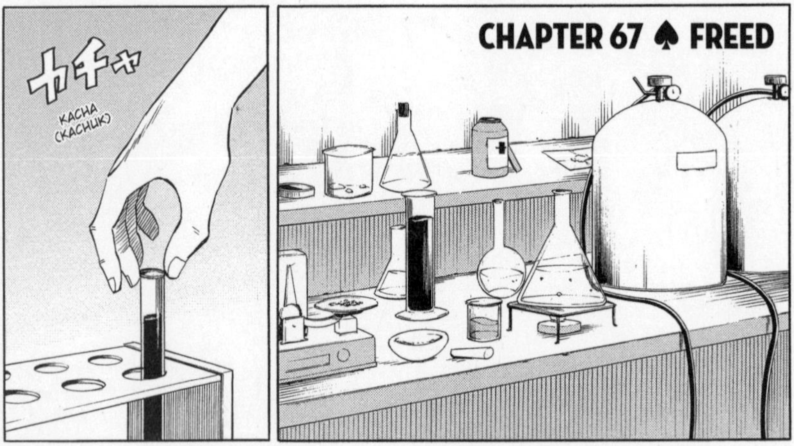
CHAPTER 67 ♠ FREED
カチャ
KACHA (KACHUK)

LEVEL OF AKIM'S MAGIC: 586,900

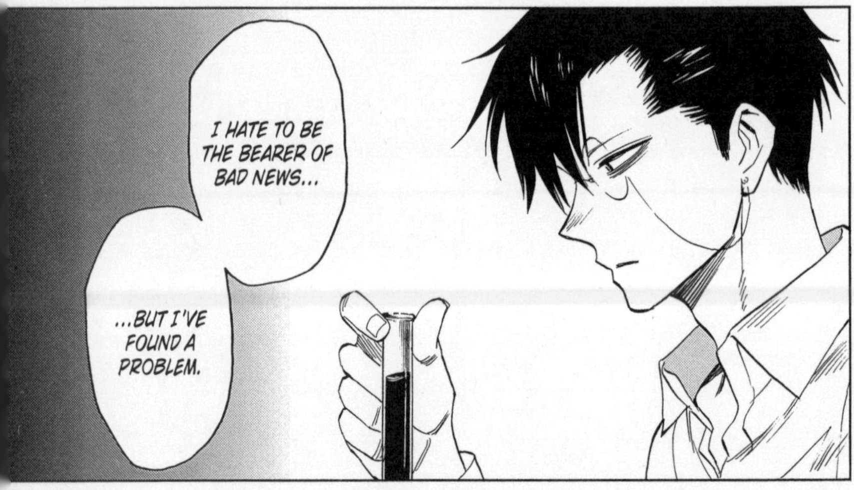
I HATE TO BE THE BEARER OF BAD NEWS...
...BUT I'VE FOUND A PROBLEM.

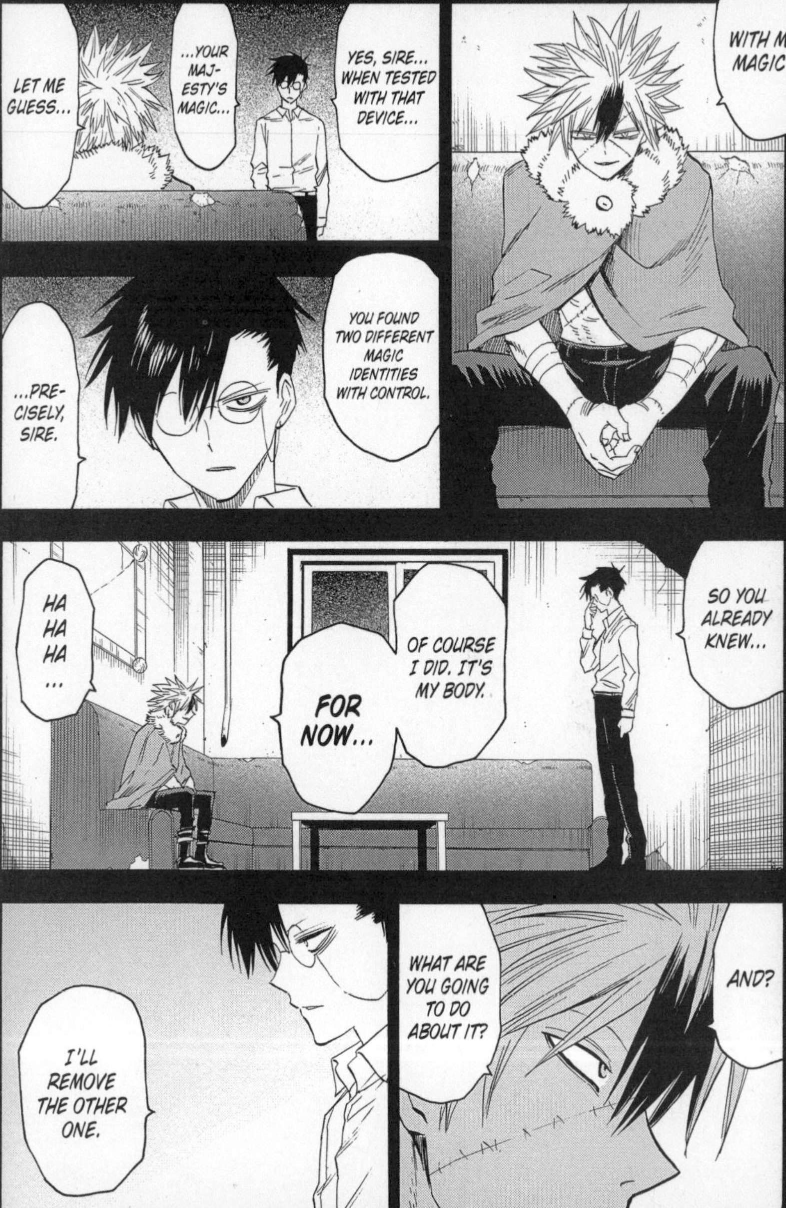
WITH MY MAGIC?
YES, SIRE... WHEN TESTED WITH THAT DEVICE...
...YOUR MAJ-ESTY'S MAGIC...
LET ME GUESS...
YOU FOUND TWO DIFFERENT MAGIC IDENTITIES WITH CONTROL.
...PRE-CISELY, SIRE.
SO YOU ALREADY KNEW...
OF COURSE I DID. IT'S MY BODY.
FOR NOW...
HA HA HA ...
AND?
WHAT ARE YOU GOING TO DO ABOUT IT?
I'LL REMOVE THE OTHER ONE.

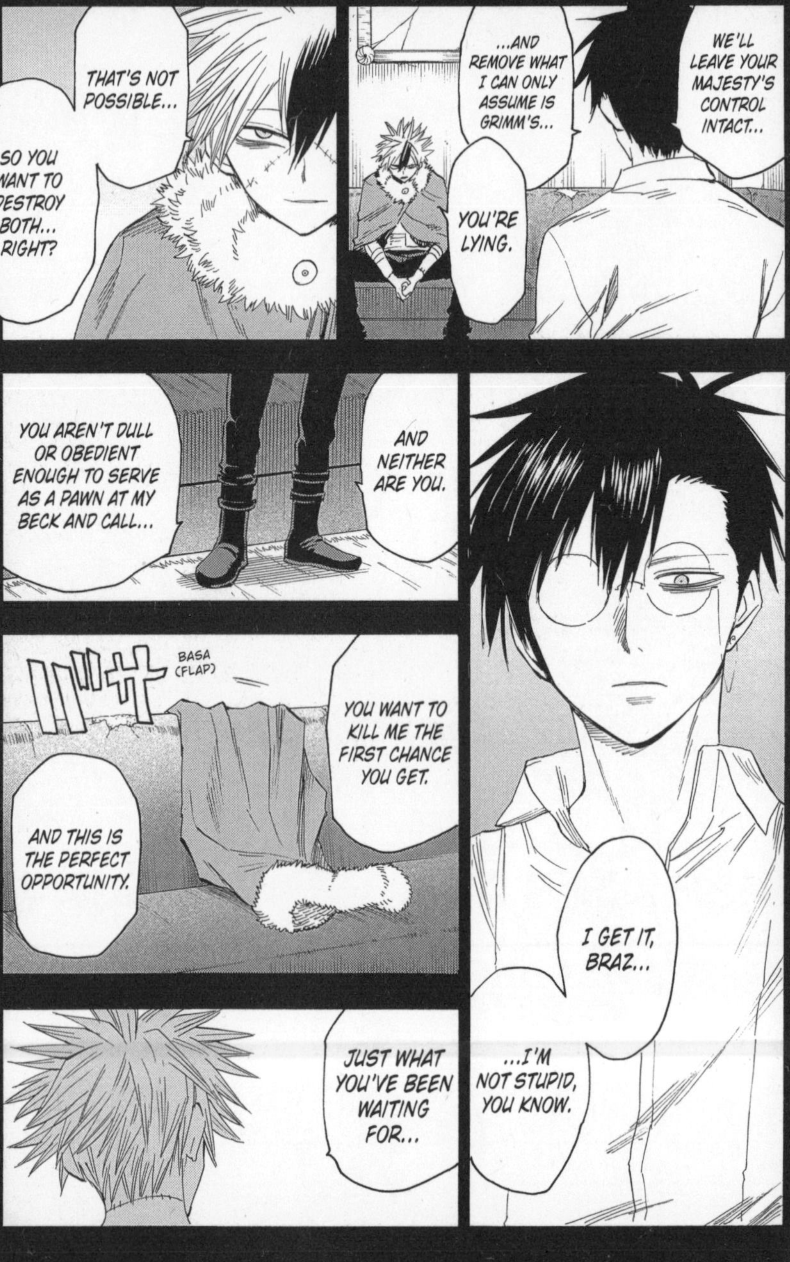
WE'LL LEAVE YOUR MAJESTY'S CONTROL INTACT...
...AND REMOVE WHAT I CAN ONLY ASSUME IS GRIMM'S...
YOU'RE LYING.
THAT'S NOT POSSIBLE...
SO YOU WANT TO DESTROY BOTH... RIGHT?
I GET IT, BRAZ...
...I'M NOT STUPID, YOU KNOW.
YOU AREN'T DULL OR OBEDIENT ENOUGH TO SERVE AS A PAWN AT MY BECK AND CALL...
AND NEITHER ARE YOU.
BASA (FLAP)
YOU WANT TO KILL ME THE FIRST CHANCE YOU GET.
AND THIS IS THE PERFECT OPPORTUNITY.
JUST WHAT YOU'VE BEEN WAITING FOR...

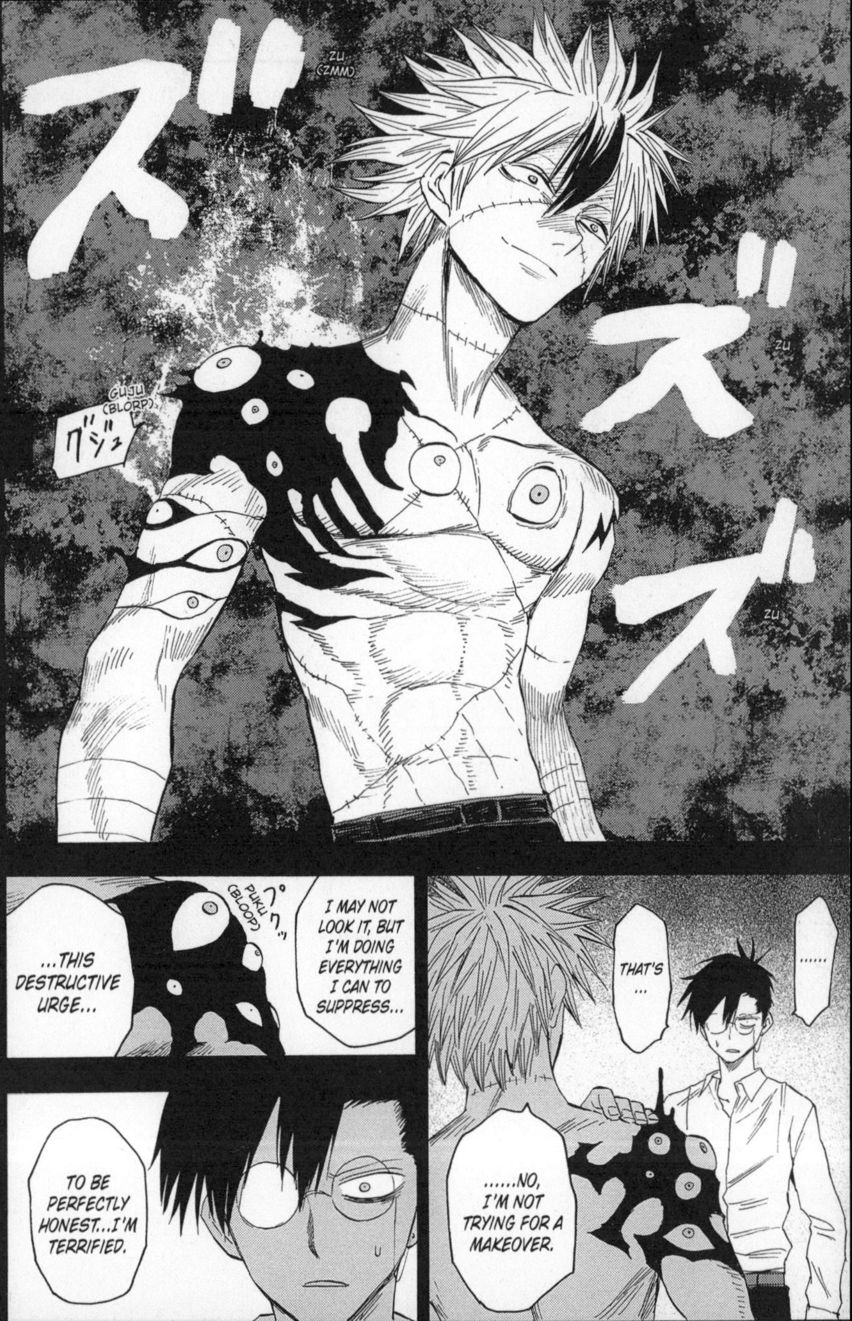
ズ
ZU (ZMM)
グジュ
GUJU (BLORP)
ズズ
ZU
ZU
プクッ
PUKU (BLOOP)
I MAY NOT LOOK IT, BUT I'M DOING EVERYTHING I CAN TO SUPPRESS...
...THIS DESTRUCTIVE URGE...
THAT'S ...
......
......NO, I'M NOT TRYING FOR A MAKEOVER.
TO BE PERFECTLY HONEST...I'M TERRIFIED.

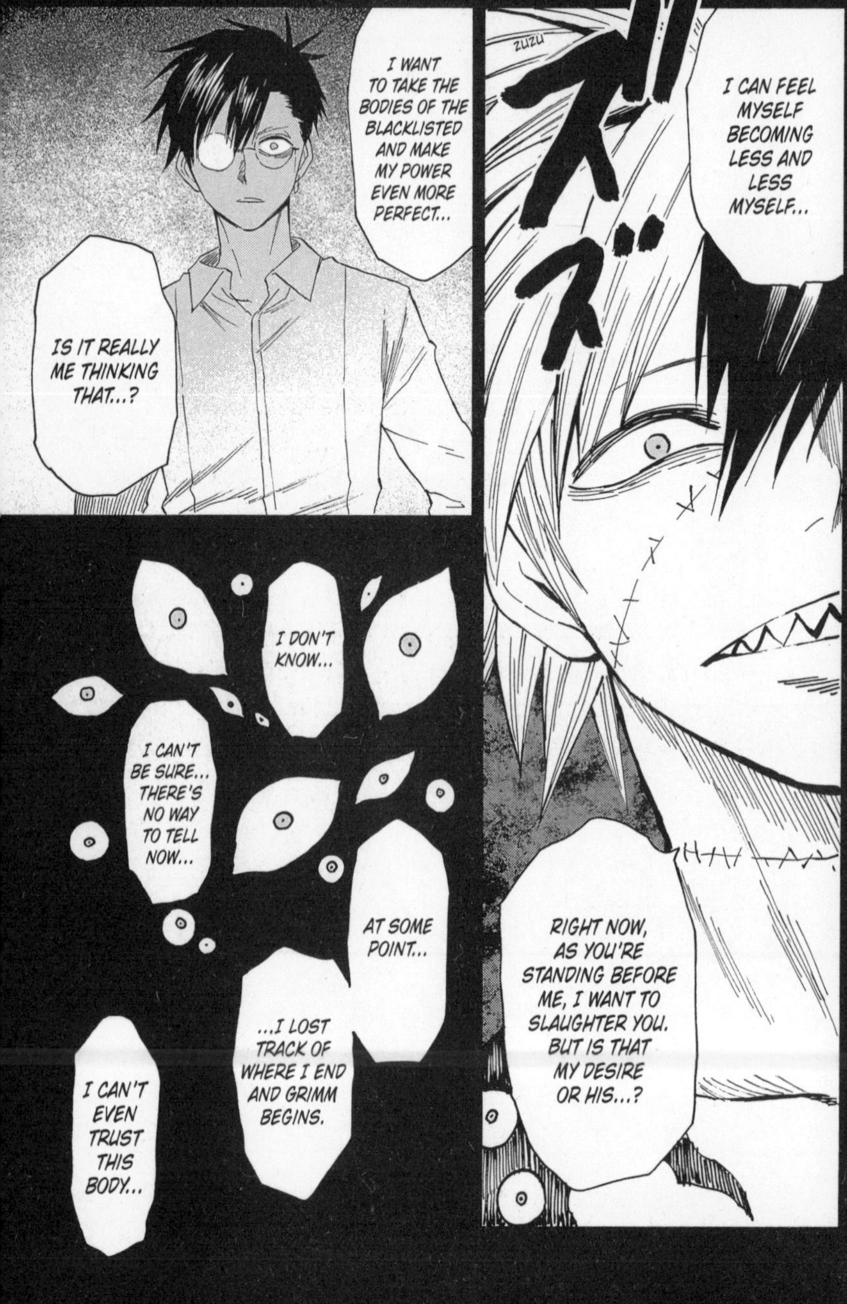
ZUZU
I CAN FEEL MYSELF BECOMING LESS AND LESS MYSELF...
RIGHT NOW, AS YOU'RE STANDING BEFORE ME, I WANT TO SLAUGHTER YOU. BUT IS THAT MY DESIRE OR HIS...?
I WANT TO TAKE THE BODIES OF THE BLACKLISTED AND MAKE MY POWER EVEN MORE PERFECT...
IS IT REALLY ME THINKING THAT...?
I DON'T KNOW...
I CAN'T BE SURE... THERE'S NO WAY TO TELL NOW...
AT SOME POINT...
...I LOST TRACK OF WHERE I END AND GRIMM BEGINS.
I CAN'T EVEN TRUST THIS BODY...

TELL ME THE TRUTH...

YOU HAVE NO INTENTION OF SAVING ME, DO YOU...?

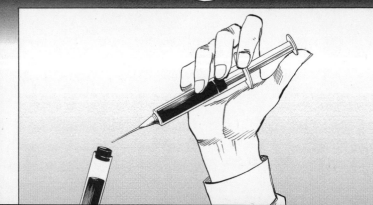

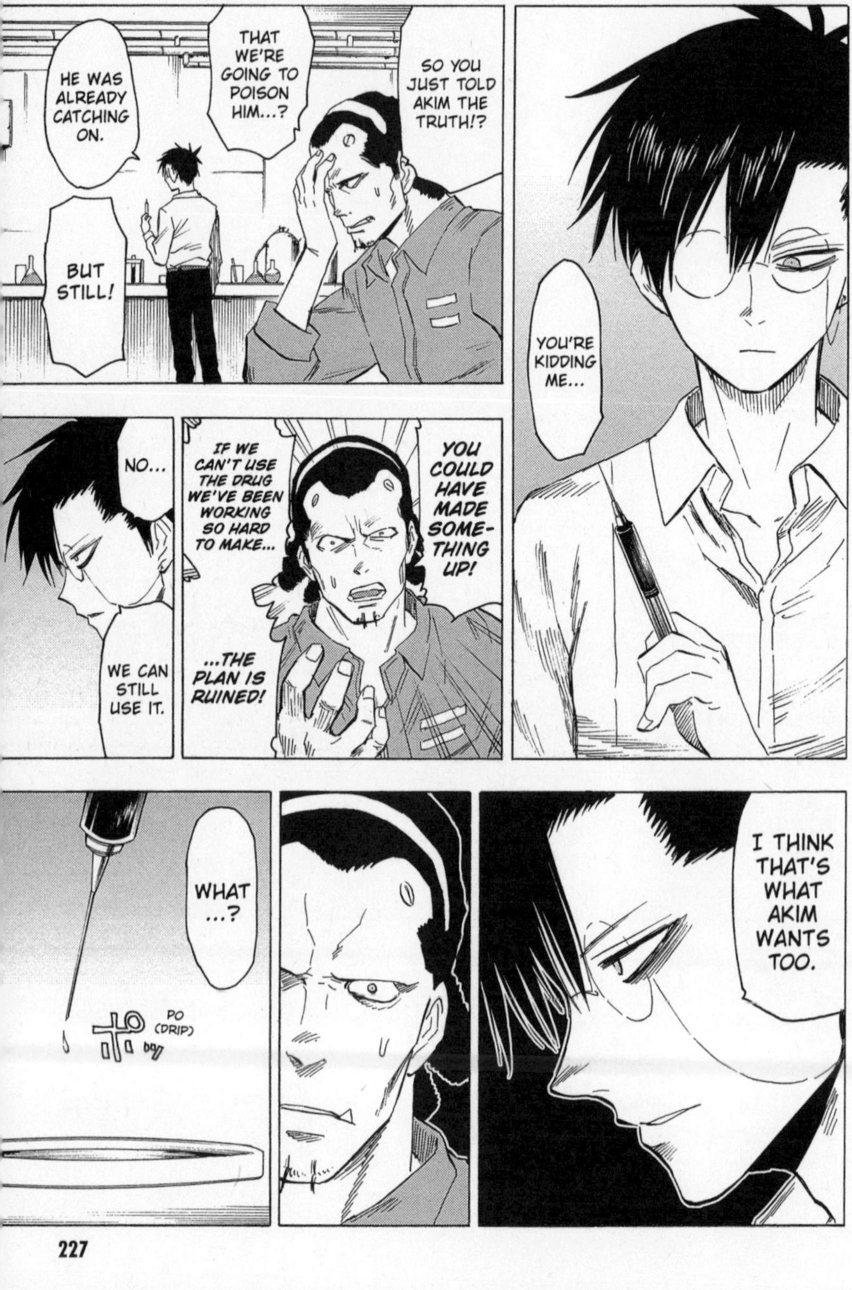
YOU'RE KIDDING ME...
SO YOU JUST TOLD AKIM THE TRUTH!?
THAT WE'RE GOING TO POISON HIM...?
HE WAS ALREADY CATCHING ON.
BUT STILL!
YOU COULD HAVE MADE SOME-THING UP!
IF WE CAN'T USE THE DRUG WE'VE BEEN WORKING SO HARD TO MAKE...
...THE PLAN IS RUINED!
NO...
WE CAN STILL USE IT.
I THINK THAT'S WHAT AKIM WANTS TOO.
WHAT ...?
PO (DRIP)

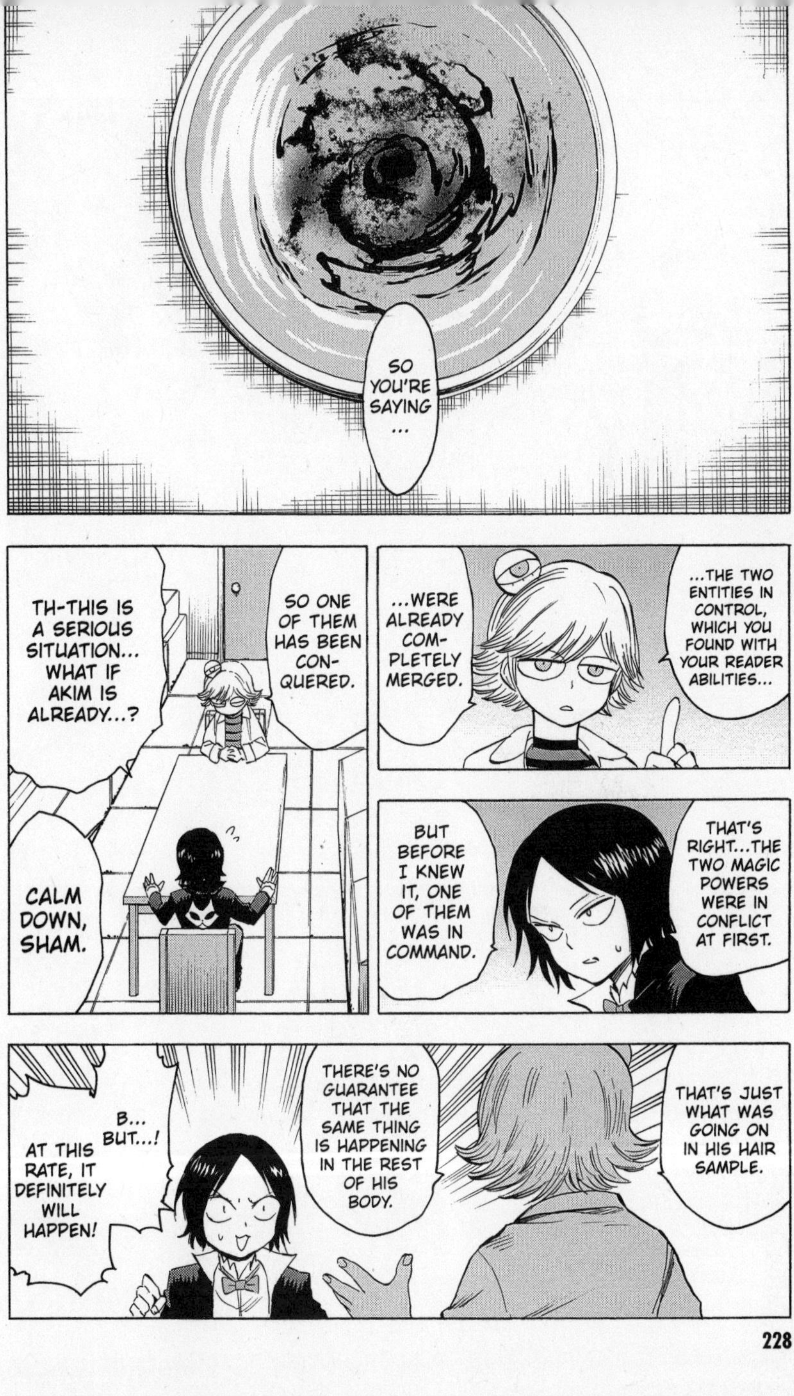
SO YOU'RE SAYING ...
...THE TWO ENTITIES IN CONTROL, WHICH YOU FOUND WITH YOUR READER ABILITIES...
...WERE ALREADY COM-PLETELY MERGED.
THAT'S RIGHT...THE TWO MAGIC POWERS WERE IN CONFLICT AT FIRST.
BUT BEFORE I KNEW IT, ONE OF THEM WAS IN COMMAND.
SO ONE OF THEM HAS BEEN CON-QUERED.
TH-THIS IS A SERIOUS SITUATION... WHAT IF AKIM IS ALREADY...?
CALM DOWN, SHAM.
THAT'S JUST WHAT WAS GOING ON IN HIS HAIR SAMPLE.
THERE'S NO GUARANTEE THAT THE SAME THING IS HAPPENING IN THE REST OF HIS BODY.
B... BUT...!
AT THIS RATE, IT DEFINITELY WILL HAPPEN!

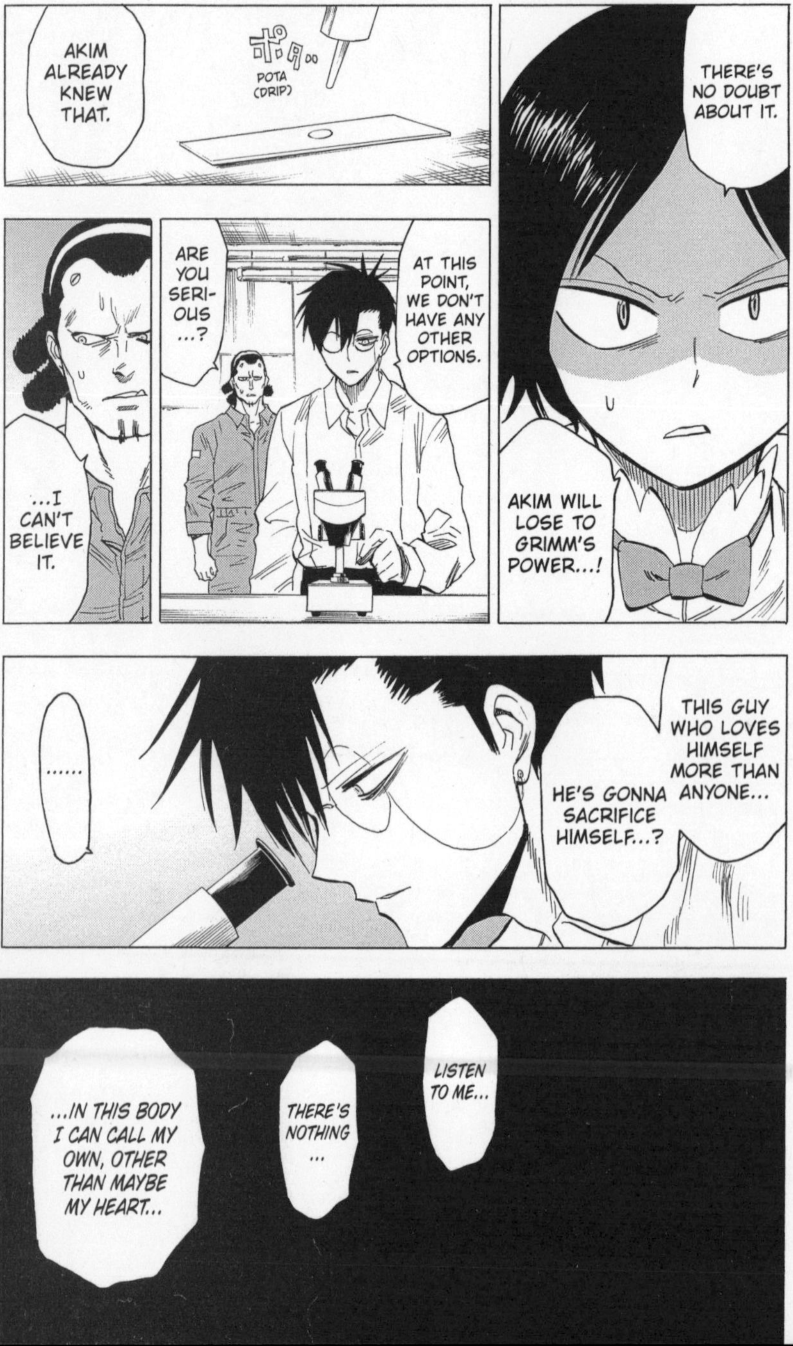
THERE'S NO DOUBT ABOUT IT.
AKIM WILL LOSE TO GRIMM'S POWER...!
ポタ
POTA (DRIP)
AKIM ALREADY KNEW THAT.
AT THIS POINT, WE DON'T HAVE ANY OTHER OPTIONS.
ARE YOU SERI-OUS ...?
...I CAN'T BELIEVE IT.
THIS GUY WHO LOVES HIMSELF MORE THAN ANYONE...
HE'S GONNA SACRIFICE HIMSELF...?
......
LISTEN TO ME...
THERE'S NOTHING ...
...IN THIS BODY I CAN CALL MY OWN, OTHER THAN MAYBE MY HEART...

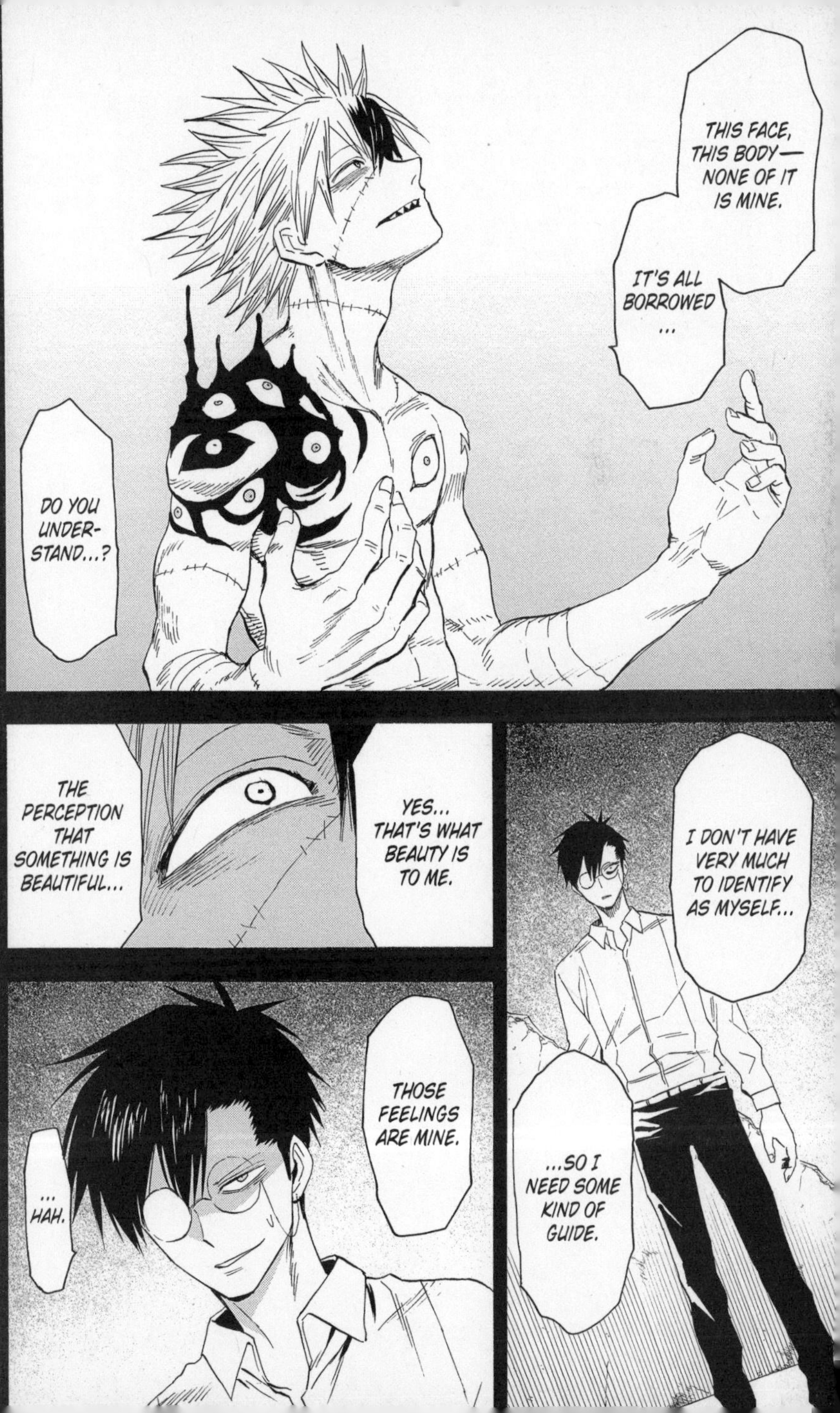
THIS FACE, THIS BODY— NONE OF IT IS MINE.
IT'S ALL BORROWED …
DO YOU UNDER-STAND…?
I DON'T HAVE VERY MUCH TO IDENTIFY AS MYSELF…
…SO I NEED SOME KIND OF GUIDE.
YES… THAT'S WHAT BEAUTY IS TO ME.
THE PERCEPTION THAT SOMETHING IS BEAUTIFUL…
THOSE FEELINGS ARE MINE.
… HAH.

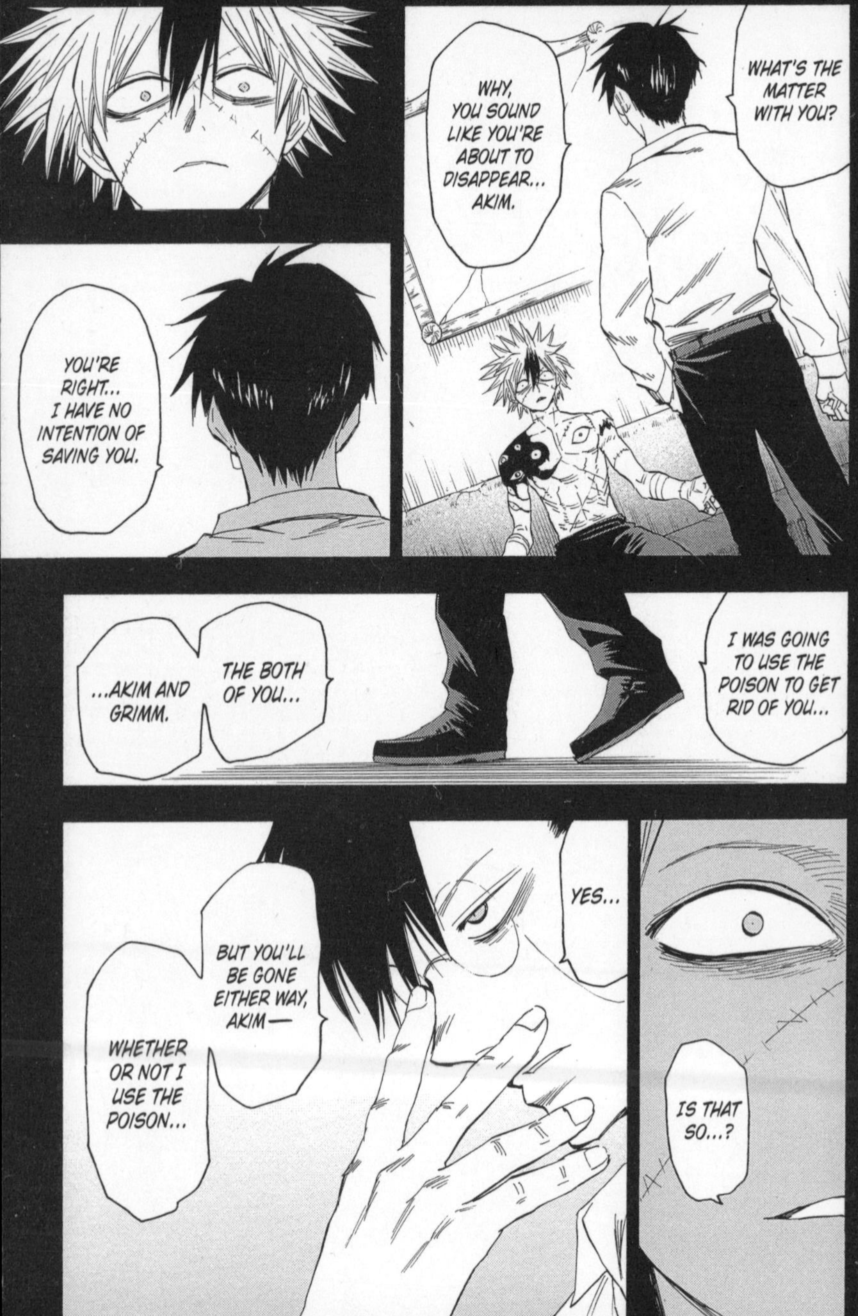
WHAT'S THE MATTER WITH YOU?
WHY, YOU SOUND LIKE YOU'RE ABOUT TO DISAPPEAR... AKIM.
YOU'RE RIGHT... I HAVE NO INTENTION OF SAVING YOU.
I WAS GOING TO USE THE POISON TO GET RID OF YOU...
THE BOTH OF YOU...
...AKIM AND GRIMM.
IS THAT SO...?
YES...
BUT YOU'LL BE GONE EITHER WAY, AKIM—
WHETHER OR NOT I USE THE POISON...

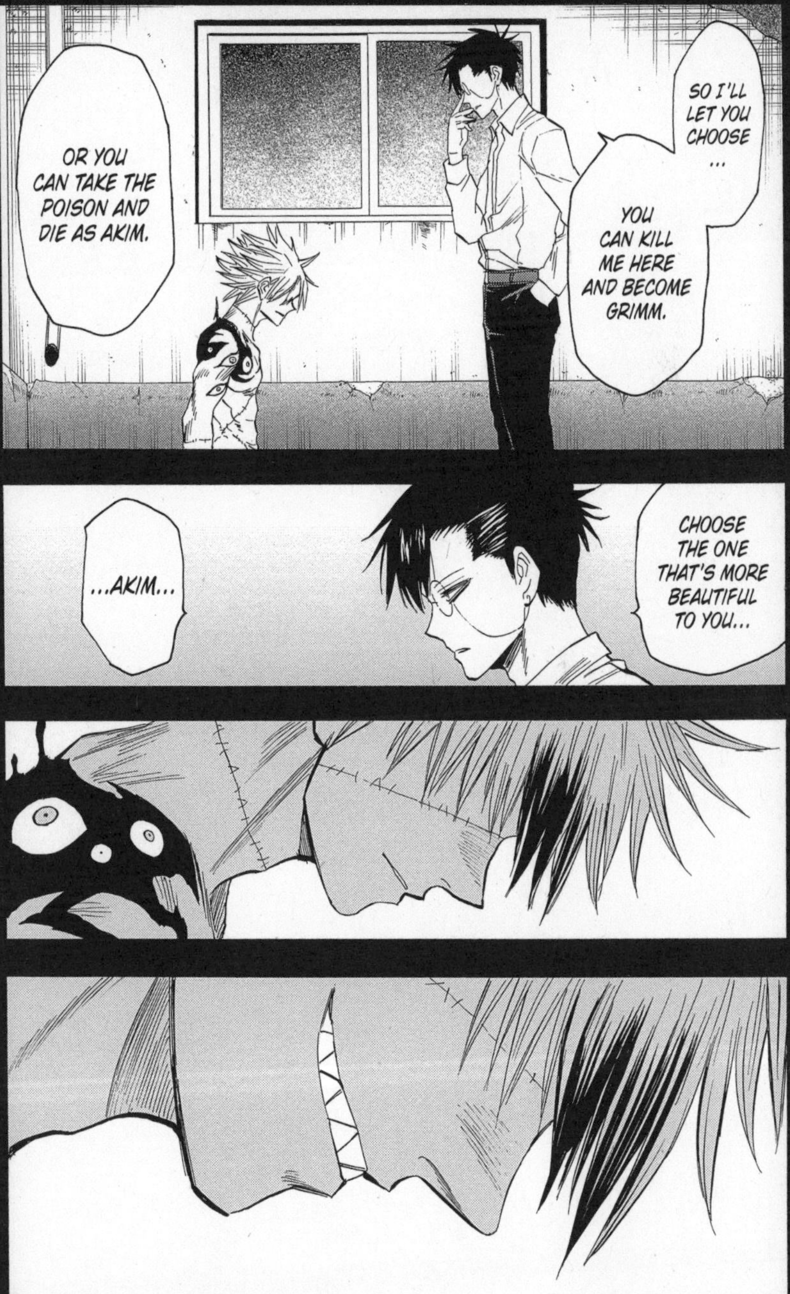
SO I'LL LET YOU CHOOSE ...
YOU CAN KILL ME HERE AND BECOME GRIMM.
OR YOU CAN TAKE THE POISON AND DIE AS AKIM.
CHOOSE THE ONE THAT'S MORE BEAUTIFUL TO YOU...
...AKIM...

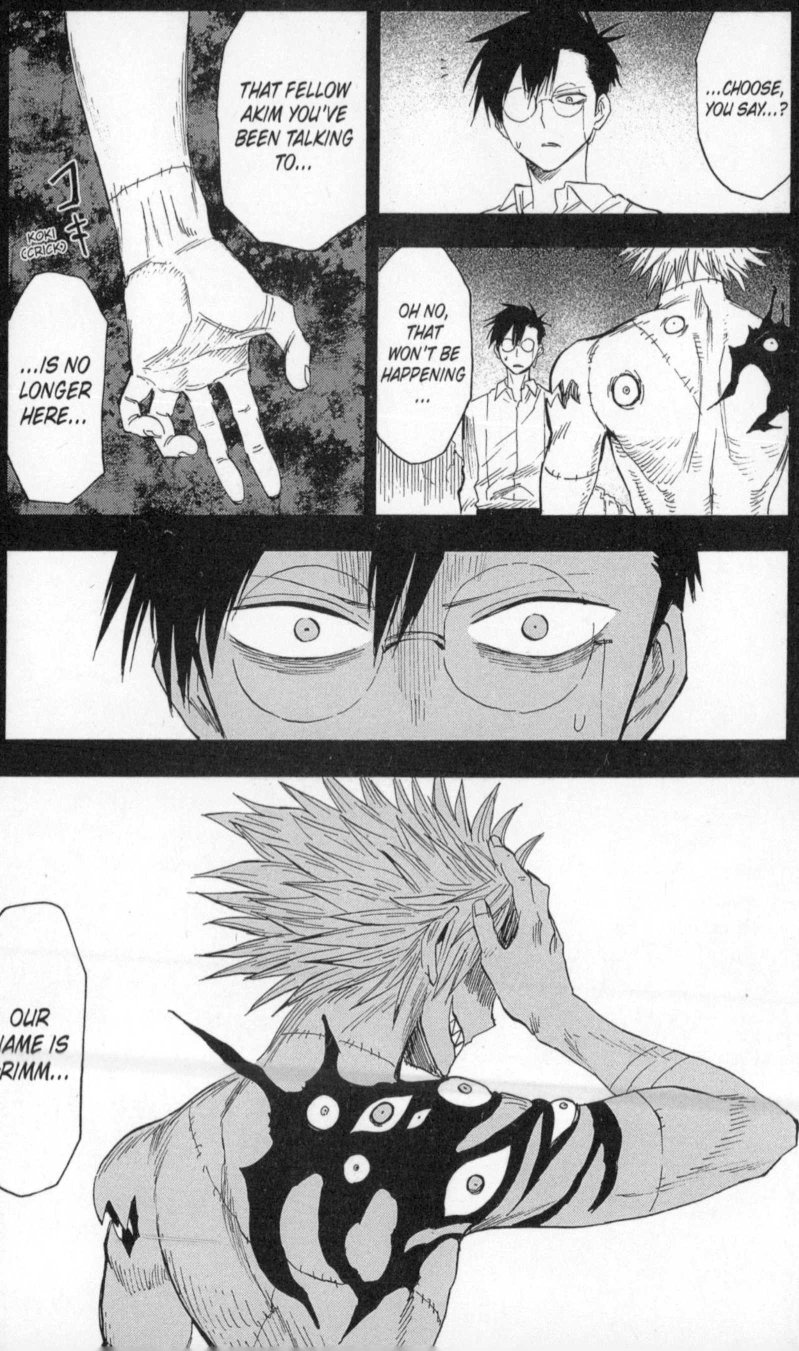
...CHOOSE, YOU SAY...?
OH NO, THAT WON'T BE HAPPENING...
THAT FELLOW AKIM YOU'VE BEEN TALKING TO...
KOKI (CRICK)
...IS NO LONGER HERE...
OUR NAME IS GRIMM...

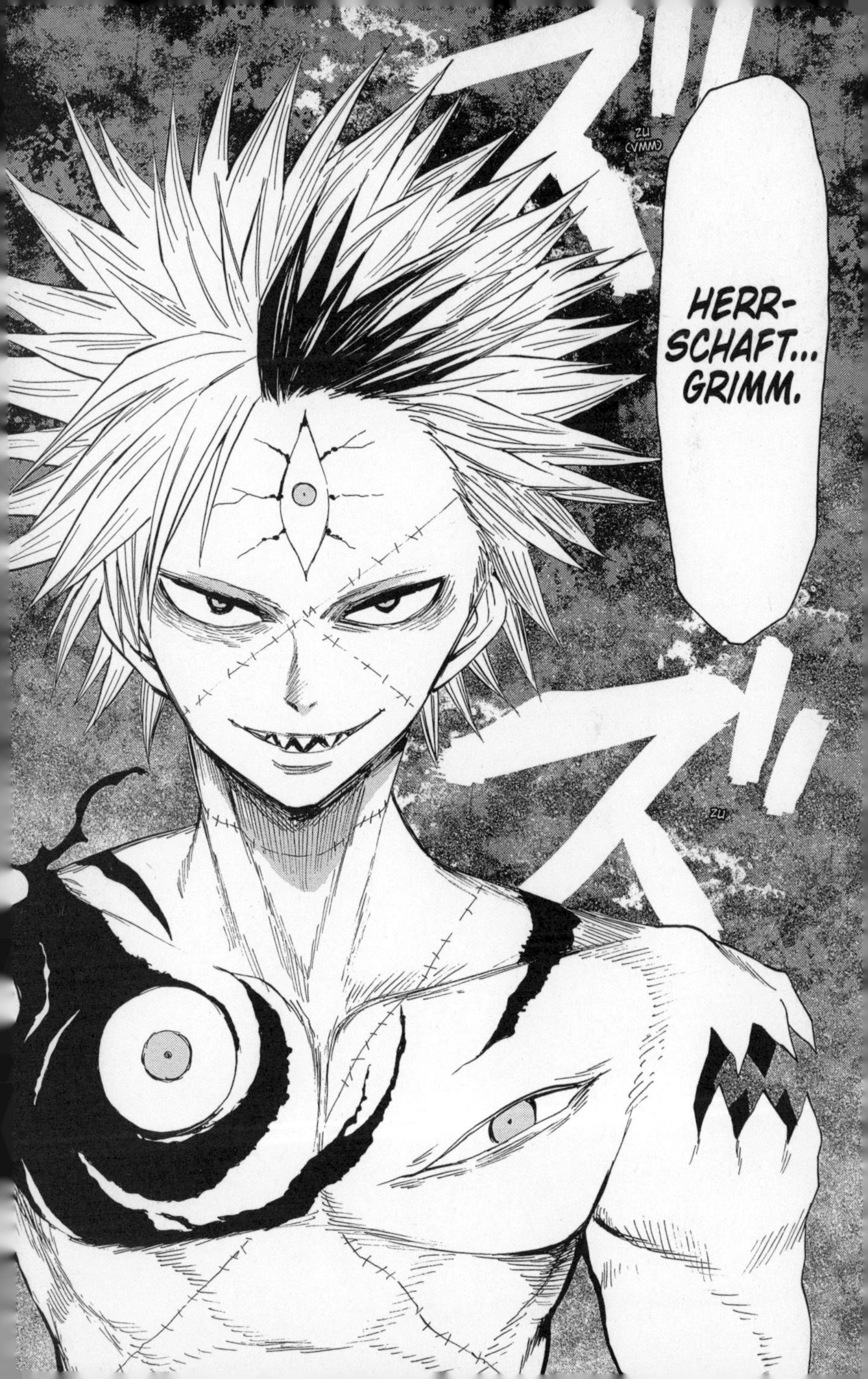
HERR-SCHAFT... GRIMM.
ZU (VMM)
ZU

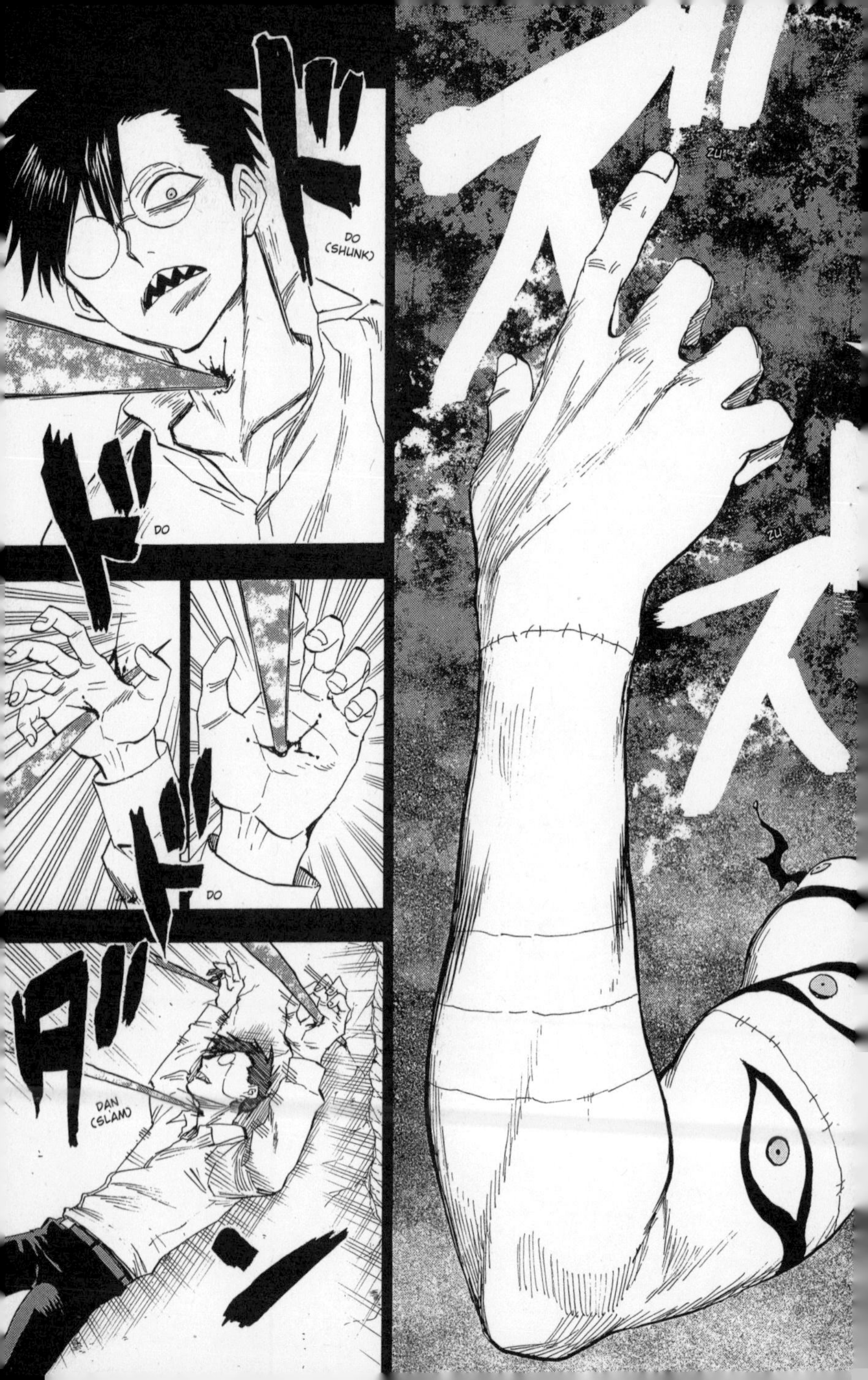
ZU
ZU
DO
(SHUNK)
DO
DO
DAN
(SLAM)

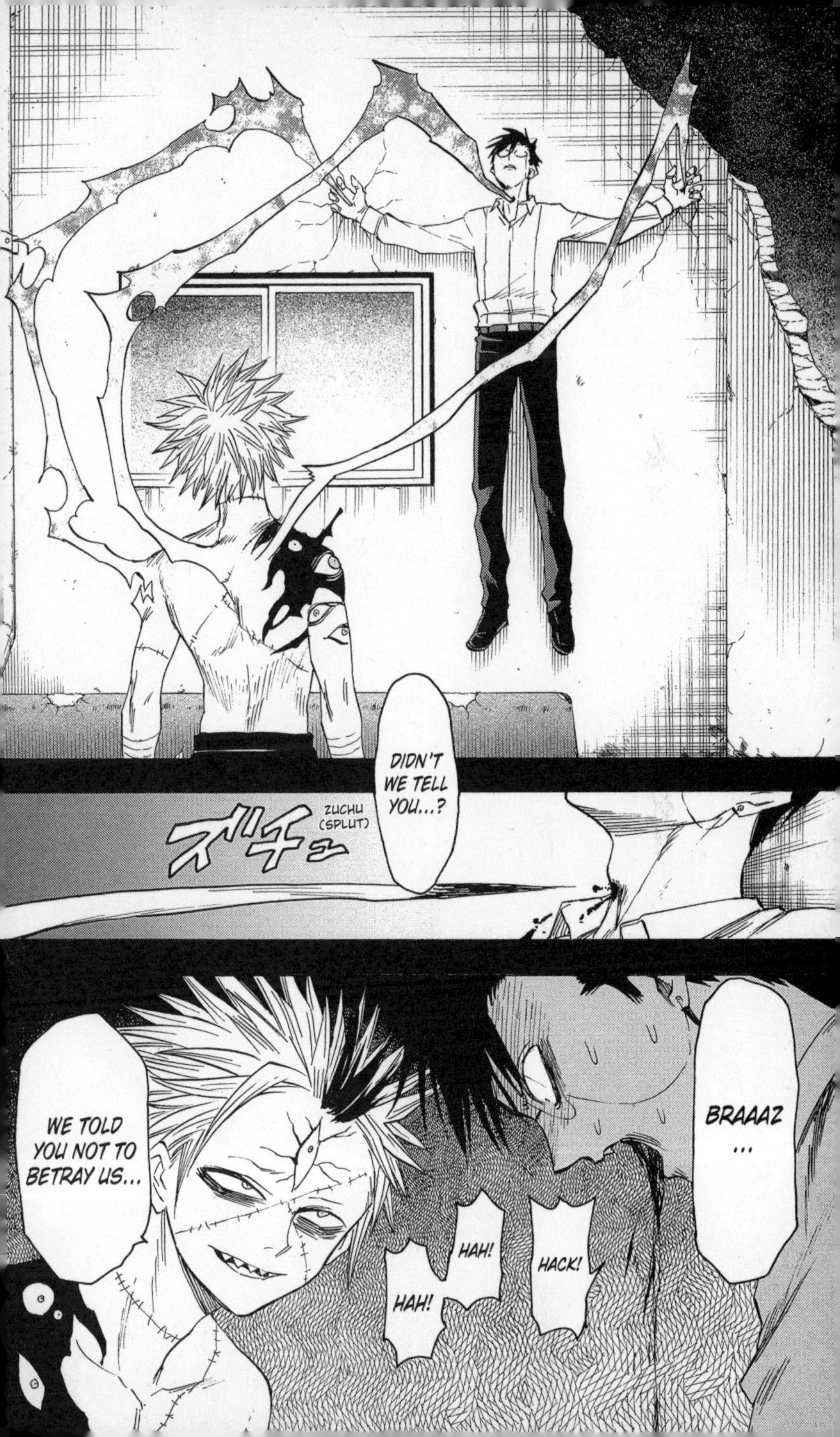
DIDN'T WE TELL YOU...?
ズチュ
ZUCHU (SPLUT)
BRAAAZ ...
HACK!
HAH!
HAH!
WE TOLD YOU NOT TO BETRAY US...

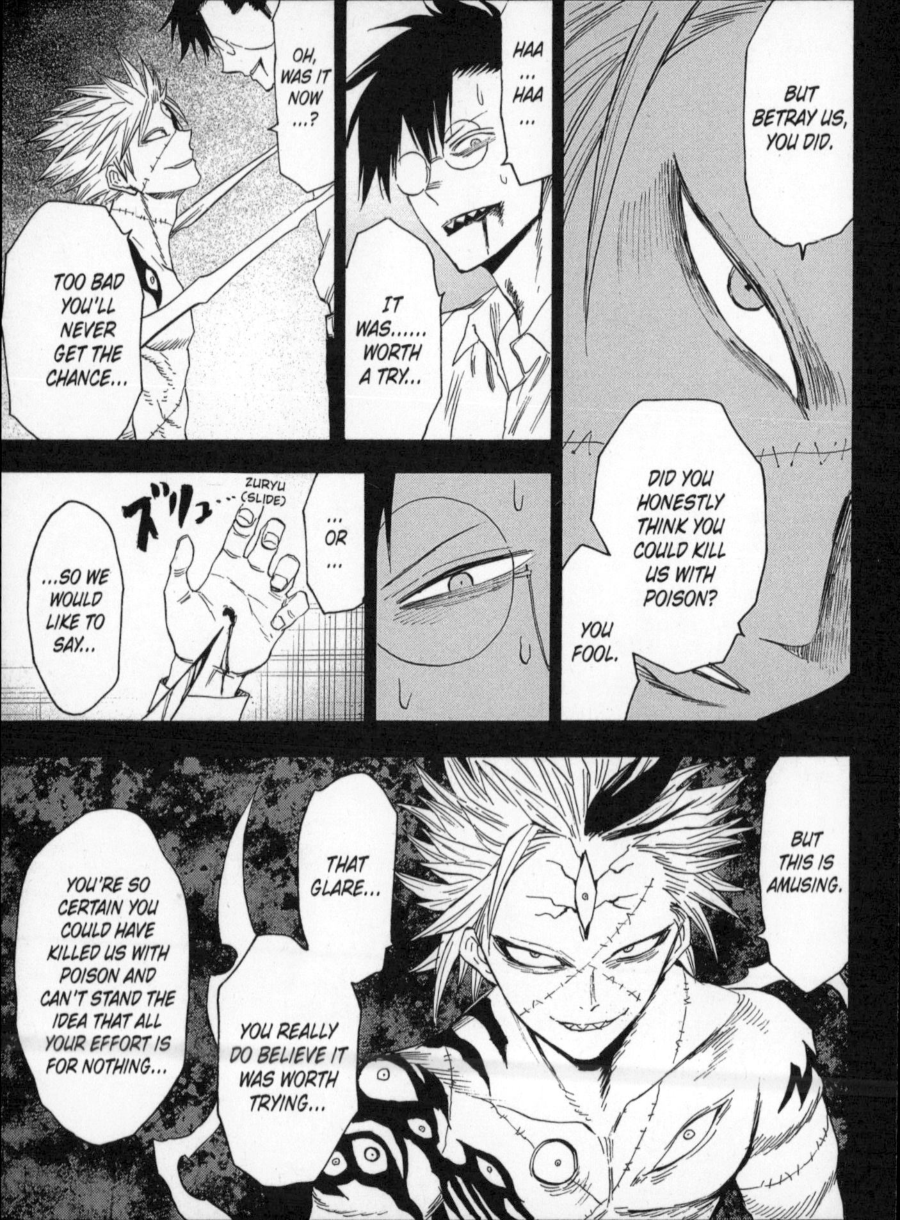
BUT BETRAY US, YOU DID.
DID YOU HONESTLY THINK YOU COULD KILL US WITH POISON?
YOU FOOL.
HAA ... HAA ...
IT WAS...... WORTH A TRY...
OH, WAS IT NOW ...?
TOO BAD YOU'LL NEVER GET THE CHANCE...
... OR ...
ZURYU (SLIDE)
...SO WE WOULD LIKE TO SAY...
BUT THIS IS AMUSING.
THAT GLARE...
YOU REALLY DO BELIEVE IT WAS WORTH TRYING...
YOU'RE SO CERTAIN YOU COULD HAVE KILLED US WITH POISON AND CAN'T STAND THE IDEA THAT ALL YOUR EFFORT IS FOR NOTHING...

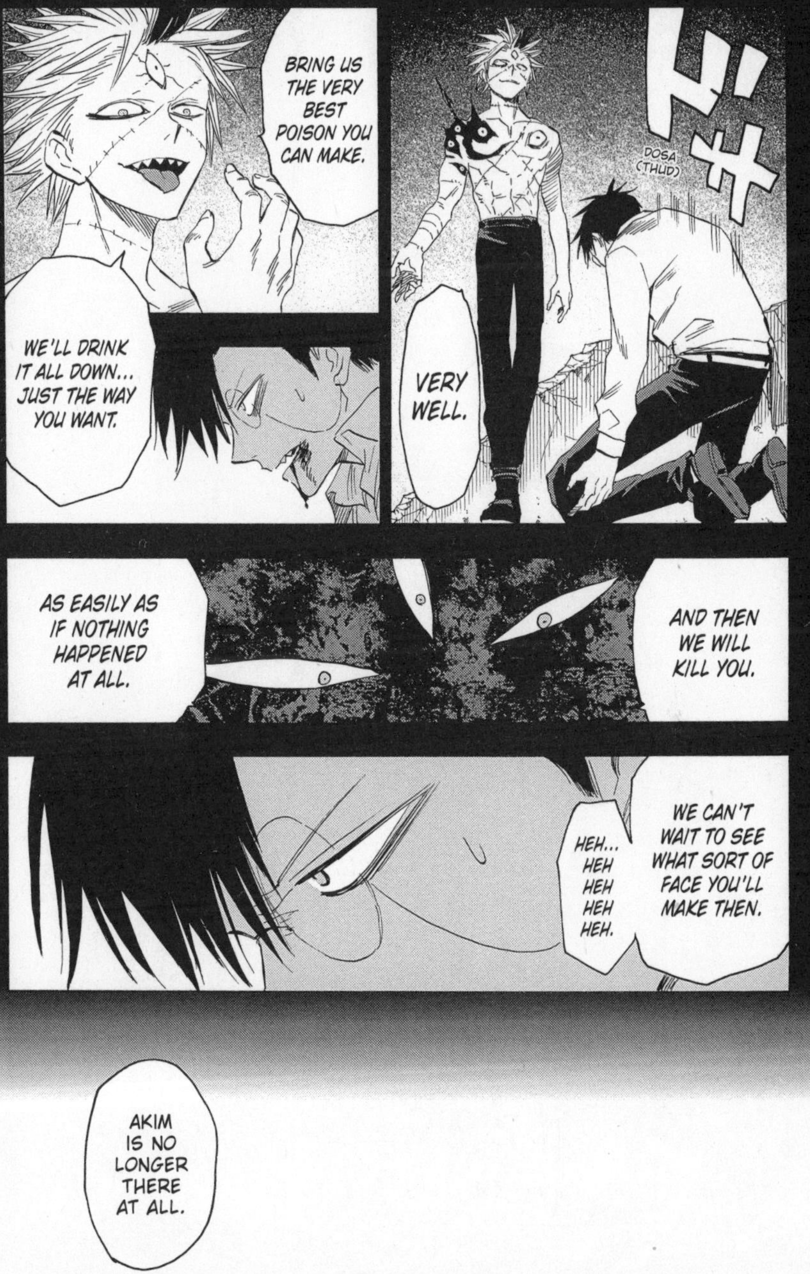
DOSA (THUD)
VERY WELL.
BRING US THE VERY BEST POISON YOU CAN MAKE.
WE'LL DRINK IT ALL DOWN... JUST THE WAY YOU WANT.
AND THEN WE WILL KILL YOU.
AS EASILY AS IF NOTHING HAPPENED AT ALL.
WE CAN'T WAIT TO SEE WHAT SORT OF FACE YOU'LL MAKE THEN.
HEH... HEH HEH HEH HEH.
AKIM IS NO LONGER THERE AT ALL.

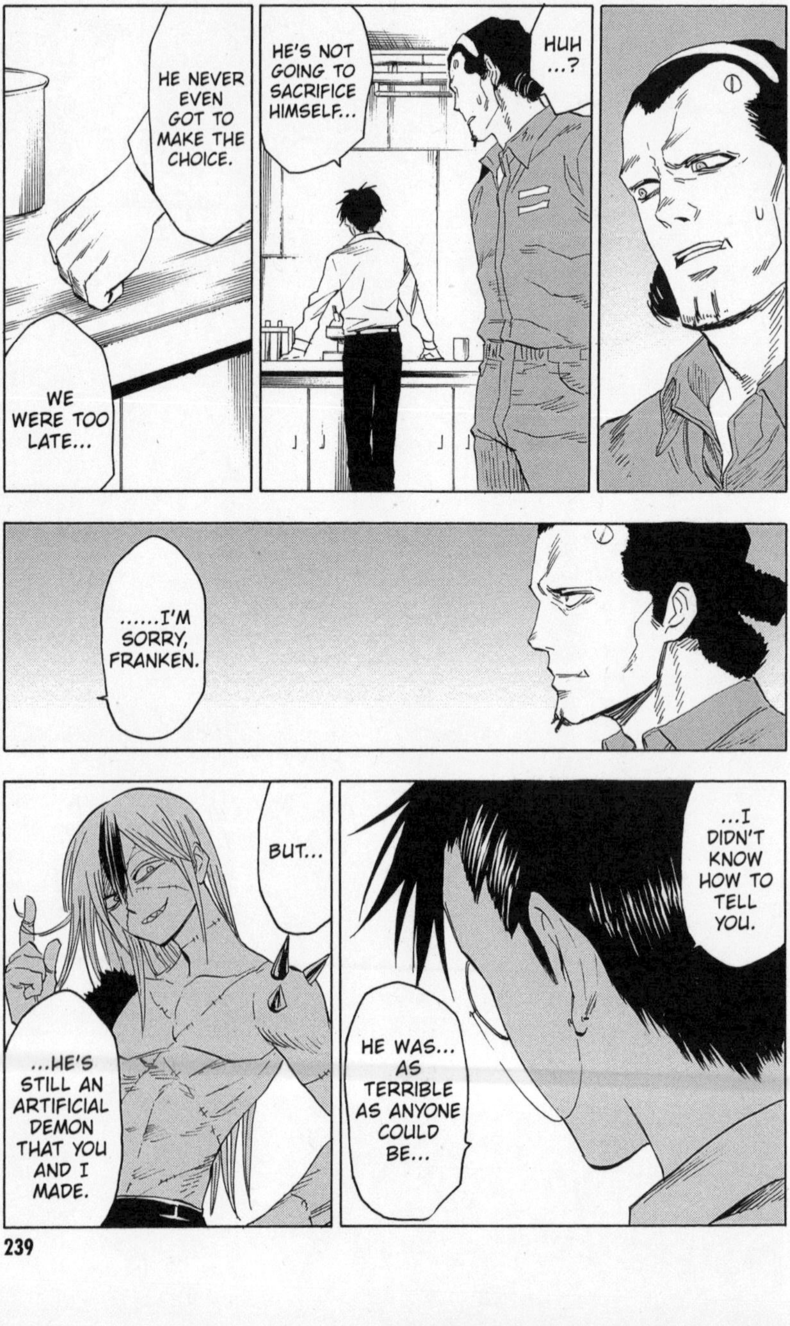
HUH ...?
HE'S NOT GOING TO SACRIFICE HIMSELF...
HE NEVER EVEN GOT TO MAKE THE CHOICE.
WE WERE TOO LATE...
......I'M SORRY, FRANKEN.
...I DIDN'T KNOW HOW TO TELL YOU.
HE WAS... AS TERRIBLE AS ANYONE COULD BE...
BUT...
...HE'S STILL AN ARTIFICIAL DEMON THAT YOU AND I MADE.

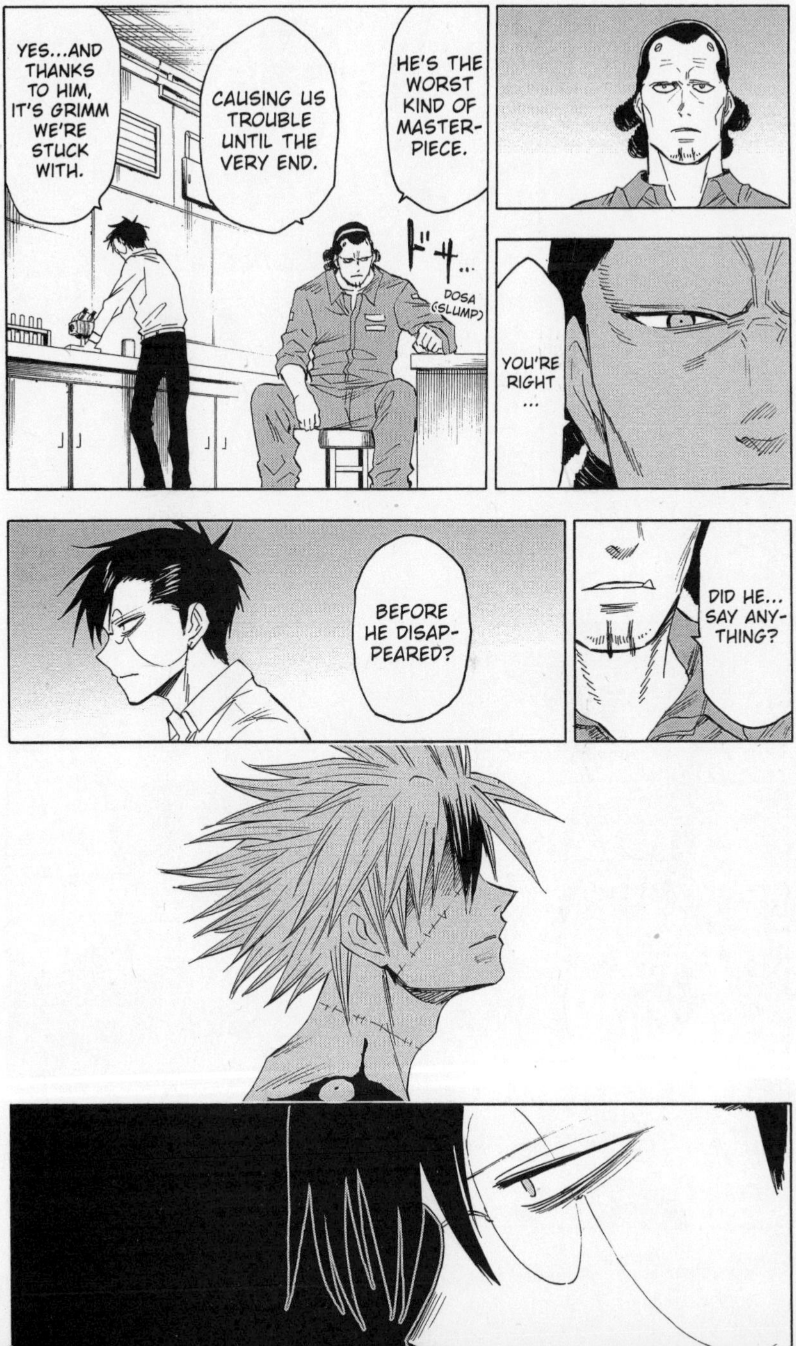
YOU'RE RIGHT ...
HE'S THE WORST KIND OF MASTER-PIECE.
CAUSING US TROUBLE UNTIL THE VERY END.
YES...AND THANKS TO HIM, IT'S GRIMM WE'RE STUCK WITH.
ドサ…
DOSA (SLUMP)
DID HE... SAY ANY-THING?
BEFORE HE DISAP-PEARED?

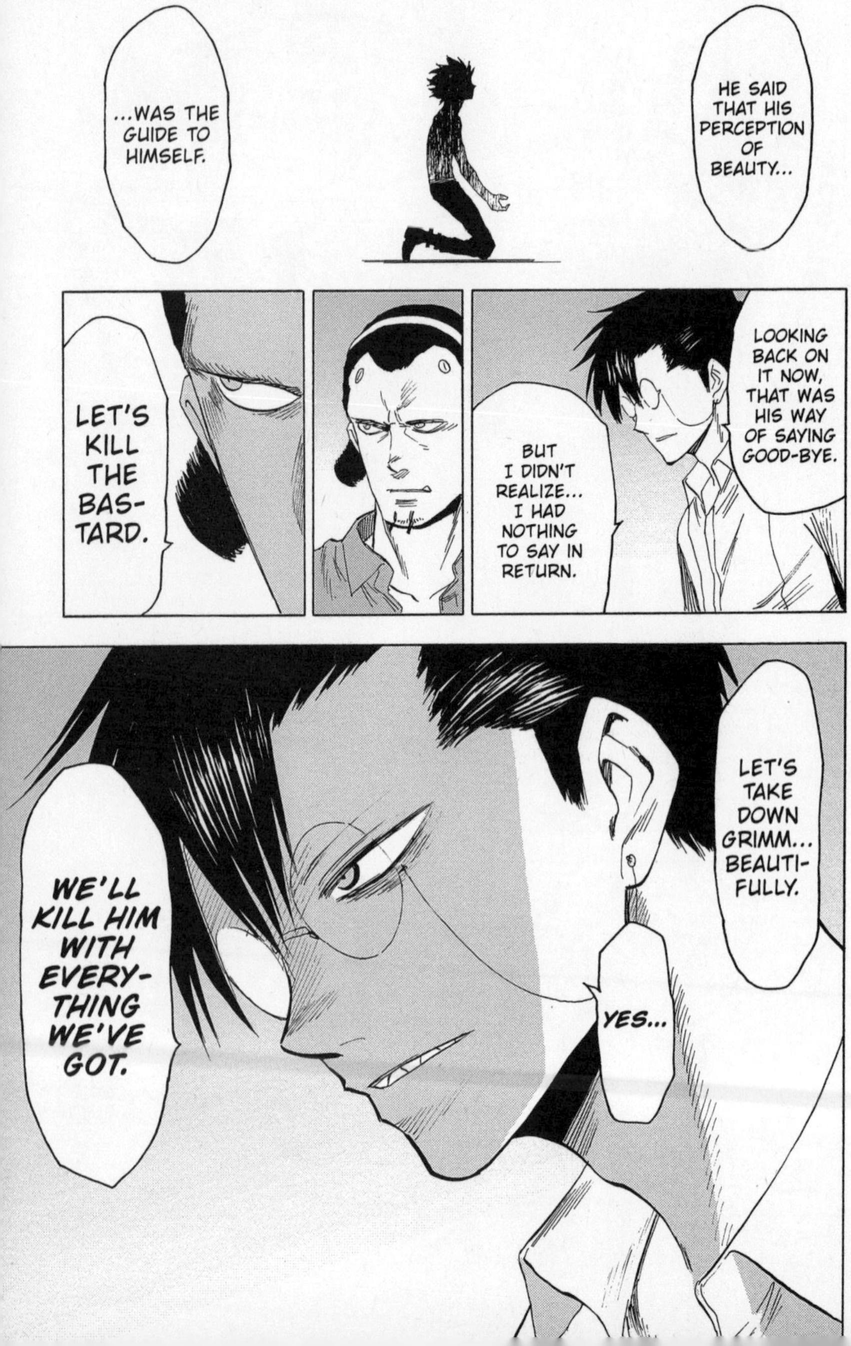
HE SAID THAT HIS PERCEPTION OF BEAUTY...
...WAS THE GUIDE TO HIMSELF.
LOOKING BACK ON IT NOW, THAT WAS HIS WAY OF SAYING GOOD-BYE.
BUT I DIDN'T REALIZE... I HAD NOTHING TO SAY IN RETURN.
LET'S KILL THE BAS-TARD.
LET'S TAKE DOWN GRIMM... BEAUTI-FULLY.
YES...
WE'LL KILL HIM WITH EVERY-THING WE'VE GOT.

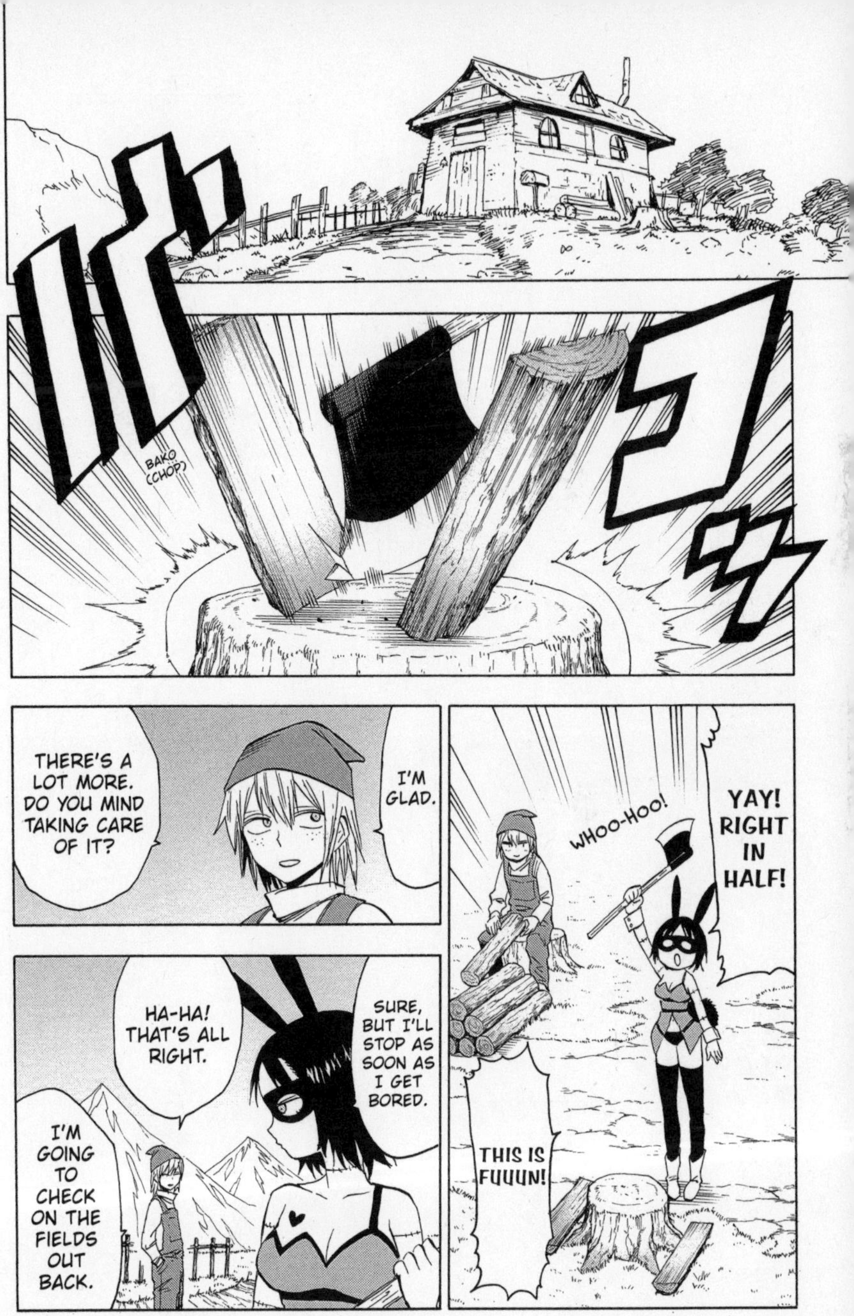
BAKO (CHOP)
YAY! RIGHT IN HALF!
WHOO-HOO!
THIS IS FUUUN!
I'M GLAD.
THERE'S A LOT MORE. DO YOU MIND TAKING CARE OF IT?
SURE, BUT I'LL STOP AS SOON AS I GET BORED.
HA-HA! THAT'S ALL RIGHT.
I'M GOING TO CHECK ON THE FIELDS OUT BACK.

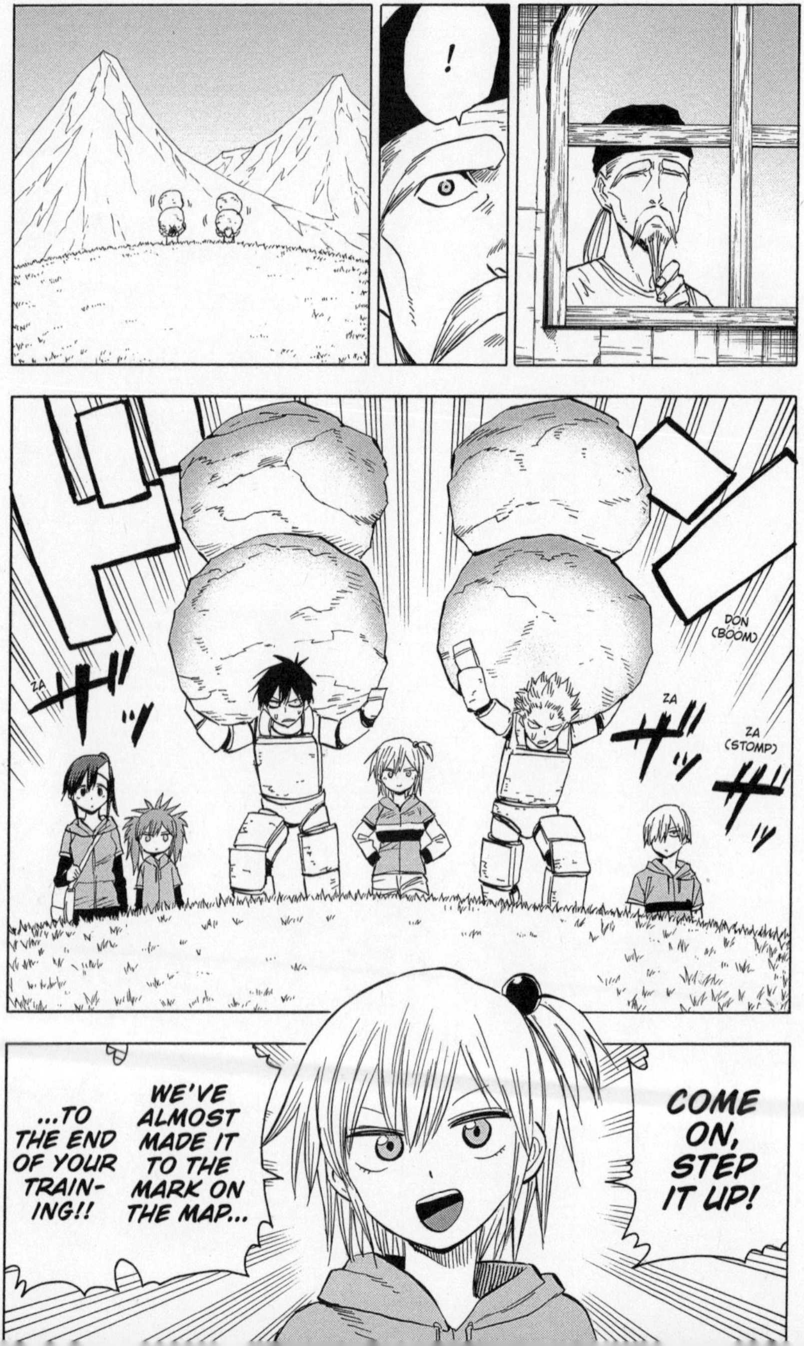
!
DON (BOOM)
ZA
ZA (STOMP)
ZA
COME ON, STEP IT UP!
WE'VE ALMOST MADE IT TO THE MARK ON THE MAP...
...TO THE END OF YOUR TRAIN-ING!!

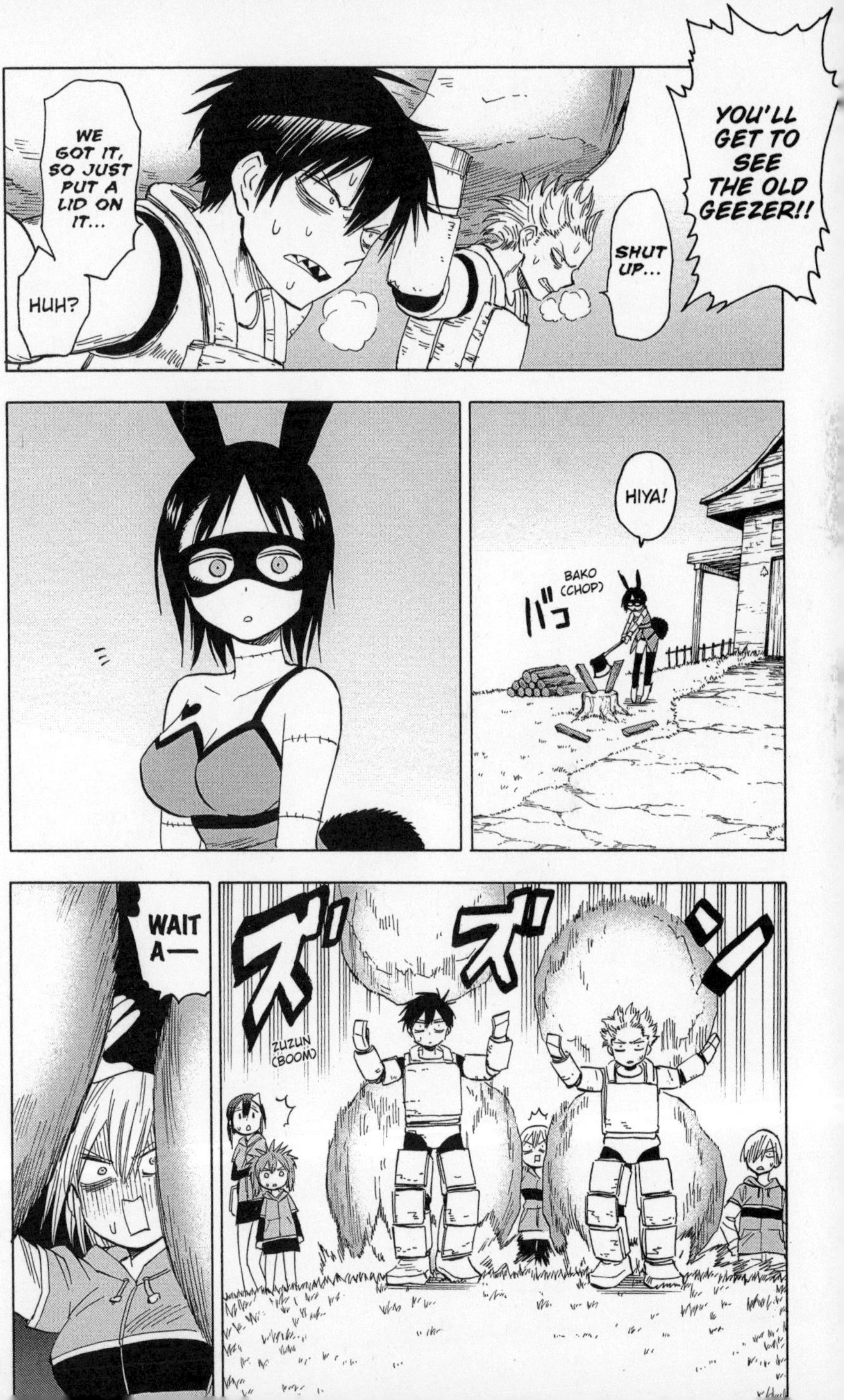
YOU'LL GET TO SEE THE OLD GEEZER!!
SHUT UP...
WE GOT IT, SO JUST PUT A LID ON IT...
HUH?
HIYA!
バコ
BAKO (CHOP)
ズズン
ZUZUN (BOOM)
WAIT A—

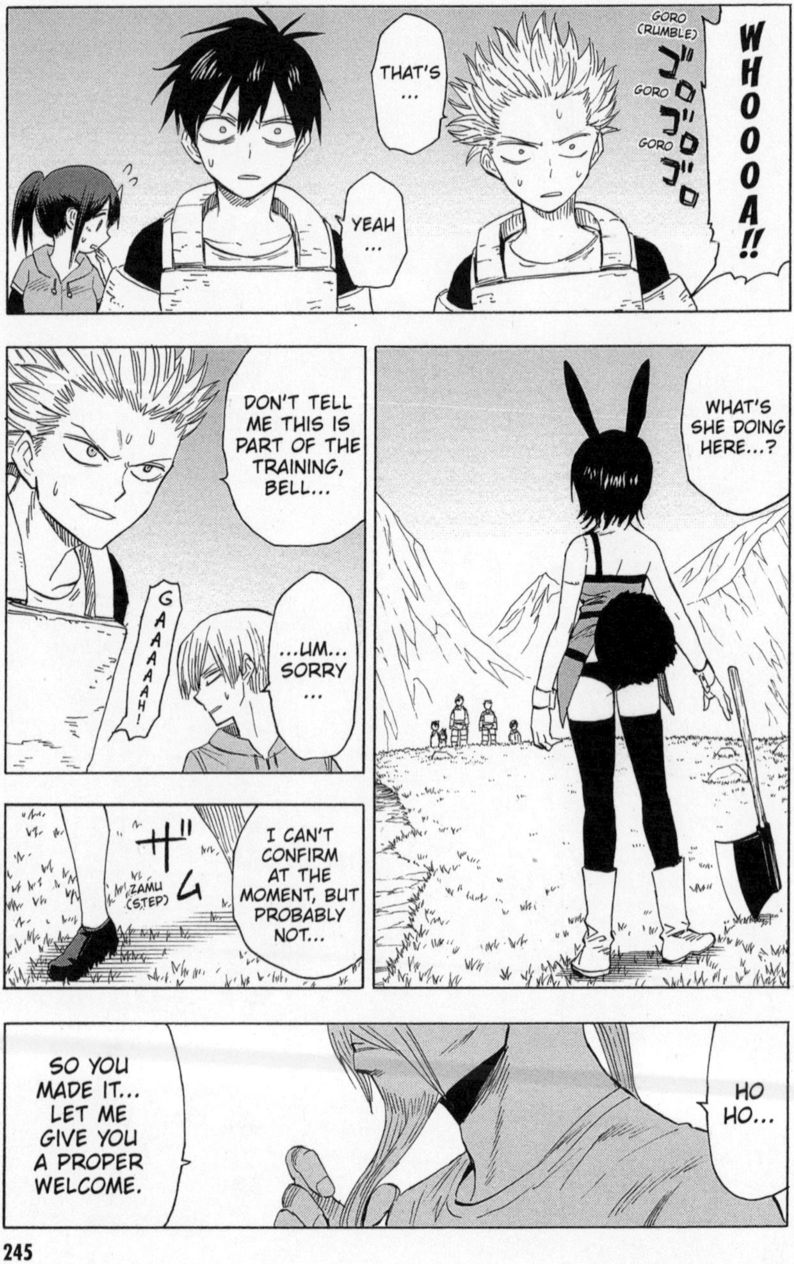
WHOOOOA!!
GORO (RUMBLE) ゴロ GORO ゴロ GORO ゴロ
THAT'S ...
YEAH ...
WHAT'S SHE DOING HERE...?
DON'T TELL ME THIS IS PART OF THE TRAINING, BELL...
GAAAAAAH!
...UM... SORRY ...
I CAN'T CONFIRM AT THE MOMENT, BUT PROBABLY NOT...
ザム ZAMU (STEP)
HO HO...
SO YOU MADE IT... LET ME GIVE YOU A PROPER WELCOME.

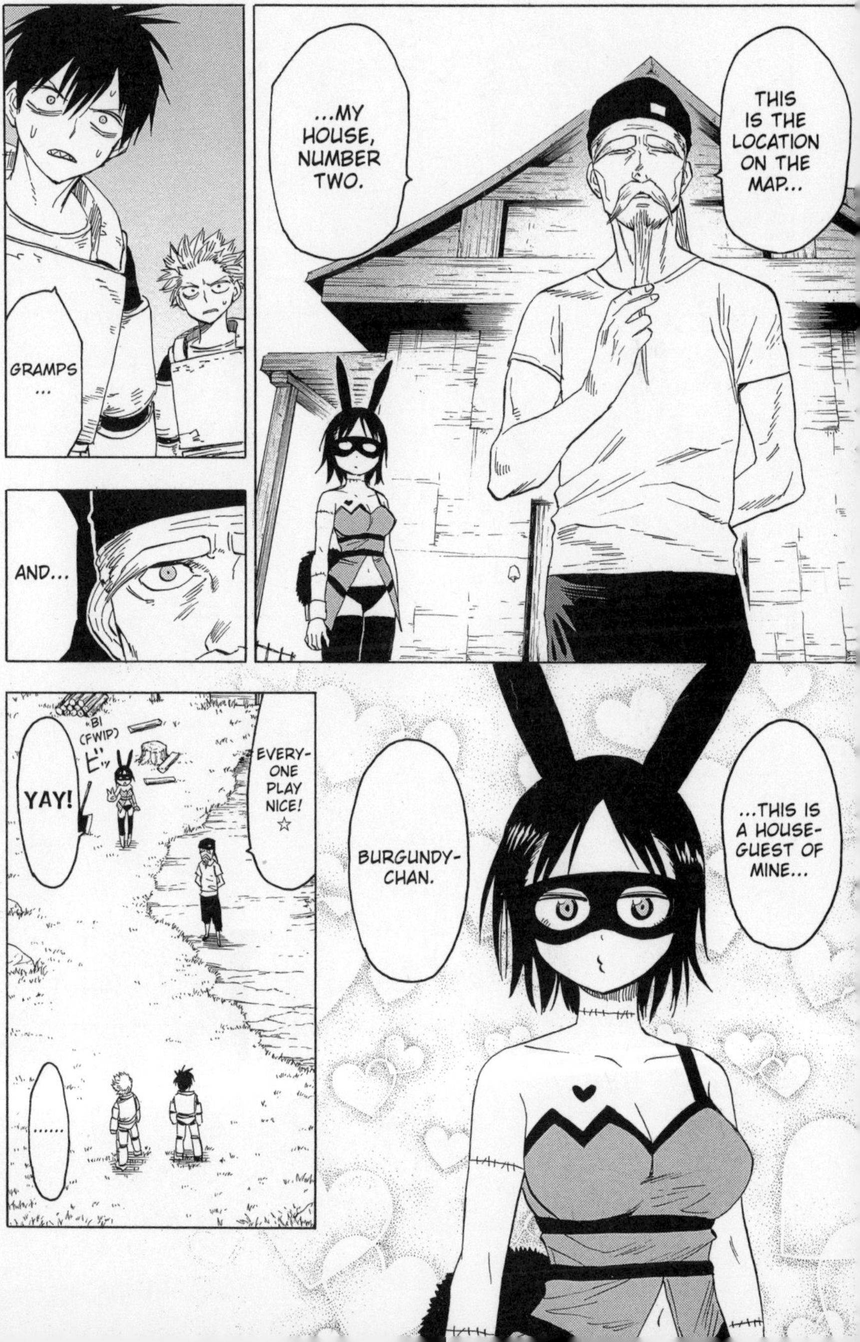
THIS IS THE LOCATION ON THE MAP...
...MY HOUSE, NUMBER TWO.
GRAMPS ...
AND...
...THIS IS A HOUSE-GUEST OF MINE...
BURGUNDY-CHAN.
EVERY-ONE PLAY NICE! ☆
BI (FWIP) ビッ
YAY!
......

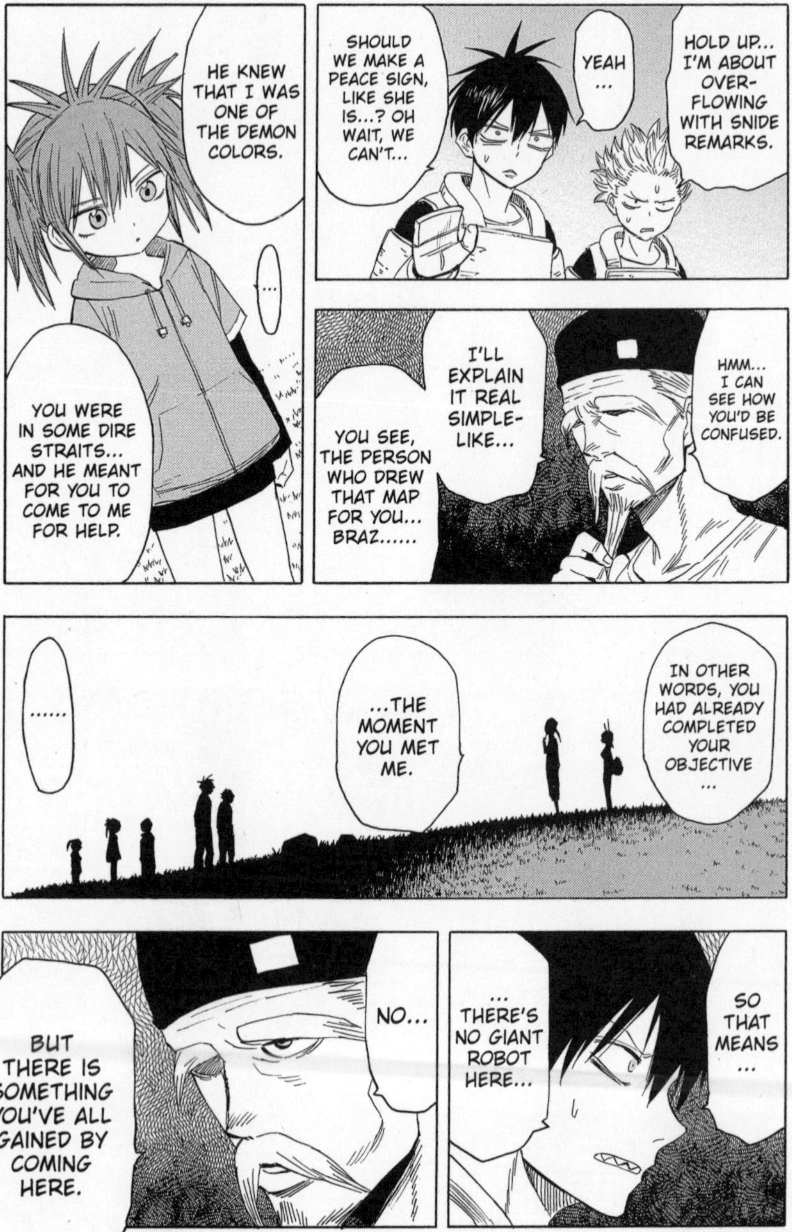
HOLD UP... I'M ABOUT OVER-FLOWING WITH SNIDE REMARKS.
YEAH ...
SHOULD WE MAKE A PEACE SIGN, LIKE SHE IS...? OH WAIT, WE CAN'T...
HMM... I CAN SEE HOW YOU'D BE CONFUSED.
I'LL EXPLAIN IT REAL SIMPLE-LIKE...
YOU SEE, THE PERSON WHO DREW THAT MAP FOR YOU... BRAZ......
HE KNEW THAT I WAS ONE OF THE DEMON COLORS.
...
YOU WERE IN SOME DIRE STRAITS... AND HE MEANT FOR YOU TO COME TO ME FOR HELP.
IN OTHER WORDS, YOU HAD ALREADY COMPLETED YOUR OBJECTIVE ...
...THE MOMENT YOU MET ME.
......
SO THAT MEANS ...
... THERE'S NO GIANT ROBOT HERE...
NO...
BUT THERE IS SOMETHING YOU'VE ALL GAINED BY COMING HERE.

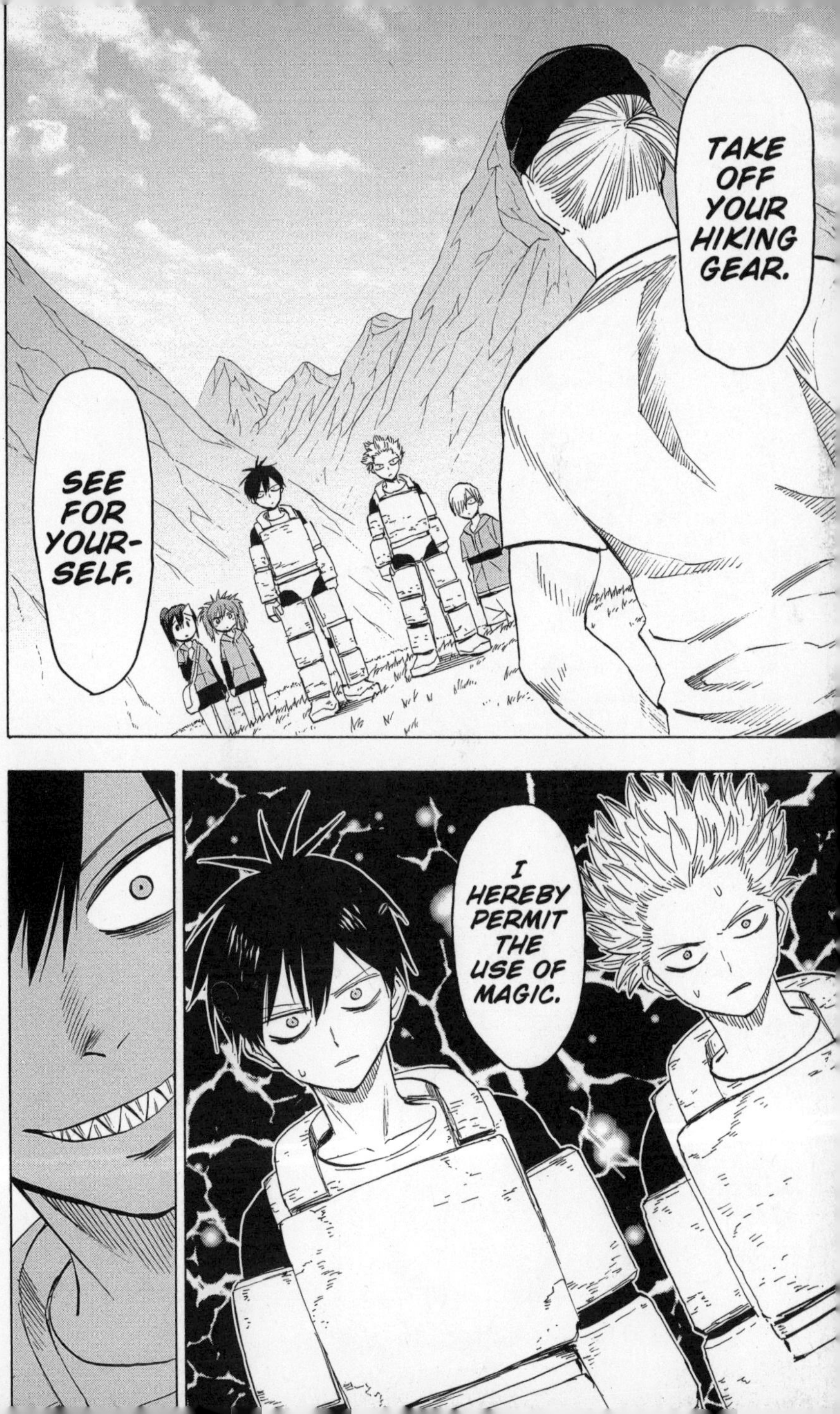
TAKE OFF YOUR HIKING GEAR.
SEE FOR YOUR-SELF.
I HEREBY PERMIT THE USE OF MAGIC.

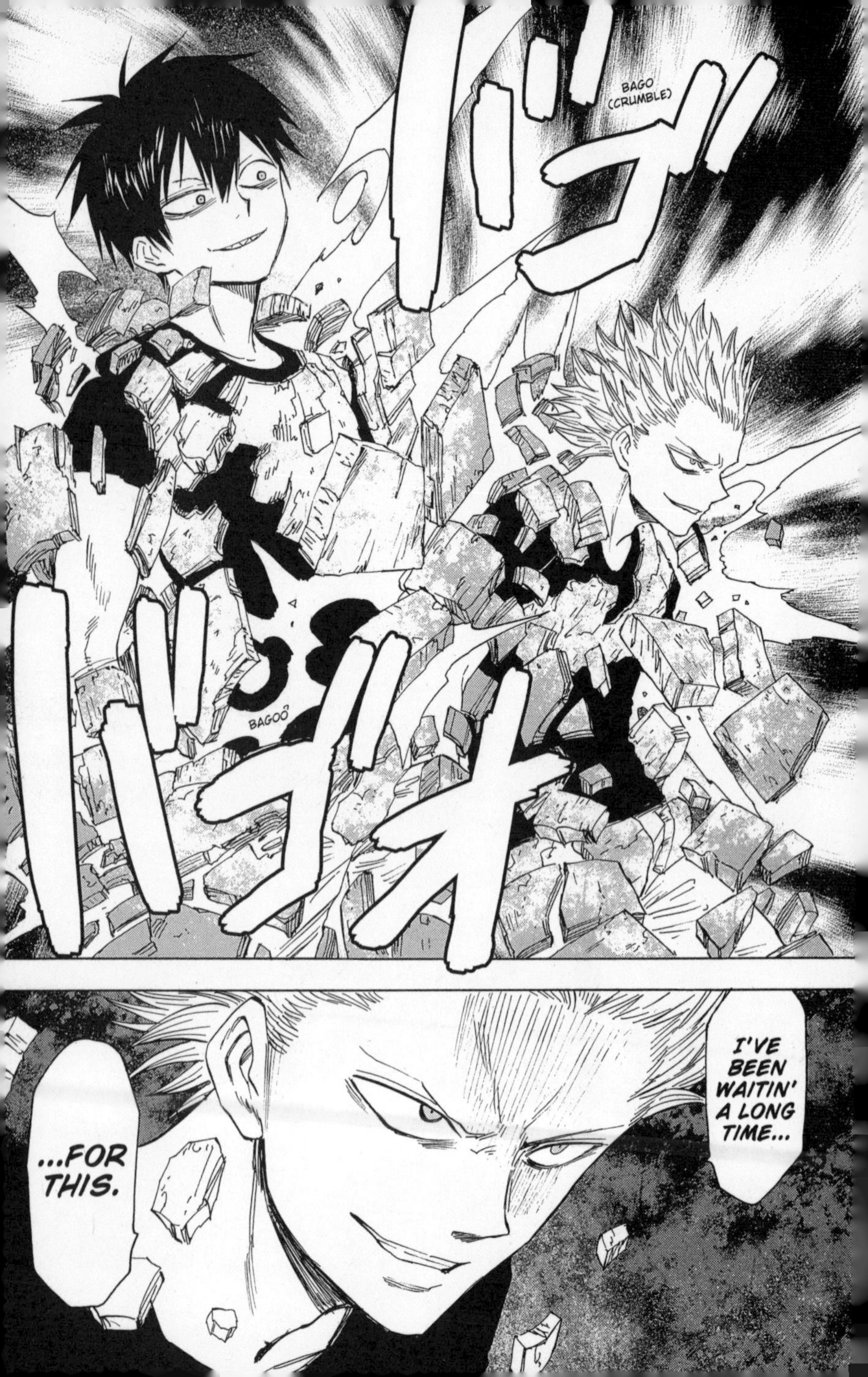
BAGO (CRUMBLE)
BAGOO
I'VE BEEN WAITIN' A LONG TIME...
...FOR THIS.

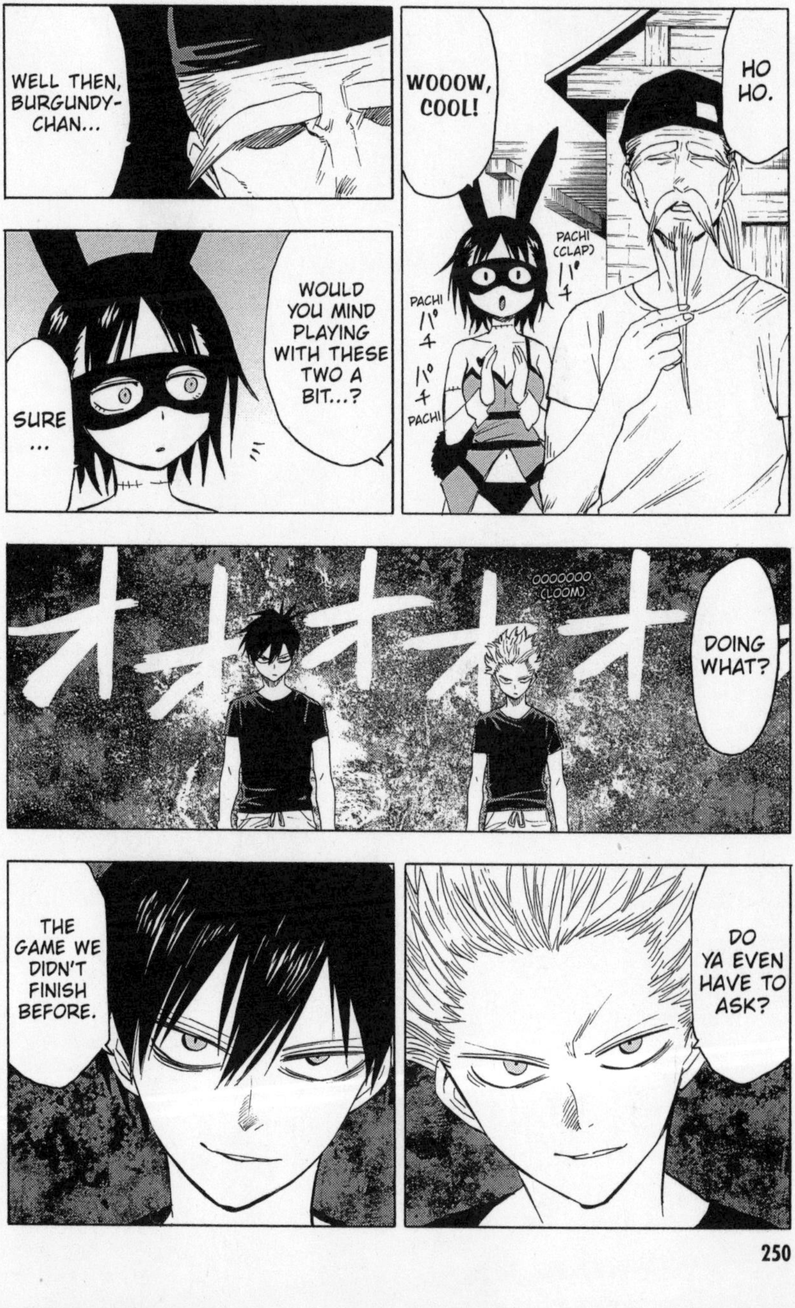
HO HO.
WOOOW, COOL!
PACHI (CLAP) パチ
PACHI パチ
パチ PACHI
WELL THEN, BURGUNDY-CHAN...
WOULD YOU MIND PLAYING WITH THESE TWO A BIT...?
SURE ...
DOING WHAT?
OOOOOOO (LOOM)
オオオオ
DO YA EVEN HAVE TO ASK?
THE GAME WE DIDN'T FINISH BEFORE.

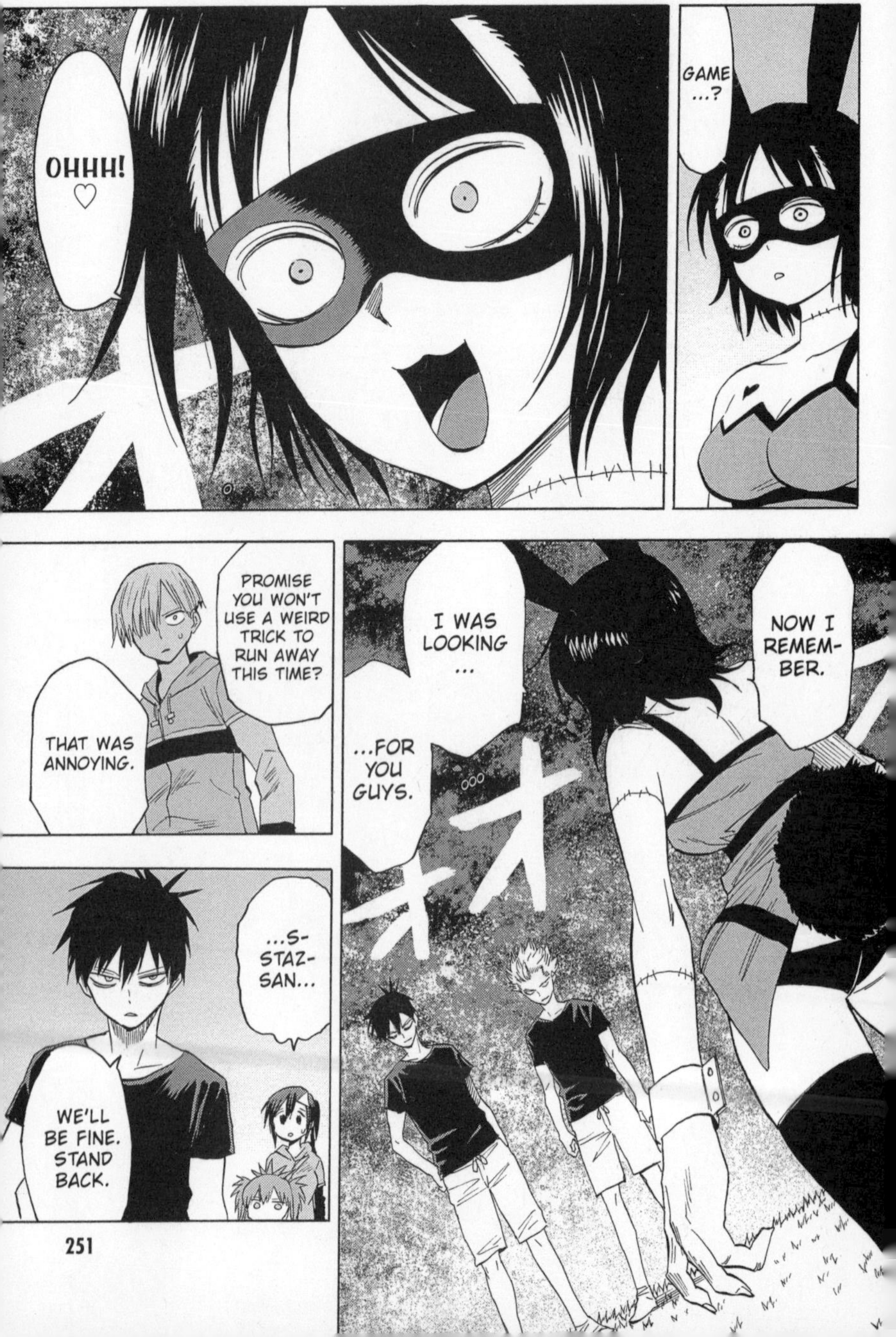
GAME ...?
OHHH! ♡
NOW I REMEMBER.
I WAS LOOKING ...
...FOR YOU GUYS.
PROMISE YOU WON'T USE A WEIRD TRICK TO RUN AWAY THIS TIME?
THAT WAS ANNOYING.
...S-STAZ-SAN...
WE'LL BE FINE. STAND BACK.

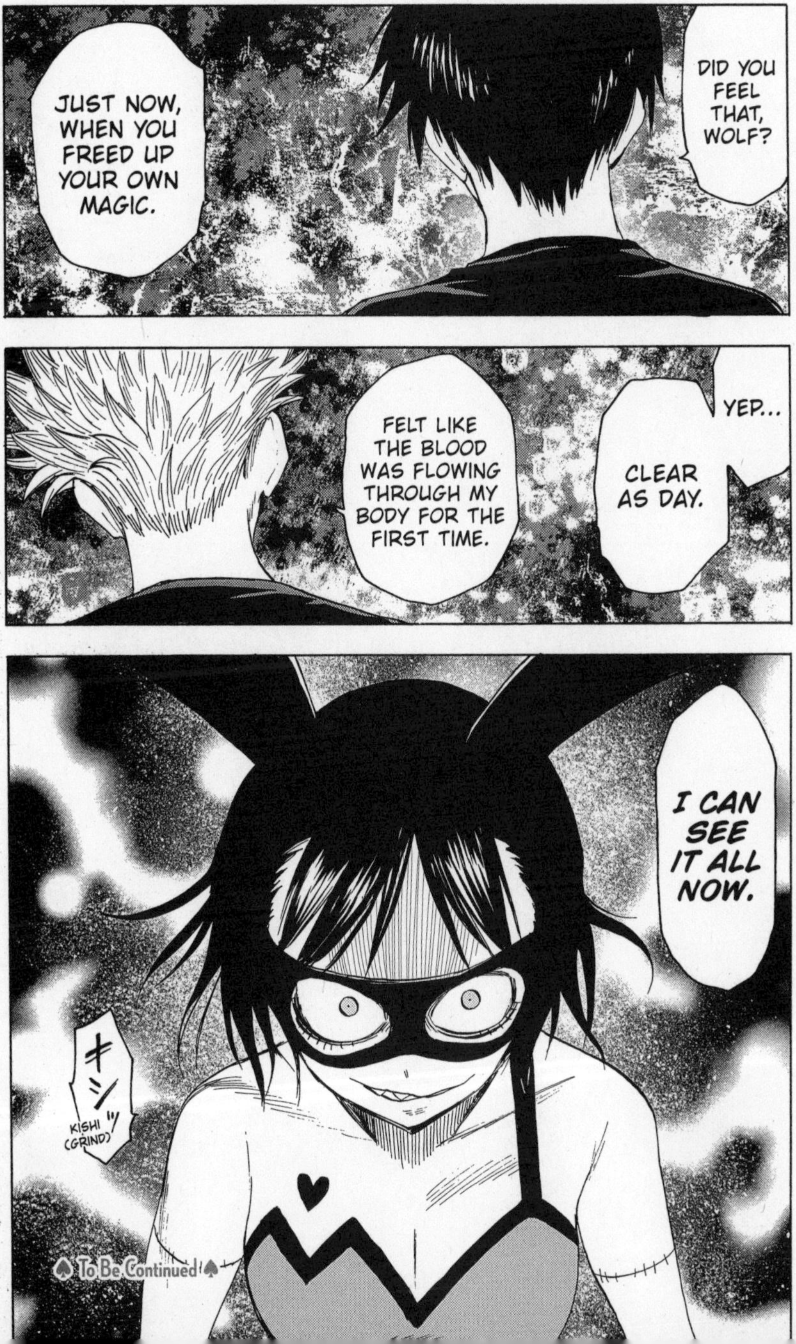
DID YOU FEEL THAT, WOLF?
JUST NOW, WHEN YOU FREED UP YOUR OWN MAGIC.
YEP...
CLEAR AS DAY.
FELT LIKE THE BLOOD WAS FLOWING THROUGH MY BODY FOR THE FIRST TIME.
I CAN SEE IT ALL NOW.
キシッ
KISHI (GRIND)
To Be Continued

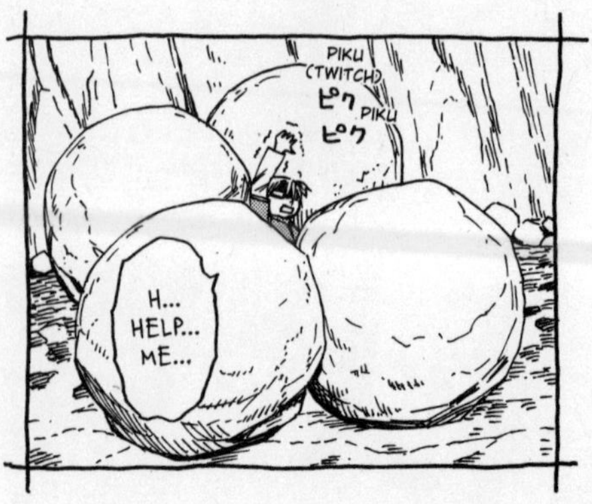
PIKU
(TWITCH)
ピク
PIKU
ピク
H...
HELP...
ME...

BLOOD LAD

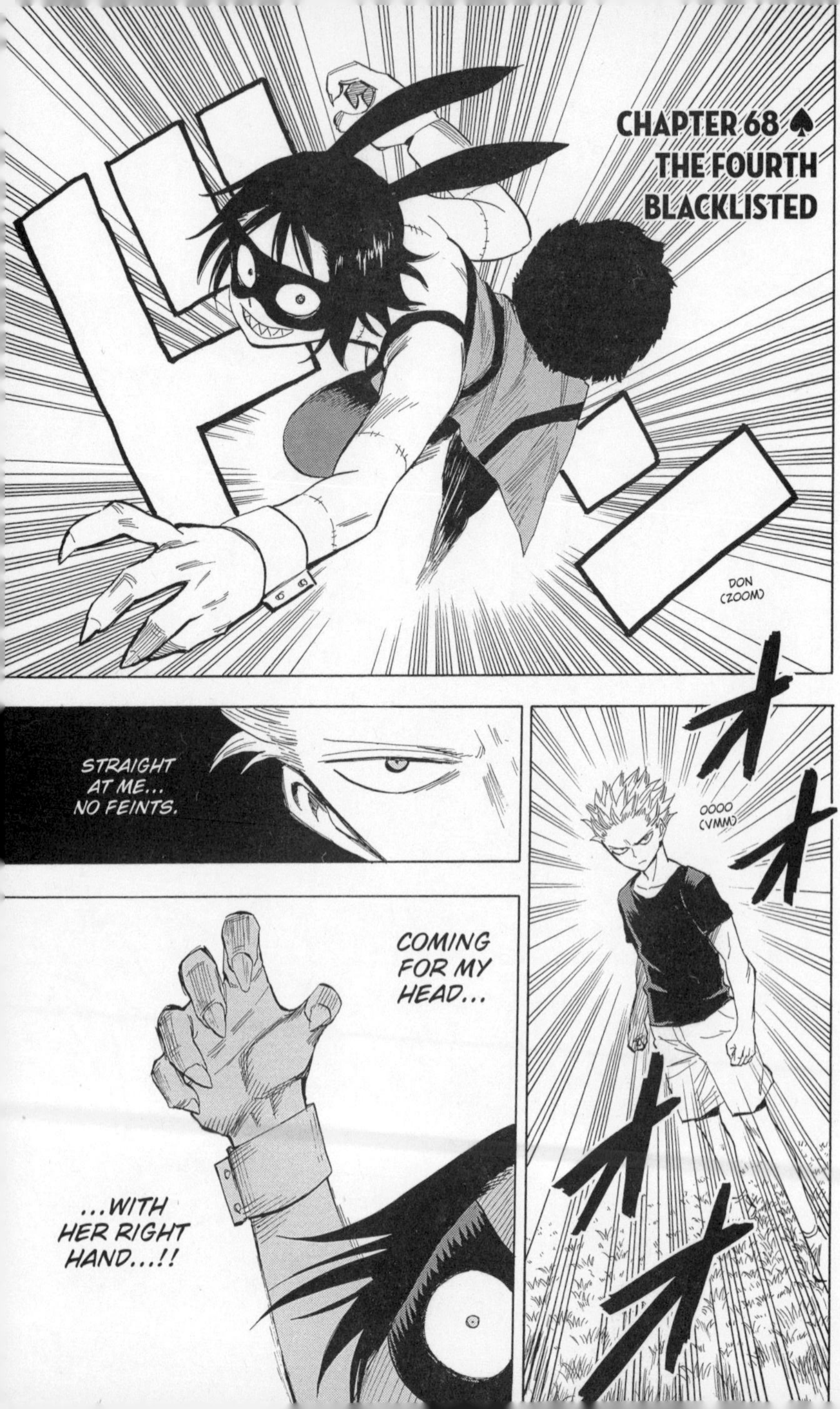
CHAPTER 68 ♠ THE FOURTH BLACKLISTED
DON (ZOOM)
OOOO (VMM)
STRAIGHT AT ME... NO FEINTS.
COMING FOR MY HEAD...
...WITH HER RIGHT HAND...!!

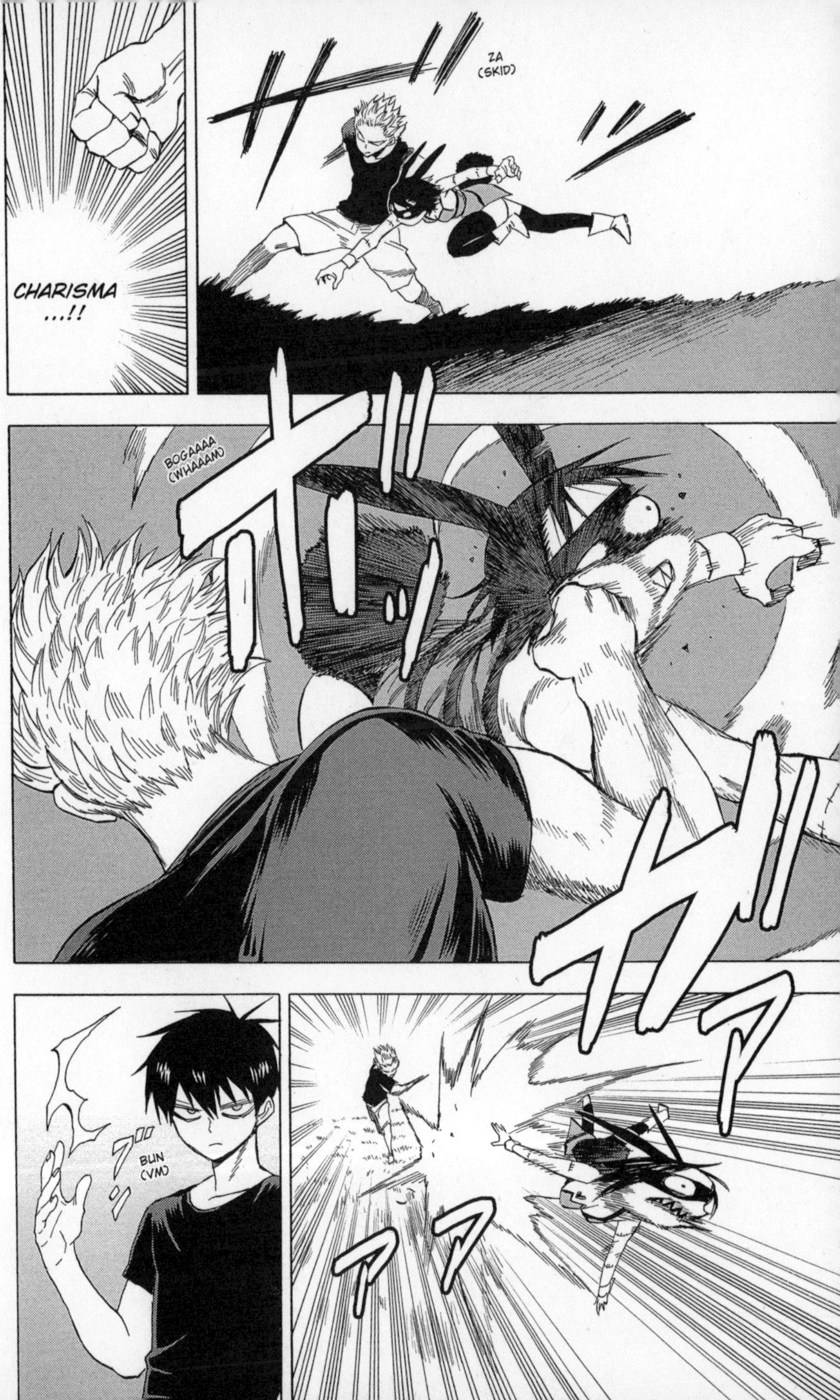
ZA
(SKID)
CHARISMA
...!!
BOGAAAA
(WHAAAM)
BUN
(VM)

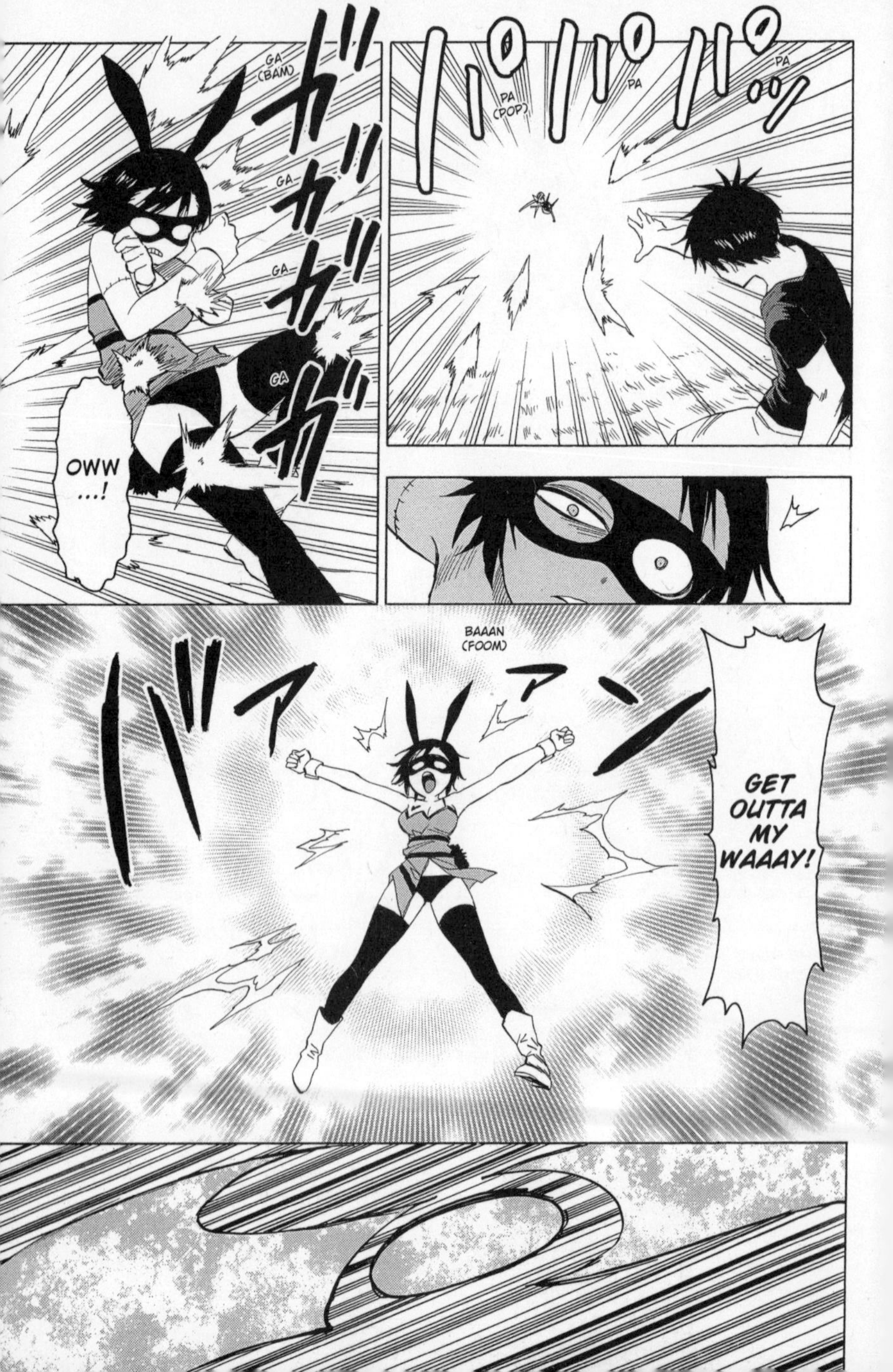
PA (POP)
PA
PA
GA (BAM)
GA
GA
GA
OWW ...!
BAAAN (FOOM)
GET OUTTA MY WAAAY!

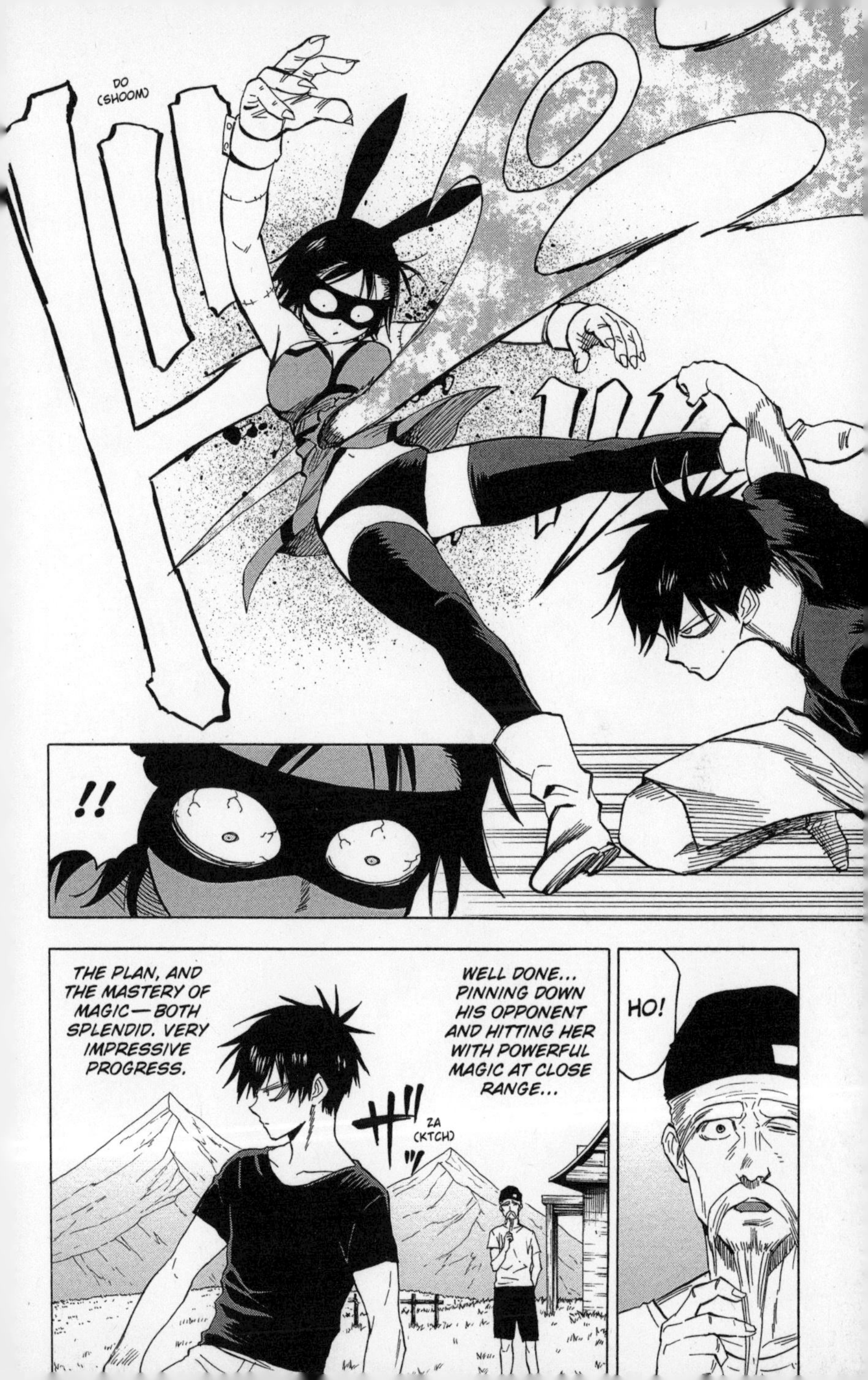
DO
(SHOOM)
!!
HO!
WELL DONE... PINNING DOWN HIS OPPONENT AND HITTING HER WITH POWERFUL MAGIC AT CLOSE RANGE...
THE PLAN, AND THE MASTERY OF MAGIC—BOTH SPLENDID. VERY IMPRESSIVE PROGRESS.
ZA
(KTCH)

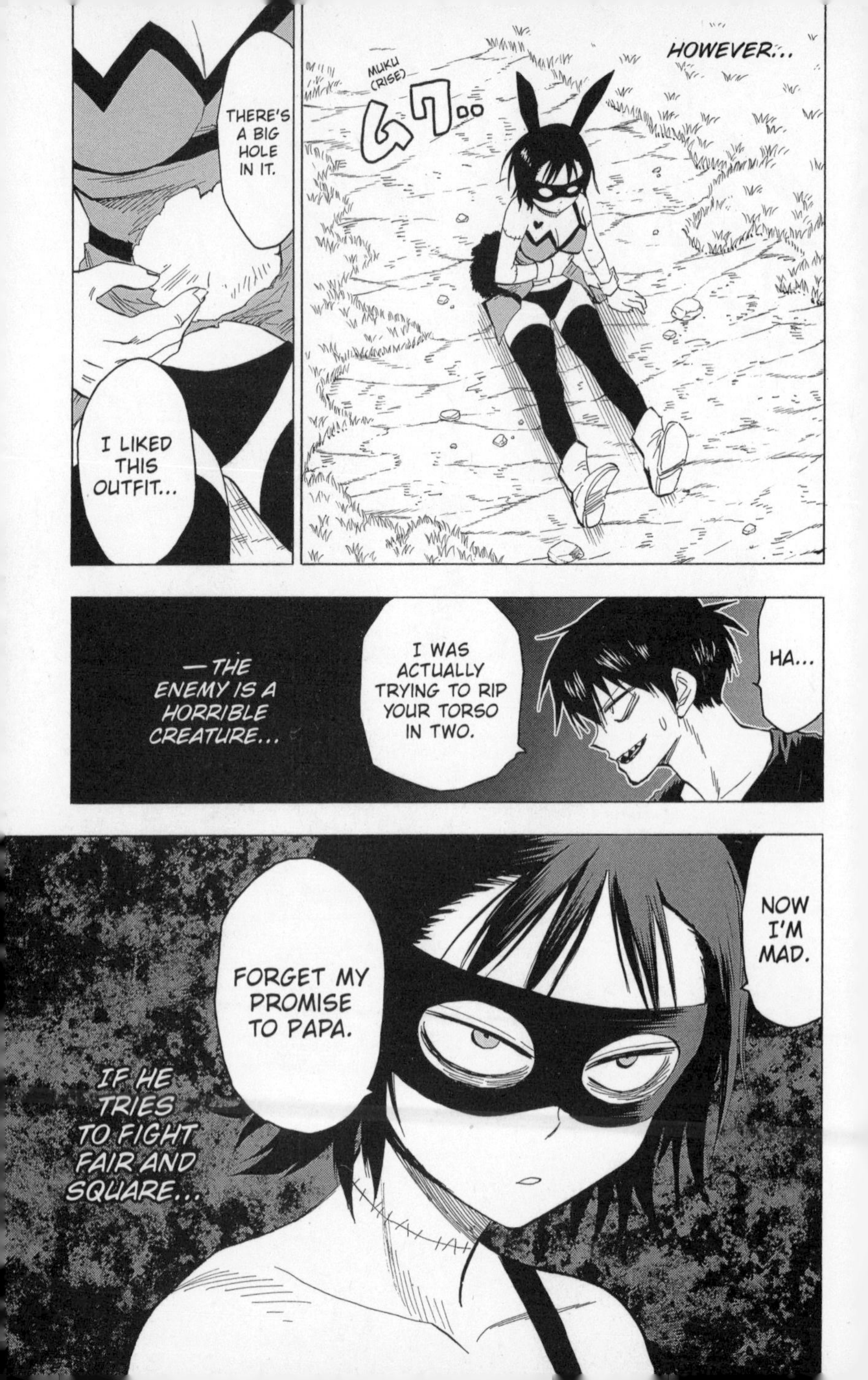
HOWEVER...
MUKU (RISE)
ムク
THERE'S A BIG HOLE IN IT.
I LIKED THIS OUTFIT...
HA...
I WAS ACTUALLY TRYING TO RIP YOUR TORSO IN TWO.
—THE ENEMY IS A HORRIBLE CREATURE...
NOW I'M MAD.
FORGET MY PROMISE TO PAPA.
IF HE TRIES TO FIGHT FAIR AND SQUARE...

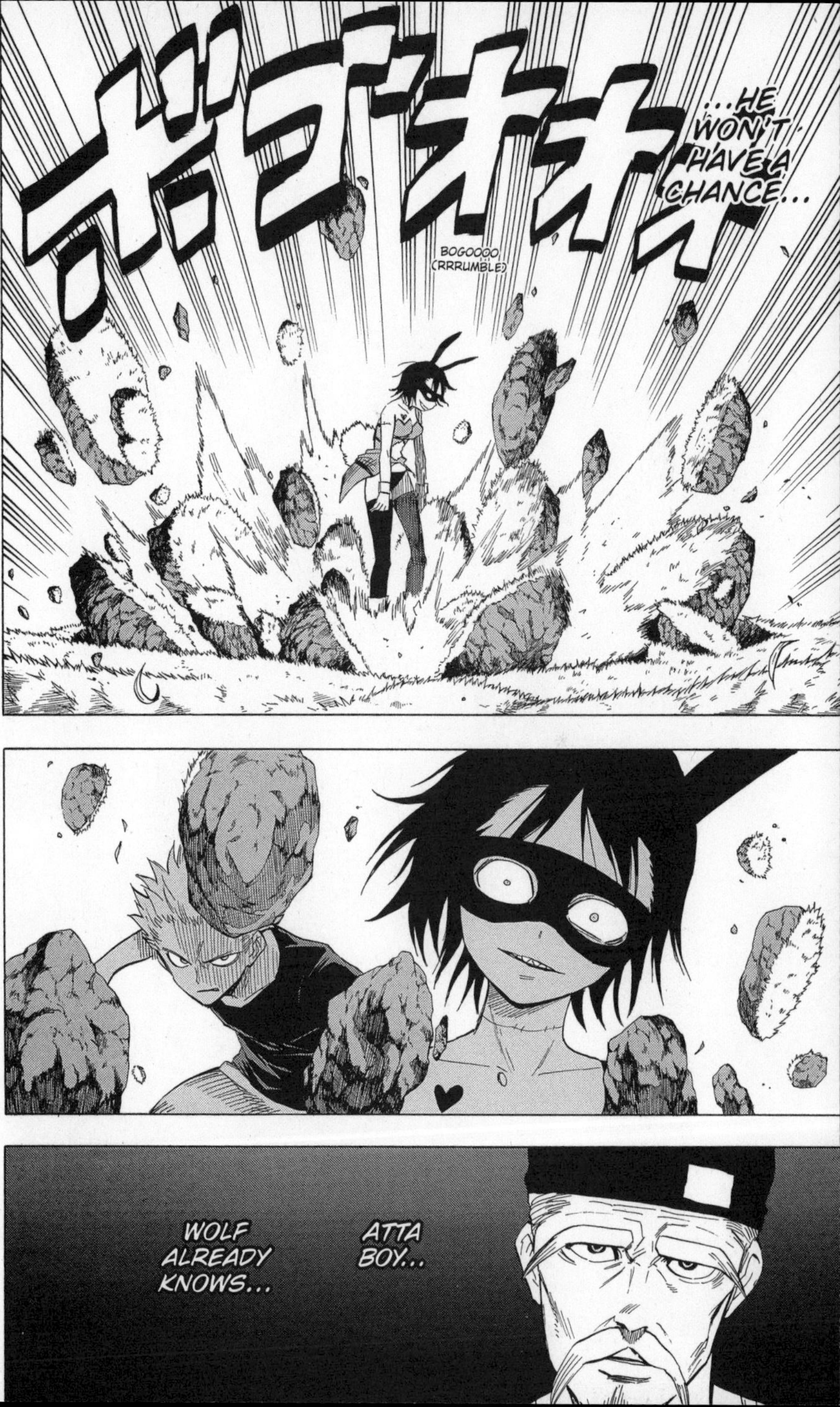
...HE WON'T HAVE A CHANCE...
BOGOOOO (RRRUMBLE)
ATTA BOY...
WOLF ALREADY KNOWS...

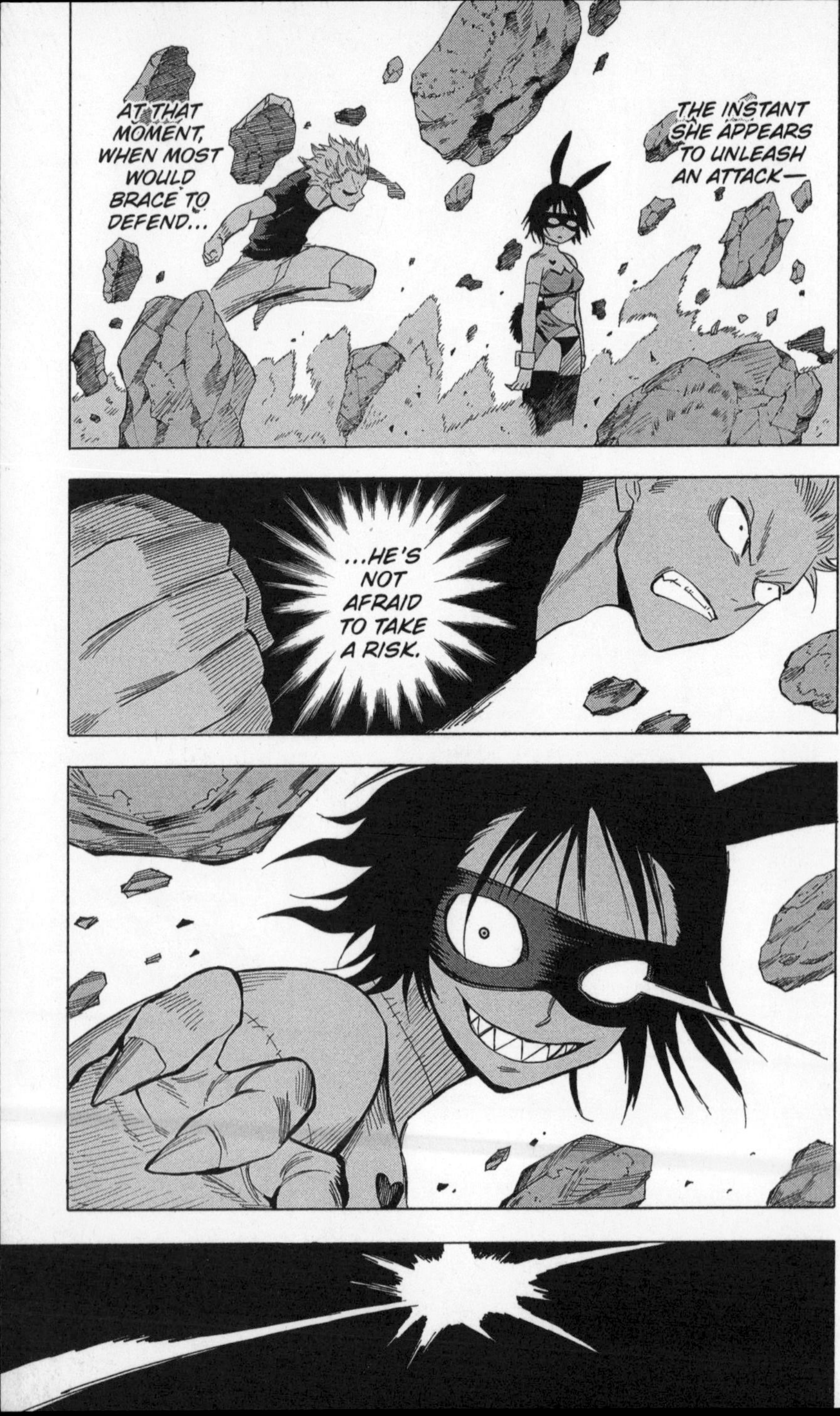
THE INSTANT SHE APPEARS TO UNLEASH AN ATTACK—
AT THAT MOMENT, WHEN MOST WOULD BRACE TO DEFEND...
...HE'S NOT AFRAID TO TAKE A RISK.

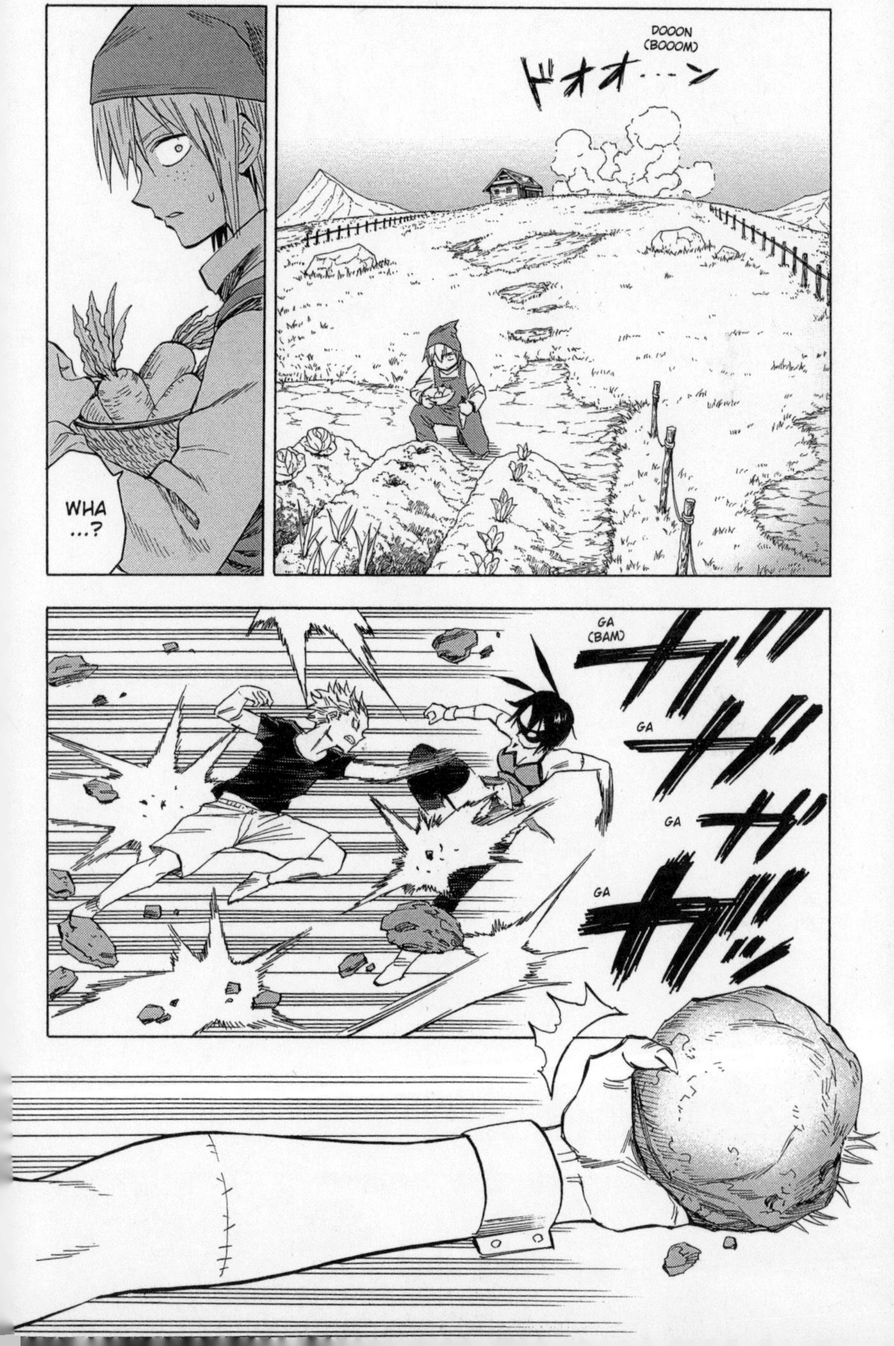
DOOON (BOOOM)
WHA ...?
GA (BAM)
GA
GA
GA

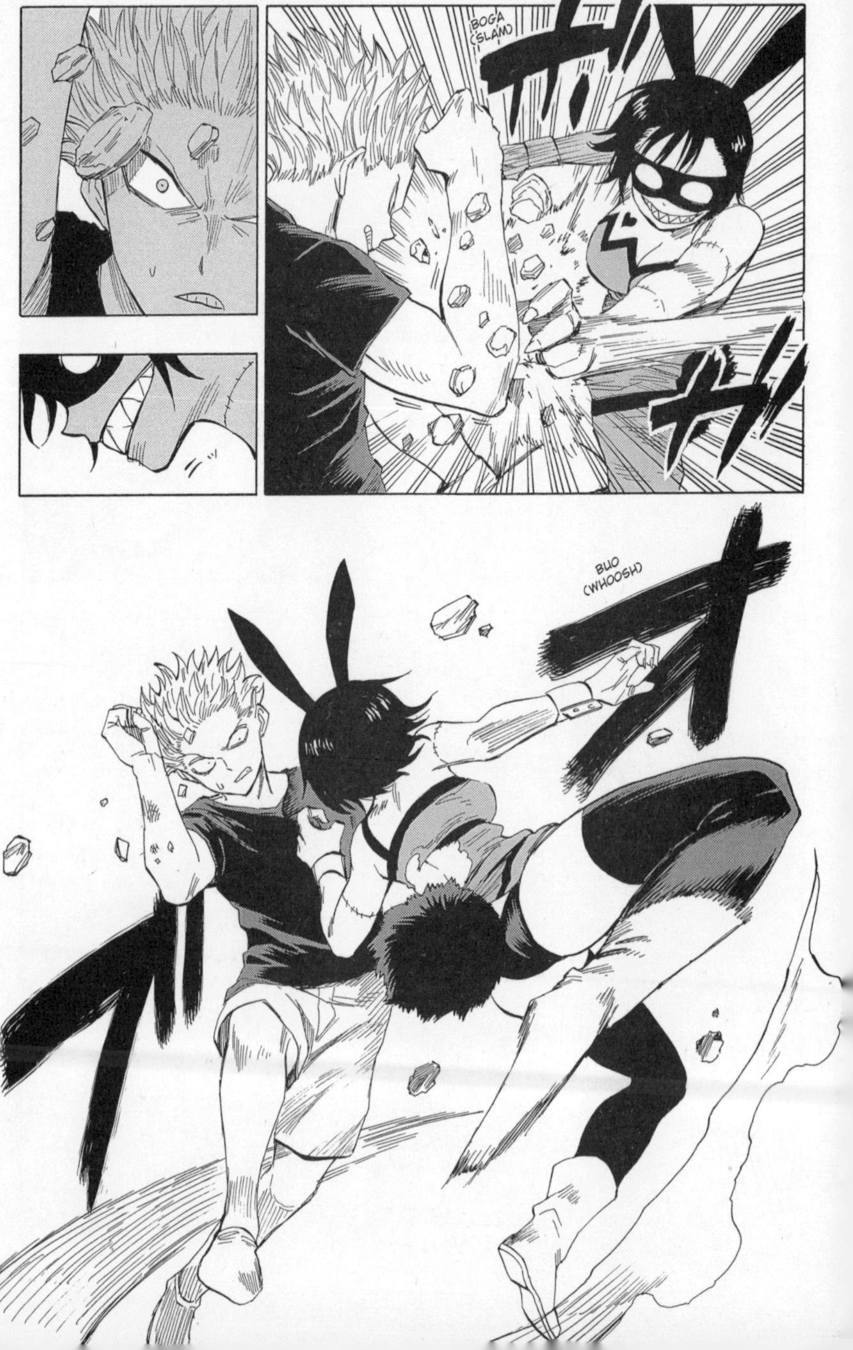
BOGA
(SLAM)
BUO
(WHOOSH)

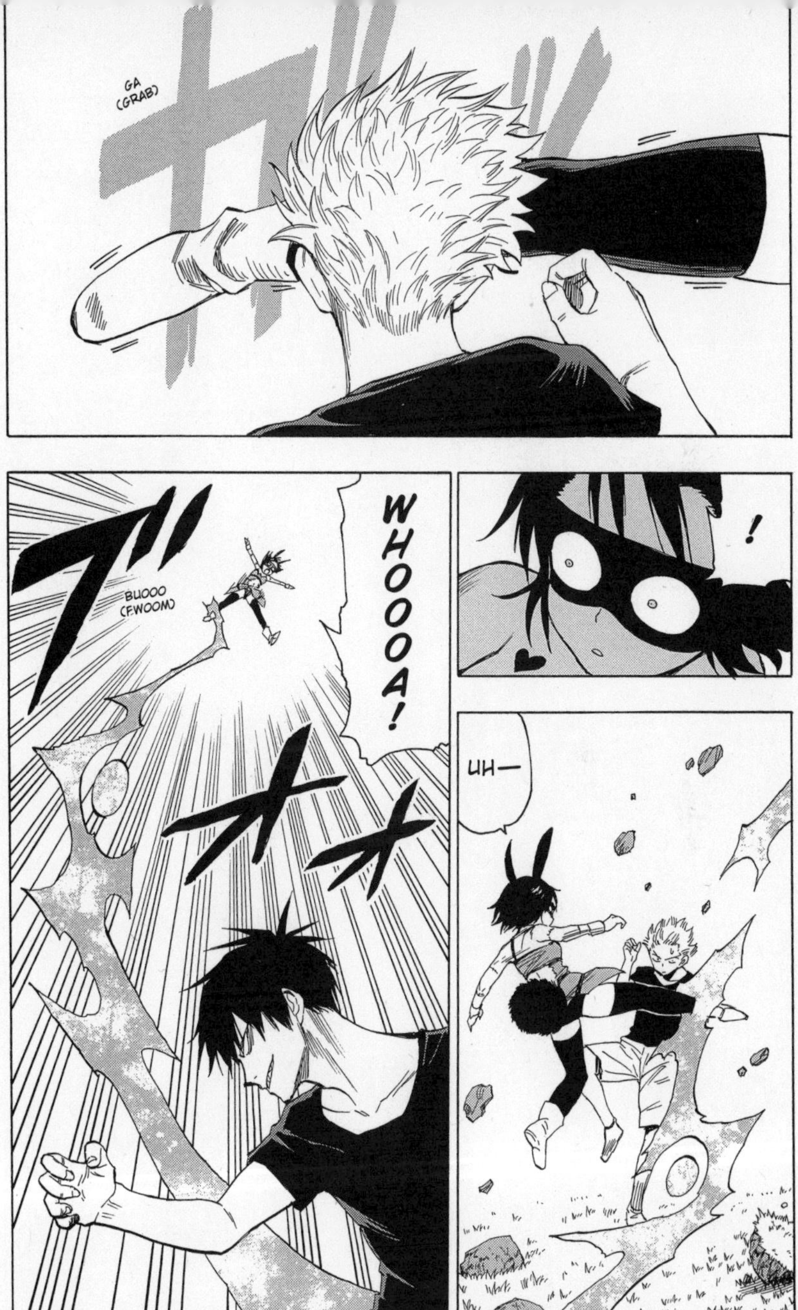
GA
(GRAB)
!
UH—
WHOOOOA!
BUOOO
(F.WOOM)

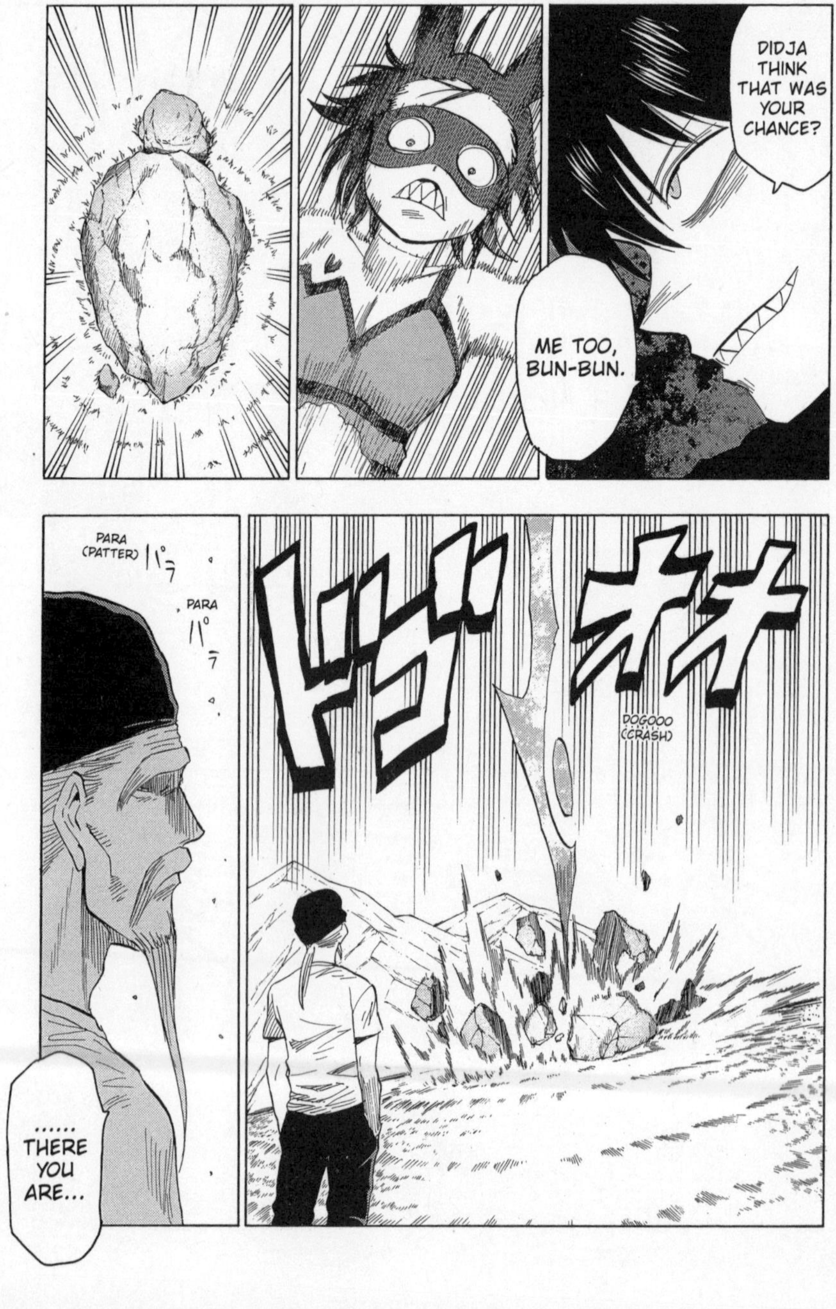
DIDJA THINK THAT WAS YOUR CHANCE?
ME TOO, BUN-BUN.
ドゴオオ
DOGOOO (CRASH)
PARA (PATTER) パラ
PARA パラ
...... THERE YOU ARE...

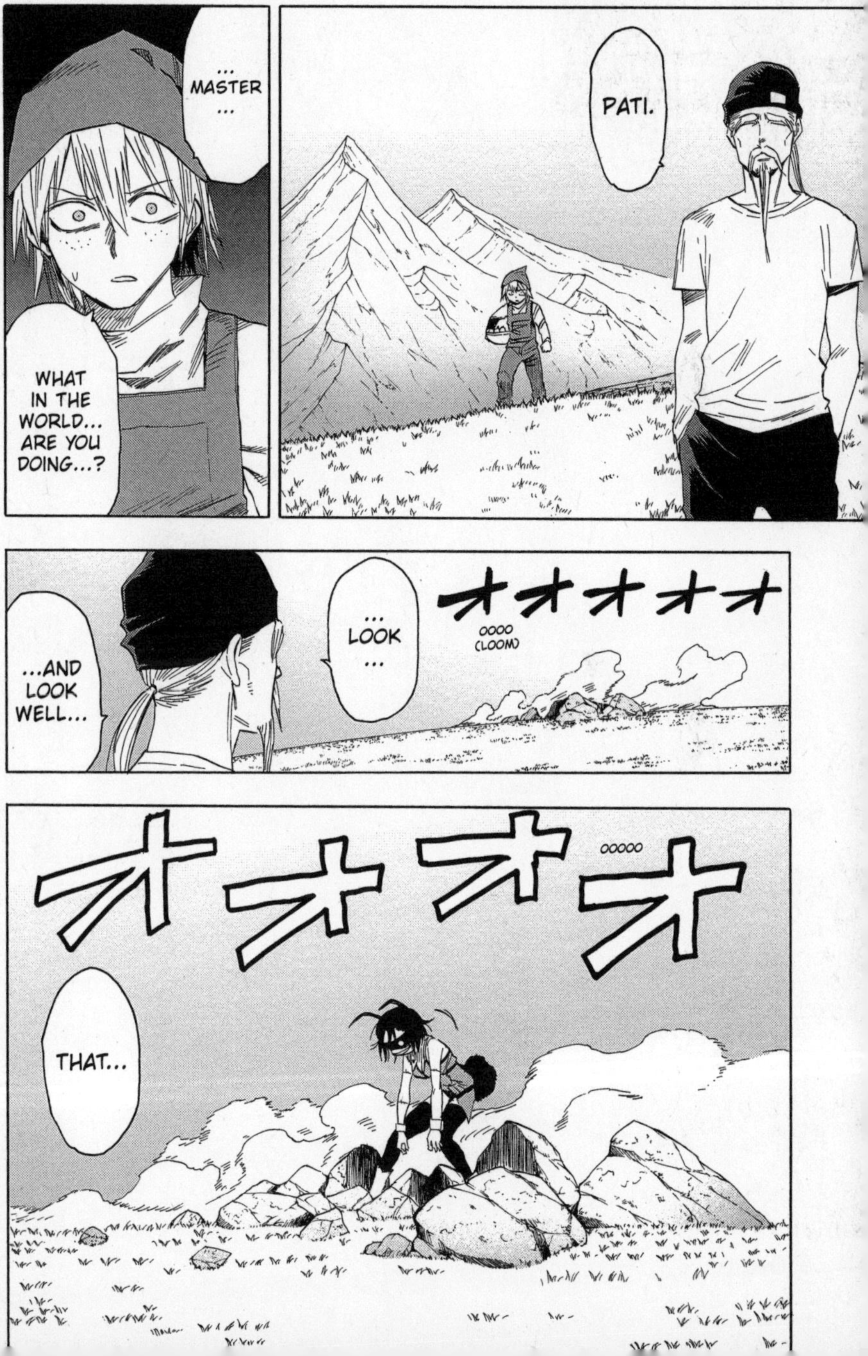
PATI.
...MASTER...
WHAT IN THE WORLD... ARE YOU DOING...?
オオオオオ
OOOO (LOOM)
...LOOK...
...AND LOOK WELL...
オオオオ
OOOOO
THAT...

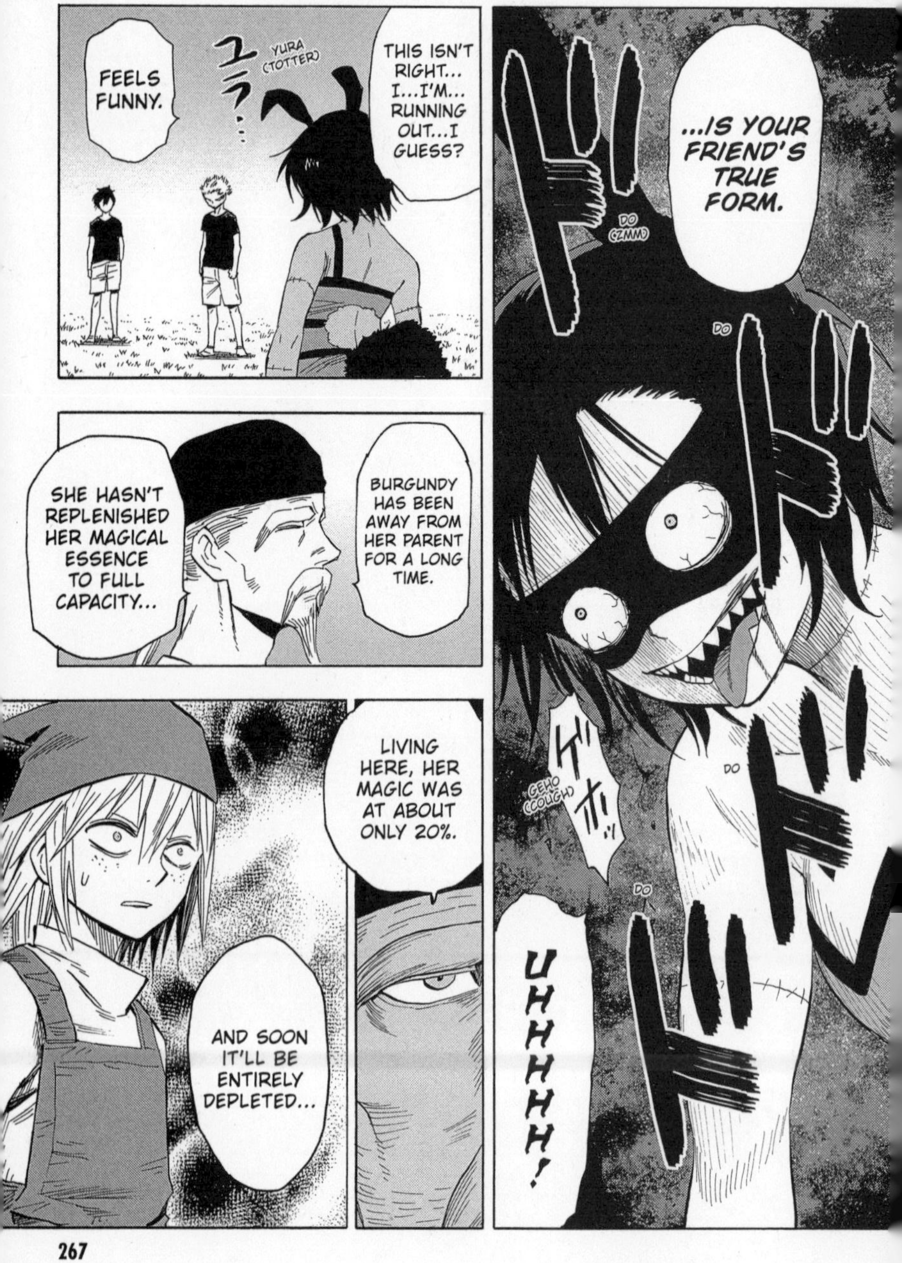
...IS YOUR FRIEND'S TRUE FORM.
DO (ZMMM)
DO
GEHO (COUGH)
DO
DO
UHHHHHH!
THIS ISN'T RIGHT... I...I'M... RUNNING OUT...I GUESS?
YURA (TOTTER)
FEELS FUNNY.
BURGUNDY HAS BEEN AWAY FROM HER PARENT FOR A LONG TIME.
SHE HASN'T REPLENISHED HER MAGICAL ESSENCE TO FULL CAPACITY...
LIVING HERE, HER MAGIC WAS AT ABOUT ONLY 20%.
AND SOON IT'LL BE ENTIRELY DEPLETED...

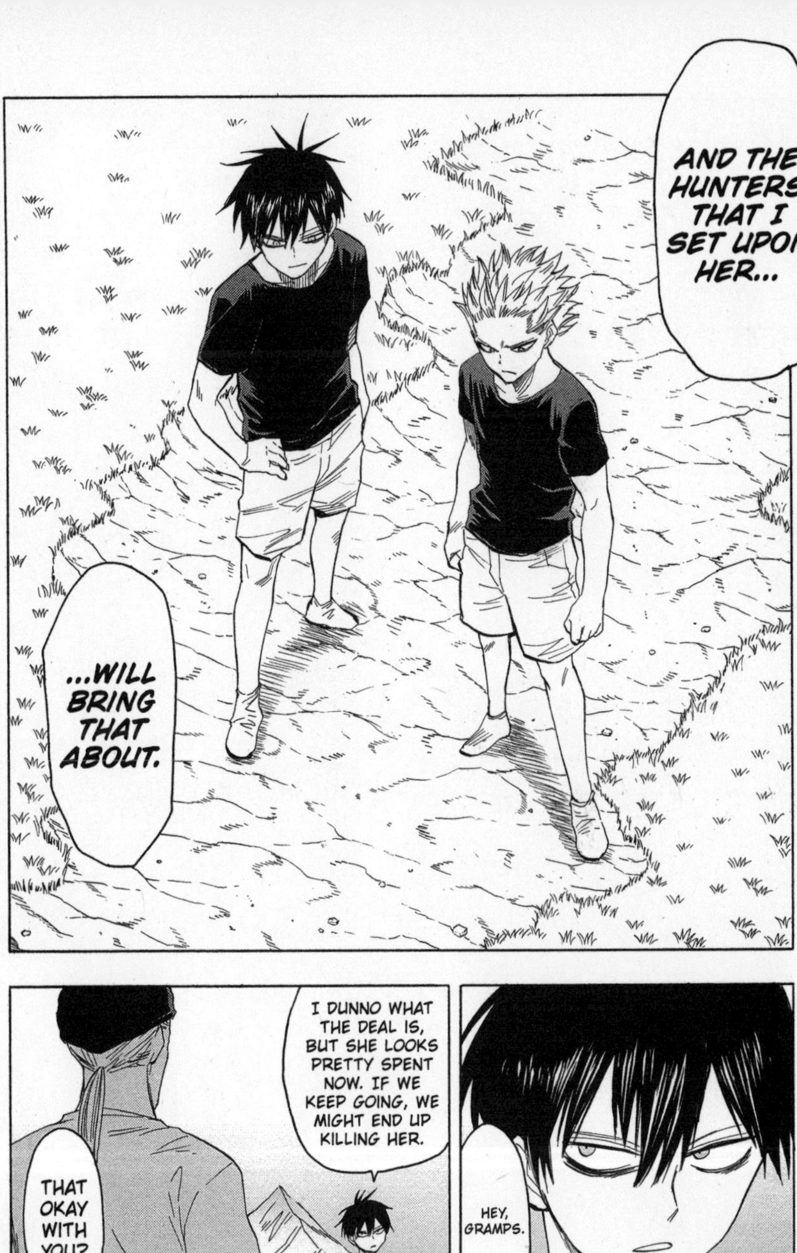
AND THE HUNTERS THAT I SET UPON HER...
...WILL BRING THAT ABOUT.
HEY, GRAMPS.
I DUNNO WHAT THE DEAL IS, BUT SHE LOOKS PRETTY SPENT NOW. IF WE KEEP GOING, WE MIGHT END UP KILLING HER.
THAT OKAY WITH YOU?

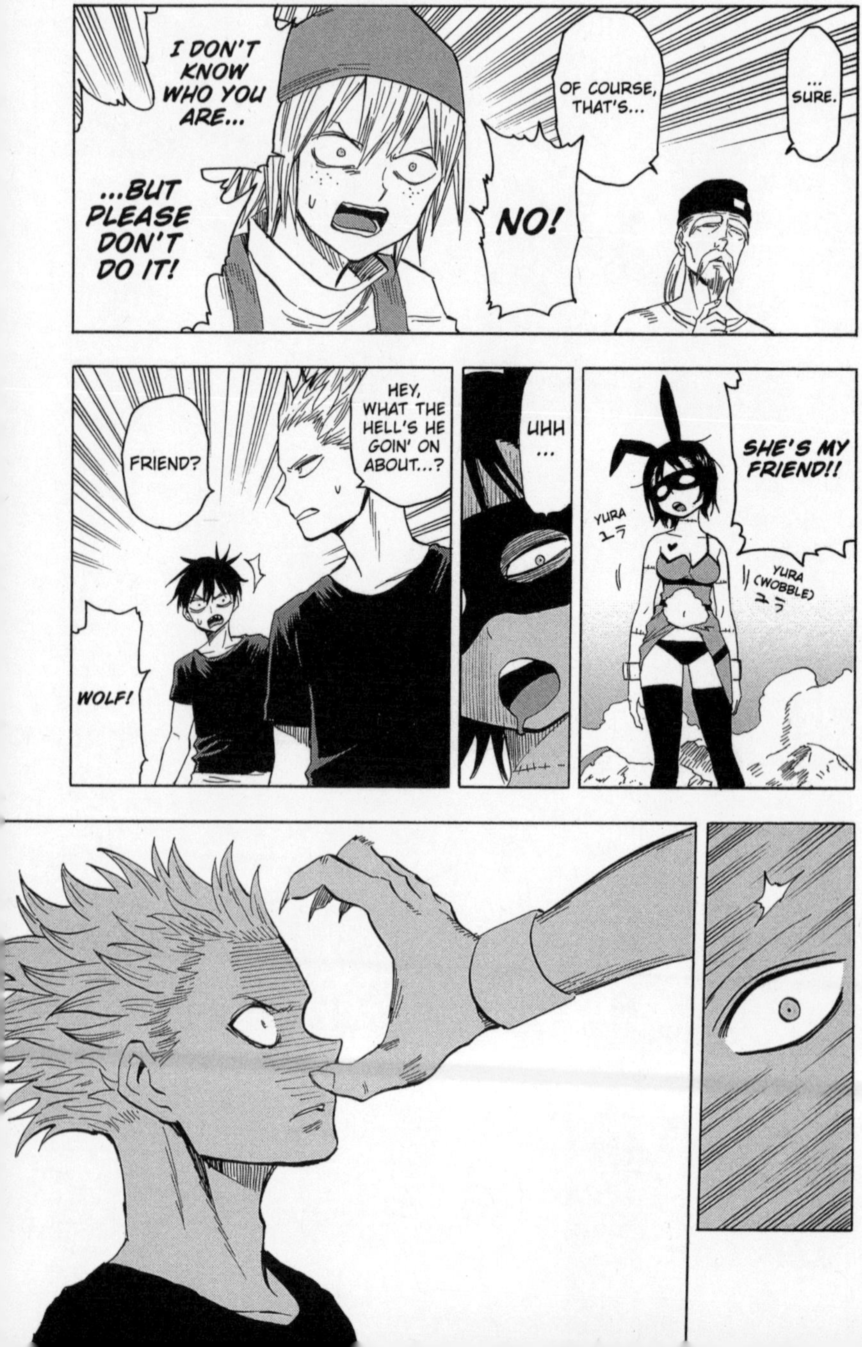

... SURE.
OF COURSE, THAT'S...
I DON'T KNOW WHO YOU ARE...
NO!
...BUT PLEASE DON'T DO IT!
SHE'S MY FRIEND!!
YURA ユラ
YURA (WOBBLE) ユラ
UHH ...
HEY, WHAT THE HELL'S HE GOIN' ON ABOUT...?
FRIEND?
WOLF!

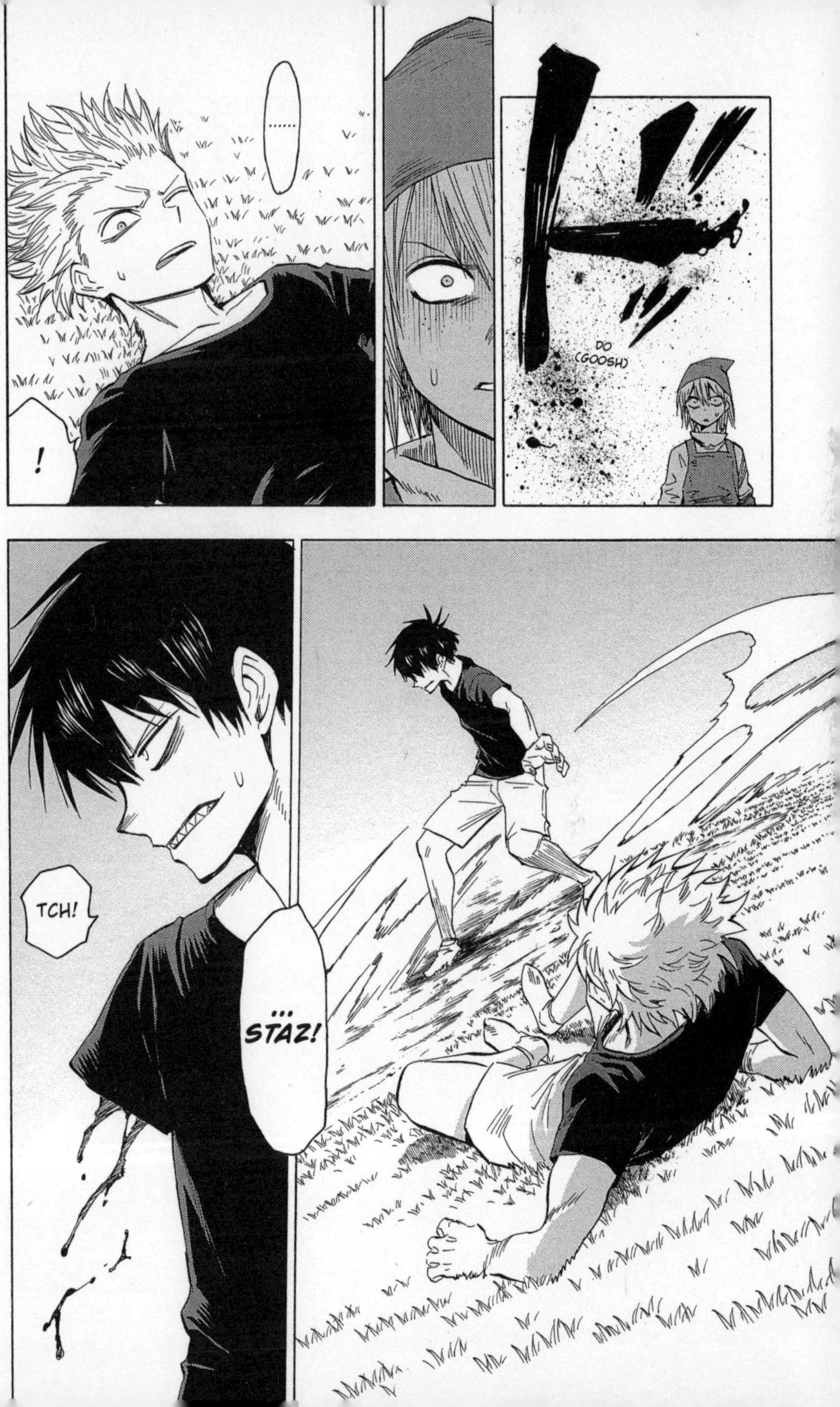
DO
(GOOSH)
……
!
…STÄZ!
TCH!

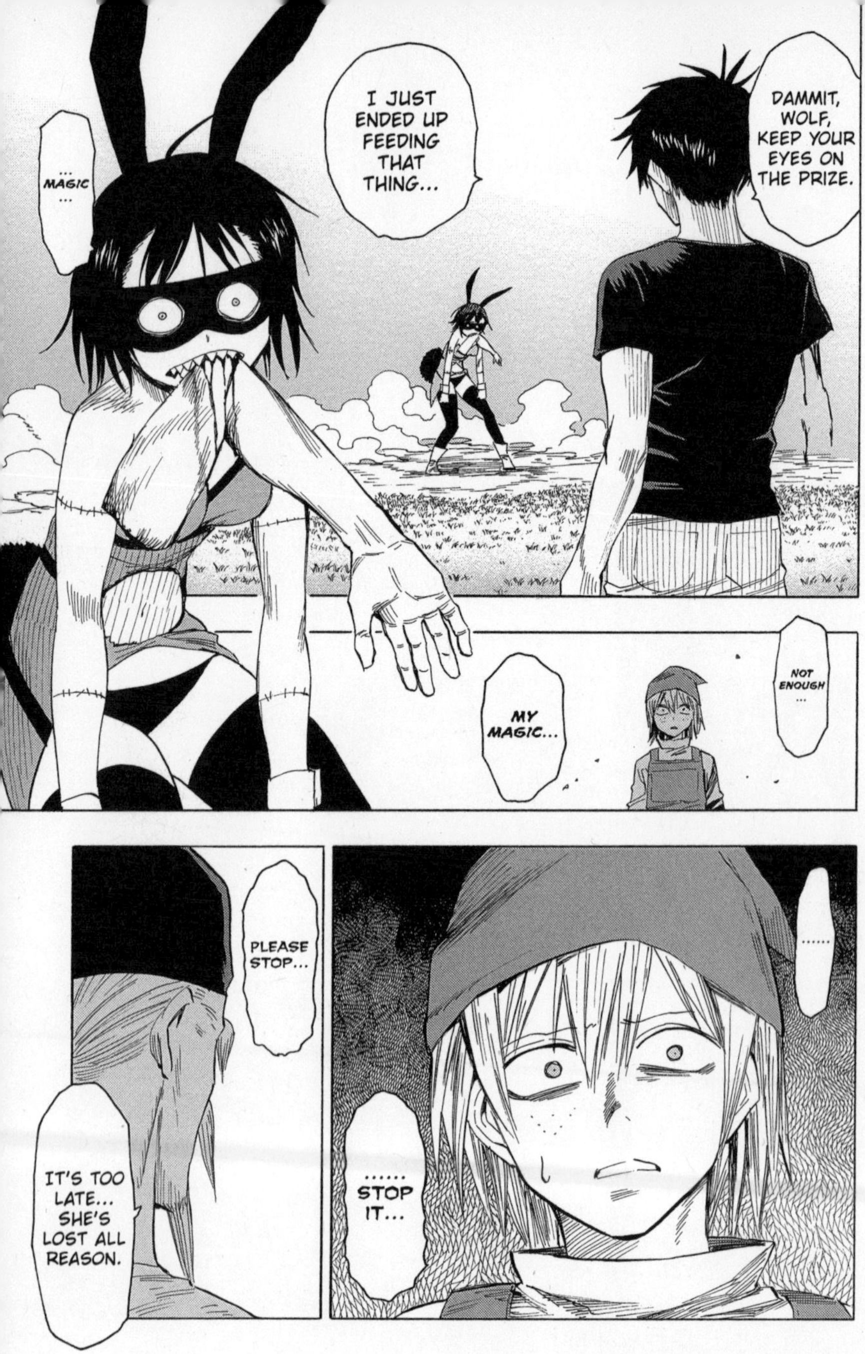
DAMMIT, WOLF, KEEP YOUR EYES ON THE PRIZE.
I JUST ENDED UP FEEDING THAT THING...
...MAGIC...
NOT ENOUGH...
MY MAGIC...
......
......STOP IT...
PLEASE STOP...
IT'S TOO LATE... SHE'S LOST ALL REASON.

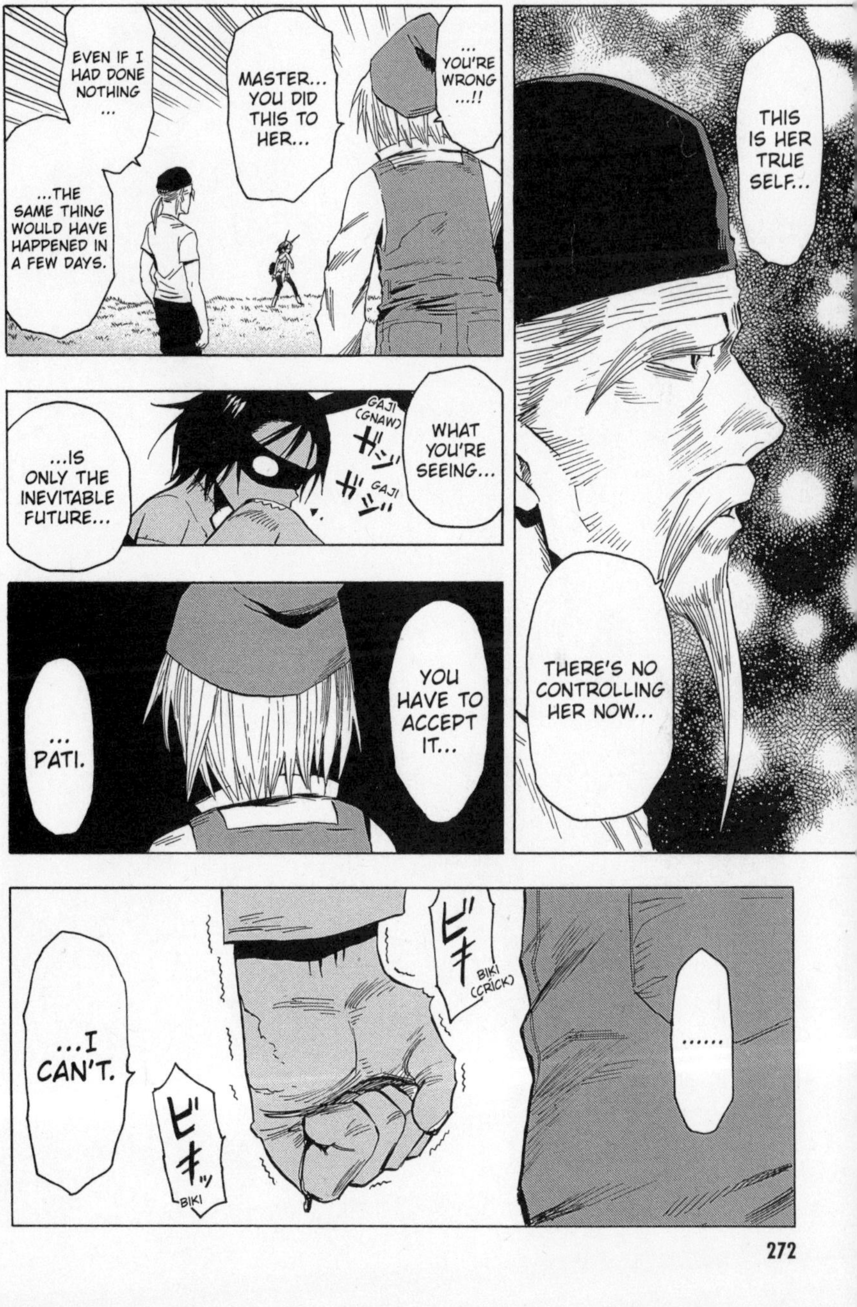
THIS IS HER TRUE SELF...
THERE'S NO CONTROLLING HER NOW...
... YOU'RE WRONG ...!!
MASTER... YOU DID THIS TO HER...
EVEN IF I HAD DONE NOTHING ...
...THE SAME THING WOULD HAVE HAPPENED IN A FEW DAYS.
WHAT YOU'RE SEEING...
GAJI (GNAW)
GAJI
...IS ONLY THE INEVITABLE FUTURE...
YOU HAVE TO ACCEPT IT...
... PATI.
......
BIKI (CRICK)
BIKI
...I CAN'T.

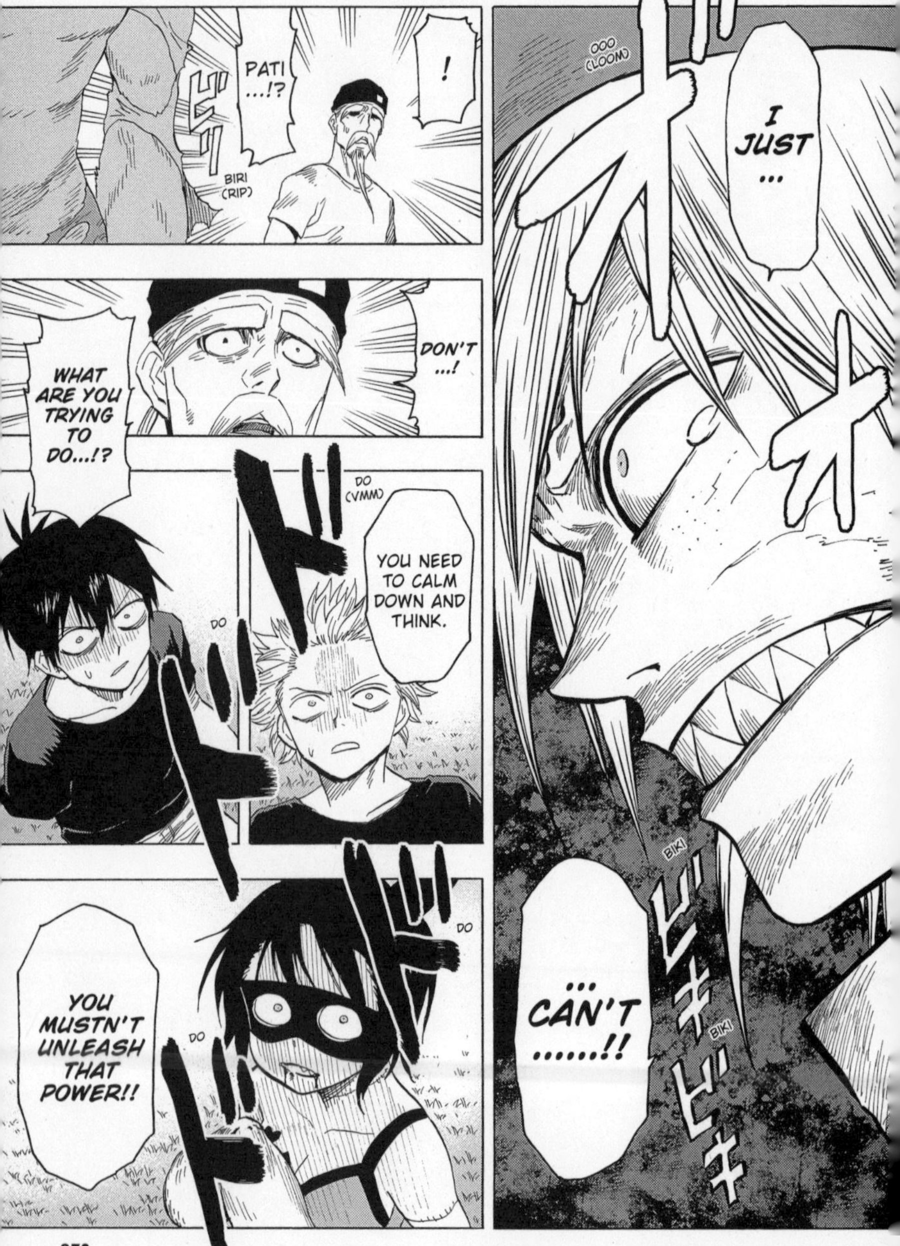
OOO (LOOM)
I JUST ...
BIKI
BIKI
... CAN'T ......!!
!
PATI ...!?
BIRI (RIP)
DON'T ...!
WHAT ARE YOU TRYING TO DO...!?
DO (VMM)
YOU NEED TO CALM DOWN AND THINK.
DO
DO
YOU MUSTN'T UNLEASH THAT POWER!!
DO

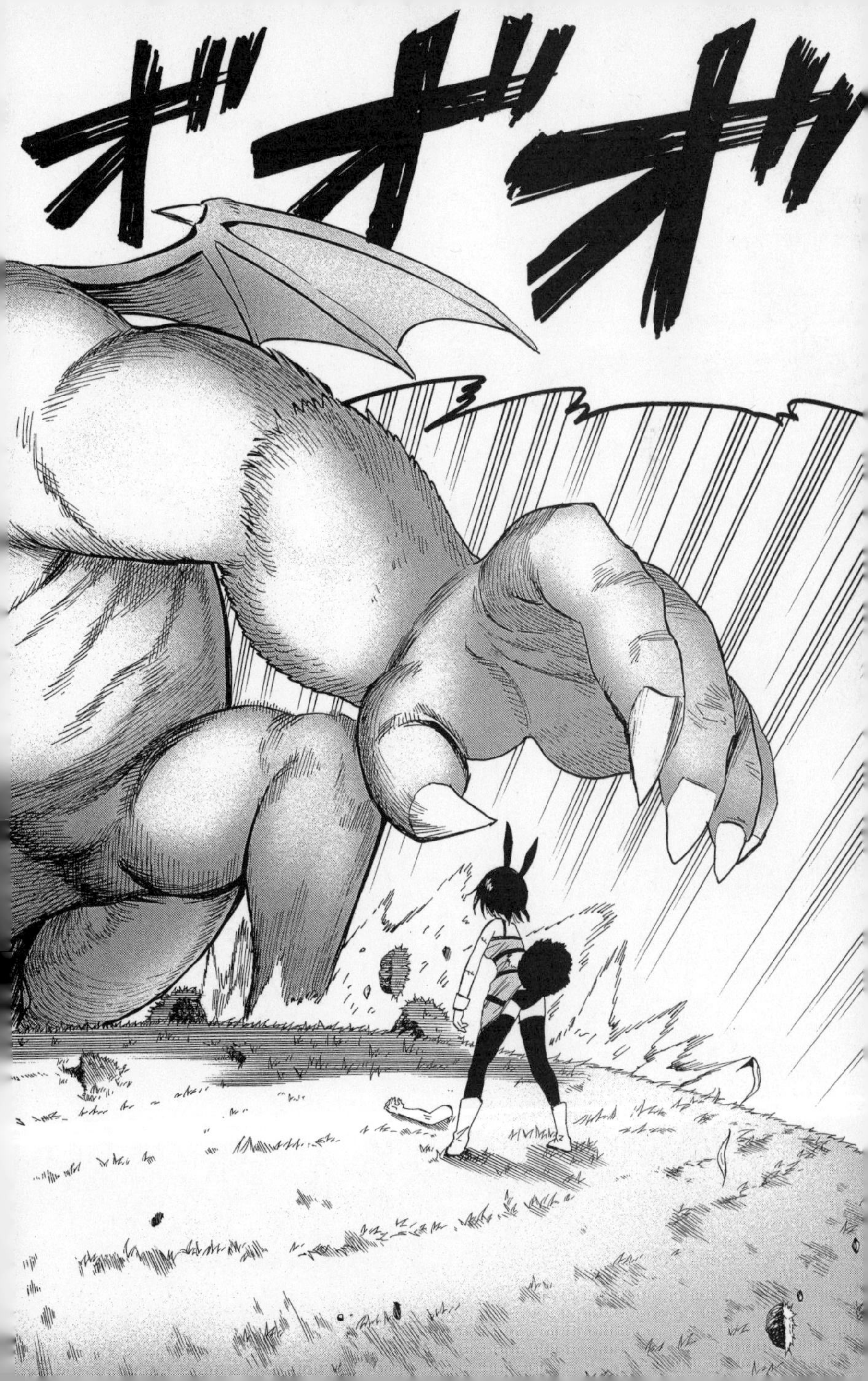
オ゛オ゛オ゛

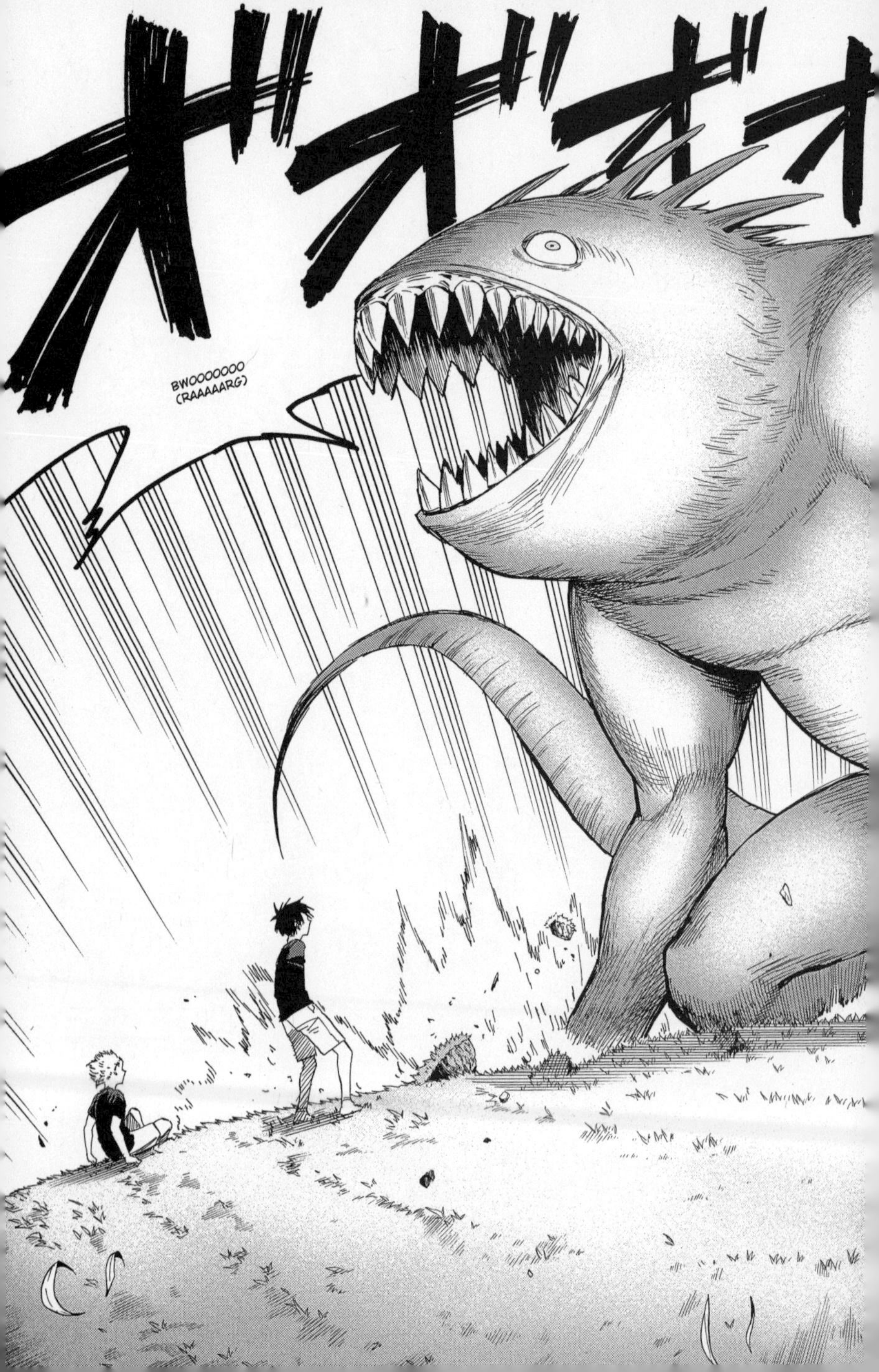
オザオザオ
BWOOOOOOO
(RAAAAARG)

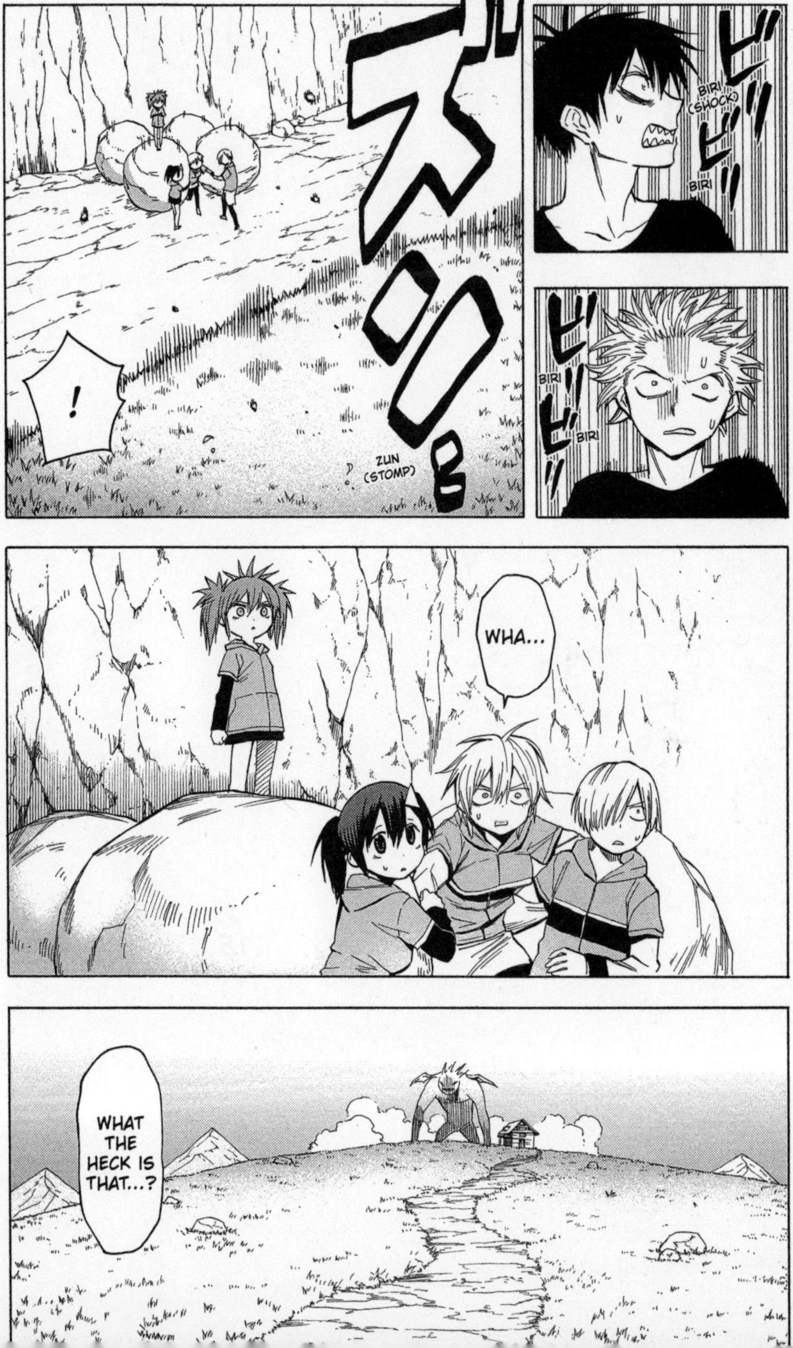
ビリビリ
BIRI (SHOCK)
BIRI
ビリビリ
BIRI
BIRI
ズン
ZUN (STOMP)
!
WHA...
WHAT THE HECK IS THAT...?

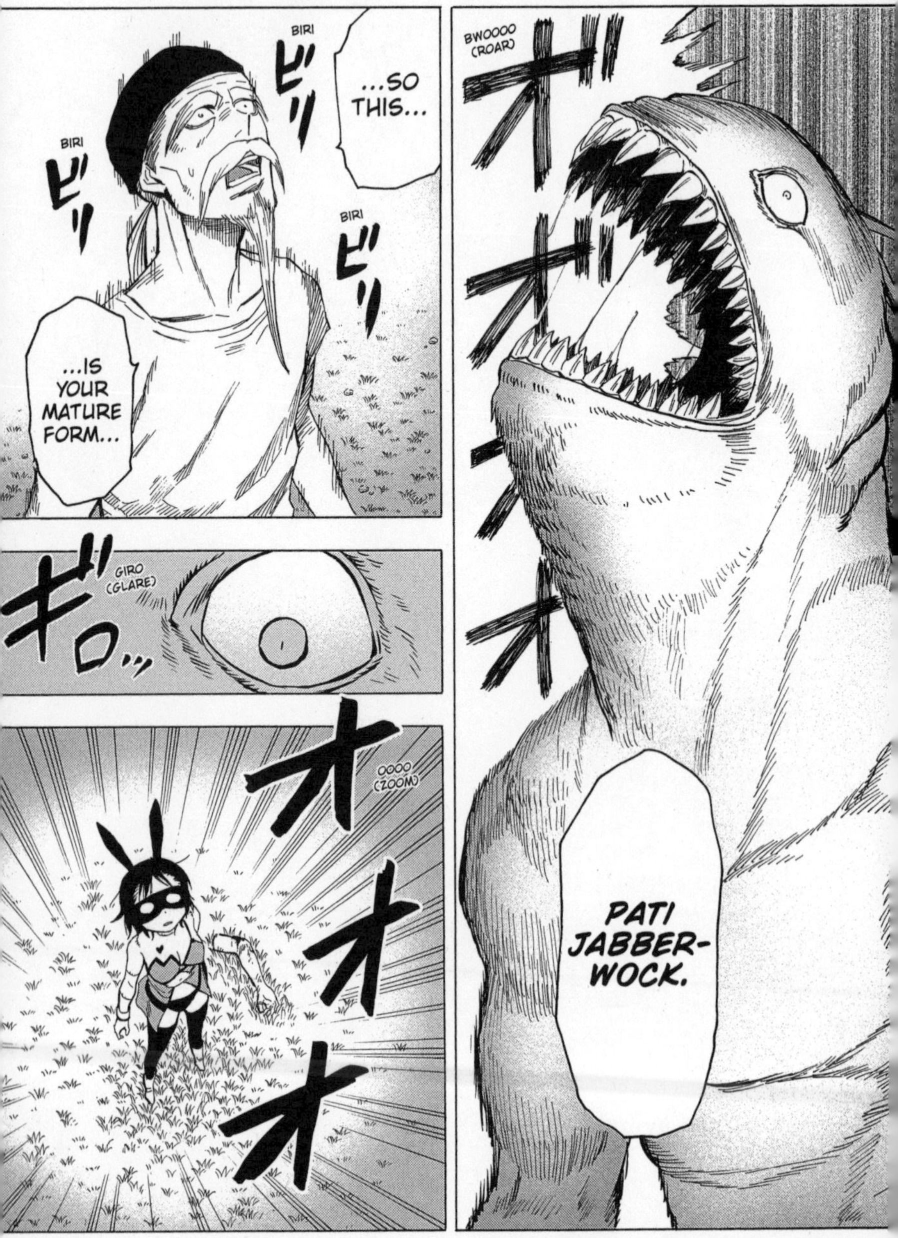
BWOOOO
(ROAR)
PATI JABBER-WOCK.
BIRI
ビリ
...SO THIS...
BIRI
ビリ
BIRI
ビリ
...IS YOUR MATURE FORM...
GIRO
(GLARE)
ギロ…
OOOO
(ZOOM)
オオオ

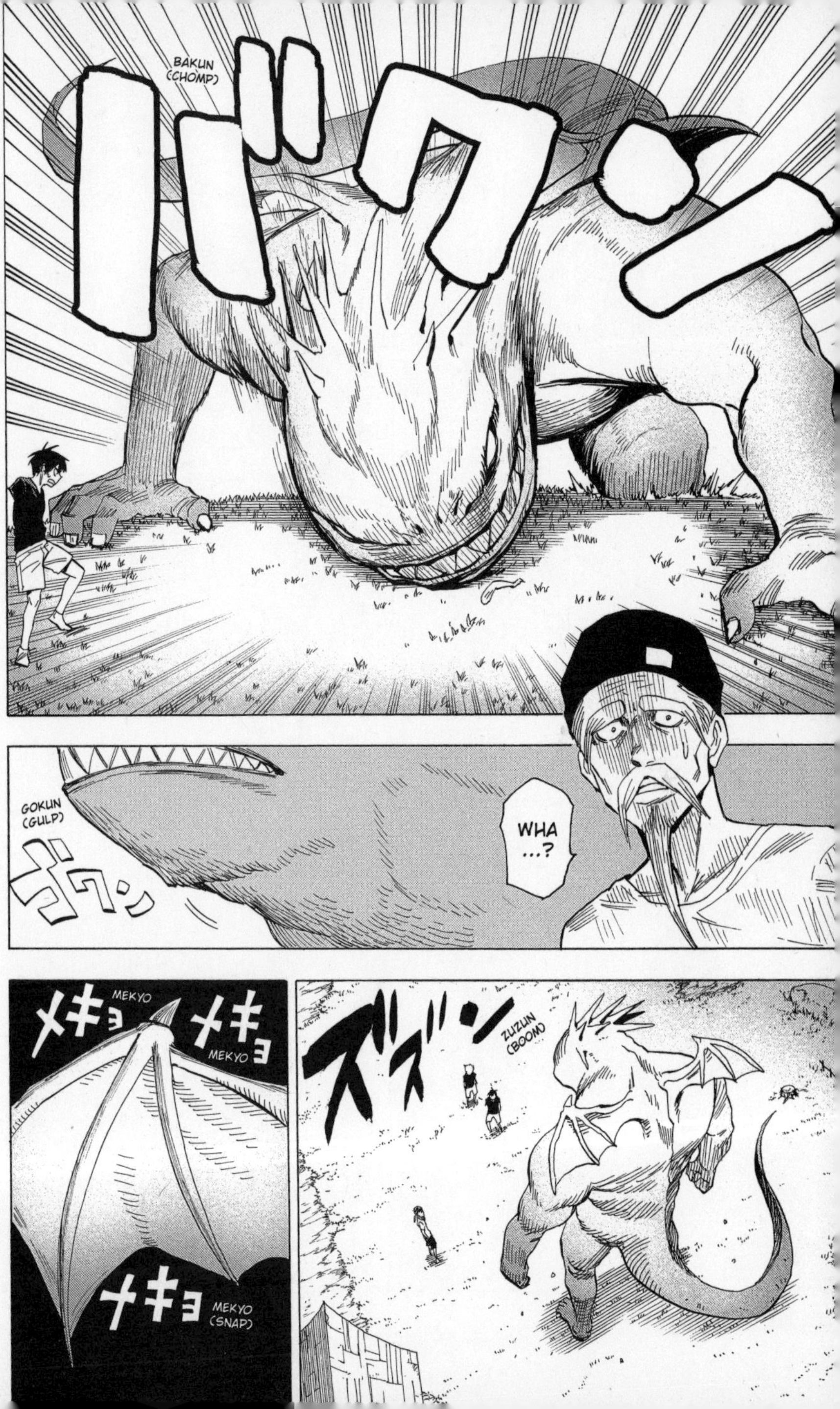

バクン
BAKUN (CHOMP)
WHA ...?
ゴクン
GOKUN (GULP)
ズズン
ZUZUN (BOOM)
メキョ
MEKYO
メキョ
MEKYO
メキョ
MEKYO (SNAP)

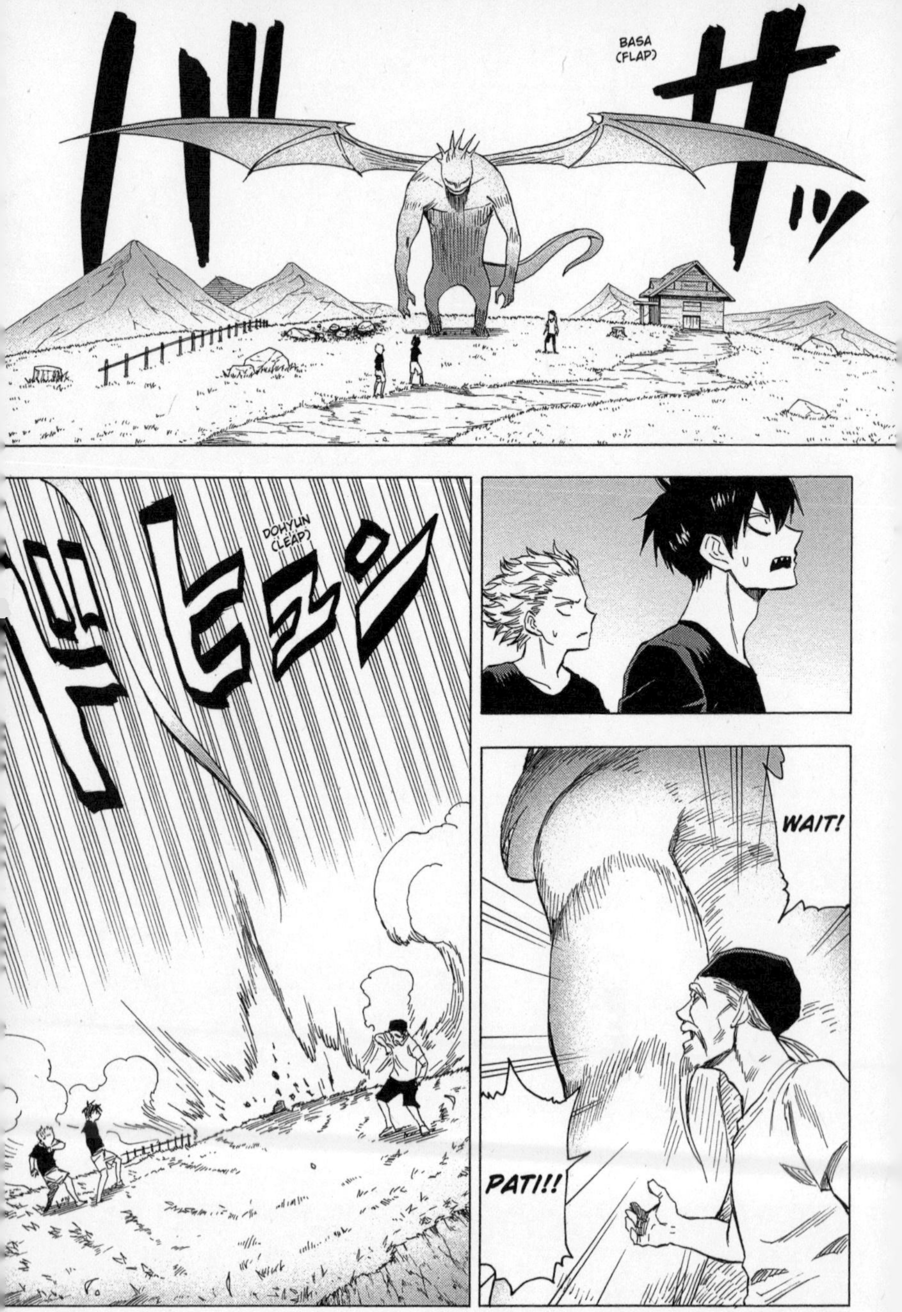
バサッ
BASA (FLAP)
WAIT!
PATI!!
ドヒュン
DOHYUN (LEAP)

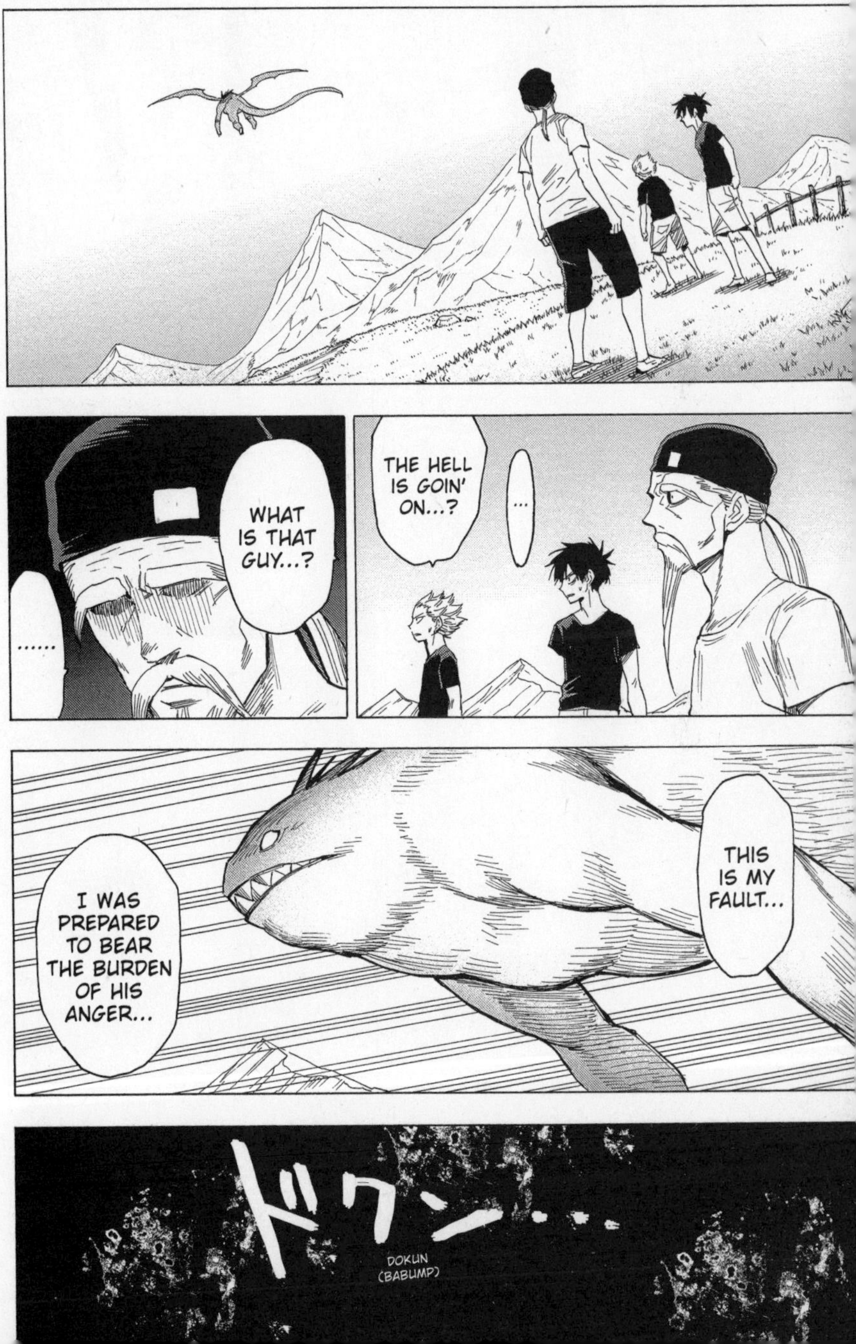
...
THE HELL IS GOIN' ON...?
WHAT IS THAT GUY...?
......
THIS IS MY FAULT...
I WAS PREPARED TO BEAR THE BURDEN OF HIS ANGER...
ドクン…
DOKUN (BABUMP)

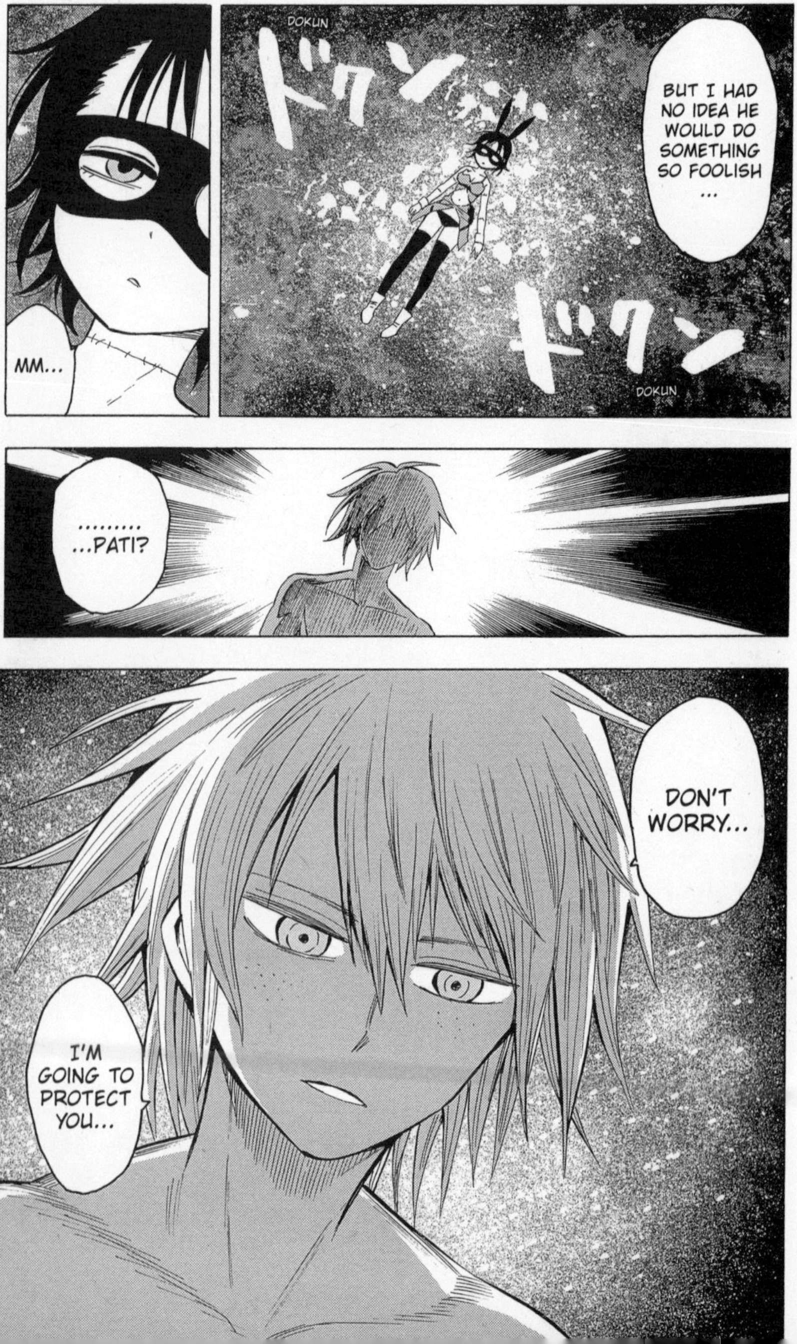
BUT I HAD NO IDEA HE WOULD DO SOMETHING SO FOOLISH ...
ドクン
DOKUN
ドクン
DOKUN
MM...
....PATI?
DON'T WORRY...
I'M GOING TO PROTECT YOU...

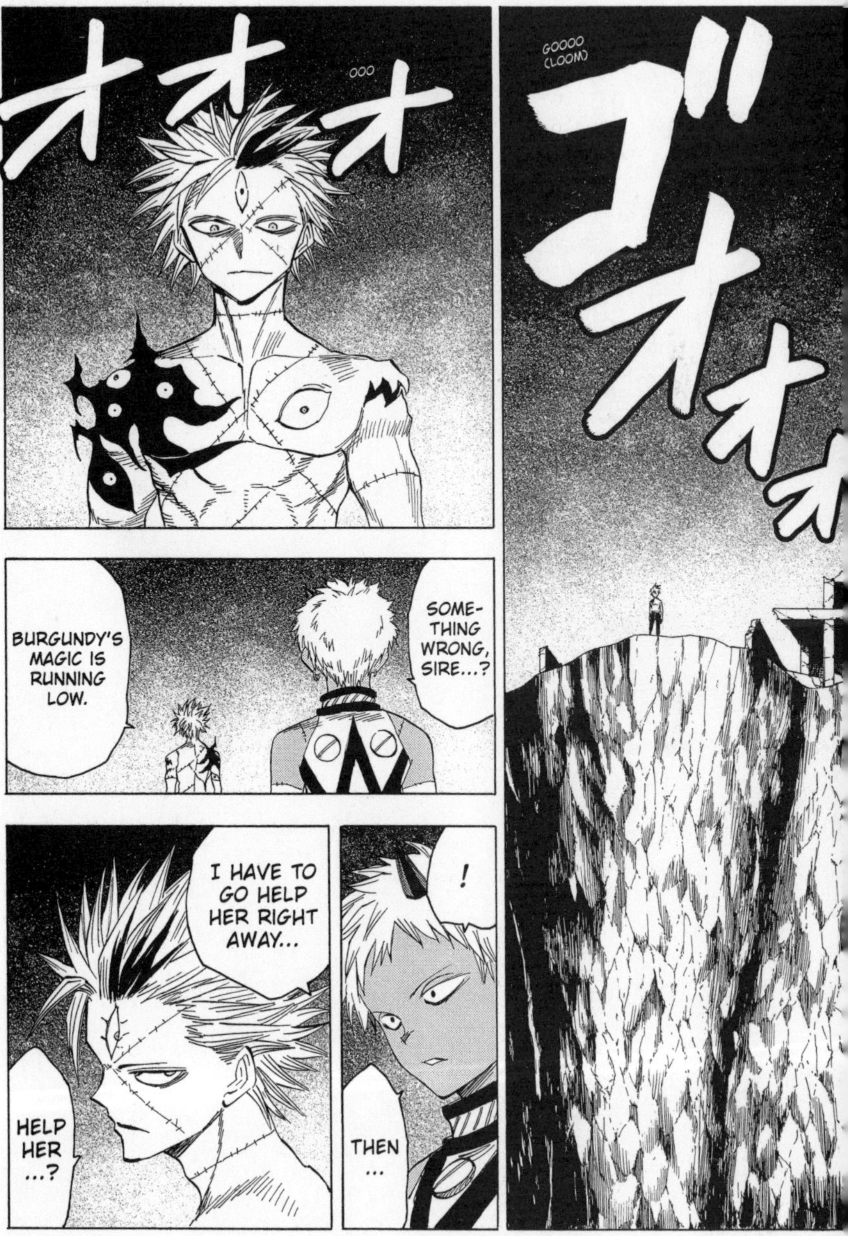
ゴオォォ
GOOOO (LOOM)
オオオ
OOO
SOME-THING WRONG, SIRE...?
BURGUNDY'S MAGIC IS RUNNING LOW.
!
THEN...
I HAVE TO GO HELP HER RIGHT AWAY...
HELP HER...?

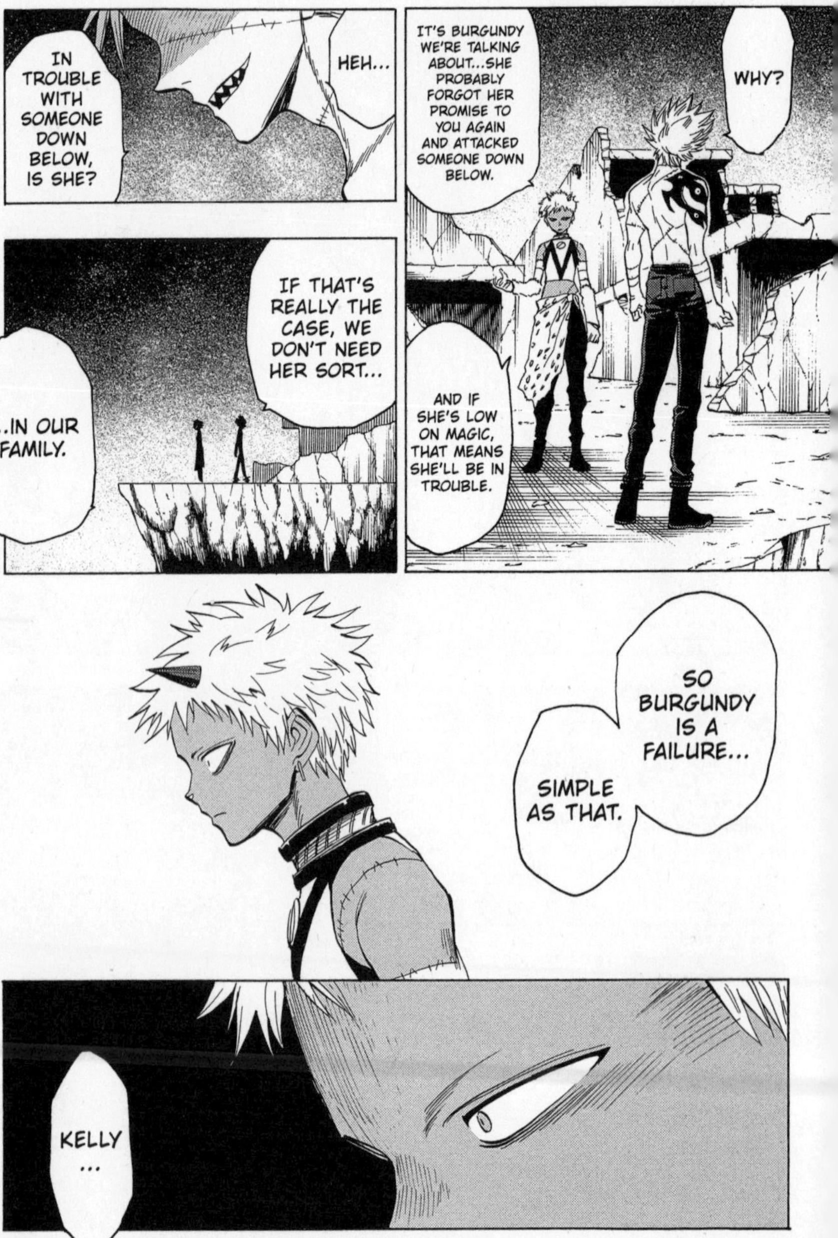
WHY?
IT'S BURGUNDY WE'RE TALKING ABOUT...SHE PROBABLY FORGOT HER PROMISE TO YOU AGAIN AND ATTACKED SOMEONE DOWN BELOW.
AND IF SHE'S LOW ON MAGIC, THAT MEANS SHE'LL BE IN TROUBLE.
HEH...
IN TROUBLE WITH SOMEONE DOWN BELOW, IS SHE?
IF THAT'S REALLY THE CASE, WE DON'T NEED HER SORT...
...IN OUR FAMILY.
SO BURGUNDY IS A FAILURE...
SIMPLE AS THAT.
KELLY ...

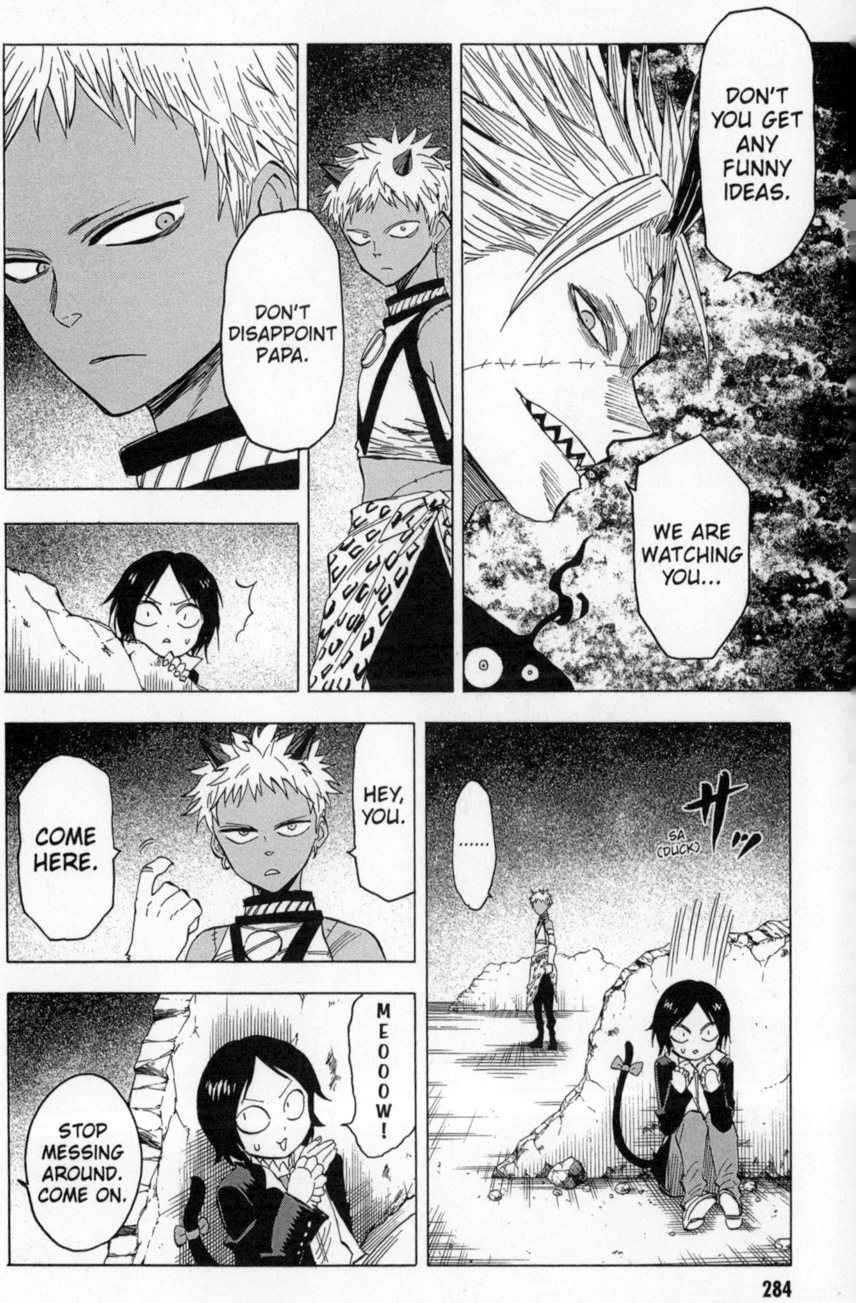
DON'T YOU GET ANY FUNNY IDEAS.
WE ARE WATCHING YOU...
DON'T DISAPPOINT PAPA.
サッ
SA (DUCK)
......
HEY, YOU.
COME HERE.
MEOOOOW!
STOP MESSING AROUND. COME ON.

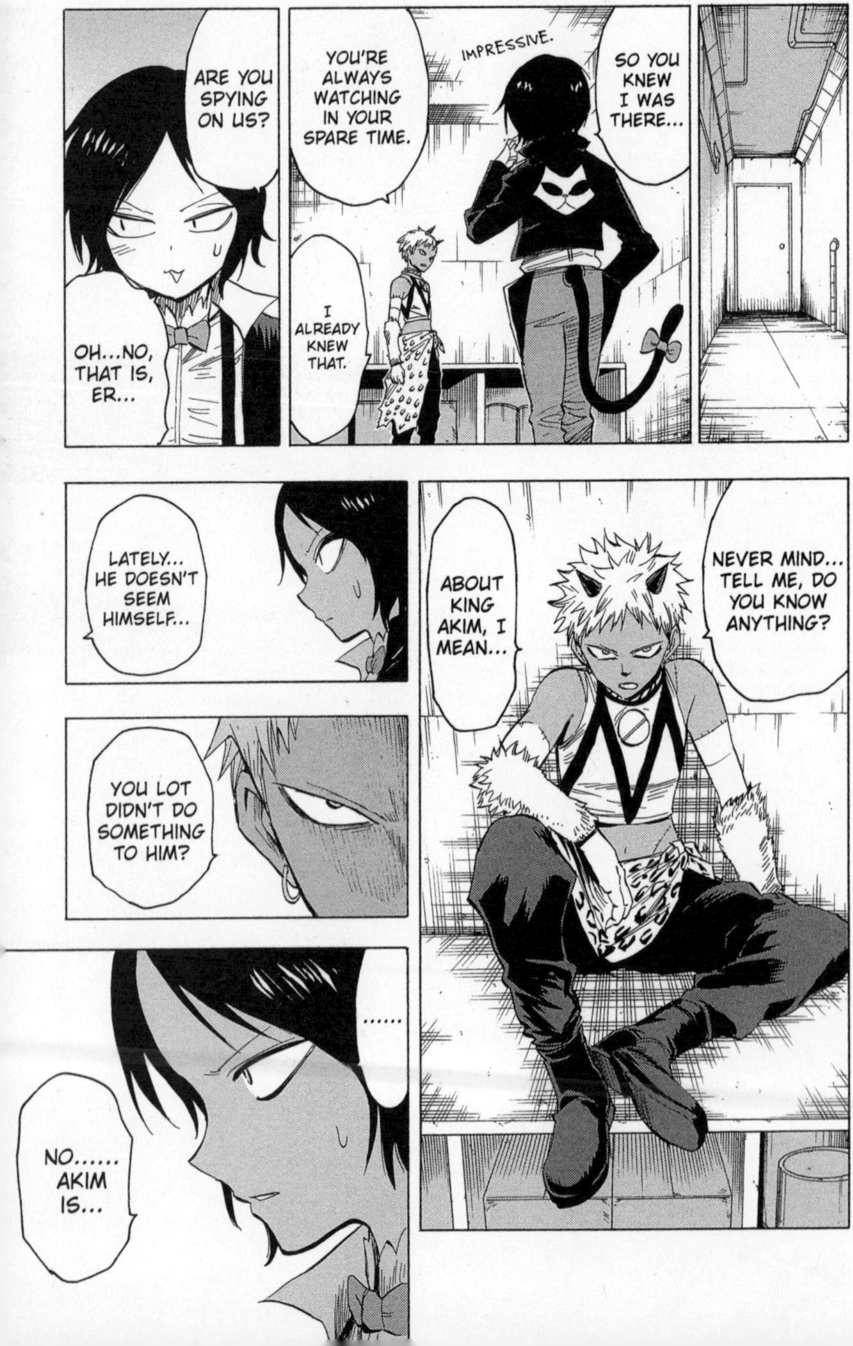
SO YOU KNEW I WAS THERE...
IMPRESSIVE.
YOU'RE ALWAYS WATCHING IN YOUR SPARE TIME.
I ALREADY KNEW THAT.
ARE YOU SPYING ON US?
OH...NO, THAT IS, ER...
NEVER MIND... TELL ME, DO YOU KNOW ANYTHING?
ABOUT KING AKIM, I MEAN...
LATELY... HE DOESN'T SEEM HIMSELF...
YOU LOT DIDN'T DO SOMETHING TO HIM?
......
NO...... AKIM IS...

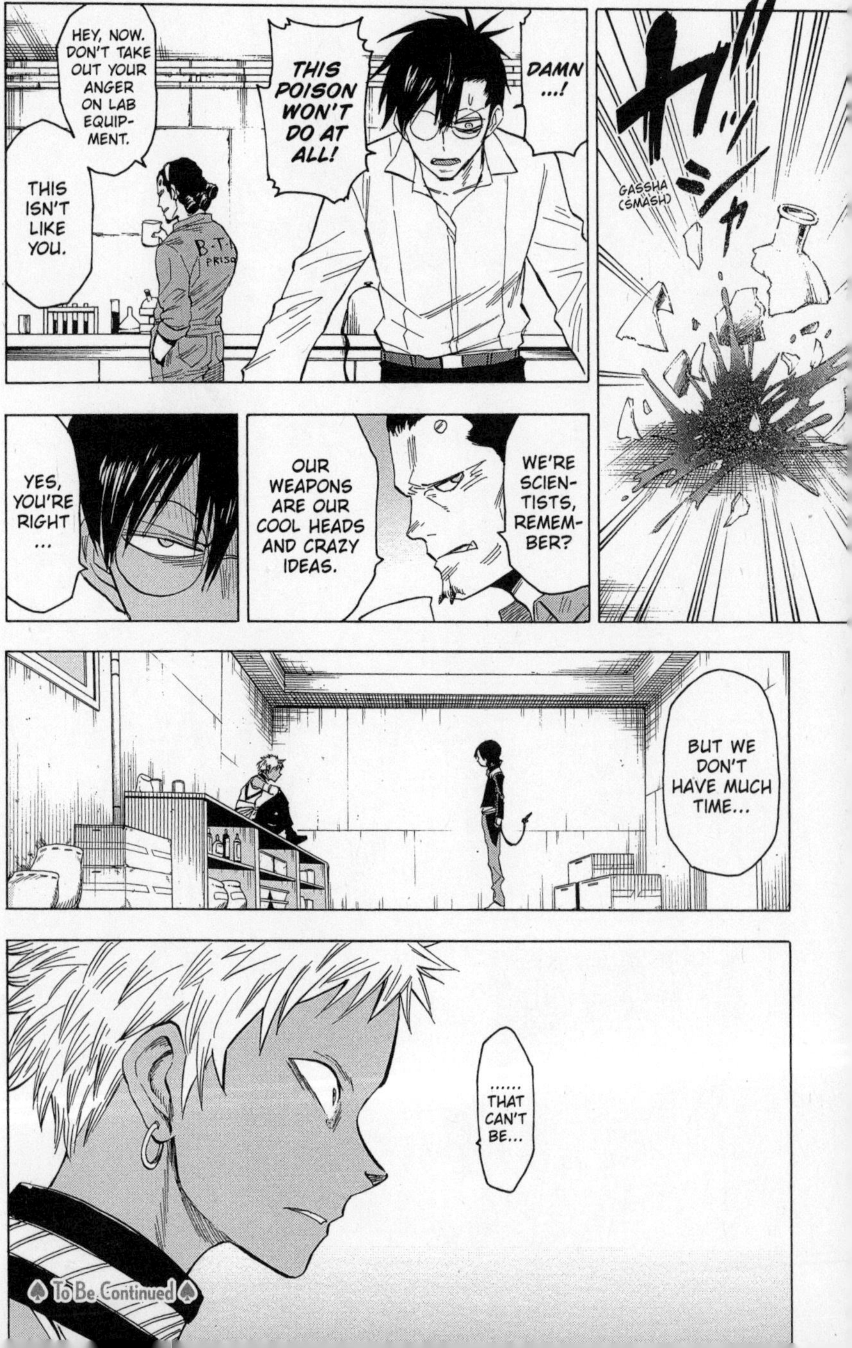
GASSHA (SMASH)
DAMN ...!
THIS POISON WON'T DO AT ALL!
HEY, NOW. DON'T TAKE OUT YOUR ANGER ON LAB EQUIPMENT.
THIS ISN'T LIKE YOU.
WE'RE SCIENTISTS, REMEMBER?
OUR WEAPONS ARE OUR COOL HEADS AND CRAZY IDEAS.
YES, YOU'RE RIGHT ...
BUT WE DON'T HAVE MUCH TIME...
...... THAT CAN'T BE...
To Be Continued

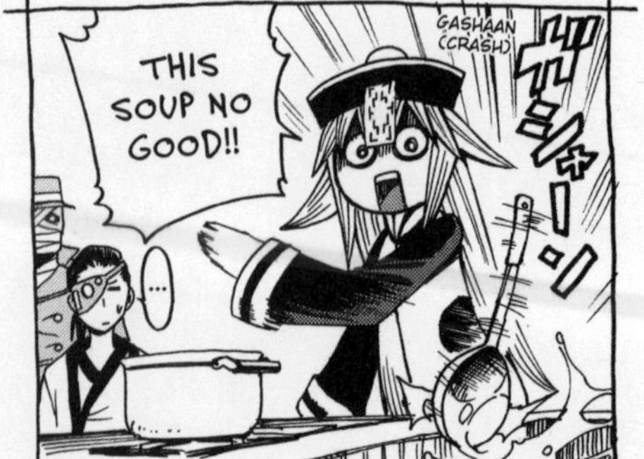
GASHAAN (CRASH)
THIS SOUP NO GOOD!!
...

BLOOD LAD

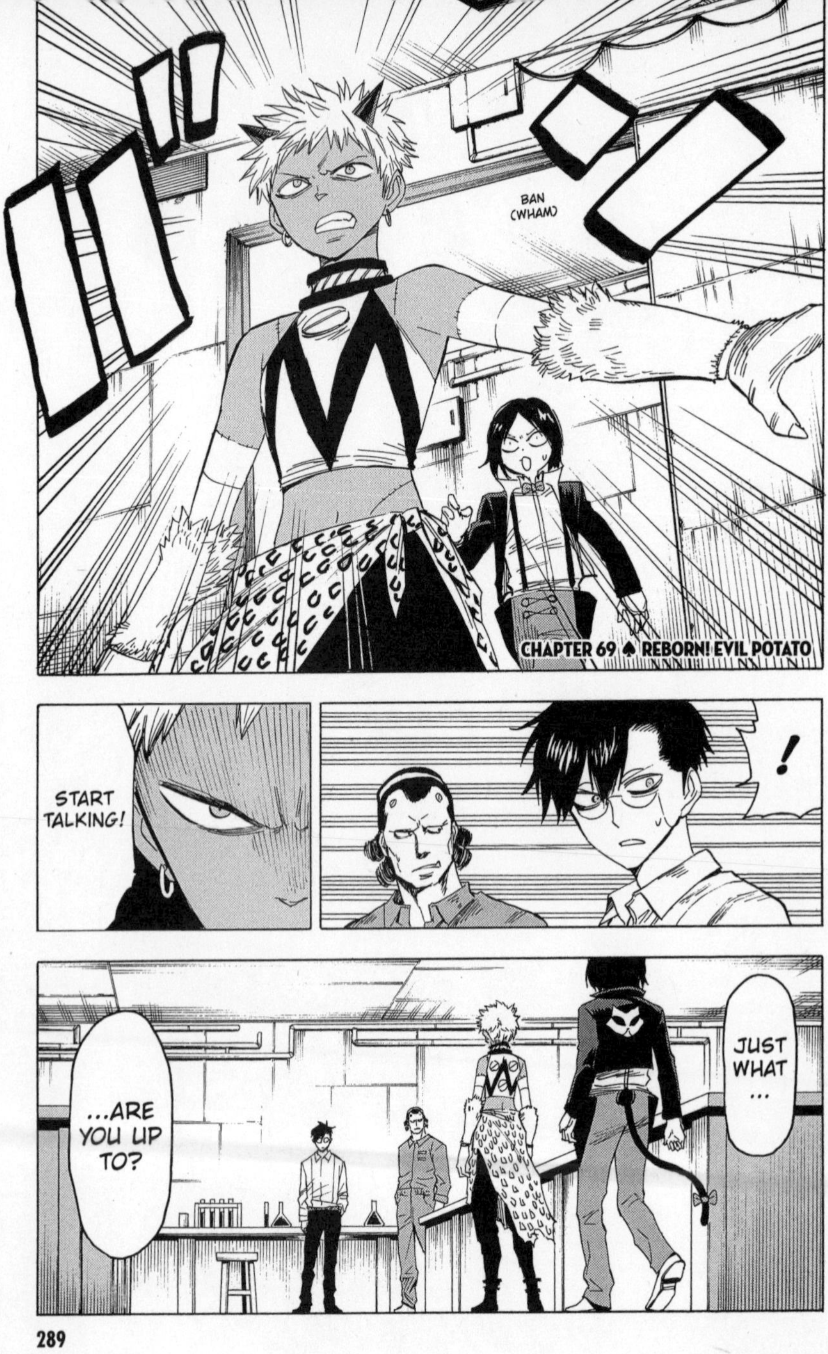
BAN
(WHAM)
CHAPTER 69 ♠ REBORN! EVIL POTATO
!
START TALKING!
JUST WHAT ...
...ARE YOU UP TO?

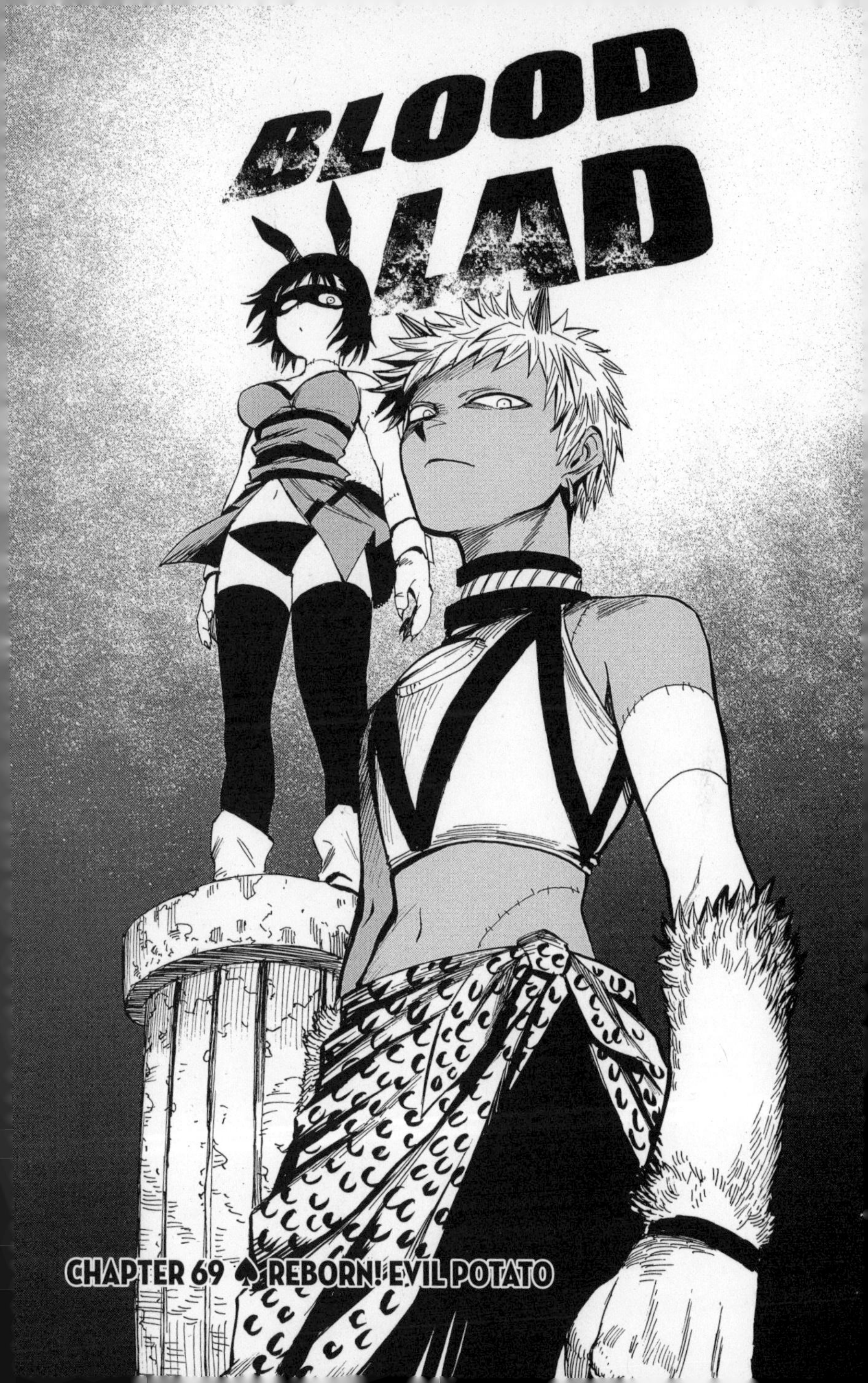
BLOOD LAD
CHAPTER 69 ♠ REBORN! EVIL POTATO

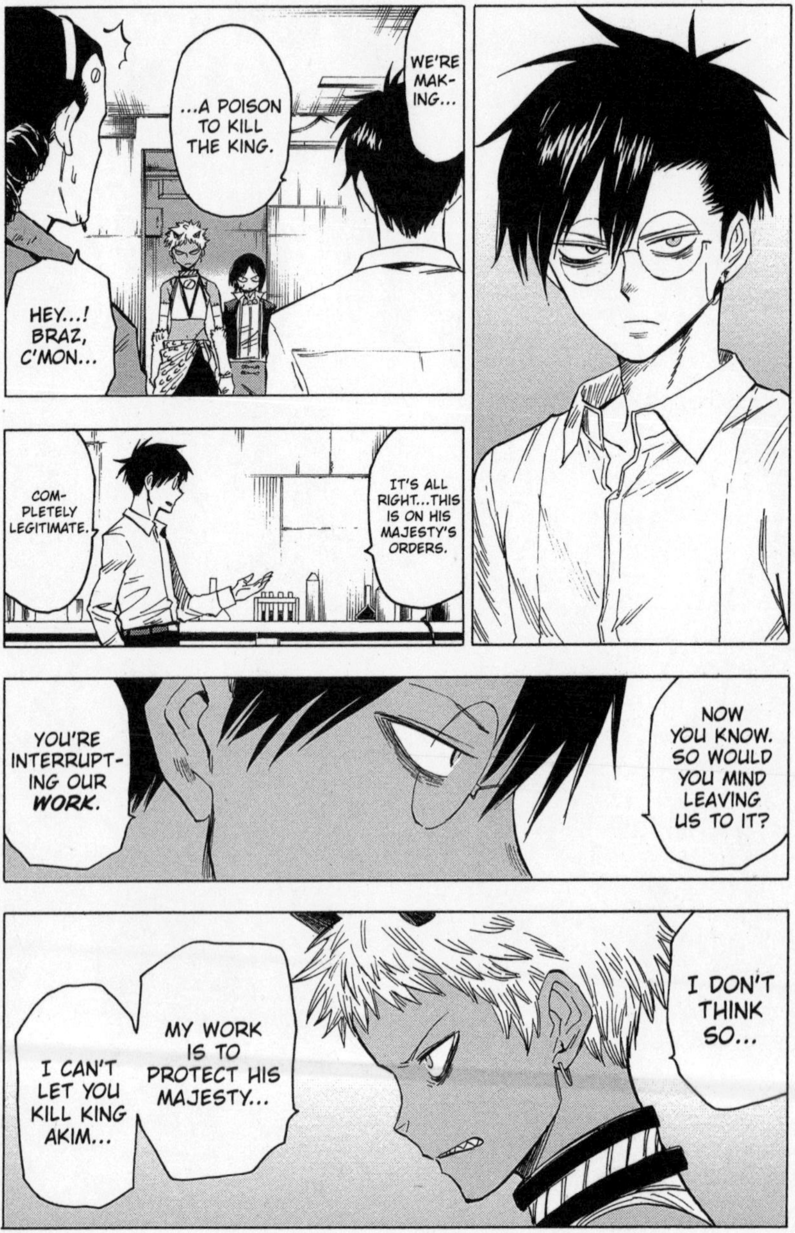
WE'RE MAK-ING...
...A POISON TO KILL THE KING.
HEY...! BRAZ, C'MON...
IT'S ALL RIGHT...THIS IS ON HIS MAJESTY'S ORDERS.
COM-PLETELY LEGITIMATE.
NOW YOU KNOW. SO WOULD YOU MIND LEAVING US TO IT?
YOU'RE INTERRUPT-ING OUR ***WORK***.
I DON'T THINK SO...
MY WORK IS TO PROTECT HIS MAJESTY...
I CAN'T LET YOU KILL KING AKIM...

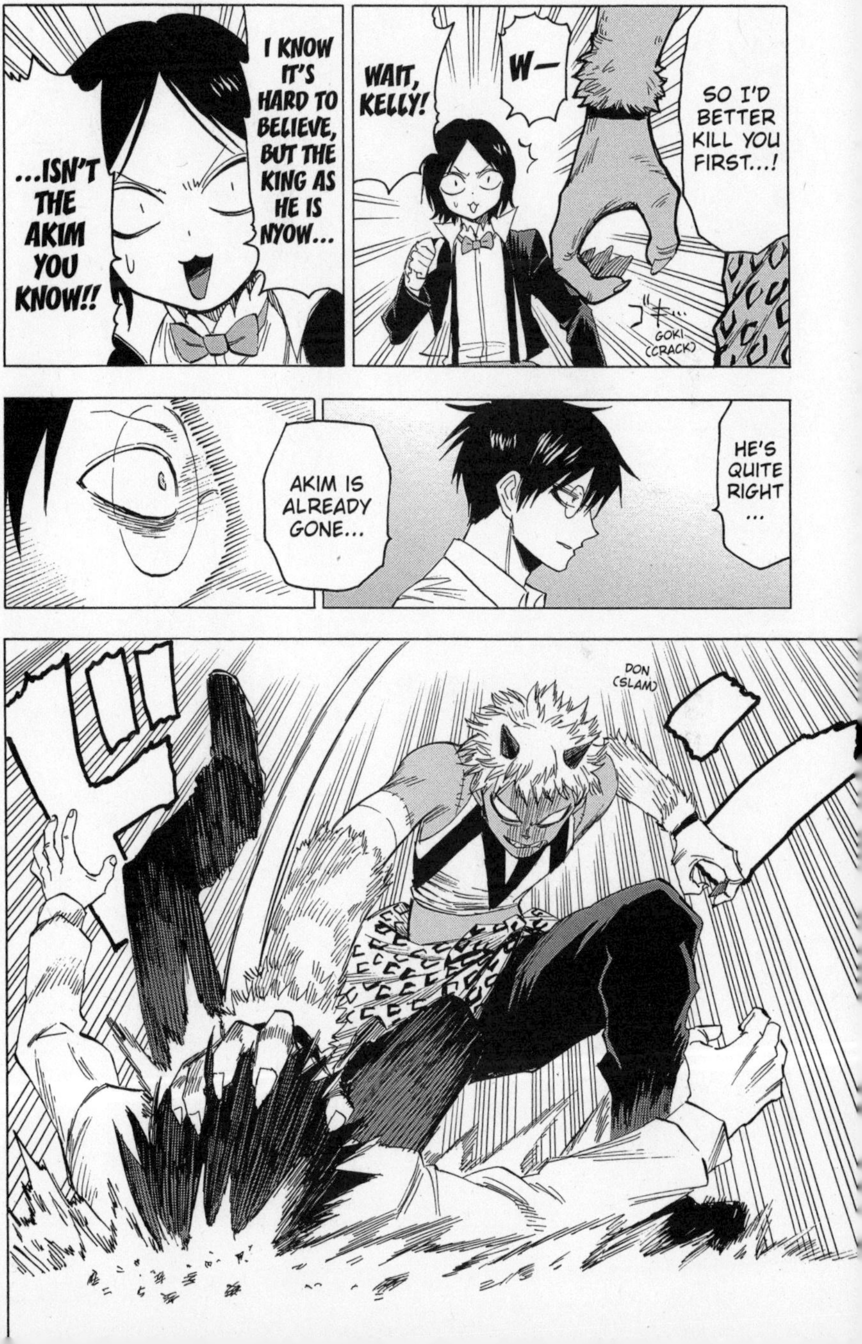
SO I'D BETTER KILL YOU FIRST...!
W—
WAIT, KELLY!
GOKI (CRACK)
I KNOW IT'S HARD TO BELIEVE, BUT THE KING AS HE IS NYOW...
...ISN'T THE AKIM YOU KNOW!!
HE'S QUITE RIGHT...
AKIM IS ALREADY GONE...
DON (SLAM)

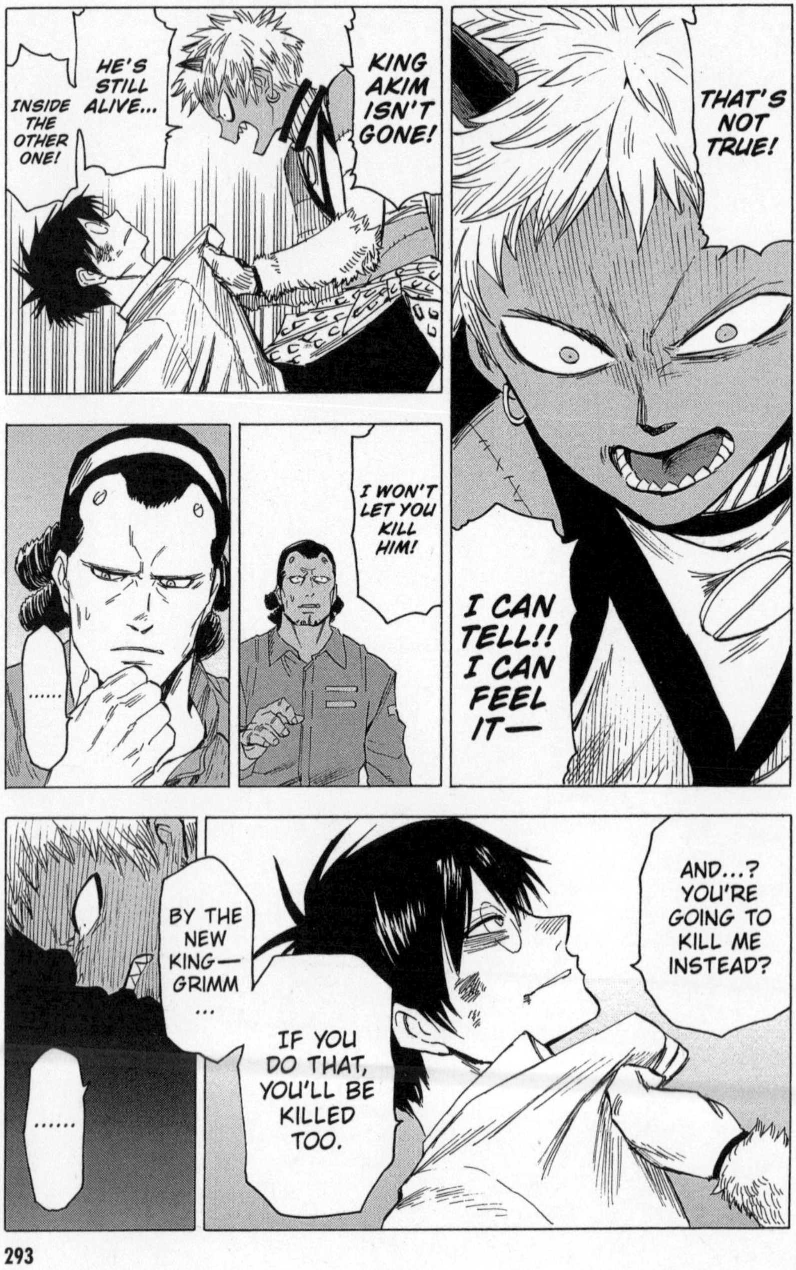
THAT'S NOT TRUE!
I CAN TELL!! I CAN FEEL IT—
KING AKIM ISN'T GONE!
HE'S STILL ALIVE...
INSIDE THE OTHER ONE!
I WON'T LET YOU KILL HIM!
......
AND...? YOU'RE GOING TO KILL ME INSTEAD?
BY THE NEW KING—GRIMM...
IF YOU DO THAT, YOU'LL BE KILLED TOO.
......

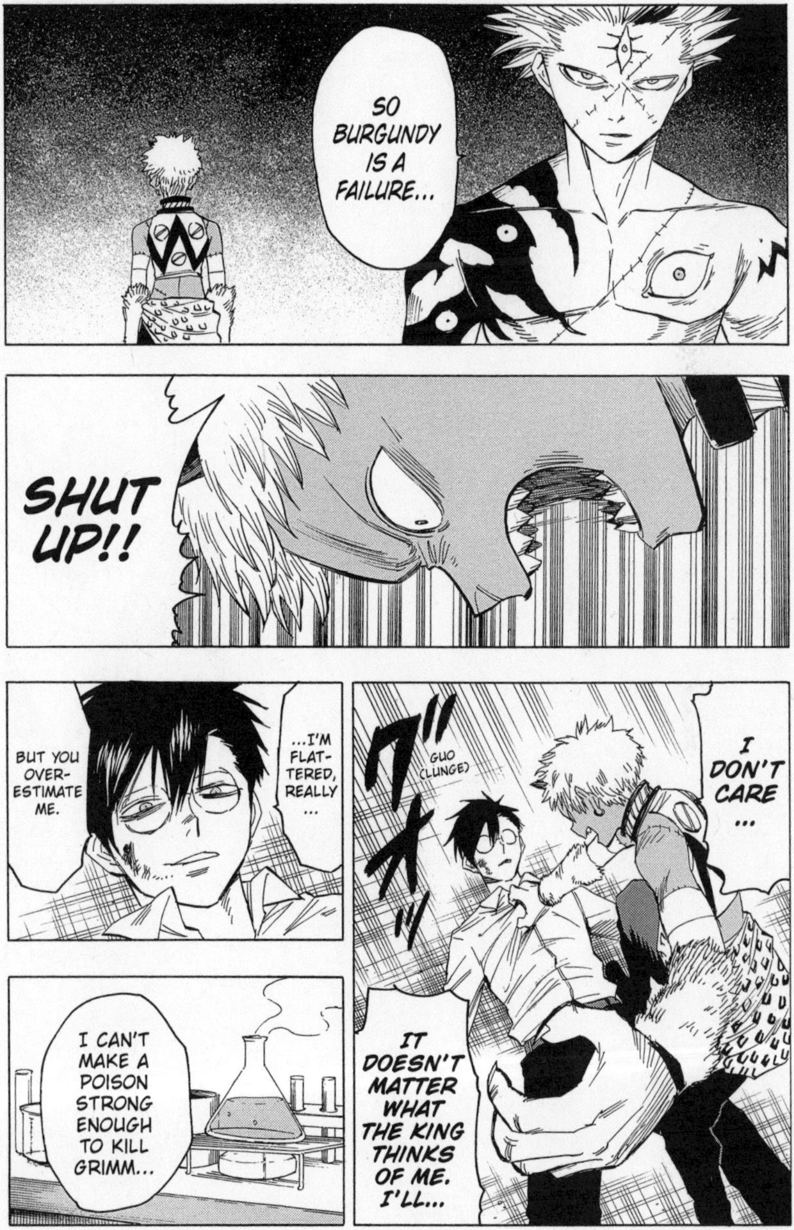
SO BURGUNDY IS A FAILURE...
SHUT UP!!
I DON'T CARE...
GUO (LUNGE)
IT DOESN'T MATTER WHAT THE KING THINKS OF ME. I'LL...
...I'M FLATTERED, REALLY...
BUT YOU OVER-ESTIMATE ME.
I CAN'T MAKE A POISON STRONG ENOUGH TO KILL GRIMM...

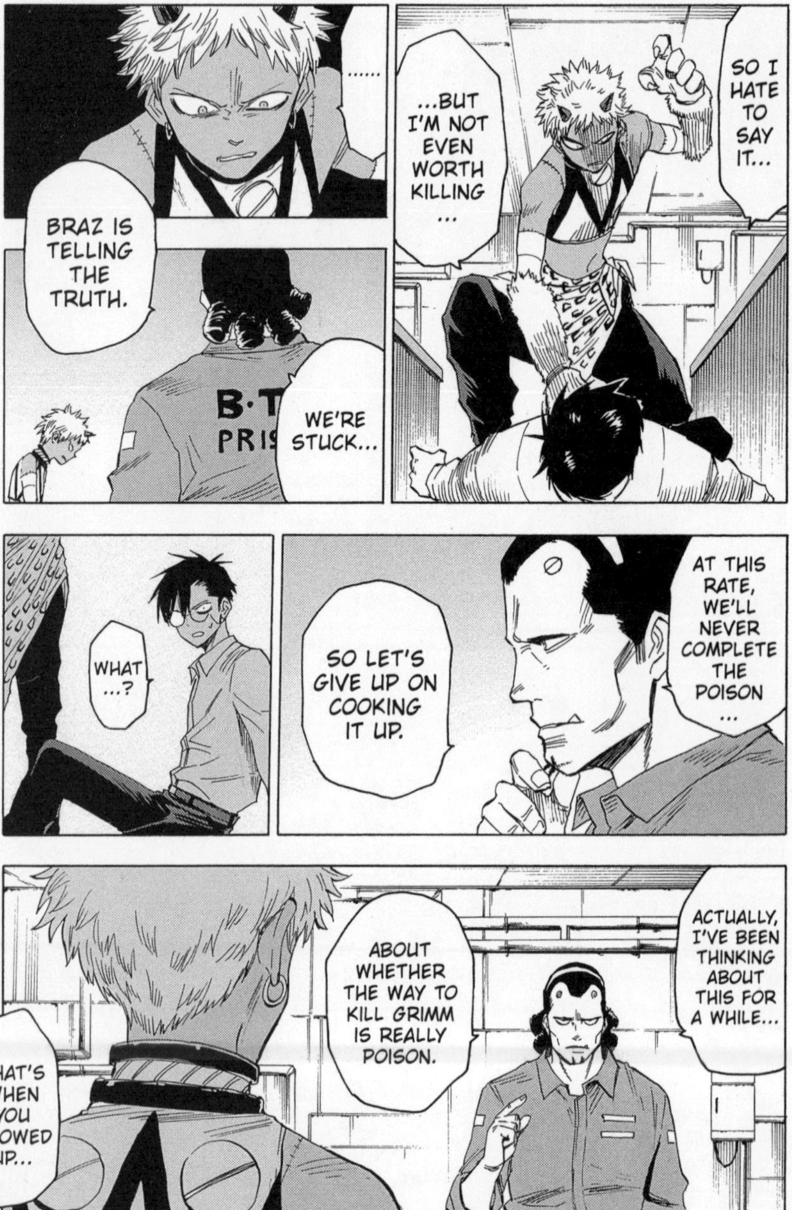
SO I HATE TO SAY IT...
...BUT I'M NOT EVEN WORTH KILLING ...
......
BRAZ IS TELLING THE TRUTH.
WE'RE STUCK...
AT THIS RATE, WE'LL NEVER COMPLETE THE POISON ...
SO LET'S GIVE UP ON COOKING IT UP.
WHAT ...?
ACTUALLY, I'VE BEEN THINKING ABOUT THIS FOR A WHILE...
ABOUT WHETHER THE WAY TO KILL GRIMM IS REALLY POISON.
THAT'S WHEN YOU SHOWED UP...

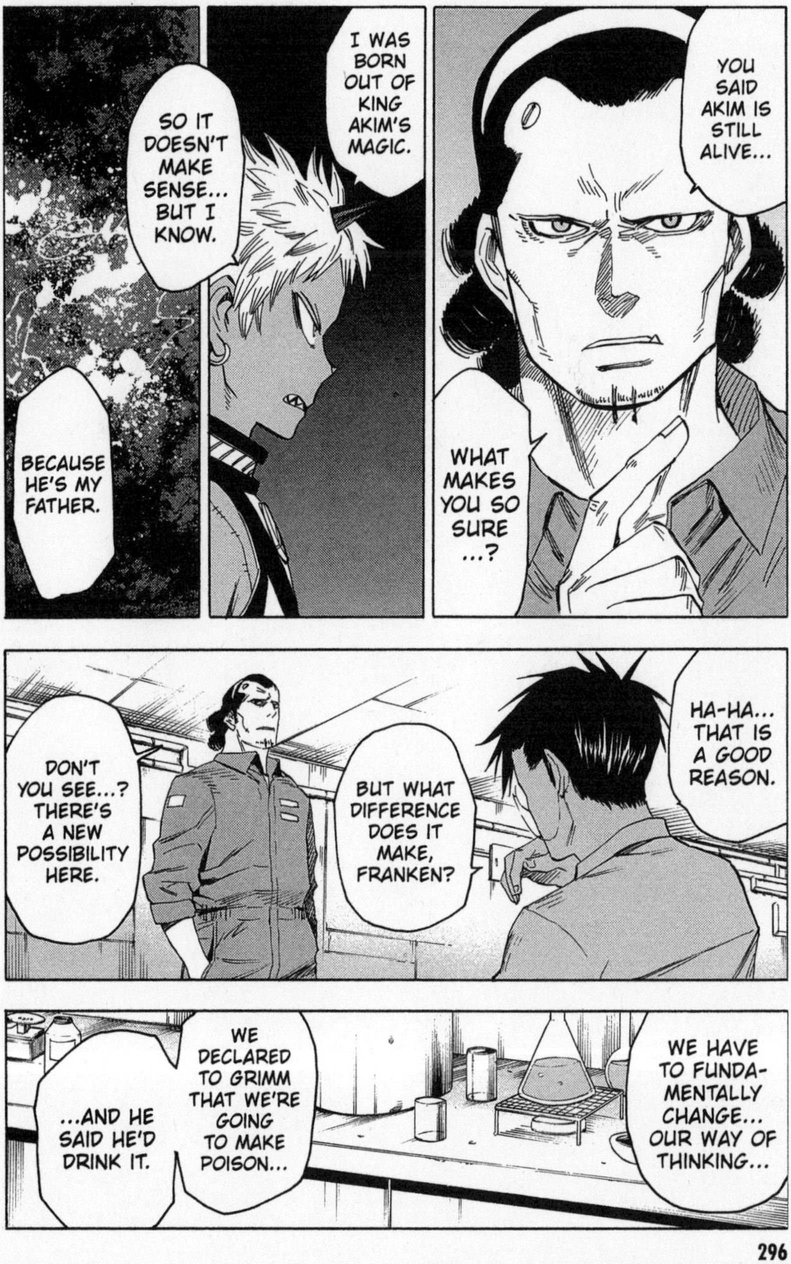
YOU SAID AKIM IS STILL ALIVE...
WHAT MAKES YOU SO SURE ...?
I WAS BORN OUT OF KING AKIM'S MAGIC.
SO IT DOESN'T MAKE SENSE... BUT I KNOW.
BECAUSE HE'S MY FATHER.
HA-HA... THAT IS A GOOD REASON.
BUT WHAT DIFFERENCE DOES IT MAKE, FRANKEN?
DON'T YOU SEE...? THERE'S A NEW POSSIBILITY HERE.
WE HAVE TO FUNDA-MENTALLY CHANGE... OUR WAY OF THINKING...
WE DECLARED TO GRIMM THAT WE'RE GOING TO MAKE POISON...
...AND HE SAID HE'D DRINK IT.

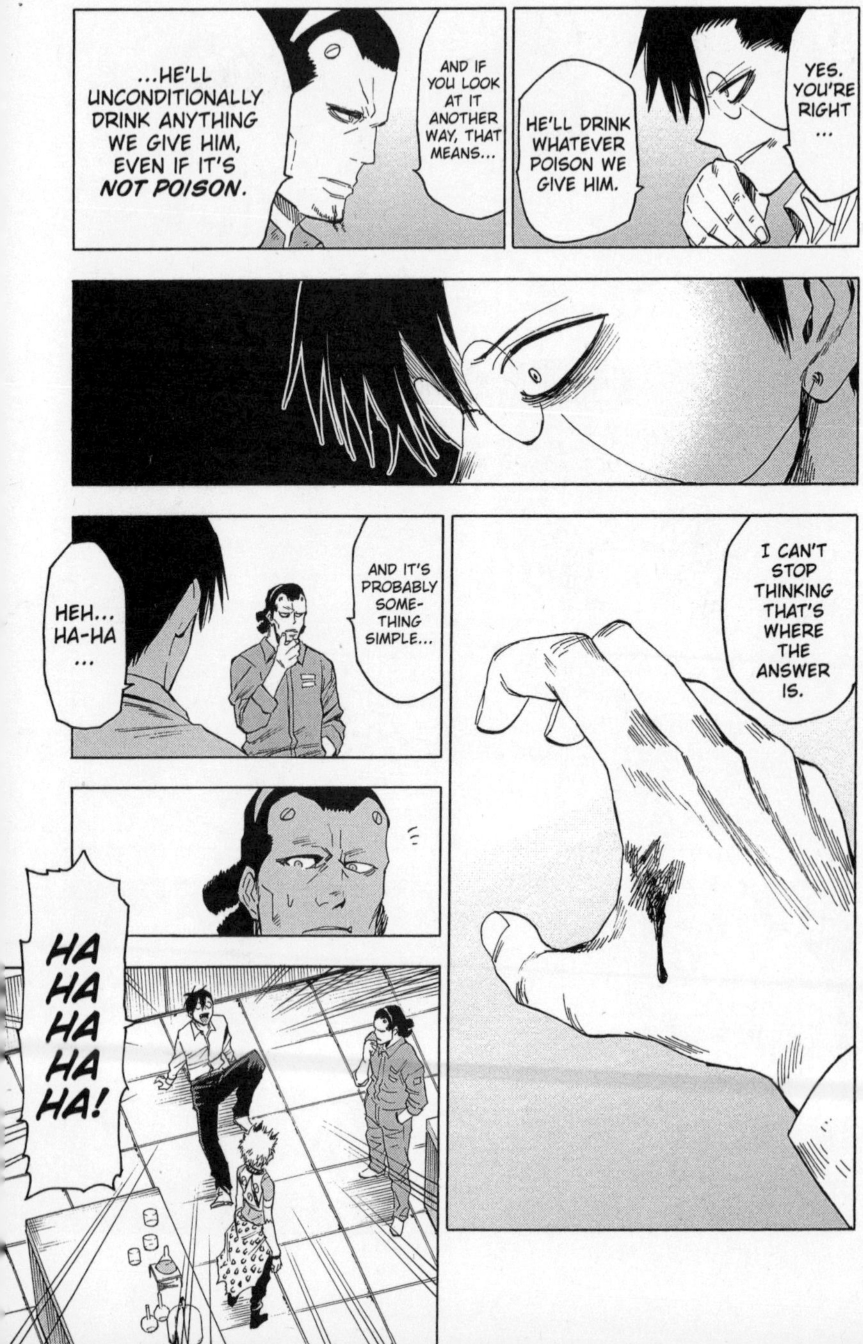
YES. YOU'RE RIGHT...
HE'LL DRINK WHATEVER POISON WE GIVE HIM.
AND IF YOU LOOK AT IT ANOTHER WAY, THAT MEANS...
...HE'LL UNCONDITIONALLY DRINK ANYTHING WE GIVE HIM, EVEN IF IT'S *NOT POISON*.
I CAN'T STOP THINKING THAT'S WHERE THE ANSWER IS.
...
AND IT'S PROBABLY SOME-THING SIMPLE...
HEH... HA-HA...
HA HA HA HA HA HA!

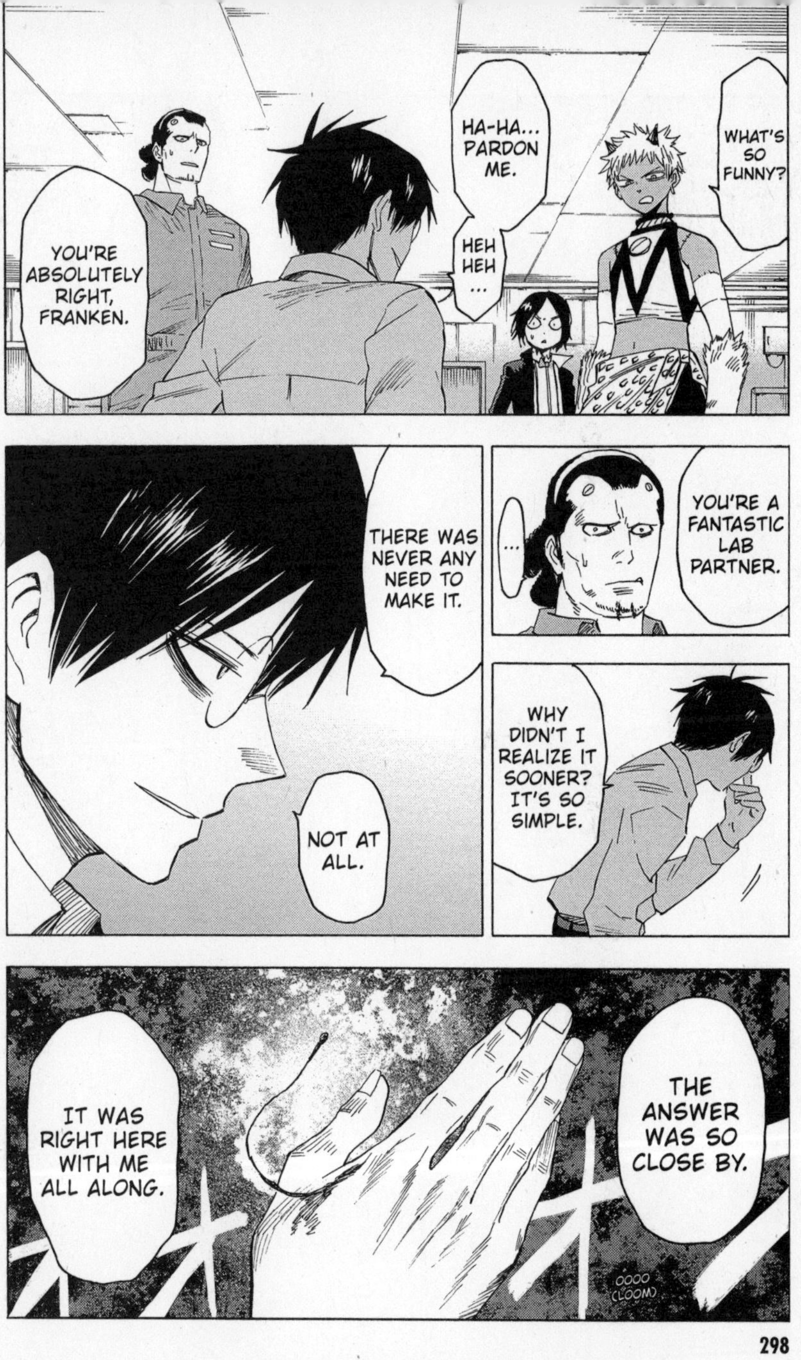
WHAT'S SO FUNNY?
HA-HA... PARDON ME.
HEH HEH ...
YOU'RE ABSOLUTELY RIGHT, FRANKEN.
YOU'RE A FANTASTIC LAB PARTNER.
...
WHY DIDN'T I REALIZE IT SOONER? IT'S SO SIMPLE.
THERE WAS NEVER ANY NEED TO MAKE IT.
NOT AT ALL.
THE ANSWER WAS SO CLOSE BY.
OOOO (LOOM)
IT WAS RIGHT HERE WITH ME ALL ALONG.

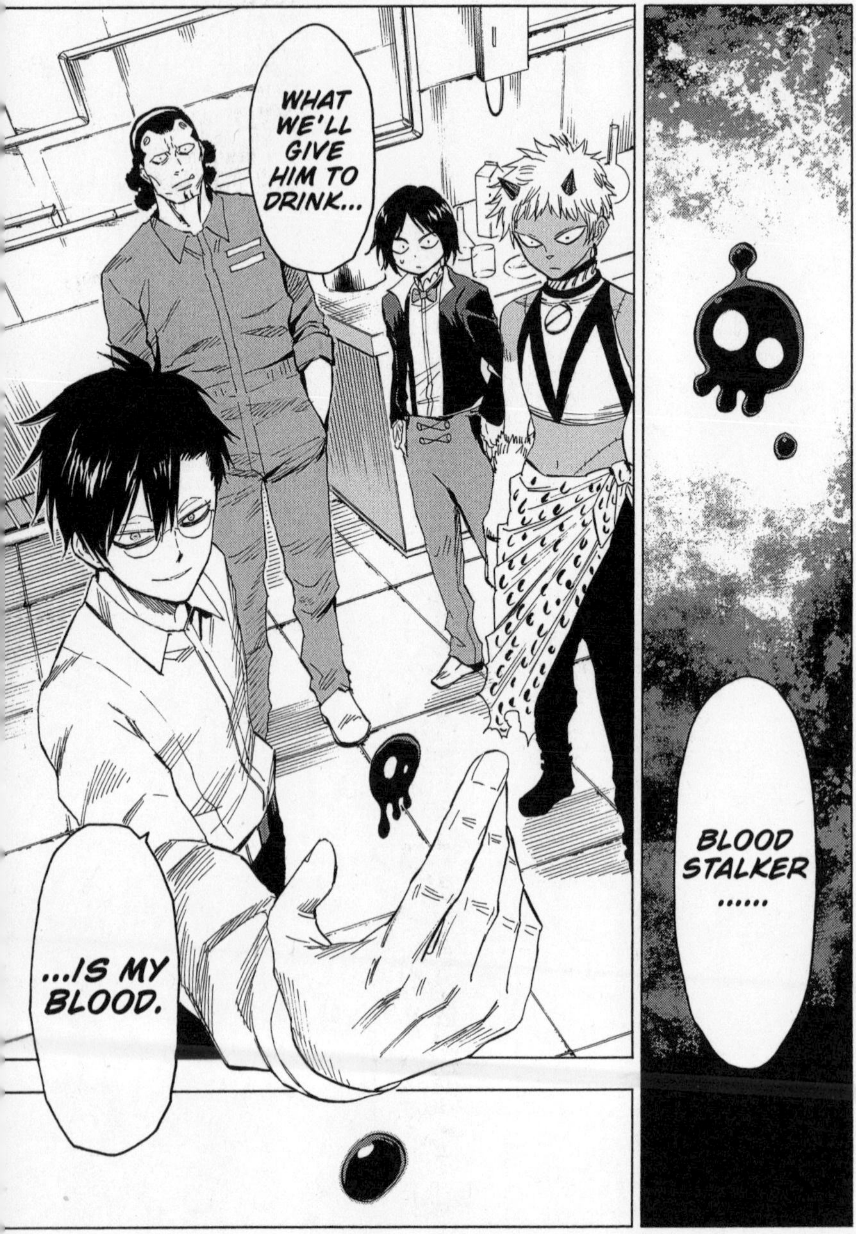
BLOOD STALKER ......
WHAT WE'LL GIVE HIM TO DRINK...
...IS MY BLOOD.

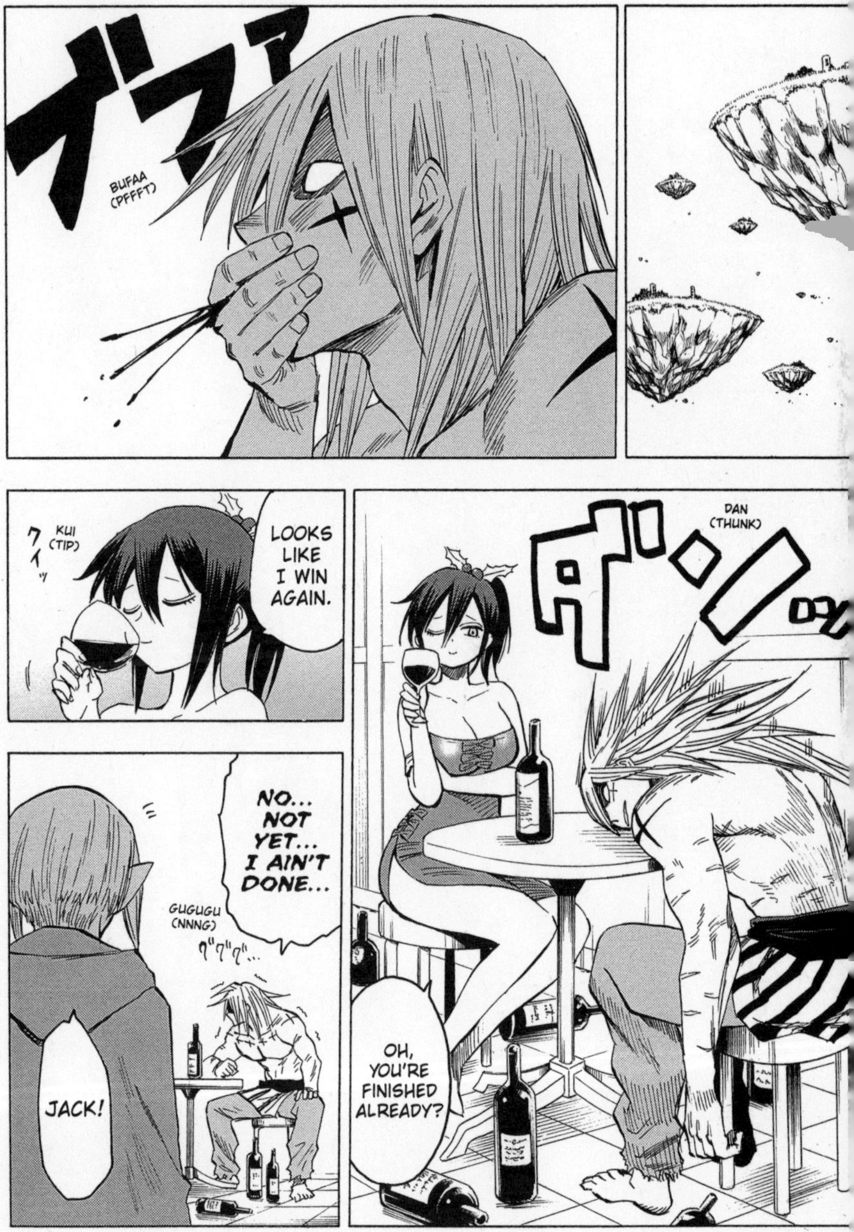
BUFAA (PFFFT)
DAN (THUNK)
OH, YOU'RE FINISHED ALREADY?
LOOKS LIKE I WIN AGAIN.
KUI (TIP)
NO... NOT YET... I AIN'T DONE...
GUGUGU (NNNG)
JACK!

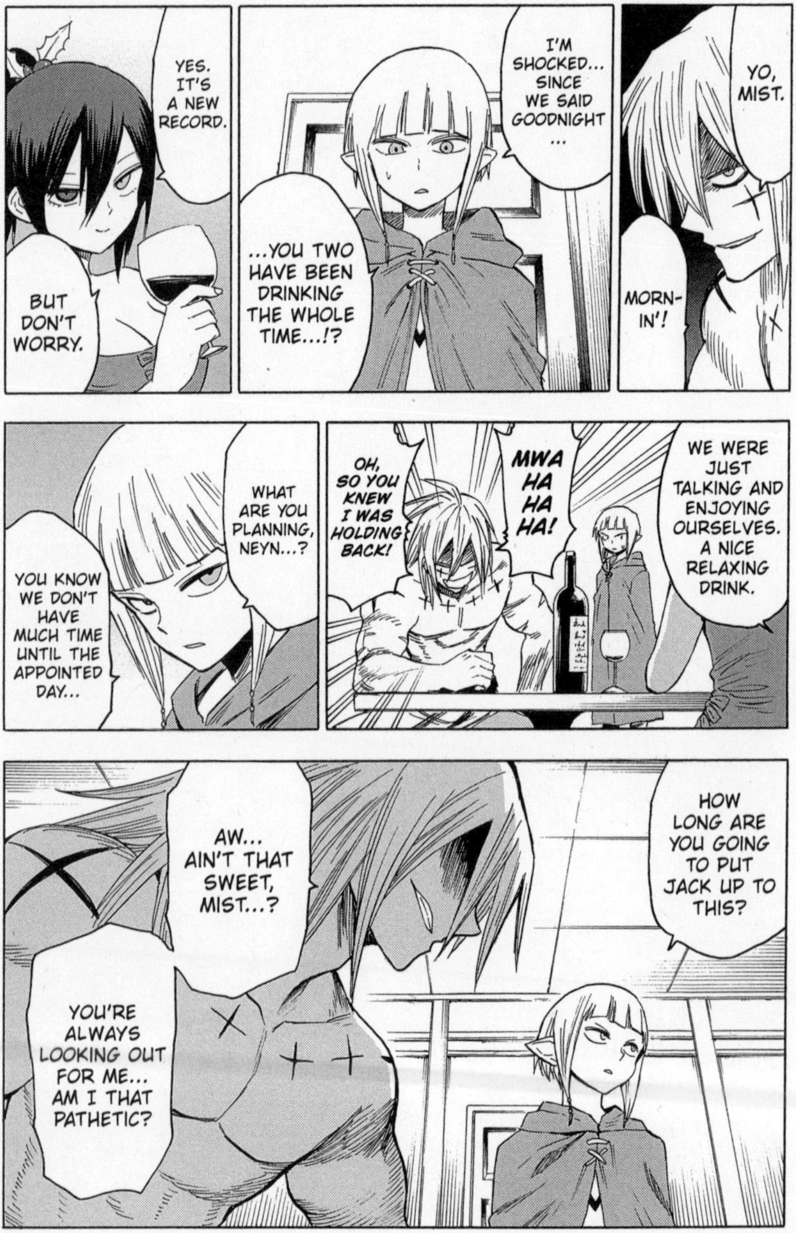
YO, MIST.
MORN-IN'!
I'M SHOCKED... SINCE WE SAID GOODNIGHT...
...YOU TWO HAVE BEEN DRINKING THE WHOLE TIME...!?
YES. IT'S A NEW RECORD.
BUT DON'T WORRY.
WE WERE JUST TALKING AND ENJOYING OURSELVES. A NICE RELAXING DRINK.
MWA HA HA HA!
OH, SO YOU KNEW I WAS HOLDING BACK!
WHAT ARE YOU PLANNING, NEYN...?
YOU KNOW WE DON'T HAVE MUCH TIME UNTIL THE APPOINTED DAY...
HOW LONG ARE YOU GOING TO PUT JACK UP TO THIS?
AW... AIN'T THAT SWEET, MIST...?
YOU'RE ALWAYS LOOKING OUT FOR ME... AM I THAT PATHETIC?

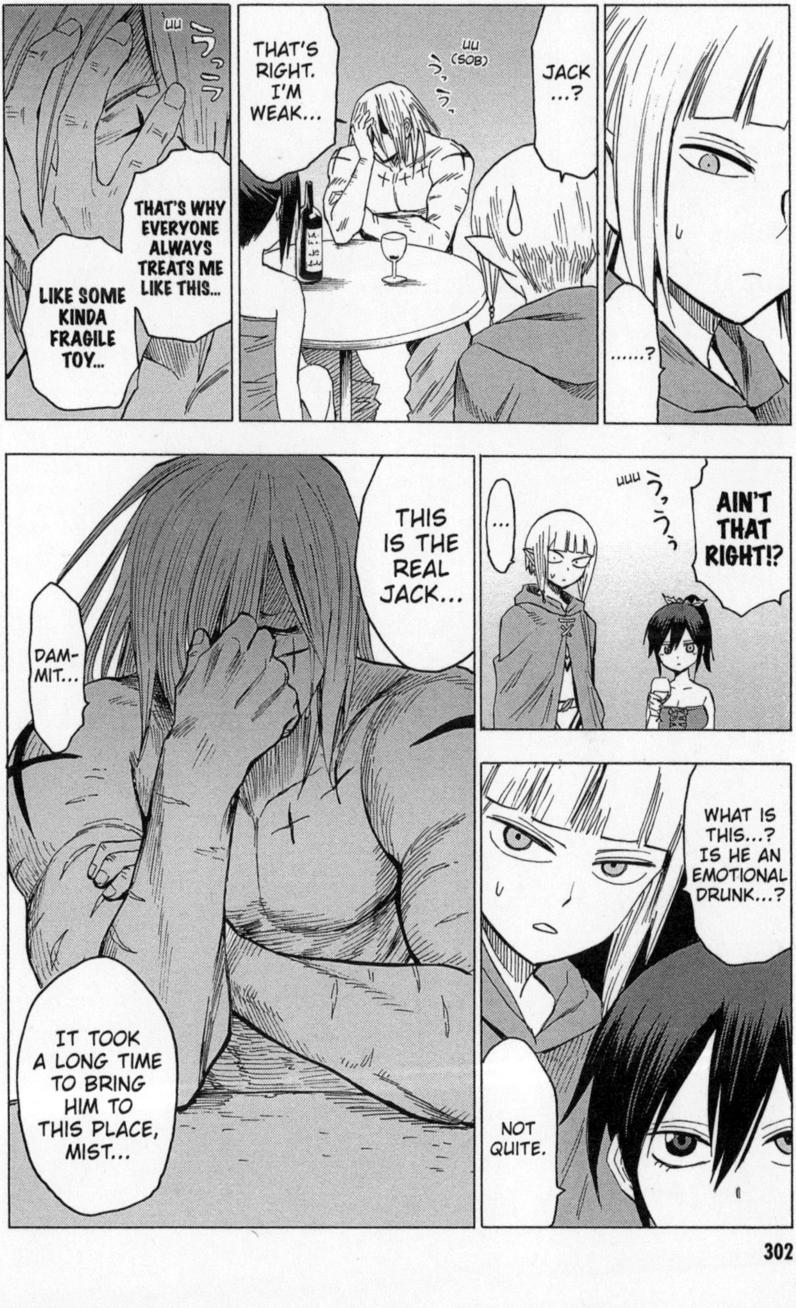
......?
JACK ...?
UU (SOB)
THAT'S RIGHT. I'M WEAK...
UU
THAT'S WHY EVERYONE ALWAYS TREATS ME LIKE THIS...
LIKE SOME KINDA FRAGILE TOY...
AIN'T THAT RIGHT!?
UUU
...
WHAT IS THIS...? IS HE AN EMOTIONAL DRUNK...?
NOT QUITE.
THIS IS THE REAL JACK...
DAM-MIT...
IT TOOK A LONG TIME TO BRING HIM TO THIS PLACE, MIST...

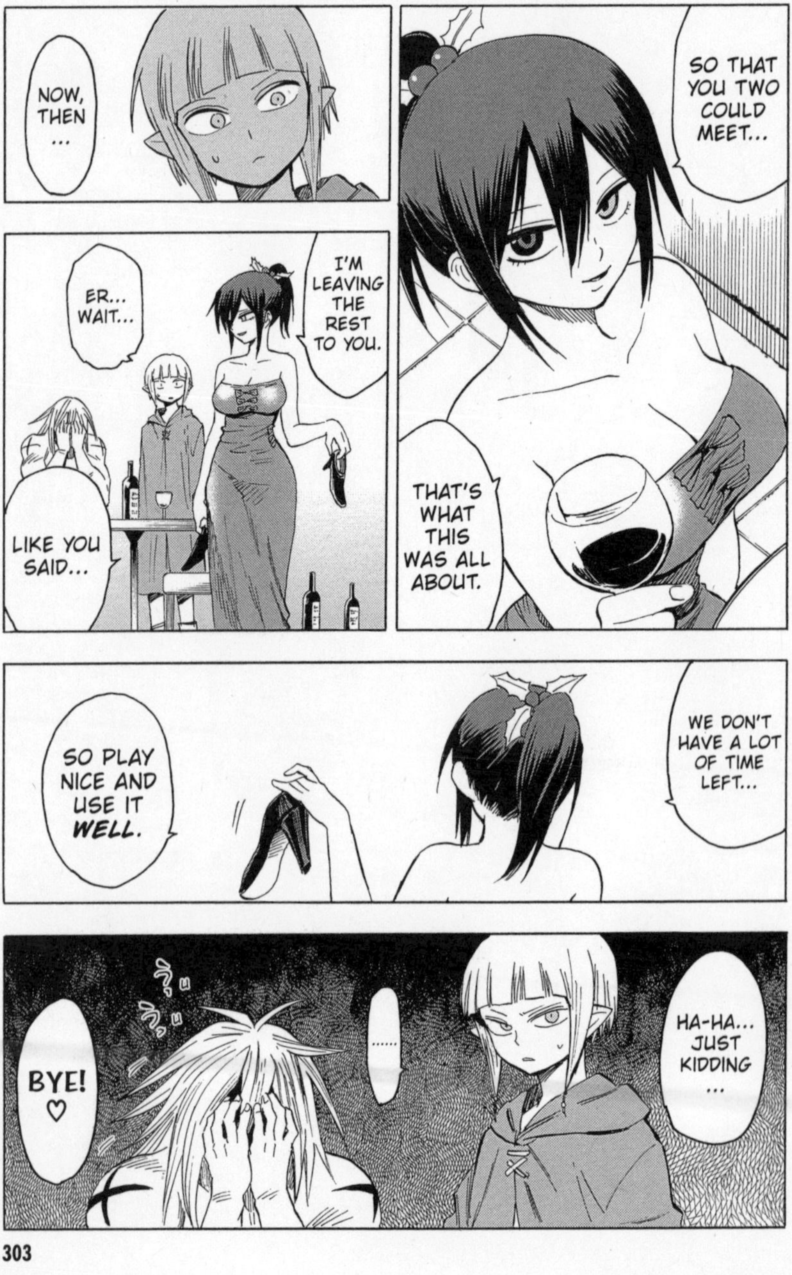
SO THAT YOU TWO COULD MEET...
THAT'S WHAT THIS WAS ALL ABOUT.
NOW, THEN ...
I'M LEAVING THE REST TO YOU.
ER... WAIT...
LIKE YOU SAID...
WE DON'T HAVE A LOT OF TIME LEFT...
SO PLAY NICE AND USE IT *WELL*.
HA-HA... JUST KIDDING ...
......
BYE! ♡

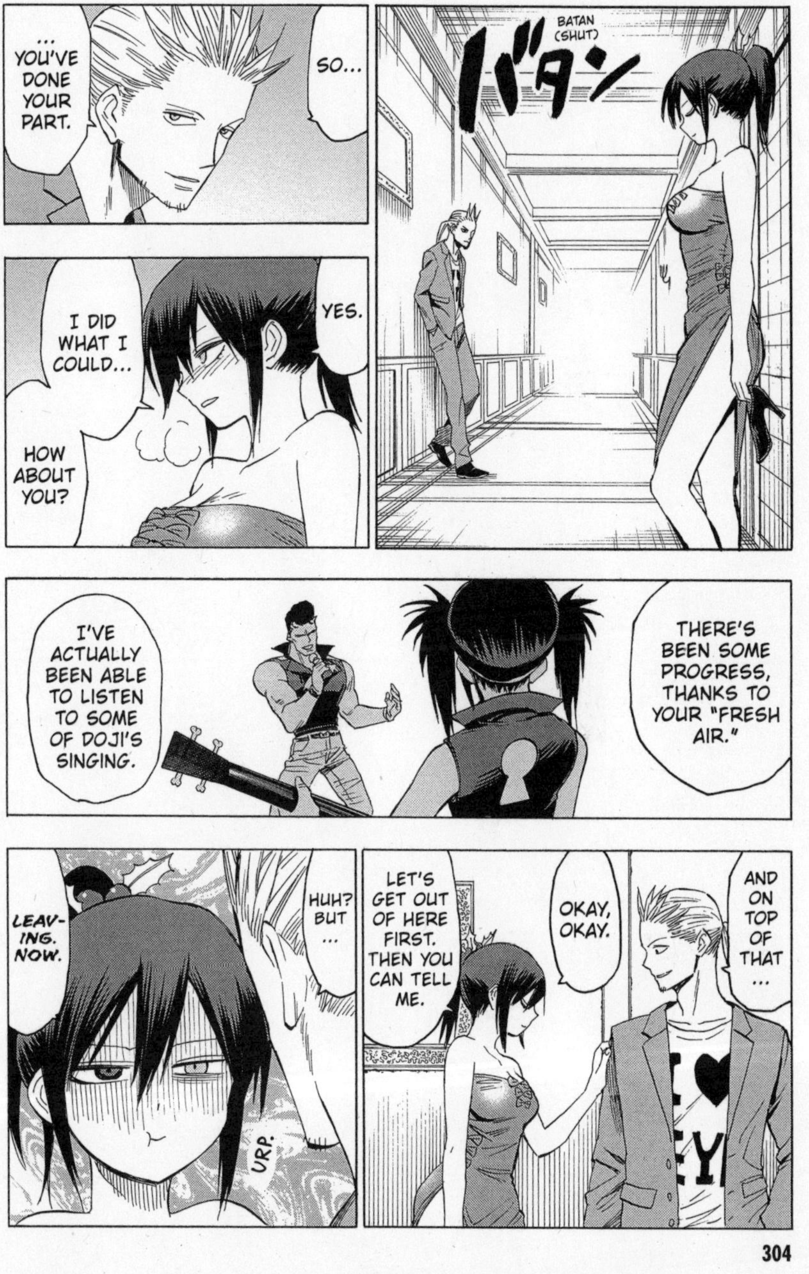
BATAN (SHUT)
バタン
SO...
...YOU'VE DONE YOUR PART.
YES.
I DID WHAT I COULD...
HOW ABOUT YOU?
THERE'S BEEN SOME PROGRESS, THANKS TO YOUR "FRESH AIR."
I'VE ACTUALLY BEEN ABLE TO LISTEN TO SOME OF DOJI'S SINGING.
AND ON TOP OF THAT...
OKAY, OKAY.
LET'S GET OUT OF HERE FIRST. THEN YOU CAN TELL ME.
HUH? BUT...
LEAVING. NOW.
URP.

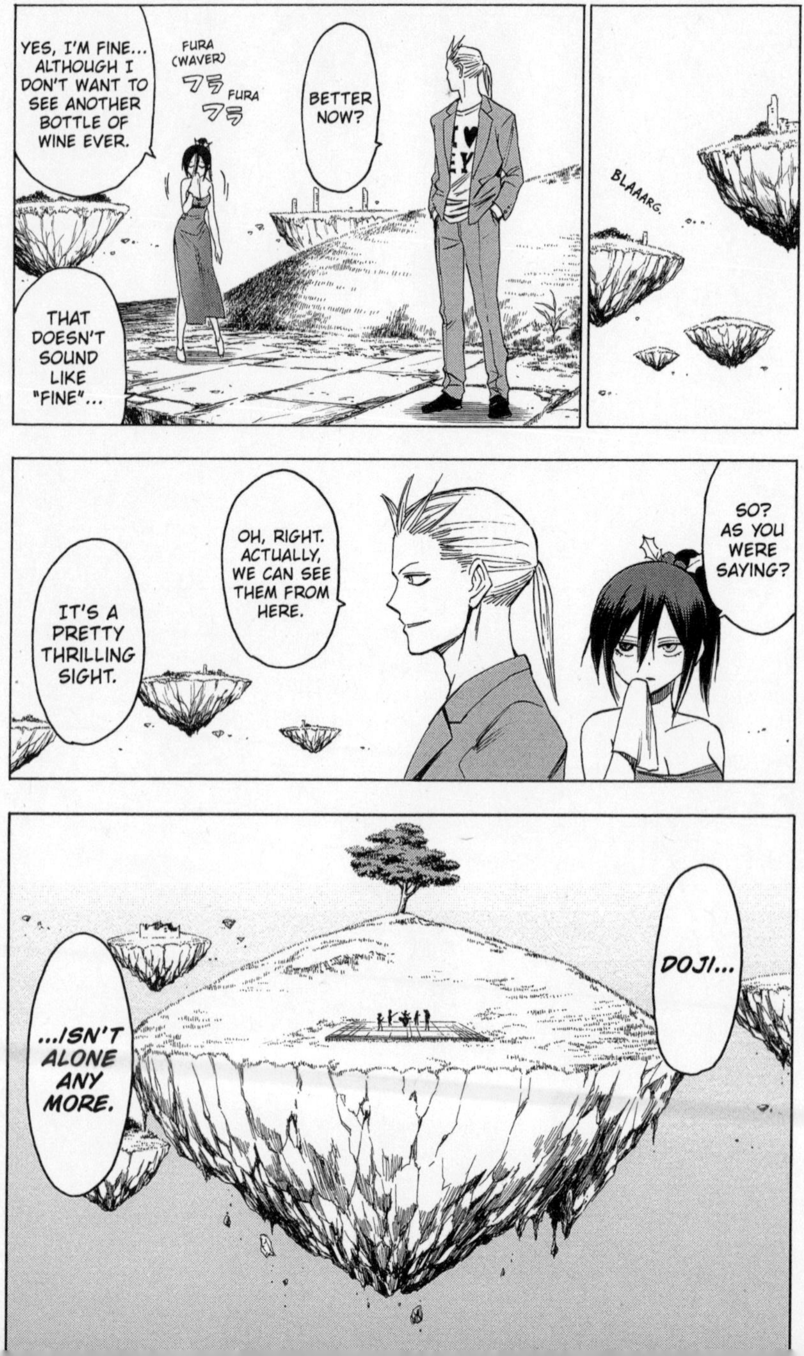
BLAAARG.
BETTER NOW?
FURA (WAVER) フラ FURA フラ
YES, I'M FINE... ALTHOUGH I DON'T WANT TO SEE ANOTHER BOTTLE OF WINE EVER.
THAT DOESN'T SOUND LIKE "FINE"...
SO? AS YOU WERE SAYING?
OH, RIGHT. ACTUALLY, WE CAN SEE THEM FROM HERE.
IT'S A PRETTY THRILLING SIGHT.
DOJI...
...ISN'T ALONE ANY MORE.

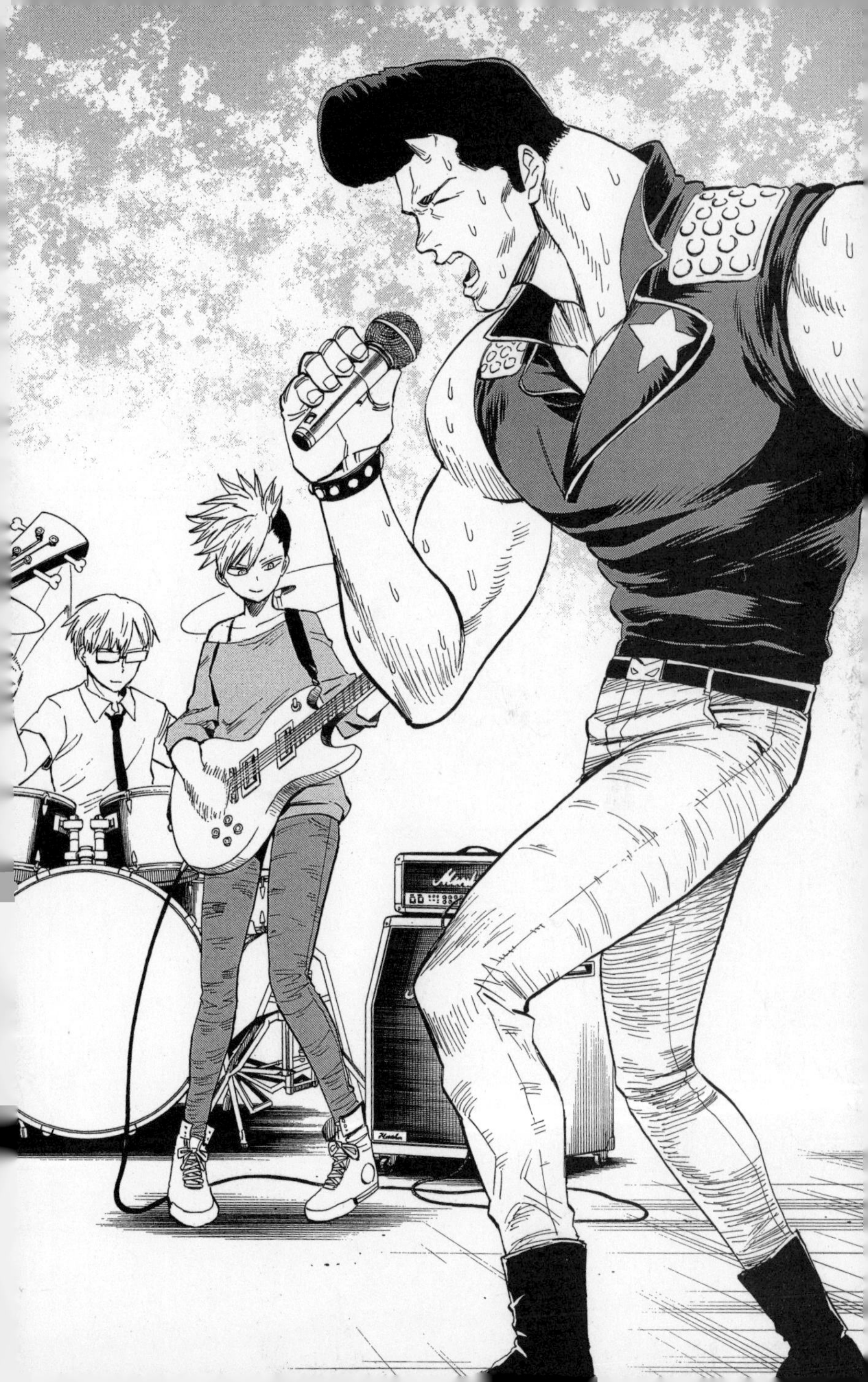

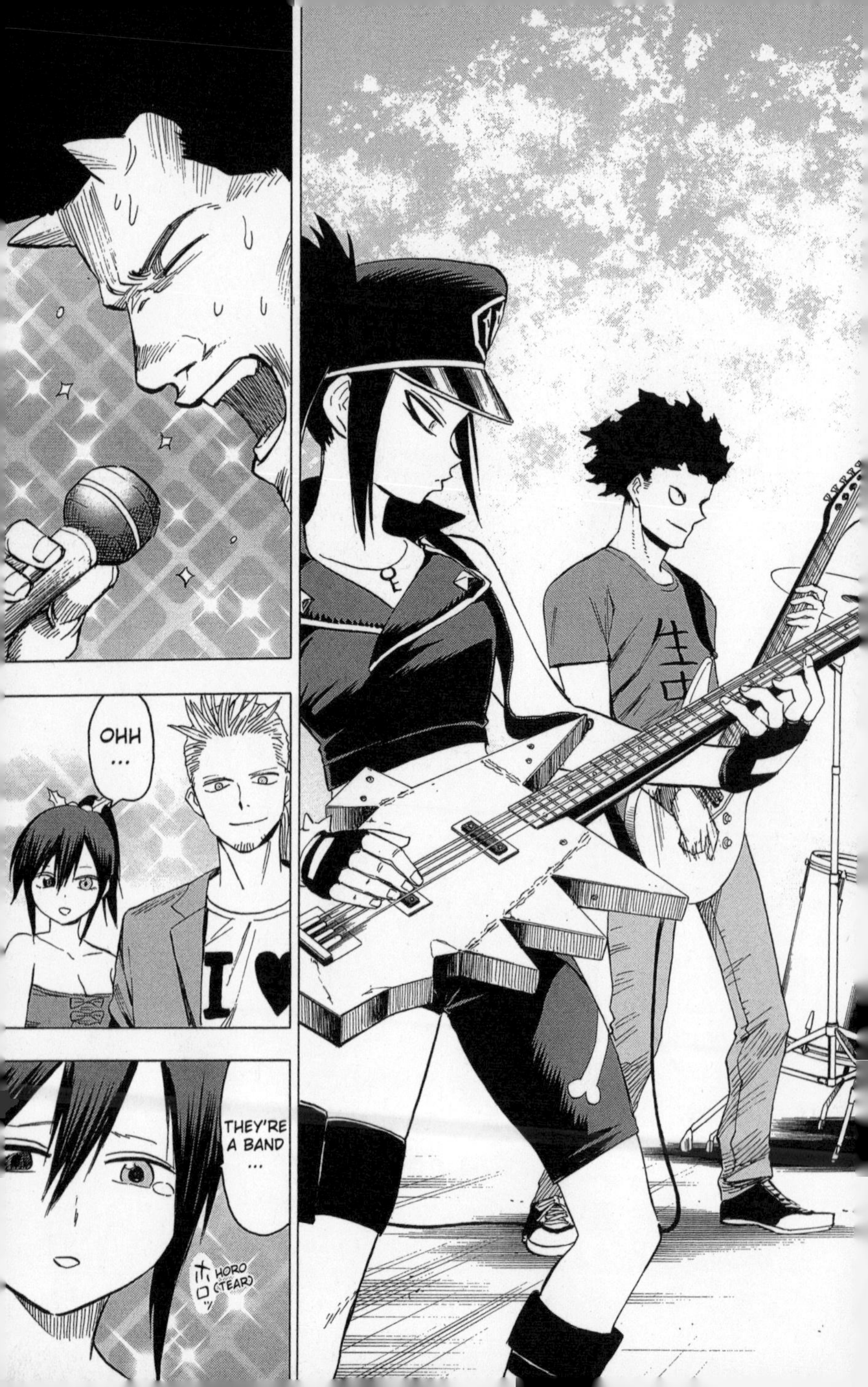
OHH
...
THEY'RE A BAND
...
ホロッ
HORO (TEAR)

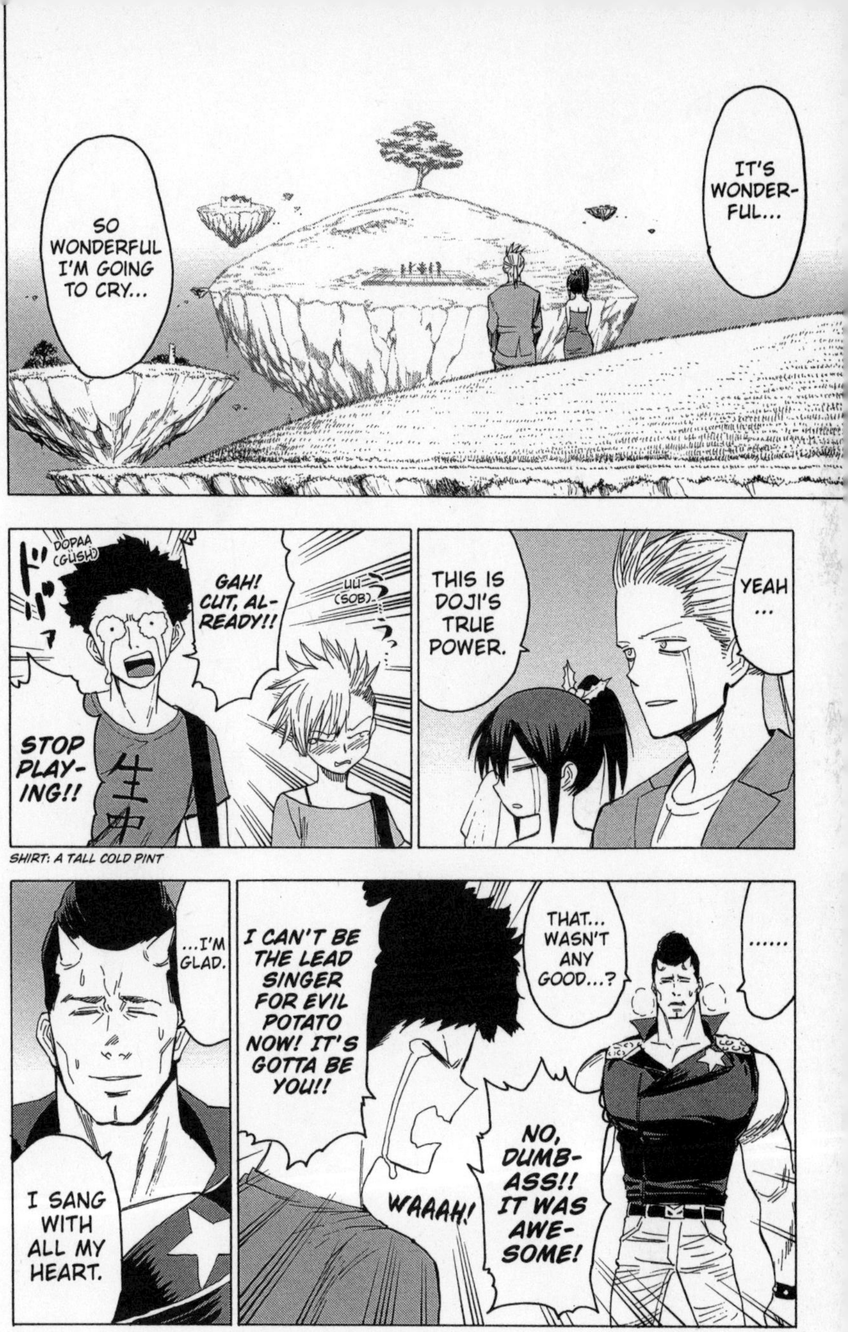
IT'S WONDERFUL...
SO WONDERFUL I'M GOING TO CRY...
YEAH...
THIS IS DOJI'S TRUE POWER.
UU (SOB)
GAH! CUT, ALREADY!!
DOPAA (GUSH)
STOP PLAYING!!
......
THAT... WASN'T ANY GOOD...?
I CAN'T BE THE LEAD SINGER FOR EVIL POTATO NOW! IT'S GOTTA BE YOU!!
NO, DUMBASS!! IT WAS AWESOME!
WAAAH!
...I'M GLAD.
I SANG WITH ALL MY HEART.

SHIRT: A TALL COLD PINT

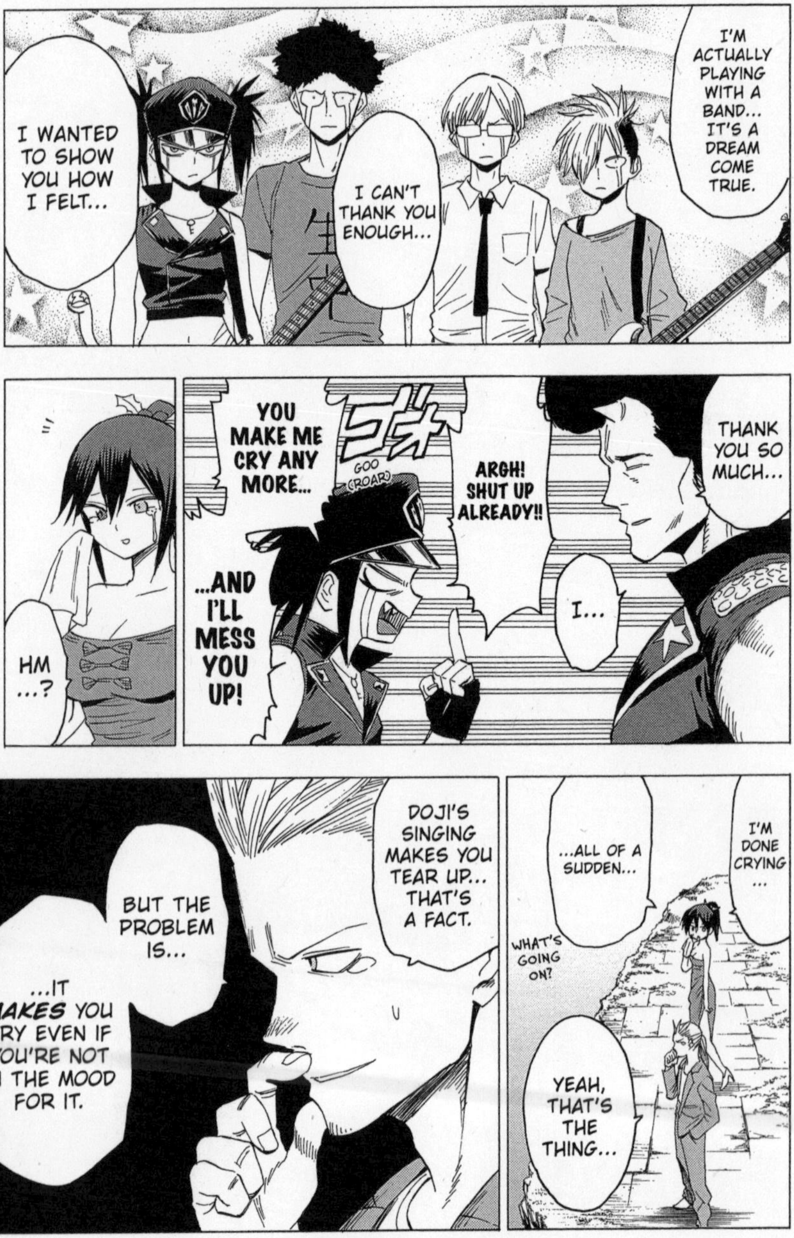
I'M ACTUALLY PLAYING WITH A BAND... IT'S A DREAM COME TRUE.
I CAN'T THANK YOU ENOUGH...
I WANTED TO SHOW YOU HOW I FELT...
THANK YOU SO MUCH...
I...
ARGH! SHUT UP ALREADY!!
GOO (ROAR)
YOU MAKE ME CRY ANY MORE...
...AND I'LL MESS YOU UP!
HM ...?
I'M DONE CRYING ...
...ALL OF A SUDDEN...
WHAT'S GOING ON?
YEAH, THAT'S THE THING...
DOJI'S SINGING MAKES YOU TEAR UP... THAT'S A FACT.
BUT THE PROBLEM IS...
...IT *MAKES* YOU CRY EVEN IF YOU'RE NOT IN THE MOOD FOR IT.

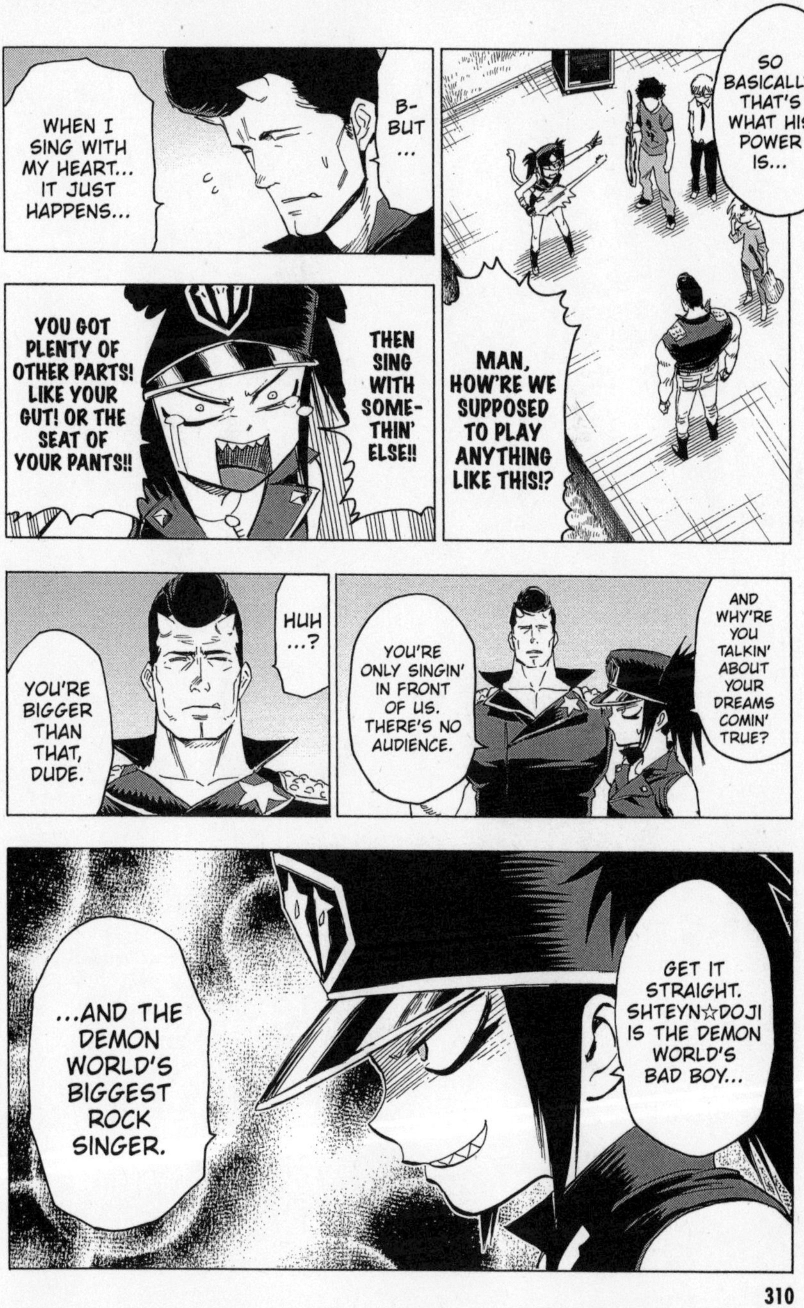
SO BASICALLY, THAT'S WHAT HIS POWER IS...
MAN, HOW'RE WE SUPPOSED TO PLAY ANYTHING LIKE THIS!?
B-BUT...
WHEN I SING WITH MY HEART... IT JUST HAPPENS...
THEN SING WITH SOME-THIN' ELSE!!
YOU GOT PLENTY OF OTHER PARTS! LIKE YOUR GUT! OR THE SEAT OF YOUR PANTS!!
AND WHY'RE YOU TALKIN' ABOUT YOUR DREAMS COMIN' TRUE?
YOU'RE ONLY SINGIN' IN FRONT OF US. THERE'S NO AUDIENCE.
HUH...?
YOU'RE BIGGER THAN THAT, DUDE.
GET IT STRAIGHT. SHTEYN☆DOJI IS THE DEMON WORLD'S BAD BOY...
...AND THE DEMON WORLD'S BIGGEST ROCK SINGER.

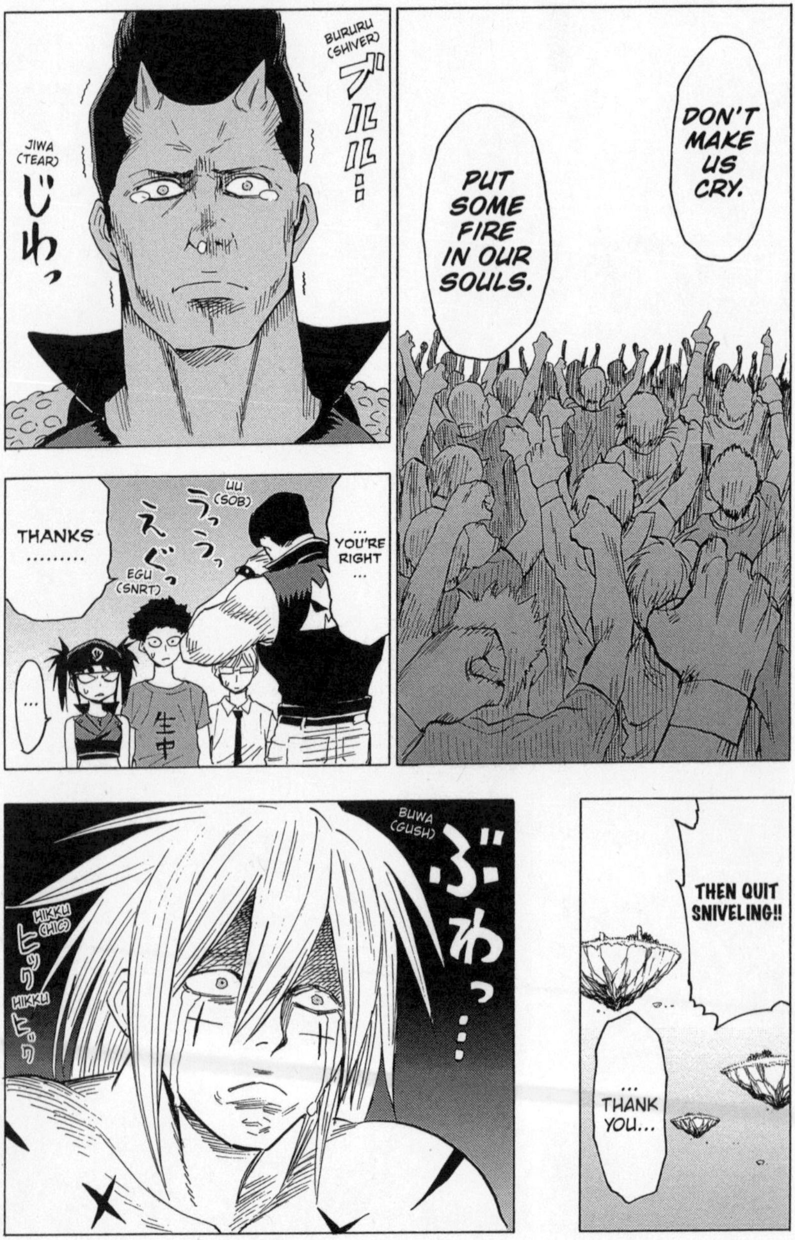
DON'T MAKE US CRY.
PUT SOME FIRE IN OUR SOULS.
BURURU (SHIVER)
ブルル!!
JIWA (TEAR)
じわっ
... YOU'RE RIGHT ...
UU (SOB)
うっうっ
EGU (SNRT)
えぐっ
THANKS ....
...
THEN QUIT SNIVELING!!
... THANK YOU...
BUWA (GUSH)
ぶわっ...
HIKKU (HIC)
ヒック
HIKKU
ヒック

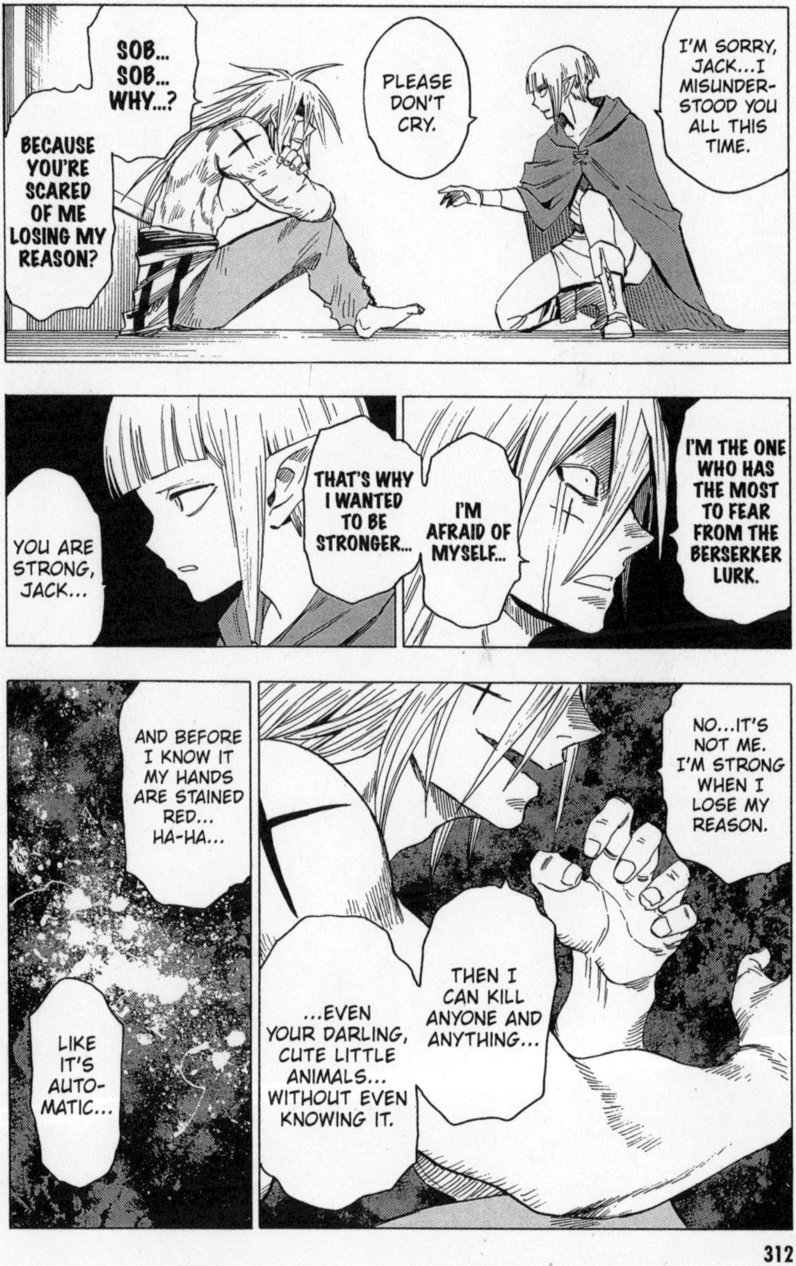
I'M SORRY, JACK...I MISUNDER-STOOD YOU ALL THIS TIME.
PLEASE DON'T CRY.
SOB... SOB... WHY...?
BECAUSE YOU'RE SCARED OF ME LOSING MY REASON?
I'M THE ONE WHO HAS THE MOST TO FEAR FROM THE BERSERKER LURK.
I'M AFRAID OF MYSELF...
THAT'S WHY I WANTED TO BE STRONGER...
YOU ARE STRONG, JACK...
NO...IT'S NOT ME. I'M STRONG WHEN I LOSE MY REASON.
THEN I CAN KILL ANYONE AND ANYTHING...
...EVEN YOUR DARLING, CUTE LITTLE ANIMALS... WITHOUT EVEN KNOWING IT.
AND BEFORE I KNOW IT MY HANDS ARE STAINED RED... HA-HA...
LIKE IT'S AUTO-MATIC...

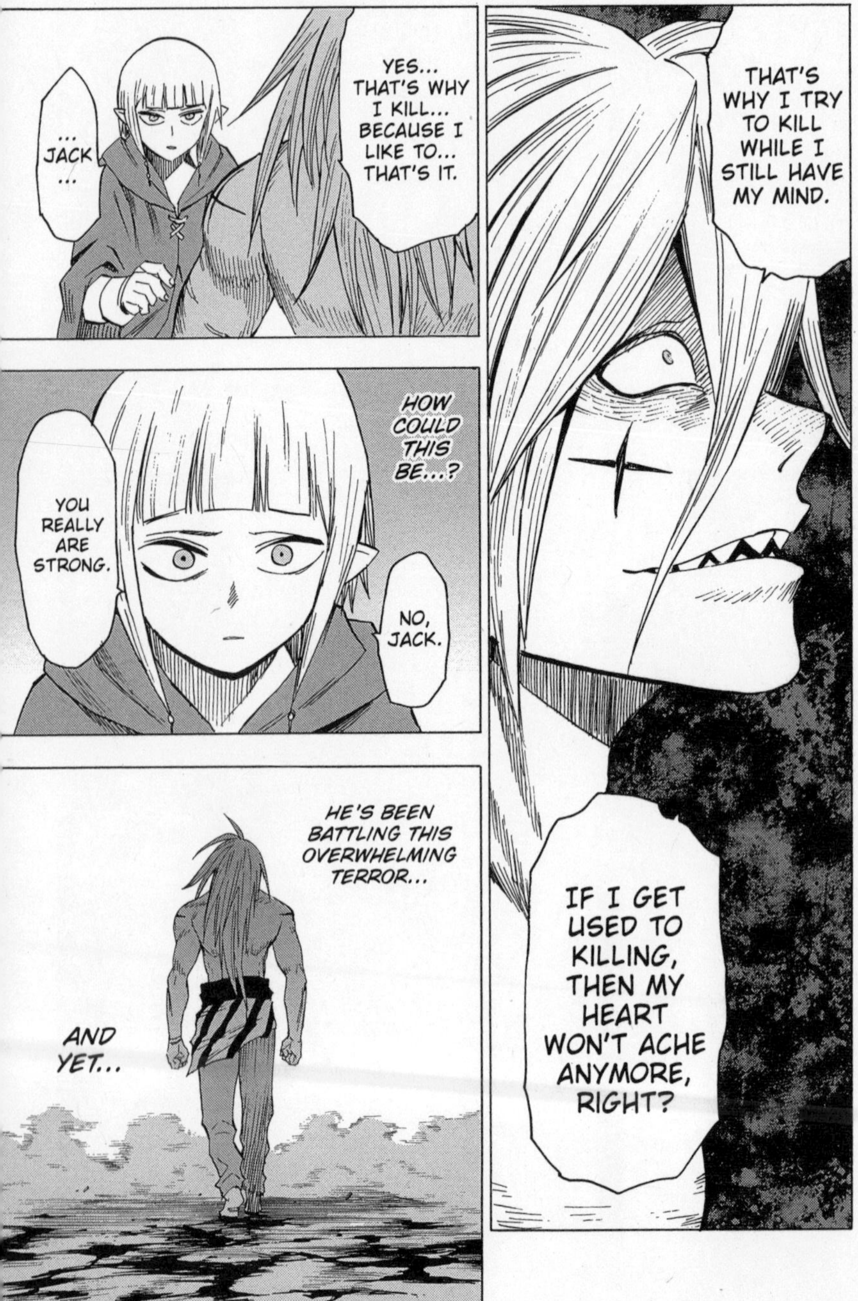
THAT'S WHY I TRY TO KILL WHILE I STILL HAVE MY MIND.
IF I GET USED TO KILLING, THEN MY HEART WON'T ACHE ANYMORE, RIGHT?
YES... THAT'S WHY I KILL... BECAUSE I LIKE TO... THAT'S IT.
... JACK ...
HOW COULD THIS BE...?
NO, JACK.
YOU REALLY ARE STRONG.
HE'S BEEN BATTLING THIS OVERWHELMING TERROR...
AND YET...

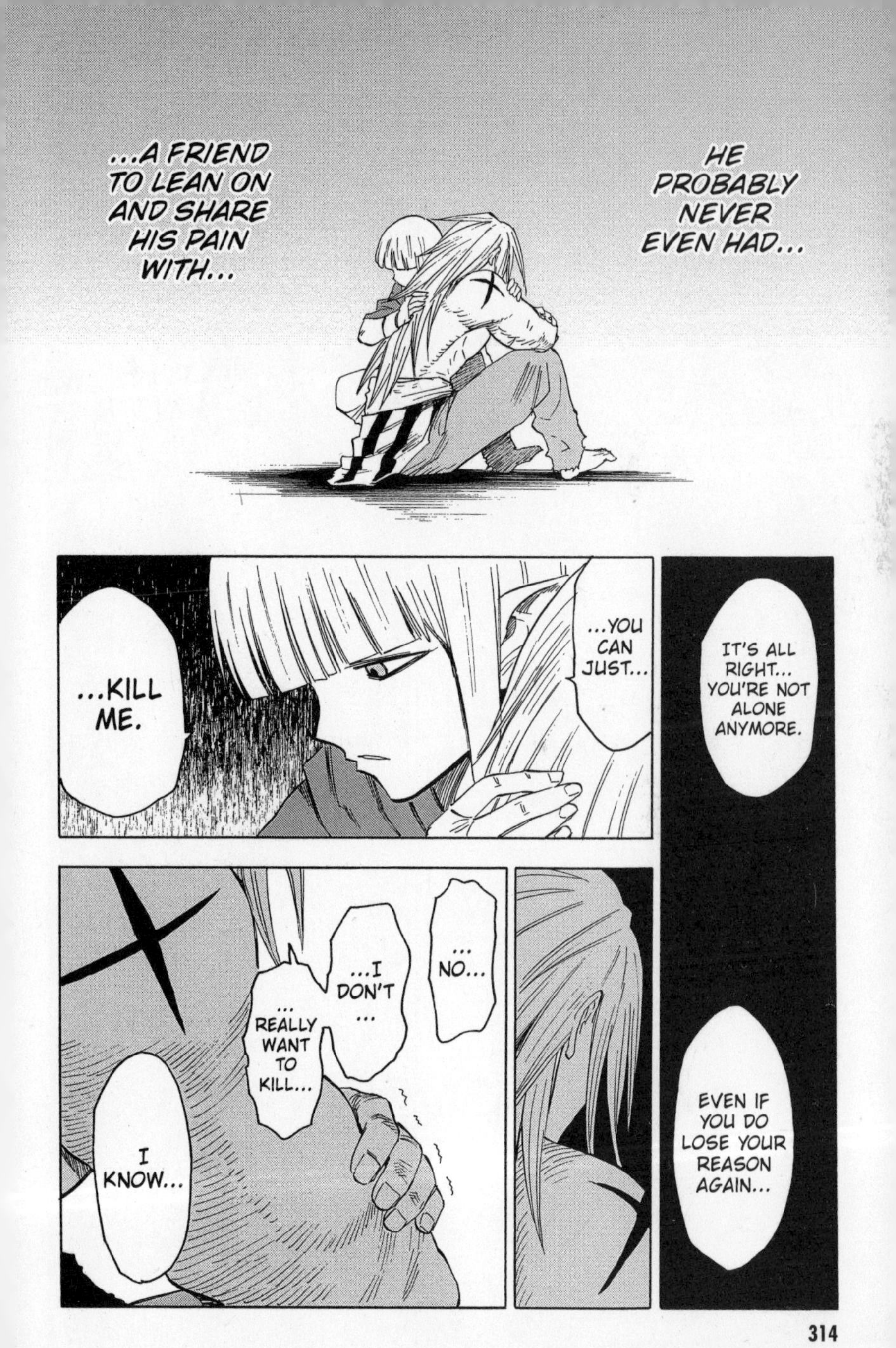
HE PROBABLY NEVER EVEN HAD...
...A FRIEND TO LEAN ON AND SHARE HIS PAIN WITH...
IT'S ALL RIGHT... YOU'RE NOT ALONE ANYMORE.
EVEN IF YOU DO LOSE YOUR REASON AGAIN...
...YOU CAN JUST...
...KILL ME.
... NO...
...I DON'T ...
... REALLY WANT TO KILL...
I KNOW...

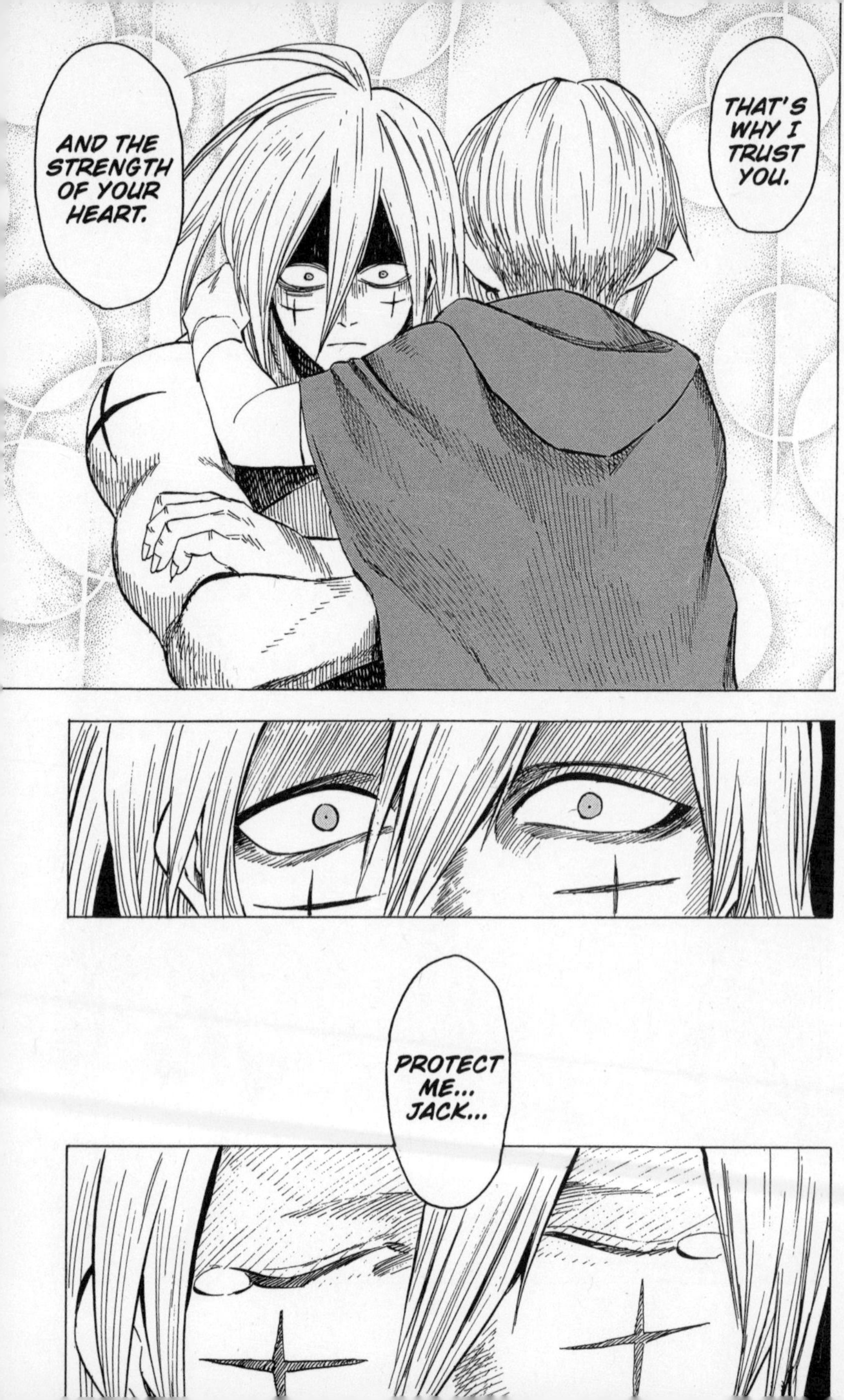
AND THE STRENGTH OF YOUR HEART.
THAT'S WHY I TRUST YOU.
PROTECT ME... JACK...

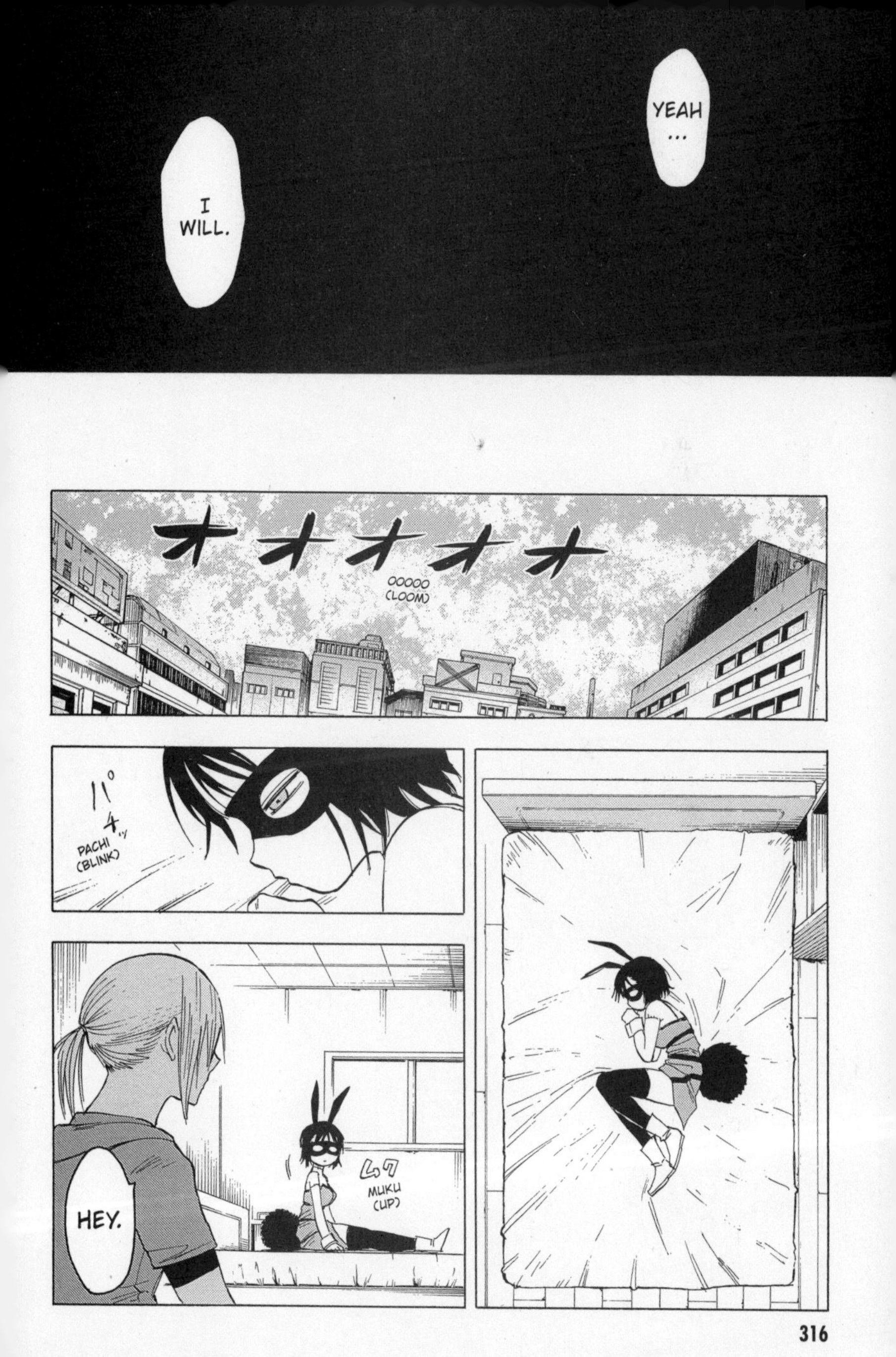
YEAH ...
I WILL.
オオオオオ
OOOOO (LOOM)
パチッ
PACHI (BLINK)
ムク
MUKU (UP)
HEY.

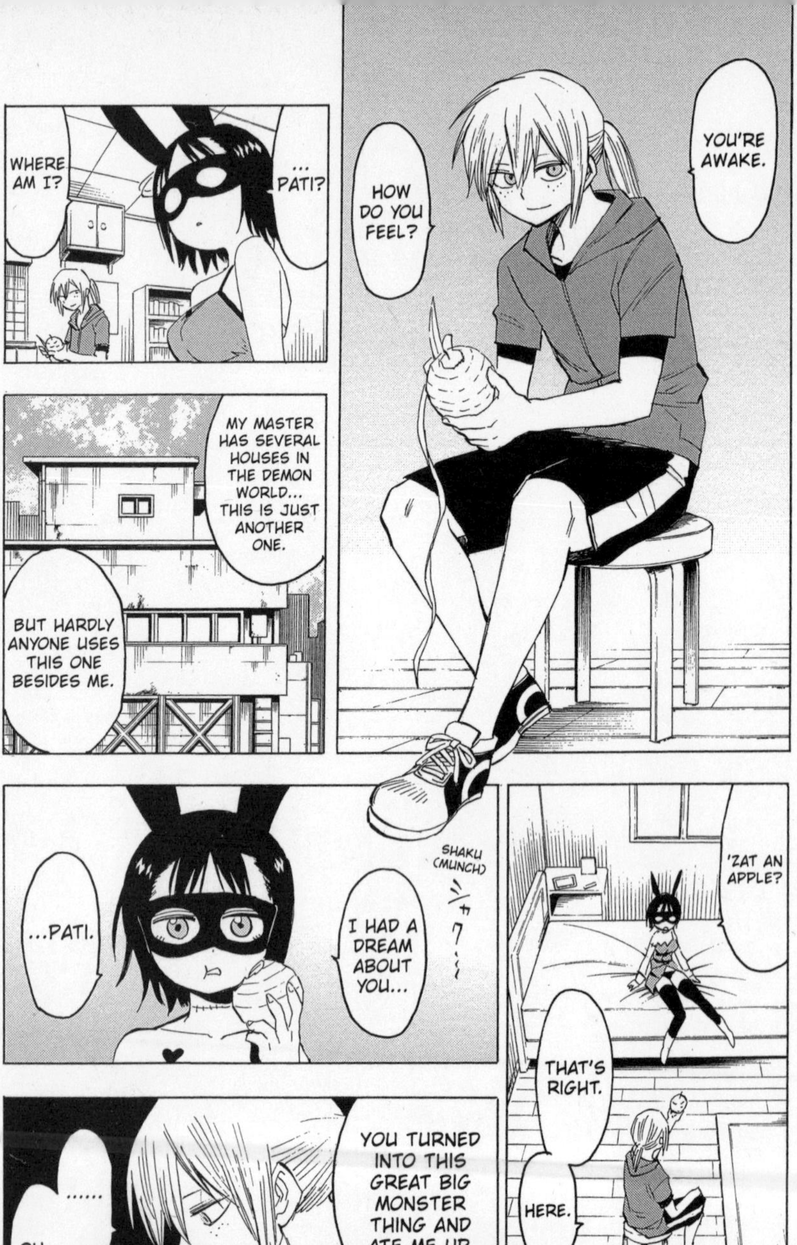

YOU'RE AWAKE.
HOW DO YOU FEEL?
... PATI?
WHERE AM I?
MY MASTER HAS SEVERAL HOUSES IN THE DEMON WORLD... THIS IS JUST ANOTHER ONE.
BUT HARDLY ANYONE USES THIS ONE BESIDES ME.
'ZAT AN APPLE?
THAT'S RIGHT.
HERE.
SHAKU (MUNCH)
シャク…
I HAD A DREAM ABOUT YOU...
...PATI.
YOU TURNED INTO THIS GREAT BIG MONSTER THING AND ATE ME UP.
......
OH...

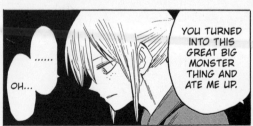

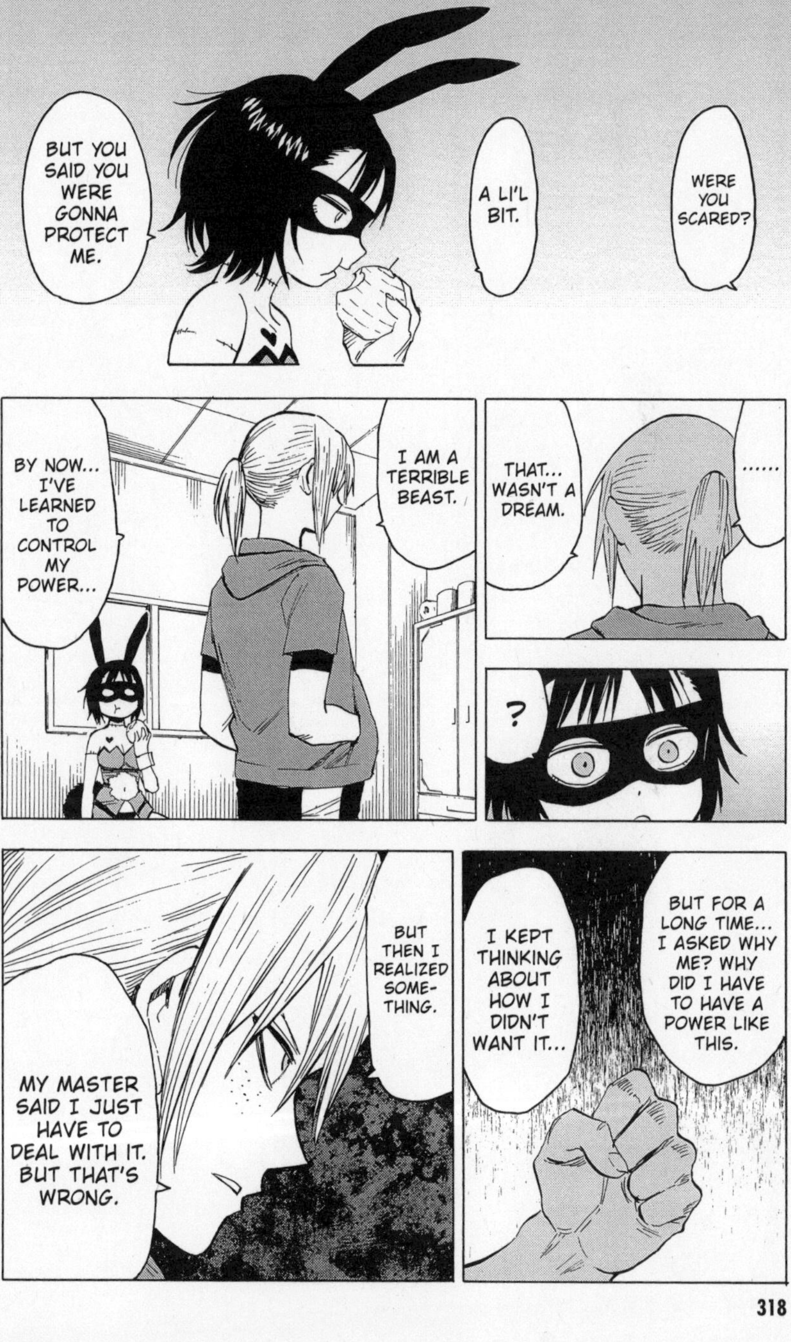
WERE YOU SCARED?
A LI'L BIT.
BUT YOU SAID YOU WERE GONNA PROTECT ME.
......
THAT... WASN'T A DREAM.
?
I AM A TERRIBLE BEAST.
BY NOW... I'VE LEARNED TO CONTROL MY POWER...
BUT FOR A LONG TIME... I ASKED WHY ME? WHY DID I HAVE TO HAVE A POWER LIKE THIS.
I KEPT THINKING ABOUT HOW I DIDN'T WANT IT...
BUT THEN I REALIZED SOME-THING.
MY MASTER SAID I JUST HAVE TO DEAL WITH IT. BUT THAT'S WRONG.

OOOOO
(LOOOM)

THERE ARE THINGS I CAN DO WITH THIS POWER.

BOKO
(BUBBLE)

BOKO

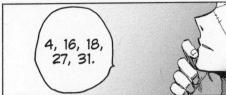

4, 16, 18, 27, 31.

7, 22, 26, 34, 38.

ROGER.

ROGER ...

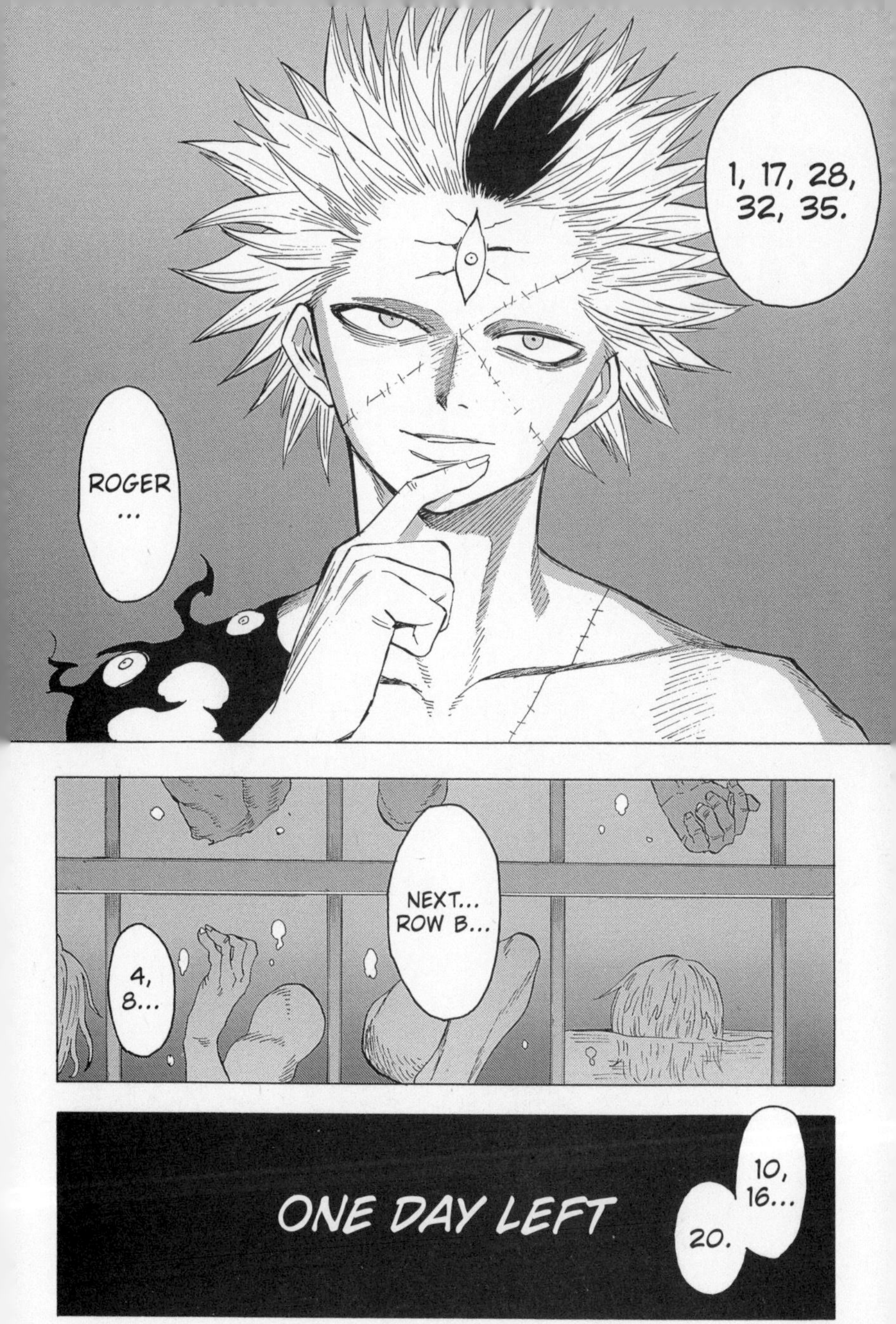

1, 17, 28, 32, 35.
ROGER ...
NEXT... ROW B...
4, 8...
10, 16...
20.
ONE DAY LEFT

♠ To Be Continued ♠

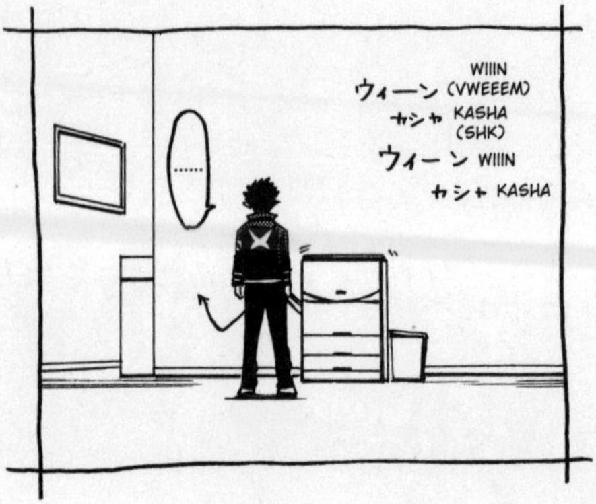
......
ウィーン WIIIN (VWEEEM)
カシャ KASHA (SHK)
ウィーン WIIIN
カシャ KASHA

BLOOD LAD

CHAPTER 70 ♠ SHOWDOWN

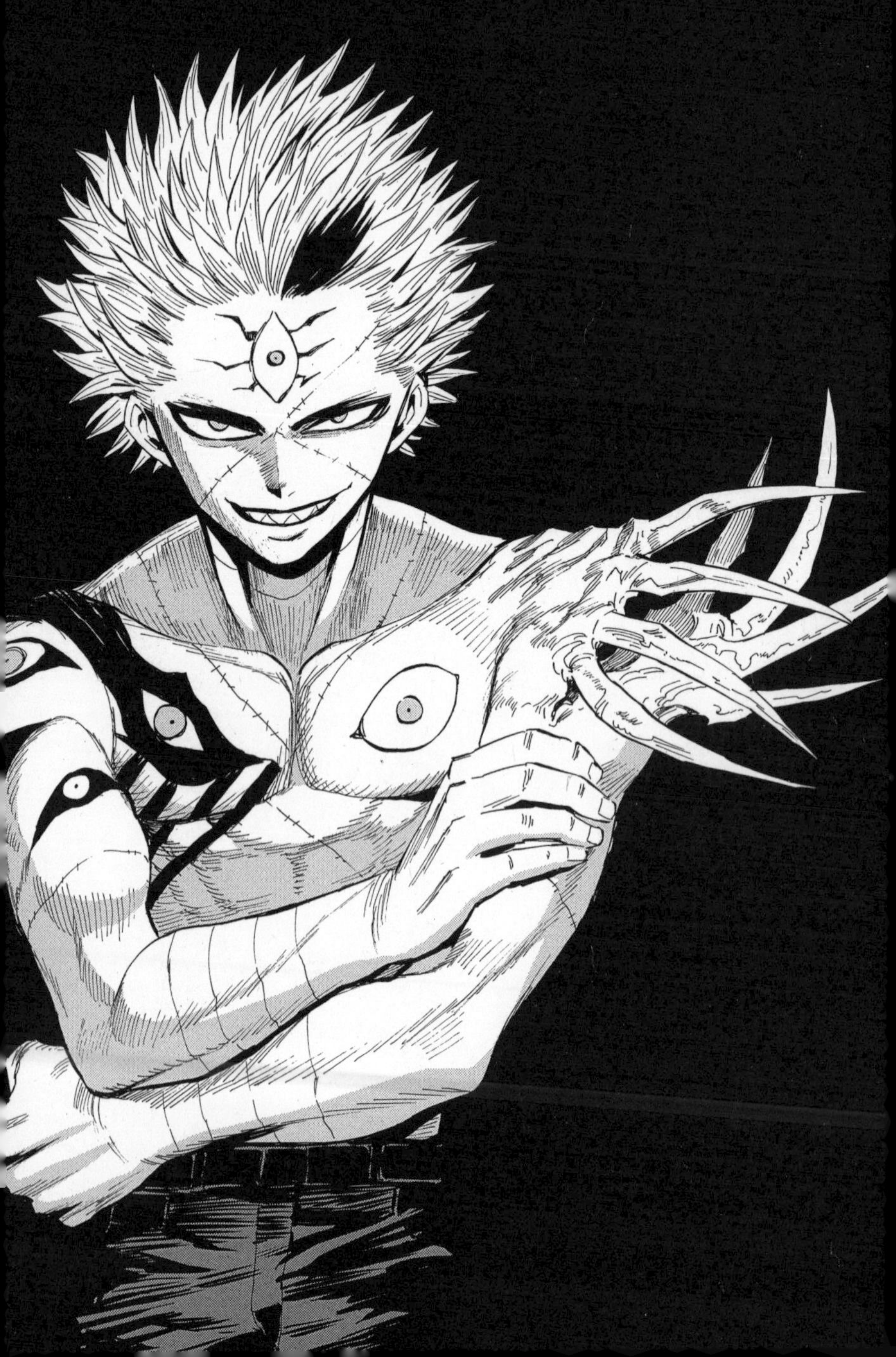

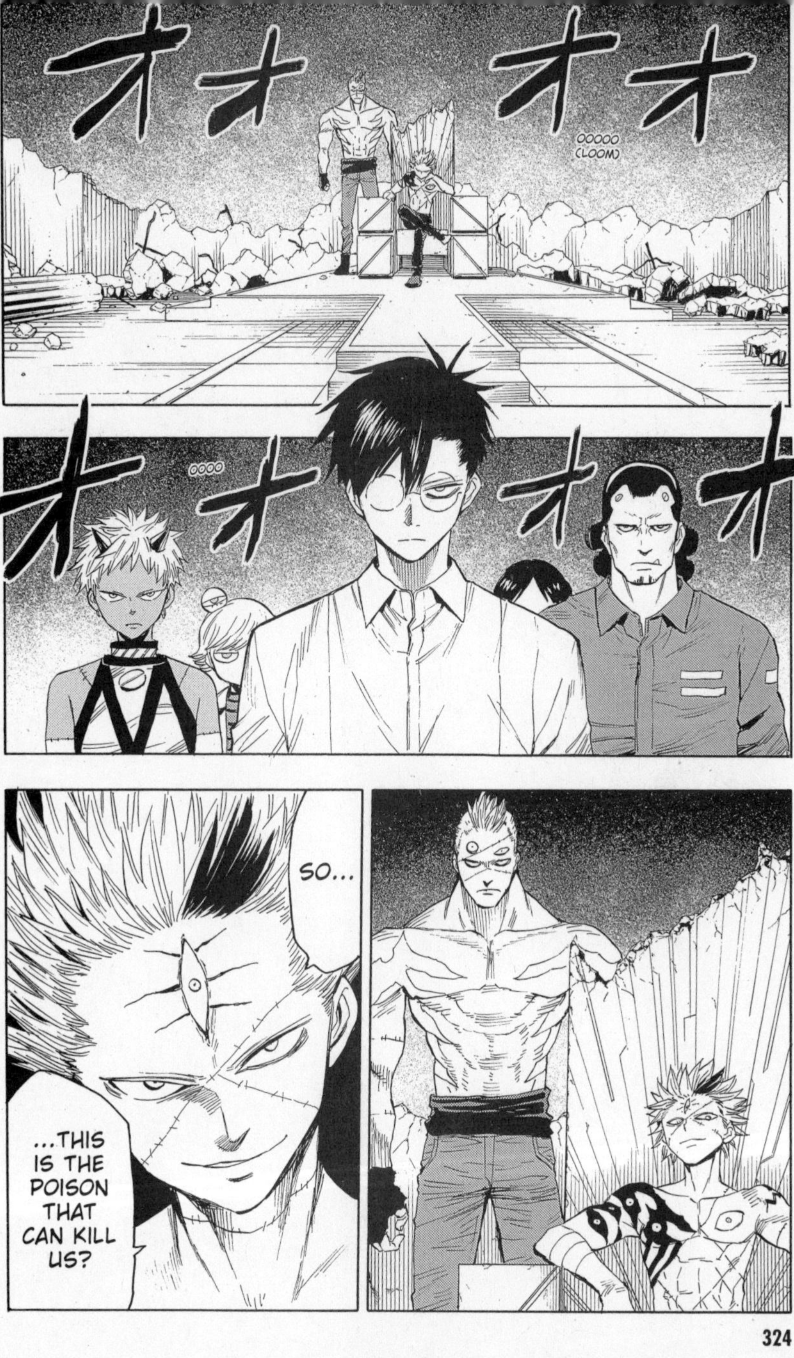
オオオオ
OOOOO (LOOM)
オオオオ
OOOO
SO...
...THIS IS THE POISON THAT CAN KILL US?

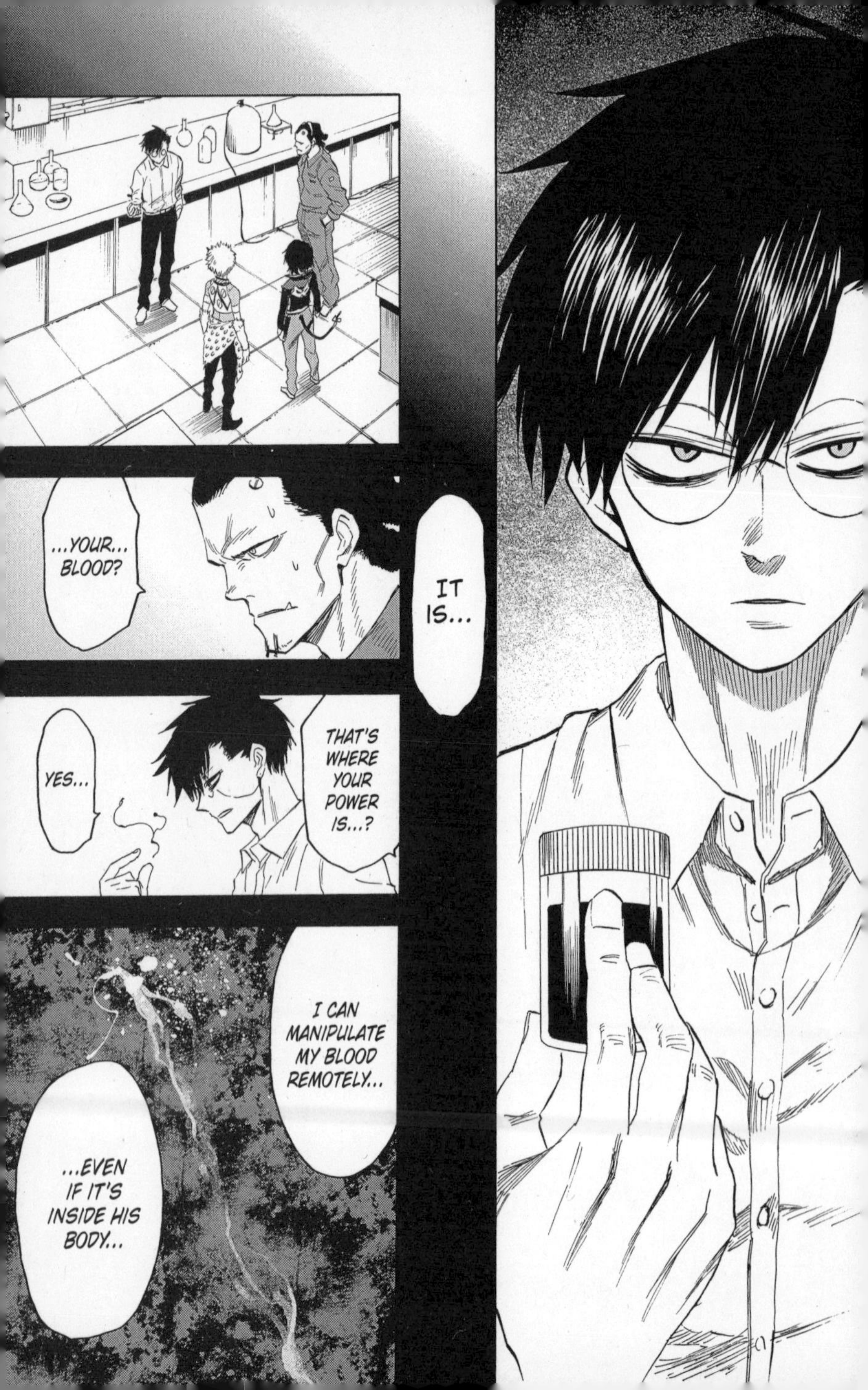
IT IS...
...YOUR... BLOOD?
THAT'S WHERE YOUR POWER IS...?
YES...
I CAN MANIPULATE MY BLOOD REMOTELY...
...EVEN IF IT'S INSIDE HIS BODY...

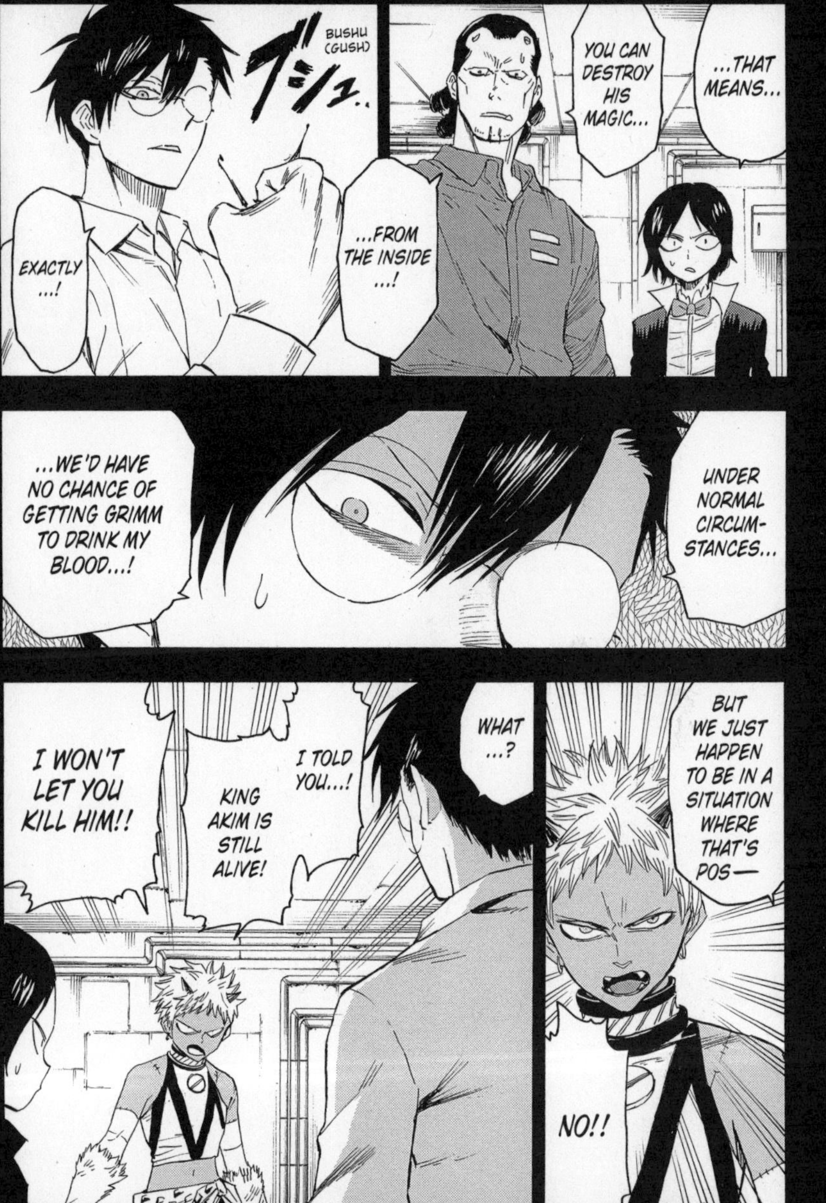
...THAT MEANS...
YOU CAN DESTROY HIS MAGIC...
...FROM THE INSIDE...!
BUSHU (GUSH)
EXACTLY...!
UNDER NORMAL CIRCUM-STANCES...
...WE'D HAVE NO CHANCE OF GETTING GRIMM TO DRINK MY BLOOD...!
BUT WE JUST HAPPEN TO BE IN A SITUATION WHERE THAT'S POS—
NO!!
WHAT...?
I TOLD YOU...!
KING AKIM IS STILL ALIVE!
I WON'T LET YOU KILL HIM!!

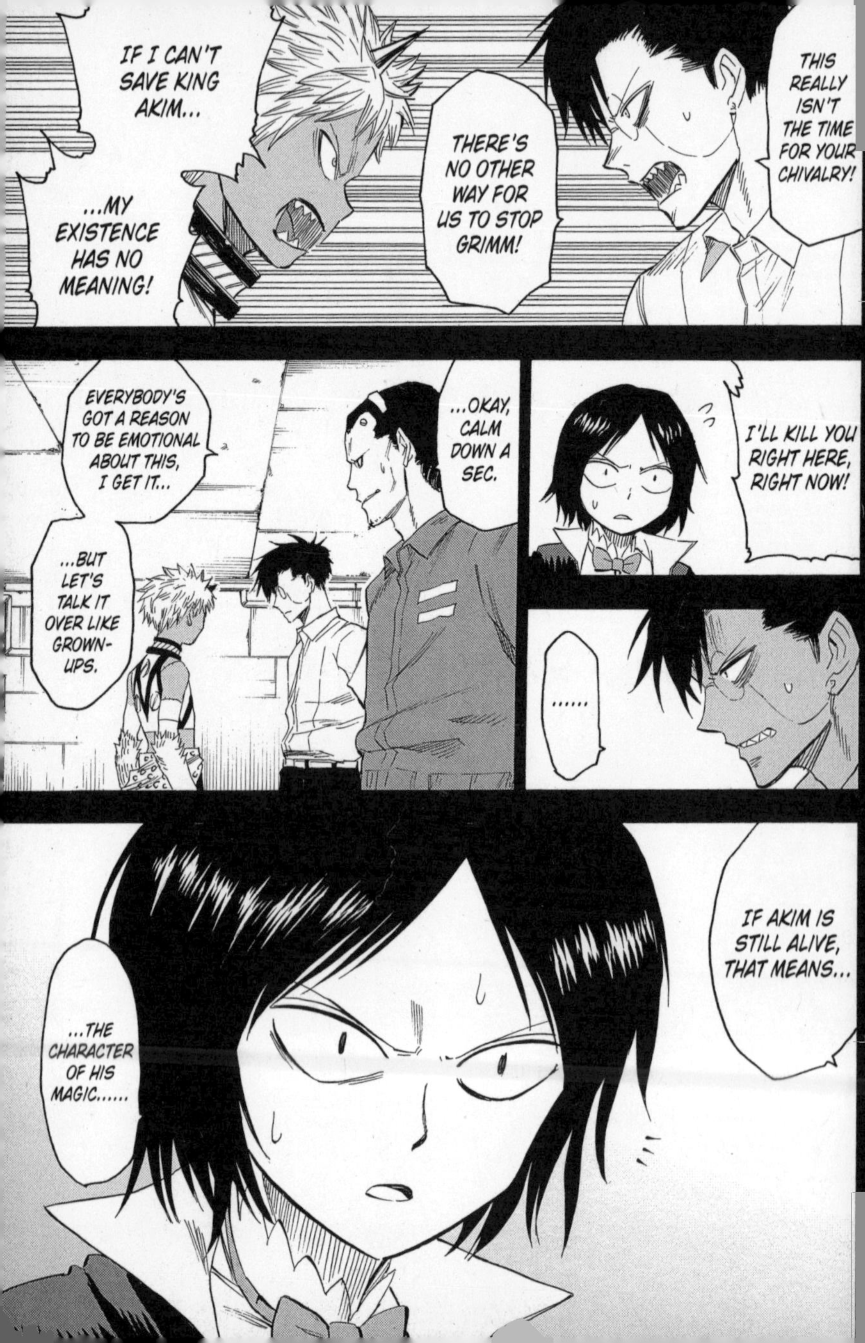

THIS REALLY ISN'T THE TIME FOR YOUR CHIVALRY!
THERE'S NO OTHER WAY FOR US TO STOP GRIMM!
IF I CAN'T SAVE KING AKIM...
...MY EXISTENCE HAS NO MEANING!
I'LL KILL YOU RIGHT HERE, RIGHT NOW!
......
...OKAY, CALM DOWN A SEC.
EVERYBODY'S GOT A REASON TO BE EMOTIONAL ABOUT THIS, I GET IT...
...BUT LET'S TALK IT OVER LIKE GROWN-UPS.
IF AKIM IS STILL ALIVE, THAT MEANS...
...THE CHARACTER OF HIS MAGIC......

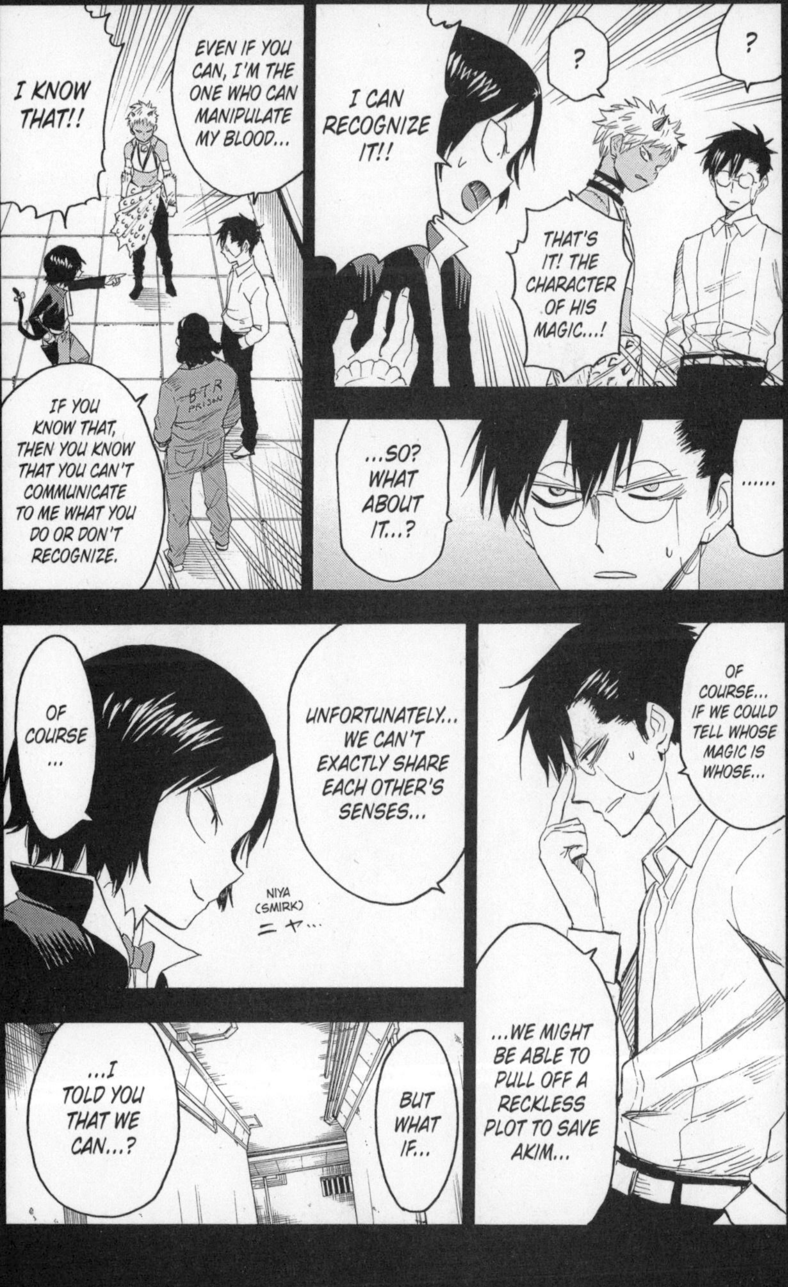
?
?
I CAN RECOGNIZE IT!!
THAT'S IT! THE CHARACTER OF HIS MAGIC...!
......
...SO? WHAT ABOUT IT...?
EVEN IF YOU CAN, I'M THE ONE WHO CAN MANIPULATE MY BLOOD...
I KNOW THAT!!
IF YOU KNOW THAT, THEN YOU KNOW THAT YOU CAN'T COMMUNICATE TO ME WHAT YOU DO OR DON'T RECOGNIZE.
OF COURSE... IF WE COULD TELL WHOSE MAGIC IS WHOSE...
...WE MIGHT BE ABLE TO PULL OFF A RECKLESS PLOT TO SAVE AKIM...
UNFORTUNATELY... WE CAN'T EXACTLY SHARE EACH OTHER'S SENSES...
NIYA (SMIRK)
ニヤ...
OF COURSE ...
BUT WHAT IF...
...I TOLD YOU THAT WE CAN...?

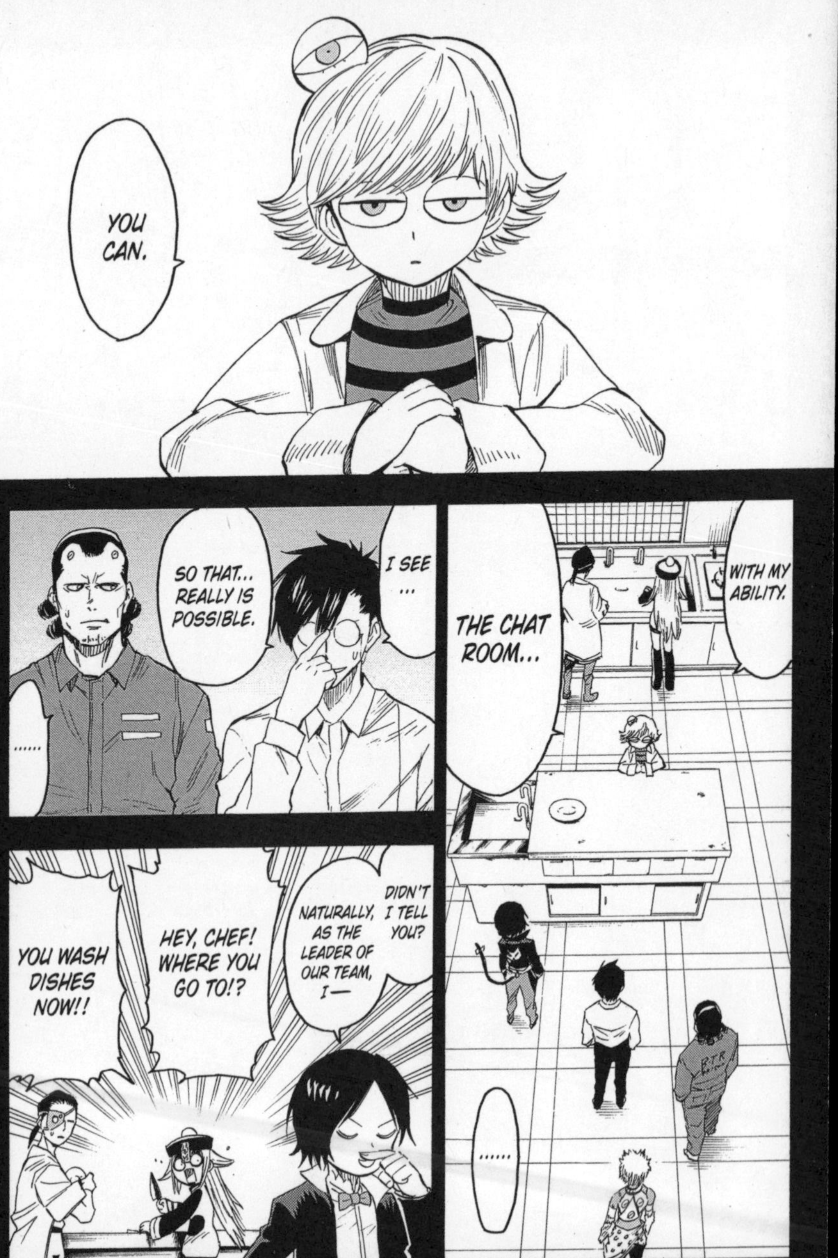
YOU CAN.
WITH MY ABILITY.
THE CHAT ROOM...
......
I SEE ...
SO THAT... REALLY IS POSSIBLE.
......
DIDN'T I TELL YOU?
NATURALLY, AS THE LEADER OF OUR TEAM, I—
HEY, CHEF! WHERE YOU GO TO!?
YOU WASH DISHES NOW!!

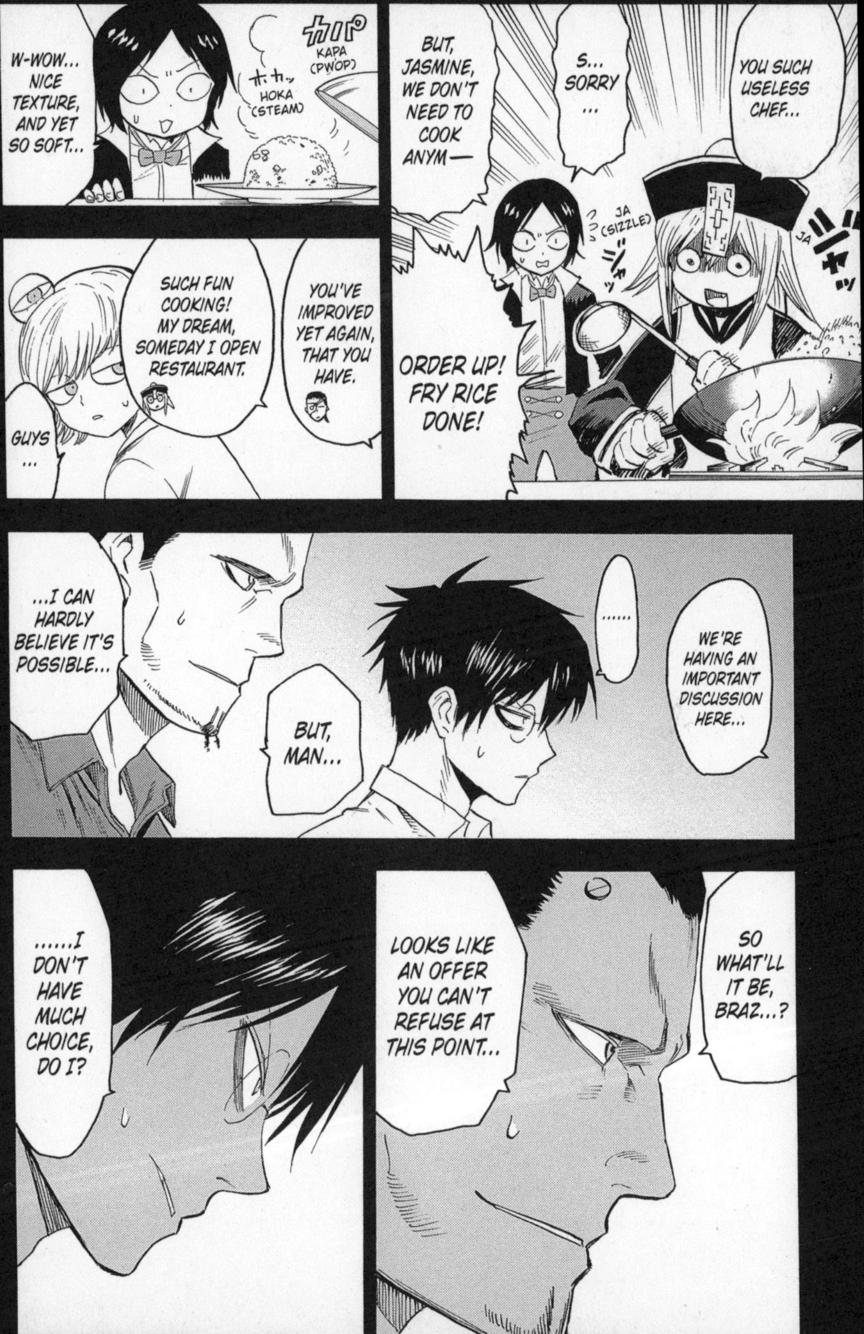
YOU SUCH USELESS CHEF...
S... SORRY ...
BUT, JASMINE, WE DON'T NEED TO COOK ANYM—
JA
JA (SIZZLE)
ORDER UP! FRY RICE DONE!
KAPA (PWOP)
HOKA (STEAM)
W-WOW... NICE TEXTURE, AND YET SO SOFT...
YOU'VE IMPROVED YET AGAIN, THAT YOU HAVE.
SUCH FUN COOKING! MY DREAM, SOMEDAY I OPEN RESTAURANT.
GUYS ...
WE'RE HAVING AN IMPORTANT DISCUSSION HERE...
......
BUT, MAN...
...I CAN HARDLY BELIEVE IT'S POSSIBLE...
SO WHAT'LL IT BE, BRAZ...?
LOOKS LIKE AN OFFER YOU CAN'T REFUSE AT THIS POINT...
......I DON'T HAVE MUCH CHOICE, DO I?

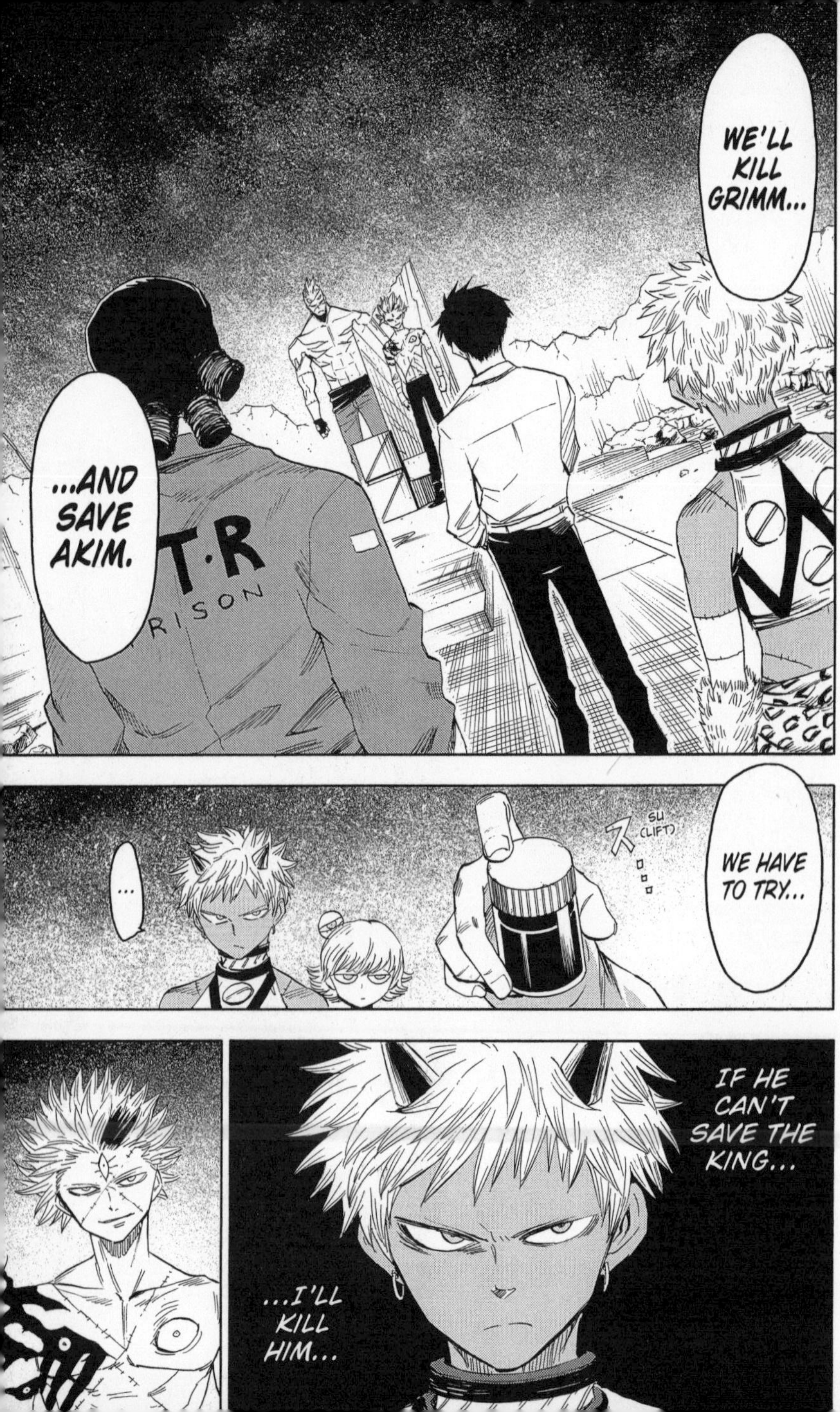
WE'LL KILL GRIMM...
...AND SAVE AKIM.
WE HAVE TO TRY...
SU (LIFT)
...
IF HE CAN'T SAVE THE KING...
...I'LL KILL HIM...

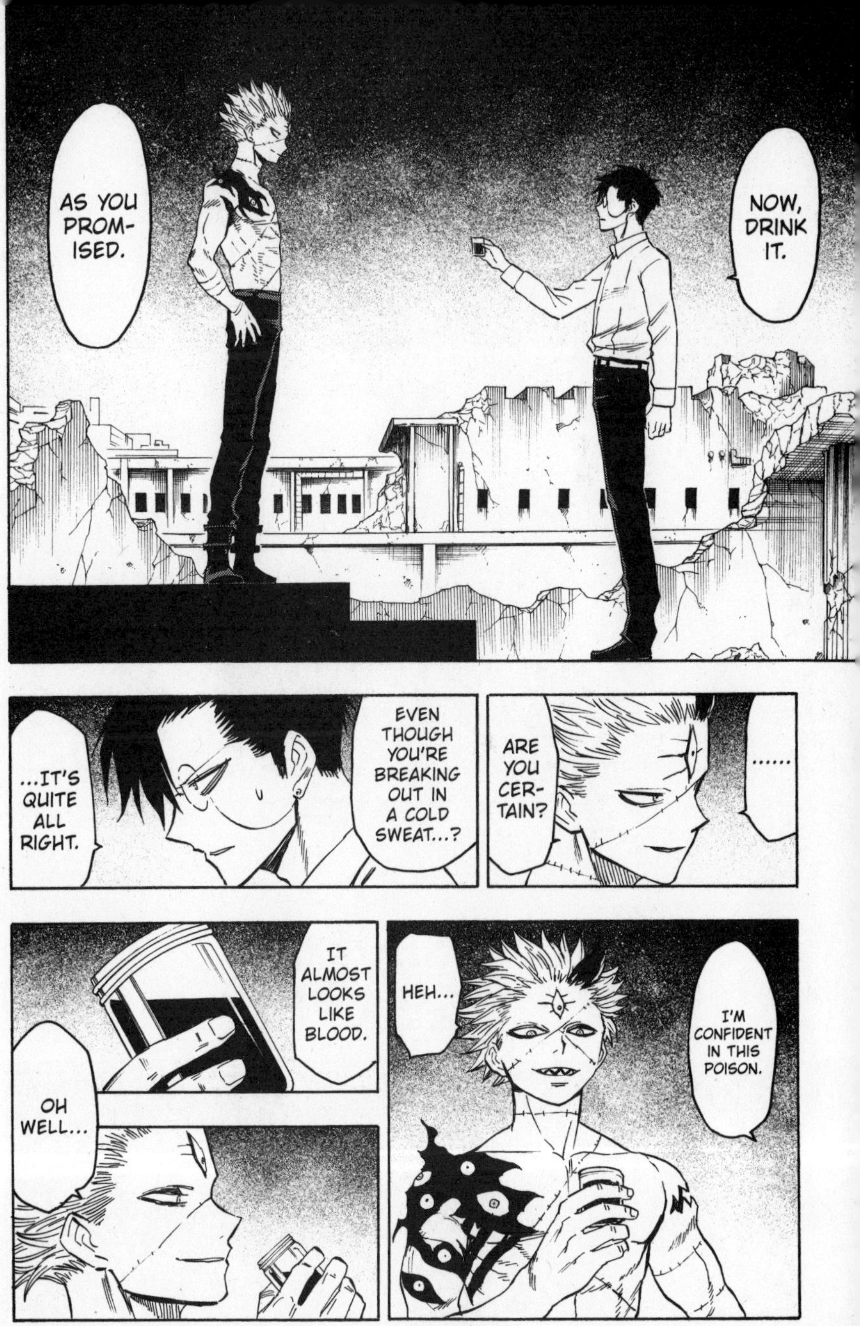
NOW, DRINK IT.
AS YOU PROMISED.
......
ARE YOU CERTAIN?
EVEN THOUGH YOU'RE BREAKING OUT IN A COLD SWEAT...?
...IT'S QUITE ALL RIGHT.
I'M CONFIDENT IN THIS POISON.
HEH...
IT ALMOST LOOKS LIKE BLOOD.
OH WELL...

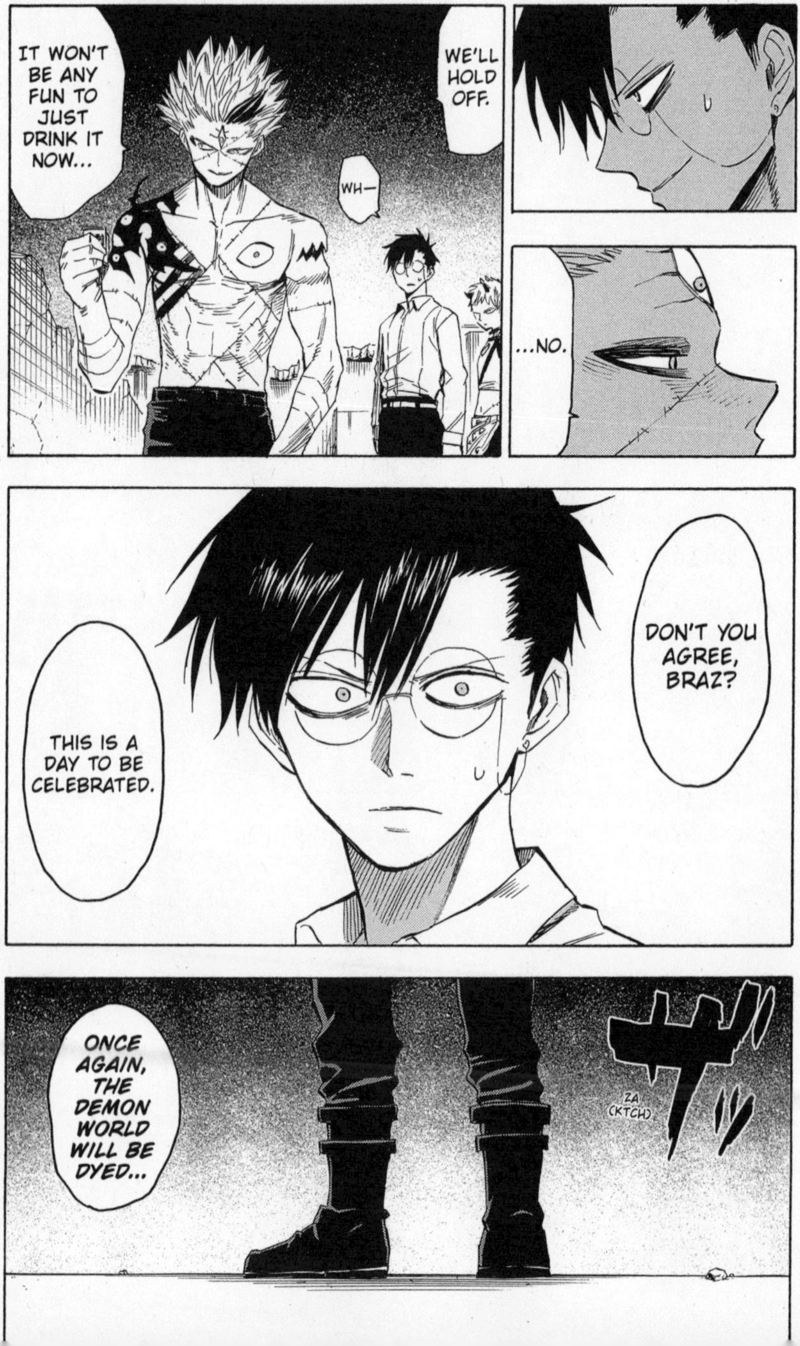
...NO.
WE'LL HOLD OFF.
IT WON'T BE ANY FUN TO JUST DRINK IT NOW...
WH—
DON'T YOU AGREE, BRAZ?
THIS IS A DAY TO BE CELEBRATED.
ZA (KTCH)
ONCE AGAIN, THE DEMON WORLD WILL BE DYED...

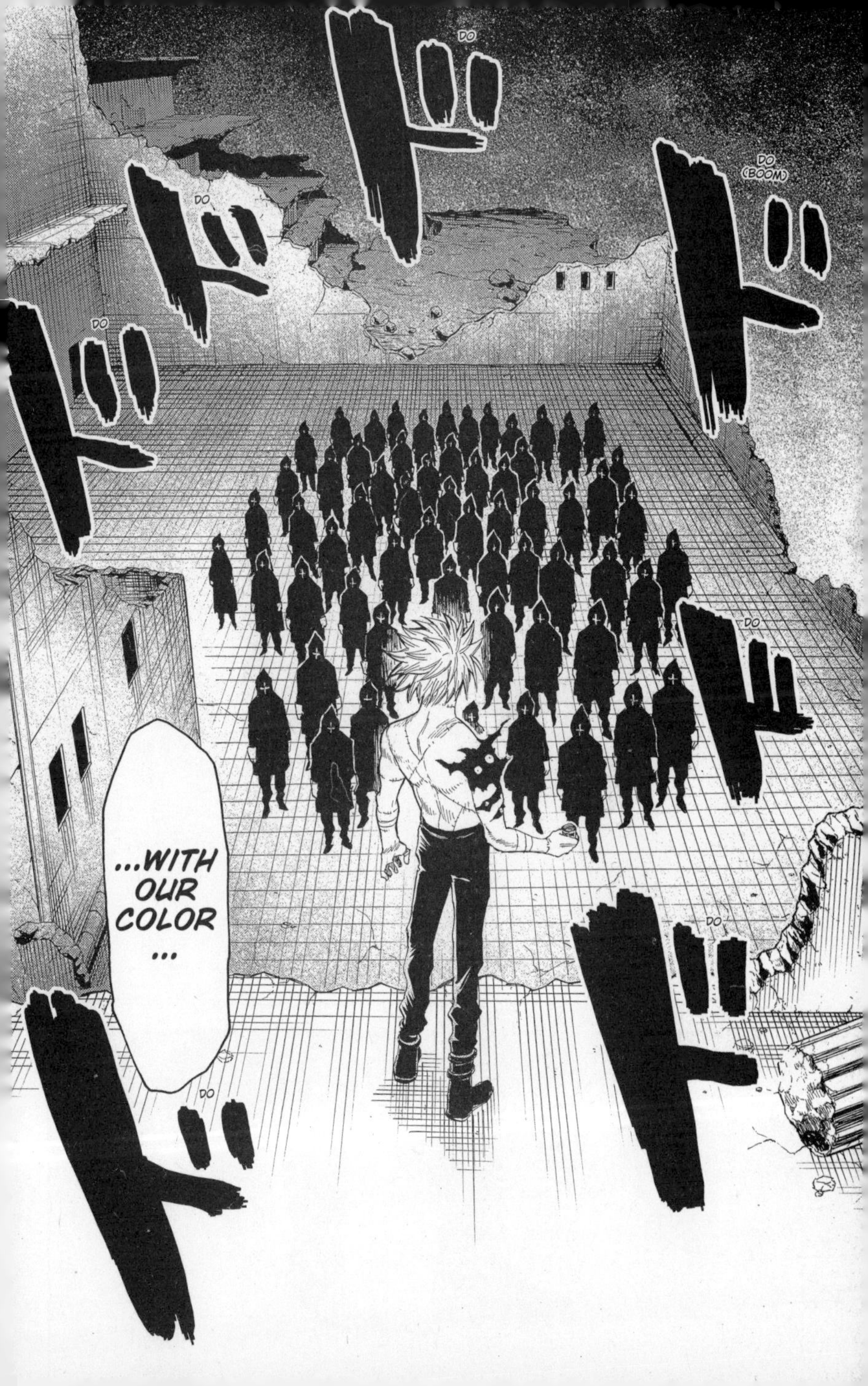

DO
DO (BOOM)
DO
DO
DO
DO
...WITH OUR COLOR ...
DO

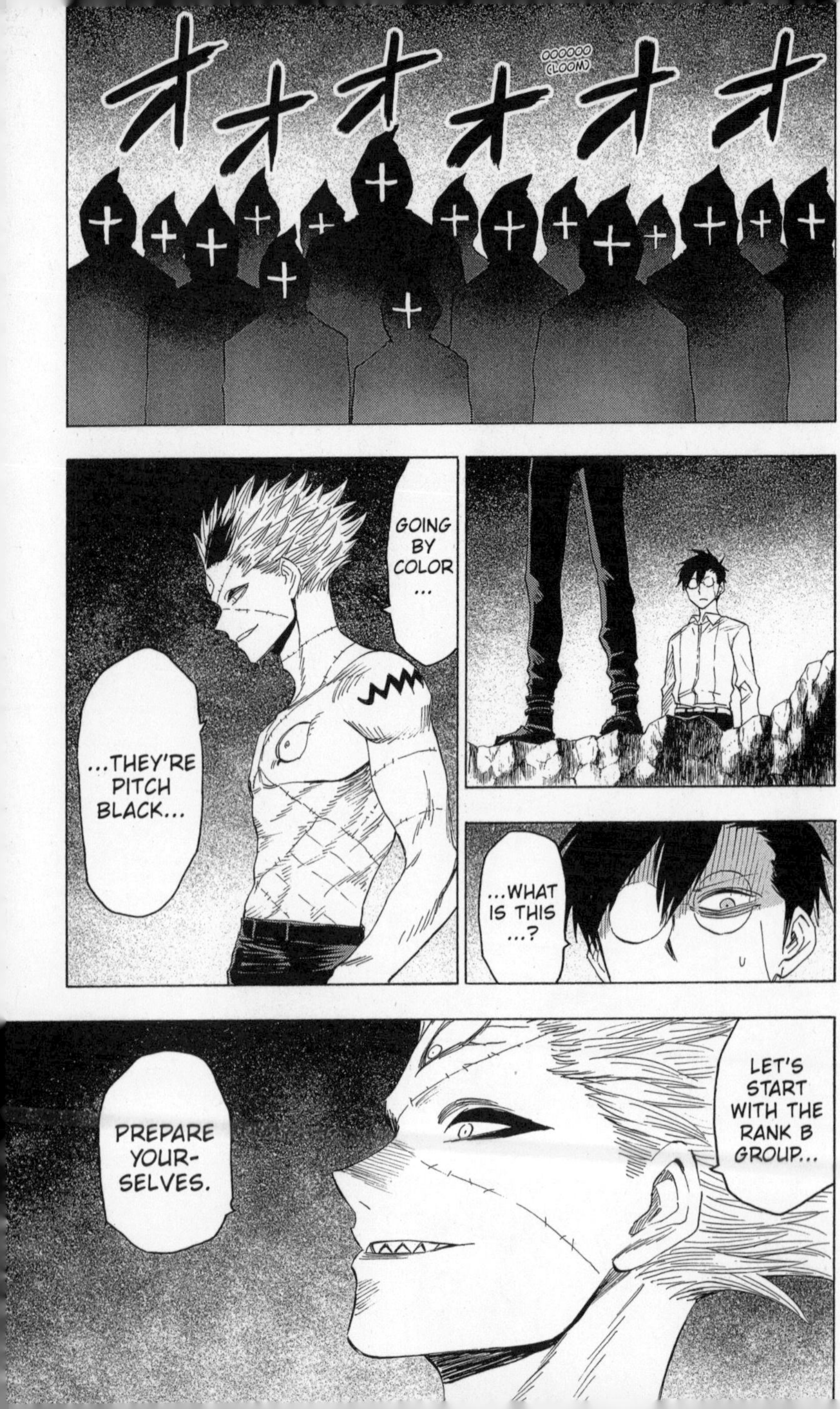
OOOOOO (LOOM)
...WHAT IS THIS ...?
GOING BY COLOR ...
...THEY'RE PITCH BLACK...
LET'S START WITH THE RANK B GROUP...
PREPARE YOUR-SELVES.

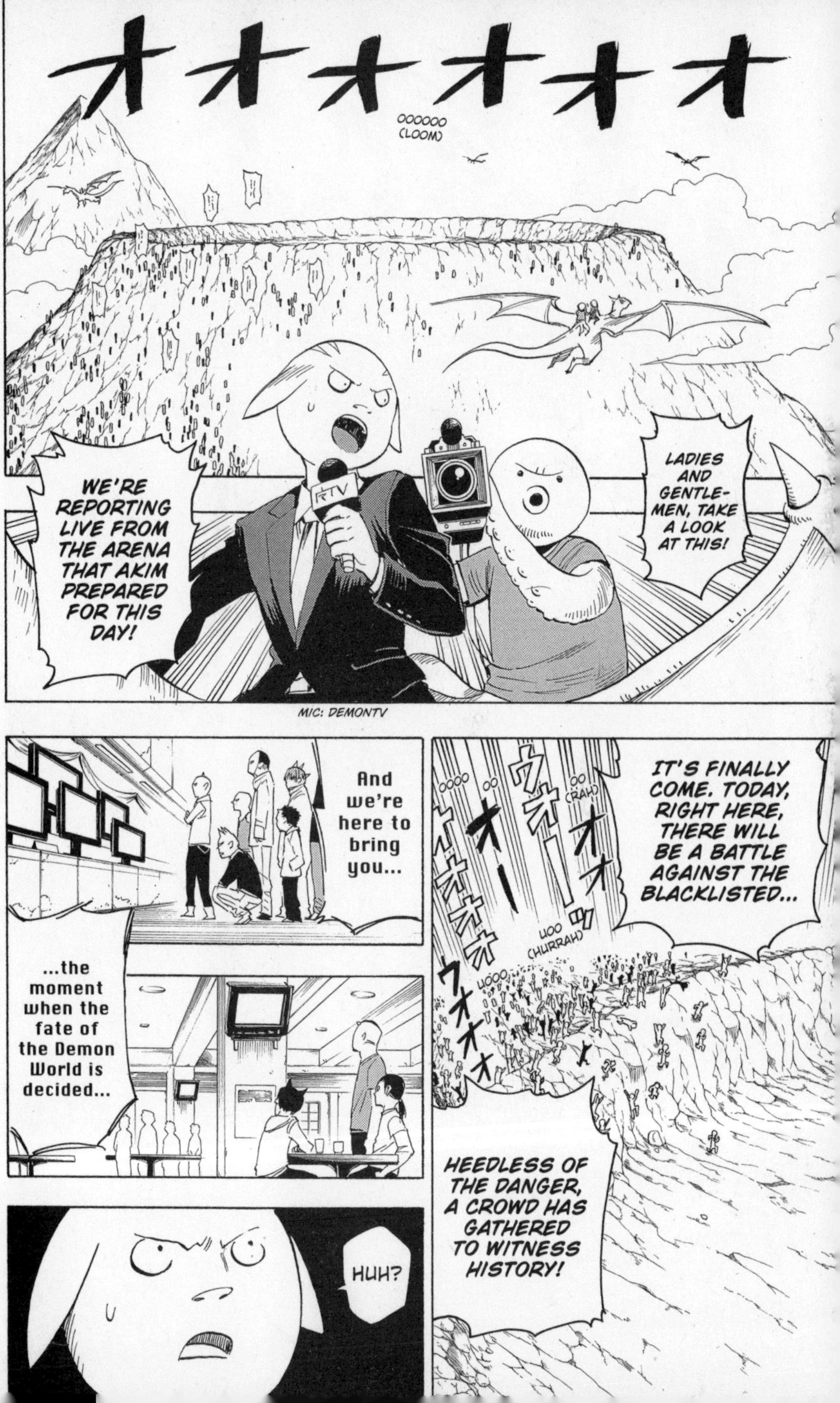
オオオオオオ
OOOOOO (LOOM)
LADIES AND GENTLEMEN, TAKE A LOOK AT THIS!
WE'RE REPORTING LIVE FROM THE ARENA THAT AKIM PREPARED FOR THIS DAY!
MIC: DEMONTV
IT'S FINALLY COME. TODAY, RIGHT HERE, THERE WILL BE A BATTLE AGAINST THE BLACKLISTED...
OO (RAH)
OO
OOOO
UOO (HURRAH)
UOOO
HEEDLESS OF THE DANGER, A CROWD HAS GATHERED TO WITNESS HISTORY!
And we're here to bring you...
...the moment when the fate of the Demon World is decided...
HUH?

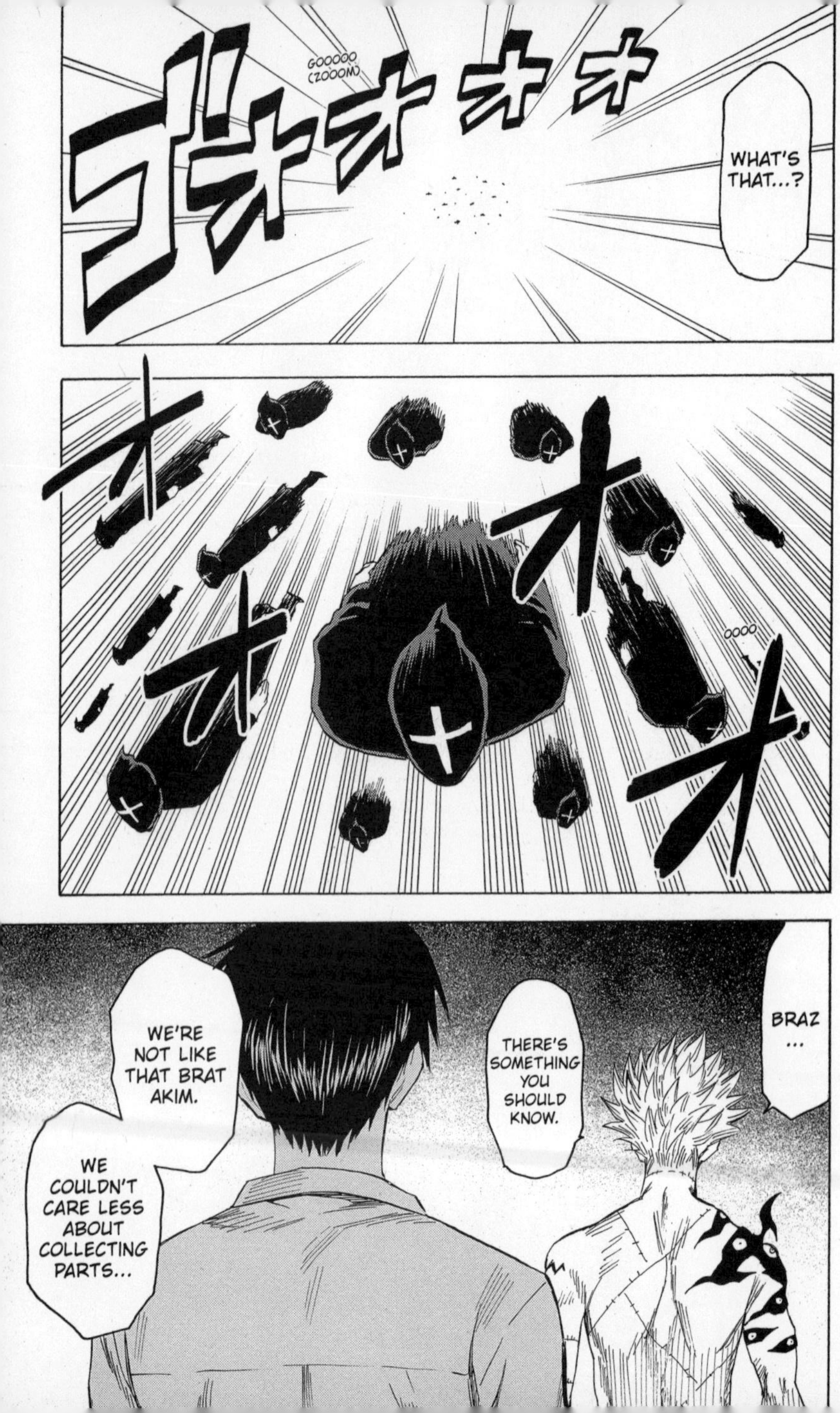
WHAT'S THAT...?
GOOOOO (ZOOOM)
OOOO
BRAZ ...
THERE'S SOMETHING YOU SHOULD KNOW.
WE'RE NOT LIKE THAT BRAT AKIM.
WE COULDN'T CARE LESS ABOUT COLLECTING PARTS...

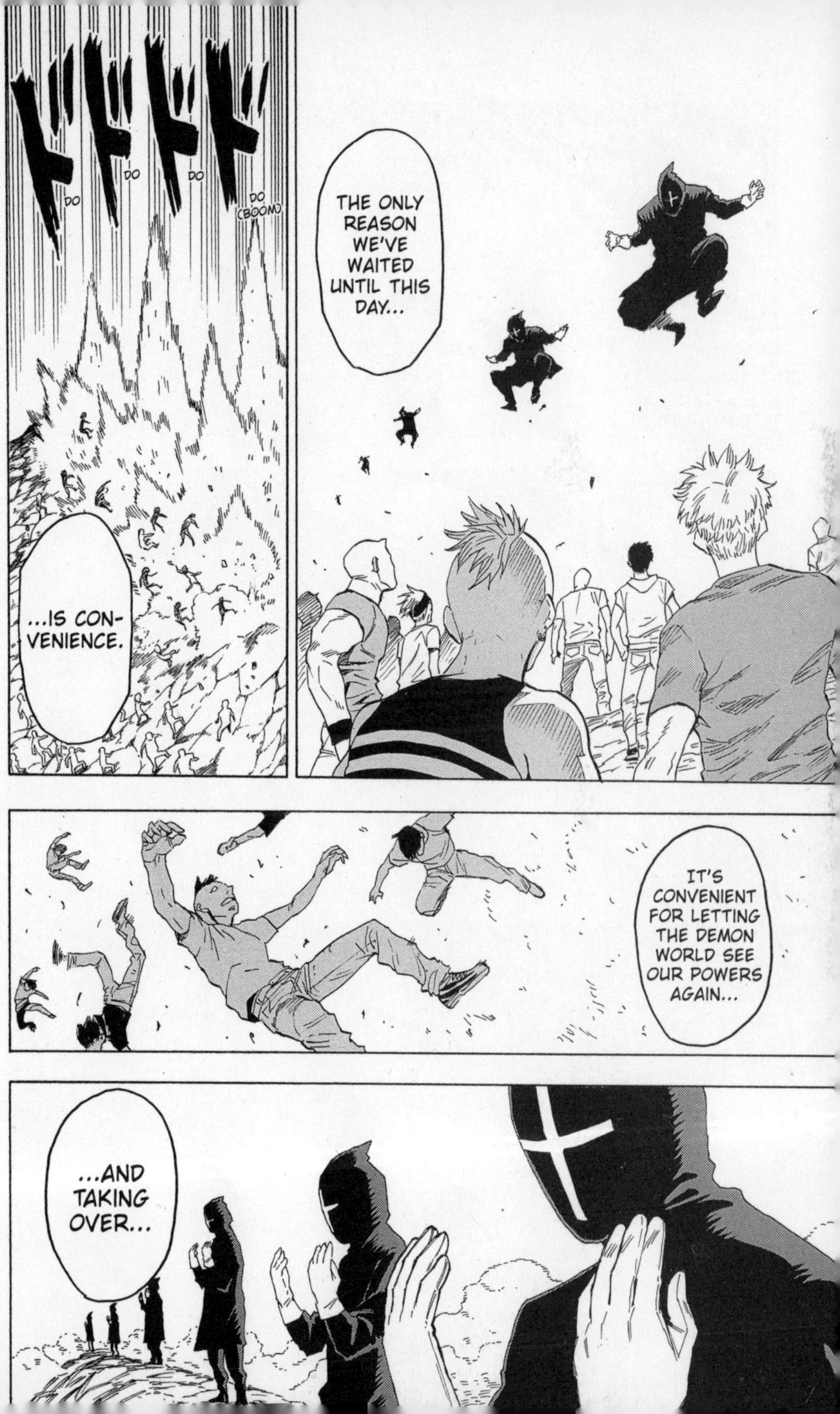
THE ONLY REASON WE'VE WAITED UNTIL THIS DAY...
ドドドドド
DO DO DO DO (BOOM)
...IS CON- VENIENCE.
IT'S CONVENIENT FOR LETTING THE DEMON WORLD SEE OUR POWERS AGAIN...
...AND TAKING OVER...

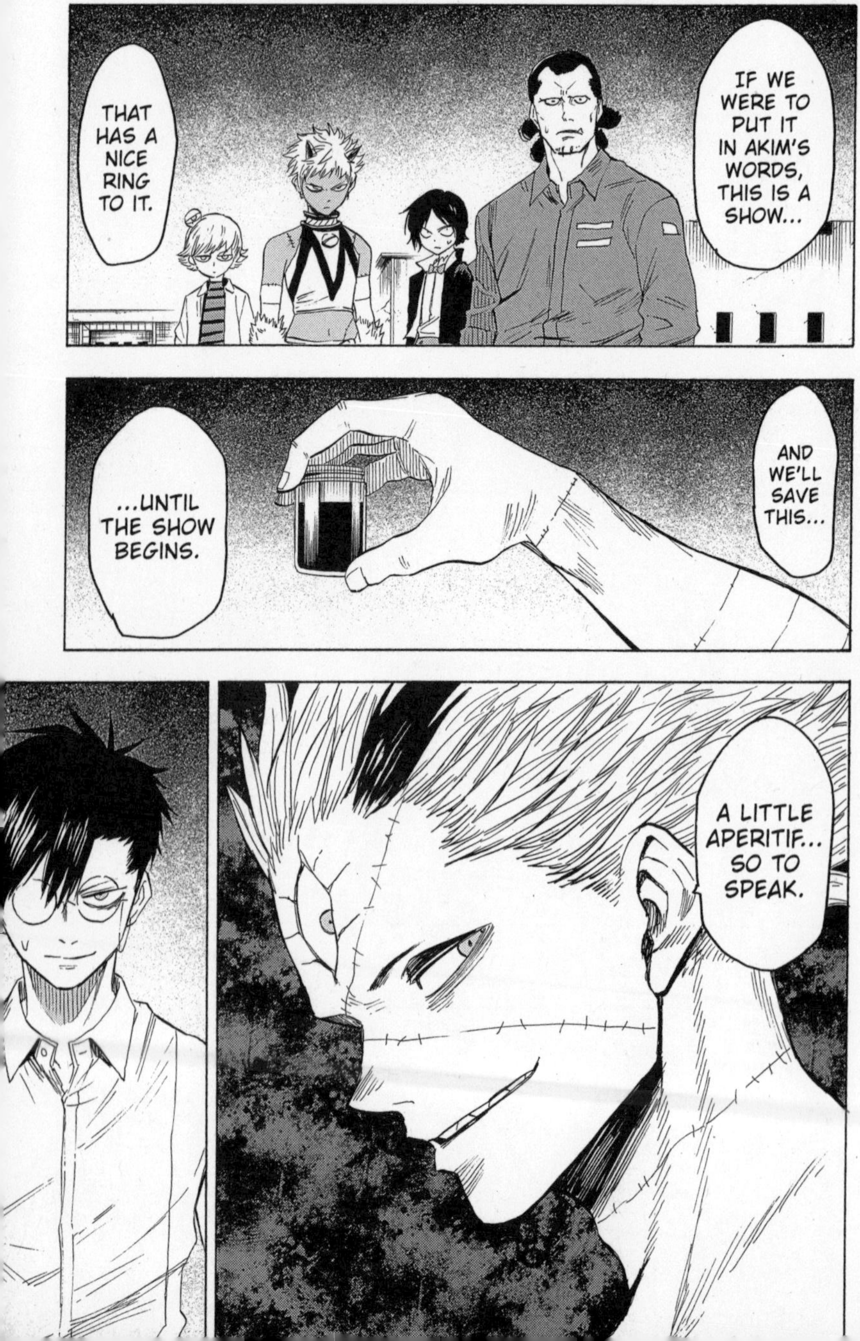
IF WE WERE TO PUT IT IN AKIM'S WORDS, THIS IS A SHOW...
THAT HAS A NICE RING TO IT.
AND WE'LL SAVE THIS...
...UNTIL THE SHOW BEGINS.
A LITTLE APERITIF... SO TO SPEAK.

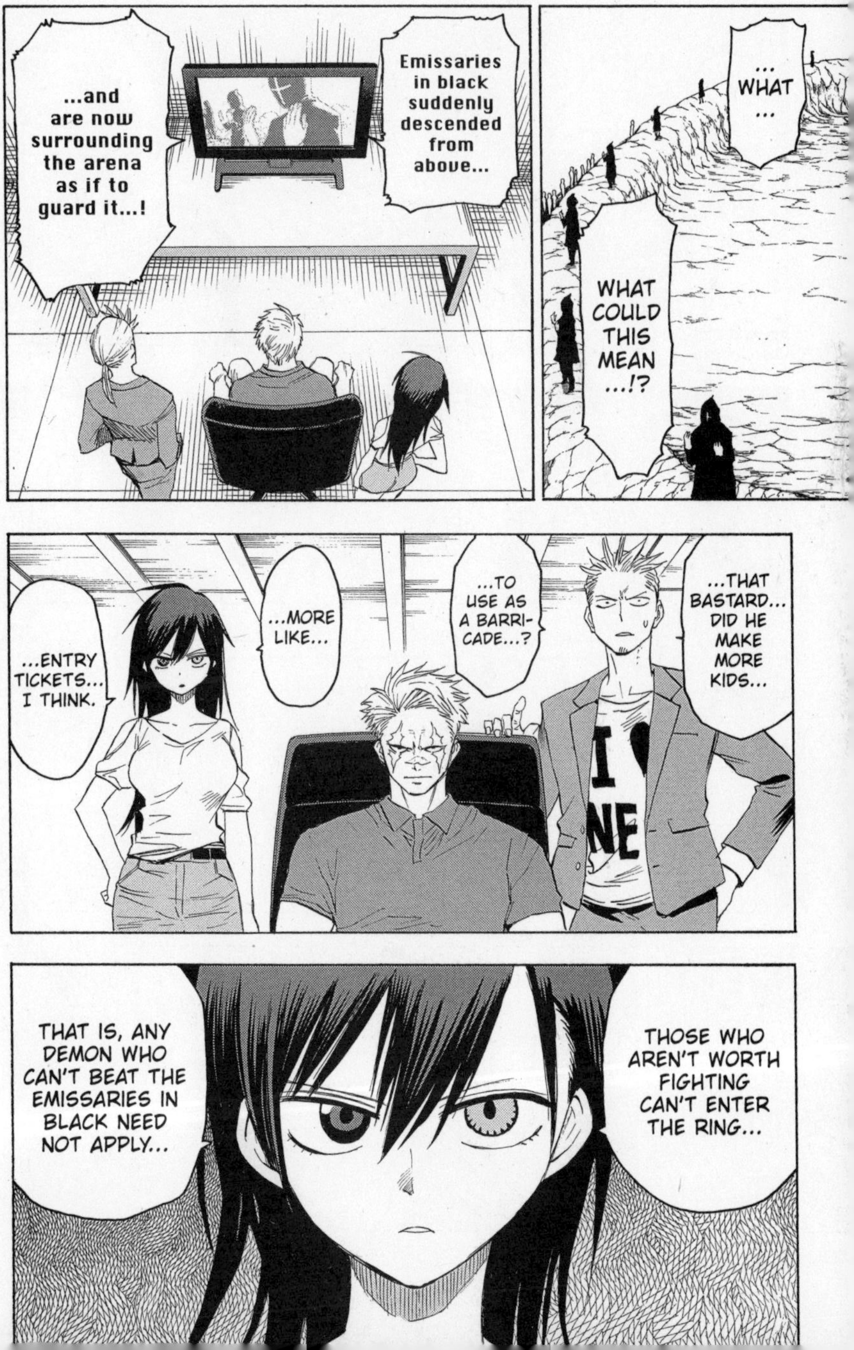
... WHAT ...
WHAT COULD THIS MEAN ...!?
Emissaries in black suddenly descended from above...
...and are now surrounding the arena as if to guard it...!
...THAT BASTARD... DID HE MAKE MORE KIDS...
...TO USE AS A BARRI-CADE...?
...MORE LIKE...
...ENTRY TICKETS... I THINK.
THOSE WHO AREN'T WORTH FIGHTING CAN'T ENTER THE RING...
THAT IS, ANY DEMON WHO CAN'T BEAT THE EMISSARIES IN BLACK NEED NOT APPLY...

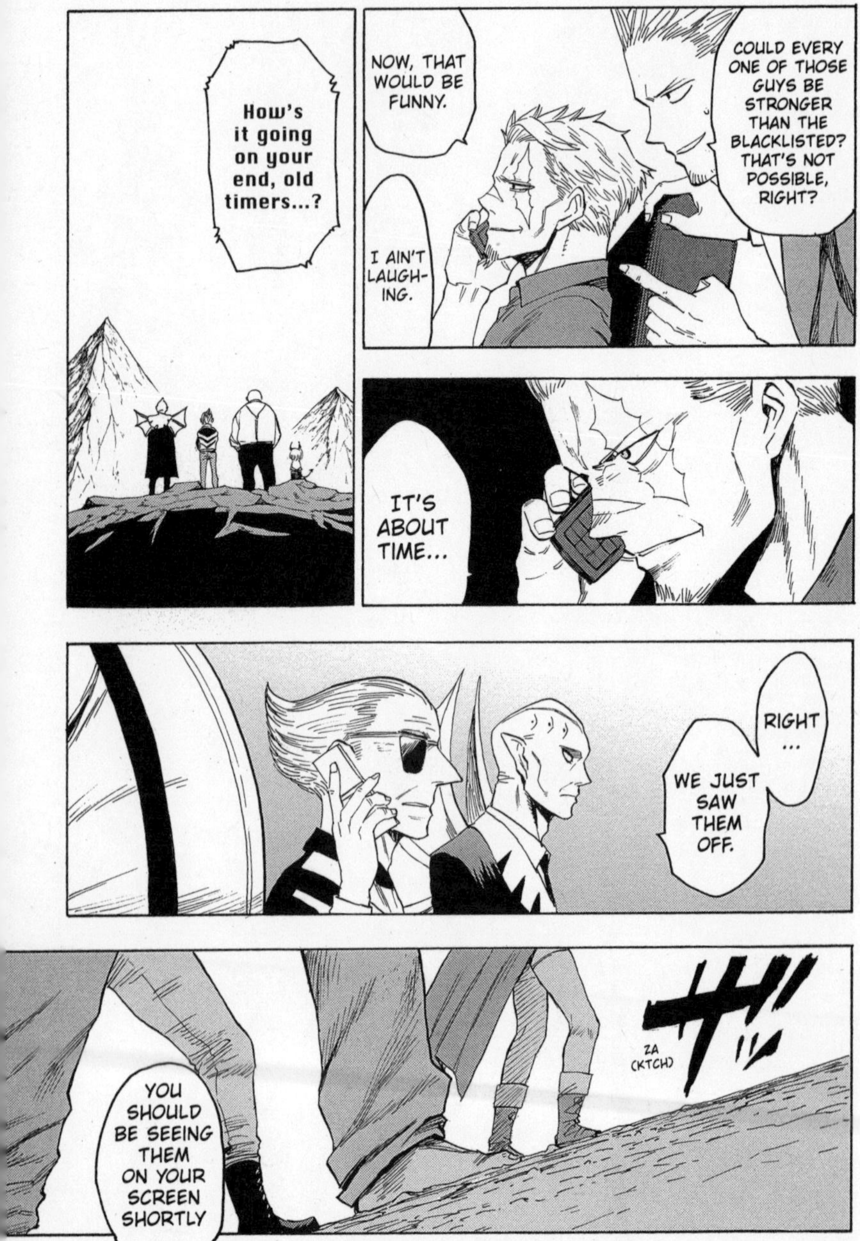

COULD EVERY ONE OF THOSE GUYS BE STRONGER THAN THE BLACKLISTED? THAT'S NOT POSSIBLE, RIGHT?
NOW, THAT WOULD BE FUNNY.
I AIN'T LAUGHING.
IT'S ABOUT TIME...
How's it going on your end, old timers...?
RIGHT... WE JUST SAW THEM OFF.
ザッ
ZA (KTCH)
YOU SHOULD BE SEEING THEM ON YOUR SCREEN SHORTLY...

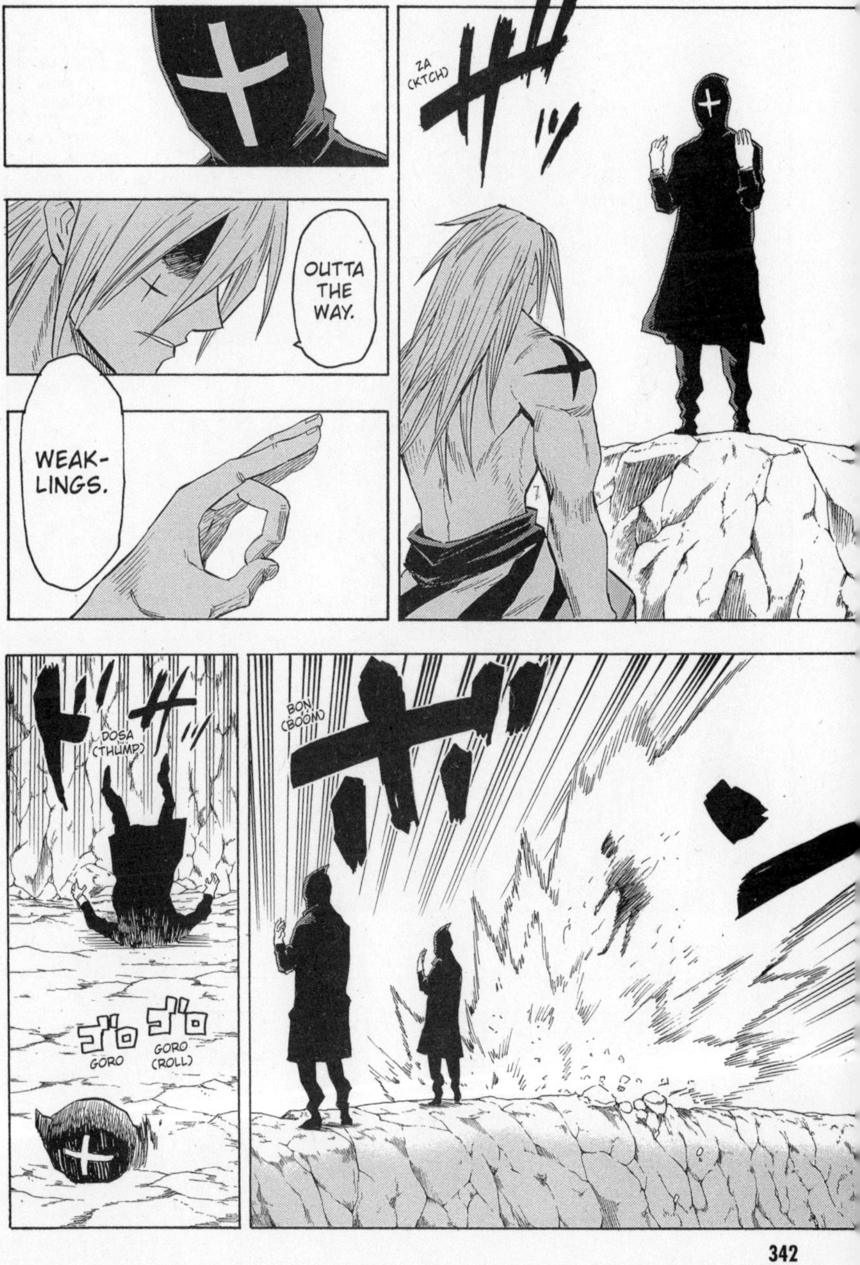
ZA
(KTCH)
OUTTA THE WAY.
WEAK-LINGS.
BON
(BOOM)
DOSA
(THUMP)
GORO
GORO
(ROLL)

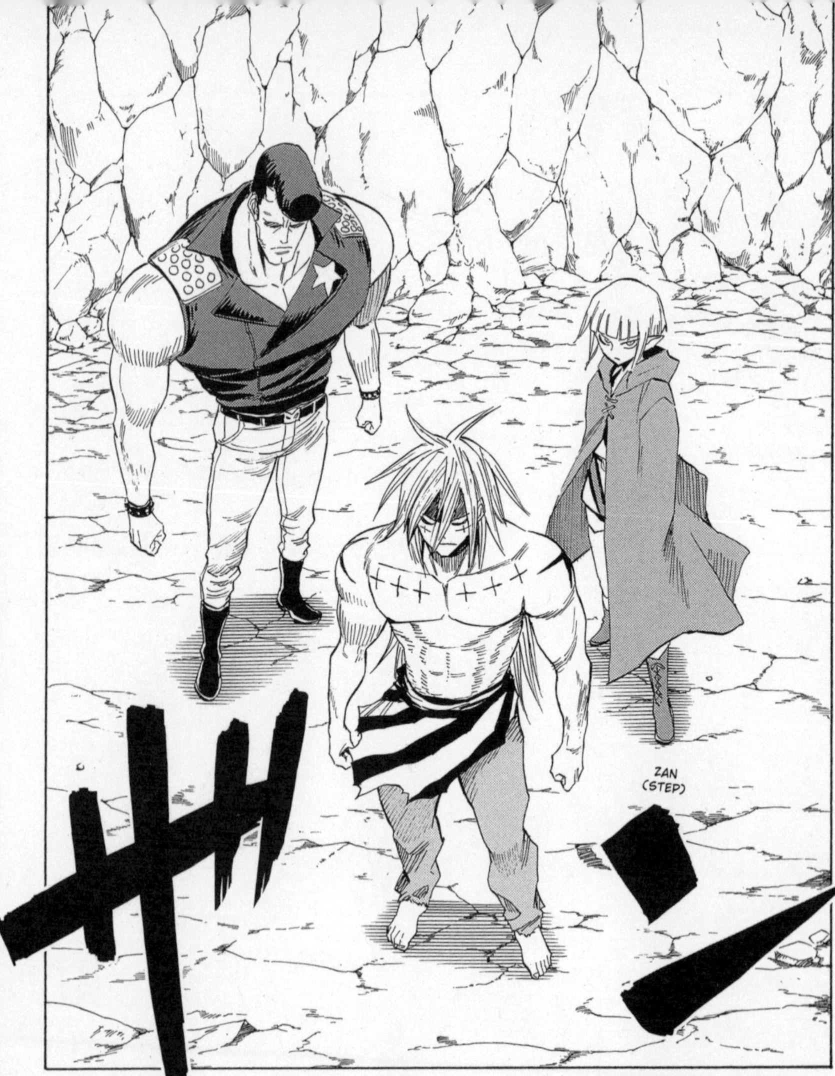
ZAN
(STEP)
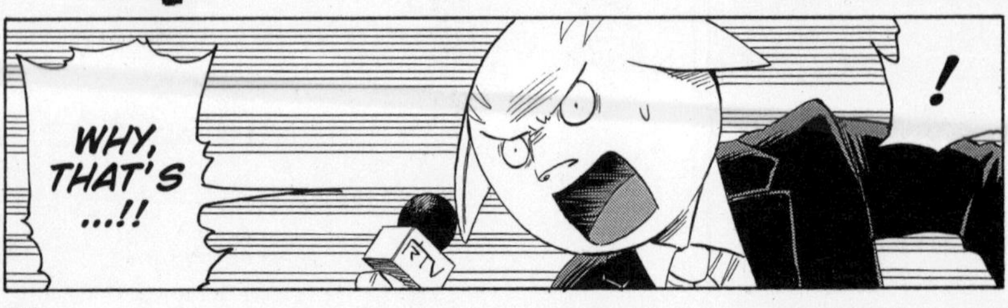
!
WHY, THAT'S ...!!

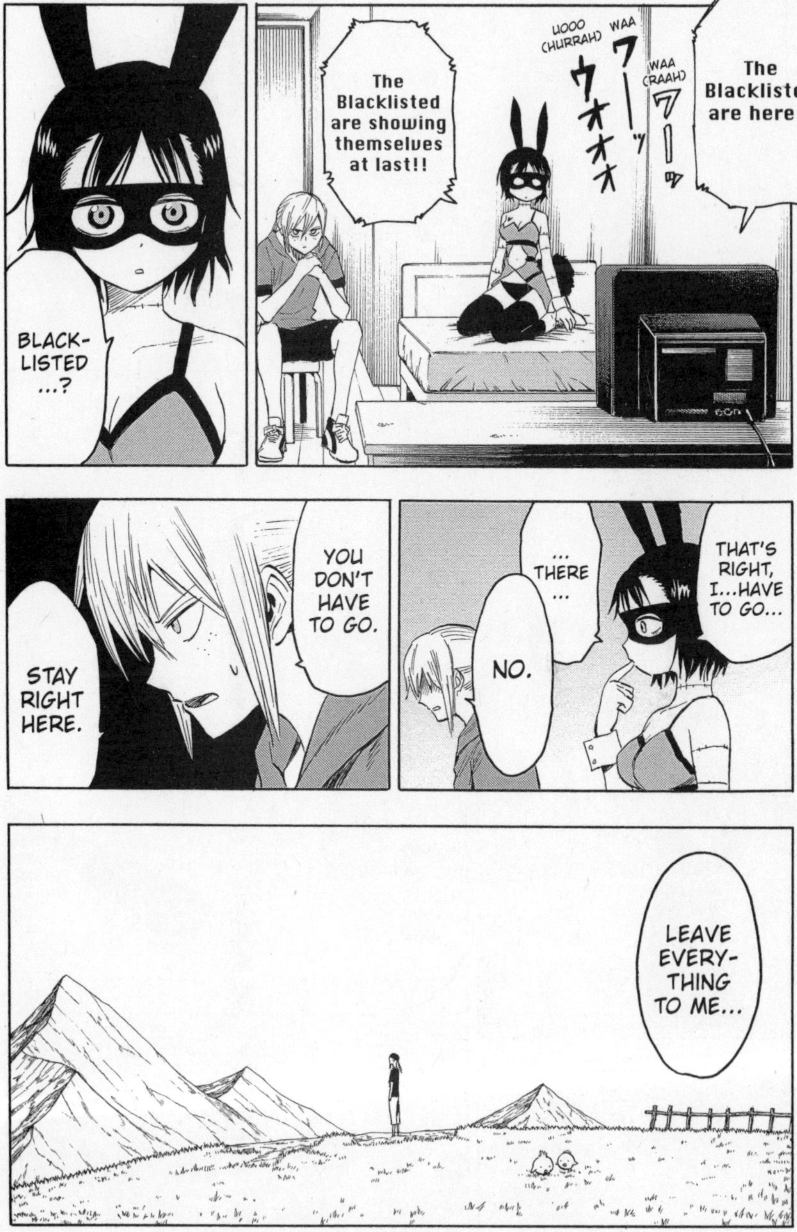
The Blacklisted are here!!
ワーッ WAA (RAAH)
ワーッ WAA
ウオオオ UOOO (HURRAH)
The Blacklisted are showing themselves at last!!
BLACK-LISTED ...?
THAT'S RIGHT, I...HAVE TO GO...
... THERE ...
NO.
YOU DON'T HAVE TO GO.
STAY RIGHT HERE.
LEAVE EVERY-THING TO ME...

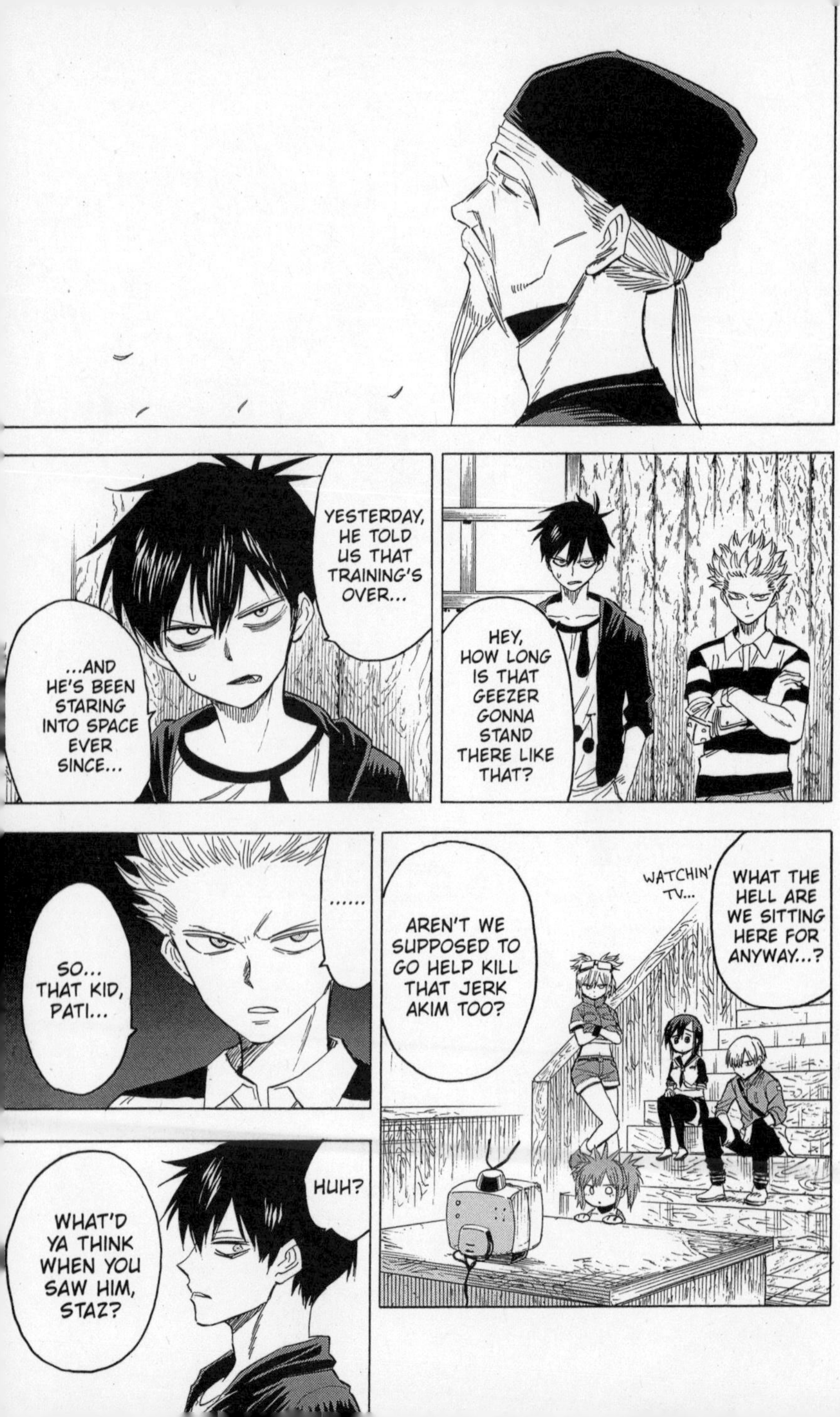
HEY, HOW LONG IS THAT GEEZER GONNA STAND THERE LIKE THAT?
YESTERDAY, HE TOLD US THAT TRAINING'S OVER...
...AND HE'S BEEN STARING INTO SPACE EVER SINCE...
WHAT THE HELL ARE WE SITTING HERE FOR ANYWAY...?
WATCHIN' TV...
AREN'T WE SUPPOSED TO GO HELP KILL THAT JERK AKIM TOO?
......
SO... THAT KID, PATI...
HUH?
WHAT'D YA THINK WHEN YOU SAW HIM, STAZ?

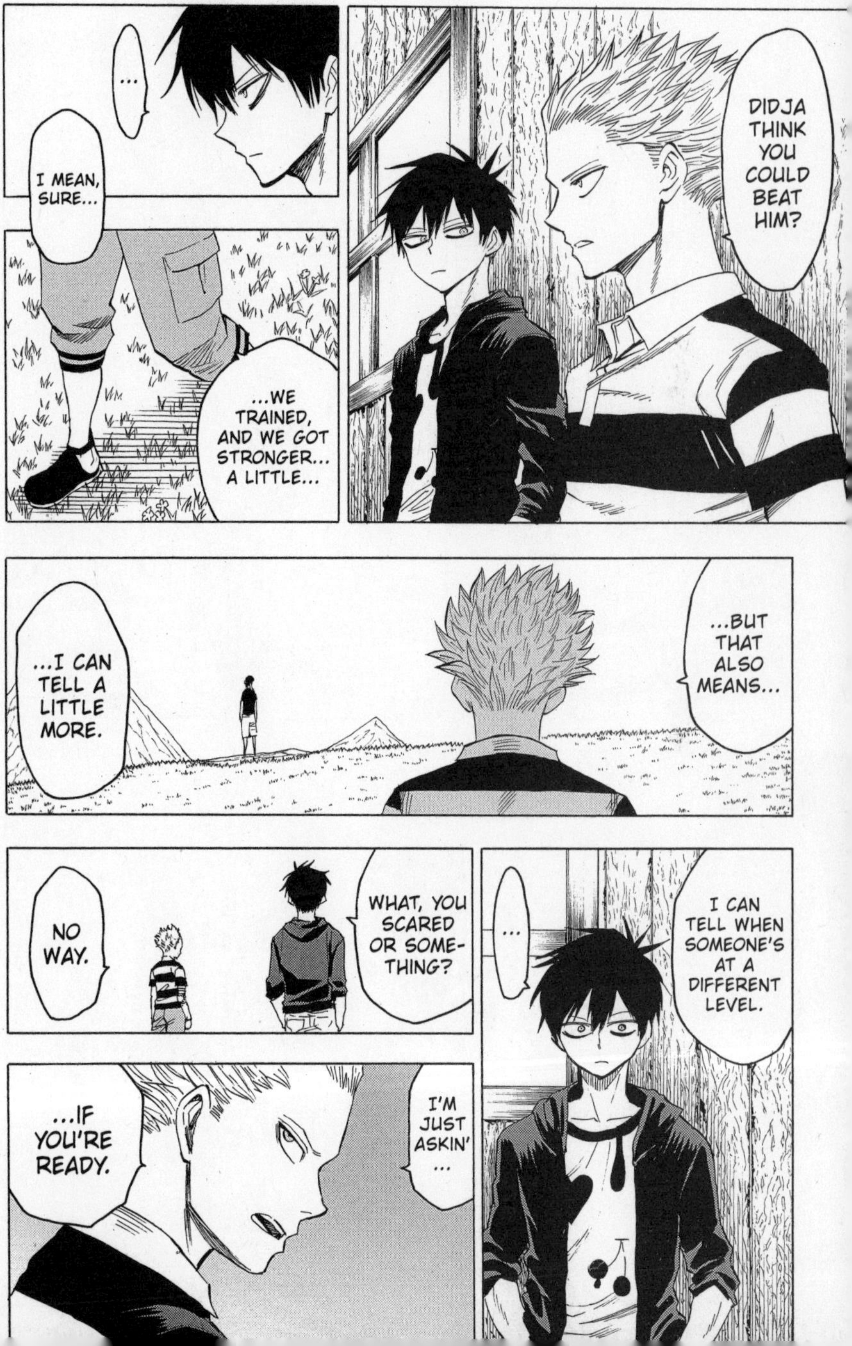
DIDJA THINK YOU COULD BEAT HIM?
...
I MEAN, SURE...
...WE TRAINED, AND WE GOT STRONGER... A LITTLE...
...BUT THAT ALSO MEANS...
...I CAN TELL A LITTLE MORE.
I CAN TELL WHEN SOMEONE'S AT A DIFFERENT LEVEL.
...
WHAT, YOU SCARED OR SOME-THING?
NO WAY.
I'M JUST ASKIN' ...
...IF YOU'RE READY.

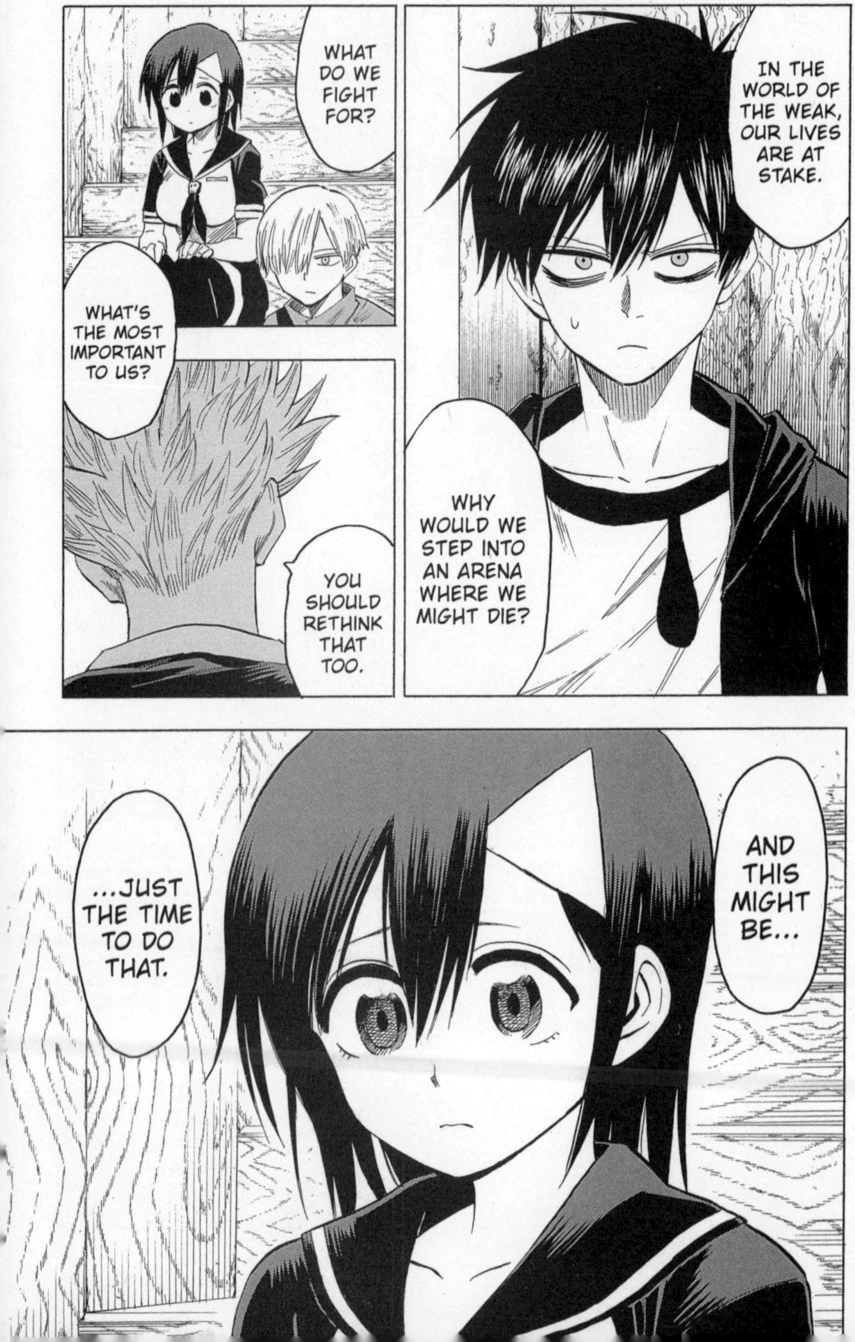
IN THE WORLD OF THE WEAK, OUR LIVES ARE AT STAKE.
WHY WOULD WE STEP INTO AN ARENA WHERE WE MIGHT DIE?
WHAT DO WE FIGHT FOR?
WHAT'S THE MOST IMPORTANT TO US?
YOU SHOULD RETHINK THAT TOO.
AND THIS MIGHT BE...
...JUST THE TIME TO DO THAT.

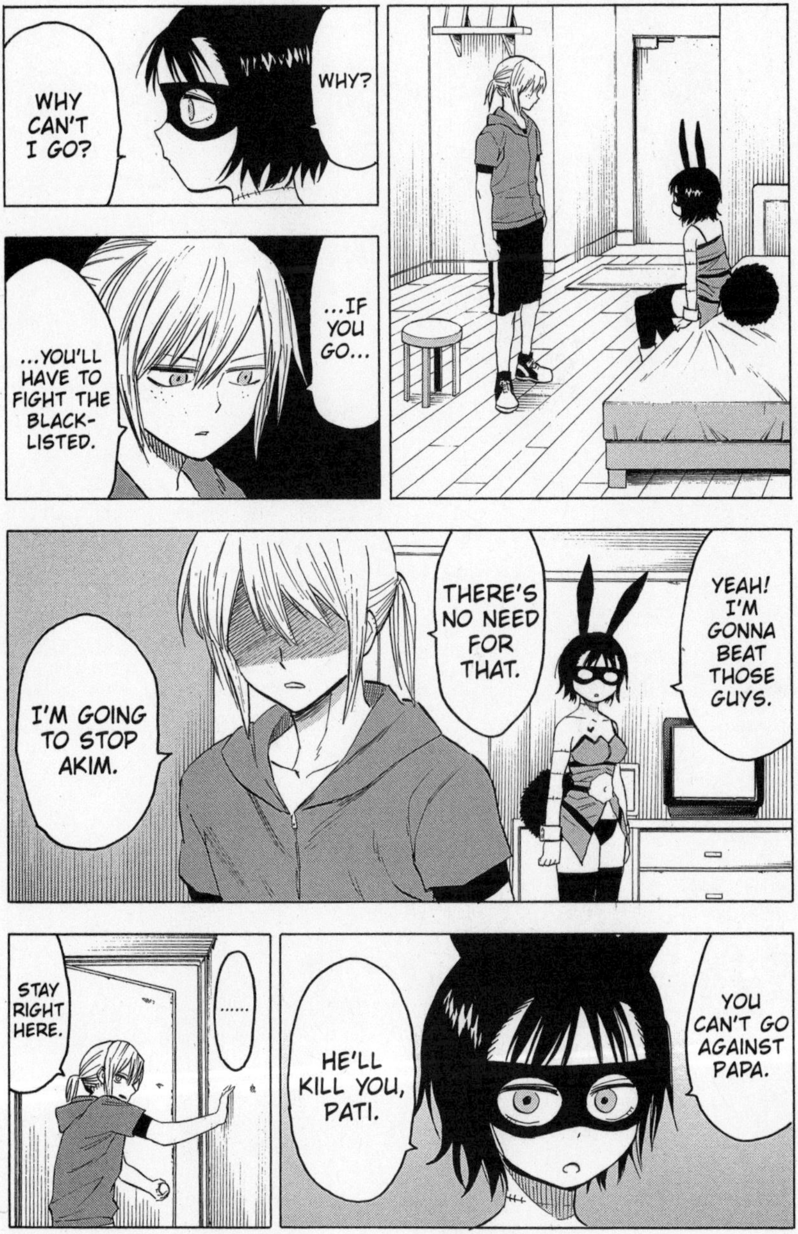
WHY?
WHY CAN'T I GO?
...IF YOU GO...
...YOU'LL HAVE TO FIGHT THE BLACK-LISTED.
YEAH! I'M GONNA BEAT THOSE GUYS.
THERE'S NO NEED FOR THAT.
I'M GOING TO STOP AKIM.
YOU CAN'T GO AGAINST PAPA.
HE'LL KILL YOU, PATI.
......
STAY RIGHT HERE.

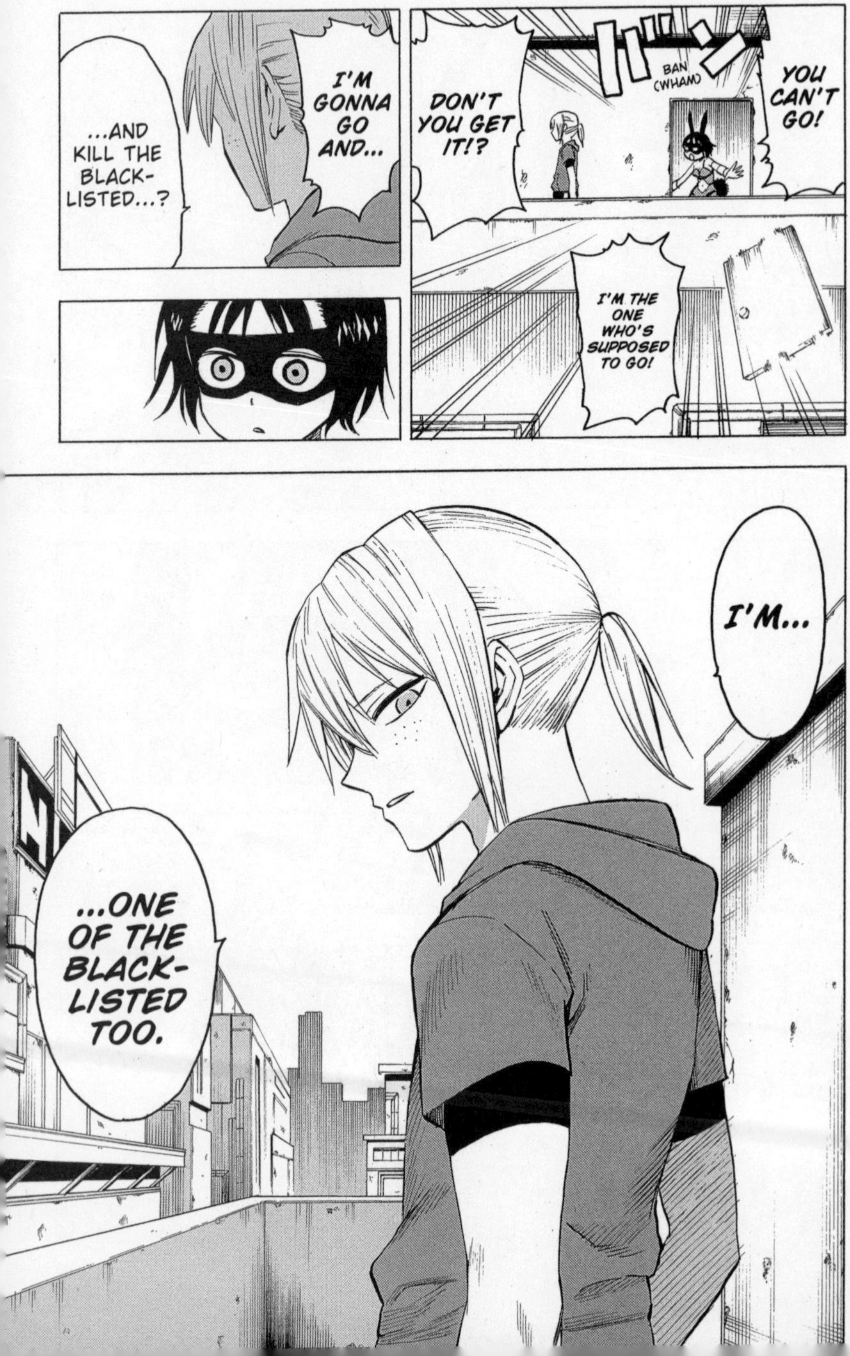
YOU CAN'T GO!
BAN (WHAM)
DON'T YOU GET IT!?
I'M THE ONE WHO'S SUPPOSED TO GO!
I'M GONNA GO AND...
...AND KILL THE BLACK-LISTED...?
I'M...
...ONE OF THE BLACK-LISTED TOO.

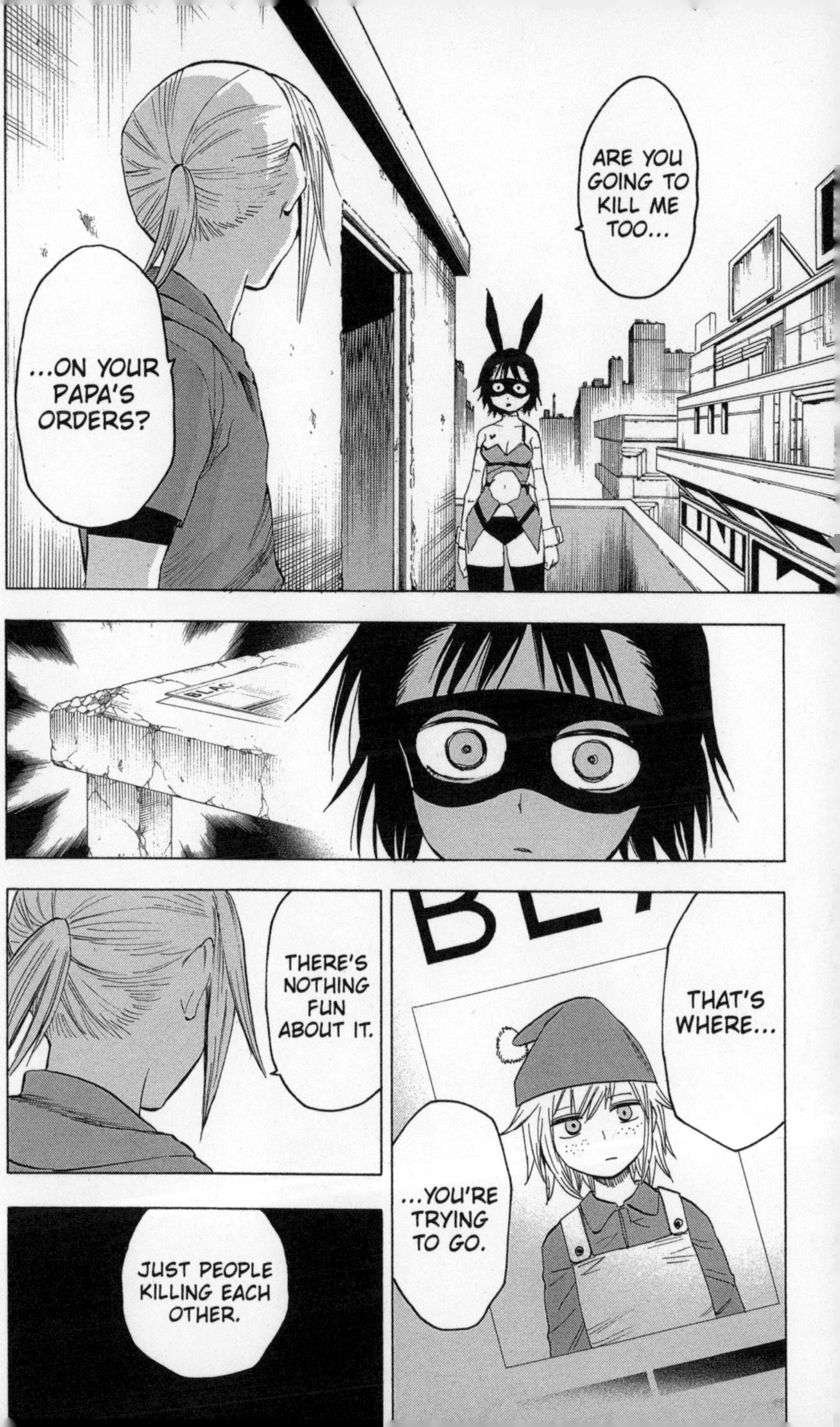
ARE YOU GOING TO KILL ME TOO...
...ON YOUR PAPA'S ORDERS?
THAT'S WHERE...
...YOU'RE TRYING TO GO.
THERE'S NOTHING FUN ABOUT IT.
JUST PEOPLE KILLING EACH OTHER.

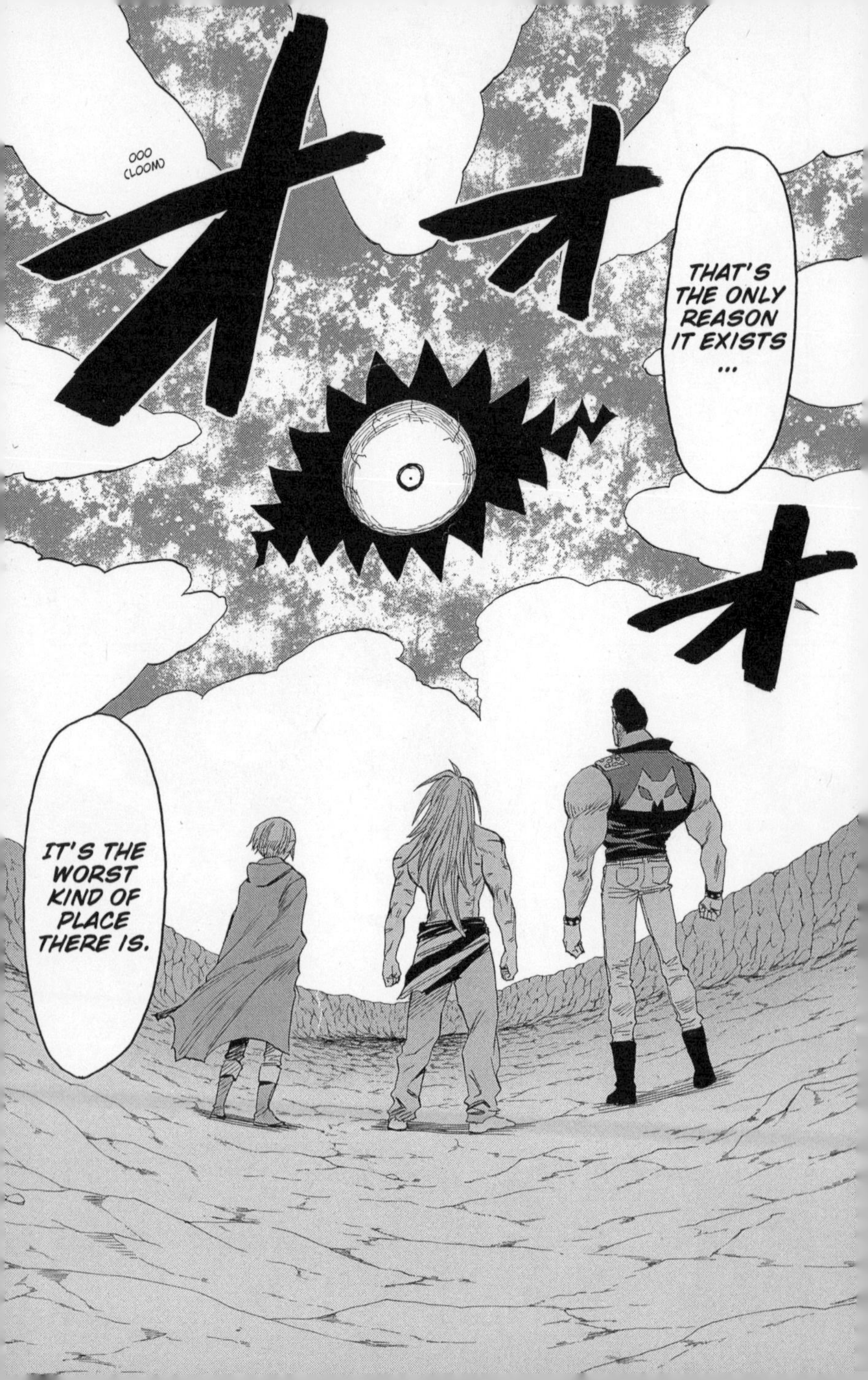
THAT'S THE ONLY REASON IT EXISTS ...
OOO (LOOM)
IT'S THE WORST KIND OF PLACE THERE IS.

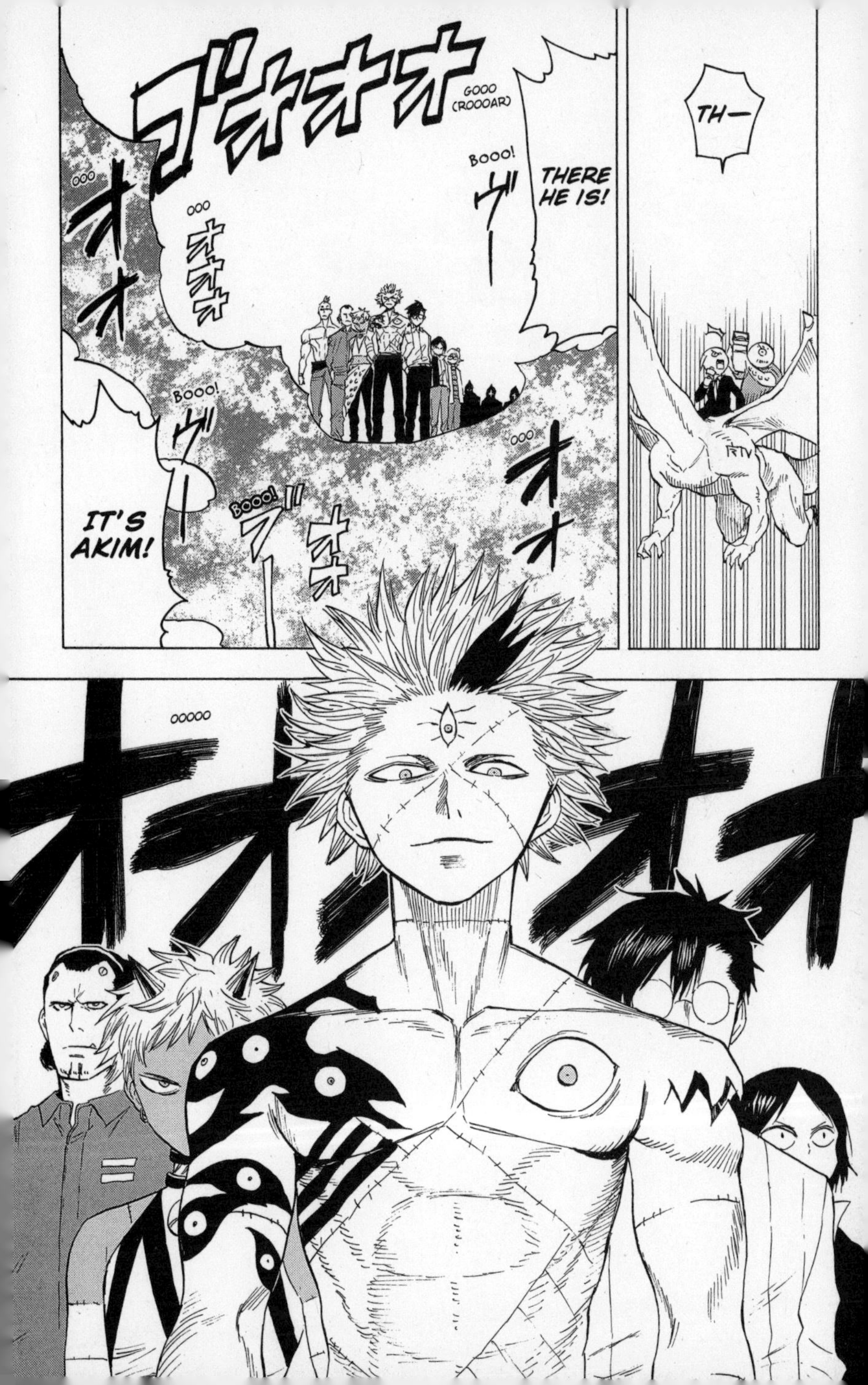
TH—
ゴォオオ
GOOO (ROOOAR)
ヴー
BOOO!
THERE HE IS!
オォォ
ooo
オオ
ooo
オオ
ooo
ブー
BOOO!
オォォ
ヴー
BOOO!
IT'S AKIM!
オオオオ
ooooo

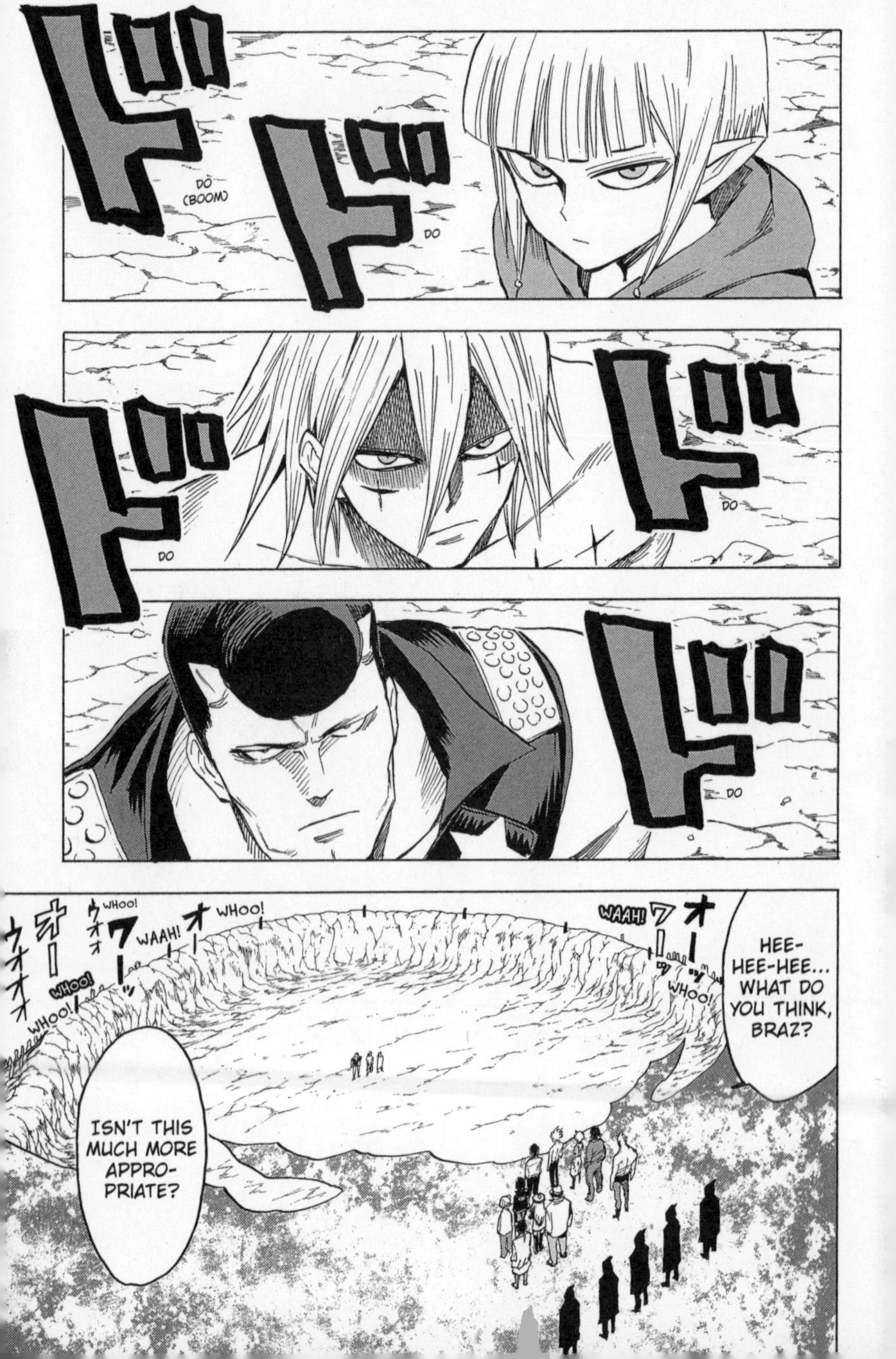
ド
DO
ド
DO (BOOM)
ド
DO
ド
DO
ド
DO
オーッ
ワーッ
WAAH!
WHOO!
HEE-HEE-HEE... WHAT DO YOU THINK, BRAZ?
オー
WHOO!
ワーッ
WAAH!
ウオオ
WHOO!
ウオオオ
WHOO!
WHOO!
ISN'T THIS MUCH MORE APPRO-PRIATE?

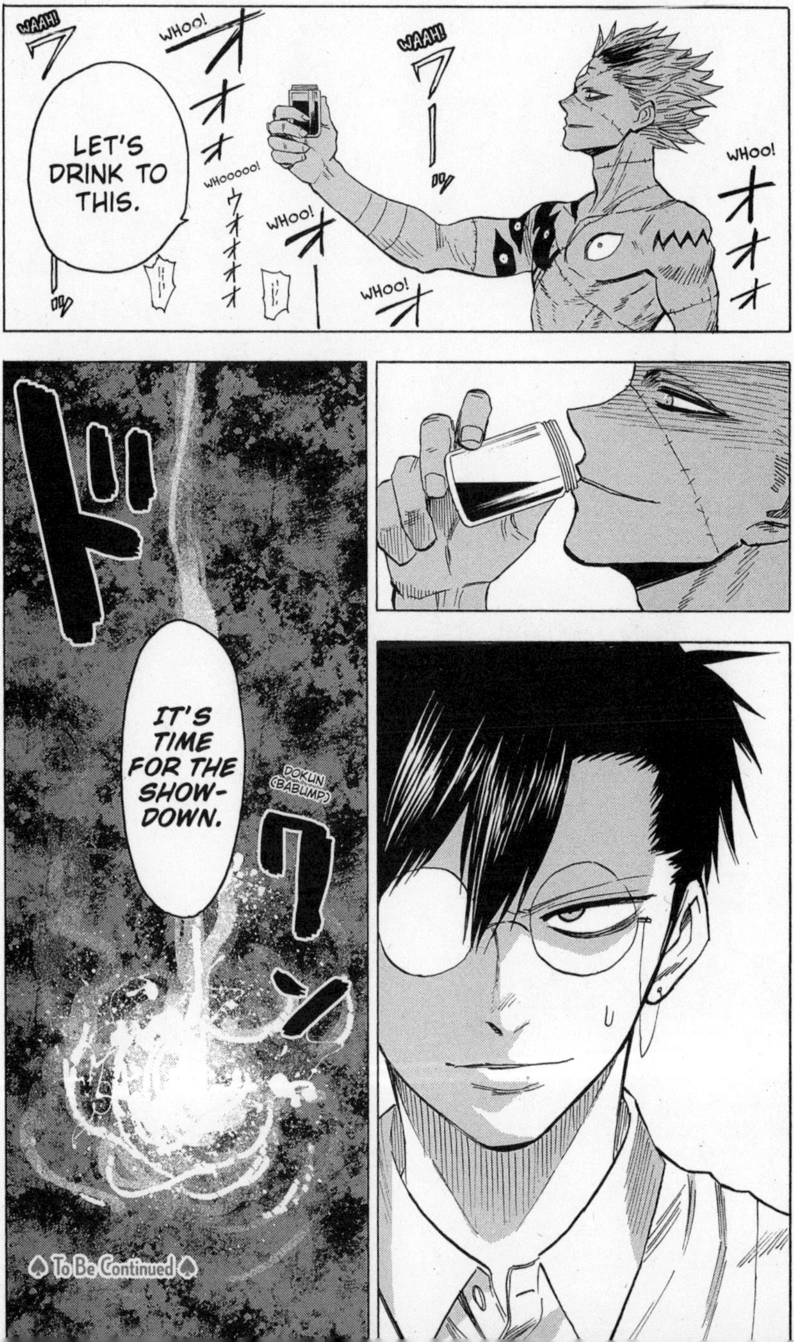
WHOO!
オオオ
WAAH!
ワー
WHOO!
オー
WHOO!
オ
WHOOOOO!
ウオオオオ
WHOO!
オオオ
LET'S DRINK TO THIS.
WAAH!
ワ
DOKUN (BABUMP)
ドクン
IT'S TIME FOR THE SHOW-DOWN.
To Be Continued

To Be Continued

BLOOD LAD

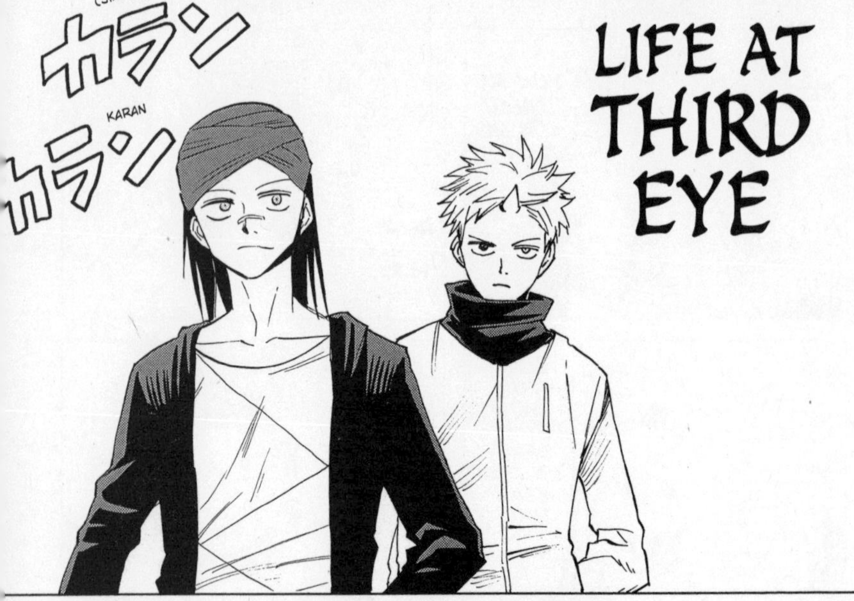
KARAN (JINGLE)
カラン
KARAN
カラン

LIFE AT THIRD EYE

THE PAIR FROM THE WEST

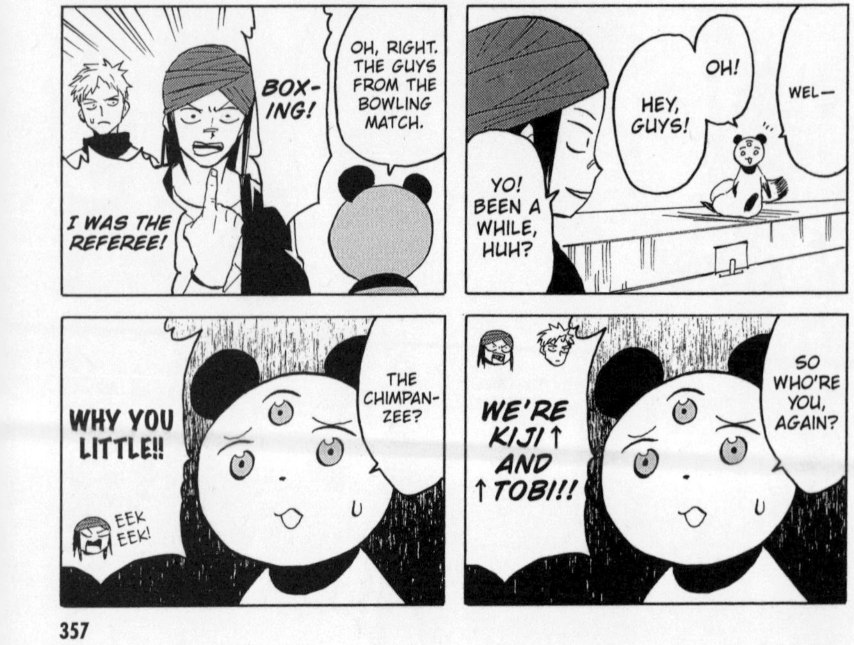
WEL—
OH!
HEY, GUYS!
YO! BEEN A WHILE, HUH?
OH, RIGHT. THE GUYS FROM THE BOWLING MATCH.
BOX-ING!
I WAS THE REFEREE!
SO WHO'RE YOU, AGAIN?
WE'RE KIJI ↑ AND ↑ TOBI!!
THE CHIMPAN-ZEE?
WHY YOU LITTLE!!
EEK EEK!

BOSS

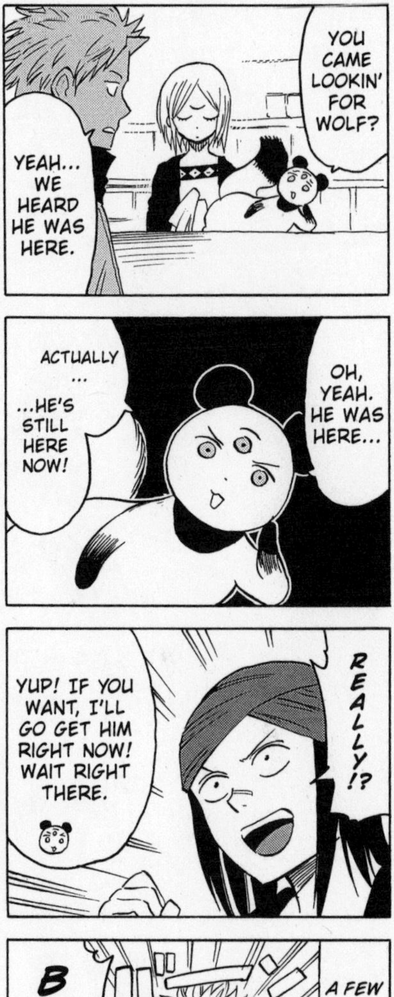

YOU CAME LOOKIN' FOR WOLF?
YEAH... WE HEARD HE WAS HERE.
OH, YEAH. HE WAS HERE...
ACTUALLY ...
...HE'S STILL HERE NOW!
REALLY!?
YUP! IF YOU WANT, I'LL GO GET HIM RIGHT NOW! WAIT RIGHT THERE.
A FEW MIN-UTES LATER —
BAAAN (TA-DAAA)
BOSS!!
モ MO

BOSS?

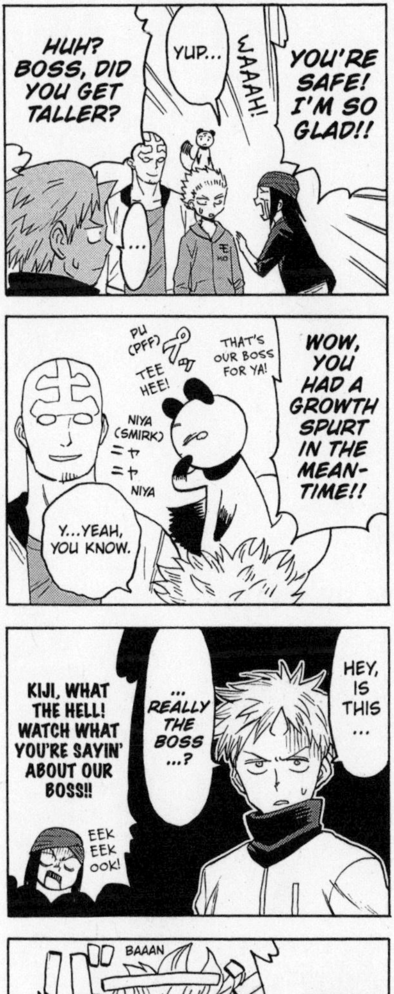

YOU'RE SAFE! I'M SO GLAD!!
WAAAAH!
YUP...
HUH? BOSS, DID YOU GET TALLER?
...
WOW, YOU HAD A GROWTH SPURT IN THE MEAN-TIME!!
THAT'S OUR BOSS FOR YA!
PU (PFF)
TEE HEE!
NIYA (SMIRK) ニヤ ニヤ NIYA
Y...YEAH, YOU KNOW.
HEY, IS THIS ...
... REALLY THE BOSS ...?
KIJI, WHAT THE HELL! WATCH WHAT YOU'RE SAYIN' ABOUT OUR BOSS!!
EEK EEK OOK!
IT'S OUR BOSS, WOLF! ISN'T IT OBVIOUS!? JUST LOOK!
BAAAN
HNNG!
NO, YOU LOOK!

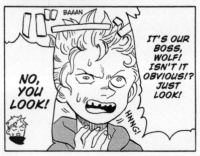

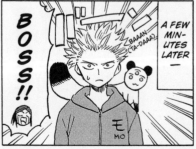

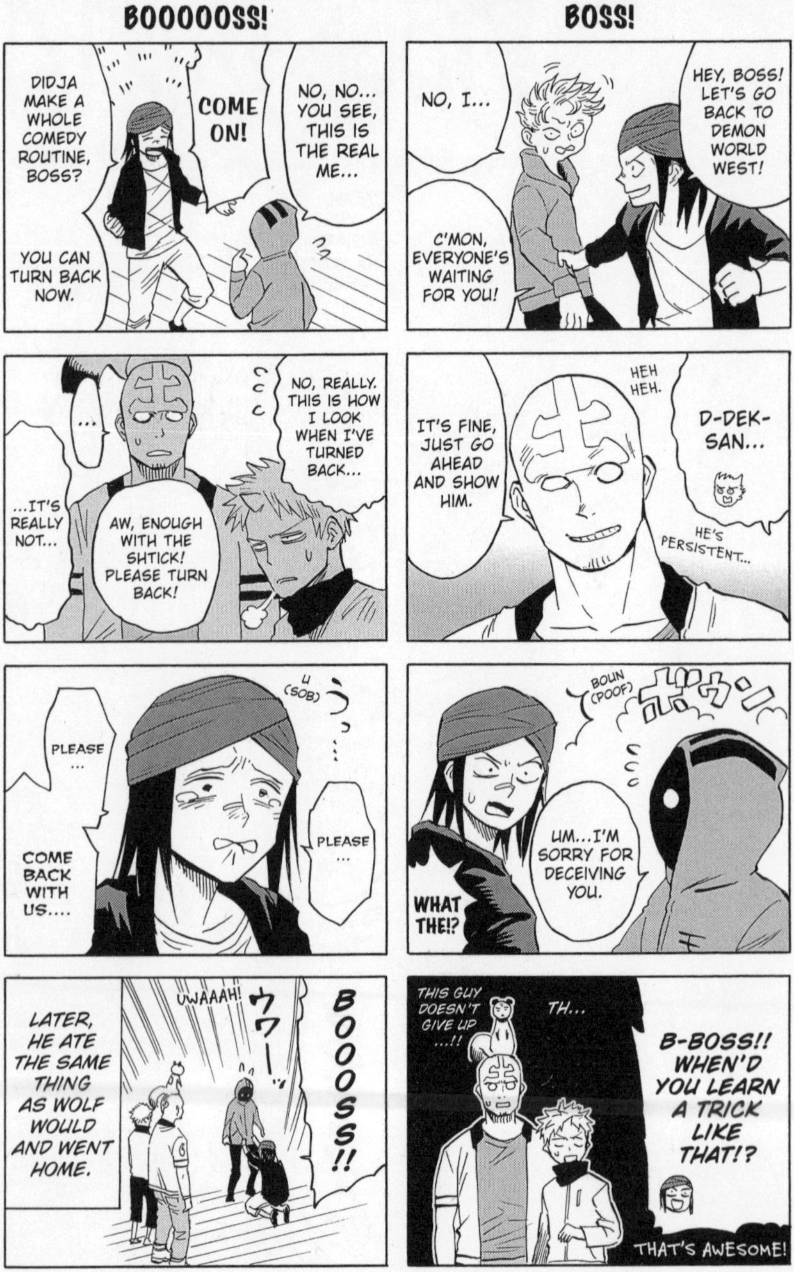
BOSS!
HEY, BOSS! LET'S GO BACK TO DEMON WORLD WEST!
NO, I...
C'MON, EVERYONE'S WAITING FOR YOU!
HEH HEH.
D-DEK-SAN...
IT'S FINE, JUST GO AHEAD AND SHOW HIM.
HE'S PERSISTENT...
ボウン
BOUN (POOF)
UM...I'M SORRY FOR DECEIVING YOU.
WHAT THE!?
B-BOSS!! WHEN'D YOU LEARN A TRICK LIKE THAT!?
TH...
THIS GUY DOESN'T GIVE UP ...!!
THAT'S AWESOME!
BOOOOOSS!
NO, NO... YOU SEE, THIS IS THE REAL ME...
COME ON!
DIDJA MAKE A WHOLE COMEDY ROUTINE, BOSS?
YOU CAN TURN BACK NOW.
NO, REALLY. THIS IS HOW I LOOK WHEN I'VE TURNED BACK...
...
AW, ENOUGH WITH THE SHTICK! PLEASE TURN BACK!
...IT'S REALLY NOT...
う
U (SOB)
PLEASE ...
PLEASE ...
COME BACK WITH US....
BOOOSS!!
ウワー
UWAAAH!
LATER, HE ATE THE SAME THING AS WOLF WOULD AND WENT HOME.
END

BLOOD LAD 14

These images appeared under the jacket of the original edition of *Blood Lad*!

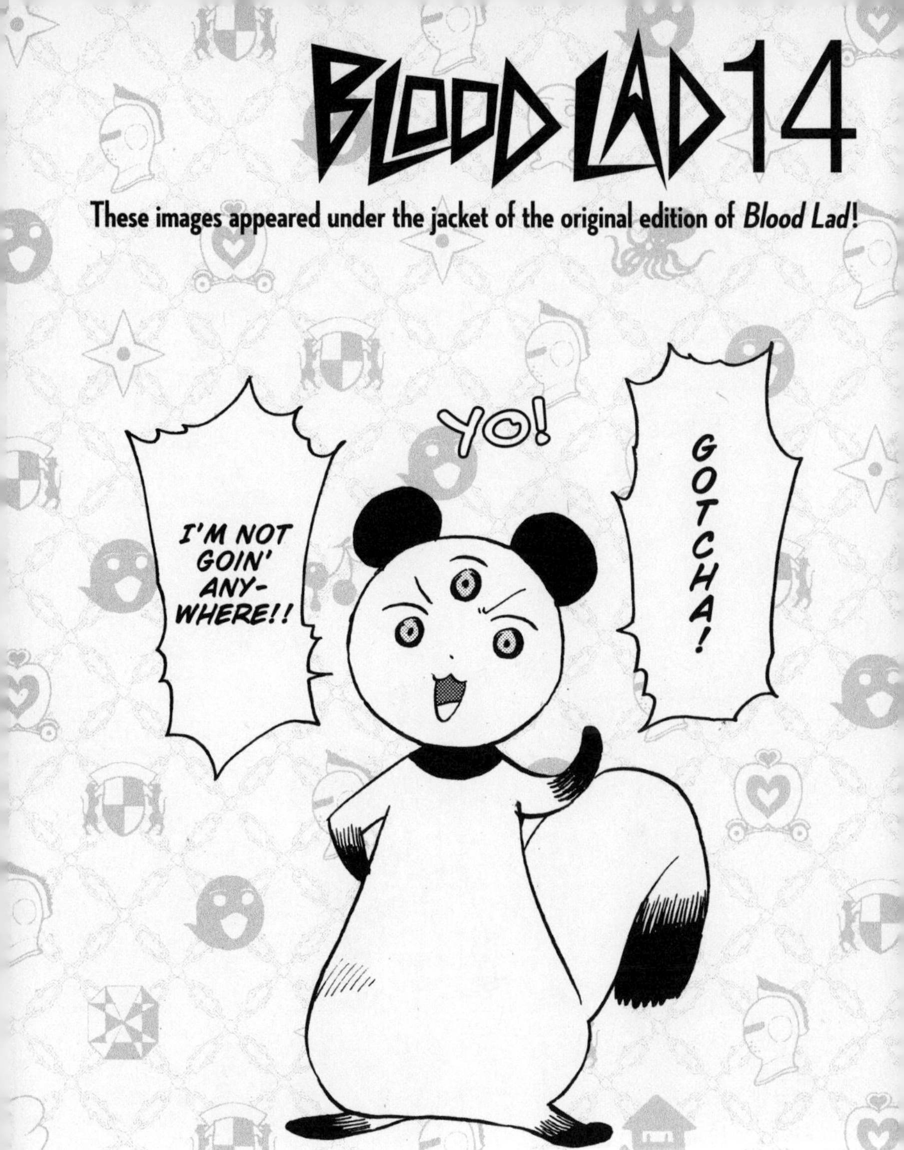
GOTCHA!
YO!
I'M NOT GOIN' ANY-WHERE!!

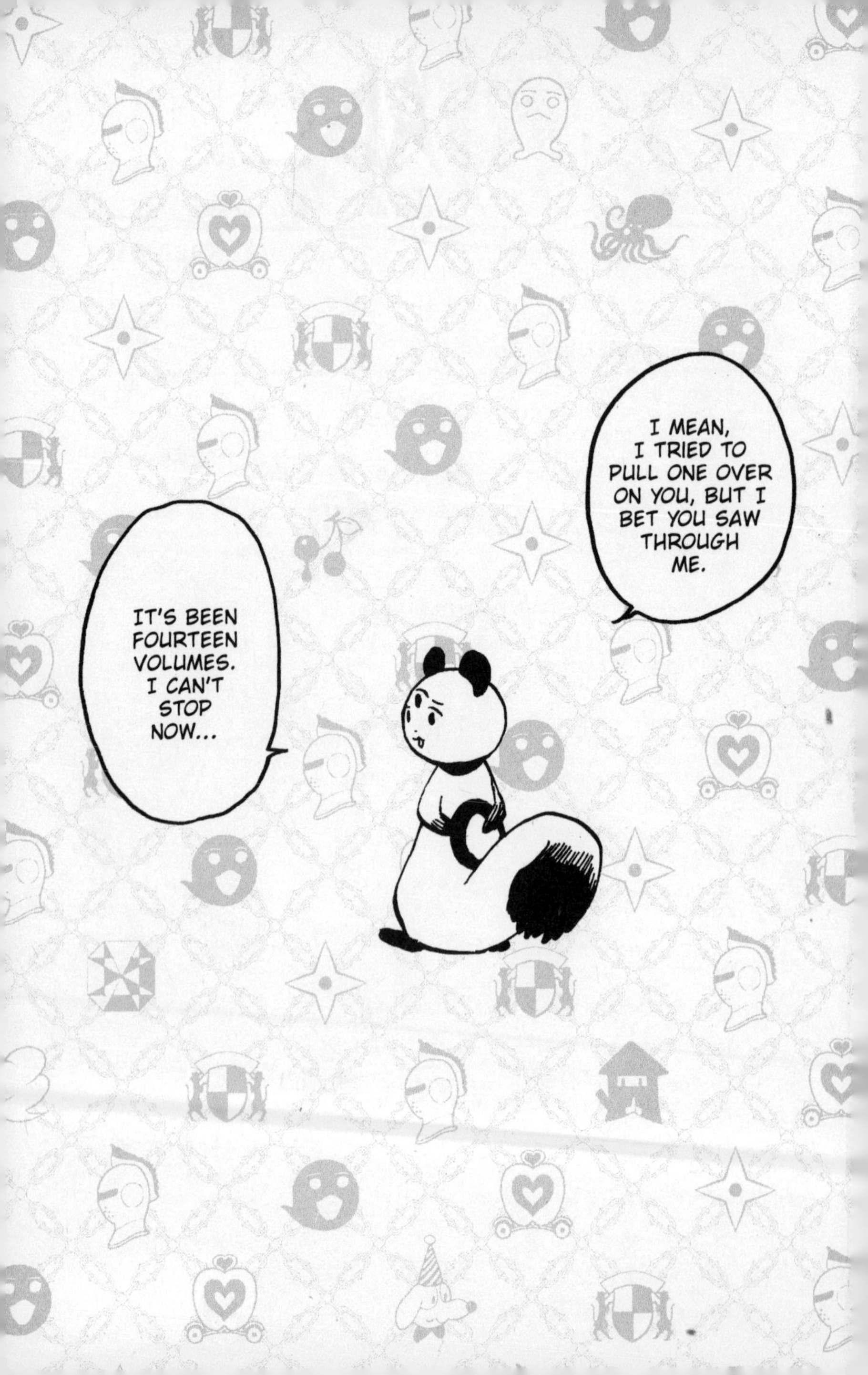
I MEAN, I TRIED TO PULL ONE OVER ON YOU, BUT I BET YOU SAW THROUGH ME.
IT'S BEEN FOURTEEN VOLUMES. I CAN'T STOP NOW...

BLOOD LAD ⑦

YUUKI KODAMA

Translation: Melissa Tanaka

Lettering: Alexis Eckerman

This book is a work of fiction. Names, characters, places, and incidents are the product of the author's imagination or are used fictitiously. Any resemblance to actual events, locales, or persons, living or dead, is coincidental.

BLOOD LAD Volumes 13 and 14 © Yuuki KODAMA 2015. First published in Japan in 2015 by KADOKAWA CORPORATION, Tokyo. English translation rights arranged with KADOKAWA CORPORATION, Tokyo, through TUTTLE-MORI AGENCY, INC., Tokyo.

English translation © 2016 by Yen Press, LLC

Yen Press
1290 Avenue of the Americas
New York, NY 10104

Visit us at yenpress.com
facebook.com/yenpress
twitter.com/yenpress
yenpress.tumblr.com
instagram.com/yenpress

Library of Congress Control Number: 2014504627

First Yen Press Edition: February 2016

Yen Press is an imprint of Yen Press, LLC.
The Yen Press name and logo are trademarks of Yen Press, LLC.

The publisher is not responsible for websites (or their content) that are not owned by the publisher.

ISBN: 978-0-316-26912-4

10 9 8 7 6 5 4 3 2

BVG

Printed in the United States of America